Chinese-English

English-Chinese

Practical Dictionary

Estabrook

Chinese-English
English-Chinese
Practical Dictionary

Yong Ho

Hippocrene Books, Inc.
New York

For information, address:
HIPPOCRENE BOOKS, INC.
171 Madison Avenue
New York, NY 10016
www.hippocrenebooks.com

Library of Congress Cataloging-in-Publication Data

Ho, Yong.
  Chinese-English English-Chinese practical dictionary / Yong
  Ho.
    p. cm.
  Includes index.
  ISBN-13: 978-0-7818-1236-8 (alk. paper)
  ISBN-10: 0-7818-1236-4
  1. Chinese language—Dictionaries—English. 2. English
language—Dictionaries—Chinese. I. Title.
PL1455.H665 2009
495.1'321—dc22

                        2008035755

Printed in the United States of America.

Contents

Guide to the Dictionary

This dictionary is written with the English-speaking student of Chinese in mind. It does not require knowledge of Chinese for the English-Chinese section other than some familiarity with Chinese phonetics, but it does presuppose an elementary knowledge of Chinese for the Chinese-English section, at least with the way strokes of characters are counted. The following is information necessary for the effective use of this dictionary:

Romanization

Of all the major writing systems in the world, Chinese is the only one that did not develop a phonetic alphabet. Its writing system is neither alphabetic nor phonetic, as it does not use romanization and its form does not bear any resemblance to the actual sound. The Chinese writing system uses a logographic script in the form of characters. All characters in this dictionary are accompanied by *pinyin*, the official system adopted in China to transcribe Chinese phonetics. For a chart listing *pinyin* and their approximate equivalents in English, please see page 13–14. The diacritical marks on *pinyin* are tone marks. For an explanation of tones and tone marks, please see page 15.

Please note that when a syllable begins with vowels a, o, and e, and is preceded by another syllable, the apostrophe (') is used to demarcate the boundary between these two syllables, e.g. *dàng'àn* and *yīng'ér*. Sometimes, the apostrophe (') is also used when the juxtaposition of two syllables can give rise to different segmentations and hence different readings, e.g. *kǔ'nǎo* (rather than *kǔn-ǎo*), *fǎn'gǎn* (rather than *fǎng-ǎn*).

Mechanics of Entries

The entries in the Chinese-English section are arranged alphabetically according to *pinyin*, but with the syllable as the unit, as is customary in most Chinese dictionaries. This is because each syllable in Chinese is a character and each character, for the most part, is a word. This ordering enables entries that share the same headword and hence the same semantic domain to be grouped together. See, for example, the following:

孔子 **kǒngzǐ** *n* Confucius
恐怖 **kǒngbù** *n* horror, terror; *adj* ghastly, horrible, terrifying; 恐怖分子 **kǒngbùfēnzǐ** *n* terrorist; 恐怖主义 **kǒngbùzhǔyì** *n* terrorism
恐吓 **kǒnghè** *v* threaten, intimidate
空白 **kòngbái** *adj* blank; *n* blank, space, gap, margin
空格 **kònggé** *n* blank, space (on a form)
控告 **kònggào** *v* accuse, charge, sue; *n* accusation

Homonymic entries are listed separately and numbered, e.g.:

bank[1] *n* 银行 yínháng; **bank account** 银行账户 yínháng zhànghù; **banker** 银行家 yínhángjiā; **banknote** 钞票 chāopiào
bank[2] *n* (*river*) 河岸 hé'àn

长[1] **zhǎng** *n* chief
长[2] **zhǎng** *v* grow, develop, come into being, begin to grow

To assist users with distinguishing different meanings of an entry, a descriptive word or phrase in italics is sometimes given in parenthesis as in the following:

basin *n* (*wash-basin*) 盆 pén; (*geo*) 盆地 péndì

Similar meanings of individual entries are separated by a comma, whereas different meanings or usages are separated by a semicolon.

How to Look Up a Chinese Word

There are mainly two ways to look up a word in a Chinese dictionary. The first and the easiest is by the alphabetic order according to *pinyin*, as that is how entries are arranged in the majority of Chinese dictionaries, including this one, but this presupposes a knowledge of character structures as well as a sufficient number of characters and their pronunciations to enable you to make an educated and intelligent guess when confronting a new word. The second approach is by the radical, the part of a character that provides semantic clues. After the radical of a character is identified, you will need to go to the section of the dictionary where all the characters with that radical are listed and count the number of the strokes of the non-radical part to find the character you are looking for. Once that character is located, you will see the page number of the entry with that character as the headword in the body of the dictionary. This is not an easy task, as it requires substantial knowledge of character formations. Native speakers of Chinese sometimes even find it difficult as many characters in Chinese do not exhibit a clearly identifiable radical. Some characters may not even have a radical.

In view of these difficulties, this dictionary adopts another method in addition to the *pinyin* approach. The new method consists of an index at the end of the book listing all the characters heading all the entries by the number of strokes such that all the characters made up of the same number of strokes are listed together. In looking up a new word, the user can simply count the total number of strokes of the initial character in the entry in the index to find the page number of the character in the body of the dictionary. This method requires familiarity on the part of the user with the way strokes are counted, but such a skill is usually taught and learned early in a Chinese class.

To make finding the right character even faster, we've grouped them by radical within each section of the index. "Single-component" characters, or characters without a radical, are listed first in the section under this scheme. Also, note that some characters may have multiple components with radicals that are difficult to identify. For easy lookup, these characters have also been lumped with single-component characters.

A Note on Major Parts of Speech in Chinese

Parts of speech in Chinese are difficult to define because of the lack of inflectional markers and the versatility of a large number of words that can assume more than one part of speech. Most words gain their parts of speech in the context of a phrase or sentence. For this reason, most Chinese dictionaries refrain from indicating the parts of speech of words. Parts of speech are indicated in this dictionary primarily for the convenience of users. They are mainly based on the frequency with which they appear syntactically in everyday language.

Parts of speech in Chinese do not always correspond with those in English such that a concept indicated by one part of speech in English can be indicated by another part of speech in Chinese. The nouns indicating time in Chinese (commonly referred to as "the time words") are a typical case in point. Nouns in Chinese can be used adverbially to indicate time, whereas the function is served by adverbs in English. One should not be surprised to see entries like the following:

刚才 **gāngcái** *n* just now, a moment ago

今后 **jīnhòu** *n* henceforth, from now on

以前 **yǐqián** *n* ago, before, formerly, previously

Nouns

Chinese does not make distinctions of number. In other words, nouns are not marked to show singular or plural.

Chinese does not make distinctions of case either. There is no opposition between *I* and *me*, *he* and *him*, *she* and *her*, *we* and *us*, and *they* and *them*.

Chinese does not have articles such as *a*, *an* and *the* in English. Definiteness and indefiniteness are mainly indicated by word order. Generally, definite items appear at the beginning of a sentence, while indefinite items appear toward the end of the sentence.

Adjectives

Adjectives in Chinese can function as predicates without a linking verb such as English *be*. For this reason, adjectives in Chinese can be considered quasi-verbs.

Another type of adjectives is attributive adjectives. They are the adjectives that are used before nouns. In Chinese, a monosyllabic adjective can directly modify a noun, but 的 *de* is needed when the adjective is disyllabic or polysyllabic. A monosyllabic attributive adjective modified by an adverb also requires the use of 的 *de* before a noun.

In this book, Chinese adjectives in the English-Chinese section have a 的 *de* after them, but not in the Chinese-English section, as is customarily the case.

Verbs

Chinese does not distinguish between first or second person and third person (such as *I speak* vs. *he speaks*), between active voice and passive voice (such as *call* vs. *be called*) and between conditional sentences and subjunctive mood (such as *if you are not coming, I'm not going* and *if I had known, I would have done it*).

Tense is conspicuously absent in Chinese. The concept of tense has two components: time (past, present, future, etc.) and aspect (manner of the action). Fortunately for students of Chinese, verbs do not present a major problem as time is expressed lexically and aspect markers are few and far between in Chinese. There are only three aspects distinguished in Chinese: indefinite, complete and continuous.

Classifiers

Classifiers are a category of words that are unique to Chinese and most other Sino-Tibetan languages, the group to which Chinese belongs. Basically, a classifier is a word that comes in between a number or a demonstrative pronoun (e.g. *this*, *that*) and a noun. They are occasionally used in English such as "a *piece* of paper," "a *school* of fish" and "two *heads* of cauliflower," but in Chinese the use of classifiers is the rule rather than the exception. What the classifiers do is to help disambiguate homophones and supply additional semantic information about the nouns they are used with. A particular classifier is usually shared by a number of nouns having the same underlying semantic features. The most commonly used classifiers in Chinese amount to less than twenty. The following is a list of the most frequently used classifiers in Chinese:

Classifier	Semantic Features	Examples
把 bǎ	objects with a handle	knife, umbrella, toothbrush, chair, flag, spade, scissors
本 běn	bound printed material	books, magazines, atlas, album
个 ge	piece; entity	person, bank, shelf, nail, school
件 jiàn	articles of furniture, luggage, etc.;	luggage, furniture
	upper body clothing	shirt, coat, jacket, sweater
块 kuài	cube-like objects	soap, cake, watch, brick, block
辆 liàng	vehicles	car, bicycle, motorcycle, truck, carriage
条 tiáo	belt-like, long objects; lower body clothing	towel, fish, street, river, snake, banner, scarf, tie, belt, pants, shorts, skirt
位 wèi	respectable person	teacher, guest, friend, doctor, customer
张 zhāng	flat, rectangular objects	map, bed, table, desk, paper
枝 zhī	long and thin objects	pencil, cigarette, rifle
只 zhī	animals; one of paired items	butterfly, cat, chicken, hand, leg, chopstick, glove, sock
座 zuò	large, solid structure	mountain, bridge, building

Pronunciation Guide

Pinyin	Approximate English Equivalent
a	as in f**a**ther
ai	as in **eye**
an	as in m**an**
ang	as in h**ung**
ao	as in n**ow**
e	as in n**ur**se
ei	as in m**a**ke
en	as in **un**der
eng	as in s**ung**
er	as in **her**
i	as in m**ee**t
i	(after z, c, s, zh, ch, sh and r is silent)
ia	as in **ya**cht
ian	as in **yen**
iang	as in **young**
iao	as in m**eow**
ie	as in **ye**s
in	as in p**in**
ing	as in p**ing**
iong	as in German **jun**ger
o	as in l**ore**
ong	as **own**
ou	as in t**ow**
u	as in r**u**de
ua	as in **wa**ddle
uai	as in **wi**de
uan	as in **wan**d
uang	as in **wah+ng**
ui	as in **weigh**
un	as in **won**der
uo	as in **wa**ll

13

Pronunciation Guide

ü	as in French t**u**
üan	**ü**+**an**
üe	**ü**+**eh**
ün	as in German gr**ün**
b	as in **b**at
c	as in ha**ts**
ch	as in **ch**arge
d	as in **d**og
f	as in **f**at
g	as in **g**o
h	as in **h**op
j	as in **j**ump
k	as in **k**ey
l	as in **l**et
m	as in **m**ap
n	as in **n**ight
p	as in **p**at
q	as in **ch**eese
r	as in **r**ay
s	as in **s**and
sh	as in **sh**arp
t	as in **t**ake
x	as in **sh**eep
z	as in car**ds**
zh	as in rou**ge**

A Guide to Tones in Chinese

Chinese is a tonal language. In Mandarin Chinese, there are four tones. Referred to as the first tone, the second tone, the third tone and the fourth tone. They are indicated respectively by the tone graphs in the following sound combinations: mā, má, mǎ, mà. The movements of these four tones are demonstrated by the following chart.

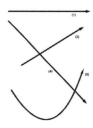

The *first tone* is called the **high level tone**. As the name suggests, it should be high, almost at the upper limit of your pitch range, and level, without any fluctuation.

The *second tone* is called the **rising tone**. It starts from the middle of your pitch range and rises.

The *third tone* is called the **falling-rising tone**. As such, it has two parts: first falling, and then rising. It moves down from the lower half of the pitch range and moves up to a point near the top.

The *fourth tone* is called the **falling tone**. It falls precipitously all the way down from the top of the pitch level.

In addition to the four tones, Mandarin Chinese has a "fifth" tone, which is actually a toneless tone. As such it is usually called the neutral tone. Its pronunciation is soft and quick. The neutral tone is not diacritically marked. It occurs with either grammatical particles or the second character of some words that do not receive stress.

Abbreviations

adj	adjective
admin	administrative
adv	adverb
anat	anatomy
arch	architecture
art	article
aux	auxiliary
sb.	somebody
sth.	something
cl	classifier
chem	chemical
conj	conjunction
elec	electricity
fig	figurative
geo	geology
gov	government
gram	grammar
interj	interjection
med	medicine
mil	military
n	noun
num	numeral
org	organization
part	particle
phr	phrase
pl	plural
pol	political
pref	prefix
prep	preposition
pron	pronoun
rel	religion
tech	technology
v	verb
zool	zoology

Chinese-English Dictionary

A

阿尔巴尼亚 **ā'ěrbāníyà** *n* Albania; 阿尔巴尼亚人
  ā'ěrbāníyàrén *n* Albanian
阿拉伯人 **ālābórén** *n* Arab; 阿拉伯语 **ālābóyǔ** *n* Arabic
阿司匹林 **āsīpīlín** *n* aspirin
阿姨 **āyí** *n* aunt
哀悼 **āidào** *n* condolences; *v* mourn
挨 **ái** *v* suffer, endure
挨打 **áidǎ** *v* take a beating, come under attack
癌症 **áizhèng** *n* cancer
矮 **ǎi** *adj* (*of stature*) short; 矮子 **ǎizi** *n* short person, dwarf
爱 **ài** *n* love, affection; *v* love, like, be fond of
爱称 **àichēng** *n* diminutive
爱尔兰 **ài'ěrlán** *n* Ireland; 爱尔兰人 **ài'ěrlánrén** *n* Irish
爱国 **àiguó** *adj* patriotic
爱好 **àihào** *v* love, like, be fond of, be keen on; *n* interest,
  hobby
爱护 **àihù** *v* cherish, treasure, take good care of
爱情 **àiqíng** *n* love
爱人 **àiren** *n* spouse
爱滋病 **àizībìng** *n* AIDS
安¹ **ān** *adj* peaceful, quiet, tranquil, calm
安² **ān** *v* install, fix, fit
安定 **āndìng** *adj* stable, settled; *v* stabilize
安家 **ānjiā** *v* settle down, set up a residence
安静 **ānjìng** *adj* quiet, peaceful
安眠药 **ānmiányào** *n* sleeping pill
安排 **ānpái** *n* arrangement; *v* arrange, plan, fix up
安全 **ānquán** *n* safety, security; *adj* safe, secure
安全带 **ānquándài** *n* seatbelt
安慰 **ānwèi** *v* comfort, console; *n* consolation
安息 **ānxī** *v* rest in peace
安息日 **ānxīrì** *n* Sabbath
安详 **ānxiáng** *adj* serene, composed
安心 **ānxīn** *v* feel at ease, set one's mind at rest
安装 **ānzhuāng** *v* install
氨 **ān** *n* ammonia
鞍 **ān** *n* saddle
岸 **àn** *n* bank, shore, coast
按 **àn** *v* press, push down; *pron* according to, in accordance
  with

按摩 **ànmó** *n/v* massage
按钮 **ànniǔ** *n* push button
按期 **ànqī** *adv* on schedule, on time
按时 **ànshí** *adv* on time, on schedule
按照 **ànzhào** *prep* according to, in accordance with, in light of, on the basis of
案件 **ànjiàn** *n* law case
案例 **ànlì** *n* case
暗 **àn** *adj* dark, dim, hidden, secret
暗藏 **àncáng** *v* hide, conceal
暗淡 **àndàn** *adj* dim, faint, gloomy
暗害 **ànhài** *v* murder, assassinate
暗杀 **ànshā** *n* assassination; *v* assassinate
暗示 **ànshì** *n* hint; *v* hint, imply
暗室 **ànshì** *n* darkroom
肮脏 **āngzāng** *adj* dirty, filthy
昂贵 **ángguì** *adj* costly, expensive
盎司 **àngsī** *n* ounce
傲慢 **àomàn** *adj* arrogant, haughty
奥地利 **àodìlì** *n* Austria; 奥地利人 **àodìlìrén** *n* Austrian
奥林匹克运动会 **àolínpǐkè yùndònghuì** *n* Olympics, Olympic games
澳大利亚 **àodàlìyà** *n* Australia; 澳大利亚人 **àodàlìyàrén** *n* Australian
澳洲 **àozhōu** *n* Australia

B

八 **bā** *num* eight
八角 **bājiǎo** *n* anise, star anise
八十 **bāshí** *num* eighty
八月 **bāyuè** *n* August
巴西 **bāxī** *n* Brazil; 巴西人 **bāxīrén** *n* Brazilian
芭蕾舞 **bālěiwǔ** *n* ballet
把 **bǎ** *prep* (*indicating the pre-verbal object is undergoing changes as a result of the action*); *cl* (*for things with handles*)
把手 **bǎshou** *n* handle
靶子 **bǎzi** *n* target
爸爸 **bàba** *n* father
罢工 **bàgōng** *n* strike; *v* go on strike
白 **bái** *adj* white, pure, plain, blank; *adv* in vain, for nothing
白菜 **báicài** *n* Chinese cabbage

白痴 **báichī** *n* idiot

白酒 **báijiǔ** *n* liquor

白人 **báirén** *n* white man or woman

白日梦 **báirìmèng** *n* pipe dream, daydream

白天 **báitiān** *n* daytime

白血病 **báixuèbìng** *n* leukemia

百 **bǎi** *n* hundred

百分比 **bǎifēnbǐ** *n* per centum, percent, percentage

百货公司 **bǎihuò gōngsī** *n* department store

百科全书 **bǎikē quánshū** *n* encyclopedia

百万 **bǎiwàn** *n* million; 百万富翁 **bǎiwàn fùwēng** *n* millionaire

百姓 **bǎixìng** *n* common people

摆 **bǎi** *v* put, place, arrange, sway, wave

摆脱 **bǎituō** *v* shake off, break away from, extricate oneself from

败 **bài** *v* be defeated, lose

败坏 **bàihuài** *v* ruin, corrupt, undermine

败退 **bàituì** *v* retreat in defeat

拜访 **bàifǎng** *v* pay a visit, call on

拜年 **bàinián** *v* pay a New Year's call, wish sb. a Happy New Year

扳机 **bānjī** *n* trigger

扳手 **bānshou** *n* spanner, wrench

扳子 **bānzi** *n* spanner, wrench

班 **bān** *n* class, squad, shift

班车 **bānchē** *n* regular bus, shuttle bus, commute bus

班机 **bānjī** *n* flight

班级 **bānjí** *n* classes

搬 **bān** *v* move, take away

搬家 **bānjiā** *v* move house

搬运 **bānyùn** *v* carry, transport; 搬运工 **bānyùngōng** *n* porter

板 **bǎn** *n* board, plank

板凳 **bǎndèng** *n* wooden bench or stool

板球 **bǎnqiú** *n* (*sport*) cricket

版 **bǎn** *n* edition, (*newspaper*) section

版本 **bǎnběn** *n* edition, version

版权 **bǎnquán** *n* copyright

版税 **bǎnshuì** *n* (*author*) royalty

办 **bàn** *v* do, handle, manage, attend to, set up, run

办法 **bànfǎ** *n* way, method, measure

办公 **bàngōng** *v* handle official business; 办公室 **bàngōngshì** *n* office; 办公时间 **bàngōng shíjiān** *n* office hour

办理 **bànlǐ** *v* handle, conduct, transact

办事 **bànshì** *v* handle business; 办事处 **bànshìchù** *n* branch office; 办事员 **bànshìyuán** *n* office worker, clerk

半 **bàn** *num* half, semi

半岛 **bàndǎo** *n* peninsula

半径 **bànjìng** *n* radius

半决赛 **bànjuésài** *n* semifinals

半路 **bànlù** *adv* halfway

半球 **bànqiú** *n* hemisphere

半天 **bàntiān** *n* a long time, quite a while

半途 **bàntú** *adv* halfway, midway

半夜 **bànyè** *n* midnight, in the middle of the night

伴 **bàn** *n* companion, partner

伴侣 **bànlǚ** *n* companion, partner, mate

伴随 **bànsuí** *v* accompany, follow

伴奏 **bànzòu** *v* (*music*) accompany

扮演 **bànyǎn** *v* play the part of, act

拌 **bàn** *v* mix, stir

帮¹ **bāng** *n* gang, band

帮² **bāng** *v* help, assist

帮忙 **bāngmáng** *v* help, give a hand, do a favor

帮派 **bāngpài** *n* faction, gang, clique

帮手 **bāngshou** *n* helper, assistant

帮助 **bāngzhù** *v* help, assist; *n* help, assistance

绑 **bǎng** *v* bind, tie

绑架 **bǎngjià** *v* kidnap, abduct

榜样 **bǎngyàng** *n* example, role model

膀子 **bǎngzi** *n* upper arm, arm

傍晚 **bàngwǎn** *n* dusk

棒 **bàng** *n* club, stick, bat; *adj* great

棒球 **bàngqiú** *n* baseball

棒子 **bàngzi** *n* stick, club, cudgel

磅 **bàng** *n* (*weight*) pound

包 **bāo** *n* bag, pack, bundle, packet, parcel; *v* wrap, surround, encircle, envelop, include, contain

包庇 **bāobì** *v* shield, harbor, cover up

包袱 **bāofu** *n* load, weight, burden

包裹 **bāoguǒ** *n* package, parcel

包含 **bāohán** *v* contain, include

包括 **bāokuò** *v* include, consist of, comprise, involve

包围 **bāowéi** *v* surround, encircle

包扎 **bāozā** *v* wrap up, bind up

包装 **bāozhuāng** *v* pack, package

包子 bāozi *n* steamed stuffed bun

剥 bāo *v* peel

薄 báo *adj* thin, flimsy, slight, meager

雹子 báozi *n* hail, hailstone

宝 bǎo *n* treasure

宝贝 bǎobèi *n* treasured object, treasure

宝贵 bǎoguì *adj* precious, valuable

宝石 bǎoshí *n* gem, precious stone

宝塔 bǎotǎ *n* pagoda

宝藏 bǎozàng *n* (*mineral*) precious deposits

饱 bǎo *v* eat one's fill

保 bǎo *v* protect, defend, keep, maintain, preserve, guarantee, ensure

保安 bǎo'ān *v* ensure public security, ensure safety;
保安人员 bǎo'ān rényuán *n* security personnel

保镖 bǎobiāo *n* bodyguard

保藏 bǎocáng *v* keep in store, preserve

保持 bǎochí *v* keep, preserve, maintain

保存 bǎocún *v* preserve, conserve, maintain

保管 bǎoguǎn *v* take care of, keep safe

保护 bǎohù *n* protection; *v* protect, safeguard

保健 bǎojiàn *n* health care

保留 bǎoliú *n* reservation; *v* reserve, retain, keep

保密 bǎomì *v* maintain secrecy, keep confidential

保姆 bǎomǔ *n* babysitter, nanny

保释 bǎoshì *v* release on bail, bail

保守 bǎoshǒu *adj* conservative

保卫 bǎowèi *v* defend, guard

保险 bǎoxiǎn *n* insurance; *adj* safe

保养 bǎoyǎng *v* maintain, keep in good repair

保障 bǎozhàng *v* ensure, guarantee, safeguard; *n* guarantee

保证 bǎozhèng *v* ensure, guarantee, pledge; *n* guarantee

堡垒 bǎolěi *n* fort, fortress

报 bào *v* report, announce, declare; *n* newspaper, periodical,
journal

报酬 bàochou *n* remuneration, reward, pay, compensation

报仇 bàochóu *v* revenge, avenge

报答 bàodá *v* repay, requite

报导 bàodǎo *v* (*news*) report, cover; *n* report

报道 bàodào *v* (*news*) report, cover; *n* report

报到 bàodào *v* report for duty, check in, register

报复 bàofù *v* retaliate, make reprisals

报告 bàogào *n/v* report
报关 bàoguān *v* declare at customs
报警 bàojǐng *v* report to the police, call the police
报名 bàomíng *v* sign up, register
报税 bàoshuì *v* file a tax return
报摊 bàotān *n* newsstand, news stall
报纸 bàozhǐ *n* newspaper
抱 bào *v* hold or carry in the arms, embrace, hug, cherish; harbor
抱负 bàofù *n* ambition, aspiration
抱歉 bàoqiàn *v* feel apologetic, regret
抱怨 bàoyuàn *n* complaint; *v* complain
暴动 bàodòng *n* insurrection, rebellion
暴风雨 bàofēngyǔ *n* storm
暴力 bàolì *n* violence, force
暴露 bàolù *v* expose, reveal
暴乱 bàoluàn *n* riot, revolt
暴行 bàoxíng *n* outrage, atrocity
暴政 bàozhèng *n* tyranny, despotic rule
爆发 bàofā *v* erupt, break out
爆炸 bàozhà *n* blast, explosion; *v* blast, blow up, explode
爆竹 bàozhú *n* firecracker
曝光 bàoguāng *n* exposure
卑鄙 bēibǐ *adj* base, contemptible, despicable
杯 bēi *n* cup, glass
杯子 bēizi *n* cup, glass
悲惨 bēicǎn *adj* miserable, tragic
悲观 bēiguān *adj* pessimistic
悲剧 bēijù *n* tragedy
悲伤 bēishāng *adj* sad, sorrowful
悲痛 bēitòng *adj* grieved, sorrowful
碑 bēi *n* stone, tablet, monument
背 bēi *v* carry on the back, bear, shoulder
背包 bēibāo *n* backpack, knapsack
北 běi *n* north
北边 běibiān *n* north, northern side
北部 běibù *n* north, northern part
北方 běifāng *n* north, northern part of a country; 北方人 běifāngrén *n* northerner
北极 běijí *n* the North Pole
贝壳 bèiké *n* (*sea*) shell
备件 bèijiàn *n* spare parts
备课 bèikè *v* (*of a teacher*) prepare lessons

备忘录 **bèiwànglù** *n* memorandum, memo
备用 **bèiyòng** *adj* spare, in reserve
背 **bèi** *n* the back of the body or an object; *v* turn away, hide sth. from
背后 **bèihòu** *n* behind, back, rear
背景 **bèijǐng** *n* background
背面 **bèimiàn** *n* the back, the reverse side, the wrong side
背叛 **bèipàn** *v* betray, defect
背弃 **bèiqì** *v* abandon, desert, renounce
背诵 **bèisòng** *v* recite
背心 **bèixīn** *n* vest, waistcoat
背约 **bèiyuē** *v* break an agreement, go back on one's word
倍 **bèi** *n* times, -fold
被 **bèi** *prep* (*passive marker*)
被单 **bèidān** *n* bedsheet
被动 **bèidòng** *adj* passive
被告 **bèigào** *n* the accused, defendant
被迫 **bèipò** *v* be compelled, be forced
被子 **bèizi** *n* comforter, quilt
奔 **bēn** *v* run quickly, hurry, hasten, rush
奔跑 **bēnpǎo** *v* run, scamper
本 **běn** *n* (*money*) capital, (*funds*) principal; *adj* this, current, present; 本地 **běndì** *n* this locality
本国 **běnguó** *n* one's own country, homeland
本来 **běnlái** *adv* originally, essentially
本领 **běnlǐng** *n* skill, ability, capability
本能 **běnnéng** *n* instinct
本质 **běnzhì** *n* essence, nature, intrinsic quality
本子 **běnzi** *n* book, notebook
本族语 **běnzúyǔ** *n* native language, mother tongue
笨 **bèn** *adj* dumb, stupid; 笨蛋 **bèndàn** *n* idiot, fool
笨重 **bènzhòng** *adj* heavy, cumbersome, unwieldy
笨拙 **bènzhuō** *adj* awkward, clumsy
崩溃 **bēngkuì** *v* collapse, crumble, fall apart, (*emotionally*) break down
绷带 **bēngdài** *n* bandage
泵 **bèng** *n* pump
逼 **bī** *v* force, compel, extort
逼迫 **bīpò** *v* force, compel, coerce
鼻孔 **bíkǒng** *n* nostril
鼻涕 **bítì** *n* nasal, mucus, snivel
鼻子 **bízi** *n* nose

比 **bǐ** *v* compare, contrast, compete, match; *prep* compared with, than

比分 **bǐfēn** *n* score

比较 **bǐjiào** *n* comparison; *v* compare, contrast; *adv* comparatively, relatively

比例 **bǐlì** *n* proportion, ratio

比利时 **bǐlìshí** *n* Belgium; 比利时人 **bǐlìshírén** *n* Belgian

比率 **bǐlǜ** *n* rate, ratio

比赛 **bǐsài** *n* competition, match, tournament; *v* compete

比喻 **bǐyù** *n* metaphor, analogy, figure of speech

比重 **bǐzhòng** *n* proportion

笔 **bǐ** *n* pen, pencil

笔法 **bǐfǎ** *n* technique of writing

笔画 **bǐhuà** *n* strokes of a Chinese character

笔迹 **bǐjì** *n* handwriting

笔记 **bǐjì** *n* notes; 笔记本 **bǐjìběn** *n* notebook

笔名 **bǐmíng** *n* pen name, pseudonym

笔译 **bǐyì** *n* written translation

鄙视 **bǐshì** *v* scorn, despise

币 **bì** *n* money, currency; 外币 **wàibì** *n* foreign currency

必定 **bìdìng** *adv* without fail, certainly

必然 **bìrán** *adj* certain, inevitable; *adv* inevitably

必修课 **bìxiūkè** *n* required course

必须 **bìxū** *adv* must, have to

必需 **bìxū** *v* be indispensable, need; 必需品 **bìxūpǐn** *n* necessity

必要 **bìyào** *adj* necessary, essential, indispensable

毕竟 **bìjìng** *adv* after all, all in all

毕生 **bìshēng** *n* all one's life, lifetime

毕业 **bìyè** *v* graduate; *n* graduation

闭塞 **bìsè** *adj* out-of-the-way, inaccessible; ill-informed

庇护 **bìhù** *v* shield, shelter

弊病 **bìbìng** *n* malady, evil, drawback, disadvantage

壁橱 **bìchú** *n* closet

壁炉 **bìlú** *n* fireplace

避 **bì** *v* avoid, evade, shun, prevent, repel

避免 **bìmiǎn** *v* avoid, refrain from, avert

避难 **bì'nàn** *v* take refuge, seek asylum; 避难所 **bì'nànsuǒ** *n* asylum, refuge, sanctuary

避孕 **bìyùn** *n* contraception; 避孕套 **bìyùntào** *n* condom; 避孕丸 **bìyùnwán** *n* birth control pill

臂 **bì** *n* arm, upper arm

边 **biān** *n* side, bound, edge
边疆 **biānjiāng** *n* border area, frontier
边界 **biānjiè** *n* boundary, border
边境 **biānjìng** *n* border, frontier
边缘 **biānyuán** *n* brink, edge, fringe, margin, verge; *adj* marginal
编 **biān** *v* weave, pleat, braid; compile, compose
编辑 **biānjí** *n* editor; *v* edit
编剧 **biānjù** *v* write a play; *n* playwright, screenwriter, scenarist
编写 **biānxiě** *v* compile, write, compose
编造 **biānzào** *v* fabricate
编者 **biānzhě** *n* editor, compiler
编织 **biānzhī** *v* knit, weave
鞭 **biān** *n* whip
鞭打 **biāndǎ** *v* whip, lash, flog, thrash
鞭炮 **biānpào** *n* firecrackers
鞭子 **biānzi** *n* whip
扁 **biǎn** *adj* flat
蝙蝠 **biǎnfú** *n* (*zool*) bat
贬低 **biǎndī** *v* belittle, depreciate, play down
贬义 **biǎnyì** *n* pejorative sense
贬值 **biǎnzhí** *v* devalue, depreciate
便饭 **biànfàn** *n* a simple meal, potluck
便服 **biànfú** *n* everyday clothes, civilian clothes
便利 **biànlì** *adj* handy, convenient
便秘 **biànmì** *n* constipation
便衣 **biànyī** *n* civilian clothes, plain clothes; plainclothesman
变 **biàn** *v* change, transform
变成 **biànchéng** *v* change into, turn into, become
变动 **biàndòng** *n* change, alteration
变化 **biànhuà** *n* change, transformation; *v* vary, change, transform
变换 **biànhuàn** *v* vary, alternate
变心 **biànxīn** *v* cease to be faithful, change heart
变压器 **biànyāqì** *n* transformer
变异 **biànyì** *n* variation
变质 **biànzhì** *v* go bad, deteriorate
遍 **biàn** *adv* all over, everywhere; *n* times, occurrences
遍及 **biànjí** *v* extend all over
辨别 **biànbié** *v* differentiate, distinguish, discriminate
辨认 **biànrèn** *v* identify

辩护 **biànhù** *v* plead, defend
辩论 **biànlùn** *n* debate; *v* argue, debate
辫子 **biànzi** *n* plait, braid, pigtail
标本 **biāoběn** *n* specimen, sample
标点 **biāodiǎn** *n* punctuation
标记 **biāojì** *n* mark, sign, symbol
标明 **biāomíng** *v* mark, indicate
标签 **biāoqiān** *n* label, tag
标题 **biāotí** *n* title, headline, caption
标语 **biāoyǔ** *n* slogan, banner
标志 **biāozhì** *n* symbol, sign, mark
标准 **biāozhǔn** *n* standard, criterion
表 **biǎo** *n* surface; (*form*) table, form, list; meter, gauge; watch
表层 **biǎocéng** *n* surface
表达 **biǎodá** *v* express
表格 **biǎogé** *n* form
表决 **biǎojué** *v* decide by vote, vote
表露 **biǎolù** *v* show, reveal
表面 **biǎomiàn** *n* surface, appearance, face
表明 **biǎomíng** *v* indicate, make clear
表情 **biǎoqíng** *n* facial expression
表示 **biǎoshì** *v* express, indicate; *n* expression, indication
表态 **biǎotài** *v* make known one's position, declare where one stands
表现 **biǎoxiàn** *n* representation, manifestation; conduct, performance; *v* express, represent, manifest
表演 **biǎoyǎn** *n* performance; *v* perform
表扬 **biǎoyáng** *v* praise, commend, compliment
别 **bié** *adj* other, another; *v* do not
别名 **biémíng** *n* alias
别人 **biérén** *n* other people, others
别针 **biézhēn** *n* safety pin, pin
别致 **biézhì** *adj* unique, unconventional
宾馆 **bīnguǎn** *n* guesthouse
冰 **bīng** *n* ice
冰雹 **bīngbáo** *n* hail, hailstone
冰川 **bīngchuān** *n* glacier
冰冷 **bīnglěng** *adj* ice-cold
冰淇淋 **bīngqílín** *n* ice cream
冰球 **bīngqiú** *n* ice hockey
冰山 **bīngshān** *n* iceberg

冰箱 **bīngxiāng** *n* refrigerator
兵 **bīng** *n* soldier
兵变 **bīngbiàn** *n* mutiny
兵力 **bīnglì** *n* military strength, armed forces, troops
兵器 **bīngqì** *n* weaponry, weapons, arms
饼 **bǐng** *n* a round flat cake
饼干 **bǐnggān** *n* biscuit, cookie, cracker
并 **bìng** *v* combine, merge, incorporate; *adv* actually, truly
并肩 **bìngjiān** *adv* shoulder to shoulder, side by side
并列 **bìngliè** *v* stand side by side, be juxtaposed
并且 **bìngqiě** *conj* and, besides, moreover, furthermore
并吞 **bìngtūn** *v* annex, merge
病 **bìng** *v* be ill, be sick; *n* disease
病床 **bìngchuáng** *n* hospital bed, sickbed
病毒 **bìngdú** *n* virus
病房 **bìngfáng** *n* (*hospital*) ward, sickroom
病假 **bìngjià** *n* sick leave
病情 **bìngqíng** *n* state of an illness, patient's condition
病人 **bìngrén** *n* patient
病愈 **bìngyù** *v* recover from an illness
拨 **bō** *v* dial, stir, poke
拨款 **bōkuǎn** *v* allocate funds
波动 **bōdòng** *v* fluctuate
波及 **bōjí** *v* spread to, involve, affect
波浪 **bōlàng** *n* wave
波折 **bōzhé** *n* twists and turns
玻璃 **bōli** *n* glass; 玻璃杯 **bōlibēi** *n* glass, tumbler
剥夺 **bōduó** *v* deprive
剥削 **bōxuē** *n* exploitation; *v* exploit
播 **bō** *v* sow; broadcast
播音 **bōyīn** *v* transmit, broadcast
播种 **bōzhǒng** *v* sow seeds
脖子 **bózi** *n* neck
伯伯 **bóbo** *n* uncle (*father's older brother*)
伯母 **bómǔ** *n* aunt (*wife of father's older brother*)
驳斥 **bóchì** *v* refute, denounce
博士 **bóshì** *n* doctor (*Ph.D.*)
博物馆 **bówùguǎn** *n* museum
搏斗 **bódòu** *n v* struggle
薄弱 **bóruò** *adj* weak, frail
薄荷 **bòhe** *n* mint
补 **bǔ** *v* mend, patch, repair, make up

补偿 **bǔcháng** *n* compensation; *v* compensate
补充 **bǔchōng** *v* supplement, replenish, complement, add
补救 **bǔjiù** *n* remedy, remediation; *v* remedy
补考 **bǔkǎo** *n* make-up examination
补课 **bǔkè** *n* make up a missed lesson
补贴 **bǔtiē** *n* subsidy, allowance
补助金 **bǔzhùjīn** *n* grant-in-aid
哺乳动物 **bǔrǔ dòngwù** *n* mammal
捕获 **bǔhuò** *v* capture
捕捉 **bǔzhuō** *v* catch, seize
不 **bù** *adv* not, no
不安 **bù'ān** *adj* uneasy, unstable, unpeaceful, restless
不必 **búbì** *v* need not, not have to
不便 **búbiàn** *adj* inconvenient
不错 **búcuò** *adj* correct, right, not bad, pretty good
不但 **búdàn** *conj* not only
不当 **búdàng** *adj* unsuitable, improper, inappropriate
不得 **bùdé** *v* must not, may not
不得不 **bùdébù** *v* have no choice but to, cannot but, must
不得已 **bùdéyǐ** *v* act against one's will, have no alternative
    but to, have to
不动产 **búdòngchǎn** *n* estate property
不断 **búduàn** *adv* incessantly, continuously
不妨 **bùfáng** *adv* there is no harm in, might as well
不公 **bùgōng** *adj* unjust, unfair
不顾 **búgù** *v* disregard
不管 **bùguǎn** *v* disregard, be in spite of, be regardless of
不规则 **bùguīzé** *adj* irregular
不过 **búguò** *adv* only, merely, no more than; *conj* but, however
不合 **bùhé** *v* not conform with, be unsuited to be, be out of
    keeping with, not get along well with
不见得 **bújiànde** *adv* not necessarily, not likely
不愧 **búkuì** *v* be worthy of, deserve to be called, prove one-
    self to be
不理 **bùlǐ** *v* refuse to acknowledge, pay no attention to,
    ignore
不利 **búlì** *adj* unfavorable, disadvantageous, detrimental
不料 **búliào** *adv* unexpectedly, to one's surprise
不列颠 **búlièdiān** *n* Britain; 不列颠人 **bùlièdiānrén** *n* Briton
不论 **búlùn** *conj* no matter … (*what, who, how, etc.*),
    whether … or …, regardless of
不能 **bùnéng** *v* cannot, must not, should not

不平 **bùpíng** *n* injustice, unfairness
不平等 **bù píngděng** *adj* unequal
不屈不挠 **bùqū bùnáo** *adj* unyielding, indomitable, tenacious
不然 **bùrán** *conj* else, otherwise, if not
不如 **bùrú** *adj* not equal to, not as good as, inferior to
不相干 **bù xiānggān** *v* be irrelevant, have nothing to do with
不行 **bùxíng** *v* will not do; be out of the question
不幸 **búxìng** *adj* unfortunate, sad; *n* misfortune, adversity
不要 **búyào** *v* don't
不用 **búyòng** *v* need not
不再 **búzài** *adv* no longer, no more
不在乎 **bú zàihu** *v* care nothing about
不止 **bùzhǐ** *adv* incessantly, without end, not limited to
不准 **bùzhǔn** *v* forbid, prohibit
布 **bù** *n* cloth, fabric
布道 **bùdào** *v* preach
布丁 **bùdīng** *n* pudding
布告 **bùgào** *n* bulletin
布局 **bùjú** *n* layout
布料 **bùliào** *n* fabric
步 **bù** *n* step, pace
步兵 **bùbīng** *n* infantry
步枪 **bùqiāng** *n* rifle
步行 **bùxíng** *v* walk, go on foot
步骤 **bùzhòu** *n* measure, step
部 **bù** *n* ministry, department; unit, part, section
部分 **bùfen** *n* part, portion, section; *adv* partly
部落 **bùluò** *n* tribe
部门 **bùmén** *n* department, branch
部长 **bùzhǎng** *n* (*gov*) minister, head of a department

C

擦 **cā** *v* rub, wipe, erase
猜 **cāi** *v* guess, speculate
猜测 **cāicè** *n* guess, conjecture, speculation
猜想 **cāixiǎng** *v* suppose, guess, suspect
猜疑 **cāiyí** *v* harbor suspicion, have misgivings
才[1] **cái** *n* ability, talent, gift
才[2] **cái** *adv* just now, then and only then, only (*before a number*)
才能 **cáinéng** *n* talent, ability
材料 **cáiliào** *n* material, data

财宝 **cáibǎo** *n* money and valuables
财产 **cáichǎn** *n* property, possessions
财富 **cáifù** *n* wealth, riches
财团 **cáituán** *n* financial group, syndicate
财务 **cáiwù** *n* financial affairs
财物 **cáiwù** *n* property, belongings
财政 **cáizhèng** *n* (*public*) finance; 财政部 **cáizhèngbù** *n* the
    Ministry of Finance; 财政年度 **cáizhèng niándù** *n* fiscal year
裁缝 **cáifeng** *n* tailor, dressmaker
裁决 **cáijué** *n* ruling, verdict
裁军 **cáijūn** *n* disarmament
裁判员 **cáipànyuán** *n* referee, umpire
采 **cǎi** *v* pick, pluck, gather
采访 **cǎifǎng** *v/n* interview
采集 **cǎijí** *v* gather, collect
采纳 **cǎinà** *v* adopt, accept (*a practice, method, etc.*)
采取 **cǎiqǔ** *v* adopt, take
采用 **cǎiyòng** *v* adopt, use, employ
采摘 **cǎizhāi** *v* pick, pluck
彩虹 **cǎihóng** *n* rainbow
彩票 **cǎipiào** *n* lottery ticket
彩色 **cǎisè** *n* multicolor, color
踩 **cǎi** *v* step on, trample
菜 **cài** *n* vegetable, greens, dish
菜场 **càichǎng** *n* food market, vegetable market
菜单 **càidān** *n* menu
菜谱 **càipǔ** *n* recipe
参观 **cānguān** *v* visit (*a place*)
参加 **cānjiā** *v* join, participate in, attend
参考 **cānkǎo** *n* reference; *v* refer to, consult
参议员 **cānyìyuán** *n* senator; 参议院 **cānyìyuàn** *n* senate
参与 **cānyù** *v* participate in
餐 **cān** *n* meal
餐馆 **cānguǎn** *n* restaurant
餐巾 **cānjīn** *n* napkin
餐具 **cānjù** *n* tableware
餐厅 **cāntīng** *n* dining room, cafeteria
餐桌 **cānzhuō** *n* dining table
残暴 **cánbào** *adj* ruthless, brutal
残废 **cánfèi** *adj* maimed, crippled, disabled
残酷 **cánkù** *adj* brutal, cruel, ruthless
蚕 **cán** *n* silkworm

惭愧 **cánkuì** *v* be ashamed
仓库 **cāngkù** *n* depot, warehouse
苍白 **cāngbái** *adj* pale
苍蝇 **cāngying** *n* fly
藏 **cáng** *v* hide, conceal
操场 **cāochǎng** *n* playground, sports ground, training ground
操纵 **cāozòng** *v* control, manipulate
操作 **cāozuò** *v* operate, manipulate
嘈杂 **cáozá** *adj* noisy
草 **cǎo** *n* grass
草稿 **cǎogǎo** *n* draft
草莓 **cǎoméi** *n* strawberry
草拟 **cǎonǐ** *v* draft
草坪 **cǎopíng** *n* lawn
草图 **cǎotú** *n* sketch, drawing
草药 **cǎoyào** *n* medicinal herbs
草原 **cǎoyuán** *n* grasslands, prairie
侧面 **cèmiàn** *n* profile, flank, side
厕所 **cèsuǒ** *n* bathroom, lavatory, restroom, toilet, washroom
测量 **cèliáng** *v* measure, survey
测试 **cèshì** *n* testing; *v* test
测验 **cèyàn** *n* quiz, test, exam
策划 **cèhuà** *v* scheme, plan, plot
策略 **cèlüè** *n* strategy, tactics
层 **céng** *n* floor; layer
曾经 **céngjīng** *adv* ever, once
差 **chā** *n* difference
差别 **chābié** *n* difference
插 **chā** *v* insert, plug in, stick in
插头 **chātóu** *n* plug
插图 **chātú** *n* illustration
插销 **chāxiāo** *n* bolt
叉子 **chāzi** *n* fork
插座 **chāzuò** *n* socket, electrical outlet
查 **chá** *v* check, examine, investigate, look up
查票员 **chápiàoyuán** *n* ticket inspector
查阅 **cháyuè** *v* look up, consult
茶 **chá** *n* tea
茶杯 **chábēi** *n* teacup
茶匙 **cháchí** teaspoon
茶馆 **cháguǎn** *n* teahouse
茶壶 **cháhú** *n* teapot

茶叶 **cháyè** *n* tea, tea leaf

察觉 **chájué** *v* detect, become aware of

差 **chà** *v* fall short of, differ from; *adj* poor, bad

差不多 **chàbùduō** *adv* almost, roughly

差事 **chāishi** *n* errand, assignment

拆 **chāi** *v* tear open, take apart, pull down, dismantle

拆除 **chāichú** *v* demolish, dismantle, remove

柴油 **cháiyóu** *n* diesel; 柴油机 **cháiyóujī** *n* diesel engine

蟾蜍 **chánchú** *n* toad

产 **chǎn** *v* produce, yield

产科 **chǎnkē** *n* obstetrics or maternity department; 产科医生 **chǎnkē yīshēng** *n* obstetrician; 产科医院 **chǎnkē yīyuàn** *n* maternity hospital

产量 **chǎnliàng** *n* output, yield

产品 **chǎnpǐn** *n* product

产生 **chǎnshēng** *v* produce, generate, result in, give birth to

产物 **chǎnwù** *n* outcome, result, product

铲子 **chǎnzi** *n* shovel

阐明 **chǎnmíng** *v* clarify, illuminate, elucidate

颤抖 **chàndǒu** *v* shiver, tremble

长 **cháng** *adj* long

长城 **chángchéng** *n* the Great Wall

长处 **chángchu** *n* strong points, advantage

长凳 **chángdèng** *n* bench

长度 **chángdù** *n* length

长方形 **chángfāngxíng** *n* rectangle

长江 **chángjiāng** *n* the Changjiang (*Yangtze River*)

长久 **chángjiǔ** *adv* for a long time, permanently

长期 **chángqī** *adj* long-range, long-term, in the long run

长统袜 **chángtǒngwà** *n* stockings, hose

长途 **chángtú** *n* long distance

长远 **chángyuǎn** *adj* long-range

肠子 **chángzi** *n* intestine

尝 **cháng** *v* taste

尝试 **chángshì** *n*; *v* attempt, try

偿还 **chánghuán** *v* repay, pay back

常 **cháng** *adv* frequently, often

常常 **chángcháng** *adv* often

常规 **chángguī** *n* routine, norm; *adj* conventional, routine

常识 **chángshí** *n* general knowledge, common sense

厂 **chǎng** *n* factory, mill, plant

场地 **chǎngdì** *n* site, space, venue

场合 **chǎnghé** *n* occasion
场面 **chǎngmiàn** *n* scene
场所 **chǎngsuǒ** *n* place, site, location
畅销 **chàngxiāo** *v* be in great demand, sell well; 畅销书 **chàngxiāoshū** *n* best-seller
倡议 **chàngyì** *v* propose; *n* proposal
唱 **chàng** *v* sing; 唱片 **chàngpiān** *n* record; 唱诗班 **chàngshībān** *n* choir
唱歌 **chànggē** *v* sing
抄 **chāo** *v* copy, transcribe; plagiarize
抄件 **chāojiàn** *n* duplicate, copy
抄写 **chāoxiě** *v* copy
钞票 **chāopiào** *n* banknote
超 **chāo** *v* exceed, surpass, overtake
超出 **chāochū** *v* go beyond, exceed
超过 **chāoguò** *v* exceed, surpass
超级 **chāojí** *adj* super; 超级大国 **chāojí dàguó** *n* superpower
超人 **chāorén** *n* superhuman
超市 **chāoshì** *n* supermarket
超越 **chāoyuè** *v* overstep, surmount
超支 **chāozhī** *v* overspend
超自然 **chāozìrán** *adj* supernatural
巢 **cháo** *n* nest
朝 **cháo** *prep* toward(s)
朝代 **cháodài** *n* dynasty
嘲弄 **cháonòng** *v* tease, deride, ridicule
嘲笑 **cháoxiào** *v* mock, sneer
潮湿 **cháoshī** *adj* damp, moist, wet
吵 **chǎo** *v* make noise, quarrel, wrangle, squabble; *adj* noisy
吵架 **chǎojià** *v* quarrel, wrangle
车 **chē** *n* vehicle
车间 **chējiān** *n* workshop
车库 **chēkù** *n* garage
车辆 **chēliàng** *n* vehicle
车票 **chēpiào** *n* train or bus ticket
车厢 **chēxiāng** *n* railway carriage
车站 **chēzhàn** *n* station
扯 **chě** *v* pull, tear
彻底 **chèdǐ** *adj* thorough; *adv* completely, entirely
撤 **chè** *v* retreat, withdraw
撤回 **chèhuí** *v* withdraw, recall
撤离 **chèlí** *v* evacuate

撤退 **chètuì** *v* retreat, withdraw
撤职 **chèzhí** *v* dismiss sb. from his post, remove sb. from office
尘土 **chéntǔ** *n* dirt, dust
沉 **chén** *v* sink; 沉没 **chénmò** *v* sink
沉默 **chénmò** *n* silence, reticence; *adj* reticent, silent
沉溺 **chénnì** *v* indulge, wallow
沉思 **chénsī** *v* contemplate, ponder, meditate, be lost in thought
沉痛 **chéntòng** *adj* grief-stricken
沉重 **chénzhòng** *adj* heavy
沉着 **chénzhuó** *adj* cool-headed, composed, calm
陈旧 **chénjiù** *adj* outmoded, obsolete, old-fashioned
陈列 **chénliè** *v* display, exhibit; 陈列室 **chénlièshì** *n* showroom
陈述 **chénshù** *n* account, statement; *v* give an account, state
衬衫 **chènshān** *n* shirt
趁 **chèn** *v* take advantage of, avail oneself of
趁机 **chènjī** *v* take advantage of the occasion, seize the chance
趁早 **chènzǎo** *adv* as early as possible
称 **chēng** *v* call
称号 **chēnghào** *n* title, designation
称呼 **chēnghu** *v* call, address; *n* address
称赞 **chēngzàn** *n/v* compliment, praise
成 **chéng** *v* accomplish, succeed, become, turn into
成本 **chéngběn** *n* cost
成分 **chéngfen** *n* ingredient, composition
成功 **chénggōng** *n* success; *v* succeed; *adj* successful
成果 **chéngguǒ** *n* achievement, positive result
成绩 **chéngjī** *n* result, achievement, success
成见 **chéngjiàn** *n* preconceived idea, prejudice
成就 **chéngjiù** *n* accomplishment, achievement
成立 **chénglì** *v* found, establish, set up
成年人 **chéngniánrén** *n* grown-up, adult
成人 **chéngrén** *n* adult
成熟 **chéngshú** *adj* mature, ripe
成为 **chéngwéi** *v* become
成语 **chéngyǔ** *n* idiom
成员 **chéngyuán** *n* member
成长 **chéngzhǎng** *v* grow up, grow to maturity
承包 **chéngbāo** *v* contract
承担 **chéngdān** *v* undertake, assume (*responsibility*)
承诺 **chéngnuò** *v* commit to, undertake
承认 **chéngrèn** *v* admit, acknowledge

诚恳 **chéngkěn** *adj* sincere
诚实 **chéngshí** *adj* honest, truthful
城 **chéng** *n* city, town
城堡 **chéngbǎo** *n* castle
城市 **chéngshì** *n* city
城镇 **chéngzhèn** *n* town
乘 **chéng** *v* ride, travel by (*plane*, *train*, *ship*); multiply
乘法 **chéngfǎ** *n* (*math*) multiplication
乘机 **chéngjī** *v* seize the opportunity
乘客 **chéngkè** *n* passenger
乘务员 **chéngwùyuán** *n* steward, flight attendant, conductor
惩罚 **chéngfá** *n* penalty, punishment; *v* penalize, punish
程度 **chéngdù** *n* extent, degree
程序 **chéngxù** *n* procedure, order, sequence; (*computer*)
    program
澄清 **chéngqīng** *v* clarify
橙色 **chéngsè** *n* orange color
橙汁 **chéngzhī** *n* orange juice
橙子 **chénzi** *n* orange
吃 **chī** *v* eat
吃惊 **chījīng** *v* be startled, be shocked, be taken aback
吃苦 **chīkǔ** *v* bear hardship
痴呆 **chīdāi** *n* dementia
痴想 **chīxiǎng** *n* wishful thinking, illusion
池塘 **chítáng** *n* pond
迟 **chí** *adj* late, slow, tardy
迟到 **chídào** *v* arrive late
迟疑 **chíyí** *v* hesitate
迟早 **chízǎo** *adv* sooner or later
持 **chí** *v* hold, carry
持久 **chíjiǔ** *adj* lasting, protracted
持续 **chíxù** *v* persist, last, go on; *adj* continued, sustained
匙子 **chízi** *n* spoon
尺 **chǐ** *n a unit of length equal to ⅓ meter*; ruler
尺寸 **chǐcùn** *n* size, measurement, dimension
尺子 **chǐzi** *n* ruler
齿轮 **chǐlún** *n* gear
耻辱 **chǐrǔ** *n* shame, disgrace, humiliation
斥责 **chìzé** *v* chide, scold, upbraid
赤道 **chìdào** *n* equator
赤脚 **chìjiǎo** *adv* barefoot
赤裸 **chìluǒ** *adj* bare

赤字 **chìzì** *n* deficit
翅膀 **chìbǎng** *n* wing
充电 **chōngdiàn** *v* charge (*a battery*)
充分 **chōngfèn** *adj* ample, abundant, sufficient; *adv* fully, sufficiently
充满 **chōngmǎn** *v* be full of, be permeated with
充足 **chōngzú** *adj* sufficient, adequate, abundant
冲 **chōng** *v* rinse, flush, charge, rush, dash
冲动 **chōngdòng** *n* impulse, urge; *adj* impulsive, impetuous
冲击 **chōngjī** *n* impact, charge, assault; *v* lash, pound
冲突 **chōngtū** *n/v* conflict
虫 **chóng** *n* insect, worm, bug
崇拜 **chóngbài** *n* adoration, worship; *v* adore, worship
崇高 **chónggāo** *adj* lofty, sublime
重 **chóng** *v* repeat, duplicate
重叠 **chóngdié** *v* overlap, superpose
重逢 **chóngféng** *v* meet again, have a reunion; *n* reunion
重复 **chóngfù** *v* repeat, duplicate
重建 **chóngjiàn** *n* reconstruction; *v* rebuild, reconstruct
重聚 **chóngjù** *n* reunion
重写 **chóngxiě** *v* rewrite
重新 **chóngxīn** *adv* again, anew, afresh
重印 **chóngyìn** *v* reprint
宠 **chǒng** *v* dote on; 宠物 **chǒngwù** *n* pet
抽 **chōu** *v* take out (*from in between*)
抽筋 **chōujīn** *v* cramp
抽空 **chōukòng** *v* manage to find time
抽水 **chōushuǐ** *v* pump water; 抽水机 **chōushuǐjī** *n* water pump
抽屉 **chōuti** *n* drawer
抽象 **chōuxiàng** *adj* abstract
抽烟 **chōuyān** *v* smoke
仇 **chóu** *n* enmity, feud
仇恨 **chóuhèn** *n* hatred
仇视 **chóushì** *v* be hostile to
仇外 **chóuwài** *n* xenophobia
愁 **chóu** *v* worry, be anxious
稠密 **chóumì** *adj* dense, thick
筹备 **chóubèi** *v* prepare, arrange
筹划 **chóuhuà** *v* plan and prepare
筹集 **chóují** *v* raise (*funds*)
酬金 **chóujīn** *n* monetary reward, remuneration
丑 **chǒu** *adj* ugly

丑角 **chǒujué** *n* clown
丑陋 **chǒulòu** *adj* ugly
丑闻 **chǒuwén** *n* scandal
臭 **chòu** *adj* smelly, stinking
臭虫 **chòuchóng** *n* bedbug
臭名昭著 **chòumíng zhāozhù** *adj* notorious
臭味 **chòuwèi** *n* stink
出 **chū** *v* go out, exit; issue, produce, put forth
出版 **chūbǎn** *v* publish; 出版社 **chūbǎnshè** *n* publishing
    house
出差 **chūchāi** *v* go on a business trip
出产 **chūchǎn** *v* produce, manufacture
出错 **chūcuò** *v* make mistakes
出发 **chūfā** *n* departure; *v* depart, set off, set out
出国 **chūguó** *v* go abroad
出汗 **chūhàn** *v* perspire, sweat
出境 **chūjìng** *v* leave the country
出口 **chūkǒu** *n* exit; export; *v* export; 出口商 **chūkǒushāng**
    n exporter
出来 **chū lái** *v* come out, emerge
出路 **chūlù** *n* way out, outlet
出门 **chūmén** *v* go out, go on a journey
出名 **chūmíng** *v* become famous
出纳员 **chūnàyuán** *n* cashier, teller
出去 **chūqù** *v* get out, go out
出色 **chūsè** *adj* outstanding, remarkable
出身 **chūshēn** *n* class origin, family background
出生 **chūshēng** *v* be born; *n* birth; 出生地 **chūshēngdì** *n*
    birthplace; 出生日期 **chūshēng rìqī** *n* date of birth;
    出生证 **chūshēngzhèng** *n* birth certificate
出售 **chūshòu** *v* sell, offer for sale
出庭 **chūtíng** *v* appear in court
出席 **chūxí** *v* attend, be present
出现 **chūxiàn** *n* appearance; *v* appear, arise, emerge
出血 **chūxuè** *v* bleed
出院 **chūyuàn** *v* be discharged from hospital
出租 **chūzū** *v* lease, hire out, let; 出租车 **chūzūchē** *n* cab,
    taxi; 出租车司机 **chūzūchē sījī** *n* taxi driver
初 **chū** *n* beginning, early part
初步 **chūbù** *adj* preliminary, tentative
初级 **chūjí** *adj* elementary (*level*)
初期 **chūqī** *n* initial stage, early days

初学者 **chūxuézhě** *n* beginner
初中 **chūzhōng** *n* junior middle school
除 **chú** *v* get rid of, eliminate, remove; *(math)* divide; 除法 **chúfǎ** *n (math)* division
除非 **chúfēi** *conj* unless, only if, only when
除了 **chúle** *prep* except; besides, in addition to
除夕 **chúxī** *n* New Year's Eve
厨房 **chúfáng** *n* kitchen
厨师 **chúshī** *n* chef, cook
橱 **chú** *n* cabinet, closet
橱窗 **chúchuāng** *n* show window, showcase
储藏 **chǔcáng** *v* store, keep; 储藏柜 **chǔcángguì** *n* cabinet; 储藏室 **chǔcángshì** *n* storeroom
储存 **chǔcún** *v* store, stockpile
储蓄 **chǔxù** *v* save, deposit; 储蓄银行 **chǔxù yínháng** *n* savings bank
处罚 **chǔfá** *v* punish, penalize
处方 **chǔfāng** *n* prescription
处境 **chǔjìng** *n* unfavorable situation, plight
处理 **chǔlǐ** *v* handle, deal with, process, treat
处女 **chǔnǚ** *n* virgin
处死 **chǔsǐ** *v* execute, put to death
处于 **chǔyú** *v* be in a certain condition or state
处置 **chǔzhì** *v* dispose of, handle, deal with
处 **chù** *n* place, bureau, department
触电 **chùdiàn** *v* get an electric shock
触犯 **chùfàn** *v* offend, violate
穿 **chuān** *v* wear, put on, be dressed in; pierce through, penetrate; cross *(road)*
穿插 **chuānchā** *v* weave, insert
穿越 **chuānyuè** *v* pass through, cut across
传 **chuán** *v* pass, pass on, relay, hand down, convey; 传话 **chuánhuà** *v* pass on a message
传播 **chuánbō** *v* spread, disseminate, propagate
传单 **chuándān** *n* leaflet, flyer
传家宝 **chuánjiābǎo** *n* family heirloom
传教士 **chuánjiàoshì** *n* missionary
传奇 **chuánqí** *n* legend, romance
传染 **chuánrǎn** *v* infect, be contagious
传染性的 **chuánrǎnxìng de** *adj* contagious, infectious
传说 **chuánshuō** *n* legend, tradition
传送 **chuánsòng** *n* transmission; *v* transmit, convey

传送带 **chuánsòngdài** *n* conveyer belt
传统 **chuántǒng** *n* tradition; *adj* traditional
传真 **chuánzhēn** *n* fax; 传真机 **chuánzhēnjī** *n* fax machine
船 **chuán** *n* boat, ship, vessel
船队 **chuánduì** *n* fleet
船坞 **chuánwù** *n* dock
船员 **chuányuán** *n* ship's crew
船长 **chuánzhǎng** *n* captain, skipper
喘 **chuǎn** *v* breathe heavily, gasp for breath
喘气 **chuǎnqì** *v* breathe deeply, pant, gasp
串 **chuàn** *n* string, cluster, bunch
疮疤 **chuāngbā** *n* scar
创伤 **chuāngshāng** *n* wound
窗户 **chuānghu** *n* window
窗帘 **chuānglián** *n* window curtain
窗台 **chuāngtái** *n* windowsill
窗子 **chuāngzi** *n* window
床 **chuáng** *n* bed
床单 **chuángdān** *n* bedsheet
闯入 **chuǎngrù** *v* intrude
创办 **chuàngbàn** *v* establish, found
创建 **chuàngjiàn** *v* found, establish
创立 **chuànglì** *v* found, establish
创始 **chuàngshǐ** *v* originate, initiate
创新 **chuàngxīn** *v* bring forth new ideas, blaze new trails; *n* innovation
创意 **chuàngyì** *n* originality
创造 **chuàngzào** *v* create; 创造者 **chuàngzàozhě** *n* creator
创作 **chuàngzuò** *v* create, produce, write
吹 **chuī** *v* blow; 吹干 **chuī gān** *v* blow dry
吹牛 **chuī niú** *v* brag, boast
吹风机 **chuīfēngjī** *n* hairdryer
炊具 **chuījù** *n* cooking utensils
垂直 **chuízhí** *adj* vertical
锤子 **chuízi** *n* hammer
春季 **chūnjì** *n* spring, springtime
春节 **chūnjié** *n* the Spring Festival, Chinese New Year
春卷 **chūnjuǎn** *n* spring roll
春联 **chūnlián** *n* Spring Festival couplets (*conveying best wishes for the year*)
春天 **chūntiān** *n* spring, springtime
纯 **chún** *adj* pure, unmixed

纯粹 **chúncuì** *adj* sheer, pure

纯正 **chúnzhèng** *adj* pure, unadulterated

唇 **chún** *n* lip

蠢 **chǔn** *adj* stupid, foolish, clumsy

戳 **chuō** *v* prick, stab

戳穿 **chuōchuān** *v* puncture, expose

绰号 **chuòhào** *n* nickname

词 **cí** *n* word

词典 **cídiǎn** *n* dictionary

词汇 **cíhuì** *n* vocabulary; 词汇表 **cíhuìbiǎo** *n* word list, glossary

词类 **cílèi** *n* parts of speech

词序 **cíxù** *n* word order

词语 **cíyǔ** *n* expression

词源 **cíyuán** *n* etymology

词组 **cízǔ** *n* phrase

瓷器 **cíqì** *n* porcelain, chinaware

瓷砖 **cízhuān** *n* tile

慈善 **císhàn** *adj* charitable, philanthropic; 慈善家 **císhànjiā** *n* philanthropist; 慈善组织 **císhàn zǔzhī** *n* charity organization

辞典 **cídiǎn** *n* dictionary

辞职 **cízhí** *v* resign (*from a position*)

磁带 **cídài** *n* (*magnetic*) tape

磁盘 **cípán** *n* (*computer*) disk

磁铁 **cítiě** *n* magnet

此 **cǐ** *pron* this

此后 **cǐhòu** *adv* after this, hereafter, henceforth

此刻 **cǐkè** *adv* this moment, now, at present

此时 **cǐshí** *n* this moment

此外 **cǐwài** *adj* besides, furthermore

次¹ **cì** *n* time

次² **cì** *adj* second-rate, inferior

次品 **cìpǐn** *n* substandard products, defective goods

次数 **cìshù** *n* number of times

次序 **cìxù** *n* order, sequence

次要 **cìyào** *adj* less important, secondary, minor

刺 **cì** *v* sting, pierce; 刺穿 **cìchuān** *v* pierce through, puncture; *n* thorn

刺激 **cìjī** *n* incentive; *v* excite, stimulate

刺客 **cìkè** *n* assassin

刺猬 **cìwei** *n* hedgehog

刺绣 **cìxiù** *n* embroidery
从 **cóng** *prep* from, through; 从不 **cóngbù** *adv* never
从此 **cóngcǐ** *adv* from this time on, from now on, from then on
从来 **cónglái** *adv* always, at all times, all along
从前 **cóngqián** *n* before, formerly, in the past
从事 **cóngshì** *v* be engaged in
匆忙 **cōngmáng** *v* hurry, rush
聪明 **cōngming** *adj* clever, intelligent, smart
丛林 **cónglín** *n* jungle
凑合 **còuhe** *adj* passable, not too bad
凑巧 **còuqiǎo** *adv* luckily, fortunately
粗 **cū** *adj* coarse, crude, rough, rude, unrefined, vulgar
粗暴 **cūbào** *adj* rude, rough, brutal
粗糙 **cūcāo** *adj* coarse, crude
粗话 **cūhuà** *n* vulgar language
粗鲁 **cūlǔ** *adj* crude, rough, rude
粗心 **cūxīn** *adj* careless
促进 **cùjìn** *v* advance, promote, boost, expedite, facilitate
促使 **cùshǐ** *v* impel, urge, spur
醋 **cù** *n* vinegar
催 **cuī** *v* rush, press, hasten, push, nudge
催促 **cuīcù** *v* urge, hasten
摧毁 **cuīhuǐ** *v* destroy
脆 **cuì** *adj* crisp
脆弱 **cuìruò** *adj* frail, weak
村民 **cūnmín** *n* villager
村子 **cūnzi** *n* village
存 **cún** *v* deposit (*money*), leave with
存款 **cúnkuǎn** *n* savings, deposit
存在 **cúnzài** *v* exist; *n* existence
寸 **cùn** *n* unit of length (=1 decimeter)
挫败 **cuòbài** *v* defeat
挫折 **cuòzhé** *n* setback
措施 **cuòshī** *n* measure
锉刀 **cuòdāo** *n* (*tool*) file
错 **cuò** *adj* wrong, incorrect, erroneous
错过 **cuòguò** *v* miss (*an opportunity, etc.*), let slip
错觉 **cuòjué** *n* illusion
错误 **cuòwù** *n* error, mistake

D

答应 **dāying** *v* answer, reply, respond, comply with, agree, promise

达成 **dáchéng** *v* reach (*an agreement*)

达到 **dádào** *v* reach, achieve, attain

答案 **dá'àn** *n* answer

答复 **dáfù** *n/v* reply

打 **dǎ** *v* beat, strike, hit, fight

打扮 **dǎban** *v* dress up, make up, deck out

打包 **dǎbāo** *v* pack

打电话 **dǎ diànhuà** *v* make a phone call

打赌 **dǎdǔ** *v* bet, wager

打断 **dǎduàn** *v* interrupt, cut short

打盹 **dǎdǔn** *n* doze off

打哈欠 **dǎhāqian;** *v* yawn

打鼾 **dǎhān** *v* snore

打滑 **dǎhuá** *v* skid

打火机 **dǎhuǒjī** *n* lighter

打击 **dǎjī** *n/v* strike, hit, attack

打架 **dǎjià** *n/v* fight, scuffle

打搅 **dǎjiǎo** *v* disturb, trouble

打开 **dǎkāi** *v* open, unfold, unwrap

打猎 **dǎliè** *v* go hunting

打喷嚏 **dǎpēntì** *v* sneeze

打破 **dǎpò** *v* break, smash

打气 **dǎqì** *v* inflate, pump up, bolster up, cheer up

打扰 **dǎrǎo** *v* bother, disturb, trouble

打扫 **dǎsǎo** *v* sweep, clean

打算 **dǎsuan** *v* intend, plan

打碎 **dǎ suì** *v* smash, break into pieces

打听 **dǎting** *v* ask about, inquire about

打印 **dǎyìn** *v* print; 打印机 **dǎyìnjī** *n* printer

打招呼 **dǎzhāohu** *v* greet, say hello

打字 **dǎzì** *v* type; 打字机 **dǎzìjī** *n* typewriter; 打字员 **dǎzìyuán** *n* typist

大 **dà** *adj* big, large

大便 **dàbiàn** *v* defecate, have a bowel movement; *n* stool, human excrement

大胆 **dàdǎn** *adj* bold, daring

大多 **dàduō** *adv* for the most part, mostly; 大多数 **dàduōshù** *n* great majority, the bulk

大方 **dàfāng** *adj* generous, liberal

大概 **dàgài** *n* general idea; *adj* general, approximate; *adv* probably, most likely

大纲 **dàgāng** *n* outline

大规模 **dàguīmó** *adj* large-scale, massive

大会 **dàhuì** *n* convention, conference

大家 **dàjiā** *pron* everybody

大理石 **dàlǐshí** *n* marble

大量 **dàliàng** *adj* a great deal of, a large number of

大陆 **dàlù** *n* continent, mainland

大麻 **dàmá** *n* marijuana, hemp

大门 **dàmén** *n* gate

大批 **dàpī** *adj* large quantities of

大气 **dàqì** *n* atmosphere

大使 **dàshǐ** *n* ambassador; 大使馆 **dàshǐguǎn** *n* embassy

大蒜 **dàsuàn** *n* garlic

大厅 **dàtīng** *n* lobby

大头针 **dàtóuzhēn** *n* pin

大西洋 **dàxīyáng** *n* the Atlantic Ocean

大象 **dàxiàng** *n* elephant

大小 **dàxiǎo** *n* size

大型 **dàxíng** *adj* large-scale, large

大选 **dàxuǎn** *n* general election

大学 **dàxué** *n* university, college; 大学生 **dàxuéshēng** *n* college student

大衣 **dàyī** *n* coat, overcoat

大意 **dàyì** *n* general idea, main points, gist

大约 **dàyuē** *adv* roughly, approximately, about

大运河 **dàyùnhé** *n* the Grand Canal

大众 **dàzhòng** *n* the masses, the people, the public

呆[1] **dāi** *adj* slow-witted, dull; 呆子 **dāizi** *n* idiot, simpleton

呆[2] **dāi** *v* stay

代[1] **dài** *n* historical period, dynasty, generation

代[2] **dài** *v* take the place of

代表 **dàibiǎo** *n* representative, deputy; representation; *v* represent, stand for; 代表大会 **dàibiǎo dàhuì** *n* congress; 代表团 **dàibiǎotuán** *n* delegation

代词 **dàicí** *n* pronoun

代号 **dàihào** *n* code

代价 **dàijià** *n* price, cost

代理 **dàilǐ** *n* agency; 代理人 **dàilǐrén** *n* agent, deputy, proxy; 代理商 **dàilǐshāng** *n* agent

代数 **dàishù** *n* algebra
代替 **dàitì** *v* replace, substitute
带 **dài** *v* bring, carry, take
带领 **dàilǐng** *v* lead, guide
带头 **dàitóu** *v* take the lead, be the first, set an example
带子 **dàizi** *n* beltstrap; band, tape
待 **dāi** *v* stay
待遇 **dàiyù** *n* treatment, remuneration, pay
贷款 **dàikuǎn** *v* provide a loan, extend credit to; *n* loan, credit
袋 **dài** *n* bag, sack
逮捕 **dàibǔ** *v* arrest
戴 **dài** *v* wear, pull on
丹麦 **dānmài** *n* Denmark; 丹麦人 **dānmàirén** *n* Dane;
    丹麦语 **dānmàiyǔ** *n* Danish
单程 **dānchéng** *adj* one way; 单程票 **dānchéngpiào** *n* one-
    way ticket
单词 **dāncí** *n* word
单调 **dāndiào** *adj* monotonous, tedious
单独 **dāndú** *adv* alone, by oneself
单方面 **dānfāngmiàn** *adj* one-sided, unilateral
单间 **dānjiān** *n* single room
单人床 **dānrénchuáng** *n* single bed
单身 **dānshēn** *adj* single, unmarried; 单身汉 **dānshēnhàn** *n*
    bachelor
单数 **dānshù** *n* (*gram*) singular
单位 **dānwèi** *n* unit, workplace
单向道 **dānxiàngdào** *n* one-way street
单一 **dānyī** *adj* unitary, single
单元 **dānyuán** *n* unit
单子 **dānzi** *n* list, bill, form
担保 **dānbǎo** *n/v* guarantee
担架 **dānjià** *n* stretcher
担任 **dānrèn** *v* serve the office of, hold the post of
担心 **dānxīn** *v* worry, feel anxious
担忧 **dānyōu** *v* worry, be anxious
耽搁 **dānge** *v/n* delay
胆 **dǎn** *n* gallbladder; guts
胆大 **dǎndà** *adj* bold, audacious
胆固醇 **dǎngùchún** *n* cholesterol
胆量 **dǎnliàng** *n* guts, courage
胆小 **dǎnxiǎo** *adj* timid, cowardly; 胆小鬼 **dǎnxiǎoguǐ** *n*
    coward

胆子 **dǎnzi** *n* courage, nerve
但是 **dànshì** *conj* but
但愿 **dànyuàn** *v* if only, wish
弹药 **dànyào** *n* ammunition
淡 **dàn** *adj* tasteless, light, bland
淡薄 **dànbó** *adj* thin, light; *v* become indifferent
淡季 **dànjì** *n* slack season
淡水 **dànshuǐ** *n* fresh water
蛋 **dàn** *n* egg
蛋白质 **dànbáizhì** *n* protein
蛋糕 **dàngāo** *n* cake
当 **dāng** *v* work as; act as
当场 **dāngchǎng** *adv* on the spot, then and there
当代 **dāngdài** *adj* contemporary
当地 **dāngdì** *adj* local
当局 **dāngjú** *n* authorities
当前 **dāngqián** *adj* present, current; *adv* currently
当然 **dāngrán** *adv* certainly, surely, of course
当时 **dāngshí** *n* at that time, then
当心 **dāngxīn** *v* take care, be careful, look out
党 **dǎng** *n* (*pol*) party; 党员 **dǎngyuán** *n* party member
档案 **dàng'àn** *n* archive, file, dossier
当 **dàng** *adj* proper, right
当做 **dàngzuò** *v* treat as, regard as, look upon as
刀 **dāo** *n* knife
刀片 **dāopiàn** *n* razor blade
刀刃 **dāorèn** *n* edge of knife
导弹 **dǎodàn** *n* missile
导师 **dǎoshī** *n* (*academic*) advisor, teacher
导演 **dǎoyǎn** *n* (*movie, play, etc.*) director
导游 **dǎoyóu** *n* tour guide
导致 **dǎozhì** *v* bring about, result in, lead to
岛 **dǎo** *n* island
倒闭 **dǎobì** *v* close down, go bankrupt
捣乱 **dǎoluàn** *v* make trouble, create a disturbance
祷告 **dǎogào** *n* prayer; *v* pray
到 **dào** *prep* to, until, up to; *v* arrive
到处 **dàochù** *adv* everywhere
到达 **dàodá** *n* arrival; *v* arrive, get to, reach
到底 **dàodǐ** *adv* at last, finally, in the end; ever, indeed
到来 **dàolái** *n* arrival, advent
到期 **dàoqī** *v* expire, be due

倒 **dào** *v* pour; reverse, be upside down, inverse
倒退 **dàotuì** *v* go backwards, retreat
盗窃 **dàoqiè** *n* theft; *v* burglarize
道 **dào** *n* road, way, path, method
道德 **dàode** *n* morality, morals, ethics; *adj* moral, ethical
道地 **dàodì** *adj* authentic, idiomatic
道教 **dàojiào** *n* Taoism
道理 **dàoli** *n* principle, truth, reason
道路 **dàolù** *n* road, way, path
道歉 **dàoqiàn** *n* apology; *v* apologize
稻草 **dàocǎo** *n* straw; 稻草人 **dàocǎorén** *n* scarecrow
稻田 **dàotián** *n* rice paddy
稻子 **dàozi** *n* paddy, rice
的 **de** *part* (*marking a modifier-modified relationship*)
地 **de** *part* (*forming adverbs*)
得 **de** *part* (*marking verbal complements*)
得 **dé** *v* get, obtain, acquire
得到 **dédào** *v* get, obtain, acquire, gain, receive
得体 **détǐ** *adj* appropriate
得罪 **dézuì** *v* offend, displease
德 **dé** *n* virtue, morals, moral character
德国 **déguó** *n* Germany; 德国人 **déguórén** *n* (*people*) German;
    德语 **déyǔ** *n* (*language*) German
得 **děi** *v* have to, need
灯 **dēng** *n* lamp, lantern, light
灯笼 **dēnglong** *n* lantern
灯谜 **dēngmí** *n* lantern riddles
灯泡 **dēngpào** *n* lightbulb
灯塔 **dēngtǎ** *n* lighthouse, beacon
登 **dēng** *v* mount, ascend; 登山 **dēngshān** *v* climb a mountain
登报 **dēngbào** *v* publish in a newspaper
登记 **dēngjì** *v* check in, register
等¹ **děng** *v* wait
等² **děng** *n* class, grade, rank
等待 **děngdài** *v* wait, await
等等 **děngděng** *adv* etc., and so on
等候 **děnghòu** *v* await, wait, expect
等级 **děngjí** *n* rank, grade, class
等同 **děngtóng** *v* equate, be equal
等于 **děngyú** *v* be equal to
凳子 **dèngzi** *n* stool, bench
低 **dī** *adj* low

低估 **dīgū** *v* underestimate
低级 **dījí** *adj* inferior, elementary, lower, vulgar
堤坝 **dībà** *n* dam, dyke
滴 **dī** *v* drip; *n* drop
的确 **díquè** *adv* indeed, certainly
敌对 **díduì** *adj* hostile, antagonistic
敌人 **dírén** *n* enemy, foe
敌视 **díshì** *v* be hostile to, adopt a hostile attitude towards
敌意 **díyì** *n* hostility, enmity, animosity
笛子 **dízi** *n* flute
迪斯科 **dísīkē** *n* disco
底 **dǐ** *n* bottom, end
底层 **dǐcéng** *n* first floor, bottom, the lowest rung
底片 **dǐpiàn** *n* (*photo*) negative
底下 **dǐxia** *n* under, below, beneath
抵达 **dǐdá** *v* arrive, reach
抵挡 **dǐdǎng** *v* withstand, keep out, ward off
抵抗 **dǐkàng** *n* resistance; *v* resist
抵押 **dǐyā** *n* mortgage; 抵押品 **dǐyāpǐn** *n* security deposit
抵制 **dǐzhì** *n/v* boycott
地 **dì** *n* earth, land, soil
地板 **dìbǎn** *n* floor, wood floor
地道[1] **dìdào** *n* tunnel
地道[2] **dìdao** *adj* authentic, idiomatic
地点 **dìdiǎn** *n* site, spot, location
地方 **dìfāng** *n* place; *adj* local
地窖 **dìjiào** *n* cellar
地雷 **dìléi** *n* land mine
地理 **dìlǐ** *n* geography
地面 **dìmiàn** *n* ground, floor
地平线 **dìpíngxiàn** *n* horizon
地球 **dìqiú** *n* earth, globe; 地球仪 **dìqiúyí** *n* globe, tellurion
地区 **dìqū** *n* area, region
地毯 **dìtǎn** *n* carpet, rug
地铁 **dìtiě** *n* subway; 地铁站 **dìtiězhàn** *n* subway station
地图 **dìtú** *n* map; 地图册 **dìtúcè** *n* atlas
地位 **dìwèi** *n* status, social standing
地下 **dìxià** *adj* subterranean, underground; 地下室 **dìxiàshì**
    n basement
地狱 **dìyù** *n* hell
地震 **dìzhèn** *n* earthquake, quake
地址 **dìzhǐ** *n* address

地质 **dìzhì** *n* geology
地中海 **dìzhōnghǎi** *n* Mediterranean Sea
地主 **dìzhǔ** *n* landowner, landlord
弟弟 **dìdi** *n* younger brother
帝国 **dìguó** *n* empire; 帝国主义 **dìguózhǔyì** *n* imperialism
递 **dì** *v* hand over, pass, give
递交 **dìjiāo** *v* hand over, present, submit
递增 **dìzēng** *v* increase progressively, increase by degrees
第 **dì** *pref* (*marker of ordinal numbers*)
颠倒 **diāndǎo** *adj* upside-down; *v* reverse
颠覆 **diānfù** *v* subvert, topple
典礼 **diǎnlǐ** *n* ceremony
典型 **diǎnxíng** *n/adj* typical
点 **diǎn** *n* o'clock, point, dot; *v* light, kindle
点菜 **diǎncài** *v* order (*food*)
点火 **diǎnhuǒ** *v* ignite
点名 **diǎnmíng** *v* call roll
点燃 **diǎnrán** *v* ignite, kindle
点头 **diǎntóu** *v* nod
点心 **diǎnxīn** *n* refreshments, snack, dim-sum
电 **diàn** *n* electricity; *adj* electric
电冰箱 **diànbīngxiāng** *n* refrigerator
电车 **diànchē** *n* tram, trolley bus
电池 **diànchí** *n* battery
电灯 **diàndēng** *n* electronic light; 电灯泡 **diàndēngpào** *n* lightbulb
电工 **diàngōng** *n* electrician
电话 **diànhuà** *n* phone, telephone; 电话簿 **diànhuàbù** *n* telephone book; 电话卡 **diànhuàkǎ** *n* phone card; 电话亭 **diànhuàtíng** *n* telephone booth
电缆 **diànlǎn** *n* cable
电流 **diànliú** *n* electric current
电路 **diànlù** *n* circuit
电脑 **diànnǎo** *n* computer
电钮 **diànniǔ** *n* push button
电视 **diànshì** *n* television; 电视机 **diànshìjī** *n* television set; 电视台 **diànshìtái** *n* TV station
电台 **diàntái** *n* radio station
电梯 **diàntī** *n* elevator
电筒 **diàntǒng** *n* flashlight
电线 **diànxiàn** *n* electrical wire
电信 **diànxìn** *n* telecommunications

电压 **diànyā** *n* voltage
电影 **diànyǐng** *n* film, movie; 电影院 **diànyǐngyuàn** *n* cinema, movie theater
电源 **diànyuán** *n* power supply
电子 **diànzǐ** *adj* electronic; *n* electronics
电子邮件 **diànzǐ yóujiàn** *n* e-mail
店 **diàn** *n* store, shop; 店主 **diànzhǔ** *n* shopkeeper, storekeeper
垫子 **diànzi** *n* cushion
雕刻 **diāokè** *v* carve; 雕刻家 **diāokèjiā** *n* sculptor
雕塑 **diāosù** *n* sculpture
雕像 **diāoxiàng** *n* statue
钓鱼 **diàoyú** *v* angle, go fishing
调¹ **diào** *v* transfer, move
调² **diào** *n* accent, tone
调查 **diàochá** *n* inquiry, investigation, survey; *v* investigate, look into, survey
调动 **diàodòng** *v* transfer, shift
调换 **diàohuàn** *v* exchange, change, switch
调遣 **diàoqiǎn** *v* maneuver, dispatch
调子 **diàozi** *n* tune, melody
掉 **diào** *v* fall, drop, lose
掉色 **diàosè** *v* lose color, fade
跌倒 **diēdǎo** *v* slip up, tumble
跌价 **diējià** *v* go down in price
钉子 **dīngzi** *n* nail
顶 **dǐng** *n* top, peak
顶点 **dǐngdiǎn** *n* zenith, culmination
顶峰 **dǐngfēng** *n* peak, summit, pinnacle
顶替 **dǐngtì** *v* take sb.'s place, replace
钉 **dìng** *v* nail, sew on
订 **dìng** *v* subscribe to, reserve, book
订单 **dìngdān** *n* order for goods, order form
订购 **dìnggòu** *v* place an order
订户 **dìnghù** *n* subscriber
订婚 **dìnghūn** *v* be engaged, be betrothed
订货 **dìnghuò** *v* order goods, place an order for goods
订书机 **dìngshūjī** *n* stapler
订正 **dìngzhèng** *v* make corrections, mend
定 **dìng** *adj* calm, stable; *v* decide, fix, set
定居 **dìngjū** *v* settle, take up residence
定期 **dìngqī** *adv* regularly, at regular intervals
定钱 **dìngqián** *n* deposit, down payment

定义 **dìngyì** *n* definition
定做 **dìngzuò** *v* have sth. made to order
丢 **diū** *v* lose (*sth.*), discard
丢脸 **diūliǎn** *v* lose face, be disgraced; *adj* disgraceful
丢弃 **diūqì** *v* discard, abandon
丢人 **diūrén** *v* lose face, be disgraced
丢失 **diūshī** *v* lose (*sth.*)
东 **dōng** *n* east
东北 **dōngběi** *n* northeast
东边 **dōngbiān** *n* east, east side
东部 **dōngbù** *n* east, eastern part
东方 **dōngfāng** *n* the East; 东方人 **dōngfāngrén** *n* easterner, Asian
东南 **dōngnán** *n* southeast
东西 **dōngxi** *n* thing, stuff, object
冬季 **dōngjì** *n* winter
冬天 **dōngtiān** *n* winter
懂 **dǒng** *v* understand
懂得 **dǒngde** *v* understand, know
董事 **dǒngshì** *n* (*board*) director, trustee; 董事会 **dǒngshìhuì** *n* board of directors
动 **dòng** *v* move, stir, act
动词 **dòngcí** *n* verb
动画片 **dònghuàpiān** *n* cartoon
动机 **dòngjī** *n* motive
动力 **dònglì** *n* drive, impetus, motivation
动脉 **dòngmài** *n* artery
动人 **dòngrén** *adj* touching, moving
动物 **dòngwù** *n* animal; 动物园 **dòngwùyuán** *n* zoo
动摇 **dòngyáo** *v* oscillate, waver
动员 **dòngyuán** *v* mobilize
动作 **dòngzuò** *n* act, move
冻 **dòng** *v* freeze
冻结 **dòngjié** *v* freeze (*salary, assets, etc.*)
洞 **dòng** *n* hole, cave
都 **dōu** *adv* all, both; even; already
斗篷 **dǒupeng** *n* cape
抖 **dǒu** *v* tremble, shiver, quiver
陡 **dǒu** *adj* steep, precipitous
陡峭 **dǒuqiào** *adj* steep
斗 **dòu** *v* fight, struggle against, contest with, contend with
斗争 **dòuzhēng** *n/v* struggle

豆腐 **dòufu** *n* tofu, bean curd
豆子 **dòuzi** *n* bean
逗号 **dòuhào** *n* comma
逗留 **dòuliú** *v* stay; stop
逗弄 **dòunong** *v* tease, kid, make fun of
都市 **dūshì** *n* city, metropolis
都市化 **dūshìhuà** *n* urbanization
毒 **dú** *n* poison, toxin; narcotics; *v* kill with poison; *adj* poisonous; malicious, cruel
毒品 **dúpǐn** *n* (*narcotics*) drug
毒药 **dúyào** *n* poison
毒液 **dúyè** *n* venom
读 **dú** *v* read; study
读本 **dúběn** *n* reader, textbook
读书 **dúshū** *v* read, study, attend school
读物 **dúwù** *n* reading matter
读者 **dúzhě** *n* reader
独 **dú** *adj* only, single, sole
独裁者 **dúcáizhě** *n* dictatorship
独唱 **dúchàng** *n/v* (*singing*) solo
独创 **dúchuàng** *n* original creation
独到 **dúdào** *adj* original
独立 **dúlì** *n* independence; *adj* independent
独木舟 **dúmùzhōu** *n* canoe
独身 **dúshēn** *adj* unmarried, single
独生女 **dúshēngnǚ** *n* only daughter
独生子 **dúshēngzǐ** *n* only son
独特 **dútè** *adj* unique
独自 **dúzì** *adv* alone, by oneself
独奏 **dúzòu** *n* (*instrumental*) solo
堵 **dǔ** *v* stop up, block up; *adj* stifled, suffocated, oppressed
堵塞 **dǔsè** *v* jam, block up, clog
赌 **dǔ** *v* bet, gamble
赌博 **dǔbó** *n* gambling; *v* gamble
赌场 **dǔchǎng** *n* casino, gambling house
肚子[1] **dǔzi** *n* triple
肚子[2] **dùzi** *n* belly, stomach, abdomen
度[1] **dù** *n* (*angles, intensity, temperature*) degree
度[2] **dù** *v* spend (*vacation, time*)
度假 **dùjià** *v* spend vacation, go on vacation
渡 **dù** *v* cross (*river*), tide over, ferry across
渡船 **dùchuán** *n* ferryboat

渡口 dùkǒu *n* ferry, pier

端午节 duānwǔjié *n* Dragon Boat Festival (*May 5th in the Chinese lunar calendar*)

短 duǎn *adj* short

短处 duǎnchu *n* shortcoming, weakness

短裤 duǎnkù *n* shorts

短跑 duǎnpǎo *n* dash, sprint

短篇小说 duǎnpiān xiǎoshuō *n* short story

短期 duǎnqī *n* short term, short time

短缺 duǎnquē *n* shortage

短袜 duǎnwà *n* socks

短语 duǎnyǔ *n* phrase

段 duàn *n* paragraph; period; section, segment

段落 duànluò *n* paragraph

断 duàn *v* disconnect, break, cut off

断绝 duànjué *v* break off; cut off; sever

断言 duànyán *n* assertion; *v* assert

锻炼 duànliàn *v* exercise, work out

堆 duī *n/v* heap, pile, stack

堆积 duījī *v* heap, pile

队 duì *n* line, queue, team

队伍 duìwu *n* procession, troops, ranks

队员 duìyuán *n* team member

对 duì *adj* correct, right; *n* pair, couple; *prep* to, versus

对比 duìbǐ *n/v* contrast

对不起 duìbùqǐ *interj* sorry, excuse me

对称 duìchèng *adj* symmetrical

对待 duìdài *v* treat

对方 duìfāng *n* the other side, the other party

对付 duìfu *v* deal with, cope with, tackle

对话 duìhuà *n* dialogue; *v* have a dialogue

对抗 duìkàng *n* confrontation; *v* resist, oppose

对立 duìlì *v* oppose, set sth. against

对面 duìmiàn *n* opposite

对手 duìshǒu *n* opponent, rival, adversary

对外 duìwài *adj* public, external, foreign

对象 duìxiàng *n* target, object

对于 duìyú *prep* in regards to, concerning, toward

对照 duìzhào *n* comparison; *v* compare

兑换 duìhuàn *v* convert, exchange; 兑换率 duìhuànlǜ *n* rate of exchange

吨 dūn *n* ton

敦促 **dūncù** *v* urge, press
蹲 **dūn** *v* crouch, squat
炖 **dùn** *v* stew
盾 **dùn** *n* shield
钝 **dùn** *adj* blunt, dull
多 **duō** *adj* many, much; *adv* more; *pref* multi-
多层 **duōcéng** *adj* multi-story, multilayer
多产 **duōchǎn** *adj* high-yielding, prolific
多国 **duōguó** *adj* multinational
多媒体 **duōméitǐ** *n* multimedia
多少 **duōshao** *pron* how many, how much
多事 **duōshì** *adj* eventful; *v* be meddlesome
多数 **duōshù** *n* majority
多样化 **duōyànghuà** *n* diversity, variety
多于 **duōyú** *v* exceed
多余 **duōyú** *adj* redundant, unnecessary, superfluous
多云 **duōyún** *adj* cloudy
多种 **duōzhǒng** *adj* multiple, many kinds of
躲 **duǒ** *v* dodge, avoid, hide
躲避 **duǒbì** *v* dodge, elude
躲藏 **duǒcáng** *v* dodge, hide out, take cover
剁 **duò** *v* chop, cut
堕落 **duòluò** *adj* corrupt; *v* (*of character*) degenerate
堕胎 **duòtāi** *n* abortion; *v* have an abortion

E

俄国 **éguó** *n* Russia; 俄国人 **éguórén** *n* (*people*) Russian;
　　俄语 **éyǔ** *n* (*language*) Russian
鹅 **é** *n* goose
额头 **étóu** *n* forehead
额外 **éwài** *adj* additional, extra
扼死 **èsǐ** *v* strangle
恶 **è** *adj* evil, malignant
恶化 **èhuà** *v* worsen, deteriorate
恶梦 **èmèng** *n* nightmare
恶魔 **èmó** *n* devil, demon
恶习 **èxí** *n* vice, bad habit
恶行 **èxíng** *n* vice, evil conduct
恶性 **èxìng** *adj* malignant
恶意 **èyì** *n* malice, spite; *adj* malignant, spiteful, vicious
恶作剧 **èzuòjù** *n* hoax, prank, mischief

饿 è *adj* hungry
饿死 èsǐ *v* starve to death
遏制 èzhì *v* stem, deter
儿童 értóng *n* children
儿子 érzi *n* son
而且 érqiě *conj* moreover, furthermore, but also
耳朵 ěrduo *n* ear
耳环 ěrhuán *n* earring
耳机 ěrjī *n* earphone, headphone
耳语 ěryǔ *n* whisper
二 èr *num* two
二重奏 èrchóngzòu *n* (*instrumental*) duet
二等 èrděng *adj* second class, second rate
二十 èrshí *num* twenty
二手 èrshǒu *adj* second-hand, used, secondary
二月 èryuè *n* February

F

发 fā *v* issue, distribute, develop
发表 fābiǎo *v* publish, issue
发愁 fāchóu *v* worry
发臭 fāchòu *v* stink
发电 fādiàn *v* generate electricity; 发电机 fādiànjī *n* generator; 发电站 fādiànzhàn *n* power plant, power station
发动机 fādòngjī *n* engine, motor
发光 fāguāng *v* shine
发明 fāmíng *n* invention; *v* invent; 发明者 fāmíngzhě *n* inventor
发怒 fānù *v* rage; be enraged
发票 fāpiào *n* invoice, receipt
发起 fāqǐ *v* launch, initiate
发起人 fāqǐrén *n* sponsor, initiator
发烧 fāshāo *v* have a fever
发射 fāshè *v* launch, project
发生 fāshēng *v* occur, happen, take place
发誓 fāshì *v* swear, vow
发送 fāsòng *v* forward, send, transmit
发现 fāxiàn *n* discovery; *v* discover, find
发行 fāxíng *v* publish, issue, distribute
发言 fāyán *v* speak, give a speech; 发言人 fāyánrén *n* spokesman, spokesperson

发音 **fāyīn** *n* pronunciation; *v* pronounce
发展 **fāzhǎn** *n* development; *v* develop
乏味 **fáwèi** *adj* dull, drab
罚 **fá** *v* penalize, punish
罚金 **fájīn** *n* fine
罚款 **fákuǎn** *v* impose a fine; *n* fine
罚球 **fáqiú** *n* penalty shot, penalty kick
阀门 **fámén** *n* valve
法 **fǎ** *n* law; way, method
法官 **fǎguān** *n* judge
法国 **fǎguó** *n* France; 法国人 **fǎguórén** *n* Frenchman, the
    French
法律 **fǎlǜ** *n* law
法庭 **fǎtíng** *n* court, tribunal
法语 **fǎyǔ** *n* (*language*) French
法院 **fǎyuàn** *n* court
发夹 **fàqiǎ** *n* hairpin
发刷 **fàshuā** *n* hairbrush
发型 **fàxíng** *n* hairstyle, hairdo
帆 **fān** *n* sail
帆布 **fānbù** *n* canvas; 帆布床 **fānbùchuáng** *n* canvas cot;
    帆布鞋 **fānbùxié** *n* canvas shoes
帆船 **fānchuán** *n* sailing-boat, sailing-ship
翻 **fān** *v* turn over, flip; translate
翻译 **fānyì** *n* interpretation, translation; translator, inter-
    preter; *v* translate, interpret
烦 **fán** *v* be annoyed, be irritated
繁 **fán** *adj* complicated
繁荣 **fánróng** *adj* booming, prosperous; *v* flourish, prosper
繁琐 **fánsuǒ** *adj* loaded down with trivial details
繁体字 **fántǐzì** *n* traditional Chinese characters
繁殖 **fánzhí** *n* reproduction; *v* reproduce, breed
凡士林 **fánshìlín** *n* vaseline
反 **fǎn** *pref* anti-; *v* counter, revolt, rebel; *adj* upside down,
    inside out
反驳 **fǎnbó** *v* retort, refute
反常 **fǎncháng** *adj* unusual, abnormal
反对 **fǎnduì** *v* object, oppose, be against; 反对党
    fǎnduìdǎng *n* opposition party; 反对派 **fǎnduìpài** *n*
    opposition faction
反而 **fǎn'ér** *adv* on the contrary, instead
反复 **fǎnfù** *adv* repeatedly, over and over again

反感 **fǎngǎn** *v* be disgusted with, take unkindly to
反攻 **fǎngōng** *v* counterattack
反悔 **fǎnhuǐ** *v* go back on one's word
反抗 **fǎnkàng** *v* revolt, resist
反馈 **fǎnkuì** *n* feedback
反面 **fǎnmiàn** *n* reverse side, opposite; *adj* negative
反叛 **fǎnpàn** *v* rebel, revolt
反应 **fǎnyìng** *n* reaction, response; *v* respond, react
反映 **fǎnyìng** *v* reflect, mirror
反语 **fǎnyǔ** *n* irony
反正 **fǎnzhèng** *adv* anyway, anyhow, in any case
反转 **fǎnzhuǎn** *v* reverse, roll back
犯 **fàn** *v* commit, violate; *n* criminal
犯法 **fànfǎ** *v* violate the law
犯规 **fànguī** *v* foul, break rules
犯人 **fànrén** *n* prisoner, convict
犯罪 **fànzuì** *v* commit a crime
饭 **fàn** *n* meal, cooked rice
饭店 **fàndiàn** *n* hotel; restaurant
饭馆 **fànguǎn** *n* restaurant
饭厅 **fàntīng** *n* dining hall, dining room, mess hall
饭碗 **fànwǎn** *n* rice bowl
饭桌 **fànzhuō** *n* dining table
范围 **fànwéi** *n* extent, range, scope
方 **fāng** *n* (*shape*) square; side
方案 **fāng'àn** *n* scheme, plan, project
方便 **fāngbiàn** *adj* convenient
方法 **fāngfǎ** *n* method, way, means
方面 **fāngmiàn** *n* aspect, regard, side
方式 **fāngshì** *n* approach, manner, fashion, mode, way
方位 **fāngwèi** *n* position, direction
方向 **fāngxiàng** *n* direction; 方向盘 **fāngxiàngpán** *n* steering wheel
方言 **fāngyán** *n* dialect
芳香 **fāngxiāng** *adj* aromatic, fragrant
防 **fáng** *v* guard against, prevent, defend
防弹 **fángdàn** *adj* bulletproof
防腐 **fángfǔ** *adj* antiseptic; 防腐剂 **fángfǔjì** *n* antiseptic, preservative
防水 **fángshuǐ** *adj* waterproof
防御 **fángyù** *n* defense; *v* defend
防止 **fángzhǐ** *v* prevent, guard against, avoid

防火墙 fánghuǒqiáng *n* fire wall
妨碍 fáng'ài *v* hinder, hamper, impede, obstruct
房 fáng *n* house
房东 fángdōng *n* landlord
房地产 fángdìchǎn *n* real estate
房间 fángjiān *n* room
房客 fángkè *n* tenant
房子 fángzi *n* house, building
仿照 fǎngzhào *v* imitate
仿制 fǎngzhì *v* imitate, be modeled on; 仿制品 fǎngzhìpǐn *n* imitation, replica, copy
访问 fǎngwèn *n/v* visit
纺 fǎng *v* spin
纺织品 fǎngzhīpǐn *n* textile
放 fàng *v* place, put, release, set free, let off
放大 fàngdà *v* amplify, enlarge, magnify
放火 fànghuǒ *v* set on fire
放假 fàngjià *v* have a holiday or vacation, have a day off
放弃 fàngqì *v* abandon, give up
放射 fàngshè *v* radiate, emit; 放射线 fàngshèxiàn *n* radioactive rays
放松 fàngsōng *v* relax, loosen
放下 fàngxià *v* put down
放心 fàngxīn *v* feel relieved, rest assured
放映 fàngyìng *v* show (*a movie*); 放映机 fàngyìngjī *n* (*film*) projector
放纵 fàngzòng *v* indulge
飞船 fēichuán *n* spaceship
飞碟 fēidié *n* unidentified flying object (*UFO*)
飞机 fēijī *n* airplane; 飞机场 fēijīchǎng *n* airport
飞行员 fēixíngyuán *n* pilot
非 fēi *pref* non-; *n* wrong
非常 fēicháng *adv* very, extremely
非得 fēiděi *v* have to, must
非法 fēifǎ *adj* illegal, unlawful
非凡 fēifán *adj* extraordinary
非人 fēirén *adj* inhuman
非正式 fēizhèngshì *adj* informal, unofficial
非洲 fēizhōu *n* Africa; 非洲人 fēizhōurén *n* African
肥 féi *adj* fat, fertile, rich; loose-fitting
肥料 féiliào *n* manure, fertilizer
肥胖 féipàng *adj* fat, corpulent, obese

肥沃 **féiwò** *adj* fertile

肥皂 **féizào** *n* soap; 肥皂剧 **féizàojù** *n* soap opera

诽谤 **fěibàng** *n/v* libel, slander

吠 **fèi** *v* bark

废 **fèi** *adj* waste, useless, disused

废除 **fèichú** *v* abolish, annul, repeal

废话 **fèihuà** *n* nonsense

废物 **fèiwù** *n* waste, garbage, trash; good-for-nothing

废墟 **fèixū** *n* ruins

废纸 **fèizhǐ** *n* waste paper

肺 **fèi** *n* lung

肺病 **fèibìng** *n* pulmonary disease, tuberculosis

肺炎 **fèiyán** *n* pneumonia

费 **fèi** *n* fee, dues, expenses, charge; *v* cost, consume

费解 **fèijiě** *adj* hard to understand, obscure

费钱 **fèiqián** *v* cost money, be costly

费时 **fèishí** *v* take time, be time-consuming

费用 **fèiyòng** *n* cost, expense

分¹ **fēn** *n* cent; minute

分² **fēn** *v* divide, separate; distribute

分辨 **fēnbiàn** *v* distinguish, differentiate

分别 **fēnbié** *v* part, leave each other; *adv* separately, respectively

分布 **fēnbù** *n* distribution; *v* distribute

分发 **fēnfā** *v* distribute, hand out

分割 **fēngē** *v* divide, carve up

分工 **fēngōng** *v* divide the work; *n* division of labor

分化 **fēnhuà** *v* split up, become divided, break up; *n* polarization

分机 **fēnjī** *n* (*telephone*) extension

分解 **fēnjiě** *v* resolve, decompose, break down, dissect

分界 **fēnjiè** *n* demarcation; 分界线 **fēnjièxiàn** *n* line of demarcation

分开 **fēnkāi** *v* separate, part; *adv* apart, separately

分类 **fēnlèi** *v* classify, sort

分离 **fēnlí** *v* separate, sever

分裂 **fēnliè** *v* split, break up

分娩 **fēnmiǎn** *n* childbirth; *v* give birth

分明 **fēnmíng** *adj* clearly, distinctly, evidently

分配 **fēnpèi** *v* distribute, allot, assign

分批 **fēnpī** *adv* in batches, in turn

分期 **fēnqī** *adv* by stages, in installments; 分期付款 **fēnqī fùkuǎn** *n* payment in installments

分歧 fēnqí *n* difference, disagreement

分清 fēnqīng *v* distinguish, draw a clear distinction between

分散 fēnsàn *v* disperse, scatter, decentralize

分数 fēnshù *n* fraction; mark, grade, score

分析 fēnxī *n* analysis; *v* analyze; 分析员 fēnxīyuán *n* analyst

分享 fēnxiǎng *v* share

分心 fēnxīn *v* divert one's attention

分行 fēnháng *n* branch bank

分钟 fēnzhōng *n* minute

分子 fēnzǐ *n* molecule

分子 fènzǐ *n* member, element

芬芳 fēnfāng *adj* fragrant, aromatic

芬兰 fēnlán *n* Finland; 芬兰人 fēnlánrén *n* Finn

坟墓 fénmù *n* grave, tomb

粉 fěn *n* powder

粉笔 fěnbǐ *n* chalk

粉红 fěnhóng *adj* pink; 粉红色 fěnhóngsè *n* pink color

粉刷 fěnshuā *v* whitewash

粉碎 fěnsuì *v* shatter, smash, crush

奋斗 fèndòu *v* struggle, fight, strive

愤恨 fènhèn *n* resentment; *v* resent

愤怒 fènnù *adj* angry, indignant

粪便 fènbiàn *n* feces

丰富 fēngfù *adj* abundant, rich

风 fēng *n* wind

风暴 fēngbào *n* storm

风度 fēngdù *n* demeanor, bearing

风格 fēnggé *n* style, manner

风光 fēngguāng *n* scenery, sight

风景 fēngjǐng *n* landscape, scenery; 风景点 fēngjǐngdiǎn *n* scenic spot

风琴 fēngqín *n* (*instrument*) organ

风趣 fēngqù *n* humor, wit; *adj* funny, witty

风水 fēngshuǐ *n* geomantic omen, *fengshui*

风俗 fēngsú *n* custom

风味 fēngwèi *n* flavor

风险 fēngxiǎn *n* risk, venture

风筝 fēngzheng *n* kite

封 fēng *v* seal; *cl* (*for letters*)

封闭 fēngbì *v* seal off, close, block out

封面 fēngmiàn *n* (*book*) cover

疯 fēng *adj* mad, insane, crazy

疯狂 fēngkuáng *adj* crazy, insane, mad
疯子 fēngzi *n* lunatic, madman, maniac
锋利 fēnglì *adj* (*knife*) sharp
蜂蜜 fēngmì *n* honey
蜂鸣器 fēngmíngqì *n* buzzer
缝 féng *v* sew
缝合 fénghé *v* sew up
缝纫机 féngrènjī *n* sewing machine
讽刺 fěngcì *v* satirize, mock
奉献 fèngxiàn *v* dedicate
佛 fó *n* Buddha; 佛教 fójiào *n* Buddhism; 佛教徒 fójiàotú *n* Buddhist
否定 fǒudìng *v* negate, deny; *adj* negative
否决 fǒujué *v* veto, vote down
否认 fǒurèn *v* deny, repudiate
否则 fǒuzé *conj* otherwise, or else
夫妇 fūfù *n* husband and wife
夫妻 fūqī *n* husband and wife
夫人 fūrén *n* Lady, Madame, wife
肤浅 fūqiǎn *adj* superficial, shallow
肤色 fūsè *n* complexion, skin color
扶 fú *v* support with the hand
扶手 fúshǒu *n* rail, handrail; 扶手椅 fúshǒuyǐ *n* armchair
扶助 fúzhù *v* help, assist, support
服 fú *n* clothes, dress; *v* take (*medicine*)
服从 fúcóng *v* obey, comply with
服丧 fúsāng *v* be in mourning
服务 fúwù *n* service; *v* serve; 服务员 fúwùyuán *n* waiter, waitress, attendant
服役 fúyì *v* enlist in the military, be on active service
服装 fúzhuāng *n* costume, clothing, uniform, dress
俘虏 fúlǔ *n* captive, captured personnel
浮 fú *v* float
浮动 fúdòng *v* be unsteady, fluctuate
幅 fú *cl* (*for pictures, paintings, etc.*)
福利 fúlì *n* benefit, welfare, well-being
抚摸 fǔmō *v* stroke
抚养 fǔyǎng *v* foster, raise, bring up
斧头 fǔtóu *n* axe
斧子 fǔzi *n* axe, hatchet
辅导 fǔdǎo *v* coach, tutor
辅音 fǔyīn *n* consonant

辅助 **fǔzhù** *v* assist; *adj* supplementary, auxiliary, subsidiary
腐败 **fǔbài** *adj* corrupt
腐烂 **fǔlàn** *adj* rotten, decomposed, putrid
腐蚀 **fǔshí** *v* corrode, etch
腐朽 **fǔxiǔ** *adj* decayed, rotten
父 **fù** *n* father
父母 **fùmǔ** *n* parents
父亲 **fùqin** *n* father
付 **fù** *v* pay
付出 **fùchū** *v* pay out, expend
付款 **fùkuǎn** *v* make a payment
付账 **fùzhàng** *v* pay a bill
妇产科 **fùchǎnkē** *n* gynecology
妇科 **fùkē** *n* gynecology; 妇科医生 **fùkē yīshēng** *n* gynecologist
妇女 **fùnǚ** *n* woman; 妇女节 **fùnǚjié** *n* Women's Day
负 **fù** *n* (*physics*) negative, minus
负担 **fùdān** *n* burden
负荷 **fùhè** *n* load
负伤 **fùshāng** *v* be wounded, be injured
负数 **fùshù** *n* negative number
负责 **fùzé** *v* be responsible for, be in charge of; *adj* conscientious; responsible
负债 **fùzhài** *v* be in debt, incur debts
附 **fù** *v* add, attach, enclose
附加 **fùjiā** *v* append, attach, add; *adj* additional
附件 **fùjiàn** *n* accessory, enclosure, appendix, attachment
附近 **fùjìn** *n* vicinity, neighborhood
附属 **fùshǔ** *adj* subsidiary, affiliated, attached
复仇 **fùchóu** *v* revenge, avenge
复发 **fùfā** *v* have a relapse, recur
复合 **fùhé** *adj* compound
复活节 **fùhuójié** *n* Easter
复数 **fùshù** *n* (*gram*) plural
复习 **fùxí** *v* review
复兴 **fùxīng** *n* renaissance; *v* revive, reinvigorate
复印 **fùyìn** *v* duplicate, xerox; 复印机 **fùyìnjī** *n* copier, copy machine
复杂 **fùzá** *adj* complex, complicated, intricate
复制 **fùzhì** *v* duplicate, reproduce; 复制品 **fùzhìpǐn** *n* replica, reproduction
副 **fù** *adj* deputy, assistant, vice

副本 **fùběn** *n* copy
副词 **fùcí** *n* adverb
副手 **fùshǒu** *n* deputy, assistant
副总统 **fùzǒngtǒng** *n* (*gov*) vice president
副作用 **fùzuòyòng** *n* side effect, by-effect
富 **fù** *adj* rich, wealthy, abundant
富有 **fùyǒu** *adj* wealthy, rich
富裕 **fùyù** *adj* prosperous, well-to-do

G

该 **gāi** *v* ought to, should, deserve
改 **gǎi** *v* change, transform, revise, correct, rectify
改变 **gǎibiàn** *n* alteration, change, transformation; *v* alter, change, transform
改革 **gǎigé** *n/v* reform
改换 **gǎihuàn** *v* change over to, change
改嫁 **gǎijià** *v* (*of a woman*) remarry
改进 **gǎijìn** *v* mend, improve
改期 **gǎiqī** *v* change the date
改日 **gǎirì** *adv* another day, some other day
改善 **gǎishàn** *v* improve
改写 **gǎixiě** *v* rewrite, adapt
改造 **gǎizào** *v* transform, reform, remold, remake
改正 **gǎizhèng** *v* correct, amend, put right
改组 **gǎizǔ** *v* reorganize
盖 **gài** *v* cover; build; *n* lid, cover
盖章 **gàizhāng** *v* affix one's seal, stamp
盖子 **gàizi** *n* lid, cap, cover
概况 **gàikuàng** *n* general situation, survey
概括 **gàikuò** *v* generalize, sum up
概念 **gàiniàn** *n* concept, notion
概述 **gàishù** *v* outline, summarize
干 **gān** *adj* dry
干杯 **gānbēi** *interj* cheers
干草 **gāncǎo** *n* hay
干旱 **gānhàn** *adj* arid, dry
干净 **gānjìng** *adj* clean, neat and tidy
干扰 **gānrǎo** *n* disturbance, obstruction; *v* interfere, disturb, obstruct
干涉 **gānshè** *n* interference, intervention; *v* interfere, meddle
干洗 **gānxǐ** *v* dry-clean

干燥 **gānzào** *adj* dry, arid
甘蓝 **gānlán** *n* broccoli
甘蔗 **gānzhè** *n* sugarcane
杆 **gān** *n* pole, rod
肝 **gān** *n* liver
肝炎 **gānyán** *n* hepatitis
肝脏 **gānzàng** *n* liver
尴尬 **gāngà** *adj* awkward, embarrassed
赶 **gǎn** *v* catch up with, overtake, make a dash for, rush for, hurry through; drive away
赶紧 **gǎnjǐn** *v* lose no time, hasten
赶快 **gǎnkuài** *adv* at once, quickly
赶上 **gǎnshàng** *v* catch up with, keep pace with
敢 **gǎn** *v* dare, have courage to
敢于 **gǎnyú** *v* dare to, be bold in, have the courage to
感到 **gǎndào** *v* feel, sense
感激 **gǎnjī** *v* feel grateful, be thankful, appreciate
感觉 **gǎnjué** *n* feeling, sensation, sense; *v* feel, sense
感冒 **gǎnmào** *n* common cold; *v* have a cold
感情 **gǎnqíng** *n* feeling, sentiment, emotion
感人 **gǎnrén** *adj* touching, moving
感想 **gǎnxiǎng** *n* impressions, reflections, thoughts
感谢 **gǎnxiè** *v* thank, be grateful
感恩节 **gǎn'ēnjié** *n* Thanksgiving Day
橄榄 **gǎnlǎn** *n* olive; 橄榄油 **gǎnlǎnyóu** *n* olive oil
橄榄球 **gǎnlǎnqiú** *n* rugby; American football
干 **gàn** *v* do, work
干劲 **gànjìn** *n* drive, vigor, enthusiasm
干线 **gànxiàn** *n* main line, trunk line
刚才 **gāngcái** *n* just now, a moment ago
刚刚 **gānggāng** *adv* a short while ago, just
缸子 **gāngzi** *n* mug
钢 **gāng** *n* steel
钢笔 **gāngbǐ** *n* pen
钢琴 **gāngqín** *n* piano
港 **gǎng** *n* port, harbor
港口 **gǎngkǒu** *n* harbor, port
杠杆 **gànggǎn** *n* lever
高 **gāo** *adj* high, tall
高潮 **gāocháo** *n* climax, high tide
高等 **gāoděng** *adj* higher; 高等教育 **gāoděng jiàoyù** *n* higher education

高地 gāodì *n* highland
高度 gāodù *n* height
高尔夫球 gāo'ěrfūqiú *n* golf; 高尔夫球场 gāo'ěrfūqiúchǎng *n* golf course
高峰 gāofēng *n* peak, summit, height
高跟鞋 gāogēnxié *n* high-heeled shoes
高贵 gāoguì *adj* noble, dignified
高级 gāojí *adj* senior, high-ranking, high-level, advanced, deluxe
高明 gāomíng *adj* brilliant, wise
高跷 gāoqiāo *n* stilt walk
高尚 gāoshàng *adj* noble, lofty
高速 gāosù *n* high speed; 高速公路 gāosù gōnglù *n* expressway
高兴 gāoxìng *adj* glad, pleased, happy
高血压 gāoxuèyā *n* hypertension, high blood pressure
高原 gāoyuán *n* plateau, highland, tableland
高中 gāozhōng *n* high school
膏药 gāoyao *n* plaster
搞 gǎo *v* do, carry on, be engaged in, produce, work out, get, get hold of
搞错 gǎocuò *v* make a mistake
搞好 gǎohǎo *v* do a good job, do well
搞坏 gǎohuài *v* damage, impair, spoil, ruin
稿子 gǎozi *n* draft, sketch, script
告别 gàobié *v* bid farewell, say good-bye
告示 gàoshi *n* official notice, bulletin; 告示牌 gàoshipái *n* billboard
告发 gàofā *v* inform against, report (*an offender*)
告诉 gàosu *v* tell, inform
告知 gàozhī *v* inform, notify
哥哥 gēge *n* older brother
胳膊 gēbo *n* arm
鸽子 gēzi *n* pigeon
割 gē *v* cut, mow
割断 gēduàn *v* sever, cut off
歌 gē *n* song
歌唱 gēchàng *v* sing; 歌唱家 gēchàngjiā *n* singer
歌词 gēcí *n* lyrics
歌剧 gējù *n* opera; 歌剧院 gējùyuàn *n* opera house
歌曲 gēqǔ *n* song
歌手 gēshǒu *n* singer, vocalist

阁楼 gélóu *n* attic

革命 gémìng *n* revolution; *adj* revolutionary; 革命者 **gémìngzhě** *n* revolutionary

革新 géxīn *n* innovation, renovation; *v* innovate, renovate

格调 gédiào *n* (*literary or artistic*) style

格式 géshì *n* form, pattern, format

格外 géwài *adv* especially, all the more

格子 gézi *n* grid, pattern in squares

隔壁 gébì *n* next door

隔阂 géhé *n* estrangement, misunderstanding

隔绝 géjué *adj* completely cut off, isolated

隔离 gélí *v* isolate, segregate

个 gè *cl* (*noun classifier*)

个案 gè'àn *n* case

个别 gèbié *adj* individual, specific

个人 gèrén *n* individual; *adj* personal

个性 gèxìng *n* personality, individuality

个子 gèzi *n* height, stature, build

各 gè *pron* each, every; *adv* separately

各位 gèwèi *n* everybody

各种各样 gèzhǒng gèyàng *adj* various, all kinds of

给 gěi *prep* for, to; *v* give, grant

根 gēn *n* root

根本 gēnběn *adj* fundamental, radical, basic, essential

根除 gēnchú *v* eradicate, uproot

根据 gēnjù *prep* according to, on the basis of; *n* basis, grounds

跟 gēn *prep* with; *v* follow

跟随 gēnsuí *v* follow

更改 gēnggǎi *v* change, alter

更换 gēnghuàn *v* change, replace

更新 gēngxīn *v* renew, update

更正 gēngzhèng *v* make corrections (*in statements or newspaper articles*)

耕 gēng *v* plough, till

耕作 gēngzuò *n* cultivation, farming

哽咽 gěngyē *v* choke with, sob

梗阻 gěngzǔ *n* obstruction; *v* block, obstruct, hamper

更 gèng *adv* still more, even more

更加 gèngjiā *adv* still, even more, all the more

工厂 gōngchǎng *n* factory

工程 gōngchéng *n* project, engineering; 工程师 **gōngchéngshī** *n* engineer

工会 **gōnghuì** *n* trade union

工匠 **gōngjiàng** *n* craftsman

工具 **gōngjù** *n* implement, tool; 工具书 **gōngjùshū** *n* reference book

工人 **gōngrén** *n* worker

工业 **gōngyè** *n* industry; 工业化 **gōngyèhuà** *adj* industrialized; *n* industrialization

工艺 **gōngyì** *n* craft

工资 **gōngzī** *n* pay, salary, wage

工作 **gōngzuò** *n* job, work; *v* work; 工作室 **gōngzuòshì** *n* studio

弓 **gōng** *n* (*weapon*) bow; 弓箭 **gōngjjiàn** *n* bow and arrow

公 **gōng** *adj* public, state-owned; metric; fair, impartial, just; male

公安 **gōng'ān** *n* public security; 公安局 **gōng'ānjú** *n* public security bureau; 公安员 **gōng'ān yuán** *n* public security officer, police

公报 **gōngbào** *n* gazette

公尺 **gōngchǐ** *n* (*measurement*) meter

公道 **gōngdao** *n* justice; *adj* fair, just, reasonable, impartial

公告 **gōnggào** *n* announcement, proclamation

公公 **gōnggong** *n* father-in-law

公共 **gōnggòng** *adj* public, common, communal; 公共汽车 **gōnggòng qìchē** *n* bus

公鸡 **gōngjī** *n* rooster

公斤 **gōngjīn** *n* kilogram

公开 **gōngkāi** *adj* open, overt, public

公里 **gōnglǐ** *n* kilometer

公立 **gōnglì** *adj* publicly established and maintained by the government

公路 **gōnglù** *n* highway

公民 **gōngmín** *n* citizen; 公民权 **gōngmínquán** *n* civil rights

公平 **gōngpíng** *adj* fair, just, impartial, equitable

公顷 **gōngqǐng** *n* hectare

公升 **gōngshēng** *n* liter

公使 **gōngshǐ** *n* envoy, minister

公式 **gōngshì** *n* (*math*) formula

公司 **gōngsī** *n* company, corporation, firm

公用 **gōngyòng** *adj* for public use, public, communal; 公用电话 **gōngyòng diànhuà** *n* public telephone, pay phone

公寓 **gōngyù** *n* apartment, flat

公园 gōngyuán *n* park
公正 gōngzhèng *adj* just, fair, impartial, fair-minded
公证 gōngzhèng *n* notarization; 公证人 gōngzhèngrén *n* notary public, notary
公众 gōngzhòng *n* public
公主 gōngzhǔ *n* princess
公文包 gōngwénbāo *n* briefcase
公务员 gōngwùyuán *n* civil servant
功 gōng *n* meritorious service, merit, achievement
功夫 gōngfu *n* ability; martial arts
功课 gōngkè *n* schoolwork, homework
功劳 gōngláo *n* meritorious service, credit
功能 gōngnéng *n* function, feature
攻击 gōngjī *n/v* attack, assault
供给 gōngjǐ *v* supply, provide, furnish
供应 gōngyìng *v* supply
宫 gōng *n* palace
宫殿 gōngdiàn *n* palace
恭敬 gōngjìng *adj* respectful
巩固 gǒnggù *v* consolidate, strengthen, solidify
拱顶 gǒngdǐng *n* vault
拱门 gǒngmén *n* arched door
供养 gòngyǎng *v* support, provide for
共 gòng *adv* together; altogether, in all, all told
共产党 gòngchǎndǎng *n* the Communist Party
共和国 gònghéguó *n* republic
共同 gòngtóng *adj* common, joint; *adv* jointly
贡品 gòngpǐn *n* tribute
贡献 gòngxiàn *n* contribution; *v* contribute
勾画 gōuhuà *v* draw the outline of, sketch
勾结 gōujié *v* collude with, collaborate with, gang up on
勾引 gōuyǐn *v* seduce
沟 gōu *n* ditch
钩子 gōuzi *n* hook
篝火 gōuhuǒ *n* bonfire
狗 gǒu *n* dog
构造 gòuzào *n* constitution, structure
购 gòu *v* buy, purchase
购买 gòumǎi *v* purchase, buy
购物中心 gòuwù zhōngxīn *n* mall, plaza, shopping center
够 gòu *adj* enough, sufficient, adequate
够格 gòugé *v* be qualified, be up to standard

估计 gūjì *n*; *v* estimate
估价 gūjià *v* appraise, evaluate
姑父 gūfu *n* uncle (*husband of father's sister*)
姑姑 gūgu *n* aunt (*father's unmarried sister*)
姑妈 gūmā *n* aunt (*father's married sister*)
姑娘 gūniang *n* girl
孤独 gūdú *adj* solitary, lonely
孤儿 gū'ér *n* orphan; 孤儿院 gū'éryuàn *n* orphanage
孤立 gūlì *adj* isolated; *v* isolate
辜负 gūfù *v* let down, fail to live up to
古 gǔ *adj* ancient, paleo-
古巴 gǔbā *n* Cuba; 古巴人 gǔbārén *n* Cuban
古代 gǔdài *n* antiquity, ancient times
古典 gǔdiǎn *adj* classical
古董 gǔdǒng *n* antique; 古董店 gǔdǒngdiàn *n* antique shop
古怪 gǔguài *adj* eccentric, odd, weird
古迹 gǔjì *n* historic site, place of historic interest
谷仓 gǔcāng *n* barn
谷物 gǔwù *n* grain
股东 gǔdōng *n* shareholder, stockholder
股份 gǔfèn *n* stock, share
股票 gǔpiào *n* stock; 股票经纪人 gǔpiào jīngjìrén *n* stock-broker; 股票市场 gǔpiào shìchǎng *n* stock market
骨干 gǔgàn *n* backbone, mainstay
骨骼 gǔgé *n* skeleton
骨科 gǔkē *n* department of orthopedics; 骨科医生 gǔkē yīshēng *n* orthopedist
骨肉 gǔròu *n* flesh and blood, kindred
骨头 gútou *n* bone
骨折 gǔzhé *n* fracture
鼓 gǔ *n* drum
鼓动 gǔdòng *v* agitate, stir up
鼓励 gǔlì *n* encouragement; *v* encourage
鼓手 gǔshǒu *n* drummer
鼓舞 gǔwǔ *v* inspire, hearten; *n* inspiration, encouragement
鼓掌 gǔzhǎng *v* applaud
固定 gùdìng *v* fasten, fix; *adj* set, fixed, regular
固体 gùtǐ *n* solid
故 gù *adj* former, old
故居 gùjū *n* former residence, former home
故事 gùshi *n* story, tale
故乡 gùxiāng *n* homeland, hometown

故意 **gùyì** *adj* deliberate, intentional; *adv* deliberately, intentionally

故障 **gùzhàng** *n* breakdown, trouble, malfunctioning

顾客 **gùkè** *n* customer

顾虑 **gùlǜ** *n* misgiving, apprehension, concern

顾问 **gùwèn** *n* advisor, consultant, counselor

雇 **gù** *v* hire, employ

雇用 **gùyòng** *v* employ, hire

雇员 **gùyuán** *n* employee

雇主 **gùzhǔ** *n* employer

瓜 **guā** *n* melon

寡妇 **guǎfu** *n* widow

挂 **guà** *v* hang, put up, hang up (*the phone*)

挂号 **guàhào** *v* register (*at a hospital*); send by registered mail; 挂号信 **guàhàoxìn** *n* registered letter

拐 **guǎi** *v* turn

拐角 **guǎijiǎo** *n* corner

拐弯 **guǎiwān** *v* turn a corner, turn

拐杖 **guǎizhàng** *n* crutch

怪 **guài** *adj* strange, odd, bizarre; *v* blame

怪物 **guàiwù** *n* monster

怪异 **guàiyì** *adj* weird

关 **guān** *v* close, shut, turn off

关闭 **guānbì** *v* shut, shut down

关怀 **guānhuái** *v* show loving care for, show concern for

关键 **guānjiàn** *n* key, crux

关节 **guānjié** *n* joint; 关节炎 **guānjiéyán** *n* arthritis

关口 **guānkǒu** *n* strategic pass, juncture

关联 **guānlián** *n* relevance, relevancy, connection

关税 **guānshuì** *n* (*customs*) duty, tariff

关头 **guāntóu** *n* juncture, moment

关系 **guānxì** *n* connection, relation, relationship

关心 **guānxīn** *n* care, concern; *v* be concerned with

关于 **guānyú** *prep* concerning, regarding, about

观察 **guānchá** *n* observation; *v* look into, observe; 观察员 **guāncháyuán** *n* observer

观点 **guāndiǎn** *n* viewpoint, standpoint

观光 **guānguāng** *n* sightseeing; *v* sightsee; 观光客 **guānguāngkè** *n* sightseer

观看 **guānkàn** *v* watch

观念 **guānniàn** *n* concept, idea, sense

观众 **guānzhòng** *n* audience, spectator

官 guān *n* official, officer
官方 guānfāng *adj* official, governmental
官僚 guānliáo *n* bureaucrat; *adj* bureaucratic; 官僚主义
　guānliáozhǔyì *n* bureaucracy
官员 guānyuán *n* officer, official
棺材 guāncai *n* coffin
鳏夫 guānfū *n* widower
管 guǎn *v* manage, run, be in charge of, control
管道 guǎndào *n* pipeline, conduit
管教 guǎnjiào *v* discipline
管理 guǎnlǐ *n* management; *v* manage, run, administer;
　管理人员 guǎnlǐ rényuán *n* managerial personnel
管制 guǎnzhì *v* control, put under survelliance
管子 guǎnzi *n* pipe, tube; 管子工 guǎnzigōng *n* plumber
管弦乐队 guǎnxián yuèduì *n* orchestra
冠军 guànjūn *n* champion
贯彻 guànchè *v* implement, carry out
贯穿 guànchuān *v* run through
贯注 guànzhù *v* concentrate on, be absorbed in
惯 guàn *v* be used to, be in the habit of; indulge, spoil
惯例 guànlì *n* convention
盥洗室 guànxǐshì *n* bathroom, lavatory
灌溉 guàngài *v* irrigate
灌木 guànmù *n* bush, shrub
灌输 guànshū *v* instill in, inculcate, imbue with
灌注 guànzhù *v* pour
罐 guàn *n* pot, can, jar
罐车 guànchē *n* tanker
罐头 guàntou *n* tin, can
罐子 guànzi *n* jar, can
光 guāng *n* light, ray; *adj* smooth, glossy, polished
光顾 guānggù *v* patronize
光滑 guānghuá *adj* smooth, glossy
光辉 guānghuī *adj* brilliant, glorious
光明 guāngmíng *adj* bright, promising
光年 guāngnián *n* light-year
光盘 guāngpán *n* compact disc, CD-ROM
光谱 guāngpǔ *n* spectrum
光荣 guāngróng *n* glory; *adj* glorious, honorable
光束 guāngshù *n* (*light*) beam
光线 guāngxiàn *n* ray
光学 guāngxué *n* optics

光泽 guāngzé *n* luster, gloss

广 guǎng *adj* wide, vast, extensive, broad

广播 guǎngbō *v* broadcast; 广播员 guǎngbōyuán *n* announcer, broadcaster

广场 guǎngchǎng *n* plaza, square

广大 guǎngdà *adj* vast, wide, broad

广泛 guǎngfàn *adj* extensive, widespread

广告 guǎnggào *n* advertisement

广阔 guǎngkuò *adj* vast, wide, broad

逛 guàng *v* stroll, ramble, roam

归 guī *v* go back to, return; belong to

归功于 guīgōng yú *v* give credit to, attribute success to

归还 guīhuán *v* give back, restore, return (*sth.*)

归纳 guīnà *v* induce, conclude, sum up

规定 guīdìng *v* stipulate, regulate; *n* regulation, stipulation

规范 guīfàn *n* standard, norm

规格 guīgé *n* specification

规划 guīhuà *v* plan

规律 guīlǜ *n* regularity

规模 guīmó *n* scale

规则 guīzé *n* rule, regulation; *adj* regular

鲑鱼 guīyú *n* salmon

轨道 guǐdào *n* orbit, track

诡计 guǐjì *n* trick, crafty plot

鬼 guǐ *n* ghost

柜台 guìtái *n* counter

柜子 guìzi *n* cupboard, cabinet

贵 guì *adj* expensive, valuable; respectable

贵宾 guìbīn *n* honored guest, distinguished guest

贵重 guìzhòng *adj* valuable, precious; 贵重物品 guìzhòng wùpǐn *n* valuables

贵族 guìzú *n* nobility

跪 guì *v* kneel

刽子手 guìzishǒu *n* hangman, executioner

滚 gǔn *v* roll; *interj* get out, get lost

棍 gùn *n* stick

棍子 gùnzi *n* rod, stick

锅 guō *n* pot, pan, cauldron

锅炉 guōlú *n* boiler

国 guó *n* state, country, nation

国防 guófáng *n* national defense; 国防部 guófángbù *n* the Ministry of National Defense

国歌 **guógē** *n* national anthem

国画 **guóhuà** *n* Chinese painting

国会 **guóhuì** *n* Congress, Parliament

国籍 **guójí** *n* nationality

国际 **guójì** *adj* international; 国际关系 **guójì guānxì** *n* international relations; 国际贸易 **guójì màoyì** *n* international trade

国家 **guójiā** *n* state, country, nation

国库 **guókù** *n* national treasury

国内 **guónèi** *adj* domestic, internal

国庆节 **guóqìngjié** *n* National Day

国外 **guówài** *adj* abroad, overseas

国王 **guówáng** *n* king

国务卿 **guówùqīng** *n* secretary of state

国务院 **guówùyuàn** (*gov*) State Department, State Council

国有化 **guóyǒuhuà** *n* nationalization

果 **guǒ** *n* fruit

果冻 **guǒdòng** *n* jelly

果断 **guǒduàn** *adj* resolute, decisive

果核 **guǒhé** *n* core

果酱 **guǒjiàng** *n* jam

果然 **guǒrán** *adv* as expected, sure enough

果肉 **guǒròu** *n* pulp

果实 **guǒshí** *n* fruit

果馅饼 **guǒxiànbǐng** *n* tart

果园 **guǒyuán** *n* orchard

果汁 **guǒzhī** *n* fruit juice

过[1] **guo** *part* (*indicating the completion of an action as well as an action that has taken place, but that does not continue up to the present*)

过[2] **guò** *v* cross, pass; spend (*time*), celebrate (*an occasion, holiday, etc.*)

过程 **guòchéng** *n* process, course

过错 **guòcuò** *n* fault, mistake

过道 **guòdào** *n* passageway, corridor

过渡 **guòdù** *n* transition

过分 **guòfèn** *adj* excessive, undue; *adv* excessively

过节 **guòjié** *v* celebrate a festival

过量 **guòliàng** *adj* excessive

过滤 **guòlǜ** *v* filter, strain; 过滤器 **guòlǜqì** *n* filter

过敏 **guòmǐn** *adj* allergic; 过敏症 **guòmǐnzhèng** *n* allergy

过期 **guòqī** *adj* overdue, expired

过去 guòqù *n* in the past, formerly; *v* pass, pass by
过时 guòshí *adj* obsolete, out of date, outdated
过早 guòzǎo *adj* premature

H

哈欠 hāqian *n* yawn
还 hái *adv* still, yet, even more, also, too, in addition;
　　passably, fairly
还是 háishì *adv* still, nevertheless, all the same; *conj* or
孩子 háizi *n* child
海 hǎi *n* sea
海岸 hǎi'àn *n* coast
海拔 hǎibá *n* elevation
海报 hǎibào *n* poster
海豹 hǎibào *n* seal
海滨 hǎibīn *n* seashore, seaside
海地 hǎidi *n* Haiti; 海地人 hǎidirén *n* Haitian
海港 hǎigǎng *n* seaport, harbor
海关 hǎiguān *n* customs
海角 hǎijiǎo *n* cape
海军 hǎijūn *n* navy
海鸥 hǎi'ōu *n* seagull
海平面 hǎipíngmiàn *n* sea level
海滩 hǎitān *n* beach
海豚 hǎitún *n* dolphin
海外 hǎiwài *adj* overseas
海湾 hǎiwān *n* bay, gulf
海味 hǎiwèi *n* seafood
海峡 hǎixiá *n* channel, strait
海洋 hǎiyáng *n* ocean
海员 hǎiyuán *n* sailor, seaman
海运 hǎiyùn *n* ocean shipping
害 hài *v* cause trouble to, harm, impair; kill, murder
害虫 hàichóng *n* pest, vermin
害处 hàichu *n* harm
害怕 hàipà *v* be frightened, be afraid
鼾声 hānshēng *n* snore
含糊 hánhu *adj* vague, ambiguous
含蓄 hánxù *adj* implicit, veiled
含义 hányì *n* implication, meaning
含有 hányǒu *v* contain

函件 **hánjiàn** *n* letters, correspondence
函授 **hánshòu** *v* teach by correspondence
函数 **hánshù** *n* (*math*) function
寒假 **hánjià** *n* winter vacation
寒冷 **hánlěng** *adj* chilly
寒暑表 **hánshǔbiǎo** *n* thermometer
罕见 **hǎnjiàn** *adj* rare
喊 **hǎn** *v* cry, shout, yell
汉堡包 **hànbǎobāo** *n* burger
汉人 **hànrén** *n* the Hans, the Han people, ethnic Chinese
汉语 **hànyǔ** *n* Chinese language
汉字 **hànzì** *n* Chinese character
汉族 **hànzú** *n* ethnic Chinese, Han nationality
汗 **hàn** *n* perspiration, sweat
汗衫 **hànshān** *n* undershirt, T-shirt
旱 **hàn** *n* dry spell, drought
旱灾 **hànzāi** *n* drought
行 **háng** *n* line, row; trade, profession, line of business
行业 **hángyè** *n* trade, profession, industry
航班 **hángbān** *n* scheduled flight
航海 **hánghǎi** *n* navigation; 航海家 **hánghǎijiā** *n* navigator
航空 **hángkōng** *n* aviation; 航空公司 **hángkōng gōngsī** *n* airline, airways; 航空邮件 **hángkōng yóujiàn** *n* airmail
航天 **hángtiān** *n* spaceflight, aerospace; 航天飞机 **hángtiān fēijī** *n* space shuttle; 航天员 **hángtiānyuán** *n* astronaut
航行 **hángxíng** *n* sailing, flight; *v* sail, fly
豪华 **háohuá** *adj* deluxe, posh
嚎叫 **háojiào** *v* howl, wail
好 **hǎo** *adj* good, fine, nice, all right, okay
好吃 **hǎochī** *adj* delicious, tasty
好处 **hǎochu** *n* benefit, advantage, gain
好多 **hǎoduō** *adj* a good many, a great deal, a lot of
好感 **hǎogǎn** *n* good opinion, favorable impression
好看 **hǎokàn** *adj* good-looking, pretty
好听 **hǎotīng** *adj* pleasant to hear
好玩儿 **hǎowánr** *adj* interesting, fun
好象 **hǎoxiàng** *v* seem, look like
好笑 **hǎoxiào** *adj* laughable, funny, ridiculous
好转 **hǎozhuǎn** *v* take a turn for the better, take a favorable turn, improve
好 **hào** *v* like, love, be fond of
好客 **hàokè** *adj* hospitable

好奇 **hàoqí** *adj* curious; 好奇心 **hàoqíxīn** *n* curiosity
好战 **hàozhàn** *adj* bellicose, warlike
号 **hào** *n* number; size; date
号码 **hàomǎ** *n* number
号召 **hàozhào** *n* call, appeal; *v* call on, appeal
浩劫 **hàojié** *n* catastrophe, calamity
耗费 **hàofèi** *v* cost, consume
耗尽 **hàojìn** *v* drain, exhaust
喝 **hē** *v* drink
喝醉 **hēzuì** *v* get drunk, get intoxicated
合 **hé** *v* close, shut; join, combine; suit, agree
合并 **hébìng** *v* combine, incorporate, merge
合唱 **héchàng** *n* chorus
合成 **héchéng** *v* synthesize, compose
合法 **héfǎ** *adj* lawful, legal, legitimate; 合法化 **héfǎhuà** *n* legalization
合格 **hégé** *adj* eligible, qualified
合伙 **héhuǒ** *v* form a partnership; 合伙人 **héhuǒrén** *n* partner
合金 **héjīn** *n* alloy
合理 **hélǐ** *adj* reasonable
合同 **hétong** *n* bond, contract
合意 **héyì** *adj* desirable
合作 **hézuò** *n* cooperation; *v* collaborate, cooperate; 合作伙伴 **hézuò huǒbàn** *n* partner
和 **hé** *conj* and; *prep* with
和蔼 **hé'ǎi** *adj* kind, affable, amiable
和解 **héjiě** *v* become reconciled
和平 **hépíng** *n* peace
和气 **héqi** *adj* gentle, kind, polite, amiable
和尚 **héshang** *n* monk
和弦 **héxián** *n* chord
和约 **héyuē** *n* peace treaty
河 **hé** *n* river
河岸 **hé'àn** *n* river bank
河边 **hébian** *n* riverside
河床 **héchuáng** *n* riverbed
河马 **hémǎ** *n* hippopotamus
核 **hé** *n* (*of fruits and nuts*) pit, stone
核实 **héshí** *v* verify, check
核桃 **hétao** *n* walnut
核武器 **héwǔqì** *n* nuclear weapon

核心 héxīn *n* core
荷花 héhuā *n* lotus
荷兰 hélán *n* Netherlands; 荷兰人 hélánrén *n* Dutch
盒子 hézi *n* box, case
鹤 hè *n* crane
黑 hēi *adj* black, dark
黑暗 hēi'àn *adj* dark
黑板 hēibǎn *n* blackboard
黑人 hēirén *n* Black people, Black
黑色 hēisè *n* black
黑市 hēishì *n* black market
痕迹 hénjī *n* mark, trace, imprint
很 hěn *adv* very, quite
狠毒 hěndú *adj* venomous, vicious
恨 hèn *v* hate
恒心 héngxīn *n* perseverance
横 héng *adj* horizontal; *n* horizontal stroke (*in a Chinese character*)
衡量 héngliáng *v* weigh, measure, judge
轰动 hōngdòng *v* cause a sensation, make a stir
轰炸 hōngzhà *v* bomb; 轰炸机 hōngzhàjī *n* bomber
哄骗 hǒngpiàn *v* coax
烘 hōng *v* dry or warm by the fire
烘烤 hōngkǎo *v* roast
烘箱 hōngxiāng *n* oven
烘干机 hōnggānjī *n* dryer
红 hóng *adj* red
红茶 hóngchá *n* black tea
红绿灯 hónglǜdēng *n* traffic light
红色 hóngsè *n* red color
红烧 hóngshāo *v* braise in soy sauce
红十字会 hóngshízìhuì *n* the Red Cross
红糖 hóngtáng *n* brown sugar
宏伟 hóngwěi *adj* magnificent, grand
洪水 hóngshuǐ *n* flood
虹 hóng *n* rainbow
喉 hóu *n* larynx, throat; 喉炎 hóuyán *n* laryngitis
喉咙 hóulóng *n* throat
猴子 hóuzi *n* monkey
吼叫 hǒujiào *v* roar
后 hòu *n* rear, back; *adv* afterwards, later
后备 hòubèi *v* reserve

后背 **hòubèi** *n* back
后边 **hòubiān** *n* in the rear, at the back, behind
后代 **hòudài** *n* descendant, offspring
后果 **hòuguǒ** *n* consequence
后悔 **hòuhuǐ** *v* regret, repent
后来 **hòulái** *adv* later, subsequently
后门 **hòumén** *n* back door
后面 **hòumian** *n* in the rear, at the back, behind
后年 **hòunián** *n* the year after next
后天 **hòutiān** *n* day after tomorrow
后退 **hòutuì** *v* retreat, draw back
后院 **hòuyuàn** *n* backyard
后缀 **hòuzhuì** *n* suffix
厚 **hòu** *adj* thick; 厚度 **hòudù** *n* thickness
候车室 **hòuchēshì** *n* (*at a railway or bus station*) waiting room
候机室 **hòujīshì** *n* airport lounge
候选人 **hòuxuǎnrén** *n* candidate
呼喊 **hūhǎn** *n* shout, call
呼救 **hūjiù** *v* call for help
呼吸 **hūxī** *n* breath; *v* breathe
呼吁 **hūyù** *v* plead, appeal
忽然 **hūrán** *adv* suddenly, all of a sudden
忽视 **hūshì** *v* neglect, ignore, overlook
狐狸 **húli** *n* fox
胡椒 **hújiāo** *n* pepper
胡说 **húshuō** *n* nonsense; *v* talk nonsense
胡桃 **hútáo** *n* walnut
胡同 **hútòng** *n* alley, lane
胡子 **húzi** *n* beard, mustache, whiskers
胡萝卜 **húluóbo** *n* carrot
壶 **hú** *n* kettle
湖 **hú** *n* lake
糊涂 **hútu** *adj* confused, muddled, bewildered
蝴蝶 **húdié** *n* butterfly
虎 **hǔ** *n* tiger
互换 **hùhuàn** *v* exchange
互联网 **hùliánwǎng** *n* Internet
互相 **hùxiāng** *adv* each other, mutually
户内 **hù'nèi** *adj/adv* indoor
户外 **hùwài** *adj/adv* outdoor
护 **hù** *v* protect, guard, shield

护理 **hùlǐ** *v* nurse

护士 **hùshi** *n* nurse

护送 **hùsòng** *v* escort

护照 **hùzhào** *n* passport

花 **huā** *n* flower

花瓣 **huābàn** *n* petal

花茶 **huāchá** *n* scented tea

花费 **huāfèi** *v* spend

花岗岩 **huāgāngyán** *n* granite

花盆 **huāpén** *n* flowerpot

花瓶 **huāpíng** *n* vase

花圈 **huāquān** *n* wreath

花商 **huāshāng** *n* florist

花生 **huāshēng** *n* peanut

花样 **huāyàng** *n* pattern, variety; trick

花园 **huāyuán** *n* garden

华丽 **huálì** *adj* gorgeous, magnificent

华侨 **huáqiáo** *n* Chinese living outside of China

滑 **huá** *adj* slippery, smooth; *v* slip, slide

滑冰 **huábīng** *n* ice-skating, skating; 滑冰场 **huábīngchǎng** *n* skating rink

滑行 **huáxíng** *v* slide, coast; 滑行车 **huáxíng chē** *n* scooter

滑雪 **huáxuě** *v* ski; 滑雪板 **huáxuěbǎn** *n* skis

划 **huá** *v* paddle, row

化 **huà** *v* change, turn, transform, convert, melt, dissolve

化肥 **huàféi** *n* chemical fertilizer

化合 **huàhé** *n* (*chemical*) combination; 化合物 **huàhéwù** *n* chemical compound

化石 **huàshí** *n* fossil

化学 **huàxué** *n* chemistry; *adj* chemical; 化学家 **huàxuéjiā** *n* chemist

化验 **huàyàn** *n* laboratory test

化妆 **huàzhuāng** *v* put on makeup, make up; 化妆品 **huàzhuāngpǐn** *n* cosmetics

化装 **huàzhuāng** *v* (*of actors*) make up, disguise oneself

划分 **huàfēn** *v* divide

划清 **huàqīng** *v* draw a clear line of demarcation, make a clear distinction

画 **huà** *n* drawing, painting, picture; *v* paint, draw

画笔 **huàbǐ** *n* paintbrush

画册 **huàcè** *n* picture album

画家 **huàjiā** *n* painter

画廊 **huàláng** *n* gallery
画像 **huàxiàng** *v* draw a portrait, portray
话 **huà** *n* word, talk, speech, dialect
话剧 **huàjù** *n* drama, play
话题 **huàtí** *n* subject of a talk, topic of conversation
怀 **huái** *n* bosom
怀念 **huáiniàn** *v* cherish the memory of
怀疑 **huáiyí** *n* disbelief, suspicion, doubt; *v* doubt, suspect
怀孕 **huáiyùn** *v* be pregnant
坏 **huài** *adj* bad; *v* go bad, spoil, break
坏处 **huàichu** *n* harm, disadvantage, detriment
坏蛋 **huàidàn** *n* bad egg, scoundrel
坏话 **huàihuà** *n* malicious remarks, vicious talk
坏人 **huàirén** *n* villain, bad guy
欢呼 **huānhū** *v* hail, cheer, acclaim
欢乐 **huānlè** *adj* happy, joyous
欢庆 **huānqìng** *v* celebrate joyously
欢送 **huānsòng** *v* see off, send off
欢喜 **huānxǐ** *adj* joyful, happy, delighted
欢迎 **huānyíng** *n/v* welcome
还 **huán** *v* return, repay, give back
还原 **huányuán** *v* return to the original condition or shape, restore
还债 **huánzhài** *v* pay one's debt, repay a debt
环 **huán** *n* ring, hoop
环节 **huánjié** *n* link
环境 **huánjìng** *n* environment, circumstances, surroundings
环球 **huánqiú** *adj* round the world
环形 **huánxíng** *adj* ringlike
缓和 **huǎnhé** *v* relax, ease up, mitigate
缓慢 **huǎnmàn** *adj* slow
缓期 **huǎnqī** *v* postpone a deadline, suspend
缓刑 **huǎnxíng** *v* reprieve, suspend a sentence
幻灯 **huàndēng** *n* slide show; 幻灯机 **huàndēngjī** *n* slide projector
幻觉 **huànjué** *n* hallucination
幻想 **huànxiǎng** *n* fantasy, illusion
幻影 **huànyǐng** *n* illusion
唤起 **huànqǐ** *v* arouse, call, recall
唤醒 **huànxǐng** *v* wake up, awaken
换 **huàn** *v* change, exchange
换车 **huànchē** *v* change trains or buses

换钱 **huànqián** *v* change money
换算 **huànsuàn** *n* (*math*) conversion
患病 **huànbìng** *v* suffer from an illness, fall ill, be ill
患者 **huànzhě** *n* sufferer, patient
荒地 **huāngdì** *n* wasteland, uncultivated land
荒废 **huāngfèi** *v* lie waste, fall into disuse, neglect
荒凉 **huāngliáng** *adj* bleak and desolate
荒谬 **huāngmiù** *adj* absurd, ridiculous
慌 **huāng** *adj* flurried, flustered, panicked
慌忙 **huāngmáng** *adv* in a great rush, in a flurry, hurriedly
慌张 **huāngzhāng** *adj* flurried, flustered, confused
皇帝 **huángdì** *n* emperor
皇后 **huánghòu** *n* empress
黄 **huáng** *adj* yellow
黄疸 **huángdǎn** *n* jaundice
黄道 **huángdào** *n* zodiac
黄蜂 **huángfēng** *n* wasp
黄瓜 **huángguā** *n* cucumber
黄河 **huánghé** *n* the Yellow River
黄昏 **huánghūn** *n* dusk
黄金 **huángjīn** *n* gold
黄色 **huángsè** *n* yellow
黄鼠狼 **huángshǔláng** *n* weasel
谎言 **huǎngyán** *n* lie
晃动 **huàngdòng** *v* shake, rock, sway
灰 **huī** *n* ash
灰尘 **huīchén** *n* dust, dirt
灰色 **huīsè** *n* gray
灰心 **huīxīn** *v* lose heart, be discouraged
恢复 **huīfù** *v* resume, renew, recover, regain, restore
挥 **huī** *v* wield, wave
挥霍 **huīhuò** *v* spend freely, squander
挥手 **huīshǒu** *v* wave one's hand, wave
挥舞 **huīwǔ** *v* wave, wield, brandish
辉煌 **huīhuáng** *adj* brilliant, splendid, glorious
回 **huí** *v* return (*to a place*), go back
回报 **huíbào** *v* repay, reciprocate
回避 **huíbì** *v* evade, dodge, avoid
回答 **huídá** *n/v* answer, reply
回顾 **huígù** *v* review, look back
回话 **huíhuà** *n* reply, answer
回声 **huíshēng** *n* echo

回收 **huíshōu** *v* reclaim, retrieve, recycle
回头 **huítóu** *v* turn one's head, turn around
回响 **huíxiǎng** *v* reverberate, echo, resound
回想 **huíxiǎng** *v* think back, recollect, recall
回信 **huíxìn** *v* write back, reply a letter; *n* a letter in reply, written reply
回忆 **huíyì** *n* recollection; *v* recall, recollect; 回忆录 **huíyìlù** *n* memoirs
悔改 **huǐgǎi** *v* repent and mend one's ways
汇报 **huìbào** *v* report, give an account of
汇款 **huìkuǎn** *v* remit money; *n* remittance
汇率 **huìlǜ** *n* exchange rate
会[1] **huì** *n* meeting, gathering, party, get-together, conference; association, society union
会[2] **huì** *v* can, know how to, be good at, be skillful in, be likely to
会场 **huìchǎng** *n* meeting-place, conference hall
会话 **huìhuà** *n* conversation
会见 **huìjiàn** *v* meet with
会谈 **huìtán** *n* talk
会堂 **huìtáng** *n* assembly, hall, auditorium
会议 **huìyì** *n* conference, meeting
会员 **huìyuán** *n* member (*of an association*)
绘画 **huìhuà** *n* drawing, painting
绘制 **huìzhì** *v* draw (*a design*)
贿赂 **huìlù** *v* bribe; *n* bribery
毁坏 **huǐhuài** *v* ruin, destroy, devastate, ravage
毁灭 **huǐmiè** *v* destroy, exterminate
毁损 **huǐsǔn** *n* damage, impair, breakage
昏暗 **hūn'àn** *adj* dim
昏倒 **hūndǎo** *v* faint
昏迷 **hūnmí** *n* coma
荤 **hūn** *n* meat or fish; 荤菜 **hūncài** *n* meat dishes
婚礼 **hūnlǐ** *n* wedding
婚姻 **hūnyīn** *n* marriage
馄饨 **húntún** *n* dumpling soup, wonton
混合 **hùnhé** *v* blend, mix, mingle
混乱 **hùnluàn** *n* chaos, confusion
混淆 **hùnxiáo** *v* confuse, mix up
混杂 **hùnzá** *v* mix, mingle
活 **huó** *v* live; *adj* living, alive, live
活动 **huódòng** *n* activity, event; *v* move about, exercise

活泼 **huópo** *adj* animate, lively
活跃 **huóyuè** *adj* active
火 **huǒ** *n* fire
火柴 **huǒchái** *n* matches
火车 **huǒchē** *n* train; 火车站 **huǒchēzhàn** *n* train station
火锅 **huǒguō** *n* hot pot
火鸡 **huǒjī** *n* turkey
火箭 **huǒjiàn** *n* rocket
火警 **huǒjǐng** *n* fire alarm
火炬 **huǒjù** *n* torch
火炉 **huǒlú** *n* stove
火炮 **huǒpào** *n* artillery
火器 **huǒqì** *n* firearm
火山 **huǒshān** *n* volcano
火腿 **huǒtuǐ** *n* ham
火星 **huǒxīng** *n* Mars
火焰 **huǒyàn** *n* blaze, flame
火药 **huǒyào** *n* gunpowder
火葬 **huǒzàng** *n* cremation; *v* cremate
伙伴 **huǒbàn** *n* partner, companion, buddy
或者 **huòzhě** *conj* or
货 **huò** *n* goods, commodity, merchandise
货币 **huòbì** *n* currency, money
货车 **huòchē** *n* freight train, truck
货船 **huòchuán** *n* cargo ship
货机 **huòjī** *n* cargo aircraft, air freighter
货物 **huòwù** *n* cargo, freight, goods
货运 **huòyùn** *n* freight transport
获得 **huòdé** *v* attain, acquire, gain, obtain
获奖 **huòjiǎng** *v* win a prize or award
获胜 **huòshèng** *v* win a victory, be victorious, triumph
获悉 **huòxī** *v* learn (*of an event*)
祸 **huò** *n* misfortune, disaster, calamity

J

几乎 **jīhū** *adv* almost, nearly, practically
讥笑 **jīxiào** *v* ridicule, sneer at, deride
击败 **jībài** *v* defeat, beat
击剑 **jījiàn** *n* fencing
击退 **jītuì** *v* repel, beat back
饥饿 **jī'è** *n* hunger, starvation

机 **jī** *n* machine, engine
机场 **jīchǎng** *n* airport
机构 **jīgòu** *n* apparatus, establishment, organization, institution
机关 **jīguān** *n* organ, office, body
机关枪 **jīguānqiāng** *n* machine-gun
机会 **jīhuì** *n* chance, opportunity
机密 **jīmì** *adj* confidential, secret, classified
机票 **jīpiào** *n* airplane ticket
机器 **jīqì** *n* machine; 机器人 **jīqìrén** *n* robot
机械 **jīxiè** *n* machinery; *adj* mechanical
机遇 **jīyù** *n* favorable circumstances, opportunity
机智 **jīzhì** *adj* quick-witted, resourceful
肌肉 **jīròu** *n* muscle
鸡 **jī** *n* chicken
鸡蛋 **jīdàn** *n* chicken egg
迹象 **jīxiàng** *n* sign, indication
积 **jī** *adj* accumulate, amass, store up
积极 **jījí** *adj* active, positive
积累 **jīlěi** *v* accumulate
积蓄 **jīxù** *v* put aside, save, accumulate
基本 **jīběn** *adj* basic, essential
基层 **jīcéng** *n* basic level, primary level, local level
基础 **jīchǔ** *n* base, basis, foundation; 基础设施 **jīchǔ shèshī** *n* infrastructure
基督 **jīdū** *n* Christ; 基督教 **jīdūjiào** *n* Christianity; 基督徒 **jīdūtú** *n* Christian
基金 **jījīn** *n* fund; 基金会 **jījīnhuì** *n* foundation
基于 **jīyú** *prep* because of, in view of, on account of, on the basis of
畸形 **jīxíng** *n* deformity, malformation; *adj* lopsided, unbalanced, abnormal
激动 **jīdòng** *adj* excited, agitated
激发 **jīfā** *v* arouse, stir up, stimulate
激光 **jīguāng** *n* laser; 激光打印机 **jīguāng dǎyìnjī** *n* laser printer
激进 **jījìn** *adj* radical
激励 **jīlì** *v* encourage, inspire, urge
激怒 **jīnù** *v* enrage, aggravate, irritate, madden, provoke
激起 **jīqǐ** *v* arouse, stir up, evoke
激情 **jīqíng** *n* passion, enthusiasm, fervor
激战 **jīzhàn** *n* fierce fighting

奇数 **jīshù** *n* odd number
疾病 **jíbìng** *n* disease, illness, sickness
及格 **jígé** *v* pass a test or an examination
及时 **jíshí** *adj* timely, in time; *adv* promptly, without delay
吉利 **jílì** *adj* lucky, auspicious
吉他 **jítā** *n* guitar; 吉他手 **jítāshǒu** *n* guitarist
吉普车 **jípǔchē** *n* jeep
吉普赛人 **jípǔsàirén** *n* Gypsy
级 **jí** *n* level, rank, grade
即将 **jíjiāng** *adv* be about to, soon
即使 **jíshǐ** *conj* even if, even though
极度 **jídù** *adv* extremely, exceedingly
极端 **jíduān** *adj* extreme; 极端主义者 **jíduānzhǔyìzhě** *n* extremist
极力 **jílì** *v* do one's utmost, spare no effort
极其 **jíqí** *adv* exceedingly, extremely
极限 **jíxiàn** *n* limit, maximum
急 **jí** *adj* impatient, anxious, urgent, pressing
急病 **jíbìng** *n* acute disease
急救 **jíjiù** *n* first aid
急流 **jíliú** *n* torrent
急忙 **jímáng** *adv* in a hurry, in haste, hurriedly, hastily
急性病 **jíxìngbìng** *n* acute disease
急躁 **jízào** *adj* impatient, irritable
急诊 **jízhěn** *n* emergency treatment; 急诊室 **jízhěnshì** *n* emergency room
集 **jí** *n* collection, anthology; *v* collect
集合 **jíhé** *v* gather, assemble
集会 **jíhuì** *n* rally, assembly
集结 **jíjié** *v* mass, build up
集市 **jíshì** *n* country fair, market
集体 **jítǐ** *n* collective; 集体主义 **jítǐzhǔyì** *n* collectivism
集团 **jítuán** *n* bloc, group
集邮 **jíyóu** *n* stamp collection
集中 **jízhōng** *v* focus, concentrate; centralize
籍贯 **jíguàn** *n* place of birth
嫉妒 **jídù** *v* envy, be jealous of
几 **jǐ** *num* how many, a few, several
几何 **jǐhé** *n* geometry
挤 **jǐ** *v* squeeze, press, cram, pack; *adj* crowded, congested
脊柱 **jǐzhù** *n* spine, backbone

脊椎 **jǐzhuī** *n* backbone, spine; 脊椎动物 **jǐzhuī dòngwù** *n* vertebrate

计划 **jìhuà** *n/v* plan

计算 **jìsuàn** *v* count, compute, calculate; 计算机 **jìsuànjī** *n* computer; 计算器 **jìsuànqì** *n* calculator

记 **jì** *v* remember, bear in mind, commit to memory, write down, record

记得 **jìde** *v* remember

记号 **jìhao** *n* mark, sign

记录 **jìlù** *v* take notes, record; *n* notes, record, minute; 纪录片 **jìlùpiàn** *n* documentary film

记忆 **jìyì** *n* memory; 记忆力 **jìyìlì** *n* the faculty of memory

记者 **jìzhě** *n* reporter, journalist; 记者招待会 **jìzhě zhāodàihuì** *n* press conference

记住 **jìzhù** *v* learn by heart, remember

纪律 **jìlǜ** *n* discipline

纪念 **jìniàn** *v* commemorate; 纪念馆 **jìniànguǎn** *n* memorial hall; 纪念碑 **jìniànbēi** *n* monument; 纪念品 **jìniànpǐn** *n* souvenir

系 **jì** *v* tie, fasten

妓女 **jìnǚ** *n* prostitute

忌妒 **jìdu** *v* envy, be jealous of

忌讳 **jìhuì** *n* taboo

技工 **jìgōng** *n* mechanic technician, skilled worker

技能 **jìnéng** *n* skill, technique

技巧 **jìqiǎo** *n* skill, technique, craftsmanship

技师 **jìshī** *n* technician

技术 **jìshù** *n* know-how, technique, technology

技艺 **jìyì** *n* feat, skill, artistry

季度 **jìdù** *n* quarter (*of a year*)

季节 **jìjié** *n* season

既然 **jìrán** *conj* since, as, now that

继承 **jìchéng** *v* inherit, succeed; 继承人 **jìchéngrén** *n* heir, successor, inheritor

继父 **jìfù** *n* stepfather

继母 **jìmǔ** *n* stepmother

继续 **jìxù** *v* continue, go on, keep on

寂静 **jìjìng** *adj* silent, quiet, still

寂寞 **jìmò** *adj* lonely, lonesome

寄 **jì** *v* send, post, mail

寄存 **jìcún** *v* deposit, leave with sb.

寄件人 **jìjiànrén** *n* sender

寄宿 **jìsù** *v* lodge; 寄宿学校 **jìsùxuéxiào** *n* boarding school

祭祀 **jìsì** *n* offer sacrifices to gods or ancestors

加 **jiā** *v* add, increase

加班 **jiābān** *v* work overtime

加倍 **jiābèi** *v* double

加长 **jiācháng** *v* lengthen

加法 **jiāfǎ** *n* (*math*) addition

加工 **jiāgōng** *v* process

加快 **jiākuài** *v* quicken, accelerate, speed up

加仑 **jiālún** *n* gallon

加拿大 **jiānádà** *n* Canada; 加拿大人 **jiānádàrén** *n* (*people*) Canadian

加强 **jiāqiáng** *v* strengthen, enhance, reinforce

加热 **jiārè** *v* heat; 加热器 **jiārèqì** *n* heater

加入 **jiārù** *v* join

加深 **jiāshēn** *v* deepen

加速 **jiāsù** *v* accelerate, speed up

加油 **jiāyóu** *v* refuel, (*fig*) make an extra effort

加油站 **jiāyóuzhàn** *n* gas station, service station

夹 **jiā** *v* clip, clamp, pinch

夹子 **jiāzi** *n* clip

家 **jiā** *n* home, family, household

家长 **jiāzhǎng** *n* parent; 家长会 **jiāzhǎnghuì** *n* parent-teacher conference

家具 **jiājù** *n* furniture

家禽 **jiāqín** *n* poultry, domestic fowl

家庭 **jiātíng** *n* family, household; 家庭主妇 **jiātíng zhǔfù** *n* housewife; 家庭作业 **jiātíng zuòyè** *n* homework

家乡 **jiāxiāng** *n* hometown

家属 **jiāshǔ** *n* family members, dependents

甲板 **jiǎbǎn** *n* deck

甲骨文 **jiǎgǔwén** *n* inscriptions on bones or tortoise shell, oracle bones

价 **jià** *n* price, value

价格 **jiàgé** *n* price

价值 **jiàzhí** *n* value, worth

驾驶 **jiàshǐ** *v* drive (*a vehicle*), steer; 驾驶员 **jiàshǐyuán** *n* driver; 驾驶执照 **jiàshǐ zhízhào** *n* driver's license

架 **jià** *n* rack, shelf

架子 **jiàzi** *n* shelf, stand, rack

假 **jiǎ** *adj* fake, phony, false, pseudo-, sham, artificial

假扮 **jiǎbàn** *v* disguise

假定 **jiǎdìng** *v* presume, suppose, assume

假如 **jiǎrú** *conj* if, supposing, in case

假设 **jiǎshè** *v* assume, suppose

假想 **jiǎxiǎng** *adj* imaginary, hypothetical

假象 **jiǎxiàng** *n* false appearance

假肢 **jiǎzhī** *n* artificial limb

假装 **jiǎzhuāng** *v* pretend, make believe, feign

假 **jià** *n* holiday, vacation, leave of absence

假期 **jiàqī** *n* vacation, period of leave

假日 **jiàrì** *n* holiday, day off

奸污 **jiānwū** *v* rape

尖 **jiān** *n* point, tip, top; *adj* pointed, piercing, sharp

尖端 **jiānduān** *adj* most advanced, sophisticated, state-of-the-art

尖锐 **jiānruì** *adj* penetrating, incisive, sharp, keen

坚持 **jiānchí** *v* adhere to, persevere in, persist in, insist on

坚定 **jiāndìng** *adj* firm, resolute, steadfast

坚固 **jiāngù** *adj* firm, solid, sturdy, strong

坚果 **jiānguǒ** *n* nut

坚强 **jiānqiáng** *adj* strong, firm, staunch

坚韧 **jiānrèn** *adj* firm and tenacious

坚硬 **jiānyìng** *adj* hard, solid

歼灭 **jiānmiè** *v* annihilate, wipe out

间 **jiān** *n* room; *cl (for rooms)*

肩 **jiān** *n* shoulder

肩膀 **jiānbǎng** *n* shoulder

艰苦 **jiānkǔ** *adj* laborious, arduous, hard

艰难 **jiānnán** *adj* difficult, hard

兼容 **jiānróng** *adj* compatible

兼职 **jiānzhí** *v* hold two or more jobs concurrently

监督 **jiāndū** *v* oversee, supervise

监禁 **jiānjìn** *v* imprison, jail

监视 **jiānshì** *v* keep watch on, keep a lookout over

监狱 **jiānyù** *n* jail, prison; 监狱长 **jiānyùzhǎng** *n* warden

监护人 **jiānhùrén** *n* guardian

煎 **jiān** *v* fry

捡 **jiǎn** *v* pick up, collect, gather

减 **jiǎn** *v* subtract, reduce, cut, decrease

减法 **jiǎnfǎ** *n* (*math*) subtraction

减肥 **jiǎnféi** *v* reduce weight

减价 **jiǎnjià** *v* reduce the price, mark down

减轻 **jiǎnqīng** *v* lighten, ease, alleviate, mitigate

减弱 **jiǎnruò** *v* weaken, abate

减少 **jiǎnshǎo** *v* decrease, diminish, lessen, reduce

剪 **jiǎn** *v* cut (*with scissors*), clip, trim

剪刀 **jiǎndāo** *n* scissors

剪纸 **jiǎnzhǐ** *n* paper-cut

检查 **jiǎnchá** *n* examination, inspection; *v* examine, inspect, look over, check up; 检查员 **jiǎncháyuán** *n* inspector; 检查站 **jiǎncházhàn** *n* checkpoint

检验 **jiǎnyàn** *v* test, examine, inspect

检阅 **jiǎnyuè** *v* review (*troops*, *etc.*)

简称 **jiǎnchēng** *n* abbreviation

简单 **jiǎndān** *adj* simple, uncomplicated, straightforward

简短 **jiǎnduǎn** *adj* brief, short

简化 **jiǎnhuà** *v* simplify

简洁 **jiǎnjié** *adj* succinct, concise, terse

简介 **jiǎnjiè** *n* brief introduction, synopsis

简历 **jiǎnlì** *n* resume, curriculum vitae

简明 **jiǎnmíng** *adj* simple and clear, concise

简体字 **jiǎntǐzì** *n* simplified Chinese character

简要 **jiǎnyào** *adj* concise and to the point

简易 **jiǎnyì** *adj* simple and easy

简直 **jiǎnzhí** *adv* simply, virtually

间谍 **jiàndié** *n* spy

间断 **jiànduàn** *adj* be disconnected, be interrupted

间隔 **jiàngé** *n* interval

间接 **jiànjiē** *adv* indirectly

间歇 **jiànxiē** *n* intermission

见 **jiàn** *v* see, catch sight of, meet with

见解 **jiànjiě** *n* view, opinion, idea

见面 **jiànmiàn** *v* meet sb., see sb.

见识 **jiànshi** *n* knowledge, experience

件 **jiàn** *n* piece, letter, paper, document; *cl* (*for clothes, furniture, tasks, etc.*)

建 **jiàn** *v* build, construct, erect, establish, set up

建交 **jiànjiāo** *v* establish diplomatic relations

建立 **jiànlì** *v* establish, set up, build, found

建设 **jiànshè** *v* construct, build; 建设性 **jiànshèxìng** *adj* constructive

建议 **jiànyì** *n* proposal, suggestion; *v* propose, suggest

建造 **jiànzào** *v* build, construct

建筑 **jiànzhù** *n* architecture, building; 建筑师 **jiànzhùshī** *n* architect

剑 jiàn *n* sword
健康 jiànkāng *n* health, physique; *adj* healthy
舰队 jiànduì *n* fleet
渐渐 jiànjiàn *adv* gradually, by degrees
溅 jiàn *v* splash, spatter
鉴别 jiànbié *v* distinguish, differentiate, discriminate, discern, identify
鉴定 jiàndìng *v* appraise, identify, authenticate
键盘 jiànpán *n* keyboard
箭 jiàn *n* arrow
箭头 jiàntóu *n* arrowhead, arrow
江 jiāng *n* river
将 jiāng *adv* be going to, be about to, will, shall
将近 jiāngjìn *adv* close to, nearly, almost
将军 jiāngjūn *n* (*military*) general
将来 jiānglái *n* future
浆果 jiāngguǒ *n* berry
缰绳 jiāngshéng *n* reins
讲 jiǎng *v* speak, say, tell, talk about, explain, interpret
讲话 jiǎnghuà *v* talk, speak, address; *n* speech, talk, address
讲究 jiǎngjiu *v* be particular about
讲课 jiǎngkè *v* teach a class, lecture
讲明 jiǎngmíng *v* explain, make clear
讲师 jiǎngshī *n* lecturer
讲座 jiǎngzuò *n* lecture
奖 jiǎng *n* award, prize; *v* reward, award
奖金 jiǎngjīn *n* bonus
奖励 jiǎnglì *v* encourage and reward, award
奖牌 jiǎngpái *n* medal
奖品 jiǎngpǐn *n* prize, trophy
奖赏 jiǎngshǎng *v* reward, award
奖学金 jiǎngxuéjīn *n* scholarship
奖章 jiǎngzhāng *n* medal
降低 jiàngdī *v* reduce, cut down, lower
降落 jiàngluò *v* descend, land, touch down
降落伞 jiàngluòsǎn *n* parachute
酱 jiàng *n* sauce, paste, jam
酱油 jiàngyóu *n* soy sauce
糨糊 jiànghu *n* paste, glue
交 jiāo *v* hand in, deliver, submit; cross, intersect; associate with, make friends
交叉 jiāochā *v* intersect, cross, alternate, stagger

交出 **jiāo chū** *v* surrender, hand over
交换 **jiāohuàn** *n/v* exchange
交际 **jiāojì** *v* communicate; *n* communication
交流 **jiāoliú** *n/v* exchange, interchange
交情 **jiāoqing** *n* friendship, friendly relation
交谈 **jiāotán** *n* conversation; *v* converse
交通 **jiāotōng** *n* traffic; 交通堵塞 **jiāotōng dǔsè** *n* traffic jam; 交通工具 **jiāotōng gōngjù** *n* means of transportation
交往 **jiāowǎng** *n* association, contact
交响乐 **jiāoxiǎngyuè** *n* symphony
交易 **jiāoyì** *n* deal, business, trade, transaction; 交易会 **jiāoyìhuì** *n* trade fair
交战 **jiāozhàn** *v* be at war, fight, clash
郊区 **jiāoqū** *n* suburbs
浇 **jiāo**¹ *v* pour liquid on, sprinkle water on
教 **jiāo**² *v* teach, instruct
教书 **jiāoshū** *v* teach (*in a school*)
胶带 **jiāodài** *n* (*sticky*) tape
胶合 **jiāohé** *v* glue
胶卷 **jiāojuǎn** *n* film
胶水 **jiāoshuǐ** *n* glue
焦点 **jiāodiǎn** *n* focus
焦急 **jiāojí** *adj* anxious, worried
礁石 **jiāoshí** *n* reef, rock
嚼 **jiáo** *v* chew
角 **jiǎo** *n* angle, corner; horn, *jiao* (*Chinese monetary unit*)
角度 **jiǎodù** *n* angle, perspective
角落 **jiǎoluò** *n* corner
绞 **jiǎo** *v* twist, wring, entangle, hang by the neck
绞刑 **jiǎoxíng** *n* death by hanging
饺子 **jiǎozi** *n* dumpling
脚 **jiǎo** *n* foot
脚本 **jiǎoběn** *n* (*movie, play, etc.*) script
脚步 **jiǎobù** *n* step, pace
脚跟 **jiǎogēn** *n* heel
脚腕 **jiǎowàn** *n* ankle
脚掌 **jiǎozhǎng** *n* sole
脚趾 **jiǎozhǐ** *n* toe
搅拌 **jiǎobàn** *n* stir, mix
搅动 **jiǎodòng** *v* stir
搅乱 **jiǎoluàn** *v* disrupt, confuse
叫 **jiào** *v* cry, shout, call; order food (*at a restaurant*)

叫喊 jiàohǎn *v* yell, shout
叫做 jiàozuò *v* be called, be known as
轿车 jiàochē *n* car
校订 jiàodìng *v* revise, proof-read
较 jiào *adv* comparatively, relatively, quite, rather
教材 jiàocái *n* textbook, teaching material
教皇 jiàohuáng *n* pope
教会 jiàohuì *n* church
教练 jiàoliàn *n* coach, instructor, trainer
教派 jiàopài *n* sect
教区 jiàoqū *n* parish
教师 jiàoshī *n* teacher
教室 jiàoshì *n* classroom
教授 jiàoshòu *n* professor
教堂 jiàotáng *n* church
教学 jiàoxué *n* teaching; 教学大纲 jiàoxué dàgāng *n* syllabus
教训 jiàoxùn *n* lesson, moral
教育 jiàoyù *n* education; *v* educate
教员 jiàoyuán *n* instructor, teacher
教科书 jiàokēshū *n* textbook
阶段 jiēduàn *n* phase, stage
接 jiē *v* meet, pick up; connect, join, put together, receive
接触 jiēchù *v* get in touch with, contact; *n* contact
接待 jiēdài *v* receive (*guests, visitors*); *n* reception; 接待员 jiēdàiyuán *n* receptionist
接管 jiēguǎn *v* take over
接见 jiējiàn *v* grant an audience to
接近 jiējìn *v* be close to, near, approach
接连 jiēlián *adv* on end, in a row, in succession
接纳 jiēnà *v* admit (*into an organization*)
接收 jiēshōu *v* receive, take over, admit
接受 jiēshòu *v* accept
接替 jiētì *v* take over, replace, succeed
接通 jiē tōng *v* put through, get connected
揭露 jiēlù *v* expose, uncover
街 jiē *n* street
街道 jiēdào *n* neighborhood, street
街角 jiējiǎo *n* corner
街头 jiētóu *n* street corner
节 jié *n* festival, holiday
节目 jiémù *n* program, item (*on a program*)
节日 jiérì *n* festival, holiday

节约 **jiéyuē** *v* economize, save
节奏 **jiézòu** *n* rhythm, pace
劫持 **jiéchí** *v* hijack, kidnap
杰出 **jiéchū** *adj* brilliant, distinguished, outstanding
杰作 **jiézuò** *n* masterpiece
结 **jié** *n* knot, tie; *v* form, forge; settle, conclude
结伴 **jiébàn** *v* go with sb.
结冰 **jiébīng** *v* freeze, ice up
结构 **jiégòu** *n* construction, framework, structure
结果 **jiéguǒ** *n* outcome, result; *adv* as a result
结合 **jiéhé** *v* integrate, combine, link
结婚 **jiéhūn** *v* get married, wed
结交 **jiéjiāo** *v* associate with, make friends with
结论 **jiélùn** *n* conclusion
结盟 **jiéméng** *v* align, ally, form an alliance with
结识 **jiéshí** *v* get to know, get acquainted with
结束 **jiéshù** *v* end, finish, conclude, close
结尾 **jiéwěi** *n* ending
结余 **jiéyú** *n* balance, surplus
捷径 **jiéjìng** *n* shortcut
睫毛 **jiémáo** *n* eyelash
截断 **jiéduàn** *v* cut off, block
截肢 **jiézhī** *n* amputation
截止 **jiézhǐ** *v* close; 截止时间 **jiézhǐ shíjiān** *n* deadline
姐夫 **jiěfu** *n* brother-in-law *(older sister's husband)*
姐姐 **jiějie** *n* older sister
解 **jiě** *v* untie, undo, allay, dispel, solve, separate
解除 **jiěchú** *v* relieve *(sb. from office)*, remove, get rid of, lift *(a ban)*
解答 **jiědá** *v* answer, explain
解冻 **jiědòng** *v* thaw, unfreeze
解毒剂 **jiědújì** *n* antidote
解放 **jiěfàng** *n* liberation, emancipation; *v* liberate, emancipate
解雇 **jiěgù** *v* dismiss, fire, lay off
解决 **jiějué** *v* resolve, settle, solve
解开 **jiěkāi** *v* undo, unfasten, unleash, untie
解散 **jiěsàn** *v* dissolve, dismiss, disband
解释 **jiěshì** *n* explanation, interpretation; *v* explain, interpret
介词 **jiècí** *n* preposition
介绍 **jièshào** *n* introduction, presentation; *v* introduce
介意 **jièyì** *v* mind, care about
戒指 **jièzhi** *n* ring

界限 **jièxiàn** *n* bounds, limits, demarcation line
借 **jiè** *v* borrow, lend
借方 **jièfāng** *n* debtor
借口 **jièkǒu** *n* excuse, pretext
借款 **jièkuǎn** *n* loan
今后 **jīnhòu** *n* henceforth, from now on
今年 **jīnnián** *n* this year
今日 **jīnrì** *n* today
今天 **jīntiān** *n* today
今晚 **jīnwǎn** *n* this evening
今夜 **jīnyè** *n* tonight
斤 **jīn** *n* Chinese measurement for weight equal to ½ kilogram
金 **jīn** *n* gold, metals
金钱 **jīnqián** *n* money
金融 **jīnróng** *n* finance
金色 **jīnsè** *adj* golden; *n* golden color
金鱼 **jīnyú** *n* goldfish
金属 **jīnshǔ** *n* metal
金子 **jīnzi** *n* gold
金字塔 **jīnzìtǎ** *n* pyramid
津贴 **jīntiē** *n* allowance, subsidy
矜持 **jīnchí** *adj* reserved, restrained
筋疲力尽 **jīnpí lìjìn** *adj* exhausted, worn out, tired
仅 **jǐn** *adv* merely, only
仅仅 **jǐnjǐn** *adv* merely, only
紧 **jǐn** *adj* tight
紧急 **jǐnjí** *adj* urgent, pressing, critical; 紧急情况 **jǐnjí qíngkuàng** *n* emergency
紧邻 **jǐnlín** *n* close neighbor
紧密 **jǐnmì** *adj* close, inseparable
紧张 **jǐnzhāng** *adj* nervous, tense, strained
谨慎 **jǐnshèn** *adj* cautious, discreet, prudent
锦标赛 **jǐnbiāosài** *n* championships
尽管 **jǐnguǎn** *prep* despite
尽量 **jìnliàng** *adv* to the best of one's ability, as far as possible
尽力 **jìnlì** *v* do all one can, try one's best
尽情 **jìnqíng** *adv* to one's heart's content
尽早 **jìnzǎo** *adv* as soon as possible
近 **jìn** *adj* near, close; *adv* almost, close to
近便 **jìnbiàn** *adj* close and convenient
近海 **jìnhǎi** *adj* offshore
近来 **jìnlái** *adv* lately, recently

近视 jìnshì *adj* near-sighted, short-sighted
近似 jìnsì *adj* approximate, similar
进 jìn *v* enter, come in
进步 jìnbù *n/v* progress, advance
进化 jìnhuà *n* evolution
进口 jìnkǒu *n* import, entrance; *v* import
进入 jìnrù *v* enter, go into
进行 jìnxíng *v* go on, be underway, carry on
进一步 jìnyībù *adv* further
晋升 jìnshēng *n* promotion (*to a higher office*); *v* promote
    (*to a higher office*)
浸 jìn *v* soak
浸洗礼 jìnxǐlǐ *n* baptism
禁忌 jìnjì *n* taboo
禁运 jìnyùn *n* embargo
禁止 jìnzhǐ *v* forbid, prohibit
京剧 jīngjù *n* Peking opera
经 jīng *n* classics, scripture
经常 jīngcháng *adv* often, frequently
经典 jīngdiǎn *n* classics
经度 jīngdù *n* longitude
经费 jīngfèi *n* funds, outlay, budget
经过 jīngguò *v* pass, go through, undergo; *prep* through;
    after; *n* process, course
经济 jīngjì *n* economy; *adj* economic; economical; 经济学
    jīngjìxué *n* economics; 经济学家 jīngjìxuéjiā *n*
    economist
经理 jīnglǐ *n* manager
经历 jīnglì *n* experience; *v* go through, undergo, experience
经验 jīngyàn *n* experience
经营 jīngyíng *v* deal, manage, run (*a business*)
经销商 jīngxiāoshāng *n* dealer
茎 jīng *n* stalk, stem
惊慌 jīnghuāng *adj* alarmed, scared, panic-stricken
惊恐 jīngkǒng *adj* terrified, panic-stricken
惊奇 jīngqí *v* be surprised, wonder
惊人 jīngrén *adj* astonishing, amazing, alarming
惊叹 jīngtàn *v* wonder, marvel, exclaim
惊吓 jīngxià *v* frighten, scare
惊异 jīngyì *adj* surprised, amazed, astonished
惊险小说 jīngxiǎn xiǎoshuō *n* thriller
精彩 jīngcǎi *adj* splendid, wonderful

精华 jīnghuá *n* essence

精力 jīnglì *n* energy, vigor

精炼 jīngliàn *v* refine, purify; 精炼厂 jīngliànchǎng *n* refinery

精美 jīngměi *adj* exquisite, elegant

精明 jīngmíng *adj* astute, shrewd, sagacious

精巧 jīngqiǎo *adj* ingenious, exquisite

精确 jīngquè *adj* precise, accurate

精神 jīngshén *n* spirit, mind, consciousness, essence

精神病 jīngshénbìng *n* mental disease, mental disorder; 精神病学 jīngshénbìngxué *n* psychiatry; 精神病院 jīngshénbìngyuàn *n* mental hospital

精通 jīngtōng *v* be proficient in, have a good command of

精细 jīngxì *adj* meticulous, fine

精心 jīngxīn *adv* meticulously, painstakingly

精选 jīngxuǎn *v* carefully select

精液 jīngyè *n* semen, sperm

精致 jīngzhì *adj* delicate, exquisite

精子 jīngzǐ *n* sperm

鲸鱼 jīngyú *n* whale

井 jǐng *n* well

景 jǐng *n* view, scenery, scene

景色 jǐngsè *n* scenery, view, scene, landscape

景泰蓝 jǐngtàilán *n* cloisonné enamel

景象 jǐngxiàng *n* sight, scene

警报 jǐngbào *n* alarm, siren

警察 jǐngchá *n* police, police officer; police force; 警察局 jǐngchájú *n* police department

警告 jǐnggào *n* warning; *v* warn, caution

警戒 jǐngjiè *v* guard against

警惕 jǐngtì *adj* alert, vigilant

警卫 jǐngwèi *n* guard

净化 jìnghuà *v* purify

净余 jìngyú *adj* net

竞赛 jìngsài *n* contest, competition, race

竞选 jìngxuǎn *v* campaign for (*office*), run for (*office*)

竞争 jìngzhēng *v* compete; *n* competition

竞技场 jìngjìchǎng *n* arena

竟然 jìngrán *adv* to one's surprise, unexpectedly

敬礼 jìnglǐ *v* salute

敬佩 jìngpèi *v* admire, esteem

敬畏 jìngwèi *v* revere, hold in awe and veneration

敬意 jìngyì *n* respect, tribute
静 jìng *adj* quiet, tranquil
静脉 jìngmài *n* vein
静止 jìngzhǐ *adj* static, motionless
镜头 jìngtóu *n* camera lens
镜子 jìngzi *n* mirror, looking-glass
窘境 jiǒngjìng *n* dilemma
纠缠 jiūchán *v* pester, nag; get entangled
纠正 jiūzhèng *v* correct, put right, redress, rectify
九 jiǔ *num* nine
九十 jiǔshí *num* ninety
九月 jiǔyuè *n* September
久 jiǔ *n* a long time
酒 jiǔ *n* liquor, wine, spirits, alcohol
酒吧 jiǔbā *n* bar
酒厂 jiǔchǎng *n* brewery, winery, distillery
酒店 jiǔdiàn *n* wineshop, liquor store
酒馆 jiǔguǎn *n* pub, tavern
酒窖 jiǔjiào *n* cellar
酒精 jiǔjīng *n* alcohol
旧 jiù *adj* (*of things*) old, used
救 jiù *v* rescue, save
救护车 jiùhùchē *n* ambulance
救火 jiùhuǒ *v* fight fire; 救火车 jiùhuǒchē *n* fire engine
救济 jiùjì *v* provide relief
救命 jiùmìng *v* save sb.'s life; *interj* Help!
救生 jiùshēng *n* lifesaving; 救生圈 jiùshēngquān *n* lifebelt;
    救生艇 jiùshēngtǐng *n* lifeboat; 救生衣 jiùshēngyī *n* life
    jacket
救灾 jiùzāi *v* provide disaster relief
就 jiù *adv* at once, right away, as early as, already, as soon
    as, right after, then, only, merely, just, exactly, precisely
就是 jiùshì *adv* even if, even
就要 jiùyào *adv* be about to, be going to, be on the verge of
就业 jiùyè *n* employment; *v* obtain employment
舅舅 jiùjiu *n* uncle (*mother's brother*)
舅母 jiùmu *n* aunt (*wife of mother's brother*)
居民 jūmín *n* dweller, inhabitant, resident
居住 jūzhù *v* live, reside, dwell
拘谨 jūjǐn *adj* overcautious, reserved
拘留 jūliú *v* detain, hold in custody
局 jú *n* office, bureau; *cl* (*game, etc.*)

局部 júbù *n* part; *adj* partial, local
局面 júmiàn *n* situation, prospects
局势 júshì *n* situation
沮丧 jǔsàng *adj* depressed, dispirited, disheartened
举 jǔ *v* lift, raise, hold up
举办 jǔbàn *v* conduct, hold (*a meeting, ceremony, etc.*)
举例 jǔlì *v* give an example, cite an instance
举手 jǔshǒu *v* raise one's hand
举行 jǔxíng *v* hold (*a meeting, ceremony, etc.*)
举止 jǔzhǐ *n* manner, bearing, conduct
举重 jǔzhòng *n* weight lifting
句法 jùfǎ *n* syntax
句号 jùhào *n* (*punctuation*) period
句子 jùzi *n* sentence
巨大 jùdà *adj* enormous, gigantic, huge, immense, massive, tremendous, vast
巨人 jùrén *n* giant
拒绝 jùjué *v* refuse, reject, turn down
具 jù *n* utensil, tool, implement
具备 jùbèi *v* possess, have
具体 jùtǐ *adj* concrete, specific, particular
俱乐部 jùlèbù *n* club
剧 jù *n* drama, play, opera
剧场 jùchǎng *n* theatre
剧团 jùtuán *n* theatrical company, opera troupe
剧院 jùyuàn *n* theatre
剧作家 jùzuòjiā *n* playwright
惧怕 jùpà *v* fear, dread
据说 jùshuō *v* it is said, they say
距离 jùlí *n* distance
飓风 jùfēng *n* hurricane
锯 jù *v* saw
锯子 jùzi *n* saw
聚 jù *v* gather
聚光灯 jùguāngdēng *n* spotlight
聚会 jùhuì *n* get-together; *v* get together
聚集 jùjí *v* gather, assemble
聚焦 jùjiāo *n* focus
捐 juān *v* contribute, donate
捐款 juānkuǎn *v* donate money
捐献 juānxiàn *v* donate, contribute
捐赠 juānzèng *v* donate, contribute

卷 **juǎn** *v* roll up; *n* roll, spool, reel
卷尺 **juǎnchǐ** *n* tape measure
卷心菜 **juǎnxīncài** *n* cabbage
卷 **juàn** *n* volume, file, dossier
卷子 **juànzi** *n* examination paper
决定 **juédìng** *n* decision; *v* decide, determine
决赛 **juésài** *n* (*sports*) final
决心 **juéxīn** *n* determination, resolution, resolve; *v* resolve
决议 **juéyì** *n* resolution
诀窍 **juéqiào** *n* knack, trick
绝对 **juéduì** *adj* absolute, unconditional; *adv* absolutely
绝食 **juéshí** *v* go on a hunger strike
绝望 **juéwàng** *v* despair
绝种 **juézhǒng** *v* become extinct, die out
觉察 **juéchá** *v* detect, become aware of
觉得 **juéde** *v* feel, think, find
爵士乐 **juéshìyuè** *n* jazz
角色 **juésè** *n* role, part
军 **jūn** *n* armed forces, army, troops; *adj* military
军队 **jūnduì** *n* armed forces, military troops
军官 **jūnguān** *n* military officer
军舰 **jūnjiàn** *n* warship, naval vessel
军人 **jūnrén** *n* soldier, serviceman
军事 **jūnshì** *n* military affairs
军衔 **jūnxián** *n* military rank
军营 **jūnyíng** *n* barracks
军装 **jūnzhuāng** *n* military uniform
君主 **jūnzhǔ** *n* monarch, sovereign; 君主政体 **junzhǔ zhèngtǐ** *n* monarchy
均等 **jūnděng** *adj* equal, impartial, fair
郡 **jùn** *n* shire, county

K

咖啡 **kāfēi** *n* coffee; 咖啡馆 **kāfēiguǎn** *n* café, coffee shop
卡车 **kǎchē** *n* truck
卡片 **kǎpiàn** *n* card
卡通 **kǎtōng** *n* cartoon
开 **kāi** *v* open, open up, turn on, start, operate, drive, run, set up; hold (*a meeting*); write out; make out (*a check*); reclaim
开车 **kāichē** *v* drive, (*of vehicles*) start, depart

开除 **kāichú** *v* dismiss, fire, expel
开刀 **kāidāo** *v* perform or have an operation
开端 **kāiduān** *n* opening, beginning
开发 **kāifā** *v* develop, open up, exploit; 开发商 **kāifāshāng** *n* developer
开关 **kāiguān** *n* switch
开花 **kāihuā** *v* bloom, blossom
开会 **kāihuì** *v* have a meeting, attend a meeting
开垦 **kāikěn** *v* reclaim, clear a wild area for cultivation
开口 **kāikǒu** *v* start to talk, begin to talk
开始 **kāishǐ** *n* beginning; *v* begin, start, embark upon
开水 **kāishuǐ** *n* boiling water, boiled water
开庭 **kāitíng** *v* open a court session, call the court to order
开头 **kāitóu** *v* start, begin; *n* beginning
开玩笑 **kāiwánxiào** *v* crack a joke
开胃 **kāiwèi** *v* whet the appetite
开心 **kāixīn** *adj* feel happy, rejoice, be delighted
开学 **kāixué** *v* school starts, term begins
开展 **kāizhǎn** *v* develop, launch, unfold, carry out
刊物 **kānwù** *n* publication
勘探 **kāntàn** *n* exploration, prospecting
看守 **kānshǒu** *v* guard, watch
砍 **kǎn** *v* chop, hack
看 **kàn** *v* look at, see, watch, read
看病 **kànbìng** *v* see a doctor, go to a doctor
看不起 **kànbuqǐ** *v* look down upon, scorn, despise
看成 **kànchéng** *v* look upon as, regard as, treat as
看穿 **kànchuān** *v* see through
看到 **kàndào** *v* see, catch sight of
看法 **kànfǎ** *n* view, opinion
看见 **kànjiàn** *v* see
看起来 **kànqǐlái** *v* look like, seem, appear
看书 **kànshū** *v* read
看医生 **kàn yīshēng** *v* go to a doctor
看做 **kànzuò** *v* look upon as, regard as
慷慨 **kāngkǎi** *adj* generous, liberal
扛 **káng** *v* carry on the shoulder
抗 **kàng** *v* resist, combat, fight
抗生素 **kàngshēngsù** *n* antibiotics
抗议 **kàngyì** *n/v* protest
考古学 **kǎogǔxué** *n* archaeology
考虑 **kǎolǜ** *v* consider

考试 **kǎoshì** *v* take an exam; *n* examination, test
拷打 **kǎodǎ** *v* torture, beat
烤 **kǎo** *v* bake, toast
烤肉 **kǎoròu** *n* barbecue
烤肉串 **kǎoròuchuàn** *n* kebab
烤箱 **kǎoxiāng** *n* oven
靠 **kào** *v* lean against, lean on, get near, near
靠近 **kàojìn** *prep* near, close to, by; *v* approach, draw near
科 **kē** *n* branch of academic study; section
科技 **kējì** *n* science and technology
科学 **kēxué** *n* science; *adj* scientific; 科学家 **kēxuéjiā** *n* scientist
蝌蚪 **kēdǒu** *n* tadpole
壳 **ké** *n* shell
咳嗽 **késou** *n/v* cough
可爱 **kě'ài** *adj* cute, lovely
可耻 **kěchǐ** *adj* disgraceful, shameful, ignominious
可观 **kěguān** *adj* considerable
可见度 **kějiàndù** *n* visibility
可敬 **kějìng** *adj* honorable, respectable
可靠 **kěkào** *adj* dependable, reliable; 可靠性 **kěkàoxìng** *n* reliability
可口可乐 **kěkǒu kělè** *n* Coca Cola
可怜 **kělián** *adj* pathetic, pitiful
可能 **kěnéng** *adj* possible, probable; *adv* possibly, maybe; 可能性 **kěnéngxìng** *n* likelihood, possibility, probability
可怕 **kěpà** *adj* awful, terrible, terrifying
可是 **kěshì** *conj* but, yet, however
可恶 **kěwù** *adj* hateful
可惜 **kěxī** *adj* it's a pity, unfortunately
可笑 **kěxiào** *adj* absurd, comic, funny, laughable, ridiculous
可信 **kěxìn** *adj* credible
可信赖 **kěxìnlài** *adj* trustworthy
可行 **kěxíng** *adj* feasible, workable
可疑 **kěyí** *adj* dubious, questionable, suspicious
可以 **kěyǐ** *aux* can, may; *adj* pretty good
渴望 **kěwàng** *v* long for, yearn for
克 **kè** *n* gram
克服 **kèfú** *v* conquer, overcome
克制 **kèzhì** *v* restrain; *n* restraint
刻 **kè** *n* quarter of an hour, moment
客 **kè** *n* guest

客观 kèguān *adj* objective
客户 kèhù *n* client
客气 kèqi *adj* polite, courteous
客人 kèrén *n* guest
客厅 kètīng *n* living room
客栈 kèzhàn *n* hostel, inn
课 kè *n* lesson, subject, course, class
课程 kèchéng *n* course, curriculum
课堂 kètáng *n* classroom
课文 kèwén *n* text
肯定 kěndìng *adj* positive, affirmative, definite, certain; *adv* certainly, definitely; *v* affirm, confirm
空 kōng *adj* empty, vacant
空调 kōngtiáo *n* air-conditioning; 空调器 kōngtiáoqì *n* air conditioner
空间 kōngjiān *n* space
空军 kōngjūn *n* airforce
空气 kōngqì *n* air
空袭 kōngxí *n* air-raid
空想 kōngxiǎng *adj* fantasy
空心 kōngxīn *adj* hollow
空虚 kōngxū *adj* hollow, empty
空中 kōngzhōng *adj* aerial, in the sky, in the air
孔子 kǒngzǐ *n* Confucius
恐怖 kǒngbù *n* horror, terror; *adj* ghastly, horrible, terrifying; 恐怖分子 kǒngbùfēnzǐ *n* terrorist; 恐怖主义 kǒngbùzhǔyì *n* terrorism
恐吓 kǒnghè *v* threaten, intimidate
恐慌 kǒnghuāng *adj* panic-stricken, scared
恐惧 kǒngjù *n* fear, dread
恐龙 kǒnglóng *n* dinosaur
恐怕 kǒngpà *adj* afraid
空白 kòngbái *adj* blank; *n* blank, space, gap, margin
空格 kònggé *n* blank, space (*on a form*)
空缺 kòngquē *n* (*job*) vacancy
空闲 kòngxián *adj* idle, free; *n* free time, spare time, leisure
控告 kònggào *v* accuse, charge, sue; *n* accusation
控制 kòngzhì *n/v* control
口 kǒu *n* mouth; opening, entrance
口才 kǒucái *n* eloquence, speechcraft
口袋 kǒudai *n* pocket
口服 kǒufú *v* take (*medicine*) orally

口供 **kǒugòng** *n* deposition, verbal confession

口号 **kǒuhào** *n* slogan

口渴 **kǒukě** *adj* thirsty

口气 **kǒuqì** *n* tone, manner of speaking

口哨 **kǒushào** *n* whistle

口授 **kǒushòu** *v* dictate

口头 **kǒutóu** *adj* oral, verbal

口味 **kǒuwèi** *n* flavor, taste

口译 **kǒuyì** *v* interpret; 口译员 **kǒuyìyuán** *n* interpreter

口音 **kǒuyīn** *n* accent

口语 **kǒuyǔ** *n* spoken language; *adj* colloquial

扣 **kòu** *v* deduct; button up, buckle; detain, arrest

扣除 **kòuchú** *v* deduct

扣留 **kòuliú** *v* detain, hold in custody

扣子 **kòuzi** *n* button

枯燥 **kūzào** *adj* dull and dry, uninteresting

哭 **kū** *v* cry, weep

哭泣 **kūqì** *v* weep, sob

苦 **kǔ** *adj* bitter

苦闷 **kǔmèn** *adj* depressed, dejected, feeling low, gloomy

库存 **kùcún** *n* stock, reserve

裤子 **kùzi** *n* pants, trousers

夸张 **kuāzhāng** *v* exaggerate; *n* exaggeration

跨 **kuà** *v* stride, bestraddle

块¹ **kuài** *n* lump, piece

快² **kuài** *adj* fast, quick, rapid

快乐 **kuàilè** *adj* happy, joyful, merry

快照 **kuàizhào** *n* snapshot

筷子 **kuàizi** *n* chopstick

会计 **kuàijì** *n* accountant

宽 **kuān** *adj* wide

宽敞 **kuānchang** *adj* spacious, roomy

宽大 **kuāndà** *adj* lenient

宽度 **kuāndù** *n* breadth, width

宽广 **kuānguǎng** *adj* broad, vast

宽容 **kuānróng** *adj* tolerant, lenient

宽松 **kuānsōng** *adj* loose

狂 **kuáng** *adj* mad, crazy; violent, wild

狂欢节 **kuánghuānjié** *n* carnival

狂热 **kuángrè** *n* fanaticism

矿 **kuàng** *n* mine, ore; 矿工 **kuànggōng** *n* miner

矿石 **kuàngshí** *n* ore

矿泉水 **kuàngquánshuǐ** *n* mineral water
矿物 **kuàngwù** *n* mineral
框架 **kuàngjià** *n* frame
昆虫 **kūnchóng** *n* insect
捆 **kǔn** *v* tie, bind
捆绑 **kǔnbǎng** *v* bind, tie up
困 **kùn** *adj* sleepy
困惑 **kùnhuò** *adj* perplexed, puzzled
困境 **kùnjìng** *n* difficult position, predicament, straits, dilemma, plight
困窘 **kùnjiǒng** *adj* embarrassed, in a difficult situation
困难 **kùnnan** *n* difficulty, hardship; *adj* difficult, tough
困扰 **kùnrǎo** *v* perplex, puzzle
扩大 **kuòdà** *v* enlarge, extend, expand
扩音器 **kuòyīnqì** *n* loudspeaker, speaker
扩展 **kuòzhǎn** *v* expand, spread, extend

L

拉 **lā** *v* drag, pull, draw, tug
拉链 **lāliàn** *n* zipper, zip fastener
垃圾 **lājī** *n* garbage, junk, refuse, rubbish, trash; 垃圾场 **lājīchǎng** *n* dump; 垃圾桶 **lājītǒng** *n* dustbin, garbage can
喇叭 **lǎba** *n* horn, trumpet
腊肠 **làcháng** *n* sausage
蜡 **là** *n* wax
蜡烛 **làzhú** *n* candle
辣 **là** *adj* hot, spicy, pungent
辣椒 **làjiāo** *n* hot pepper, chili
来 **lái** *v* come
来到 **lái dào** *n* arrival; *v* come, arrive
来回 **láihuí** *adv* to and fro, back and forth; 来回票 **láihuípiào** *n* round-trip ticket
来历 **láilì** *n* origin, source, background, past history
来源 **láiyuán** *n* source, origin
拦截 **lánjié** *v* intercept
拦阻 **lánzǔ** *v* block, hold back, obstruct
蓝 **lán** *adj* blue
蓝色 **lánsè** *n* blue color
篮球 **lánqiú** *n* basketball
篮子 **lánzi** *n* basket
阑尾炎 **lánwěiyán** *n* appendicitis

懒 **lǎn** *adj* lazy
懒惰 **lǎnduò** *adj* lazy
滥用 **lànyòng** *v* abuse, misuse
狼 **láng** *n* wolf
朗诵 **lǎngsòng** *v* recite, deliver a recitation
浪 **làng** *n* wave; 浪花 **lànghuā** *n* spray, spindrift
浪费 **làngfèi** *v* waste; *adj* wasteful
浪漫 **làngmàn** *adj* romantic
劳动 **láodòng** *n/v* labor, work; 劳动节 **láodòngjié** *n* Labor Day; 劳动力 **láodònglì** *n* work force
劳驾 **láojià** *interj* excuse me (*used when asking for help*)
牢 **láo** *n* jail, prison; *adj* firm, sturdy
牢房 **láofáng** *n* prison, cell, prison ward
牢固 **láogù** *adj* firm, secure
老 **lǎo** *adj* old, aged, of long standing
老板 **lǎobǎn** *n* boss
老虎 **lǎohǔ** *n* tiger
老练 **lǎoliàn** *adj* seasoned, experienced
老人 **lǎorén** *n* old person, the aged, the old
老师 **lǎoshī** *n* teacher
老式 **lǎoshì** *adj* old-fashioned
老鼠 **lǎoshǔ** *n* rat, mouse
老套 **lǎotào** *n* stereotype
了 **le** *part* (*indicating a new situation or the completion of an action*)
老乡 **lǎoxiāng** *n* fellow-townsman, fellow-villager
乐观 **lèguān** *adj* optimistic; 乐观主义者 **lèguānzhǔyìzhě** *n* optimist
乐趣 **lèqù** *n* delight, pleasure, joy
乐意 **lèyì** *v* be ready, be willing; *adj* pleased, happy
雷 **léi** *n* thunder; mine
雷达 **léidá** *n* radar
肋骨 **lèigǔ** *n* rib
泪 **lèi** *n* tear, teardrop; 泪水 **lèishuǐ** *n* tear, teardrop
类 **lèi** *n* kind, type, category
类别 **lèibié** *n* category, kind, type
类似 **lèisì** *adj* similar, analogous
类推 **lèituī** *v* analogize, reason by analogy
类型 **lèixíng** *n* type
冷 **lěng** *adj* cold
冷餐 **lěngcān** *n* buffet
冷藏 **lěngcáng** *v* refrigerate, deep freeze

冷淡 lěngdàn *adj* icy, cold, indifferent
冷盘 lěngpán *n* cold dish, hors d'oeuvres
厘米 límǐ *n* centimeter
梨子 lízi *n* pear
离 lí *prep* off, away from; *v* leave, part from
离别 líbié *v* part, leave, bid farewell
离合器 líhéqì *n* (*machine*) clutch
离婚 líhūn *v* divorce
离开 líkāi *v* depart, get away, leave
离奇 líqí *adj* odd, bizarre
离弃 líqì *v* desert, abandon
离题 lítí *v* digress from the subject, stray from the point
犁 lí *n/v* plough
黎明 límíng *n* dawn, daybreak
篱笆 líba *n* fence
礼 lǐ *n* ceremony, rite; courtesy, etiquette, manners; gift
礼貌 lǐmào *n* courtesy, manners; *adj* polite
礼炮 lǐpào *n* salvo, gun salute
礼品 lǐpǐn *n* gift, present
礼物 lǐwù *n* gift, present
李子 lǐzi *n* plum
里 lǐ *prep* in, inside; *n* lining
里边 lǐbian *n* in, inside
里程碑 lǐchéngbēi *n* milestone
里面 lǐmiàn *n* in, inside, interior
俚语 lǐyǔ *n* slang
理发 lǐfà *v* cut hair; 理发店 lǐfàdiàn *n* barber shop; 理发师 lǐfàshī *n* barber
理解 lǐjiě *n* comprehension, understanding; *v* understand
理科 lǐkē *n* science department in a college; science subject
理论 lǐlùn *n* theory
理事 lǐshì *n* board member, trustee; 理事会 lǐshìhuì *n* council, board of directors
理想 lǐxiǎng *n* idea; *adj* ideal; 理想主义 lǐxiǎngzhǔyì *n* idealism
理性 lǐxìng *n* reason; *adj* rational
理由 lǐyóu *n* reason, grounds
理智 lǐzhì *n* reason, sense
力量 lìliàng *n* force, power, strength
力学 lìxué *n* (*science*) mechanics
历程 lìchéng *n* course
历史 lìshǐ *n* history; 历史学家 lìshǐxuéjiā *n* historian

历险 **lìxiǎn** *v* adventure
厉害 **lìhai** *adj* severe, sharp, fierce, terrible
立场 **lìchǎng** *n* position, stance, standpoint
立法 **lìfǎ** *n* legislation; *v* legislate
立方 **lìfāng** *n* (*math*) cube
立即 **lìjí** *adv* immediately, at once, promptly
立刻 **lìkè** *adv* at once, immediately, instantly, right away
立体 **lìtǐ** *adj* three-dimensional, stereoscopic
立志 **lìzhì** *v* be resolved, be determined
立足点 **lìzúdiǎn** *n* footing, standpoint, stand
利率 **lìlǜ** *n* interest rate
利润 **lìrùn** *n* gain, profit
利息 **lìxī** *n* (*banking*) interest
利益 **lìyì** *n* benefit, interest, profit
利用 **lìyòng** *v* utilize, use, make use of
沥青 **lìqīng** *n* pitch, asphalt
例会 **lìhuì** *n* regular meeting
例如 **lìrú** *v* for example, for instance, such as
例外 **lìwài** *n* exception
例证 **lìzhèng** *n* illustration, exemplification
例子 **lìzi** *n* example, instance, case
栗子 **lìzi** *n* chestnut
粒子 **lìzǐ** *n* particle
连词 **liáncí** *n* (*gram*) conjunction
连接 **liánjiē** *v* join, link
连累 **liánlěi** *v* incriminate, implicate, get sb. into trouble
连续 **liánxù** *v* continue
连衣裙 **liányīqún** *n* dress
帘子 **liánzi** *n* curtain
联邦 **liánbāng** *n* federation; *adj* federal
联合 **liánhé** *v* unite, ally, join
联合国 **liánhéguó** *n* the United Nations
联结 **liánjié** *v* connect, bind, tie, join
联盟 **liánméng** *n* alliance, federation, league, union
联系 **liánxì** *v* contact, relate; *n* contact, relation
联想 **liánxiǎng** *v* associate, connect in the mind
廉价 **liánjià** *n* low price
脸 **liǎn** *n* face
脸红 **liǎnhóng** *v* blush
脸色 **liǎnsè** *n* complexion, look, facial expression
练 **liàn** *v* practice
练习 **liànxí** *n/v* exercise, practice

恋爱 **liàn'ài** *n/v* love
恋人 **liànrén** *n* sweetheart
链环 **liànhuán** *n* link
链子 **liànzi** *n* chain
良心 **liángxīn** *n* conscience
凉 **liáng** *adj* cool
凉爽 **liángshuǎng** *adj* nice and cool
凉鞋 **liángxié** *n* sandals
梁 **liáng** *n* (*arch*) beam
量 **liáng** *v* measure
粮食 **liángshi** *n* grain
两面派 **liǎngmiànpài** *n* double dealer
亮 **liàng** *adj* bright, shining
谅解 **liàngjiě** *v* understand; *n* understanding
量 **liàng** *n* amount, quantity 量词 **liàngcí** *n* (*gram*) classifier, measure word
疗法 **liáofǎ** *n* therapy, treatment
疗养 **liáoyǎng** *v* recuperate, convalesce
聊 **liáo** *v* chat; 聊天 **liáotiān** *v* chat
料想 **liàoxiǎng** *v* expect, think, presume
料子 **liàozi** *n* material for making clothes
列 **liè** *v* list, arrange, line up; *n* row, file, rank
列车 **lièchē** *n* train; 列车长 **lièchēzhǎng** *n* train conductor
列举 **lièjǔ** *v* enumerate, list
劣 **liè** *adj* bad, inferior, of low quality
劣质 **lièzhì** *adj* of poor quality
烈士 **lièshì** *n* martyr
猎 **liè** *v* hunt
猎人 **lièrén** *n* hunter
裂缝 **lièfèng** *n* crack, rift, split, crevice
裂开 **lièkāi** *v* split open
裂口 **lièkǒu** *n* gap, rift, crack
邻近 **línjìn** *adj* neighboring, near, close to, adjacent to
邻居 **línjū** *n* neighbor
林荫道 **línyīndào** *n* boulevard, avenue
临时 **línshí** *adj* provisional, temporary; *adv* temporarily
淋浴 **línyù** *n* shower
吝啬 **lìnsè** *adj* mean, miserly, stingy
灵感 **línggǎn** *n* inspiration
灵魂 **línghún** *n* soul
灵活 **línghuó** *adj* flexible, nimble, agile, elastic
灵敏 **língmǐn** *adj* sensitive, keen, agile, acute

灵巧 língqiǎo *adj* dexterous, nimble, skillful, ingenious

凌乱 língluàn *adj* in disorder, in a mess

铃 líng *n* bell

零 líng *n* nil, nought, zero

零售 língshòu *n/v* retail; 零售商 língshòushāng *n* retailer

零用钱 língyòngqián *n* pocket money

领 lǐng *v* lead, usher; receive; claim

领带 lǐngdài *n* tie

领导 lǐngdǎo *v* lead; *n* leader, leadership; 领导人 lǐngdǎorén *n* leader

领会 lǐnghuì *v* grasp, comprehend

领事 lǐngshì *n* consul; 领事馆 lǐngshìguǎn *n* consulate

领土 lǐngtǔ *n* territory

领悟 lǐngwù *v* comprehend, grasp

领袖 lǐngxiù *n* leader

领养 lǐngyǎng *v* adopt (*a child*)

领子 lǐngzi *n* collar

另 lìng *adj* another, other

另外 lìngwài *adv* in addition, moreover, besides

溜冰 liūbīng *v* skate; 溜冰场 liūbīngchǎng *n* skating rink; 溜冰鞋 liūbīngxié *n* skate

刘海 liúhǎi *n* fringe; bang

浏览 liúlǎn *v* browse, glance over, skim through

流 liú *v* flow, run

流产 liúchǎn *v* miscarry; *n* miscarriage

流传 liúchuán *v* spread, circulate, hand down

流动 liúdòng *v* flow, go from place to place; *adj* fluid

流放 liúfàng *v* banish, send into exile

流汗 liúhàn *v* sweat

流浪 liúlàng *v* roam about, lead a vagrant life; 流浪汉 liúlànghàn *n* tramp, vagrant

流利 liúlì *adj* fluent

流失 liúshī *v* drain, run off, discharge, be wasted away

流逝 liúshì *v* (*of time*) lapse, pass

流线型 liúxiànxíng *n* streamline

流星 liúxīng *n* meteor

流行 liúxíng *adj* in vogue, popular, fashionable; 流行病 liúxíngbìng *n* epidemic disease

流行性 liúxíngxìng *adj* epidemic; 流行性感冒 liúxíngxìng gǎnmào *n* flu, influenza

流血 liúxuè *v* shed blood, bleed

流言 liúyán *n* gossip, rumor

留 liú *v* stay, remain; reserve, keep

留心 liúxīn *v* be careful, take care, be observant

留学 liúxué *v* study abroad; 留学生 liúxuéshēng *n* student studying abroad

留言 liúyán *v* leave a message; *n* message

留意 liúyì *v* look out, keep one's eyes open

柳树 liǔshù *n* willow tree

六 liù *num* six

六十 liùshí *num* sixty

六月 liùyuè *n* June

龙 lóng *n* dragon

龙头 lóngtóu *n* faucet, tap

龙虾 lóngxiā *n* lobster

笼子 lóngzi *n* cage

聋 lóng *adj* deaf

聋哑人 lóngyǎrén *n* deaf-mute

垄断 lǒngduàn *v* monopolize; *n* monopoly

楼 lóu *n* building; floor

楼梯 lóutī *n* stairs, staircase

搂抱 lǒubào *v* cuddle, hug

漏 lòu *v* leak

漏洞 lòudòng *n* leak, hole

漏斗 lòudǒu *n* funnel

露面 lòumiàn *v* turn up, make an appearance

炉子 lúzi *n* stove, furnace

颅骨 lúgǔ *n* skull

鲁莽 lǔmǎng *adj* reckless, rash

露水 lùshuǐ *n* dew

露出 lùchū *v* show, reveal, surface

露天 lùtiān *adv* in the open, outdoors

露营 lùyíng *v* camp, encamp

陆地 lùdì *n* land

陆军 lùjūn *n* army

陆路 lùlù *n* land route

陆续 lùxù *adv* one after another, in succession

录取 lùqǔ *v* admit, enroll, accept

录像 lùxiàng *v* videotape; 录像带 lùxiàngdài *n* videotape; 录像机 lùxiàngjī *n* video recorder

录音 lùyīn *v* record (*sounds*); 录音机 lùyīnjī *n* tape recorder

录用 lùyòng *v* employ, hire

鹿 lù *n* deer

路 lù *n* road

路标 **lùbiāo** *n* road sign
路灯 **lùdēng** *n* street lamp
路线 **lùxiàn** *n* route, itinerary
驴子 **lúzi** *n* donkey
旅程 **lǚchéng** *n* journey, itinerary
旅费 **lǚfèi** *n* traveling expenses, fare
旅馆 **lǚguǎn** *n* hotel
旅行 **lǚxíng** *v/n* travel, tour, journey; 旅行指南 **lǚxíng zhǐnán** *n* guidebook; 旅行支票 **lǚxíng zhīpiào** *n* traveler's check; 旅行社 **lǚxíngshè** *n* travel agency
旅游 **lǚyóu** *v* tour; 旅游业 **lǚyóuyè** *n* tourism, tourist industry, travel industry
铝 **lǚ** *n* aluminum
履历 **lǚlì** *n* curriculum vitae
履行 **lǚxíng** *v* fulfill, perform
律师 **lùshī** *n* attorney, lawyer, counselor
率 **lǜ** *n* rate, ratio
绿 **lǜ** *adj* green
绿化 **lǜhuà** *v* make green by planting trees, flowers etc., afforest
绿色 **lǜsè** *n* green color
绿洲 **lǜzhōu** *n* oasis
乱 **luàn** *adj* in disorder, in a turmoil, chaotic, messy; *n* disorder, upheaval, chaos
卵子 **luǎnzǐ** *n* ovum, egg
伦理 **lúnlǐ** *n* ethics, moral principles
轮班 **lúnbān** *v* be on duty, be in shift, be in rotation
轮廓 **lúnkuò** *n* outline, profile, contour
轮流 **lúnliú** *v* alternate, rotate, take turns
轮胎 **lúntāi** *n* tire
轮椅 **lúnyǐ** *n* wheelchair
轮子 **lúnzi** *n* wheel
论点 **lùndiǎn** *n* argument, thesis
论坛 **lùntán** *n* forum, tribune
论文 **lùnwén** *n* thesis, dissertation, paper
罗盘 **luópán** *n* compass
逻辑 **luóji** *n* logic
螺栓 **luóshuān** *n* bolt
螺丝刀 **luósīdāo** *n* screwdriver
螺丝钉 **luósīdīng** *n* screw
螺旋桨 **luóxuánjiǎng** *n* propeller
裸体 **luǒtǐ** *adj* naked, nude

骆驼 **luòtuo** *n* camel
落 **luò** *v* drop, fall, go down, decline
落后 **luòhòu** *v* lag behind; *adj* backward

M

妈妈 **māma** *n* mother
抹布 **mābù** *n* rag
麻烦 **máfan** *n* problem, trouble; *v* trouble
麻木 **mámù** *adj* apathetic
麻疹 **mázhěn** *n* measles
麻醉 **mázuì** *n* anesthesia; 麻醉师 **mázuìshī** *n* anesthetist
马 **mǎ** *n* horse
马车 **mǎchē** *n* horse-drawn carriage, cart
马拉松 **mǎlāsōng** *n* marathon
马来西亚 **mǎláixīyà** *n* Malaysia; 马来西亚人 **mǎláixīyàrén**
  n Malaysian
马力 **mǎlì** *n* horsepower
马铃薯 **mǎlíngshǔ** *n* potato
马上 **mǎshàng** *adv* right away, at once, immediately
马戏团 **mǎxìtuán** *n* circus
码头 **mǎtou** *n* wharf, dock, quay, pier
蚂蚁 **mǎyǐ** *n* ant
骂 **mà** *v* curse, swear, call names, scold
埋怨 **mányuàn** *v* complain
埋葬 **máizàng** *v* bury
买 **mǎi** *v* buy, purchase; 买方 **mǎifāng** *n* buyer
麦克风 **màikèfēng** *n* microphone
麦子 **màizi** *n* wheat
卖 **mài** *v* sell; 卖方 **màifāng** *n* seller
卖弄 **màinong** *v* show off
脉搏 **màibó** *n* pulse
馒头 **mántou** *n* steamed bun, steamed bread
满 **mǎn** *adj* full, filled, packed
满意 **mǎnyì** *adj* satisfied, pleased
满足 **mǎnzú** *adj* satisfied, content; *v* satisfy, meet (*the needs
  of*), fulfill (*requirements*)
慢 **màn** *adj* slow
慢走 **mànzǒu** *interj* good-bye, take care
漫画 **mànhuà** *n* cartoon, caricature
忙 **máng** *adj* busy, occupied
忙碌 **mánglù** *adj* hectic, busy

盲 **máng** *adj* blind; 盲人 **mángrén** *n* the blind

盲目 **mángmù** *adj* (*fig*) blind

猫 **māo** *n* cat

猫头鹰 **māotóuyīng** *n* owl

毛 **máo** *n* hair; wool

毛笔 **máobǐ** *n* brush pen

毛发 **máofà** *n* hair

毛巾 **máojīn** *n* towel

毛皮 **máopí** *n* fur

毛线 **máoxiàn** *n* yarn; 毛线衣 **máoxiànyī** *n* sweater

矛 **máo** *n* spear

矛盾 **máodùn** *n* contradiction; *adj* contradictory

锚 **máo** *n* anchor

冒充 **màochōng** *v* pretend to be, pass sb. or sth. off as

冒犯 **màofàn** *v* offend

冒号 **màohào** *n* (*gram*) colon

冒险 **màoxiǎn** *v* take a risk, take chances

贸易 **màoyì** *n* trade; 贸易公司 **màoyì gōngsī** *n* trade company, import/export company

帽子 **màozi** *n* cap, hat

没 **méi** *adv* not

没有 **méiyǒu** *v* not have, there is not, be without

玫瑰 **méigui** *n* rose

眉毛 **méimao** *n* brow, eyebrow

梅 **méi** *n* plum; 梅花 **méihuā** *n* plum blossom; (*playing cards*) club

媒介 **méijiè** *n* medium

媒人 **méirén** *n* matchmaker, go-between

媒体 **méitǐ** *n* media

煤 **méi** *n* coal

煤矿 **méikuàng** *n* coal mine

煤气 **méiqì** *n* gas

霉 **méi** *n* mold, mildew

每 **měi** *adj* every, each, per

美 **měi** *n* beauty; *adj* beautiful, pretty

美德 **měidé** *n* virtue, moral excellence

美国 **měiguó** *n* America, the United States; 美国人 **měiguórén** *n* American

美好 **měihǎo** *adj* nice, happy

美景 **měijǐng** *n* beautiful scenery, bright prospect

美丽 **měilì** *adj* beautiful

美术 **měishù** *n* fine arts

美味 **měiwèi** *n* delicious food
美学 **měixué** *n* aesthetics
美元 **měiyuán** *n* U. S. dollar
美洲 **měizhōu** *n* (*the continent*) America
妹夫 **mèifu** *n* brother-in-law (*younger sister's husband*)
妹妹 **mèimei** *n* younger sister
魅力 **mèilì** *n* charm
门 **mén** *n* door, gate
门槛 **ménkǎn** *n* threshold
门口 **ménkǒu** *n* doorway
门廊 **ménláng** *n* porch
门牌 **ménpái** *n* house number
门票 **ménpiào** *n* admission fee, entrance ticket
门厅 **méntīng** *n* entrance, hall, vestibule
门诊 **ménzhěn** *n* outpatient service; 门诊所 **ménzhěnsuǒ** *n* clinic
猛 **měng** *adv* suddenly, with a rush
猛烈 **měngliè** *adj* vigorous, violent, fierce
梦 **mèng** *n* dream
梦想 **mèngxiǎng** *v* dream of, vainly hope; *n* fond dream, wishful thinking
迷路 **mílù** *v* lose one's way, get lost
迷人 **mírén** *adj* enchanting, charming
迷失 **míshī** *v* lose, get lost
迷信 **míxìn** *n* superstition; *adj* superstitious
米 **mǐ** *n* (*measurement*) meter, (*raw*) rice
米饭 **mǐfàn** *n* (*cooked*) rice
米糕 **mǐgāo** *n* rice cake
米酒 **mǐjiǔ** *n* rice wine, sake
米色 **mǐsè** *n* cream color
秘密 **mìmì** *n/adj* secret; 秘密警察 **mìmì jǐngchá** *n* secret police
秘书 **mìshū** *n* secretary
密 **mì** *adj* dense
密度 **mìdù** *n* density
密封 **mìfēng** *v* seal up, seal airtight
密集 **mìjí** *adj* intensive, concentrated
密码 **mìmǎ** *n* code, password
密谋 **mìmóu** *n* plot; *v* conspire, plot
密切 **mìqiè** *adj* close, intimate; *adv* closely
密探 **mìtàn** *n* secret agent, spy
蜜蜂 **mìfēng** *n* bee

蜜月 **mìyuè** *n* honeymoon

绵羊 **miányáng** *n* sheep

棉 **mián** *n* cotton

棉花 **miánhuā** *n* cotton

棉塞 **miánsāi** *n* tampon

免除 **miǎnchú** *v* waive, exempt, relieve

免费 **miǎnfèi** *adj* free of charge; *adv* gratis

免税 **miǎnshuì** *adj* duty-free, tax-free; *v* exempt from taxation

免疫 **miǎnyì** *n* immunity (*from disease*)

勉励 **miǎnlì** *v* encourage, urge

勉强 **miǎnqiǎng** *adj* reluctant, inadequate, unconvincing;
    adv reluctantly, grudgingly; *v* do with difficulty, force sb.
    to do sth.

腼腆 **miǎntiǎn** *adj* shy

面[1] **miàn** *n* face, surface; side, aspect

面[2] **miàn** *n* flour; noodles

面包 **miànbāo** *n* bread; 面包店 **miànbāodiàn** *n* bakery;
    面包师 **miànbāoshī** *n* baker

面对 **miànduì** *v* face, confront

面粉 **miànfěn** *n* flour

面积 **miànjī** *n* area

面颊 **miànjiá** *n* cheek

面具 **miànjù** *n* mask

面临 **miànlín** *v* be faced with, be confronted with

面纱 **miànshā** *n* veil

面试 **miànshì** *n* oral quiz, audition, interview

面谈 **miàntán** *v* interview, speak with sb. face to face

面条 **miàntiáo** *n* noodles

面团 **miàntuán** *n* dough

面子 **miànzi** *n* (*fig*) face

苗 **miáo** *n* seedling

苗条 **miáotiao** *adj* slender, slim

描 **miáo** *v* trace, copy

描绘 **miáohuì** *v* portray, depict, describe

描写 **miáoxiě** *v* portray, depict, describe; *n* description

瞄准 **miáozhǔn** *v* take aim, aim

藐视 **miǎoshì** *v* despise, look down upon

庙 **miào** *n* temple

庙会 **miàohuì** *n* temple fair

灭火 **mièhuǒ** *v* put out a fire; 灭火器 **mièhuǒqì** *n* fire
    extinguisher

灭绝 **mièjué** *v* exterminate, become extinct

民 **mín** *n* people, folk
民歌 **míngē** *n* folk song
民间 **mínjiān** *adj* folk, nongovernmental
民俗 **mínsú** *n* folk custom, folkways
民意 **mínyì** *n* public opinion; 民意测验 **mínyì cèyàn** *n* public opinion poll
民乐 **mínyuè** *n* folk music
民主 **mínzhǔ** *n* democracy; *adj* democratic
民族 **mínzú** *n* nation, nationality; 民族主义 **mínzúzhǔyì** *n* nationalism
敏感 **mǐngǎn** *adj* sensitive
敏捷 **mǐnjié** *adj* agile, nimble, quick
敏锐 **mǐnruì** *adj* acute, sharp, keen
名称 **míngchēng** *n* name (*of an object*)
名词 **míngcí** *n* noun
名片 **míngpiàn** *n* name card, business card
名人 **míngrén** *n* celebrity, famous personality
名声 **míngshēng** *n* reputation
名言 **míngyán** *n* well-known saying, celebrated dictum, famous quote
名誉 **míngyù** *n* reputation, fame, honor
名字 **míngzi** *n* name
明亮 **míngliàng** *adj* bright, light, well-lit
明确 **míngquè** *v* make clear; *adj* definite, explicit, specific
明天 **míngtiān** *n* tomorrow
明显 **míngxiǎn** *adj* apparent, evident, obvious
明信片 **míngxìnpiàn** *n* postcard
明智 **míngzhì** *adj* wise, sensible
命令 **mìnglìng** *n/v* command, order
命运 **mìngyùn** *n* destiny, fate
模范 **mófàn** *n* an exemplary person or thing, role model, fine example
模仿 **mófǎng** *v* imitate, model, copy
模糊 **móhu** *adj* vague, dim, misty, obscure, blurred
模拟 **mónǐ** *v* simulate, imitate
模式 **móshì** *n* pattern, model
模型 **móxíng** *n* model
摩天大楼 **mótiān dàlóu** *n* skyscraper
摩托车 **mótuōchē** *n* motorbike, motorcycle
磨光 **móguāng** *v* polish
蘑菇 **mógu** *n* mushroom
魔鬼 **móguǐ** *n* devil, demon, monster

魔力 **mólì** *n* magic power

魔术 **móshù** *n* magic; 魔术师 **móshùshī** *n* magician

陌生 **mòshēng** *adj* strange, unfamiliar; 陌生人 **mòshēngrén** *n* stranger

莫名其妙 **mòmíng qímiào** *adj* be baffled, inexplicable, odd

漠不关心 **mòbù guānxīn** *adj* indifferent, unconcerned

墨水 **mòshuǐ** *n* ink

墨西哥 **mòxīgē** *n* Mexico; 墨西哥人 **mòxīgērén** *n* Mexican

谋杀 **móushā** *v* murder

某 **mǒu** *pron* certain

某某 **mǒumǒu** *pron* so-and-so

某人 **mǒurén** *pron* somebody, a certain person

模子 **múzi** *n* mold

母鸡 **mǔjī** *n* hen

母亲 **mǔqīn** *n* mother

母语 **mǔyǔ** *n* mother tongue

拇指 **mǔzhǐ** *n* thumb

木 **mù** *n* wood

木板 **mùbǎn** *n* board, plank

木材 **mùcái** *n* timber, wood, lumber

木柴 **mùchái** *n* firewood

木匠 **mùjiàng** *n* carpenter

木偶 **mù'ǒu** *n* puppet

木头 **mùtou** *n* wood, log, timber

目标 **mùbiāo** *n* aim, goal, object, objective, target

目的 **mùdì** *n* purpose, aim, goal, objective, end

目的地 **mùdìdì** *n* destination

目光 **mùguāng** *n* sight, vision, view

目击 **mùjī** *v* witness; 目击者 **mùjīzhě** *n* eyewitness, witness

目录 **mùlù** *n* catalog, table of contents

目前 **mùqián** *adv* at present, at the moment

牧场 **mùchǎng** *n* pasture, pasture land, grazing land

牧师 **mùshī** *n* clergyman, pastor, minister

墓 **mù** *n* tomb, grave

墓碑 **mùbēi** *n* tombstone, gravestone

墓地 **mùdì** *n* cemetery, graveyard

穆斯林 **mùsīlín** *n* Muslim

N

拿 **ná** *v* take, hold, bring, fetch

哪 **nǎ** *pron* which

哪里 **nǎli** *pron* what place
内 **nèi** *n* inner, inside, within
内部 **nèibù** *n* interior, inside; *adj* internal
内地 **nèidì** *n* inland, interior, hinterland
内阁 **nèigé** *n* (*gov*) cabinet
内科 **nèikē** *n* internal medicine; 内科医师 **nèikē yīshī** *n* physician
内裤 **nèikù** *n* underpants
内容 **nèiróng** *n* content, substance
内胎 **nèitāi** *n* (*tire*) inner tube
内心 **nèixīn** *n* heart, innermost being
内行 **nèiháng** *n* expert, professional
内衣 **nèiyī** *n* underclothes, underwear
内在 **nèizài** *adj* inherent, intrinsic
内脏 **nèizàng** *n* internal organs
内战 **nèizhàn** *n* civil war
那 **nà** *pron* that
那些 **nàxiē** *pron* those
奶酪 **nǎilào** *n* cheese
奶油 **nǎiyóu** *n* cream
氖 **nǎi** *n* neon
耐力 **nàilì** *n* endurance, stamina
耐心 **nàixīn** *n* patience; *adj* patient
耐性 **nàixìng** *n* patience, endurance
耐用 **nàiyòng** *adj* durable
男 **nán** *adj* male
男孩 **nánhái** *n* boy
男朋友 **nánpéngyou** *n* boyfriend
男人 **nánrén** *n* man
男生 **nánshēng** *n* schoolboy
男巫 **nánwū** *n* wizard
男性 **nánxìng** *n* male
男主角 **nánzhǔjiǎo** *n* (*movie, play, etc.*) hero, protagonist
男子气 **nánzǐqì** *n* masculinity
南 **nán** *n* south
南边 **nánbiān** *n* south, southern side
南部 **nánbù** *n* south, southern part
南方 **nánfāng** *n* south, southern part of a country; *adj* southern; 南方人 **nánfāngrén** *n* southerner
南瓜 **nánguā** *n* pumpkin
南极 **nánjí** *n* the South Pole
难 **nán** *adj* hard, difficult

难得 **nándé** *adv* rarely, seldom
难点 **nándiǎn** *n* difficult point, difficulty
难怪 **nánguài** *adv* no wonder
难过 **nánguò** *adj* feel sorry, feel bad
难看 **nánkàn** *adj* ugly
难受 **nánshòu** *adj* feel ill, feel unhappy, feel uncomfortable
难题 **nántí** *n* difficult problem
难忘 **nánwàng** *adj* memorable, unforgettable
难为情 **nánwéiqíng** *adj* embarrassed, ashamed
难以 **nányǐ** *adj* difficult to do; 难以理解 **nányǐ lǐjiě** *adj* incomprehensible; 难以忍受 **nányǐ rěnshòu** *adj* unbearable; 难以形容 **nányǐ xíngróng** *adj* indescribable; 难以置信 **nányǐ zhìxìn** *adj* inconceivable, unbelievable
难民 **nànmín** *n* refugee
恼怒 **nǎonù** *adj* vexed, angry, furious
恼人 **nǎorén** *adj* annoying, irritating
脑 **nǎo** *n* brain
闹鬼 **nàoguǐ** *v* be haunted
闹事 **nàoshì** *v* make trouble
闹钟 **nàozhōng** *n* alarm clock
嫩 **nèn** *adj* tender, delicate
能 **néng** *v* can, be able to, be capable of; *n* energy; 太阳能 **tàiyángnéng** *n* solar energy; 原子能 **yuánzǐnéng** *n* atomic energy
能干 **nénggàn** *v* competent, able, capable
能够 **nénggòu** *v* can, be able to, be capable to
能力 **nénglì** *n* ability, capacity, capability, power
能量 **néngliàng** *n* energy
能源 **néngyuán** *n* energy source
泥 **ní** *n* mud
泥泞 **nínìng** *adj* muddy
泥土 **nítǔ** *n* earth, soil
你 **nǐ** *pron* you
你的 **nǐde** *pron* your, yours
你们 **nǐmen** *pron* (*pl*) you
你们的 **nǐmende** *pron* (*pl*) yours
你自己 **nǐ zìjǐ** *pron* yourself
匿名 **nìmíng** *adj* anonymous
溺爱 **nì'ài** *v* spoil (*a child*), dote on (*a child*)
年 **nián** *n* year, age
年代 **niándài** *n* age, time, decade
年级 **niánjí** *n* (*school*) grade, year

年龄 **niánlíng** *n* age

年青 **niánqīng** *adj* young

年轻 **niánqīng** *adj* young; 年轻人 **niánqīngrén** *n* young person/people

黏土 **niántǔ** *n* clay

碾 **niǎn** *v* grind, crush, flatten

念 **niàn** *v* read, read aloud

鸟 **niǎo** *n* bird

鸟巢 **niǎocháo** *n* bird nest

鸟嘴 **niǎozuǐ** *n* beak

尿 **niào** *n* urine

尿布 **niàobù** *n* diaper

捏 **niē** *v* pinch

宁静 **níngjìng** *adj* peaceful, tranquil, quiet

柠檬 **níngméng** *n* lemon; 柠檬汁 **níngméngzhī** *n* lemonade

凝视 **níngshì** *v* gaze, stare

拧 **nǐng** *v* twist, wring, pinch, tweak

宁可 **nìngkě** *adv* would rather

宁愿 **nìngyuàn** *adv* would rather

牛 **niú** *n* ox, cow, bull

牛奶 **niúnǎi** *n* milk

牛排 **niúpái** *n* steak

牛肉 **niúròu** *n* beef

牛仔 **niúzǎi** *n* cowboy

牛仔裤 **niúzǎikù** *n* jeans

纽带 **niǔdài** *n* link, tie, bond

纽扣 **niǔkòu** *n* button

农场 **nóngchǎng** *n* farm

农村 **nóngcūn** *n* countryside

农历 **nónglì** *n* the lunar calendar

农民 **nóngmín** *n* farmer, peasant

农业 **nóngyè** *n* agriculture, farming

浓厚 **nónghòu** *adj* dense, thick, intense

浓缩 **nóngsuō** *v* concentrate

弄 **nòng** *v* do, make, handle

奴隶 **núlì** *n* slave; 奴隶制 **núlìzhì** *n* slavery

努力 **nǔlì** *adv* hard, diligently; *v* strive; *n* effort

女 **nǚ** *adj* female

女儿 **nǚ'ér** *n* daughter

女孩 **nǚhái** *n* girl

女朋友 **nǚpéngyou** *n* girlfriend

女人 **nǚrén** *n* woman

女神 **nǚshén** *n* goddess
女生 **nǚshēng** *n* schoolgirl
女士 **nǚshì** *n* lady, madam
女王 **nǚwáng** *n* queen
女巫 **nǚwū** *n* witch
女性 **nǚxìng** *n* female
女婿 **nǚxù** *n* son-in-law
女主角 **nǚzhǔjué** *n* (*in a movie, play, etc.*) heroine, female protagonist
女主人 **nǚzhǔrén** *n* hostess
虐待 **nüèdài** *v* abuse, maltreat, ill-treat, mistreat
虐待狂 **nuèdàikuáng** *n* sadism
暖和 **nuǎnhuo** *adj* warm
挪威 **nuówēi** *n* Norway; 挪威人 **nuówēirén** *n* Norwegian
诺言 **nuòyán** *n* promise
懦夫 **nuòfū** *n* coward

O

欧盟 **ōuméng** *n* European Union
欧元 **ōuyuán** *n* euro
欧洲 **ōuzhōu** *n* Europe; 欧洲人 **ōuzhōurén** *n* European
呕吐 **ǒutù** *v* vomit, throw up
偶尔 **ǒu'ěr** *adv* occasionally
偶然 **ǒurán** *adj* accidental, fortuitous, chance; *adv* accidently, by chance
偶数 **ǒushù** *n* even number
偶像 **ǒuxiàng** *n* idol

P

爬 **pá** *v* climb, crawl
爬行 **páxíng** *v* crawl, creep; 爬行动物 **páxíng dòngwù** *n* reptile
扒手 **páshǒu** *n* pickpocket
怕 **pà** *v* fear, dread, be afraid of
拍 **pāi** *v* pat, clap, slap; take a picture, shoot; *n* bat, racket
拍打 **pāidǎ** *v* pat, slap
拍卖 **pāimài** *n/v* auction
拍手 **pāishǒu** *v* clap, applaud
拍照 **pāizhào** *v* take a picture
拍子 **pāizi** *n* bat, racket; (*music*) beat
排 **pái** *n* row, line; *v* arrange, put in order

排斥 **páichì** *v* repel, exclude, reject
排除 **páichú** *v* eliminate, exclude
排练 **páiliàn** *n* rehearsal; *v* rehearse
排列 **páiliè** *v* arrange, put in order
排气管 **páiqìguǎn** *n* exhaust pipe
排球 **páiqiú** *n* volleyball
排外 **páiwài** *adj* exclusive, antiforeign
牌坊 **páifāng** *n* memorial archway
牌子 **páizi** *n* sign, brand, trademark
派 **pài** *v* dispatch, send; *n* school of thought; (political) wing
派别 **pàibié** *n* faction, wing
派遣 **pàiqiǎn** *v* dispatch, send
攀登 **pāndēng** *v* climb, scale
盘子 **pánzi** *n* dish, plate
判断 **pànduàn** *n* judgment; *v* judge, decide
叛变 **pànbiàn** *v* turn traitor, defect
叛乱 **pànluàn** *n* armed rebellion
叛逆 **pànnì** *n* treason
叛徒 **pàntú** *n* traitor
盼望 **pànwàng** *v* hope for, long for, look forward to
庞大 **pángdà** *adj* huge, enormous, gigantic
旁边 **pángbiān** *n* side
旁观者 **pángguānzhě** *n* onlooker, bystander
螃蟹 **pángxiè** *n* crab
膀胱 **pángguāng** *n* bladder
胖 **pàng** *adj* fat
抛 **pāo** *v* throw, toss
抛弃 **pāoqì** *v* abandon, forsake
咆哮 **páoxiāo** *v* roar
炮 **pào** *n* cannon
炮兵 **pàobīng** *n* artilleryman, cannoneer
炮弹 **pàodàn** *n* (*artillery*) shell
炮轰 **pàohōng** *v* shell, bombard
跑 **pǎo** *v* run; run away, escape
跑步 **pǎobù** *v* run, double time
跑道 **pǎodào** *n* racetrack, runway, track
泡 **pào** *n* bubble
泡沫 **pàomò** *n* foam, froth
陪 **péi** *v* accompany, escort
陪审团 **péishěntuán** *n* jury
陪审员 **péishěnyuán** *n* juror
陪同 **péitóng** *v* accompany, escort

培养 **péiyǎng** *v* cultivate, foster, train
配额 **pèi'é** *n* quota
配合 **pèihé** *v* coordinate, assist
配偶 **pèi'ǒu** *n* spouse
喷 **pēn** *v* spurt, spout, gush, spray, sprinkle
喷气式飞机 **pēnqìshì fēijī** *n* jet plane
喷泉 **pēnquán** *n* fountain
喷射 **pēnshè** *v* spray, spurt
喷嚏 **pēntì** *n* sneeze
盆 **pén** *n* basin, tub
盆地 **péndì** *n* (*geo*) basin
烹饪 **pēngrèn** *n* cuisine, cooking
烹调 **pēngtiáo** *v* cook; *n* cuisine
朋友 **péngyou** *n* friend
棚子 **péngzi** *n* shed, shack
篷车 **péngchē** *n* caravan
膨胀 **péngzhàng** *n* inflation; *v* swell, expand, inflate
捧 **pěng** *v* hold or carry in both hands
碰 **pèng** *v* bump, touch
碰撞 **pèngzhuàng** *v* bump, collide, crash
批 **pī** *n* batch
批发 **pīfā** *n* wholesale; 批发商 **pīfāshāng** *n* distributor, wholesaler
批评 **pīpíng** *n* criticism; *v* criticize
批准 **pīzhǔn** *v* approve, ratify; *n* approval
劈 **pī** *v* split, chop, cleave
皮 **pí** *n* skin, hide, leather
皮包 **píbāo** *n* leather bag
皮带 **pídài** *n* strap, leather belt
皮肤 **pífū** *n* skin
皮革 **pígé** *n* leather
皮箱 **píxiāng** *n* leather suitcase, trunk
皮鞋 **píxié** *n* leather shoes
皮影 **píyǐng** *n* shadow puppet
皮衣 **píyī** *n* leather jacket
疲倦 **píjuàn** *adj* tired
疲劳 **píláo** *adj* tired; *n* fatigue
啤酒 **píjiǔ** *n* beer
脾气 **píqi** *n* temper
屁 **pì** *n* (*bowels*) wind, fart
屁股 **pìgu** *n* backside, buttocks
偏 **piān** *adj* inclined to one side, leaning; partial, prejudiced

偏爱 **piān'ài** *n* preference; *v* prefer
偏激 **piānjī** *adj* extreme
偏见 **piānjiàn** *n* bias, prejudice
偏僻 **piānpì** *adj* remote, out-of-the-way
偏头痛 **piāntóutòng** *n* migraine
偏远 **piānyuǎn** *adj* remote, faraway
便宜 **piányi** *adj* cheap, inexpensive
骗 **piàn** *v* deceive, fool
骗子 **piànzi** *n* imposter, swindler
片 **piàn** *n* piece, slice, card
漂 **piāo** *v* float, drift
飘 **piāo** *v* float (*in the air*), flutter
漂白 **piǎobái** *v* bleach; 漂白剂 **piǎobáijì** *n* bleach
漂亮 **piàoliang** *adj* pretty, good-looking, handsome, beautiful
票 **piào** *n* ticket
票房 **piàofáng** *n* box office, ticket office
瞥见 **piējiàn** *v* glimpse, catch sight of
拼 **pīn** *v* put together, piece together, patch
拼音 **pīnyīn** *n* pinyin (*Chinese transcription system*)
拼写 **pīnxiě** *n* spelling; *v* spell
贫乏 **pínfá** *adj* poor, short, lacking
贫瘠 **pínjí** *adj* barren, infertile, sterile
贫困 **pínkùn** *adj* poor, impoverished; *n* poverty
贫穷 **pínqióng** *adj* needy, poor
贫血 **pínxuè** *n* anemia
贫民窟 **pínmínkū** *n* slum
频道 **píndào** *n* (*TV*) channel
频繁 **pínfán** *adj* frequent
频率 **pínlǜ** *n* frequency
品尝 **pǐncháng** *v* savor, taste, sample
品脱 **pǐntuō** *n* pint
乒乓球 **pīngpāngqiú** *n* table tennis, ping-pong
平 **píng** *adj* flat, level, even, smooth
平常 **píngcháng** *adj* common, ordinary, so-so; *adv* generally, usually
平等 **píngděng** *n* equality; *adj* equal
平方 **píngfāng** *n* (*math*) square
平分 **píngfēn** *v* divide equally
平衡 **pínghéng** *v; n* balance
平静 **píngjìng** *adj* calm, quiet, tranquil
平均 **píngjūn** *adj* average, mean
平民 **píngmín** *n* the common people

平时 **píngshí** *n* usually, day-to-day, in normal times
平坦 **píngtǎn** *adj* (*of land, roads, etc.*) flat, level, even, smooth
平稳 **píngwěn** *adj* smooth and steady
平行 **píngxíng** *adj* parallel
平庸 **píngyōng** *adj* mediocre, commonplace
平原 **píngyuán** *n* plain
评 **píng** *v* comment, evaluate
评价 **píngjià** *v* evaluate, appraise; *n* evaluation
评论 **pínglùn** *n* comment, commentary; *v* remark, comment;
   评论家 **pínglùnjiā** *n* critic, commentator
评语 **píngyǔ** *n* comment, remark
凭借 **píngjiè** *v* rely on, depend on
凭证 **píngzhèng** *n* voucher, proof, evidence, certificate
苹果 **píngguǒ** *n* apple
屏幕 **píngmù** *n* screen
瓶塞 **píngsāi** *n* cork; 瓶塞钻 **píngsāizuàn** *n* corkscrew
瓶子 **píngzi** *n* bottle
坡 **pō** *n* slope
婆婆 **pópo** *n* mother-in-law (*husband's mother*)
迫害 **pòhài** *n* persecution; *v* persecute
迫切 **pòqiè** *adj* urgent, pressing
迫使 **pòshǐ** *v* force, compel
破 **pò** *v* break, damage; *adj* broken, damaged, torn, worn out
破产 **pòchǎn** *v* go bankrupt
破坏 **pòhuài** *v* destroy, wreck, undermine, do great damage
   to; *n* destruction
破裂 **pòliè** *v* burst, crack, fracture
破晓 **pòxiǎo** *v* dawn
破折号 **pòzhéhào** *n* (*punctuation*) dash
铺 **pū** *v* spread, lay, pave
仆人 **púrén** *n* servant
葡萄 **pútáo** *n* grape; 葡萄园 **pútáoyuán** *n* vineyard
葡萄酒 **pútáojiǔ** *n* wine
葡萄牙 **pútáoyá** *n* Portugal; 葡萄牙人 **pútáoyárén** *n* (*people*)
   Portuguese; 葡萄牙语 **pútáoyáyǔ** *n* (*language*) Portuguese
葡萄柚 **pútáoyòu** *n* grapefruit
菩萨 **púsà** *n* Boddhisattva
朴素 **púsù** *adj* (*of life*) simple, plain
普遍 **pǔbiàn** *adj* universal, widespread, general, common
普通 **pǔtōng** *adj* common, ordinary
普通话 **pǔtōnghuà** *n* Mandarin
瀑布 **pùbù** *n* waterfall

Q

七 **qī** *num* seven
七十 **qīshí** *num* seventy
七月 **qīyuè** *n* July
妻子 **qīzi** *n* wife
期 **qī** *n* (*magazine*) issue; a period of time, duration, phase
期待 **qīdài** *v* look forward to, expect
期间 **qījiān** *n* duration, span
期刊 **qīkān** *n* periodical
期望 **qīwàng** *n* expectation; *v* anticipate, expect
期限 **qīxiàn** *n* time limit, deadline
欺骗 **qīpiàn** *v* cheat, deceive, trick
漆 **qī** *n* lacquer, paint; *v* paint
其实 **qíshí** *adv* actually, in fact, as a matter of fact
其他 **qítā** *adj* the other, the rest
其中 **qízhōng** *n* thereinto, of which, of whom
奇怪 **qíguài** *adj* odd, peculiar, queer, strange
奇迹 **qíjì** *n* miracle, wonder
奇妙 **qímiào** *adj* marvelous, wonderful, miraculous
奇异 **qíyì** *adj* queer, strange, odd
歧视 **qíshì** *n* discrimination; *v* discriminate against
祈求 **qíqiú** *v* pray for
崎岖 **qíqū** *adj* rugged
骑 **qí** *v* ride
骑士 **qíshì** *n* knight
旗 **qí** *n* flag, banner
旗袍 **qípáo** *n* cheongsam (*Chinese-style dress*)
乞丐 **qǐgài** *n* beggar
乞求 **qǐqiú** *v* beg
企图 **qǐtú** *n/v* attempt
企业 **qǐyè** *n* enterprise, business
启发 **qǐfā** *v* arouse, inspire, enlighten
启示 **qǐshì** *n* inspiration, revelation
起床 **qǐchuáng** *v* get up, get out of bed
起飞 **qǐfēi** *v* (*plane*) take off
起航 **qǐháng** *v* set sail
起居室 **qǐjūshì** *n* living room
起身 **qǐshēn** *v* get up, leave, set out
起诉 **qǐsù** *v* sue, prosecute; 起诉人 **qǐsùrén** *n* plaintiff,
    prosecutor; 起诉书 **qǐsùshū** *n* indictment

起义 qǐyì *n* uprising, insurrection, revolt
起源 qǐyuán *n* origin; *v* originate
起重机 qǐzhòngjī *n* (*machine*) crane
气 qì *n* gas, air, breath
气愤 qìfèn *adj* indignant, furious
气候 qìhòu *n* climate
气流 qìliú *n* air current, airflow
气泡 qìpào *n* air bubble
气球 qìqiú *n* balloon
气味 qìwèi *n* odor, scent, smell
弃置 qìzhì *v* discard, throw aside
汽 qì *n* steam
汽车 qìchē *n* automobile, car
汽车旅馆 qìchē lǚguǎn *n* motel
汽油 qìyóu *n* gas, gasoline, petrol
契约 qìyuē *n* deed, contract, pact
器官 qìguān *n* (*body*) organ
千 qiān *n* thousand
牵连 qiānlián *v* implicate, involve sb. (*in trouble*)
牵涉 qiānshè *v* involve, concern
铅笔 qiānbǐ *n* pencil
谦恭 qiāngōng *adj* modest and courteous
谦逊 qiānxùn *adj* humble, modest, unassuming
签名 qiānmíng *n* signature; *v* sign one's name, autograph
签证 qiānzhèng *n* visa
前 qián *adj* front, preceding, former
前边 qiánbian *n* in front, ahead
前额 qián'é *n* forehead
前进 qiánjìn *n* advance, progress; *v* advance, go ahead, march
前面 qiánmian *n* in front, ahead
前年 qiánnián *n* the year before last, two years ago
前提 qiántí *n* premise
前天 qiántiān *n* day before yesterday
前途 qiántú *n* future, prospect
前往 qiánwǎng *v* head for, bound for, leave for
前夕 qiánxī *n* eve
前线 qiánxiàn *n* battlefront, frontline
虔诚 qiánchéng *adj* pious, devout
钱 qián *n* money
钱包 qiánbāo *n* purse, wallet
钱柜 qiánguì *n* cash register, money-box
潜力 qiánlì *n* potential

潜水 **qiánshuǐ** *n* diving; *v* dive; 潜水员 **qiánshuǐyuán** *n* diver

潜艇 **qiántǐng** *n* submarine

潜在 **qiánzài** *adj* potential, latent

浅 **qiǎn** *adj* shallow

谴责 **qiǎnzé** *v* condemn, damn, denounce

欠 **qiàn** *v* owe

歉意 **qiànyì** *n* regret, apology

枪 **qiāng** *n* gun, rifle, firearm

枪手 **qiāngshǒu** *n* gunman

强 **qiáng** *adj* powerful, strong

强大 **qiángdà** *adj* formidable, mighty, powerful, strong

强盗 **qiángdào** *n* bandit, robber

强调 **qiángdiào** *n* emphasis, stress; *v* emphasize, stress, underline

强度 **qiángdù** *n* intensity, strength

强加 **qiángjiā** *v* impose, force

强奸 **qiángjiān** *v* rape; 强奸犯 **qiángjiānfàn** *n* rapist

强有力 **qiángyǒulì** *adj* forceful, strong

强制 **qiángzhì** *adj* compulsory; *v* force, compel, coerce

强壮 **qiángzhuàng** *adj* robust, strong, sturdy

墙 **qiáng** *n* wall

墙壁 **qiángbì** *n* wall

墙纸 **qiángzhǐ** *n* wallpaper

抢 **qiǎng** *v* rob, snatch, grab

抢夺 **qiǎngduó** *v* grab, snatch, seize

抢劫 **qiǎngjié** *v* rob, plunder

抢救 **qiǎngjiù** *v* rescue, salvage, save

敲 **qiāo** *v* knock

敲诈 **qiāozhà** *v* blackmail, extort

锹 **qiāo** *n* spade

桥 **qiáo** *n* bridge

桥牌 **qiáopái** *n* (*cards*) bridge

巧 **qiǎo** *adj* artful, skillful; coincidental

巧合 **qiǎohé** *n* coincidence

巧克力 **qiǎokèlì** *n* chocolate

切 **qiē** *v* cut, slice

切断 **qiēduàn** *v* sever, cut off

茄子 **qiézi** *n* eggplant

窃取 **qièqǔ** *v* usurp, steal

亲 **qīn** *v* kiss; *adj* intimate, close, dear

亲爱 **qīn'ài** *adj* dear, loving

亲近 **qīnjìn** *adj* close, intimate

亲密 **qīnmì** *adj* close, intimate

亲戚 **qīnqi** *n* relatives

亲切 **qīnqiè** *adj* kind, affable

亲人 **qīnrén** *n* close relatives

亲自 **qīnzì** *adv* personally, in person

侵略 **qīnlüè** *n* aggression, invasion; *v* invade; 侵略者 **qīnlüèzhě** *n* invader

侵扰 **qīnrǎo** *v* invade and harass

侵蚀 **qīnshí** *n* erosion; *v* erode

钦佩 **qīnpèi** *n* admiration; *v* admire

勤勉 **qínmiǎn** *adj* diligent, assiduous

寝具 **qǐnjù** *n* bedding

寝室 **qǐnshì** *n* bedroom

青春 **qīngchūn** *n* youth, youthfulness; 青春期 **qīngchūnqī** *n* puberty

青年 **qīngnián** *n* youth, young people

青少年 **qīngshàonián** *n* teenagers, youngsters

青蛙 **qīngwā** *n* frog

轻 **qīng** *adj* light, gentle; *adv* gently, lightly

轻率 **qīngshuài** *adj* indiscreet, rash, hasty

轻蔑 **qīngmiè** *adj* scornful, disdainful, contemptuous

轻松 **qīngsōng** *adj* easy, relaxed

轻微 **qīngwēi** *adj* slight, light

倾向 **qīngxiàng** *n* inclination, trend, tendency; *v* be inclined to, prefer

倾斜 **qīngxié** *v* incline, tilt, slant

清 **qīng** *adj* clear

清楚 **qīngchu** *adj* clear, distinct; *adv* clearly, plainly

清单 **qīngdān** *n* detailed list, inventory

清洁 **qīngjié** *adj* clean; 清洁工 **qīngjiégōng** *n* cleaner

清明节 **qīngmíngjié** *n* Tomb-sweeping Day (*April 4th or 5th*)

清漆 **qīngqī** *n* varnish

清醒 **qīngxǐng** *adj* sober, clear-headed

清真寺 **qīngzhēnsì** *n* mosque

情 **qíng** *n* feeling, affection

情报 **qíngbào** *n* intelligence

情感 **qínggǎn** *n* emotion, feeling, affection

情节 **qíngjié** *n* (*story*) plot

情景 **qíngjǐng** *n* scene, situation, scenario

情况 **qíngkuàng** *n* condition, situation

情形 **qíngxing** *n* situation, circumstances, state of affairs

情绪 **qíngxù** *n* mood, sentiment

晴朗 **qínglǎng** *adj* sunny

请 **qǐng** *v* (*polite*) please, request, ask, invite

请客 **qǐngkè** *v* treat (*sb. to a meal, etc.*)

请求 **qǐngqiú** *n* request; *v* ask for, petition, request

请愿 **qǐngyuàn** *v* petition

庆祝 **qìngzhù** *v* celebrate

穷 **qióng** *adj* poor

穷人 **qióngrén** *n* poor people

秋千 **qiūqiān** *n* swing

秋季 **qiūjì** *n* autumn, fall

秋天 **qiūtiān** *n* autumn, fall

囚犯 **qiúfàn** *n* prisoner, convict

求 **qiú** *v* beg, entreat

求助 **qiúzhù** *v* seek help

球 **qiú** *n* ball

球场 **qiúchǎng** *n* (*sports*) court, field

球队 **qiúduì** *n* (*sports*) team

球门 **qiúmén** *n* (*sports*) goal

球拍 **qiúpāi** *n* racket

球体 **qiútǐ** *n* sphere

区 **qū** *n* district, ward, area, region, zone

区别 **qūbié** *n* difference, distinction; *v* distinguish, differentiate

区域 **qūyù** *n* region, area

曲线 **qūxiàn** *n* curve

驱逐 **qūzhú** *v* banish, expel; 驱逐出境 **qūzhú chūjìng** *v* deport

驱逐舰 **qūzhújiàn** *n* destroyer

屈服 **qūfú** *v* give in, surrender, yield

躯干 **qūgàn** *n* torso

趋势 **qūshì** *n* trend, tendency

趋向 **qūxiàng** *v* tend to, incline to; *n* trend

渠道 **qúdào** *n* channel

曲调 **qǔdiào** *n* melody, tune

曲子 **qǔzi** *n* song, melody, tune

取得 **qǔdé** *v* gain, acquire, obtain

取消 **qǔxiāo** *v* cancel, call off

取保金 **qǔbǎojīn** *n* bail

去 **qù** *v* go, leave

圈 **quān** *n* circle, ring

全 **quán** *n* entire, whole, complete

全部 **quánbù** *n* entirety, all

全国 **quánguó** *n* the whole country; *adj* national
全国性 **quánguóxìng** *adj* nationwide, national
全面 **quánmiàn** *adj* comprehensive, overall
全民 **quánmín** *n* entire population
全球 **quánqiú** *n* the whole world; 全球化 **quánqiúhuà** *n* globalization
全体 **quántǐ** *adj* all, entire, whole
全职 **quánzhí** *adj* full-time
权 **quán** *n* right, power
权利 **quánlì** *n* right
权威 **quánwēi** *n* authority
拳击 **quánjī** *n* boxing; 拳击手 **quánjīshǒu** *n* boxer
拳头 **quántóu** *n* fist
痊愈 **quányù** *v* fully recover (*from an illness*)
劝 **quàn** *v* advise, urge, try to persuade
劝告 **quàngào** *v* advise, urge, admonish
缺 **quē** *v* lack, be short of
缺点 **quēdiǎn** *n* drawback, defeat; shortcoming, flaw, imperfection
缺乏 **quēfá** *v* lack, be short of
缺口 **quēkǒu** *n* gap, breach
缺席 **quēxí** *adj* absent
缺陷 **quēxiàn** *n* flaw, shortcoming
确定 **quèdìng** *v* determine, define; *adj* definite, certain
确切 **quèqiè** *adj* exact, definite, precise
确认 **quèrèn** *v* confirm, affirm
确实 **quèshí** *adv* indeed, really
群 **qún** *n* flock, crowd, group
群众 **qúnzhòng** *n* the masses

R

然而 **rán'ér** *conj* however, yet, but
然后 **ránhòu** *adv* afterwards, then
燃料 **ránliào** *n* fuel
燃烧 **ránshāo** *v* blaze, burn, kindle
染 **rǎn** *v* dye
染料 **rǎnliào** *n* dye, dyestuff
让 **ràng** *v* let, allow, make (*sb. do sth.*), give way, yield
饶恕 **ráoshù** *v* forgive, pardon
扰乱 **rǎoluàn** *v* harass, disturb
绕道 **ràodào** *v* make a detour

惹恼 rěnǎo *v* annoy

热 rè *adj* hot

热带 rèdài *n* the tropics; *adj* tropical

热切 rèqiè *adj* eager, fervent, earnest; *adv* eagerly, earnestly

热情 rèqíng *n* enthusiasm, zeal, warmth; *adj* warm, enthusiastic

人 rén *n* man, human being, person, people

人道 réndào *adj* humane; 人道主义 réndàozhǔyì *n* humanitarianism

人格 réngé *n* personality, character

人口 rénkǒu *n* population; 人口普查 rénkǒu pǔchá *n* census

人类 rénlèi *n* humanity, mankind; 人类学 rénlèixué *n* anthropology

人力 rénlì *n* manpower; 人力资源 rénlì zīyuán *n* human resources

人们 rénmen *n* people

人权 rénquán *n* human rights

人群 rénqún *n* crowd

人寿保险 rénshòu bǎoxiǎn *n* life insurance

人物 rénwù *n* character, cast

人行道 rénxíngdào *n* pavement, sidewalk

人行横道 rénxíng héngdào *n* pedestrian crossing

人员 rényuán *n* personnel

人造 rénzào *adj* man-made, synthetic, artificial

人质 rénzhì *n* hostage

仁慈 réncí *adj* humane, kind

忍受 rěnshòu *v* bear, put up with, tolerate

认出 rènchū *v* recognize

认得 rènde *v* know, recognize

认可 rènkě *v* approve; *n* approval

认识 rènshi *v* know, recognize

认为 rènwéi *v* deem, believe

认真 rènzhēn *adj* serious, earnest; *adv* seriously, earnestly

任 rèn *v* assume a post, take up a job; let, allow, give free rein to

任何 rènhé *adj* any; 任何地方 rènhé dìfāng *adv* anywhere; 任何人 rènhé rén *pron* anyone; 任何时候 rènhé shíhou *adv* anytime; 任何事 rènhé shì *pron* anything

任命 rènmìng *v* appoint; *n* appointment

任务 rènwu *n* assignment, task

扔 rēng *v* cast, fling, throw, discard

仍然 réngrán *adv* nonetheless, still

日 **rì** *n* sun; day
日本 **rìběn** *n* Japan; 日本人 **rìběnrén** *n* (*people*) Japanese
日常 **rìcháng** *adj* day-to-day, routine
日出 **rìchū** *n* sunrise
日记 **rìjì** *n* diary, journal
日历 **rìlì** *n* calendar
日落 **rìluò** *n* sunset
日期 **rìqī** *n* date
日语 **rìyǔ** *n* (*language*) Japanese
日志 **rìzhì** *n* log, record
日子 **rìzi** *n* day, date
荣誉 **róngyù** *n* honor
容量 **róngliàng** *n* capacity
容貌 **róngmào** *n* features, looks
容器 **róngqì** *n* container, vessel
容忍 **róngrěn** *v* tolerate
容易 **róngyì** *adj* easy
溶解 **róngjiě** *v* melt, dissolve
熔炉 **rónglú** *n* furnace
熔岩 **róngyán** *n* lava
融化 **rónghuà** *v* thaw, melt
冗长 **rǒngcháng** *adj* lengthy
冗余 **rǒngyú** *adj* redundant
柔和 **róuhé** *adj* soft, gentle, mild
柔软 **róuruǎn** *adj* velvet, soft
肉 **ròu** *n* flesh, meat
肉汁 **ròuzhī** *n* gravy
如 **rú** *v* like, as, as if; *conj* if
如此 **rúcǐ** *adv* so, such, in this way, like this
如果 **rúguǒ** *conj* if
如何 **rúhé** *adv* how
儒教 **rújiào** *n* Confucianism
蠕虫 **rúchóng** *n* worm
蠕动 **rúdòng** *v* wriggle
乳房 **rǔfáng** *n* breast
乳头 **rǔtóu** *n* nipple
乳制品 **rǔzhìpǐn** *n* dairy products
入 **rù** *v* enter; join
入口 **rùkǒu** *n* entrance
入门 **rùmén** *n* elementary course; *v* learn the rudiments of a
  subject
入场券 **rùchǎngquàn** *n* admission ticket

软 **ruǎn** *adj* soft
软管 **ruǎnguǎn** *n* tube
软件 **ruǎnjiàn** *n* software
瑞典 **ruìdiǎn** *n* Sweden; 瑞典人 **ruìdiǎnrén** *n* Swede, Swedish
瑞士 **ruìshì** *n* Switzerland; 瑞士人 **ruìshìrén** *n* Swiss
闰年 **rùnnián** *n* leap-year
润肤霜 **rùnfūshuāng** *n* moisturizing cream
润滑剂 **rùnhuájì** *n* lubricant
弱 **ruò** *adj* weak
弱点 **ruòdiǎn** *n* vulnerability, weakness

S

洒 **sǎ** *v* sprinkle, scatter
塞 **sāi** *v* stuff, fill in, squeeze in
塞子 **sāizi** *n* plug, cork, stopper
赛马 **sàimǎ** *n* horse racing, racehorse; 赛马场 **sàimǎchǎng** *n* racecourse, racetrack
赛跑 **sàipǎo** *n* race
三 **sān** *num* three
三角 **sānjiǎo** *n* triangle
三角形 **sānjiǎoxíng** *n* triangle
三明治 **sānmíngzhì** *n* sandwich
三十 **sānshí** *num* thirty
三月 **sānyuè** *n* March
伞 **sǎn** *n* umbrella
伞兵 **sǎnbīng** *n* paratroops
散 **sàn** *v* disseminate, scatter
散布 **sànbù** *v* spread (*rumors, etc.*)
散步 **sànbù** *v* take a walk, stroll
散发 **sànfā** *v* distribute, give out, send forth, emit
嗓音 **sǎngyīn** *n* voice
骚乱 **sāoluàn** *n* riot
骚扰 **sāorǎo** *v* annoy, harass
扫 **sǎo** *v* sweep
扫描 **sǎomiáo** *v* scan; 扫描器 **sǎomiáoqì** *n* scanner
嫂子 **sǎozi** *n* sister-in-law (*older brother's wife*)
扫帚 **sàozhou** *n* broom
色 **sè** *n* color
色情 **sèqíng** *adj* pornographic
森林 **sēnlín** *n* forest
杀害 **shāhài** *v* slay, kill, murder

杀手 **shāshǒu** *n* killer
杀死 **shāsǐ** *v* kill, put to death
沙丁鱼 **shādīngyú** *n* sardine
沙拉 **shālā** *n* salad
沙漠 **shāmò** *n* desert
沙子 **shāzi** *n* sand
刹车 **shāchē** *v* brake
鲨鱼 **shāyú** *n* shark
傻 **shǎ** *adj* silly
傻瓜 **shǎguā** *n* fool
傻笑 **shǎxiào** *v* giggle
晒斑 **shàibān** *n* sunburn
晒太阳 **shàitàiyáng** *v* sunbathe
山 **shān** *n* hill, mountain
山崩 **shānbēng** *n* landslide
山顶 **shāndǐng** *n* crest, peak, summit
山洞 **shāndòng** *n* cave
山谷 **shāngǔ** *n* valley
山脉 **shānmài** *n* mountain range
山羊 **shānyáng** *n* goat
删除 **shānchú** *v* delete, cross out
煽动 **shāndòng** *v* incite
闪电 **shǎndiàn** *n* lightning
闪光 **shǎnguāng** *n* flash of light, gleam; *v* gleam, glisten, glitter; 闪光灯 **shǎnguāngdēng** *n* flash, photoflash
闪烁 **shǎnshuò** *v* glitter, twinkle
扇形 **shànxíng** *adj* fan-shaped
扇子 **shànzi** *n* fan
善 **shàn** *adj* kind, good, friendly
善良 **shànliáng** *adj* kindhearted, good and honest
善意 **shànyì** *n* goodwill, good intention
擅长 **shàncháng** *v* specialize in, be good at
赡养费 **shànyǎngfèi** *n* alimony
伤 **shāng** *n* wound, injury; *v* wound, injure
伤疤 **shāngbā** *n* scar
伤残 **shāngcán** *n* disability; *adj* disabled
伤害 **shānghài** *v* hurt, harm, injure
伤痕 **shānghén** *n* scar
伤亡 **shāngwáng** *n* casualty
商标 **shāngbiāo** *n* trademark
商店 **shāngdiàn** *n* shop, store

商品 **shāngpǐn** *n* merchandise, goods, commodity, wares;
　商品交易会 **shāngpǐn jiāoyìhuì** *n* trade fair
商人 **shāngrén** *n* businessman, businessperson, merchant
商业 **shāngyè** *n* business, commerce
赏 **shǎng** *v* grant a reward, award
赏识 **shǎngshí** *v* appreciate, recognize the worth of
上 **shàng** *adj* upper, upward; last, previous, preceding; *v* go
　up, board, get on
上班 **shàngbān** *v* go to work
上边 **shàngbian** *n* above, over, on, on top of, on the surface of
上车 **shàngchē** *v* get on (*a bus, train, etc.*)
上床 **shàngchuáng** *v* go to bed
上帝 **shàngdì** *n* God
上光 **shàngguāng** *v* polish
上级 **shàngjí** *n* superior
上面 **shàngmian** *n* above, over, on, on top of, on the surface of
上坡 **shàngpō** *v* go uphill
上升 **shàngshēng** *v* go up, rise, increase
上诉 **shàngsù** *v* appeal
上午 **shàngwǔ** *n* morning
上校 **shàngxiào** *n* colonel
上学 **shàngxué** *v* go to school
上衣 **shàngyī** *n* jacket
上瘾 **shàngyǐn** *v* become addicted
烧 **shāo** *v* burn, cook, bake
烧烤 **shāokǎo** *v* grill, roast, toast; *n* barbecue
烧伤 **shāoshāng** *n* burn
勺 **sháo** *n* spoon
少 **shǎo** *adj* little, few
少数 **shǎoshù** *n* few, handful, minority
少数民族 **shǎoshù mínzú** *n* ethnic minority
少年 **shàonián** *n* juvenile, youngster
奢侈 **shēchǐ** *n* luxury; *adj* luxurious; 奢侈品 **shēchǐpǐn** *n*
　luxury product
舌头 **shétou** *n* tongue
蛇 **shé** *n* serpent, snake
设备 **shèbèi** *n* facility, equipment
设计 **shèjì** *n/v* design; 设计师 **shèjìshī** *n* designer
设立 **shèlì** *v* set up, establish
设施 **shèshī** *n* facilities
设想 **shèxiǎng** *v* conceive, imagine, assume; *n* tentative plan
设置 **shèzhì** *v* set up, install

社会 shèhuì *n* society; *adj* social; 社会主义 shèhuìzhǔyì *n* socialism

社论 shèlùn *n* editorial

社区 shèqū *n* community

射击 shèjī *v* shoot, fire

涉及 shèjí *v* involve, relate to

涉水 shèshuǐ *v* wade

赦免 shèmiǎn *v* pardon (*a criminal*)

摄影 shèyǐng *n* photography; 摄影师 shèyǐngshī *n* photographer

谁 shéi (*also pronounced as* shuí) *pron* who

谁的 shéide (*also pronounced as* shuíde) *pron* whose

申请 shēnqǐng *n* application; *v* apply

伸展 shēnzhǎn *v* extend, stretch

身份 shēnfen *n* status, identity

身份证 shēnfènzhèng *n* ID card

身体 shēntǐ *n* body, health

呻吟 shēnyín *v* groan, moan

绅士 shēnshì *n* gentleman

深 shēn *adj* deep

深度 shēndù *n* depth

深刻 shēnkè *adj* profound

深思 shēnsī *v* think deeply about, ponder deeply over

神 shén *n* god; *adj* divine

神话 shénhuà *n* myth, mythology

神经 shénjīng *n* nerve; 神经过敏 shénjīng guòmǐn *n* neuroticism; *adj* neurotic, oversensitive

神秘 shénmì *adj* mysterious

神圣 shénshèng *adj* holy, sacred

神志 shénzhì *n* consciousness

审查 shěnchá *v* examine, investigate

审判 shěnpàn *n* trial

审慎 shěnshèn *adj* cautious, careful

审问 shěnwèn *n* interrogation; *v* interrogate

审讯 shěnxùn *n* interrogation; *v* interrogate

审阅 shěnyuè *v* review and approval

肾脏 shènzàng *n* kidney

甚至 shènzhì *adv* even

升 shēng *n* liter; *v* rise, go up

生 shēng *adj* raw, uncooked; strange, unfamiliar

生病 shēngbìng *v* become sick, fall ill

生产 **shēngchǎn** *n* production; *v* produce; 生产者 **shēngchǎnzhě** *n* producer

生词 **shēngcí** *n* new word; 生词表 **shēngcíbiǎo** *n* list of new words, glossary

生长 **shēngzhǎng** *n* growth; *v* grow

生存 **shēngcún** *n* survival; *v* exist, survive

生动 **shēngdòng** *adj* vivid, lively

生活 **shēnghuó** *n* life, living, livelihood; 生活方式 **shēnghuó fāngshì** *n* lifestyle, way of life; 生活水平 **shēnghuó shuǐpíng** *n* standard of living

生计 **shēngjì** *n* livelihood

生命 **shēngmìng** *n* life; 生命力 **shēngmìnglì** *n* vitality

生日 **shēngrì** *n* birthday

生态学 **shēngtàixué** *n* ecology; *adj* ecological

生物 **shēngwù** *n* living things; 生物学 **shēngwùxué** *n* biology

生锈 **shēngxiù** *adj* rusty

生涯 **shēngyá** *n* career, profession

生意 **shēngyì** *n* business

生育 **shēngyù** *v* breed, reproduce; *n* reproduction

生殖 **shēngzhí** *n* reproduction; *v* reproduce; 生殖器 **shēngzhíqì** *n* genital, reproductive organ

声 **shēng** *n* sound, voice

声称 **shēngchēng** *v* allege, claim

声调 **shēngdiào** *n* (*pitch*) tone

声名 **shēngmíng** *n* reputation

声明 **shēngmíng** *n* statement

声音 **shēngyīn** *n* sound, voice

绳索 **shéngsuǒ** *n* cord

绳子 **shéngzi** *n* rope

省¹ **shěng** *n* province

省² **shěng** *v* save, economize, omit, leave out

胜 **shèng** *v* win

胜利 **shènglì** *n* triumph, victory; *v* win a victory; 胜利者 **shènglìzhě** *n* victor

圣诞节 **shèngdànjié** *n* Christmas

圣地 **shèngdì** *n* holy land, sacred place

圣经 **shèngjīng** *n* Bible

圣人 **shèngrén** *n* saint

盛会 **shènghuì** *n* gala

剩余 **shèngyú** *n* surplus, remainder, residual

尸体 **shītǐ** *n* corpse, dead body

失败 **shībài** *n* defeat, failure; *v* fail, be defeated

失眠 **shīmián** *v* suffer from insomnia
失明 **shīmíng** *v* lose one's sight, go blind
失去 **shīqù** *v* lose, be missing
失事 **shīshì** *v* (*airplane, ship, etc.*) crash, wreck
失望 **shīwàng** *n* disappointment; *adj* disappointed
失业 **shīyè** *n* unemployment; *adj* out of work, unemployed
失踪 **shīzōng** *v* disappear, go missing
诗 **shī** *n* poem, poetry; 诗人 **shīrén** *n* poet
诗歌 **shīgē** *n* poem, poetry
施肥 **shīféi** *v* fertilize
狮子 **shīzi** *n* lion
湿气 **shīqì** *n* moisture
湿润 **shīrùn** *adj* humid, wet, damp
十 **shí** *num* ten
十分 **shífēn** *adv* quite, very, extremely
十二月 **shí'èryuè** *n* December
十一月 **shíyīyuè** *n* November
十月 **shíyuè** *n* October
十字架 **shízìjià** *n* cross
十字路口 **shízì lùkǒu** *n* crossroads, intersection
什么 **shénme** *pron* what
石灰 **shíhuī** *n* lime
石窟 **shíkū** *n* grotto
石头 **shítou** *n* stone, rock
石油 **shíyóu** *n* petroleum
时代 **shídài** *n* era, age, times, epoch
时间 **shíjiān** *n* time; 时间表 **shíjiānbiǎo** *n* timetable, schedule
时刻 **shíkè** *n* moment
时髦 **shímáo** *adj* stylish, fashionable
时期 **shíqī** *n* period
时尚 **shíshàng** *n* fashion, vogue
时态 **shítài** *n* (*gram*) tense
时兴 **shíxīng** *adj* fashionable, popular
识别 **shíbié** *v* identify
实 **shí** *adj* solid, true, real
实际 **shíjì** *n* reality; *adj* practical, realistic, real, actual
实践 **shíjiàn** *n/v* practice
实例 **shílì** *n* instance, case, example
实现 **shíxiàn** *n* realization; *v* materialize, realize
实行 **shíxíng** *v* implement, carry out
实验室 **shíyànshì** *n* laboratory; lab

实用 **shíyòng** *adj* practical
食品 **shípǐn** *n* food, foodstuff
食物 **shíwù** *n* food
食欲 **shíyù** *n* appetite
士兵 **shìbīng** *n* soldier
士气 **shìqì** *n* morale
世纪 **shìjì** *n* century
世界 **shìjiè** *n* world
市 **shì** *n* city, municipality
市场 **shìchǎng** *n* bazaar, market
市长 **shìzhǎng** *n* mayor
市政 **shìzhèng** *n* municipality; *adj* municipal; 市政厅
    shìzhèngtīng *n* city hall
示威 **shìwēi** *v* demonstrate, protest; 示威游行 **shìwēi**
    yóuxíng *n* march, demonstration
式样 **shìyàng** *n* pattern, style, model
事 **shì** *n* thing, matter, affair
事故 **shìgù** *n* accident
事件 **shìjiàn** *n* incident
事实 **shìshí** *n* fact, truth; 事实上 **shìshí shàng** *adv* in fact, in
    reality, actually
事务 **shìwù** *n* general affairs, work, routine
事业 **shìyè** *n* career
势利 **shìli** *adj* snobbish
视觉 **shìjué** *n* vision; *adj* optical, visual
视力 **shìlì** *n* eyesight, vision
试 **shì** *v* try, test
试验 **shìyàn** *n/v* experiment, test
室 **shì** *n* room
室内 **shìnèi** *adj* indoor, interior
室温 **shìwēn** *n* room temperature
是 **shì** *adv* yes, right; *v* be
是否 **shìfǒu** *conj* whether or not
适当 **shìdàng** *adj* suitable, proper, appropriate
适度 **shìdù** *adj* moderate
适合 **shìhé** *v* fit, suit; *adj* suitable
释放 **shìfàng** *v* release, set free
誓言 **shìyán** *n* oath, vow
收 **shōu** *v* receive, accept
收到 **shōudào** *v* receive
收回 **shōuhuí** *v* take back, retrieve, recall
收获 **shōuhuò** *n* harvest, gain

收集 **shōují** *v* collect
收据 **shōujù** *n* receipt
收款员 **shōukuǎnyuán** *n* cashier
收容所 **shōuróngsuǒ** *n* asylum
收入 **shōurù** *n* income, revenue, earnings
收缩 **shōusuō** *v* shrink, contract
收养 **shōuyǎng** *v* adopt (*a child*)
收益 **shōuyì** *n* gain, benefit
收音机 **shōuyīnjī** *n* radio
手 **shǒu** *n* hand
手臂 **shǒubì** *n* arm
手表 **shǒubiǎo** *n* watch
手册 **shǒucè** *n* handbook, manual
手电筒 **shǒudiàntǒng** *n* flashlight, torch
手稿 **shǒugǎo** *n* manuscript
手工 **shǒugōng** *n* handwork; *adv* by hand; 手工艺
   shǒugōngyì *n* handicraft
手机 **shǒujī** *n* cell phone
手铐 **shǒukào** *n* handcuffs
手榴弹 **shǒuliúdàn** *n* grenade
手帕 **shǒupà** *n* handkerchief
手枪 **shǒuqiāng** *n* pistol
手势 **shǒushì** *n* gesture
手术 **shǒushù** *n* operation, surgery; 手术室 **shǒushùshì** *n*
   operating room
手套 **shǒutào** *n* glove
手提包 **shǒutíbāo** *n* handbag
手提箱 **shǒutíxiāng** *n* suitcase
手续 **shǒuxù** *n* procedure, formalities
手艺 **shǒuyì** *n* craft, skill
手语 **shǒuyǔ** *n* sign language
手掌 **shǒuzhǎng** *n* palm
手杖 **shǒuzhàng** *n* cane, walking stick
手指 **shǒuzhǐ** *n* finger
手镯 **shǒuzhuó** *n* bracelet
守门员 **shǒuményuán** *n* goalkeeper
守卫 **shǒuwèi** *v* guard
首都 **shǒudū** *n* capital of a country
首先 **shǒuxiān** *adv* firstly
首要 **shǒuyào** *adj* chief, of primary importance
受 **shòu** *v* suffer, be subject to; receive, accept; stand,
   endure, bear

受欢迎 **shòu huānyíng** *adj* popular
受贿 **shòuhuì** *v* accept a bribe
受苦 **shòukǔ** *v* suffer
受伤 **shòushāng** *v* be injured, be wounded
狩猎 **shòuliè** *n* hunting
兽 **shòu** *n* beast
兽皮 **shòupí** *n* hide
兽医 **shòuyī** *n* vet, veterinary surgeon, veterinary medicine
售 **shòu** *v* sell
售货员 **shòuhuòyuán** *n* salesman, salesperson
售票处 **shòupiàochù** *n* ticket office
授 **shòu** *v* award
授权 **shòuquán** *n* authorization; *v* authorize
瘦 **shòu** *adj* lean, thin, skinny
书 **shū** *n* book; 书店 **shūdiàn** *n* bookshop, bookstore
书法 **shūfǎ** *n* calligraphy
书架 **shūjià** *n* bookcase, bookshelf
书面 **shūmiàn** *adj* written; 书面语言 **shūmiàn yǔyán** *n* written language
书桌 **shūzhuō** *n* desk
叔叔 **shūshu** *n* uncle (*father's younger brother*)
梳子 **shūzi** *n* comb
疏忽 **shūhu** *n* neglect, negligence; *v* neglect
舒适 **shūshì** *adj* comfortable, cozy
输入 **shūrù** *v* input, enter (*data*), import
输血 **shūxuè** *v* transfuse; *n* blood transfusion
蔬菜 **shūcài** *n* vegetable
赎回 **shúhuí** *v* redeem
赎金 **shújīn** *n* ransom
熟 **shú** *adj* ripe; cooked; familiar
熟练 **shúliàn** *adj* skillful, skilled, experienced
熟人 **shúrén** *n* acquaintance
熟悉 **shúxī** *adj* familiar
数 **shǔ** *v* count
鼠 **shǔ** *n* mouse
属相 **shǔxiàng** *n* animals symbolizing the Twelve Branches used to designate years according to the Chinese lunar calendar
属于 **shǔyú** *v* belong to
术语 **shùyǔ** *n* term, terminology
束 **shù** *n* bunch, bouquet
树 **shù** *n* tree

143

树干 **shùgàn** *n* trunk
树篱 **shùlí** *n* hedge
树立 **shùlì** *v* erect, set up, establish
树林 **shùlín** *n* woods, forest
树皮 **shùpí** *n* bark
树叶 **shùyè** *n* leaf
树枝 **shùzhī** *n* branch
竖 **shù** *v* erect; *adj* vertical, upright; *n* vertical stroke (*in a Chinese character*)
竖起 **shùqǐ** *v* erect, hold up
数 **shù** *n* number
数据 **shùjù** *n* data; 数据库 **shùjùkù** *n* database
数量 **shùliàng** *n* amount, quantity
数码 **shùmǎ** *adj* digital
数学 **shùxué** *n* mathematics
数字 **shùzì** *n* digit, figure, number, numeral
漱口 **shùkǒu** *v* rinse one's mouth, gargle
刷 **shuā** *v* brush, paint
刷子 **shuāzi** *n* brush
衰老 **shuāilǎo** *adj* senile
衰落 **shuāiluò** *v* decline
衰弱 **shuāiruò** *adj* feeble, weak, fragile
衰退 **shuāituì** *v* degenerate, decline
摔倒 **shuāidǎo** *v* fall, fumble, lose one's balance
摔跤 **shuāijiāo** *n* wrestling; *v* wrestle; fall
涮羊肉 **shuànyángròu** *n* dip-boiled mutton slices
双 **shuāng** *adj* double, dual, twin; even; *n* pair
双胞胎 **shuāngbāotāi** *n* twins
双人床 **shuāngrénchuáng** *n* double bed
双人间 **shuāngrénjiān** *n* (*hotel*) double room
双语 **shuāngyǔ** *adj* bilingual; *n* dual language
谁 **shuí** (*also pronounced* **shéi**) *pron* who
谁的 **shuíde** (*also pronounced* **shéide**) *pron* whose
水 **shuǐ** *n* water
水坝 **shuǐbà** *n* dam
水果 **shuǐguǒ** *n* fruit
水壶 **shuǐhú** *n* kettle, watering can, canteen
水坑 **shuǐkēng** *n* puddle
水库 **shuǐkù** *n* reservoir
水墨画 **shuǐmòhuà** *n* Chinese brush drawing, ink and wash painting
水泥 **shuǐní** *n* cement

水牛 shuǐniú *n* water buffalo

水泡 shuǐpào *n* blister, bubble

水平 shuǐpíng *n* level, standard, proficiency; *adj* horizontal, level

水手 shuǐshǒu *n* sailor, seaman

水灾 shuǐzāi *n* flood

税 shuì *n* tax, duty

税收 shuìshōu *n* tax revenue

睡 shuì *v* sleep

睡袋 shuìdài *n* sleeping bag

睡觉 shuìjiào *v* sleep

睡衣 shuìyī *n* pajamas

顺便 shùnbiàn *adv* conveniently, in passing

顺从 shùncóng *v* comply with, be obedient to, submit to

顺序 shùnxù *n* sequence, order; *adv* in proper order, in turn

说 shuō *v* say, speak, talk, utter

说服 shuōfú *v* convince, persuade

说话 shuōhuà *v* say, speak, talk

说谎 shuōhuǎng *v* lie

说明 shuōmíng *v* explain, illustrate, show; *n* explanation; 说明书 shuōmíngshū *n* (*a booklet of*) directions, technical manual

丝绸 sīchóu *n* silk

司法 sīfǎ *n* administration of justice; 司法部 sīfǎbù *n* Ministry of Justice; 司法权 sīfǎquán *n* judicial power

司机 sījī *n* chauffeur, driver

司令 sīlìng *n* commander, commanding officer

司仪 sīyí *n* master of ceremony

私 sī *adj* private, personal, secret; illicit, illegal

私利 sīlì *n* self-interest

私人 sīrén *adj* private, personal

私下 sīxià *adv* privately, secretly

思考 sīkǎo *v* reflect on, think deeply, ponder over

思念 sīniàn *v* miss, think of, long for

撕 sī *v* tear

死 sǐ *v* die; *adj* dead

死亡 sǐwáng *n* death, doom

死刑 sǐxíng *n* death penalty, capital punishment

四 sì *num* four

四十 sìshí *num* forty

四月 sìyuè *n* April

饲养 sìyǎng *v* raise (*animals*)

寺庙 **sìmiào** *n* temple

松 **sōng** *adj* loose, slack; *v* loosen, slacken, relax

松树 **sōngshù** *n* pine tree

耸人听闻 **sǒngréntīngwén** *adj* sensational

送 **sòng** *v* deliver; give as a present; see sb. off

送货 **sònghuò** *v* deliver goods

搜 **sōu** *v* search

搜捕 **sōubǔ** *v* manhunt

搜索 **sōusuǒ** *v* search for, hunt for

搜寻 **sōuxún** *n* search for, look for, seek

苏打 **sūdá** *n* soda; 苏打水 **sūdǎshuǐ** *n* soda water

苏格兰 **sūgélán** *n* Scotland; 苏格兰人 **sūgélánrén** *n* Scot

苏醒 **sūxǐng** *v* regain consciousness, come to

诉苦 **sùkǔ** *v* vent grievances

诉讼 **sùsòng** *n* lawsuit, litigation

素 **sù** *n* vegetable; *adj* (*of color*) plain, simple

素菜 **sùcài** *n* vegetable dish

素食 **sùshí** *n* vegetarian diet; *adj* vegetarian; 素食者 **sùshízhě** *n* vegetarian

速度 **sùdù** *n* speed, pace, rate, velocity

宿舍 **sùshè** *n* dormitory

塑料 **sùliào** *n*/*adj* plastic

塑造 **sùzào** *v* mold, portray

酸 **suān** *n* acid; *adj* sour

酸奶 **suānnǎi** *n* yogurt

算 **suàn** *v* calculate, compute, figure out

算盘 **suànpán** *n* abacus

算术 **suànshù** *n* arithmetic

虽然 **suīrán** *conj* though, although

随 **suí** *v* follow, comply with, adapt to; let sb. do as he likes

随笔 **suíbǐ** *n* informal essay

随便 **suíbiàn** *adj* casual, random; *v* do as you like

随员 **suíyuán** *n* attaché

碎 **suì** *adj* fragmentary, broken

碎片 **suìpiàn** *n* fragment, scrap

隧道 **suìdào** *n* tunnel

孙女 **sūnnǚ** *n* granddaughter

孙子 **sūnzi** *n* grandson

损害 **sǔnhài** *v* harm, injure, damage

损坏 **sǔnhuài** *v* damage, injure

损失 **sǔnshī** *n* loss, damage; *v* lose

梭子 **suōzi** *n* shuttle

缩短 **suōduǎn** *v* shorten
缩写 **suōxiě** *n* abbreviation; *v* abbreviate
所 **suǒ** *n* place
所以 **suǒyǐ** *conj* so, therefore
所有 **suǒyǒu** *v* own, possess; *n* all; 所有格 **suǒyǒugé** *n* (*gram*) possessive case; 所有权 **suǒyǒuquán** *n* ownership; 所有人 **suǒyǒurén** *n* possessor, owner
索取 **suǒqǔ** *v* ask for, demand, exact
索引 **suǒyǐn** *n* index
琐碎 **suǒsuì** *adj* trivial, trifling
锁 **suǒ** *n/v* lock

T

T恤衫 **T-xùshān** *n* tee-shirt, T-shirt
他 **tā** *pron* he, him
他的 **tāde** *pron* his
他们 **tāmen** *pron* they, them
他们的 **tāmende** *pron* their, theirs
她 **tā** *pron* she, her
她的 **tāde** *pron* her, hers
它 **tā** *pron* it
它的 **tāde** *pron* its
它们 **tāmen** *pron* (*nonhuman*) they
塔 **tǎ** *n* tower, pagoda
踏 **tà** *v* step on, tread
踏板 **tàbǎn** *n* pedal, footboard
台 **táijiē** *n* platform, stage, terrace
台阶 **táijiē** *n* step, a flight of steps
太 **tài** *adv* too, excessively, very, extremely
太空 **tàikōng** *n* outer space; 太空船 **tàikōngchuán** *n* spacecraft, spaceship
太平间 **tàipíngjiān** *n* mortuary
太平洋 **tàipíngyáng** *n* Pacific Ocean
太太 **tàitai** *n* Mrs. , wife
太阳 **tàiyáng** *n* sun
太阳镜 **tàiyángjìng** *n* sunglasses
太阳能 **tàiyángnéng** *n* solar energy
态度 **tàidu** *n* attitude
坍塌 **tāntā** *v* collapse, cave in
贪婪 **tānlán** *adj* greedy
摊位 **tānwèi** *n* stall, booth

谈 **tán** *v* talk, chat, negotiate

谈判 **tánpàn** *n* negotiation; *v* negotiate

弹 **tán** *v* spring, bounce; play (*piano, guitar, etc.*)

坦白 **tǎnbái** *n* confession; *v* confess, own up; *adj* honest, frank, candid

坦克 **tǎnkè** *n* (*mil*) tank

坦率 **tǎnshuài** *adj* outspoken, straightforward, candid, frank

毯子 **tǎnzi** *n* blanket

叹息 **tànxī** *v* sigh, heave a sigh

探雷器 **tànléiqì** *n* mine, detector; *n* exploration

探索 **tànsuǒ** *v* explore, probe

探险家 **tànxiǎnjiā** *n* explorer

汤 **tāng** *n* soup

汤匙 **tāngchí** *n* spoon

汤面 **tāngmiàn** *n* noodle soup

糖 **táng** *n* sugar

糖果 **tángguǒ** *n* candy, sweets

糖浆 **tángjiāng** *n* syrup

糖尿病 **tángniàobìng** *n* diabetes

倘若 **tǎngruò** *conj* if, in case, supposing

躺 **tǎng** *v* lie, recline

逃 **táo** *v* run away, escape, flee

逃犯 **táofàn** *n* escaped criminal

逃跑 **táopǎo** *v* flee, escape, run away

逃脱 **táotuō** *v* succeed in escaping, get clear of

逃亡 **táowáng** *v* succeed in escaping, go into exile

桃子 **táozi** *n* peach

桃树 **táoshù** *n* peach tree

陶瓷 **táocí** *n* ceramics, pottery, porcelain

陶工 **táogōng** *n* potter

陶器 **táoqì** *n* pottery, earthware

淘气 **táoqì** *adj* naughty, mischievous

讨 **tǎo** *v* demand, ask for

讨价还价 **tǎojià huánjià** *v* bargain, haggle

讨论 **tǎolùn** *n* discussion; *v* discuss

讨厌 **tǎoyàn** *adj* disgusting, disagreeable, nasty; *v* be annoyed with, be disgusted with

套 **tào** *n* set, collection

套间 **tàojiān** *n* suite

套装 **tàozhuāng** *n* (*clothes*) suit

特别 **tèbié** *adj* particular, special, specially designated; *adv* especially, particularly, specially

特点 **tèdiǎn** *n* characteristic, trait, feature, specialty
特定 **tèdìng** *adj* specific, specified
特技 **tèjì** *n* stunt, special effects
特遣部队 **tèqiǎn bùduì** *n* (*mil*) task force
特区 **tèqū** *n* special region
特权 **tèquán** *n* privilege
特色 **tèsè** *n* characteristic, trait, feature
特赦 **tèshè** *n* special amnesty, special pardon
特殊 **tèshū** *adj* special, particular, peculiar
特务 **tèwu** *n* secret agent, spy
特有 **tèyǒu** *adj* peculiar, characteristic, unique
疼 **téng** *adj* painful, sore
疼痛 **téngtòng** *n* ache, pain; *adj* painful, sore
梯子 **tīzi** *n* ladder
踢 **tī** *v* kick
啼 **tí** *v* crow
提 **tí** *v* lift, raise; mention, put forth
提倡 **tíchàng** *v* advocate, promote, encourage
提供 **tígòng** *v* furnish, provide, offer
提交 **tíjiāo** *v* submit (*a document, proposal, etc.*)
提名 **tímíng** *n* nomination; *v* nominate
提起 **tíqǐ** *v* mention, speak of
提神 **tíshén** *v* refresh oneself
提示 **tíshì** *v* prompt, hint
提问 **tíwèn** *v* raise questions
提醒 **tíxǐng** *v* remind
题目 **tímù** *n* topic, title
体 **tǐ** *n* (*calligraphy, etc.*) style
体操 **tǐcāo** *n* gymnastics
体格 **tǐgé** *n* (*body*) constitution; 体格检查 **tǐgé jiǎnchá** *n* health checkup, physical examination
体积 **tǐjī** *n* volume
体贴 **tǐtiē** *adj* thoughtful, considerate
体验 **tǐyàn** *v* experience
体育 **tǐyù** *n* sports, physical education, physical training; 体育场 **tǐyùchǎng** *n* stadium; 体育馆 **tǐyùguǎn** *n* gymnasium, gym
剃 **tì** *v* shave
替 **tì** *v* replace, take the place of, substitute
替换 **tì** *v* replace, displace
替罪羊 **tìzuìyáng** *n* scapegoat
天 **tiān** *n* sky, heaven; day; season; weather

天才 **tiāncái** *n* genius, talent
天花板 **tiānhuābǎn** *n* ceiling
天空 **tiānkōng** *n* heaven, sky
天平 **tiānpíng** *n* scales
天气 **tiānqì** *n* weather
天然 **tiānrán** *adj* natural
天生 **tiānshēng** *adj* inherent, innate
天使 **tiānshǐ** *n* angel
天堂 **tiāntáng** *n* heaven, paradise
天线 **tiānxiàn** *n* antenna
天真 **tiānzhēn** *n* naïve
天主教 **tiānzhǔjiào** *n* Catholicism; 天主教徒 **tiānzhǔjiàotú**
  n Catholic
田 **tián** *n* field, farmland; 田野 **tiányě** *n* field; 田野调查
  tiányě diàochá *n* fieldwork
甜 **tián** *adj* sweet
舔 **tiǎn** *v* lick
挑 **tiāo** *v* pick, choose, select
调 **tiáo** *v* adjust
调焦 **tiáojiāo** *v* focus
调节 **tiáojié** *v* regulate, adjust; *n* regulation
调解 **tiáojiě** *n* mediation; *v* mediate
调停 **tiáotíng** *v* mediate, intervene; 调停者 **tiáotíngzhě** *n*
  mediator
调整 **tiáozhěng** *v* adjust, rectify; *n* adjustment, rectification
挑衅 **tiǎoxìn** *v* provoke
挑战 **tiǎozhàn** *n/v* challenge
条 **tiáo** *cl* (*for belt-like objects*)
条件 **tiáojiàn** *n* condition, term
条纹 **tiáowén** *n* streak, stripe
条约 **tiáoyuē** *n* pact
跳 **tiào** *v* jump, leap, bounce
跳伞 **tiàosǎn** *v* parachute
跳水 **tiàoshuǐ** *v* dive
跳舞 **tiàowǔ** *v* dance
跳跃 **tiàoyuè** *v* jump, leap
跳蚤 **tiàozǎo** *n* flea
铁 **tiě** *n* iron
铁轨 **tiěguǐ** *n* rail
铁路 **tiělù** *n* railway, railroad
听 **tīng** *v* listen, hear
听力 **tīnglì** *n* hearing

听任 **tīngrèn** *v* allow, let sb. do as he pleases
听写 **tīngxiě** *n* dictation
听众 **tīngzhòng** *n* audience
停 **tíng** *v* stop, halt, pause; 停车场 **tíngchēchǎng** *n* parking lot
停车 **tíngchē** *v* park, pull up
停顿 **tíngdùn** *v* stop, halt, pause, stall
停工 **tínggōng** *v* stop work, shut down
停火 **tínghuǒ** *v* cease fire, stop fighting
停留 **tíngliú** *v* stay, stop over
停战 **tíngzhàn** *n* truce, armistice
停止 **tíngzhǐ** *v* cease, stop, halt, suspend
通 **tōng** *adj* open, through; *v* lead to, be connected; understand, know; *n* authority, expert
通常 **tōngcháng** *adj* usual, general, normal; *adv* generally, usually, normally
通风 **tōngfēng** *v* ventilate; *adj* well-ventilated
通过 **tōngguò** *v* pass, get past; *adj* adopted (*a resolution, etc.*); *prep* through, by means of
通货 **tōnghuò** *n* currency; 通货膨胀 **tōnghuò péngzhàng** *n* inflation
通奸 **tōngjiān** *n* adultery
通路 **tōnglù** *n* thoroughfare, passageway
通信 **tōngxìn** *v* correspond; *n* correspondence
通讯 **tōngxùn** *n* communication, news report; 通讯录 **tōngxùnlù** *n* directory; 通讯社 **tōngxùnshè** *n* news agency, press agency; 通讯员 **tōngxùnyuán** *n* correspondent
通知 **tōngzhī** *n* announcement, notice; *v* inform, notify
同盟 **tóngméng** *n* alliance, league;
同情 **tóngqíng** *n* pity, sympathy; *v* pity, sympathize, show sympathy for
同时 **tóngshí** *adv* simultaneously, at the same time, in the meantime
同事 **tóngshì** *n* associate, colleague
同性恋 **tóngxìngliàn** *n* gay, homosexual
同学 **tóngxué** *n* classmate, fellow student
同样 **tóngyàng** *adj* same, similar; *adv* in the same way, likewise
同一 **tóngyī** *adj* identical, same
同意 **tóngyì** *n* consent; *v* consent, agree
铜 **tóng** *n* copper, bronze
童年 **tóngnián** *n* childhood
瞳孔 **tóngkǒng** *n* (*eye*) pupil

统计 **tǒngjì** *n* statistics; *v* add up, count

统治 **tǒngzhì** *v* govern, reign, rule, dominate; *n* domination, rule; 统治者 **tǒngzhìzhě** *n* ruler

桶 **tǒng** *n* barrel, bucket, tub

痛 **tòng** *v* ache, pain

痛哭 **tòngkū** *v* wail, cry

痛苦 **tòngkǔ** *n* misery, pain, bitter suffering, torment; *adj* painful

偷 **tōu** *v* steal; *adv* stealthily, secretly

头 **tóu** *n* head; top; end; beginning

头发 **tóufa** *n* hair

头盔 **tóukuī** *n* helmet

头脑 **tóunǎo** *n* mind, brains

头痛 **tóutòng** *n* headache

投 **tóu** *v* throw, fling, hurl, project

投标 **tóubiāo** *v* submit a tender, enter a bid

投机 **tóujī** *v* speculate; 投机主义 **tóujīzhǔyì** *n* opportunism

投降 **tóuxiáng** *v* surrender; *n* capitulation

投票 **tóupiào** *v* vote, cast a vote

投入 **tóurù** *v* throw in, put into

投射 **tóushè** *v* project; (*basketball*) shoot

投掷 **tóuzhì** *v* throw, hurl

投资 **tóuzī** *n* investment; *v* invest; 投资者 **tóuzīzhě** *n* investor

骰子 **tóuzi** *n* dice

透 **tòu** *v* penetrate, pass through, seep through; *adv* fully, thoroughly

透镜 **tòujìng** *n* lens

透明 **tòumíng** *adj* transparent

透视 **tòushì** *n* perspective; fluoroscopy

秃 **tū** *adj* bald; 秃子 **tūzi** *n* bald person

秃鹫 **tūjiù** *n* vulture

突出 **tūchū** *adj* prominent, outstanding; *v* highlight, give prominence to

突破 **tūpò** *v* break through; *n* breakthrough

突然 **tūrán** *adv* suddenly, all of a sudden, abruptly

突袭 **tūxí** *n* surprise attack

图 **tú** *n* diagram, chart, graph, drawing

图表 **túbiǎo** *n* diagram, chart, graph

图画 **túhuà** *n* drawing, picture, painting

图解 **tújiě** *n* illustration via a diagram or a graph

图书馆 **túshūguǎn** *n* library; 图书馆员 **túshūguǎnyuán** *n* librarian

图像 **túxiàng** *n* image, picture

图章 **túzhāng** *n* seal, stamp

徒劳 **túláo** *adj* futile, in vain

途径 **tújìng** *n* approach, way, channel

屠夫 **túfū** *n* butcher

屠杀 **túshā** *v* slaughter, massacre, butcher

屠宰 **túzǎi** *v* slaughter, butcher; 屠宰场 **túzǎichǎng** *n* slaughterhouse

土 **tǔ** *n* soil, earth; *adj* local, native

土产 **tǔchǎn** *n* local product

土地 **tǔdì** *n* land, soil

土耳其 **tǔ'ěrqí** *n* Turkey; 土耳其人 **tǔ'ěrqírén** *n* Turk; 土耳其语 **tǔ'ěrqíyǔ** *n* (*language*) Turkish

土壤 **tǔrǎng** *n* soil

吐 **tǔ** *v* spit

吐气 **tǔqì** *v* exhale

兔 **tù** *n* rabbit

团 **tuán** *n* group, delegation

团结 **tuánjié** *v* unite, rally; *adj* united

团聚 **tuánjù** *v* reunite

团体 **tuántǐ** *n* organization, group

推 **tuī** *v* push, shove

推测 **tuīcè** *n* speculation, guess; *v* speculate, guess, infer

推迟 **tuīchí** *v* defer, postpone, put off

推动 **tuīdòng** *v* push, urge; 推动力 **tuīdònglì** *n* impetus, urge, motive

推翻 **tuīfān** *v* overthrow

推荐 **tuījiàn** *v* recommend; *n* recommendation; 推荐信 **tuījiànxìn** *n* recommendation letter

推理 **tuīlǐ** *n* deduction, inference; *v* deduce, infer

推算 **tuīsuàn** *v* calculate, reckon

推托 **tuītuō** *v* evade, shirk

推诿 **tuīwěi** *v* shift reponsibility

推销 **tuīxiāo** *v* promote sales, market; 推销员 **tuīxiāoyuán** *n* salesman

腿 **tuǐ** *n* leg

退 **tuì** *v* withdraw, quit, retreat; give back, refund

退出 **tuìchū** *v* withdraw, quit, back out

退还 **tuìhuán** *v* return, send back

退款 **tuìkuǎn** *n/v* refund

退伍 **tuìwǔ** *v* be demobilized, be discharged from active military service; 退伍军人 **tuìwǔ jūnrén** *n* veteran

退休 **tuìxiū** *v* retire; *adj* retired; 退休金 **tuìxiūjīn** *n* pension

褪色 **tuìsè** *v* (*color*) fade

吞 **tūn** *v* swallow, gulp down

吞食 **tūnshí** *v* devour, swallow

臀部 **túnbù** *n* buttocks

托 **tuō** *v* ask sb. to do sth., entrust

托儿所 **tuō'érsuǒ** *n* nursery, daycare center

托盘 **tuōpán** *n* tray

拖 **tuō** *v* drag, tow

拖车 **tuōchē** *n* trailer

拖拉机 **tuōlājī** *n* tractor

拖鞋 **tuōxié** *n* slipper

脱 **tuō** *v* (*clothes*) take off, cast off

脱离 **tuōlí** *v* separate from, break away from, be divorced from

唾沫 **tuòmo** *n* spittle, saliva

W

挖 **wā** *v* dig

歪 **wāi** *adj* askew, crooked

歪曲 **wāiqū** *v* distort; *n* distortion

外 **wài** *adj* outer, outward, outside; foreign, external

外边 **wàibian** *n* outside, out, exterior; surface

外表 **wàibiǎo** *n* façade, surface, outward appearance

外部 **wàibù** *adj* exterior, external

外公 **wàigōng** *n* grandfather (*maternal*)

外观 **wàiguān** *n* outward appearance, exterior

外国 **wàiguó** *n* foreign country; *adj* foreign; 外国人 **wàiguórén** *n* foreigner

外汇 **wàihuì** *n* foreign exchange

外交 **wàijiāo** *n* foreign affairs, diplomacy; *adj* diplomatic; 外交部长 **wàijiāo bùzhǎng** *n* foreign minister; 外交官 **wàijiāoguān** *n* diplomat; 外交关系 **wàijiāoguānxì** *n* diplomatic relations

外科 **wàikē** *n* surgical department; 外科医生 **wàikē yīshēng** *n* surgeon

外面 **wàimian** *n* outside, out; exterior, surface

外婆 **wàipó** *n* grandmother (*maternal*)

外侨 **wàiqiáo** *n* alien, foreign national

外伤 **wàishāng** *n* trauma

外甥 **wàisheng** *n* nephew (*sister's son*)
外甥女 **wàishēngnǚ** *n* niece (*sister's daughter*)
外孙 **wàisūn** *n* grandson (*daughter's son*)
外孙女 **wàisūnnǚ** *n* granddaughter (*daughter's daughter*)
外形 **wàixíng** *n* external form, appearance
外祖父 **wàizǔfù** *n* grandfather (*maternal*)
外祖母 **wàizǔmǔ** *n* grandmother (*maternal*)
弯曲 **wānqū** *adj* curved, bent
完 **wán** *v* finish, complete, use up, run out
完成 **wánchéng** *v* accomplish, complete, fulfill
完美 **wánměi** *adj* perfect
完全 **wánquán** *adj* complete, whole; *adv* quite, completely, fully, entirely
完整 **wánzhěng** *adj* complete, intact
玩 **wán** *v* play, have fun, enjoy
玩具 **wánjù** *n* toy
玩偶 **wán'ǒu** *n* doll
玩笑 **wánxiào** *n* joke, jest
顽固 **wángù** *adj* obstinate, stubborn
顽皮 **wánpí** *adj* mischievous, naughty
挽回 **wǎnhuí** *v* retrieve, redeem
晚 **wǎn** *adj* late; *n* evening, night
晚餐 **wǎncān** *n* supper, dinner
晚饭 **wǎnfàn** *n* supper, dinner
晚年 **wǎnnián** *n* old age
晚期 **wǎnqī** *n* (*of disease*) later period, advanced stage
晚上 **wǎnshang** *n* evening
碗 **wǎn** *n* bowl
碗橱 **wǎnchú** *n* cupboard
王 **wáng** *n* king
王冠 **wángguān** *n* royal crown
王国 **wángguó** *n* kingdom
王室 **wángshì** *n* royal family, imperial court
王子 **wángzǐ** *n* prince
网 **wǎng** *n* net, web
网络 **wǎngluò** *n* network
网球 **wǎngqiú** *n* tennis; 网球场 **wǎngqiúchǎng** *n* tennis court
往 **wǎng** *prep* in the direction of, toward
往返票 **wǎngfǎnpiào** *n* return ticket, round-trip ticket
往往 **wǎngwǎng** *adv* often, frequently
忘 **wàng** *v* forget
忘恩负义 **wàng'ēn fùyì** *adj* ungrateful

忘记 wàngjì *v* forget
望 wàng *v* gaze into the distance, look over, look far ahead
望远镜 wàngyuǎnjìng *n* telescope, binoculars
危害 wēihài *v* jeopardize, harm, endanger
危机 wēijī *n* crisis, peril
危险 wēixiǎn *n* danger, hazard; *adj* dangerous, hazardous, risky
威尔士 wēi'ěrshì *n* Wales
威力 wēilì *n* might, power
威士忌 wēishìjì *n* whiskey, whisky
威望 wēiwàng *n* prestige
威胁 wēixié *n* menace, threat; *v* threaten
威严 wēiyán *adj* dignified, stately, majestic
微风 wēifēng *n* breeze
微弱 wēiruò *adj* faint, feeble, weak
微小 wēixiǎo *adj* tiny, small, little
微笑 wēixiào *n*; *v* smile
微型 wēixíng *adj* miniature, mini-
为 wèi *prep* for, in the interest of, for the benefit of
为了 wèile *prep* for, for the sake of, in order to
为什么 wèishénme *adv* why
围 wéi *v* enclose, surround
围攻 wéigōng *v* besiege, lay siege to, jointly attack
围巾 wéijīn *n* scarf
围棋 wéiqí *n* I-go, the game of go
围裙 wéiqún *n* apron
违法 wéifǎ *v* break the law; *adj* illegal
违反 wéifǎn *v* violate, infringe, run counter to
违抗 wéikàng *v* defy, disobey
唯恐 wéikǒng *v* fear
唯一 wéiyī *adj* sole, only
维持 wéichí *v* maintain, sustain, preserve, keep
维生素 wéishēngsù *n* vitamin
伪君子 wěijūnzǐ *n* hypocrite
伪善 wěishàn *adj* hypocritical
伪造 wěizào *v* fabricate, forge, feign, falsify, counterfeit
伪装 wěizhuāng *v* disguise, pretend
尾巴 wěiba *n* tail
纬度 wěidù *n* latitude
委员 wěiyuán *n* committee member; 委员会 wěiyuánhuì *n* committee, commission, council
卫兵 wèibīng *n* guard, bodyguard

卫生 **wèishēng** *n* sanitation, hygiene; *adj* sanitary, hygienic;
　　卫生纸 **wèishēngzhǐ** *n* toilet paper
卫星 **wèixīng** *n* satellite
未 **wèi** *adv* not, not yet, no
未婚 **wèihūn** *adj* unmarried, single; 未婚夫 **wèihūnfū** *n*
　　fiancé; 未婚妻 **wèihūnqī** *n* fiancée
未来 **wèilái** *adj* future, time to come
未知 **wèizhī** *adj* unknown
位于 **wèiyú** *v* be located at, be situated at, lie in
位置 **wèizhi** *n* location, position
位子 **wèizi** *n* seat; position
味道 **wèidao** *n* flavor, taste
胃 **wèi** *n* stomach
胃口 **wèikǒu** *n* appetite
胃痛 **wèitòng** *n* stomachache
喂 **wèi** *v* feed
温 **wēn** *adj* warm, lukewarm, tepid; *n* temperature
温度 **wēndù** *n* temperature; 温度计 **wēndùjì** *n*
　　thermometer
温和 **wēnhé** *adj* temperate, mild, moderate
温暖 **wēnnuǎn** *adj* warm; *n* warmth
温室 **wēnshì** *n* greenhouse
温顺 **wēnshùn** *adj* meek, docile, tame
文 **wén** *n* language; writing; *adj* civil, gentle, refined
文房四宝 **wénfángsìbǎo** *n* the four treasures of the study
　　(writing brush, ink stick, ink slab, and paper)
文化 **wénhuà** *n* culture
文集 **wénjí** *n* collected works
文件 **wénjiàn** *n* document, papers; 文件夹 **wénjiànjiā** *n*
　　folder
文具 **wénjù** *n* stationery; 文具店 **wénjùdiàn** *n* stationer,
　　stationery store
文盲 **wénmáng** *n* illiterate person; illiteracy
文明 **wénmíng** *n* civilization; *adj* civil, civilized
文凭 **wénpíng** *n* diploma
文学 **wénxué** *n* literature; 文学家 **wénxuéjiā** *n* man of letters
文雅 **wényǎ** *adj* elegant, cultured, refined
文章 **wénzhāng** *n* article, essay
纹身 **wénshēn** *n/v* tattoo
闻 **wén** *v* smell
蚊子 **wénzi** *n* mosquito
吻 **wěn** *v/n* kiss

稳 wěn *adj* stable, steady
稳定 wěndìng *adj* stable, steady; 稳定性 wěndìngxìng *n* stability
问 wèn *v* ask
问号 wènhào *n* question mark
问卷 wènjuàn *n* questionnaire
问题 wèntí *n* matter, problem, question, issue
蜗牛 wōniú *n* snail
我 wǒ *pron* I, me
我的 wǒde *pron* mine, my
我们 wǒmen *pron* we, us
我们的 wǒmende *pron* our, ours
我们自己 wǒmen zìjǐ *pron* ourselves
我自己 wǒ zìjǐ *pron* myself
卧室 wòshì *n* bedroom
握 wò *v* hold in hand
握手 wòshǒu *v* shake hands
乌鸦 wūyā *n* crow
污点 wūdiǎn *n* stain
污秽 wūhuì *adj* filthy, foul, squalid
污染 wūrǎn *n* pollution, contamination; *v* contaminate, pollute
屋顶 wūdǐng *n* roof
屋子 wūzi *n* house
无 wú *v* not have, there is not; *adv* no, not, without
无常 wúcháng *adj* uncertain
无耻 wúchǐ *adj* shameless
无处 wúchù *adv* nowhere
无辜 wúgū *adj* innocent
无关 wúguān *adj* unrelated
无家可归 wújiā kěguī *adj* homeless
无价 wújià *adj* invaluable, priceless
无可救药 wúkě jiùyào *adj* incurable
无礼 wúlǐ *adj* impolite, insolent
无力 wúlì *adj* powerless
无论何时 wúlùn héshí *conj* whenever, no matter when
无论哪个 wúlùn nǎgè *pron* whichever
无论哪里 wúlùn nǎli *adv* wherever, no matter where
无论如何 wúlùn rúhé *adv* anyhow, anyway, no matter how
无论什么 wúlùn shénme *pron* whatever
无论谁 wúlùn shuí *pron* whoever, no matter whom

无能 **wúnéng** *adj* incapable; 无能为力 **wúnéng wéilì** *adj* powerless, helpless

无情 **wúqíng** *adj* ruthless, merciless

无趣 **wúqù** *adj* uninteresting, boring

无人 **wúrén** *pron* nobody

无数 **wúshù** *adj* countless, numerous

无私 **wúsī** *adj* selfless, unselfish

无条件 **wútiáojiàn** *adj* unconditional

无畏 **wúwèi** *adj* fearless

无瑕 **wúxiá** *adj* immaculate, flawless

无限 **wúxiàn** *adj* infinite, limitless, unlimited

无效 **wúxiào** *adj* ineffective, invalid, void

无形 **wúxíng** *adj* invisible

无疑 **wúyí** *adv* doubtless, undoubtedly

无意 **wúyì** *v* have no intention of doing; *adv* inadvertently, unwittingly; 无意识 **wúyìshí** *adj* unconscious

无用 **wúyòng** *adj* futile, useless

无知 **wúzhī** *adj* ignorant, uneducated

无止境 **wúzhǐjìng** *adj* endless

无助 **wúzhù** *adj* helpless

无罪 **wúzuì** *adj* innocent

五 **wǔ** *num* five

五十 **wǔshí** *num* fifty

五月 **wǔyuè** *n* May

午餐 **wǔcān** *n* lunch

午饭 **wǔfàn** *n* lunch

午宴 **wǔyàn** *n* luncheon

午夜 **wǔyè** *n* midnight

武 **wǔ** *n* force; *adj* military

武器 **wǔqì** *n* arms, weapon

武术 **wǔshù** *n* martial art

武装 **wǔzhuāng** *adj* armed; 武装力量 **wǔzhuāng lìliàng** *n* armed forces, military force

侮辱 **wǔrǔ** *n/v* insult

舞 **wǔ** *n* dance

舞蹈 **wǔdǎo** *n* dance; 舞蹈家 **wǔdǎojiā** *n* dancer

舞会 **wǔhuì** *n* (*dance*) ball

舞台 **wǔtái** *n* stage

舞厅 **wǔtīng** *n* ballroom

物 **wù** *n* thing, object

物理 **wùlǐ** *n* physics; 物理学家 **wùlǐxuéjiā** *n* physicist

物体 **wùtǐ** *n* object

物质 wùzhì *n* matter, substance
误会 wùhuì *v* misunderstand; *n* misunderstanding
误算 wùsuàn *v* miscalculate; *n* miscalculation
误用 wùyòng *v* misuse
雾 wù *n* fog

X

X射线 X-shèxiàn *n* X-ray
西 xī *n* west
西班牙 xībānyá *n* Spain; 西班牙人 xībānyárén *n* (*people*)
　　Spanish; 西班牙语 xībānyáyǔ *n* (*language*) Spanish
西北 xīběi *n* northwest
西边 xībian *n* west, west side
西部 xībù *n* west, western part
西方 xīfāng *n* West; 西方人 xīfāngrén *n* Westerner
西瓜 xīguā *n* watermelon
西红柿 xīhóngshì *n* tomato
西南 xīnán *n* southwest
西装 xīzhuāng *n* suit
吸 xī *v* suck, inhale
吸气 xīqì *v* breathe in, inhale
吸管 xīguǎn *n* drinking straw
吸收 xīshōu *v* absorb, accept
吸血鬼 xīxuèguǐ *n* vampire
吸烟 xīyān *v* smoke
吸引 xīyǐn *v* attract, draw; 吸引力 xīyǐnlì *n* gravity; appeal,
　　attraction; 吸引人 xīyǐnrén *adj* appealing, attractive
希望 xīwàng *n/v* hope, wish
希伯来语 xībóláiyǔ *n* Hebrew
牺牲 xīshēng *v/n* sacrifice
稀 xī *adj* thin, watery
稀薄 xībó *adj* (*of air*) thin
稀少 xīshǎo *adj* rare, few, scarce
稀释 xīshì *v* dilute
锡 xī *n* tin
熄火 xīhuǒ *v* (*engine*) stall
熄灭 xīmiè *v* extinguish, put out (*fire*)
蜥蜴 xīyì *n* lizard
膝盖 xīgài *n* knee
蟋蟀 xīshuài *n* cricket
习惯 xíguàn *n* habit, custom; *v* be used to

习俗 xísú *n* custom
袭击 xíjī *v* raid, strike
媳妇 xífù *n* daughter-in-law
洗 xǐ *v* wash
洗涤 xǐdí *v* wash
洗发液 xǐfàyè *n* shampoo
洗劫 xǐjié *v* loot, ransack
洗衣店 xǐyīdiàn *n* laundry
洗衣房 xǐyīfáng *n* laundry room
洗衣粉 xǐyīfěn *n* washing powder
洗澡 xǐzǎo *v* take a bath/shower
喜爱 xǐ'ài *v* favor, like
喜欢 xǐhuan *v* like
喜剧 xǐjù *n* comedy; 喜剧演员 xǐjù yǎnyuán *n* comedian
喜庆 xǐqìng *adj* festive; *v* celebrate
戏 xì *n* drama, opera
戏剧 xìjù *n* drama
戏弄 xìnòng *v* kid
戏曲 xìqǔ *n* traditional opera
系 xì *n* (*college*) department, faculty; 系主任 xìzhǔrèn *n* (*college*) department chair
系列 xìliè *n* series
系统 xìtǒng *n* system; 系统软件 xìtǒng ruǎnjiàn *n* system software
细 xì *adj* thin, slender; fine, delicate, exquisite; meticulous, detailed
细胞 xìbāo *n* cell
细节 xìjié *n* detail, particular
细菌 xìjūn *n* bacteria, germ
虾 xiā *n* shrimp
瞎 xiā *adj* blind
瑕疵 xiácī *n* defect
峡谷 xiágǔ *n* gorge, valley
狭窄 xiázhǎi *adj* narrow
下 xià *v* go down; *adj* next; *adv* down
下边 xiàbian *n* below, under, underneath
下面 xiàmian *n* below, under, underneath; next, following
下车 xiàchē *v* get off (*a bus, train, etc.*)
下沉 xiàchén *v* sink
下船 xiàchuán *v* disembark, get off (*a boat or ship*)
下蛋 xiàdàn *v* lay an egg
下定义 xiàdìngyì *v* define

下颚 xià'è *n* chin
下级 xiàjí *n* subordinate
下降 xiàjiàng *v* descend
下落 xiàluò *n* whereabouts
下坡 xiàpō *v* go downhill
下属 xiàshǔ *n* subordinate
下水道 xiàshuǐdào *n* sewer
下午 xiàwǔ *n* afternoon
下星期 xiàxīngqī *n* next week
下雪 xiàxuě *v* snow
下一 xiàyī *adj* next
下雨 xiàyǔ *v* rain
下载 xiàzǎi *v* download
下周 xiàzhōu *adv* next week
吓唬 xiàhu *v* frighten, scare
夏季 xiàjì *n* summer, summertime
夏天 xiàtiān *n* summer
先 xiān *adv* first, earlier
先进 xiānjìn *adj* advanced
先生 xiānsheng *n* mister (Mr.), sir; husband
先天 xiāntiān *adj* congenital, inborn
先知 xiānzhī *n* prophet
纤维 xiānwéi *n* fiber
闲 xián *adj* not busy, idle, unoccupied
闲暇 xiánxiá *n* leisure
咸 xián *adj* salty
嫌疑犯 xiányífàn *n* suspect
显得 xiǎnde *v* look, appear
显而易见 xiǎn'ér yìjiàn *adj* conspicuous, obvious
显露 xiǎnlù *v* reveal, unfold
显然 xiǎnrán *adv* evidently, obviously
显示 xiǎnshì *v* show, reveal
显微镜 xiǎnwēijìng *n* microscope
显著 xiǎnzhù *adj* distinctive, notable, noteworthy
县 xiàn *n* county; 县城 xiànchéng *n* county seat
现成 xiànchéng *adj* on hand, ready-made
现存 xiàncún *adj* present, existing
现代 xiàndài *adj* modern; 现代化 xiàndàihuà *v* modernize;
    n modernization
现今 xiànjīn *adv* nowadays
现金 xiànjīn *n* cash

想法 xiǎngfa

现实 **xiànshí** *n* reality; *adj* realistic; 现实主义 **xiànshízhǔyì** *n* realism
现象 **xiànxiàng** *n* phenomenon
现有 **xiànyǒu** *adj* existing
现在 **xiànzài** *n* now, present
线 **xiàn** *n* line, string, thread
线索 **xiànsuǒ** *n* clue
限制 **xiànzhì** *v* confine, limit, restrict; *n* restriction, limitation
宪法 **xiànfǎ** *n* constitution
宪章 **xiànzhāng** *n* charter
陷阱 **xiànjǐng** *n* trap
陷入 **xiànrù** *v* plunge, get into
馅饼 **xiànbǐng** *n* pie
羡慕 **xiànmù** *v* envy, admire
献词 **xiàncí** *n* dedication
乡村 **xiāngcūn** *n* country, village
乡下 **xiāngxià** *n* rural area, countryside
相当 **xiāngdāng** *adv* quite, rather, fairly
相等 **xiāngděng** *adj* equal, equivalent
相对 **xiāngduì** *adv* relatively
相反 **xiāngfǎn** *adj* contrary
相互 **xiānghù** *adv* one another, mutually
相配 **xiāngpèi** *v* match
相似 **xiāngsì** *n* resemblance, similarity; *adj* alike, similar
相同 **xiāngtóng** *adj* same
相像 **xiāngxiàng** *n* likeness
相信 **xiāngxìn** *v* believe
香 **xiāng** *adj* fragrant, aromatic, scented
香槟酒 **xiāngbīnjiǔ** *n* champagne
香草 **xiāngcǎo** *n* vanilla
香肠 **xiāngcháng** *n* sausage
香港 **xiānggǎng** *n* Hong Kong
香蕉 **xiāngjiāo** *n* banana
香料 **xiāngliào** *n* spice
香水 **xiāngshuǐ** *n* perfume
香味 **xiāngwèi** *n* scent
香烟 **xiāngyān** *n* cigarette
箱子 **xiāngzi** *n* chest, trunk, box
详细 **xiángxì** *adj* detailed
享受 **xiǎngshòu** *v* enjoy; *n* enjoyment
想 **xiǎng** *v* think, miss; would like
想法 **xiǎngfa** *n* idea, thought

想象 xiǎngxiàng *v* fancy, imagine; 想象力 xiǎngxiànglì *n* imagination

想要 xiǎngyào *v* desire, wish

相貌 xiàngmào *n* looks

相片 xiāngpiàn *n* photo

相声 xiàngsheng *n* comic dialog

向 xiàng *prep* in the direction of, toward(s)

向导 xiàngdǎo *n* guide

项链 xiàngliàn *n* necklace

项目 xiàngmù *n* item; project

像 xiàng *v* resemble, take after; *prep* such as, like; *n* image, portrait

象 xiàng *n* elephant

象鼻子 xiàngbízi *n* trunk

象棋 xiàngqí *n* Chinese chess

象牙 xiàngyá *n* ivory

象征 xiàngzhēng *v* stand for, symbolize; *n* symbol

橡胶 xiàngjiāo *n* rubber

橡皮 xiàngpí *n* rubber; 橡皮图章 xiàngpí túzhāng *n* rubber stamp

橡皮圈 xiàngpíquān *n* rubber band

橡树 xiàngshù *n* oak

肖像 xiāoxiàng *n* portrait

削 xiāo *v* peel

消沉 xiāochén *adj* depressed

消毒 xiāodú *v* sterilize, disinfect

消防车 xiāofángchē *n* fire engine

消防队 xiāofángduì *n* fire brigade, fire department; 消防队员 xiāofáng duìyuán *n* fireman

消防站 xiāofángzhàn *n* fire station

消费 xiāofèi *v* consume; 消费者 xiāofèizhě *n* consumer

消耗 xiāohào *n* consumption; *v* consume

消化 xiāohuà *v* digest; 消化不良 xiāohuà bùliáng *n* indigestion

消灭 xiāomiè *v* annihilate, wipe out, eliminate

消遣 xiāoqiǎn *n* diversion, pastime, recreation, relaxation

消散 xiāosàn *v* clear off, scatter

消失 xiāoshī *v* disappear, vanish

消息 xiāoxi *n* news

萧条 xiāotiáo *n* depression; recession; *adj* desolate, bleak

销路 xiāolù *n* market

销子 xiāozi *n* peg

小 xiǎo *adj* little, small

小报 xiǎobào *n* tabloid
小册子 xiǎocèzi *n* booklet, brochure, pamphlet
小吃 xiǎochī *n* snack; 小吃店 xiǎochīdiàn *n* snack bar
小丑 xiǎochǒu *n* clown
小道 xiǎodào *n* trail; 小道消息 xiǎodào xiāoxi *n* hearsay, the grapevine
小贩 xiǎofàn *n* vendor, peddler
小费 xiǎofèi *n* gratuity, tip
小孩 xiǎohái *n* kid, child
小伙子 xiǎohuǒzi *n* lad, chap
小鸡 xiǎojī *n* chick
小姐 xiǎojie *n* Miss, young lady
小路 xiǎolù *n* path
小麦 xiǎomài *n* wheat
小猫 xiǎomāo *n* kitten
小牛 xiǎoniú *n* calf
小品 xiǎopǐn *n* skit
小时 xiǎoshí *n* hour
小说 xiǎoshuō *n* fiction, novel; 小说家 xiǎoshuōjiā *n* novelist
小提琴 xiǎotíqín *n* violin
小偷 xiǎotōu *n* burglar, thief
小巷 xiǎoxiàng *n* alley, lane
小心 xiǎoxīn *v* beware, look out; *adj* careful, cautious
小学 xiǎoxué *n* elementary school, primary school
哮喘 xiàochuǎn *n* asthma
效果 xiàoguǒ *n* effect
效劳 xiàoláo *v* work for, be at sb.'s service
效率 xiàolǜ *n* efficiency
效应 xiàoyìng *n* effect
校园 xiàoyuán *n* campus
校长 xiàozhǎng *n* (*of schools*) headmaster, principal, president
笑 xiào *v* laugh, laugh at, ridicule; *n* laughter
笑话 xiàhua *n* joke, jest
笑声 xiàoshēng *n* laughter
歇斯底里 xiēsīdǐlǐ *adj* hysterical
协会 xiéhuì *n* association
协调 xiétiáo *v* coordinate
协议 xiéyì *n* agreement
协助 xiézhù *v* assist; *n* assistance
邪恶 xié'è *n* depravity; *adj* evil, wicked
邪魔 xiémó *n* demon

斜 **xié** *adj* inclined, slanting, tilted
斜坡 **xiépō** *n* slope
斜体 **xiétǐ** *n* italics
携带 **xiédài** *v* carry
鞋子 **xiézi** *n* shoe
写 **xiě** *v* write
写作 **xiězuò** *v* compose, write
泄露 **xièlòu** *v* divulge, let out, leak
泻药 **xièyào** *n* laxative
卸货 **xièhuò** *v* unload
亵渎 **xièdú** *v* desecrate
谢 **xiè** *v* thank
谢绝 **xièjué** *v* decline with thanks
谢谢 **xièxie** *v* thank, thank you
邂逅 **xièhòu** *v/n* encounter
心 **xīn** *n* heart, mind, feeling; core, center
心理 **xīnlǐ** *n* state of mind; 心理学 **xīnlǐxué** *n* psychology;
    adj psychological; 心理学家 **xīnlǐxuéjiā** *n* psychologist
心情 **xīnqíng** *n* mood, state of mind
心虚 **xīnxū** *adj* with a guilty conscience, lacking in self-
    confidence
心脏 **xīnzàng** *n* heart; 心脏病 **xīnzàngbìng** *n* heart disease
辛苦 **xīnkǔ** *adj* hard, laborious; *v* work hard
辛辣 **xīnlà** *adj* spicy
新 **xīn** *adj* new
新郎 **xīnláng** *n* bridegroom, groom
新年 **xīnnián** *n* New Year
新娘 **xīnniáng** *n* bride
新生 **xīnshēng** *n* new student
新闻 **xīnwén** *n* news; 新闻界 **xīnwénjiè** *n* the press;
    新闻广播 **xīnwén guǎngbō** *n* newscast; 新闻播音员
    xīnwén bōyīnyuán *n* newscaster; newsreader; 新闻记者
    xīnwén jìzhě *n* journalist; 新闻业 **xīnwényè** *n* journalism
新西兰 **xīnxīlán** *n* New Zealand; 新西兰人 **xīnxīlánrén** *n*
    New Zealander
新鲜 **xīnxiān** *adj* fresh
信 **xìn** *n* (*mail*) letter
信封 **xìnfēng** *n* envelope
信号 **xìnhào** *n* signal
信赖 **xìnlài** *v* trust
信念 **xìnniàn** *n* belief
信任 **xìnrèn** *n/v* trust

信使 xìnshǐ *n* courier, messenger
信息 xìnxī *n* information, message
信箱 xìnxiāng *n* letterbox, mailbox
信心 xìnxīn *n* confidence
信仰 xìnyǎng *n* belief, faith
信用 xìnyòng *n* credit; 信用卡 xìnyòngkǎ *n* credit card
兴奋 xīngfèn *adj* excited, thrilled; 兴奋剂 xīngfènjì *n*
   stimulant
兴建 xīngjiàn *v* build, construct
兴旺 xīngwàng *adj* thriving, booming
星 xīng *n* star
星期 xīngqī *n* week
星期二 xīngqī'èr *n* Tuesday
星期六 xīngqīliù *n* Saturday
星期三 xīngqīsān *n* Wednesday
星期四 xīngqīsì *n* Thursday
星期天 xīngqītiān *n* Sunday
星期五 xīngqīwǔ *n* Friday
星期一 xīngqīyī *n* Monday
猩红 xīnghóng *adj* scarlet
行 xíng *adj* all right
行动 xíngdòng *n* action, deeds
行贿 xínghuì *v* bribe
行李 xíngli *n* baggage, luggage
行人 xíngrén *n* pedestrian
行为 xíngwéi *n* behavior, deed, conduct
行星 xíngxīng *n* planet
行凶 xíngxiōng *v* commit physical assault or murder
行政 xíngzhèng *n* administration; *adj* administrative
形成 xíngchéng *v* form, fashion
形容 xíngróng *adj* describe; *n* description; 形容词
   xíngróngcí *n* adjective
形式 xíngshì *n* form, format
形势 xíngshì *n* situation
形象 xíngxiàng *n* image
形状 xíngzhuàng *n* shape
醒 xǐng *v* wake up, be awake
醒来 xǐnglái *v* wake up
醒目 xǐngmù *adj* striking, eye-catching
兴趣 xìngqù *n* interest
杏 xìng *n* apricot
杏仁 xìngrén *n* almond

杏子 **xìngzi** *n* apricot
姓 **xìng** *n* surname, family name
幸存 **xìngcún** *v* survive; 幸存者 **xìngcúnzhě** *n* survivor
幸福 **xìngfú** *n* happiness; *adj* happy
幸运 **xìngyùn** *adj* fortunate, lucky; *adv* fortunately, luckily
性 **xìng** *n* sex; nature, character, disposition; property, quality
性别 **xìngbié** *n* gender, sex
性病 **xìngbìng** *n* venereal disease
性感 **xìnggǎn** *adj* sexy
性交 **xìngjiāo** *n* sexual intercourse
性质 **xìngzhì** *n* property, nature
凶 **xiōng** *adj* fierce, ferocious
凶恶 **xiōng'è** *adj* fiendish, atrocious
凶猛 **xiōngměng** *adj* fierce, savage
凶手 **xiōngshǒu** *n* murderer, killer
汹涌 **xiōngyǒng** *adj* turbulent, tempestuous
胸 **xiōng** *n* chest
胸怀 **xiōnghuái** *n* mind, heart; vision
胸罩 **xiōngzhào** *n* bra, brassiere
雄 **xióng** *adj* male; 雄性 **xióngxìng** *n* male
雄辩 **xióngbiàn** *adj* eloquent
熊 **xióng** *n* bear
休会 **xiūhuì** *v* adjourn
休假 **xiūjià** *v* take a vacation, go on vacation
休克 **xiūkè** *v* (*med*) shock
休息 **xiūxi** *n* break, rest; *v* rest, relax; 休息室 **xiūxīshì** *n* lounge
修 **xiū** *v* mend, repair
修补 **xiūbǔ** *v* patch, repair, mend
修复 **xiūfù** *v* renovate, restore
修改 **xiūgǎi** *v* modify, alter
修剪 **xiūjiǎn** *v* clip, trim
修理 **xiūlǐ** *v* fix, mend, repair; 修理工 **xiūlǐgōng** *n* mechanic
羞耻 **xiūchǐ** *n* shame
羞辱 **xiūrǔ** *n* humiliation
袖口 **xiùkǒu** *n* cuff
袖子 **xiùzi** *n* sleeve
虚 **xū** *adj* diffident, timid; false, nominal; weak, in poor health
虚构 **xūgòu** *v* fabricate, make up; *adj* fictitious, fictional
虚假 **xūjiǎ** *adj* false, sham
虚荣心 **xūróngxīn** *n* vanity
虚弱 **xūruò** *v* weak, fragile
需求 **xūqiú** *n* demand, requirement

需要 xūyào *n* requirement, need; *v* require, need
许多 xǔduō *adj* much, many
许可 xǔkě *v* permit, allow; 许可证 xǔkězhèng *n* permit
叙述 xùshù *v* narrate, relate
畜棚 xùpéng *n* barn
续集 xùjí *n* sequel
酗酒 xùjiǔ *v* drink excessively
嗅 xiù *v* sniff
宣布 xuānbù *v* announce, declare, proclaim
宣传 xuānchuán *v* publicize; *n* publicity
宣判 xuānpàn *v* sentence
喧嚣 xuānxiāo *adj* noisy; *v/n* clamor
悬挂 xuánguà *v* hang, suspend
悬崖 xuányá *n* cliff
旋律 xuánlǜ *n* melody
旋钮 xuánniǔ *n* knob
旋转 xuánzhuǎn *v* revolve, rotate, spin
选 xuǎn *v* choose, select
选集 xuǎnjí *n* anthology
选举 xuǎnjǔ *v* elect; *n* election; 选举人 xuǎnjǔrén *n* voter
选民 xuǎnmín *n* voter
选票 xuǎnpiào *n* ballot
选手 xuǎnshǒu *n* (*sports*) player
选择 xuǎnzé *n* choice, option, selection; *v* choose, opt for, select
炫耀 xuànyào *v* show off
眩晕 xuànyūn *adj* dizzy; *n* dizziness
靴子 xuēzi *n* boot
学 xué *v* study, learn
学费 xuéfèi *n* tuition
学会 xuéhuì *n* (*academic*) association
学历 xuélì *n* curriculum vitae
学年 xuénián *n* academic year
学期 xuéqī *n* academic term, semester
学生 xuésheng *n* pupil, student
学识 xuéshí *n* learning, wisdom
学士 xuéshì *n* bachelor's degree
学术 xuéshù *adj* academic
学徒 xuétú *n* apprentice
学位 xuéwèi *n* academic degree
学习 xuéxí *n* study; *v* study, learn
学校 xuéxiào *n* school

学院 **xuéyuàn** *n* academy, college, institute
学者 **xuézhě** *n* scholar
雪 **xuě** *n* snow
雪貂 **xuědiāo** *n* ferret
雪橇 **xuěqiāo** *n* sled, sledge
雪茄 **xuějiā** *n* cigar
血 **xuè** *n* blood
血管 **xuèguǎn** *n* blood vessel
血型 **xuèxíng** *n* blood type
血液 **xuèyè** *n* blood
寻求 **xúnqiú** *v* quest, seek, look for
寻找 **xúnzhǎo** *v* search, seek, look for
巡逻 **xúnluó** *n/v* patrol
巡洋舰 **xúnyángjiàn** *n* (*ship*) cruiser
询问 **xúnwèn** *n* inquiry; *v* enquire, inquire
循环 **xúnhuán** *v* circulate, cycle
训练 **xùnliàn** *n* training; *v* coach, train
迅速 **xùnsù** *adj* prompt, quick, rapid, speedy, swift; *adv*
    quickly, rapidly

Y

压 **yā** *v* press, weigh down
压倒 **yādǎo** *v* overpower, overwhelm, prevail over
压力 **yālì** *n* pressure, stress
压迫 **yāpò** *v* oppress; *n* oppression
压碎 **yāsuì** *v* crush
压缩 **yāsuō** *v* compress, cut down
压抑 **yāyì** *adj* depressed, inhibited
压榨 **yāzhà** *v* squeeze, press
压制 **yāzhì** *v* suppress, stifle
押金 **yājīn** *n* security, deposit
鸦片 **yāpiàn** *n* opium
鸭子 **yāzi** *n* duck
牙 **yá** *n* tooth
牙齿 **yáchǐ** *n* tooth
牙膏 **yágāo** *n* toothpaste
牙科 **yákē** *n* dentistry; dental department
牙签 **yáqiān** *n* toothpick
牙刷 **yáshuā** *n* toothbrush
牙痛 **yátòng** *n* toothache
牙医 **yáyī** *n* dentist

牙龈 **yáyín** *n* gums
芽 **yá** *n* bud, sprout, shoot
哑 **yǎ** *adj* dumb
哑巴 **yǎba** *n* mute
哑铃 **yǎlíng** *n* dumbbell
亚军 **yàjūn** *n* runner-up
亚洲 **yàzhōu** *n* Asia; 亚洲人 **yàzhōurén** *n* Asian
咽喉 **yānhóu** *n* throat
烟 **yān** *n* smoke; cigarette
烟草 **yāncǎo** *n* tobacco
烟囱 **yāncōng** *n* chimney
烟斗 **yāndǒu** *n* pipe
烟灰缸 **yānhuīgāng** *n* ashtray
烟火 **yānhuǒ** *n* fireworks
烟雾 **yānwù** *n* smoke, mist, smog
胭脂 **yānzhi** *n* rouge
淹没 **yānmò** *v* submerge, inundate
淹死 **yānsǐ** *v* to drown
腌肉 **yānròu** *n* bacon
延长 **yáncháng** *v* prolong, lengthen, extend
延迟 **yánchí** *v* delay, postpone, put off
延缓 **yánhuǎn** *v* delay
延期 **yánqī** *v* postpone, defer, put off
延伸 **yánshēn** *v* reach, stretch, extend
延误 **yánwù** *v* incur loss through delay
延续 **yánxù** *v* continue, go on, last
严 **yán** *adj* rigorous, strict
严格 **yángé** *adj* rigorous, strict; *adv* strictly
严寒 **yánhán** *n* severe cold, bitter cold
严谨 **yánjǐn** *adj* rigorous, strict
严禁 **yánjìn** *v* strictly forbid
严峻 **yánjùn** *adj* stern, severe, rigorous, grim
严厉 **yánlì** *adj* severe, stern, harsh
严密 **yánmì** *adj* tight, close
严肃 **yánsù** *adj* grave, serious, solemn
严重 **yánzhòng** *adj* critical, grave, grievous, severe
言论 **yánlùn** *n* opinion on public affairs
言行 **yánxíng** *n* words and deeds, statements and actions
言语 **yányǔ** *n* spoken language, speech
岩洞 **yándòng** *n* cave
岩石 **yánshí** *n* rock
沿海 **yánhǎi** *adj* coastal

沿着 yánzhe *prep* along; *v* follow

炎热 yánrè *adj* scorching, blazing, sweltering, burning hot

炎症 yánzhèng *n* inflammation

研究 yánjiū *v* research; 研究生 yánjiūshēng *n* graduate student; 研究生院 yánjiūshēngyuàn *n* graduate school; 研究所 yánjiūsuǒ *n* research institute; 研究员 yánjiūyuán *n* researcher

研讨会 yántǎohuì *n* seminar, symposium

盐 yán *n* salt

颜料 yánliào *n* pigment, dyestuff

颜色 yánsè *n* color

掩蔽 yǎnbì *v* shelter, mask

掩盖 yǎngài *v* cover, conceal

掩护 yǎnhù *v* shield, cover

掩埋 yǎnmái *v* bury

眼光 yǎnguāng *n* sight, insight, vision

眼界 yǎnjiè *n* field of vision, outlook

眼睛 yǎnjing *n* eye

眼镜 yǎnjìng *n* eyeglasses, spectacles

眼泪 yǎnlèi *n* tear

眼珠 yǎnzhū *n* eyeball

演 yǎn *v* act, perform; 演员 yǎnyuán *n* actor, performer

演变 yǎnbiàn *n* evolution; *v* evolve

演出 yǎnchū *v* perform; *n* performance

演化 yǎnhuà *v* evolve; *n* evolution

演讲 yǎnjiǎng *n* address, lecture; *v* give a lecture, make a speech; 演讲人 yǎnjiǎngrén *n* speaker

演示 yǎnshì *v* demonstrate; *n* demonstration

演说 yǎnshuō *n* speech; *v* deliver a speech

演习 yǎnxí *n* maneuvre, exercise

演戏 yǎnxì *v* put on a play, act in a play

厌恶 yànwù *v* detest, abhor, be disgusted with

厌烦 yànfán *v* be sick of, be fed up

厌倦 yànjuàn *adj* be weary of, be tired of

砚台 yàntái *n* ink stone, ink slab

宴会 yànhuì *n* banquet, feast

验血 yànxuè *v* do a blood test

验证 yànzhèng *v* validate

谚语 yànyǔ *n* proverb, saying

燕子 yànzi *n* swallow

赝品 yànpǐn *n* fake product, counterfeit product

秧歌舞 yānggē wǔ *n* yangge dance

扬声器 **yángshēngqì** *n* loudspeaker

羊 **yáng** *n* sheep

羊羔 **yánggāo** *n* lamb

羊毛 **yángmáo** *n* wool

羊肉 **yángròu** *n* mutton, (*meat*) lamb

阳 **yáng** *n* sun; 阳性 **yángxìng** *n* (*med*) positive

阳光 **yángguāng** *n* sunlight, sunshine

阳历 **yánglì** *n* solar calendar

阳台 **yángtái** *n* balcony, terrace

洋 **yáng** *n* ocean; *adj* foreign

洋葱 **yángcōng** *n* onion

仰视 **yǎngshì** *v* look up

仰泳 **yǎngyǒng** *n* (*sport*) backstroke

养 **yǎng** *v* raise, grow, rear; *adj* foster, adoptive

养家 **yǎngjiā** *v* support one's family

养育 **yǎngyù** *v* bring up, rear

养殖 **yǎngzhí** *v* breed

氧气 **yǎngqì** *n* oxygen

痒 **yǎng** *v* itch, tickle; *adj* itchy

样品 **yàngpǐn** *n* sample, specimen

样式 **yàngshì** *n* style, (*clothes*) cut

样子 **yàngzi** *n* appearance, shape, manner, style, cut

妖怪 **yāoguài** *n* monster, goblin, demon

要求 **yāoqiú** *v* request, demand, require, claim; *n* requirement, demand

腰 **yāo** *n* waist

邀请 **yāoqǐng** *n* invitation; *v* invite; 邀请信 **yāoqǐngxìn** *n* invitation letter

谣言 **yáoyán** *n* rumor

摇 **yáo** *v* rock, shake

摇摆 **yáobǎi** *v* sway, swing, rock, vacillate

摇动 **yáodòng** *v* rock, shake

摇滚乐 **yáogǔnyuè** *n* rock 'n' roll

摇晃 **yáohuàng** *v* rock, sway, shake

摇篮 **yáolán** *n* cradle

摇头 **yáotóu** *v* shake one's head

遥控 **yáokòng** *v/n* remote control

遥远 **yáoyuǎn** *adj* distant, remote

咬 **yǎo** *v* bite

药 **yào** *n* drug, medicine

药草 **yàocǎo** *n* herbal medicine

药店 **yàodiàn** *n* drugstore, pharmacy

药方 **yàofāng** *n* prescription
药房 **yàofáng** *n* dispensary, drugstore, pharmacy
药剂师 **yàojìshī** *n* pharmacist
药量 **yàoliàng** *n* dose, dosage
药片 **yàopiàn** *n* tablet, pill
药品 **yàopǐn** *n* medicine, drug
药水 **yàoshuǐ** *n* liquid medicine
药丸 **yàowán** *n* pill
药物 **yàowù** *n* medicine, pharmaceuticals
要 **yào** *v* want, wish, desire, need, require
要不 **yàobù** *conj* otherwise, or else, or; 要不是 **yàobùshì**
    conj if it were not for, but for
要点 **yàodiǎn** *n* main point, essentials, gist
要害 **yàohài** *n* vital part, crucial point
要紧 **yàojǐn** *adj* important, essential, critical
要么 **yàome** *conj* or, either ... or ...
要塞 **yàosài** *n* fort, fortress, fortification
要素 **yàosù** *n* element, factor
要闻 **yàowén** *n* important news, front-page story
钥匙 **yàoshi** *n* key
椰子 **yēzi** *n* coconut
爷爷 **yéye** *n* grandfather (*paternal*)
也 **yě** *adv* also, too
也许 **yěxǔ** *adv* maybe, perhaps
野 **yě** *adj* wild, undomesticated
野餐 **yěcān** *n* picnic
野草 **yěcǎo** *n* weeds
野果 **yěguǒ** *n* wild fruit
野蛮 **yěmán** *adj* savage, uncivilized
野生 **yěshēng** *adj* wild
野兽 **yěshòu** *n* wild beast, wild animal
野外 **yěwài** *n* open country, field
野心 **yěxīn** *n* ambition
野营 **yěyíng** *n* camping
业绩 **yèjī** *n* achievement, performance
业务 **yèwù** *n* vocational work, professional work, business
业余 **yèyú** *n* spare time, after-hours; *adj* amateur;
    业余爱好者 **yèyú àihàozhě** *n* amateur
叶子 **yèzi** *n* leaf
页 **yè** *n* page
夜 **yè** *n* night
夜班 **yèbān** *n* night shift

夜景 yèjǐng *n* night scene
夜里 yèlǐ *n* night
夜晚 yèwǎn *n* night
夜校 yèxiào *n* night school
夜总会 yèzǒnghuì *n* nightclub
液体 yètǐ *n* fluid, liquid; *adj* liquid
腋窝 yèwō *n* armpit
一 yī *num* one
一般 yībān *adj* general, average; *adv* generally, usually
一半 yībàn *n* half
一边 ... 一边 yībiān ... yībiān *conj* while, as, at the same time, simultaneously
一辈子 yībèizi *n* all one's life, throughout one's life, a lifetime
一尘不染 yīchén bùrǎn *adj* spotless
一旦 yīdàn *conj* once
一道 yīdào *adv* together, side by side, alongside
一等 yīděng *adj* first-class
一点儿 yīdiǎnr *n* a little, a bit
一定 yīdìng *adv* surely, certainly; *adj* certain
一对 yīduì *n* couple, pair
一概 yīgài *adv* one and all, without exception, totally
一共 yīgòng *adv* altogether, in all, all told
一块儿 yīkuàir *adv* at the same place, together
一律 yīlǜ *adv* all without exception
一模一样 yīmú yīyàng *adj* exactly alike
一瞥 yīpiē *n* glimpse
一起 yīqǐ *adv* together
一切 yīqiè *n* all, every, everything
一生 yīshēng *n* lifetime, one's whole life
一时 yīshí *adv* for a short while, temporarily, momentarily
一丝不苟 yīsī bùgǒu *adj* meticulous
一下 yīxià *adv* briefly, for a short while
一些 yīxiē *num* some, a number of, a certain amount
一心 yīxīn *adv* wholeheartedly, heart and soul, of one mind
一月 yīyuè *n* January
一再 yīzài *adv* time and again, again and again, repeatedly
一直 yīzhí *adv* straight, all along
伊斯兰教 yīsīlánjiào *n* Islam
衣橱 yīchú *n* wardrobe
衣服 yīfu *n* clothes, clothing, garment
衣架 yījià *n* hanger
衣领 yīlǐng *n* collar

衣帽间 yīmàojiān *n* checkroom
医疗 yīliáo *n* medical treatment; *adj* medical
医生 yīshēng *n* doctor
医务室 yīwùshì *n* dispensary, clinic
医学 yīxué *n* medical science; 医学院 yīxuéyuàn *n* medical school
医药 yīyào *n* medicine; 医药费 yīyàofèi *n* medical expenses
医院 yīyuàn *n* hospital
医治 yīzhì *v* cure, treat, heal
依据 yījù *prep* according to, in the light of, on the basis of, judging by; *n* basis, foundation, grounds
依靠 yīkào *v* depend on, rely on
依赖 yīlài *v* rely on
依偎 yīwēi *v* cuddle
依照 yīzhào *prep* according to, in accordance with
仪表 yíbiǎo *n* appearance, bearing; meter, instrument
仪器 yíqì *n* instrument
仪式 yíshì *n* rite, ritual, ceremony
仪仗队 yízhàngduì *n* honor guard
姨夫 yífu *n* uncle (*husband of mother's sister*)
姨妈 yímā *n* aunt (*mother's married sister*)
姨子 yízi *n* sister-in-law (*wife's sister*)
移 yí *v* move, shift, change
移动 yídòng *adj* mobile, portable; 移动电话 yídòng diànhuà *n* mobile phone
移居 yíjū *v* migrate; resettle
移民 yímín *n* immigrant
移植 yízhí *v* transplant
遗产 yíchǎn *n* heritage, legacy, inheritance
遗传 yíchuán *n* heredity; *adj* hereditary; 遗传学 yíchuánxué *n* genetics
遗骸 yíhái *n* remains
遗憾 yíhàn *n* regret; *adj* regretful
遗迹 yíjī *n* historical site
遗留 yíliú *v* leave behind, hand down
遗漏 yílòu *n* omission; *v* omit, leave out
遗弃 yíqì *v* abandon, forsake, desert
遗失 yíshī *v* lose (sth.)
遗物 yíwù *n* things left behind by the deceased
遗址 yízhǐ *n* ruins, relics, historical site
遗嘱 yízhǔ *n* testament, will
疑惑 yíhuò *v* feel uncertain, not be convinced

疑问 yíwèn *n* query, doubt, question
已婚 yǐhūn *adj* married
已经 yǐjīng *adv* already
已知 yǐzhī *adj* known, given
以便 yǐbiàn *conj* so that, in order to, so as to, with the aim of
以后 yǐhòu *n* after, afterwards, later, hereafter
以及 yǐjí *conj* as well as, along with, and
以来 yǐlái *n* since
以免 yǐmiǎn *conj* in order to avoid, so as not to, lest
以内 yǐnèi *n* within, less than
以前 yǐqián *n* ago, before, formerly, previously
以上 yǐshàng *n* more than, above, over, above-mentioned, foregoing
以外 yǐwài *n* beyond, outside, other than
以为 yǐwéi *v* think, believe, feel
以下 yǐxià *n* below, under; the following
椅子 yǐzi *n* chair
义务 yìwù *n* obligation; *adj* voluntary
亿 yì *n* a hundred million
艺人 yìrén *n* actor; artisan, artist
艺术 yìshù *n* art; 艺术家 yìshùjiā *n* artist
议案 yì'àn *n* proposal, motion
议程 yìchéng *n* agenda
议会 yìhuì *n* council, parliament
议价 yìjià *v* bargain
议论 yìlùn *v* comment, talk about, discuss; *n* discussion, commentary
议题 yìtí *n* topic for discussion
议员 yìyuán *n* assemblyman, congressman
议院 yìyuàn *n* House, parliament
异常 yìcháng *adj* unusual, abnormal
异物 yìwù *n* foreign matter, foreign body
异议 yìyì *n* dissention, objection
抑郁 yìyù *adj* depressed, despondent, gloomy
抑制 yìzhì *v* curb, restrain; *n* restraint
译文 yìwén *n* translated text, translation
译者 yìzhě *n* translator
易 yì *adj* easy
易挥发 yìhuīfā *adj* volatile
易接近 yìjiējìn *adj* accessible
易燃 yìrán *adj* inflammable

易受 yìshòu *adj* liable to; 易受攻击 yìshòu gōngjī *adj* vulnerable; 易受影响 yìshòu yǐngxiǎng *adj* susceptible

易碎 yìsuì *adj* fragile

疫苗 yìmiáo *n* vaccine

意大利 yìdàlì *n* Italy; 意大利人 yìdàlìrén *n* (*people*) Italian; 意大利语 yìdàlìyǔ *n* (*language*) Italian

意见 yìjian *n* comment, opinion

意识 yìshí *n* consciousness, awareness; 意识到 yìshí dào *v* realize, become aware of

意思 yìsi *n* meaning, sense

意图 yìtú *n* intent, intention

意外 yìwài *adj* unexpected, surprising

意味 yìwèi *n* meaning, significance, implication; 意味着 yìwèi zhe *v* mean, imply

意义 yìyì *n* meaning, significance

意愿 yìyuàn *n* wish, desire, aspiration

意志 yìzhì *n* will, volition

溢出 yìchū *v* overflow, run over, spill

毅力 yìlì *n* willpower, stamina

因此 yīncǐ *adv* hence, therefore, thus

因而 yīn'ér *adv* consequently, therefore

因素 yīnsù *n* factor

因为 yīnwèi *conj* because; *prep* because of, due to

阴 yīn *adj* overcast, cloudly; hidden, secret; 阴性 yīnxìng *n* (*med*) negative

阴暗 yīn'àn *adj* dark, gloomy

阴道 yīndào *n* vagina

阴沟 yīngōu *n* sewer

阴茎 yīnjīng *n* penis

阴历 yīnlì *n* lunar calendar

阴凉 yīnliáng *adj* shady and cool

阴谋 yīnmóu *n* conspiracy, intrigue, scheme

阴天 yīntiān *n* overcast sky, cloudy day

阴险 yīnxiǎn *adj* sinister, insidious, treacherous

阴影 yīnyǐng *n* shadow

荫 yīn *n* shade

荫凉 yīnliáng *adj* shady and cool

音 yīn *n* sound

音标 yīnbiāo *n* phonetic symbol

音带 yīndài *n* soundtrack

音调 yīndiào *n* tone

音符 yīnfú *n* (*music*) note

音高 **yīngāo** *n* (*music*) pitch

音阶 **yīnjiē** *n* (*music*) scale

音节 **yīnjié** *n* syllable

音乐 **yīnyuè** *n* music; 音乐会 **yīnyuèhuì** *n* concert; 音乐家 **yīnyuèjiā** *n* musician

音量 **yīnliàng** *n* (*sound*) volume

淫秽 **yínhuì** *adj* obscene, bawdry

淫猥 **yínwěi** *adj* lewd

银 **yín** *n* silver

银河 **yínhé** *n* the Milky Way

银行 **yínháng** *n* bank; 银行家 **yínhángjiā** *n* banker

银子 **yínzi** *n* silver

引发 **yǐnfā** *v* trigger

引号 **yǐnhào** *n* quotation marks

引进 **yǐnjìn** *n* introduction; *v* introduce, import

引力 **yǐnlì** *n* gravitation, gravitational force

引起 **yǐnqǐ** *v* cause, give rise to

引擎 **yǐnqíng** *n* engine

引文 **yǐnwén** *n* quotation

引用 **yǐnyòng** *v* quote, cite

引诱 **yǐnyòu** *v* seduce, entice

饮料 **yǐnliào** *n* beverage

饮食 **yǐnshí** *n* diet

隐蔽 **yǐnbì** *v* conceal, take cover

隐藏 **yǐncáng** *v* hide, conceal

隐患 **yǐnhuàn** *n* hidden trouble, hidden danger

隐讳 **yǐnhuì** *v* avoid mentioning, taboo

隐晦 **yǐnhuì** *adj* obscure, veiled

隐居 **yǐnjū** *v* live in seclusion, withdraw from society and live in solitude, be a hermit

隐瞒 **yǐnmán** *v* conceal, hide

隐私 **yǐnsī** *n* privacy

隐形眼镜 **yǐnxíng yǎnjìng** *n* contact lens

隐喻 **yǐnyù** *n* metaphor

瘾 **yǐn** *n* addiction, habitual craving

印 **yìn** *v* print, engrave; *n* seal, stamp, chop; print, mark

印度 **yìndù** *n* India; 印度人 **yìndùrén** *n* (*people*) Indian

印刷 **yìnshuā** *n* printing; *v* print; 印刷工 **yìnshuāgōng** *n* (*worker*) printer; 印刷机 **yìnshuājī** *n* printing machine, printing press

印象 **yìnxiàng** *n* impression

印章 **yìnzhāng** *n* seal, stamp

应当 yīngdāng *aux* should, ought to
应得 yīngdé *adj* deserved, due
应该 yīnggāi *aux* should, ought to
应有 yīngyǒu *adj* due, proper, deserved
英镑 yīngbàng *n* pound sterling
英尺 yīngchǐ *n* (*measurement*) foot
英寸 yīngcùn *n* inch
英国 yīngguó *n* Britain, England, Great Britain, United Kingdom; 英国人 yīngguórén *n* (*people*) British, Englishman
英俊 yīngjùn *adj* handsome
英里 yīnglǐ *n* mile
英明 yīngmíng *adj* wise, brilliant
英亩 yīngmǔ *n* acre
英文 yīngwén *n* (*language*) English
英雄 yīngxióng *n* hero
英勇 yīngyǒng *adj* valiant, heroic
英语 yīngyǔ *n* (*language*) English
婴儿 yīng'ér *n* baby, infant
樱花 yīnghuā *n* oriental cherry
樱桃 yīngtáo *n* cherry
鹦鹉 yīngwǔ *n* parrot
鹰 yīng *n* eagle
迎 yíng *v* go to meet, welcome, greet
迎接 yíngjiē *v* welcome, greet
盈利 yínglì *n* profit, gain
盈余 yíngyú *n* surplus
萤火虫 yínghuǒchóng *n* firefly, glowworm
营地 yíngdì *n* campsite, campground
营房 yíngfáng *n* barracks
营救 yíngjiù *v* rescue
营养 yíngyǎng *n* nourishment; 营养不良 yíngyǎng bùliáng *n* malnutrition
营业 yíngyè *v* conduct business, open for business; 营业时间 yíngyè shíjiān *n* business hours
赢 yíng *v* win
赢利 yínglì *v* profit, gain
影片 yǐngpiàn *n* film, movie
影响 yǐngxiǎng *n* impact, influence; *v* affect, influence
影印 yǐngyìn *v* photocopy; 影印本 yǐngyìnběn *n* photocopy; 影印机 yǐngyìnjī *n* photocopier
影院 yǐngyuàn *n* cinema, movie theater
影子 yǐngzi *n* shadow

应付 yìngfù *v* deal with, cope with
应用 yìngyòng *v* apply, use; *n* application, use
应急 yìngjí *v* meet an urgent need, meet an emergency
硬 yìng *adj* (*of objects*) hard
硬币 yìngbì *n* coin
硬件 yìngjiàn *n* hardware
硬盘 yìngpán *n* hard disk
拥抱 yōngbào *n/v* hug, embrace
拥护 yōnghù *v* support
拥挤 yōngjǐ *adj* crowded, congested
拥有 yōngyǒu *v* own, possess
庸俗 yōngsú *adj* vulgar
永恒 yǒnghéng *adj* eternal
永久 yǒngjiǔ *adj* everlasting, permanent, perpetual
永远 yǒngyuǎn *adv* forever
泳裤 yǒngkù *n* swimming trunks
泳衣 yǒngyī *n* swimsuit
勇敢 yǒnggǎn *adj* brave, valiant
勇气 yǒngqì *n* courage
踊跃 yǒngyuè *adj* enthusiastic, eager; *adv* enthusiastically, eagerly
佣金 yòngjīn *n* commission
用 yòng *v* use, make use of, apply
用处 yòngchu *n* use
用法 yòngfǎ *n* use, usage
用功 yònggōng *adj* hardworking, diligent, studious
用户 yònghù *n* user, consumer
用具 yòngjù *n* appliance
用力 yònglì *adv* exert oneself, put forth one's strength
用途 yòngtú *n* use, purpose
用心 yòngxīn *adv* diligently, attentively; *n* motive, intention
优点 yōudiǎn *n* merit, strong point
优惠 yōuhuì *adj* preferential, favorable
优良 yōuliáng *adj* fine, good
优美 yōuměi *adj* graceful
优柔寡断 yōuróu guǎduàn *adj* irresolute, indecisive
优势 yōushì *n* advantage, superiority
优胜者 yōushèngzhě *n* winner
优先 yōuxiān *n* priority
优秀 yōuxiù *adj* excellent
优雅 yōuyǎ *adj* elegant
优异 yōuyì *adj* excellent, outstanding, exceedingly good

优越 yōuyuè *n* superiority; *adj* superior
优质 yōuzhì *adj* high quality, high grade
忧愁 yōuchóu *adj* sad, depressed
忧虑 yōulǜ *n* anxiety, concern; *adj* anxious
幽魂 yōuhún *n* ghost
幽静 yōujìng *adj* quiet and secluded, peaceful
幽灵 yōulíng *n* phantom
幽默 yōumò *n* humor; *adj* humorous
悠久 yōujiǔ *adj* long, long-standing, age-old
悠闲 yōuxián *adj* leisurely
尤其 yóuqí *adv* especially, particularly
由此 yóucǐ *adv* from this, therefrom, thus
由来 yóulái *n* origin
由于 yóuyú *prep* owing to, due to, thanks to
犹太教 yóutàijiào *n* Judaism
犹太人 yóutàirén *n* Jew
犹豫 yóuyù *v* hesitate
邮编 yóubiān *n* zip code
邮差 yóuchāi *n* mailman, postman
邮戳 yóuchuō *n* postmark
邮寄 yóujì *v* mail
邮件 yóujiàn *n* mail
邮局 yóujú *n* post office
邮票 yóupiào *n* stamp
邮箱 yóuxiāng *n* mailbox, postbox
邮政编码 yóuzhèng biānmǎ *n* postal code
邮政信箱 yóuzhèng xìnxiāng *n* post box
邮资 yóuzī *n* postage
油 yóu *n* oil, grease; *adj* oily, greasy
油画 yóuhuà *n* oil painting
油井 yóujǐng *n* oil well
油轮 yóulún *n* oil tanker
油腻 yóunì *adj* greasy, oily
油漆 yóuqī *n* paint
油田 yóutián *n* oilfield
油箱 yóuxiāng *n* gas tank
油炸 yóuzhà *v* deep fry
油脂 yóuzhī *n* grease
铀 yóu *n* uranium
游 yóu *v* swim; tour
游击队 yóujīduì *n* guerrilla
游击战 yóujīzhàn *n* guerrilla war

游客 yóukè *n* tourist
游览 yóulǎn *v* go sightseeing, tour
游艇 yóutǐng *n* yacht
游玩 yóuwán *v* amuse oneself, play
游戏 yóuxì *n* game
游行 yóuxíng *n/v* parade
游泳 yóuyǒng *v* swim; *n* swimming; 游泳池 yóuyǒngchí *n* swimming pool; 游泳衣 yóuyǒngyī *n* bathing suit
友爱 yǒu'ài *n* friendly affection, fraternal love
友好 yǒuhǎo *adj* friendly
友情 yǒuqíng *n* friendly sentiments, friendship
友善 yǒushàn *n* friendliness; *adj* friendly
友谊 yǒuyì *n* friendship
有 yǒu *v* have, there is/are
有的 yǒude *adj* some
有点儿 yǒudiǎnr *adv* somewhat, rather, a bit
有毒 yǒudú *adj* poisonous, toxic, venomous
有关 yǒuguān *v* have to do with, be related to
有害 yǒuhài *adj* harmful
有机 yǒujī *adj* organic
有礼 yǒulǐ *adj* courteous, polite
有理 yǒulǐ *adj* reasonable, justified in the right to, rational
有力 yǒulì *adj* potent, vigorous
有利 yǒulì *adj* advantageous; 有利可图 yǒulì kětú *adj* profitable, lucrative
有名 yǒumíng *adj* famous
有趣 yǒuqù *adj* fun, interesting
有时 yǒushí *adv* sometimes
有限 yǒuxiàn *adj* limited
有线电视 yǒuxiàn diànshì *n* cable TV
有效 yǒuxiào *adj* effective, valid; 有效期 yǒuxiàoqī *n* term of validity
有些 yǒuxiē *adj* some; *adv* somewhat
有益 yǒuyì *adj* profitable, beneficial, useful
有意 yǒuyì *v* have a mind to, be inclined to; *adv* intentionally, deliberately, purposely
有意思 yǒuyìsi *adj* fun, interesting
有用 yǒuyòng *adj* helpful, useful
有罪 yǒuzuì *adj* guilty
又 yòu *adv* again; 又 … 又 … yòu … yòu … *conj* both … and
右 yòu *n* (*opposite of left*) right
右边 yòubian *n* (*opposite of left*) right

右面 **yòumian** *n* (*opposite of left*) right
右手 **yòushǒu** *n* right hand
右翼 **yòuyì** *n* right wing
幼儿园 **yòu'éryuán** *n* kindergarten
幼稚 **yòuzhì** *adj* young, childish, naive
诱导 **yòudǎo** *v* guide, lead, induce
诱拐 **yòuguǎi** *v* abduct
诱惑 **yòuhuò** *n* temptation; *v* lure, tempt, seduce
诱饵 **yòumǐ** *n* bait
迂回 **yūhuí** *adj* circuitous, tortuous, roundabout
于 **yú** *prep* in, at, on
于是 **yúshì** *conj* and, then, thereupon, hence, consequently,
     as a result
余地 **yúdì** *n* leeway, margin, room, latitude
余下 **yúxià** *adj* remaining
鱼 **yú** *n* fish
鱼饵 **yúěr** *n* bait
鱼鳞 **yúlín** *n* fish scales
鱼露 **yúlù** *n* fish sauce
娱乐 **yúlè** *n* entertainment; 娱乐界 **yúlèjiè** *n* show business
渔民 **yúmín** *n* fisherman
愉快 **yúkuài** *adj* cheerful, delighted, entertaining, pleasant
愚蠢 **yúchǔn** *adj* stupid, foolishly
愚昧 **yúmèi** *adj* ignorant, benighted
愚弄 **yúnòng** *v* fool
舆论 **yúlùn** *n* public opinion
与 **yǔ** *conj* and
宇航员 **yǔhángyuán** *n* astronaut, spaceman
宇宙 **yǔzhòu** *n* universe
羽毛 **yǔmáo** *n* feather
雨 **yǔ** *n* rain
雨季 **yǔjì** *n* rainy season
雨伞 **yǔsǎn** *n* umbrella
雨水 **yǔshuǐ** *n* rainwater, rainfall
雨衣 **yǔyī** *n* raincoat
语法 **yǔfǎ** *n* grammar
语气 **yǔqì** *n* tone, manner of speaking, mood
语态 **yǔtài** *n* (*gram*) voice
语文 **yǔwén** *n* Chinese
语言 **yǔyán** *n* language; 语言学 **yǔyánxué** *n* linguistics;
     语言学家 **yǔyánxuéjiā** *n* linguist
语音 **yǔyīn** *n* pronunciation; 语音学 **yǔyīnxué** *n* phonetics

玉 **yù** *n* jade
玉米 **yùmǐ** *n* corn
郁闷 **yùmèn** *adj* gloomy, depressed
狱卒 **yùzú** *n* jailer, prison guard
浴缸 **yùgāng** *n* bathtub
浴室 **yùshì** *n* bathroom, shower room
浴衣 **yùyī** *n* bathrobe
预报 **yùbào** *n/v* forecast
预备 **yùbèi** *v* prepare, get ready; *adj* preparatory, probational
预测 **yùcè** *n/v* forecast
预订 **yùdìng** *v* reserve, make a reservation
预定 **yùdìng** *v* fix in advance, predetermine, schedule
预防 **yùfáng** *v* prevent
预付款 **yùfùkuǎn** *n* (*money*) advance
预告 **yùgào** *v* announce in advance; *n* advance notice
预计 **yùjì** *v* calculate in advance, estimate
预见 **yùjiàn** *v* foresee
预料 **yùliào** *n* anticipation; *v* anticipate
预谋 **yùmóu** *adj* premeditated; *n* premeditation
预期 **yùqī** *v* anticipate, expect
预赛 **yùsài** *n* preliminary contest, trial match
预算 **yùsuàn** *n* budget
预习 **yùxí** *v* (*of students*) prepare lessons before class
预言 **yùyán** *v* predict, foretell; *n* prophecy
预演 **yùyǎn** *n* (*movie, performance, etc.*) preview, rehearsal
预约 **yùyuē** *n* appointment; *v* make an appointment
预兆 **yùzhào** *n* omen, presage
欲望 **yùwàng** *n* desire, lust
寓所 **yùsuǒ** *n* residence, abode, dwelling place
寓言 **yùyán** *n* fable, allegory, parable
寓意 **yùyì** *n* implied meaning, moral
遇到 **yùdào** *v* encounter, run into
遇见 **yùjiàn** *v* meet, run into
遇难 **yùnàn** *v* die in an accident, be murdered
遇险 **yùxiǎn** *v* meet with a mishap, be in danger, be in distress
愈合 **yùhé** *v* heal
冤屈 **yuānqū** *n* wrongful treatment, injustice
冤枉 **yuānwang** *v* wrong, treat unjustly; *adj* not worthwhile
渊博 **yuānbó** *adj* broad and profound, erudite
渊源 **yuānyuán** *n* origin, source
元旦 **yuándàn** *n* New Year's Day
元件 **yuánjiàn** *n* element, component

元帅 **yuánshuài** *n* marshal
元素 **yuánsù** *n* element
元宵节 **yuánxiāojié** *n* Lantern Festival (*Jan. 15th in the Chinese lunar calendar*)
元音 **yuányīn** *n* vowel
员 **yuán** *n* person, member
员工 **yuángōng** *n* staff, employee
园丁 **yuándīng** *n* gardener
园林 **yuánlín** *n* gardens
园艺 **yuányì** *n* gardening; 园艺师 **yuányìshī** *n* gardener
原材料 **yuáncáiliào** *n* raw materials
原稿 **yuángǎo** *n* manuscript, master copy
原告 **yuángào** *n* accuser, plaintiff
原来 **yuánlái** *adj* original, former; *adv* so, turn out to be
原理 **yuánlǐ** *n* principle; workings
原谅 **yuánliàng** *n* forgiveness, pardon; *v* forgive, pardon
原料 **yuánliào** *n* material
原木 **yuánmù** *n* log
原始 **yuánshǐ** *adj* original, primitive
原文 **yuánwén** *n* original text, the original
原先 **yuánxiān** *adj* former, original
原型 **yuánxíng** *n* prototype
原因 **yuányīn** *n* cause, reason
原则 **yuánzé** *n* principle
原著 **yuánzhù** *n* original work
原状 **yuánzhuàng** *n* original state, previous condition
原子核 **yuánzǐhé** *n* nuclear
原作 **yuánzuò** *n* original work
圆 **yuán** *adj* round, circular
圆顶 **yuándǐng** *n* dome
圆规 **yuánguī** *n* compass
圆滑 **yuánhuá** *adj* slick
圆满 **yuánmǎn** *adv* successful, satisfactory; *adv* satisfactorily
圆圈 **yuánquān** *n* circle
圆心 **yuánxīn** *n* the center of a circle
圆形 **yuánxíng** *adj* circular, round
圆周 **yuánzhōu** *n* circumference
圆珠笔 **yuánzhūbǐ** *n* ballpoint pen
圆柱 **yuánzhù** *n* cylinder
圆锥 **yuánzhuī** *n* circular cone, taper
援救 **yuánjiù** *n/v* rescue
援助 **yuánzhù** *n/v* aid

缘分 **yuánfèn** *n* lot or luck by which people are brought together, fate

缘故 **yuángù** *n* cause, reason

缘由 **yuányóu** *n* cause, reason

源泉 **yuánquán** *n* source, fountainhead

源头 **yuántóu** *n* source, fountainhead

猿 **yuán** *n* ape

猿猴 **yuánhóu** *n* apes and monkeys

远 **yuǎn** *adj* far, remote

远程 **yuǎnchéng** *adj* long-range, long-distance; 远程教育 **yuǎnchéng jiàoyù** *n* distance learning

远大 **yuǎndà** *adj* long-range, ambitious

远方 **yuǎnfāng** *n* distant place

远古 **yuǎngǔ** *n* remote antiquity

远见 **yuǎnjiàn** *n* foresight, vision

远景 **yuǎnjǐng** *n* perspective, vista

远离 **yuǎnlí** *adj* far away from

远视 **yuǎnshì** *n* long sight, farsightedness; hyperopia, hypermetropia

远征 **yuǎnzhēng** *n* expedition; *v* go on an expedition

远足 **yuǎnzú** *n* outing, hiking

怨恨 **yuànhèn** *n* bitterness, resentment

怨言 **yuànyán** *n* complaint

院士 **yuànshì** *n* academician

院子 **yuànzi** *n* courtyard, yard

愿望 **yuànwàng** *n* wish

愿意 **yuànyì** *v* be willing, be ready

约 **yuē** *v* make an appointment, arrange

约定 **yuēdìng** *v* (*of time*) arrange, agree on

约会 **yuēhuì** *n* appointment, date; *v* set up an appointment

约束 **yuēshù** *v* keep within bounds, restrain, bind

月 **yuè** *n* month; moon

月饼 **yuèbǐng** *n* moon cake

月光 **yuèguāng** *n* moonlight

月经 **yuèjīng** *n* menstruation

月亮 **yuèliang** *n* moon

月票 **yuèpiào** *n* monthly ticket

月球 **yuèqiú** *n* the moon

月台 **yuètái** *n* (*railway*) platform

乐队 **yuèduì** *n* band, orchestra; 乐队指挥 **yuèduì zhǐhuī** *n* conductor, bandmaster

乐谱 **yuèpǔ** *n* music score

乐器 **yuèqì** *n* musical instrument
乐曲 **yuèqǔ** *n* musical composition, music
乐团 **yuètuán** *n* philharmonic, orchestra
岳父 **yuèfù** *n* father-in-law (*wife's father*)
岳母 **yuèmǔ** *n* mother-in-law (*wife's mother*)
阅读 **yuèdú** *n* reading; *v* read
阅览 **yuèlǎn** *v* read; 阅览室 **yuèlǎnshì** *n* reading room
越发 **yuèfā** *adv* all the more, even more
越轨 **yuèguǐ** *v* exceed the bounds, transgress
越过 **yuèguò** *v* cross, surmount
越来越 **yuèláiyuè** *adv* more and more, increasingly
晕倒 **yūndǎo** *v* fall in a faint
云 **yún** *n* cloud
匀称 **yúnchèn** *adj* symmetrical
允诺 **yǔnnuò** *n/v* promise
允许 **yǔnxǔ** *n* permission; *v* allow, permit
陨石 **yǔnshí** *n* aerolite, stony meteorite
孕妇 **yùnfù** *n* pregnant woman
孕育 **yùnyù** *v* be pregnant with, breed
运 **yùn** *n* fortune, luck, fate; *v* ship, transport
运动 **yùndòng** *n* campaign; sports, exercise; motion, movement; 运动场 **yùndòngchǎng** *n* sports ground, stadium, field; 运动会 **yùndònghuì** *n* sports meet; 运动衫 **yùndòngshān** *n* sport shirt; 运动鞋 **yùndòngxié** *n* sneaker, gym shoes; 运动员 **yùndòngyuán** *n* athlete, sportsman; 运动装 **yùndòngzhuāng** *n* sportswear
运费 **yùnfèi** *n* shipping charge
运河 **yùnhé** *n* canal
运气 **yùnqi** *n* fortune, luck
运输 **yùnshū** *n/v* transport
运送 **yùnsòng** *v* convey, transport, ship
运算 **yùnsuàn** *n* (*math*) operation
运行 **yùnxíng** *v* move, be in motion, operate
运用 **yùnyòng** *v* utilize, apply, put to use; *n* application
晕车 **yùnchē** *v* be carsick
晕船 **yùnchuán** *v* be seasick
晕机 **yùnjī** *v* be airsick
韵律 **yùnlǜ** *n* meter (*in verse*), rules of rhyming, rhyme scheme
韵文 **yùnwén** *n* verse
熨 **yùn** *v* iron; 熨斗 **yùndǒu** *n* (*clothes*) iron

Z

杂 zá *adj* miscellaneous, sundry, mixed

杂烩 záhuì *n* a stew of various ingredients, mixed stew; hodgepodge

杂货 záhuò *n* grocery; 杂货店 záhuòdiàn *n* grocery store

杂技 zájì *n* acrobatics

杂乱 záluàn *adj* mixed and disorderly, in a jumble, messy

杂务 záwù *n* chore

杂志 zázhì *n* journal, magazine

灾害 zāihài *n* calamity, disaster

灾难 zāinàn *n* disaster, calamity

灾区 zāiqū *n* disaster area

栽 zāi *v* plant, grow, raise

栽培 zāipéi *v* cultivate, grow; foster, train, groom

栽种 zāizhòng *v* plant, grow

宰杀 zǎishā *v* slaughter, butcher

再 zài *adv* again, anew, once more

再见 zàijiàn *interj* good-bye, bye, bye-bye

再三 zàisān *adv* repeatedly

再生 zàishēng *n* rebirth

再说 zàishuō *v* put off until sometime later, what's more, besides

在 zài *prep* at, in, on

在场 zàichǎng *v* be on the scene, be on the spot, be present

在乎 zàihu *v* care about, mind, take to heart

在于 zàiyú *v* lie in, rest with, be determined by, depend on

咱们 zánmen *pron* we (*includes both the speaker and the person or persons spoken to*)

暂时 zànshí *n* temporarily

暂停 zàntíng *n/v* pause

赞成 zànchéng *v* approve of, agree with, endorse

赞美 zànměi *v* eulogize, sing the praise of; 赞美诗 zànměishī *n* hymn

赞赏 zànshǎng *v* appreciate, admire

赞同 zàntóng *v* approve of, agree with, endorse

赞扬 zànyáng *v* speak highly of, praise, commend

赞助 zànzhù *v* sponsor; 赞助人 zànzhùrén *n* sponsor, patron

脏 zāng *adj* dirty

葬 zàng *v* bury

葬礼 zànglǐ *n* funeral

遭到 zāodào *v* suffer, meet with, encounter

遭受 **zāoshòu** *v* suffer, meet with, encounter

遭殃 **zāoyāng** *v* suffer a disaster

遭遇 **zāoyù** *v* meet with, encounter, run up against; *n* bitter experience, hard lot

糟糕 **zāogāo** *interj* how terrible, what bad luck, too bad

糟蹋 **zāotà** *v* waste, ruin, spoil, trample on, ravage

凿 **záo** *v* chisel; 凿子 **záozi** *n* chisel

早 **zǎo** *adj/adv* early

早安 **zǎo'ān** *interj* good morning

早餐 **zǎocān** *n* breakfast

早晨 **zǎochén** *n* (*early*) morning

早点 **zǎodiǎn** *n* (*light*) breakfast

早饭 **zǎofàn** *n* breakfast

早年 **zǎonián** *n* one's early years

早期 **zǎoqī** *n* early stage, early phase

早上 **zǎoshang** *n* morning

早晚 **zǎowǎn** *n* morning and evening; *adv* sooner or later

早先 **zǎoxiān** *n* previously

枣 **zǎo** *n* Chinese date

澡盆 **zǎopén** *n* bathtub

造 **zào** *v* build, make

造成 **zàochéng** *v* cause, lead to

造反 **zàofǎn** *v* rise in rebellion, rebel, revolt

造句 **zàojù** *v* make sentences

造谣 **zàoyáo** *v* start a rumor

噪声 **zàoshēng** *n* noise

责备 **zébèi** *v* blame, reproach

责骂 **zémà** *v* scold, rebuke, dress down

责任 **zérèn** *n* responsibility

责问 **zéwèn** *v* call to account, take to task

贼 **zéi** *n* thief

怎么 **zěnme** *adv* how

怎么了 **zěnmele** *phr* what's wrong?, what's the matter?

怎么样 **zěnmeyàng** *phr* how is it?, what do you think?

怎样 **zěnyàng** *adv* how

增补 **zēngbǔ** *v* augment, supplement

增光 **zēngguāng** *v* add luster to, do credit to, add to the prestige of

增加 **zēngjiā** *v* increase, multiply

增进 **zēngjìn** *v* further, promote

增强 **zēngqiáng** *v* boost, strengthen

增添 **zēngtiān** *v* add, increase

增长 zēngzhǎng *n* growth; *v* grow

增值 zēngzhí *v* appreciate in value; 增值税 zēngzhíshuì *n* value-added tax

憎恨 zēnghèn *v* detest; *n* hatred

憎恶 zēngwù *v* loathe, abhor

赠 zèng *v* give as a gift

赠送 zèngsòng *v* present, give as a gift

扎 zhā *v* tie

扎实 zhāshi *adj* sturdy, strong, solid, down-to-earth

闸 zhá *n* brake

闸门 zhámén *n* floodgate

眨眼 zhǎyǎn *v* blink, wink

诈骗 zhàpiàn *n* fraud; *v* swindle

炸 zhà *v* bomb, blow up, blast

炸弹 zhàdàn *n* bomb

炸药 zhàyào *n* explosive, dynamite

榨取 zhàqǔ *v* squeeze, extort

摘 zhāi *v* pick, pluck, cull, select

摘录 zhāilù *v* extract, excerpt; *n* extracts, excerpts

摘要 zhāiyào *n* digest, summary

债 zhài *n* debt

债权人 zhàiquánrén *n* creditor

债券 zhàiquàn *n* bond

债务人 zhàiwùrén *n* debtor

沾污 zhānwū *v* defile, smear

毡 zhān *n* felt

粘 zhān *v* glue, stick, paste; 粘贴 zhāntiē *v* stick, paste

展出 zhǎnchū *v* put on display, be on show, exhibit

展开 zhǎnkāi *v* unfold, unroll, unwind

展览 zhǎnlǎn *n* exhibition; *v* exhibit

展示 zhǎnshì *n* demonstration, display; *v* demonstrate, display

展望 zhǎnwàng *v* look into the future, look ahead; *n* forecast, prospect

展现 zhǎnxiàn *v* unfold before one's eyes, emerge

崭新 zhǎnxīn *adj* brand new

占 zhàn *v* occupy, seize, take; make up, account for

占据 zhànjù *v* occupy

占领 zhànlǐng *n* occupation; *v* occupy; 占领者 zhànlǐngzhě *n* occupier

占线 zhànxiàn *v* (*of phone lines*) be busy

占有 zhànyǒu *v* possess, own, have

战场 zhànchǎng *n* battlefield, battleground, battlefront
战斗 zhàndòu *n/v* combat, fight; 战斗机 zhàndòujī *n* fighter plane
战犯 zhànfàn *n* war criminal
战俘 zhànfú *n* prisoner of war
战绩 zhànjī *n* military successes
战舰 zhànjiàn *n* warship
战利品 zhànlìpǐn *n* booty, spoil, trophy
战略 zhànlüè *n* strategy; 战略性 zhànlüèxìng *adj* strategic
战胜 zhànshèng *v* prevail, win over, defeat
战时 zhànshí *n* wartime
战士 zhànshì *n* fighter, soldier
战术 zhànshù *n* tactic
战线 zhànxiàn *n* battle line, battlefront, front
战役 zhànyì *n* battle, campaign
战友 zhànyǒu *n* comrade-in-arms, battle companion
战争 zhànzhēng *n* war, warfare
站 zhàn *n* station, stop; *v* stand; 站起来 zhàn qǐlái *v* stand up
站岗 zhàngǎng *v* stand guard, stand sentry
站台 zhàntái *n* (*railway*) platform
蘸 zhàn *v* dip
张 zhāng *cl* (*for flat things such as beds, tables, paper, etc.*)
张贴 zhāngtiē *v* post
章 zhāng *n* (*book*) chapter
章程 zhāngchéng *n* charter, bylaws, statute
章节 zhāngjié *n* chapters and sections
章鱼 zhāngyú *n* octopus
蟑螂 zhāngláng *n* cockroach
长¹ zhǎng *n* chief
长² zhǎng *v* grow, develop, come into being, begin to grow; 长大 zhǎngdà *v* grow up
长辈 zhǎngbèi *n* elder generation, senior
涨 zhǎng *v* rise, inflate
涨潮 zhǎngcháo *n* rising tide
涨价 zhǎngjià *v* rise in prices
掌管 zhǎngguǎn *v* be in charge of, administer
掌声 zhǎngshēng *n* clapping, applause
掌握 zhǎngwò *v* master, grasp, command
丈 zhàng *n* Chinese measurement for length equal to 3.33 meters
丈夫 zhàngfu *n* husband
丈母娘 zhàngmǔ'niáng *n* mother-in-law (*wife's mother*)

丈人 **zhàngren** *n* father-in-law (*wife's father*)
帐篷 **zhàngpeng** *n* tent
胀 **zhàng** *v* expand, swell, be bloated, be full
账 **zhàng** *n* account
账单 **zhàngdān** *n* bill, check
账户 **zhànghù** *n* account
障碍 **zhàng'ài** *n* barrier, obstacle, obstruction
朝阳 **zhāoyáng** *n* the rising sun, the morning sun
招 **zhāo** *v* enroll, recruit, enlist
招标 **zhāobiāo** *v* invite tenders, invite bids
招待 **zhāodài** *v* entertain, play host to
招呼 **zhāohu** *v* call, hail, greet
招牌 **zhāopai** *n* shop sign, signboard
招聘 **zhāopìn** *v* invite applications for a job
招生 **zhāoshēng** *v* enroll new students, recruit students
招手 **zhāoshǒu** *v* beckon, wave
招致 **zhāozhì** *v* incur, beget, lead to
着火 **zháohuǒ** *v* catch fire, be on fire
着急 **zháojí** *v* worry, feel anxious
着凉 **zháoliáng** *v* catch cold, catch a chill
着迷 **zháomí** *v* be fascinated, be captivated
找 **zhǎo** *v* look for, seek
找到 **zhǎodào** *v* find
找回 **zhǎohuí** *v* recover (*a lost item*)
找钱 **zhǎoqián** *v* (*money*) give change
沼泽 **zhǎozé** *n* marsh, swamp, bog
召唤 **zhàohuàn** *v* summon; *n* call
召回 **zhàohuí** *v* recall (*a person, e.g., diplomat*)
召集 **zhàojí** *v* summon, gather
召开 **zhàokāi** *v* convene, convoke
兆头 **zhàotou** *n* sign, omen
照 **zhào** *v* shine, reflect; shoot (*a picture*)
照常 **zhàocháng** *adv* as usual
照顾 **zhàogù** *v* attend to, look after, take care of
照旧 **zhàojiù** *adv* as before, as usual
照看 **zhàokàn** *v* look after, attend to, keep an eye on
照亮 **zhàoliàng** *v* illuminate
照料 **zhàoliào** *v* attend to, take care of
照明 **zhàomíng** *v* illuminate
照片 **zhàopiàn** *n* photo, picture
照像 **zhàoxiàng** *v* take a picture; 照像机 **zhàoxiàngjī** *n* camera

照耀 zhàoyào *v* shine
罩 zhào *v* cover, overspread, wrap; *n* cover, shade, hood
肇事 zhàoshì *v* cause trouble, cause an accident
着 zhe *part* (*indicating continuing state*)
遮蔽 zhēbì *v* hide from view, cover, screen, obstruct, block
遮挡 zhēdǎng *v* shelter from, keep out
遮掩 zhēyǎn *v* cover, overspread, cover up, hide, conceal
蜇 zhé *v* sting
折 zhé *v* fold
折叠 zhédié *v* fold; 折叠椅 zhédiéyǐ *n* folding chair
折合 zhéhé *v* convert into, be equivalent to
折扣 zhékòu *n* discount
折磨 zhémo *n* ordeal, torture; *v* torture
折算 zhésuàn *v* convert
折纸 zhézhǐ *v* paper folding; *n* origami
哲学 zhéxué *n* philosophy; 哲学家 zhéxuéjiā *n* philosopher
这 zhè *pron* this
这次 zhècì *pron* this time
这儿 zhèr *n* here
这里 zhèlǐ *n* here
这么 zhème *adv* so, such, like this
这些 zhèxiē *pron* these
这样 zhèyàng *pron* such
针 zhēn *n* needle
针对 zhēnduì *v* be directed against, be aimed at
针尖 zhēnjiān *n* the point of a needle, pinpoint
针灸 zhēnjiǔ *n* acupuncture
针头 zhēntóu *n* syringe needle
针织 zhēnzhī *adj* knitting
侦察 zhēnchá *n* reconnaissance, spying; *v* spy; 侦察员 zhēncháyuán *n* scout
侦探 zhēntàn *n* detective
珍爱 zhēn'ài *v* treasure, love dearly, be very fond of
珍宝 zhēnbǎo *n* jewelery, treasure
珍藏 zhēncáng *v* collect (*rare books, art treasures, etc.*)
珍贵 zhēnguì *adj* valuable, precious
珍奇 zhēnqí *adj* rare
珍惜 zhēnxī *v* treasure, value, cherish
珍珠 zhēnzhū *n* pearl
真 zhēn *adj* real, true
真诚 zhēnchéng *adj* sincere
真的 zhēnde *adv* really; 真的吗? zhēnde ma? *interj* really?

真菌 **zhēnjūn** *n* fungus

真空 **zhēnkōng** *n* vacuum; 真空吸尘器 **zhēnkōng xīchénqì** *n* vacuum cleaner

真理 **zhēnlǐ** *n* truth

真实 **zhēnshí** *adj* authentic, true, real

真相 **zhēnxiàng** *n* truth, the real facts, the actual state of affairs

真心 **zhēnxīn** *adj* wholehearted, heartfelt, sincere

真正 **zhēnzhèng** *adj* genuine, true, real

榛子 **zhēnzi** *n* hazel, hazelnut

诊断 **zhěnduàn** *n* diagnosis; *v* diagnose

诊所 **zhěnsuǒ** *n* clinic

诊治 **zhěnzhì** *v* make a diagnosis and give treatment

枕头 **zhěntou** *n* pillow; 枕头套 **zhěntóutào** *n* pillowcase

疹 **zhěn** *n* rash

振动 **zhèndòng** *n* vibration; *v* vibrate

振奋 **zhènfèn** *v* rouse oneself, hearten, inspire

振兴 **zhènxīng** *v* develop vigorously, promote

振作 **zhènzuò** *v* bestir oneself

镇定 **zhèndìng** *adj* calm, cool, composed, unruffled; 镇定剂 **zhèndìngjì** *n* tranquilizer

镇静 **zhènjìng** *adj* calm, cool, composed, unruffled

镇痛 **zhèntòng** *v* ease pain

镇压 **zhènyā** *v* suppress, repress, crack down

震动 **zhèndòng** *v* shock, shake, quake

震撼 **zhènhàn** *v* shake, shock

震惊 **zhènjīng** *v* shock, astonish

争 **zhēng** *v* strive, vie, fight

争辩 **zhēngbiàn** *v* argue, debate, contend

争吵 **zhēngchǎo** *v* quarrel, wrangle, squabble

争端 **zhēngduān** *n* dispute, conflict

争论 **zhēnglùn** *n* argument; *v* argue

争取 **zhēngqǔ** *v* strive for, fight for

争议 **zhēngyì** *n* dispute, controversy

争执 **zhēngzhí** *n/v* dispute

征 **zhēng** *v* recruit, enlist, solicit

征服 **zhēngfú** *n* conquest; *v* conquer

征募 **zhēngmù** *v* recruit, enlist

征求 **zhēngqiú** *v* solicit, seek, ask for

征税 **zhēngshuì** *v* levy, tax

蒸 **zhēng** *v* steam; 蒸汽 **zhēngqì** *n* steam

蒸发 **zhēngfā** *v* evaporate

蒸气 zhēngqì *n* vapor

症结 zhēngjié *n* crux, sticking point

拯救 zhěngjiù *n* salvation; *v* salvage

整 zhěng *adj* whole, entire

整顿 zhěngdùn *v* rectify, consolidate, reorganize

整个 zhěnggè *adj* entire, whole

整洁 zhěngjié *adj* neat, tidy

整理 zhěnglǐ *v* put in order, straighten out, arrange, sort out

整齐 zhěngqí *adj* in good order, neat, tidy

整数 zhěngshù *n* integer, whole number, round number

整体 zhěngtǐ *n* whole, entirety

整修 zhěngxiū *v* rebuild, renovate, recondition

整治 zhěngzhì *v* renovate, repair, dredge (*a river, etc.*), fix

挣 zhèng *v* earn

正 zhèng *adv* just; right; *adj* upright, honest; *n* (*physics*) positive, plus

正常 zhèngcháng *adj* normal; *adv* normally

正当 zhèngdāng *adj* proper, appropriate, legitimate

正方形 zhèngfāngxíng *n* (*shape*) square

正规 zhèngguī *adj* regular, standard

正好 zhènghǎo *adv* just in time, just right, just enough, as it happens

正经 zhèngjing *adj* decent, respectable, honest, serious

正面 zhèngmiàn *n* façade, front, the right side; *adj* positive; *adv* directly

正派 zhèngpài *adj* decent, upright, honest

正确 zhèngquè *adj* correct, right

正式 zhèngshì *adj* formal, official; *adv* formally, officially

正视 zhèngshì *v* face squarely, face up to, look squarely at

正数 zhèngshù *n* positive number

正文 zhèngwén *n* text

正义 zhèngyì *n* justice

正在 zhèngzài *adv* in the process of, in the course of

正直 zhèngzhí *adj* honest, upright, fair-minded

证 zhèng *n* certificate, card, ID

证件 zhèngjiàn *n* credentials, papers, ID

证据 zhèngjù *n* evidence, proof

证明 zhèngmíng *n* certificate, proof; *v* prove, bear out, certify

证券 zhèngquàn *n* bond, security; 证券交易所 zhèngquàn jiāoyìsuǒ *n* stock exchange

证人 zhèngrén *n* witness

证实 **zhèngshí** *v* confirm, verify, substantiate
证书 **zhèngshū** *n* certificate, credentials
郑重 **zhèngzhòng** *adj* serious, solemn, earnest; *adv* seriously, solemnly, earnestly
政变 **zhèngbiàn** *n* coup
政策 **zhèngcè** *n* policy
政党 **zhèngdǎng** *n* political party
政府 **zhèngfǔ** *n* government
政客 **zhèngkè** *n* politician
政权 **zhèngquán** *n* political power, regime
政体 **zhèngtǐ** *n* government polity
政治 **zhèngzhì** *n* politics; 政治家 **zhèngzhìjiā** *n* politician, statesman
症状 **zhèngzhuàng** *n* symptom
只 **zhī** *cl* (*for animals, one of a pair of things, etc.*)
枝 **zhī** *n* branch; *cl* (*for slender items*)
之后 **zhīhòu** *n* later, after, afterwards
之前 **zhīqián** *n* before, prior to, ago
支撑 **zhīchēng** *v* prop; prop up, sustain
支持 **zhīchí** *n* backing, support, bolster; *v* back up, support; 支持者 **zhīchízhě** *n* supporter
支出 **zhīchū** *v* pay, expend, disburse; *n* expenses, expenditure, outlay
支付 **zhīfù** *v* pay
支流 **zhīliú** *n* tributary, branch
支配 **zhīpèi** *n* domination; *v* dominate; *adj* dominant
支票 **zhīpiào** *n* check; 支票本 **zhīpiàoběn** *n* checkbook
支援 **zhīyuán** *v* support, assist, aid, back up
汁 **zhī** *n* juice
芝麻 **zhīma** *n* sesame
知道 **zhīdao** *v* know
知己 **zhījǐ** *adj* intimate, understanding
知觉 **zhījué** *n* consciousness, perception
知名 **zhīmíng** *adj* well-known, noted, celebrated, famous
知识 **zhīshi** *n* knowledge
知心 **zhīxīn** *adj* intimate, understanding
织 **zhī** *v* weave, knit
织物 **zhīwù** *n* fabric
肢 **zhī** *n* limb
肢解 **zhījiě** *n* dismemberment; *v* dismember
肢体 **zhītǐ** *n* limbs
脂肪 **zhīfáng** *n* fat

蜘蛛 **zhīzhū** *n* spider
执行 **zhíxíng** *v* execute, implement, carry out
执照 **zhízhào** *n* license
执政 **zhízhèng** *v* be in power, be in office, be at the helm of the state
侄女 **zhínǚ** *n* niece (*brother's daughter*)
侄子 **zhízi** *n* nephew (*brother's son*)
直 **zhí** *adj/adv* straight
直尺 **zhíchǐ** *n* ruler
直到 **zhídào** *conj/prep* until
直观 **zhíguān** *adj* directly perceived through the senses, audiovisual; *n* direct observation
直角 **zhíjiǎo** *n* right angle
直接 **zhíjiē** *adj* direct; *adv* directly
直径 **zhíjìng** *n* diameter
直觉 **zhíjué** *n* intuition
直立 **zhílì** *adj* upright
直升机 **zhíshēngjī** *n* helicopter
直率 **zhíshuài** *adj* candor
直线 **zhíxiàn** *n* straight line
直言 **zhíyán** *n* blunt words
直至 **zhízhì** *conj* till, until, up to
值 **zhí** *v* be worth; *n* value
值班 **zhíbān** *v* be on duty
值得 **zhíde** *v* deserve; *adj* worthy, worthwhile
值钱 **zhíqián** *adj* valuable
职称 **zhíchēng** *n* job title, professional titles and ranks
职工 **zhígōng** *n* staff and workers
职位 **zhíwèi** *n* position, post
职务 **zhíwù** *n* position, post
职业 **zhíyè** *n* occupation, profession, vocation
职员 **zhíyuán** *n* clerk, staffer
职责 **zhízé** *n* duty, responsibility
植树 **zhíshù** *n* tree planting; *v* plant trees; 植树节 **zhíshùjié** *n* Tree-planting Day, Arbor Day
植物 **zhíwù** *n* plant; 植物人 **zhíwùrén** *n* person in a vegetated state
殖民 **zhímín** *v* colonize; 殖民地 **zhímíndì** *n* colony
止 **zhǐ** *v* stop, cease
止境 **zhǐjìng** *n* end, limit
止咳 **zhǐké** *v* relieve a cough
止痛药 **zhǐtòngyào** *n* painkiller

止血 **zhǐxuè** *v* stop bleeding
只 **zhǐ** *adv* only
只好 **zhǐhǎo** *adv* have to, be forced to
只是 **zhǐshì** *adv* merely, only, just, simply
只要 **zhǐyào** *conj* so long as, as long as
只有 **zhǐyǒu** *conj* only when
纸 **zhǐ** *n* paper
纸盒 **zhǐhé** *n* carton
纸浆 **zhǐjiāng** *n* pulp
纸片 **zhǐpiàn** *n* slip of paper
纸箱 **zhǐxiāng** *n* carton
纸张 **zhǐzhāng** *n* paper
指 **zhǐ** *v* point; 指出 **zhǐchū** *v* indicate, point out
指导 **zhǐdǎo** *n* guidance; *v* guide, instruct
指点 **zhǐdiǎn** *v* give directions, show how
指定 **zhǐdìng** *v* appoint, assign, designate
指挥 **zhǐhuī** *n* command; *v* conduct, direct, command
指甲 **zhǐjia** *n* nail
指控 **zhǐkòng** *v* accuse, charge
指南 **zhǐnán** *n* guidebook; 指南针 **zhǐnánzhēn** *n* compass
指派 **zhǐpài** *v* assign
指使 **zhǐshǐ** *v* incite, instigate
指示 **zhǐshì** *n* direction, instruction; *v* direct, instruct
指数 **zhǐshù** *n* index number
指头 **zhǐtou** *n* finger
指望 **zhǐwàng** *v* bank on, count on; *n* prospect, hope
指纹 **zhǐwén** *n* fingerprint
指责 **zhǐzé** *n* accusation; *v* accuse, ensure, criticize
指针 **zhǐzhēn** *n* indicator, pointer, needle, guiding principle
至多 **zhìduō** *adv* at most
至高无上 **zhìgāo wúshàng** *adj* supreme, paramount
至关重要 **zhìguān zhòngyào** *adj* of utmost importance
至今 **zhìjīn** *n* up to now, to this day, so far
至少 **zhìshǎo** *adv* at least
至于 **zhìyú** *conj* as for, as to
志气 **zhìqì** *n* aspiration, ambition
志愿 **zhìyuàn** *n* aspiration, wish; *v* volunteer; 志愿者
    zhìyuànzhě *n* volunteer
制裁 **zhìcái** *v* sanction, punish
制度 **zhìdù** *n* system, institution
制服 **zhìfú** *n* uniform
制药 **zhìyào** *v* manufacture medicines

制约 zhìyuē *v* restrict, condition
制造 zhìzào *v* make, manufacture; 制造商 zhìzàoshāng *n* manufacturer; 制造业 zhìzàoyè *n* manufacturing
制止 zhìzhǐ *v* check, curb, prevent, stop
制作 zhìzuò *v* make, manufacture
治 zhì *v* rule, govern, administer, manage; (*med*) treat, cure; control, harness
治安 zhì'ān *n* public order, public security
治理 zhìlǐ *v* govern, harness, bring under control, put in order
治疗 zhìliáo *n* therapy, treatment; *v* treat, cure
治愈 zhìyù *v* cure, heal
质地 zhìdì *n* texture
质量 zhìliàng *n* quality
质朴 zhìpǔ *adj* simple and unadorned, unaffected, plain
秩序 zhìxù *n* order
致力 zhìlì *v* dedicate, devote
致命 zhìmìng *adj* deadly, fatal, lethal, mortal
致使 zhìshǐ *v* bring about, lead to
致谢 zhìxiè *v* express one's thanks, extend thanks
致意 zhìyì *v* send one's best regards, send one's greetings
窒息 zhìxī *v* stifle, suffocate
智慧 zhìhuì *n* wisdom, wits
智力 zhìlì *n* intellect, intelligence
智谋 zhìmóu *n* resourcefulness
智囊团 zhì'nángtuán *n* the brain trust, think tank
置 zhì *v* place, put, install, set up
中 zhōng *n* middle, center; in, among, amidst
中部 zhōngbù *n* center, central section, middle part
中餐 zhōngcān *n* Chinese food; lunch
中产阶级 zhōngchǎn jiējí *n* middle class
中等 zhōngděng *adj* medium, medium-sized
中东 zhōngdōng *n* Middle East
中断 zhōngduàn *n* disruption, interruption; *v* disrupt, interrupt
中饭 zhōngfàn *n* lunch
中风 zhòngfēng *n* stroke, apoplexy
中国 zhōngguó *n* China; 中国人 zhōngguórén *n* (*people*) Chinese
中级 zhōngjí *adj* intermediate (*level*)
中间 zhōngjiān *n* middle, midst
中介 zhōngjiè *n* intermediary, medium, agent

中立 **zhōnglì** *adj* neutral
中年 **zhōngnián** *n* middle age; 中年人 **zhōngniánrén** *n* middle-aged person
中秋节 **zhōngqiūjié** *n* Mid-autumn Festival, Moon Festival
中士 **zhōngshì** *n* sergeant
中世纪 **zhōngshìjì** *n* Middle Ages
中途 **zhōngtú** *adv* midway, on the way
中文 **zhōngwén** *n* Chinese language
中午 **zhōngwǔ** *n* noon, noontime
中心 **zhōngxīn** *n* center
中型 **zhōngxíng** *adj* medium-sized, middle-sized
中学 **zhōngxué** *n* secondary school, middle school
中央 **zhōngyāng** *n* center; central government
中药 **zhōngyào** *n* traditional Chinese medicine
中医 **zhōngyī** *n* traditional Chinese medical science; doctor of traditional Chinese medicine
中止 **zhōngzhǐ** *v* discontinue, suspend, break off
中转 **zhōngzhuǎn** *v* (*bus, train, or plane*) transfer
忠 **zhōng** *adj* loyal, faithful
忠诚 **zhōngchéng** *n* loyalty; *adj* loyal
忠告 **zhōnggào** *n* advice
忠实 **zhōngshí** *adj* faithful
忠于 **zhōngyú** *v* be true to, be loyal to, be faithful to, stick by
终点 **zhōngdiǎn** *n* end point, terminal point, destination; 终点站 **zhōngdiǎnzhàn** *n* terminus
终端 **zhōngduān** *n* terminal
终结 **zhōngjié** *n* end, final stage
终究 **zhōngjiū** *adv* eventually, in the end, after all
终身 **zhōngshēn** *adj* lifelong, all one's life
终于 **zhōngyú** *adv* at last
终止 **zhōngzhǐ** *v* terminate
钟 **zhōng** *n* bell, clock
衷心 **zhōngxīn** *adj* heartfelt, wholehearted, cordial
肿块 **zhǒngkuài** *n* lump; tumor
肿瘤 **zhǒngliú** *n* tumor
肿胀 **zhǒngzhàng** *adj* swollen
种 **zhǒng** *n* kind, sort, type
种类 **zhǒnglèi** *n* kind, sort, species, variety
种种 **zhǒngzhǒng** *adj* all sorts of, a variety of
种子 **zhǒngzi** *n* seed
种族 **zhǒngzú** *n* race; 种族灭绝 **zhǒngzú mièjué** *n* genocide; 种族清洗 **zhǒngzú qīngxǐ** *n* ethnic cleansing; 种族主义

zhǒngzúzhǔyì *n* racism; 种族主义者 **zhǒngzúzhǔyìzhě** *n* racist

种 **zhòng** *v* plant, grow

种地 **zhòngdì** *v* cultivate land, till the land

种田 **zhòngtián** *v* till the land, farm

种植 **zhòngzhí** *v* plant, grow

中毒 **zhòngdú** *v* be poisoned

中奖 **zhòngjiǎng** *v* win a prize in a lottery

中意 **zhòngyì** *v* be to one's liking, catch the fancy of

仲裁 **zhòngcái** *v* arbitrate; *n* arbitration

仲夏 **zhòngxià** *n* midsummer

众多 **zhòngduō** *adj* multitudinous, numerous

众人 **zhòngrén** *n* everybody

众所周知 **zhòngsuǒ zhōuzhī** *adj* well-known, known to all

众议院 **zhòngyìyuàn** *n* House of Representatives

重 **zhòng** *adj* heavy, weighty

重大 **zhòngdà** *adj* important, major

重点 **zhòngdiǎn** *n* focus, emphasis

重读 **zhòngdú** *v* stress, accentuate

重工业 **zhònggōngyè** *n* heavy industry

重力 **zhònglì** *n* gravity

重量 **zhòngliàng** *n* weight

重任 **zhòngrèn** *n* important task, heavy responsibility

重视 **zhòngshì** *v* attach importance to, pay attention to, value

重要 **zhòngyào** *adj* important, significant; 重要性 **zhòngyàoxìng** *n* significance

重音 **zhòngyīn** *n* stress, accent

重罪 **zhòngzuì** *n* felony

州 **zhōu** *n* state (*of the U.S. fifty states*); 州长 **zhōuzhǎng** *n* governor

州际 **zhōujì** *adj* interstate

周 **zhōu** *n* week; 周末 **zhōumò** *n* weekend; 周日 **zhōurì** *n* weekday

周长 **zhōucháng** *n* circumference, perimeter

周到 **zhōudào** *adj* thoughtful, considerate

周刊 **zhōukān** *n* weekly

周密 **zhōumì** *adj* careful, thorough, meticulous

周年 **zhōunián** *n* anniversary

周期 **zhōuqī** *n* cycle, period

周围 **zhōuwéi** *n* surroundings

周折 **zhōuzhé** *v* twists and turns, setbacks

周转 **zhōuzhuǎn** *n* (*financial*) turnover; *v* (*financial*) turn over

洲 zhōu *n* continent

洲际 zhōujì *adj* intercontinental

粥 zhōu *n* porridge

肘 zhǒu *n* elbow

咒骂 zhòumà *v* curse, swear, revile

咒语 zhòuyǔ *n* curse

皱纹 zhòuwén *n* wrinkle

珠宝 zhūbǎo *n* pearls and jewels, jewelry; 珠宝商 zhūbǎoshāng *n* jeweler

珠子 zhūzi *n* beads

猪 zhū *n* hog, pig

猪排 zhūpái *n* pork chop

猪圈 zhūjuàn *n* sty

猪肉 zhūròu *n* pork

猪油 zhūyóu *n* lard

竹笋 zhúsǔn *n* bamboo shoots

竹子 zhúzi *n* bamboo

逐步 zhúbù *adv* step by step, progressively

逐渐 zhújiàn *adv* gradually, by degrees

逐日 zhúrì *adv* day by day

逐一 zhúyī *adv* one by one

逐字 zhúzì *adv* literally, word for word

主 zhǔ *n* host; owner, master; person concerned

主办 zhǔbàn *v* (*of events*) hold, sponsor

主编 zhǔbiān *n* chief editor, editor-in-chief

主持 zhǔchí *v* take charge of, preside over, chair

主导 zhǔdǎo *adj* leading, dominant, guiding

主动 zhǔdòng *adj* active; on one's own initiative

主妇 zhǔfù *n* homemaker, housewife

主观 zhǔguān *adj* subjective

主见 zhǔjiàn *n* one's own view, one's own judgment

主角 zhǔjué *n* leading role, protagonist

主教 zhǔjiào *n* bishop

主力 zhǔlì *n* main force, main strength of an army

主权 zhǔquán *n* sovereign rights, sovereignty

主人 zhǔrén *n* host, master, owner

主任 zhǔrèn *n* director

主食 zhǔshí *n* (*food*) staple

主题 zhǔtí *n* theme, subject matter

主席 zhǔxí *n* chair, chairman

主修 zhǔxiū *n* major; *v* major in

主演 zhǔyǎn *v* act the leading role (*in a play or film*)

主要 zhǔyào *adj* leading, main, primary, prime, principal

主义 zhǔyì *n* doctrine, -ism

主意 zhǔyi *n* idea

主语 zhǔyǔ *n* (*gram*) subject

主张 zhǔzhāng *n* proposition, opinion; *v* advocate

主旨 zhǔzhǐ *n* substance, purport, gist

煮 zhǔ *v* boil, cook

嘱咐 zhǔfù *v* enjoin, tell, exhort

嘱托 zhǔtuō *v* entrust

瞩目 zhǔmù *v* fix one's eyes upon, focus one's attention upon

住 zhù *v* live, reside, stay

住处 zhùchù *n* residence, dwelling, quarters

住房 zhùfáng *n* housing, lodgings

住口 zhùkǒu *v* shut up, stop talking

住所 zhùsuǒ *n* dwelling, place, residence, domicile

住宅 zhùzhái *n* dwelling, residence

助 zhù *v* help, assist

助长 zhùzhǎng *v* encourage, abet, foster

助词 zhùcí *n* auxiliary word

助教 zhùjiào *n* assistant lecturer, teaching assistant

助理 zhùlǐ *n* assistant

助手 zhùshǒu *n* assistant, aide, helper

助产士 zhùchǎnshì *n* midwife

注册 zhùcè *v* enroll, register

注定 zhùdìng *v* be doomed, be destined

注解 zhùjiě *v* annotate; *n* annotation

注明 zhùmíng *v* give clear indication of

注射 zhùshè *v* inject; 注射器 zhùshèqì *n* syringe

注视 zhùshì *v* gaze, watch

注释 zhùshì *n* explanatory note, annotation; *v* annotate

注销 zhùxiāo *v* cancel, write off

注意 zhùyì *v* note, notice, pay attention to, mind

注重 zhùzhòng *v* lay stress on, pay attention to, attach importance to

贮藏 zhùcáng *v* store up, lay in

贮存 zhùcún *v* stock, reserve

驻地 zhùdì *n* (*embassy, troops, etc.*) station, encampment; (*gov*) seat

驻军 zhùjūn *n* garrison

柱子 zhùzi *n* pillar

祝 zhù *v* wish

祝福 zhùfú *v* wish happiness to, bless

祝贺 **zhùhè** *v* congratulate; *n* congratulation
祝酒 **zhùjiǔ** *v* propose a toast
祝愿 **zhùyuàn** *v* wish, offer best wishes; *n* wish
著名 **zhùmíng** *adj* noted, well-known, renowned
著作 **zhùzuò** *n* (*book*) work, writings
抓 **zhuā** *v* catch, arrest; scratch
抓紧 **zhuājǐn** *v* clutch, hold fast
抓住 **zhuāzhù** *v* clutch, grab, grasp, seize
爪子 **zhuǎzi** *n* claw
专长 **zhuāncháng** *n* specialty, expertise
专攻 **zhuāngōng** *v* specialize
专家 **zhuānjiā** *n* expert, specialist
专刊 **zhuānkān** *n* (*magazine, etc.*) special issue, monograph
专栏 **zhuānlán** *n* (*newspaper*) column
专利 **zhuānlì** *n* patent
专门 **zhuānmén** *adj* special; *adv* specially
专题 **zhuāntí** *n* special subject, special topic
专心 **zhuānxīn** *adj* attentive, concentrated; 专心致志
  zhuānxīn zhìzhì *adj* wholly absorbed, with single-
  minded devotion
专业 **zhuānyè** *n* major, specialty; *adj* professional; 专业知识
  zhuānyè zhīshi *n* expertise, professional knowledge;
  专业人士 **zhuānyè rénshì** *n* professional
专一 **zhuānyī** *adj* single-minded, concentrated
专用 **zhuānyòng** *adj* for a special purpose
专政 **zhuānzhèng** *n* dictatorship
专职 **zhuānzhí** *adj* full-time
砖 **zhuān** *n* brick
砖头 **zhuāntou** *n* brick
转 **zhuǎn** *v* turn; transfer
转变 **zhuǎnbiàn** *n* change, transformation, turnabout; *v*
  change, transform
转达 **zhuǎndá** *v* pass on, convey
转动 **zhuǎndòng** *v* turn, revolve, rotate
转告 **zhuǎngào** *v* pass on (*word*), relay (*a message*)
转化 **zhuǎnhuà** *v* transform, change; *n* transformation, change
转换 **zhuǎnhuàn** *v* convert, change, transform
转交 **zhuǎnjiāo** *v* pass on, deliver to
转弯 **zhuǎnwān** *v* turn corner, make turn
转向 **zhuǎnxiàng** *v* turn round, change direction
转眼 **zhuǎnyǎn** *adv* in the twinkling of an eye, in an instant,
  in a flash

转移 **zhuǎnyí** *v* shift, transfer, divert
转帐 **zhuǎnzhàng** *v* transfer (*money*)
转折 **zhuǎnzhé** *n* a turn in the course of events; transition (*in an essay*); 转折点 **zhuǎnzhédiǎn** *n* turning point
赚 **zhuàn** *v* earn
赚钱 **zhuànqián** *v* make money
传记 **zhuànjì** *n* biography
篆刻 **zhuànkè** *n* seal cutting
庄稼 **zhuāngjia** *n* crop
庄严 **zhuāngyán** *adj* solemn, stately
庄园 **zhuāngyuán** *n* estate, manor
庄重 **zhuāngzhòng** *adj* serious, grave, solemn
桩 **zhuāng** *n* stake
装 **zhuāng** *v* make believe, pretend, disguise; load, mount, install
装扮 **zhuāngbàn** *v* impersonate, disguise, masquerade
装备 **zhuāngbèi** *n* gear, equipment; *v* equip, fit out
装订 **zhuāngdìng** *v* bind
装满 **zhuāngmǎn** *v* fill, fill up
装配 **zhuāngpèi** *v* assemble
装饰 **zhuāngshì** *v* decorate, deck, adorn; 装饰物 **zhuāngshìwù** *n* ornament
装修 **zhuāngxiū** *v* fix up (*a house, etc.*), renovate
装载 **zhuāngzài** *v* load, (*of cart, truck, train, etc.*) carry
装置 **zhuāngzhì** *n* installation, fitting
壮大 **zhuàngdà** *v* grow in strength, expand, strengthen
壮观 **zhuàngguān** *adj* spectacular
壮丽 **zhuànglì** *adj* majestic, magnificent, splendid
状况 **zhuàngkuàng** *n* circumstance, status, condition
状态 **zhuàngtài** *n* state, condition, state of affairs
状语 **zhuàngyǔ** *n* adverbial
撞 **zhuàng** *v* ram, dash against, crash, bump
追 **zhuī** *v* chase, pursue
追捕 **zhuībǔ** *n* manhunt
追悼 **zhuīdào** *v* mourn for
追赶 **zhuīgǎn** *v* chase, run after, pursue
追求 **zhuīqiú** *n* pursuit; *v* pursue
追上 **zhuī shàng** *v* overtake, catch up
追随 **zhuīsuí** *v* follow
追逐 **zhuīzhú** *v* chase
追踪 **zhuīzōng** *v* trace, pursue
坠毁 **zhuìhuǐ** *v* crash

坠落 zhuìluò *v* (*of airplanes*) crash

准 zhǔn *v* allow, grant, permit; *adj* accurate, exact

准备 zhǔnbèi *v* prepare; *n* preparation

准确 zhǔnquè *adj* accurate

准时 zhǔnshí *adv* on time, punctually

准许 zhǔnxǔ *v* permit, allow

准则 zhǔnzé *n* norm, guideline, rule

卓绝 zhuōjué *adj* unsurpassed, outstanding, of the highest degree

卓越 zhuōyuè *adj* prominent, superb, salient

卓著 zhuōzhù *adj* distinguished, outstanding, eminent

拙劣 zhuōliè *adj* clumsy, inferior

桌布 zhuōbù *n* tablecloth

桌面 zhuōmiàn *n* desktop

桌子 zhuōzi *n* table, desk

着陆 zhuólù *v* (*airplane*) land

着落 zhuóluò *n* whereabouts

着手 zhuóshǒu *v* commence, set about

着想 zhuóxiǎng *v* consider (*the interests of sb. or sth.*)

着重 zhuózhòng *v* stress, emphasize

咨询 zīxún *n* consultation; *v* consult

姿势 zīshì *n* posture, gesture

姿态 zītài *n* stance

资本 zīběn *n* (*money*) capital; 资本家 zīběnjiā *n* capitalist; 资本主义 zīběnzhǔyì *n* capitalism

资产阶级 zīchǎn jiējí *n* the capitalist class, the bourgeoisie

资格 zīgé *n* qualification, eligibility

资金 zījīn *n* funds, capital

资历 zīlì *n* qualifications, credentials

资料 zīliào *n* data, information, reference material

资源 zīyuán *n* resource

资助 zīzhù *v* aid, subsidize; *n* financial aid, subsidy

子 zǐ *n* child, son

子弹 zǐdàn *n* bullet

子弟 zǐdì *n* children, juniors

子宫 zǐgōng *n* womb

子女 zǐnǚ *n* sons and daughters, children

子孙 zǐsūn *n* descendants, offspring

仔细 zǐxì *adj* careful; *adv* carefully

姊妹 zǐmèi *n* sisters

紫色 zǐsè *n* purple color

字 zì *n* Chinese character

字典 zìdiǎn *n* dictionary
字迹 zìjī *n* handwriting
字母 zìmǔ *n* letters of an alphabet; 字母表 zìmǔbiǎo *n* alphabet
字幕 zìmù *n* subtitle, caption
字体 zìtǐ *n* font, script, typeface; style of calligraphy
自 zì *pron* self, oneself, one's own; *prep* from, since
自白 zìbái *n* confession
自卑 zìbēi *v* feel oneself inferior, be self-abased
自从 zìcóng *prep* ever since
自动 zìdòng *adj* automatic; *adv* automatically; 自动化 zìdònghuà *n* automation
自发 zìfā *adj* spontaneous
自费 zìfèi *adv* at one's own expense
自负 zìfù *adj* conceited, overconfident
自豪 zìháo *n* pride; *adj* proud
自己 zìjǐ *pron* self, oneself
自给 zìjǐ *v* self-sufficient, self-supporting; 自给自足 zìjǐ zìzú *adj* self-sufficient
自夸 zìkuā *v* boast, brag
自来水 zìláishuǐ *n* running water, tap water
自立 zìlì *v* stand on one's own two feet, support oneself, earn one's own living
自满 zìmǎn *adj* complacent, conceited
自然 zìrán *n* nature; *adj* natural, spontaneous; *adv* naturally
自杀 zìshā *n* suicide; *v* commit suicide
自身 zìshēn *n* self, oneself
自首 zìshǒu *v* turn oneself in, confess one's crime, give oneself up
自私 zìsī *adj* selfish
自卫 zìwèi *n* self-defence
自习 zìxí *v* study on one's own, study independently, teach oneself
自信 zìxìn *n* self-confidence; *adj* self-confident
自行车 zìxíngchē *n* bicycle
自由 zìyóu *n* freedom, liberty; *adj* free; 自由主义 zìyóuzhǔyì *n* liberalism; 自由主义者 zìyóu zhǔyìzhě *n* liberal
自愿 zìyuàn *v* act voluntarily
自制 zìzhì *v* make by oneself; *n* self-control, self-restraint
自治 zìzhì *v* self-govern, self-rule; 自治区 zìzhìqū *n* autonomous region
自主 zìzhǔ *v* be one's own master, take the initiative

自传 **zìzhuàn** *n* autobiography
自助餐 **zìzhùcān** *n* buffet
自尊 **zìzūn** *n* self-respect, self-esteem
恣意 **zìyì** *adv* recklessly, willfully
宗教 **zōngjiào** *n* religion
宗派 **zōngpài** *n* faction, sect
宗旨 **zōngzhǐ** *n* aim, purpose, mission
综合 **zōnghé** *v* integrate, synthesize
棕榈 **zōnglǘ** *n* palm
棕色 **zōngsè** *n* brown color
踪迹 **zōngjī** *n* trace
踪影 **zōngyǐng** *n* trace, sign
总 **zǒng** *adj* general, overall, total
总部 **zǒngbù** *n* headquarters
总共 **zǒnggòng** *adv* altogether, in all, in total
总和 **zǒnghé** *n* sum, total, sum total
总计 **zǒngjì** *v* total, amount to
总结 **zǒngjié** *v* summarize, sum up; *n* summary
总经理 **zǒngjīnglǐ** *n* general manager
总理 **zǒnglǐ** *n* premier, prime minister
总是 **zǒngshì** *adv* always
总数 **zǒngshù** *n* sum, total
总体 **zǒngtǐ** *n* totality
总统 **zǒngtǒng** *n* (*gov*) president
总之 **zǒngzhī** *adv* in a word, in short
纵然 **zòngrán** *conj* even if, even though
纵容 **zòngróng** *v* connive, wink at
粽子 **zòngzi** *n* a pyramid-shaped dumpling made of glutinous
    rice wrapped in bamboo or reed leaves
走 **zǒu** *v* walk; leave
走开 **zǒu kāi** *v* go away
走廊 **zǒuláng** *n* corridor, hallway, veranda
走路 **zǒulù** *v* walk, go on foot
走失 **zǒushī** *v* go astray
走私 **zǒusī** *v* smuggle; *n* smuggling; 走私者 **zǒusīzhě** *n*
    smuggler
走运 **zǒuyùn** *v* be in luck, have good luck
奏 **zòu** *v* (*music instrument*) play, perform, strike up
奏效 **zòuxiào** *v* be successful, achieve the desired result
租 **zū** *v* rent; 租金 **zūjīn** *n* rent
租约 **zūyuē** *n* lease
足 **zú** *adj* enough, sufficient

足 zú *n* foot
足够 zúgòu *adj* enough, sufficient
足迹 zújī *n* footmark, footprint
足球 zúqiú *n* soccer
足智多谋 zúzhì duōmóu *adj* resourceful
诅咒 zǔzhòu *v* curse, damn
阻碍 zǔ'ài *v* hinder, obstruct; *n* hindrance, obstruction
阻挡 zǔdǎng *v* bar, obstruct
阻拦 zǔlán *v* stop, obstruct, hinder
阻力 zǔlì *n* obstruction, resistance
阻挠 zǔnáo *v* obstruct, thwart, stand in the way
阻塞 zǔsè *v* block, obstruct, clog
阻止 zǔzhǐ *v* deter, prevent
组 zǔ *n* group; *v* organize
组成 zǔchéng *v* form, make up, compose
组合 zǔhé *v* make up, combine; *n* combination
组织 zǔzhī *n* organization; *v* organize
组装 zǔzhuāng *v* assemble
祖辈 zǔbèi *n* ancestors, forefathers
祖传 zǔchuán *adj* handed down from one's ancestors
祖父 zǔfù *n* grandfather (*paternal*)
祖国 zǔguó *n* homeland, native country
祖母 zǔmǔ *n* grandmother (*paternal*)
祖先 zǔxiān *n* ancestors, forefathers
钻 zuān *v* drill
钻孔 zuànkǒng *v* bore, drill
钻石 zuànshí *n* diamond
嘴 zuǐ *n* mouth
嘴巴 zuǐba *n* mouth
嘴唇 zuǐchún *n* lip
最 zuì *adv* most
最初 zuìchū *adv* originally, initially, at first
最高 zuìgāo *adj* supreme, tallest, highest
最好 zuìhǎo *adj* best
最后 zuìhòu *adv* finally, lastly, ultimately; *adj* final, ultimate;
　　最后通牒 zuìhòu tōngdié *n* ultimatum
最坏 zuìhuài *adj* worst
最近 zuìjìn *adv* lately, recently; shortly; *adj* latest, up-to-date
最终 zuìzhōng *adv* finally, ultimately
罪 zuì *n* crime, guilt, sin
罪犯 zuìfàn *n* convict, criminal
罪魁 zuìkuí *n* ringleader, culprit

罪孽 **zuìniè** *n* sin
罪人 **zuìrén** *n* guilty person, offender, sinner
罪行 **zuìxíng** *n* criminal act
罪证 **zuìzhèng** *n* evidence of a crime
罪状 **zuìzhuàng** *n* facts about a crime, charges in an indictment
醉 **zuì** *v* be drunk
醉酒 **zuìjiǔ** *adj* drunk
尊敬 **zūnjìng** *n* reverence, respect; *v* honor, look up to, respect; *adj* honored, respected
尊严 **zūnyán** *n* dignity
尊重 **zūnzhòng** *n/v* respect
遵守 **zūnshǒu** *v* conform, observe
遵循 **zūnxún** *v* follow, adhere to
遵照 **zūnzhào** *v* obey, conform to, comply with, act in accordance with
琢磨 **zuómó** *v* polish, refine
昨天 **zuótiān** *n* yesterday
昨晚 **zuówǎn** *n* last night
左 **zuǒ** *n* left
左边 **zuǒbian** *n* left
左轮手枪 **zuǒlún shǒuqiāng** *n* revolver
左面 **zuǒmiàn** *n* the left side
左派 **zuǒpài** *n* the Left, the left wing, Leftist
左手 **zuǒshǒu** *n* left hand
左翼 **zuǒyì** *adj* left-wing; 左翼分子 **zuǒyì fēnzǐ** *n* left-winger
左右 **zuǒyòu** *v* master, control, influence; *n* more or less
作 **zuò** *v* write, compose; do, make; pretend, affect; act as, become
作罢 **zuòbà** *v* drop (*a matter*), forget it
作弊 **zuòbì** *v* cheat (*in an exam*)
作操 **zuòcāo** *v* do gymnastics, do exercises
作对 **zuòduì** *v* set oneself against, oppose
作法 **zuòfǎ** *n* way of doing things, practice
作废 **zuòfèi** *v* become invalid
作风 **zuòfēng** *n* style of work, way of doing things
作家 **zuòjiā** *n* author, writer
作假 **zuòjiǎ** *v* counterfeit, falsify, cheat, play tricks, behave affectedly
作料 **zuóliào** *n* condiments, seasoning
作呕 **zuò'ǒu** *v* become nauseous
作品 **zuòpǐn** *n* works, production

作曲 **zuòqǔ** *v* write music, compose; 作曲家 **zuòqǔjiā** *n* composer

作为 **zuòwéi** *prep* as

作文 **zuòwén** *n* composition, essay

作业 **zuòyè** *n* schoolwork, homework

作用 **zuòyòng** *n* function, role, effect

作者 **zuòzhě** *n* author, writer

作证 **zuòzhèng** *v* testify

作主 **zuòzhǔ** *v* decide, take the responsibility for a decision

做 **zuò** *v* do, make

做饭 **zuòfàn** *v* cook

做梦 **zuòmèng** *v* dream

坐 **zuò** *v* sit; travel by (*bus, train, plane, etc.*)

坐垫 **zuòdiàn** *n* cushion

坐落 **zuòluò** *v* be situated, be located

座谈 **zuòtán** *v* have an informal discussion; 座谈会 **zuòtánhuì** *n* informal discussion

座位 **zuòwèi** *n* seat

English–Chinese
Dictionary

A

a; an *art* 一 yī

abandon *v* 放弃 fàngqì, 抛弃 pāoqì, 摒弃 bìngqì

abate *v* 减少 jiǎnshǎo, 减轻 jiǎnqīng; **abatement** *n* 减轻 jiǎnqīng, 折扣 zhékòu

abbreviate *v* 缩写 suōxiě, 缩短 suōduǎn; **abbreviation** *n* 缩写 suōxiě

abdomen *n* 腹部 fùbù

abduct *v* 诱拐 yòuguǎi

abhor *v* 憎恶 zēngwù, 痛恨 tònghèn; **abhorrence** *n* 痛恨 tònghèn, 憎恶 zēngwù

abide *v* (*abide by*) 遵守 zūnshǒu

ability *n* 能力 nénglì; **to the best of one's ability** 尽最大的努力 jìn zuìdà de nǔlì

able *adj* 有能力的 yǒu nénglì de

abnormal *adj* 反常的 fǎncháng de

aboard *adv* 在船上 zài chuán shàng

abolish *v* 废止 fèizhǐ, 废除 fèichú; **abolition** *n* 废除 fèichú

abomination *n* 憎恨 zēnghèn; **abominable** *adj* 讨厌的 tǎoyàn de

abortion *n* 堕胎 duòtāi

about *prep* (*approximately*) 大约 dàyuē; (*regarding*) 关于 guānyú

above *prep* 在 ... 上 zài ... shàng

abreast *adv* 并肩地 bìngjiān de, 并排地 bìngpái de; **keep abreast of** *or* **with** 跟上 gēnshàng, 不落后于 bù luòhòu yú

abroad *adv* 在国外 zài guówài

abrupt *adj* 突然的 tūrán de

absence *n* 缺席 quēxí; **absent** *adj* 缺席的 quēxí de; **absent-minded** *adj* 心不在焉的 xīnbùzàiyān de

absolute *adj* 绝对的 juéduì de; **absolutely** *adv* 绝对地 juéduì de

absorb *v* 吸收 xīshōu; **be absorbed in** 专心于 zhuānxīn yú, 沉浸于 chénjìn yú

abstain *v* 禁绝 jìnjué, 放弃 fàngqì, 弃权 qìquán; **abstinence** *n* 节制 jiézhì

abstraction *n* 提取 tíqǔ; **abstract** *adj* 抽象的 chōuxiàng de

absurd *adj* 荒谬的 huāngmiù de, 可笑的 kěxiào de

abundance *n* 丰富 fēngfù; **abundant** *adj* 丰富的 fēngfù de, 大量的 dàliàng de

abuse *v/n* 虐待 nüèdài; 滥用 lànyòng

abyss *n* 深渊 shēnyuān; **abysmal** *adj* 深不可测的 shēnbùkěcè de

academy *n* 学院 xuéyuàn; **academic** *adj* 学术的 xuéshù de

accent *n* 口音 kǒuyīn; 重音 zhòngyīn

accept *v* 接受 jiēshòu; **acceptance** *n* 接受 jiēshòu; **acceptable** *adj* 可接受的 kě jiēshòu de

access *n* 通路 tōnglù; *v* 接进 jiējìn; **accessible** *adj* 易接近的 yì jiējìn de

accessory *n* 附件 fùjiàn

accident *n* 事故 shìgù; **by accident** 偶然地 ǒurán de, 无意地 wúyì de; **accidentally** *adv* 偶然地 ǒurán de

acclaim *v* 欢呼 huānhū; 称赞 chēngzàn

acclimatize *v* (使) 适应新环境 (shǐ) shìyìng xīn huánjìng

accommodate *v* 供应 gōngyìng; (使) 适应 (shǐ) shìyìng; 为… 提供方便 wèi … tígòng fāngbiàn; **accommodation** *n* 住处 zhùchù

accompany *v* 陪同 péitóng, 陪伴 péibàn

accomplice *n* 同谋者 tóngmóuzhě

accomplish *v* 完成 wánchéng; **accomplishment** *n* 成就 chéngjiù

accord *v* 给予 jǐyǔ, 授予 shòuyǔ; 符合 fúhé; **of one's own accord** 主动的 zhǔdòng de, 自愿的 zìyuàn de; **in accordance with** 根据 gēnjù; **according to** 根据 gēnjù

account *n* (*bank, etc.*) 账户 zhànghù; (*narrative*) 陈述 chénshù; **on account of** 由于 yóuyú, 因为 yīnwèi; **take into account** 考虑到 kǎolǜ dào; **account for** (*explain*) 解释 jiěshì; (*make up*) 占 zhàn; **accountant** *n* 会计 kuàijì

accumulate *v* 积累 jīlěi

accuracy *n* 准确 zhǔnquè; **accurate** *adj* 准确的 zhǔnquè de

accuse *v* 谴责 qiǎnzé, 指控 zhǐkòng; **accused** *n* 被告 bèigào; **accusation** *n* 谴责 qiǎnzé, 指控 zhǐkòng

accustom *v* (使) 习惯于 (shǐ) xíguàn yú

ache *v* 痛 tòng

achieve *v* 取得 qǔdé; **achievement** *n* 成就 chéngjiù

acid *n* 酸 suān; **acidic** *adj* 酸的 suān de

acknowledge *v* (*admit*) 承认 chéngrèn; (*thank*) 鸣谢 míngxiè; **acknowledgement** *n* (*admission*) 承认 chéngrèn; (*thanks*) 鸣谢 míngxiè

acoustics *n* 声学 shēngxué; **acoustic** *adj* 音响的 yīnxiǎng de

acquaint *v* (使) 熟知 (shǐ) shúzhī; **be acquainted with** 和 … 熟悉 hé … shúxī; **acquaintance** *n* 熟人 shúrén

acquire *v* 获得 huòdé; **acquisition** *n* 获得 huòdé

acquit *v* 赦免无罪 shèmiǎn wúzuì; **acquittal** *n* 赦免 shèmiǎn

acre *n* 英亩 yīngmǔ

acrid *adj* 辛辣的 xīnlà de, 刻薄的 kèbó de

acrobat *n* 杂技演员 zájì yǎnyuán; **acrobatics** *n* 杂技 zájì

across *prep* 在 ... 对面 zài ... duìmiàn; *adv* 在对面 zài duìmiàn; 从一边到另一边 cóng yībiān dào lìngyībiān

act *n* 行为 xíngwéi, 行动 xíngdòng, 举动 jǔdòng; 法案 fǎ'àn; (*opera*) 幕 mù; *v* 行动 xíngdòng; **actor** *n* 演员 yǎnyuán; **actress** *n* 女演员 nǚyǎnyuán

action *n* 行动 xíngdòng; **bring an action against** 控告 kònggào; **out of action** 不再起作用 bùzài qǐ zuòyòng

activity *n* 活动 huódòng; **active** *adj* 活跃的 huóyuè de, 积极的 jījí de

actual *adj* 实际的 shíjì de; **actually** *adv* 实际上 shíjìshang; 竟然 jìngrán

actuate *v* 开动 kāidòng

acupuncture *n* 针灸 zhēnjiǔ; **acupuncturist** *n* 针灸师 zhēnjiǔshī

acute *adj* 敏锐的 mǐnruì de; 急性的 jíxìng de

adamant *adj* 坚决的 jiānjué de

adapt *v* (使) 适应 (shǐ) shìyìng; (*book, play*) 改编 gǎibiān; **adaptation** *n* 适应 shìyìng; **adapter** *n* (*elec*) 转接器 zhuǎnjiēqì, 变压器 biànyāqì; **adaptable** *adj* 易于适应的 yìyú shìyìng de

add *v* 加 jiā, 添 tiān; **add up** 加起来 jiā qǐlái; 说得通 shuō de tōng; **addition** *n* 增加 zēngjiā; **additional** *adj* 附加的 fùjiā de, 额外的 éwài de

addict *n* 有瘾的人 yǒuyǐn de rén; **be addicted to** 对 ... 上瘾 duì ... shàngyǐn; **addiction** *n* 瘾 yǐn; **addictive** *adj* 使人上瘾的 shǐ rén shàngyǐn de

additive *n* 添加剂 tiānjiājì

address *v* 对 ... 发表演说 duì ... fābiǎo yǎnshuō; 写信给 xiěxìn gěi; 对付 duìfu, 处理 chǔlǐ; *n* (*speech*) 演讲 yǎnjiǎng; (*letter*) 地址 dìzhǐ

adept *adj* 熟练的 shúliàn de

adequate *adj* 充分的 chōngfèn de, 足够的 zúgòu de

adhere *v* 遵循 zūnxún; 坚持 jiānchí

adhesive *adj* 粘的 zhān de

adjacent *adj* 邻近的 línjìn de

adjective *n* 形容词 xíngróngcí

adjourn *v* 延期 yánqī; **adjournment** *n* 休会 xiūhuì, 延期 yánqī

adjust *v* 调整 tiáozhěng; **adjustment** *n* 调整 tiáozhěng

administer *v* 执行 zhíxíng, 实施 shíshī; **administration** *n* 行政部门 xíngzhèng bùmén; (*government*) 政府 zhèngfǔ; **administrator** *n* 行政官员 xíngzhèng guānyuán; **administrative** *adj* 行政的 xíngzhèng de

admiral *n* 海军上将 hǎijūn shàngjiàng

admire *v* 敬佩 jìngpèi; **admiration** *n* 仰慕 yǎngmù, 钦佩 qīnpèi

admit *v* (*acknowledge*) 承认 chéngrèn; (*accept*) 录取 lùqǔ; **admission** *n* (*acknowledgment*) 承认 chéngrèn; (*acceptance*) 录取 lùqǔ; (*ticket*) 入场费 rùchǎngfèi

adolescence *n* 青春期 qīngchūnqī

adopt *v* (*child*) 收养 shōuyǎng; 采纳 cǎi'nà; **adoption** *n* 采用 cǎiyòng; (*child*) 收养 shōuyǎng; **adopted** *adj* (*child*) 收养的 shōuyǎng de

adore *v* 爱慕 àimù; **adoration** *n* 爱慕 àimù

adorn *v* 装饰 zhuāngshì

adrift *adv* 漂浮着 piāofú zhe

adult *n* 成人 chéngrén

adulterate *v* 掺杂 chānzá

adultery *n* 通奸 tōngjiān

advance *n* (*progress*) 前进 qiánjìn; (*money*) 预付款 yùfùkuǎn

advantage *n* 优势 yōushì; **take advantage of** 利用 lìyòng; 占便宜 zhànpiányi; **advantageous** *adj* 有利的 yǒulì de, 有益的 yǒuyì de

advent *n* 出现 chūxiàn; 到来 dàolái

adventure *n* 历险 lìxiǎn

adverb *n* 副词 fùcí

adversary *n* 敌手 díshǒu

adversity *n* 不幸 bùxìng; **adverse** *adj* 敌对的 díduì de

advertise *v* 做广告 zuò guǎnggào; **advertisement** *n* 广告 guǎnggào

advise *v* 劝告 quàngào, 建议 jiànyì; **adviser/advisor** *n* 顾问 gùwèn; (*academic*) 导师 dǎoshī; **advice** *n* 忠告 zhōnggào, 建议 jiànyì; **advisable** *adj* 明智的 míngzhì de

advocate *v* 提倡 tíchàng; *n* 提倡者 tíchàngzhě

aerial *n* 天线 tiānxiàn; *adj* 空中的 kōngzhōng de

aeronautics *n* 航空学 hángkōngxué

aesthetics *n* 美学 měixué; **aesthetic** *adj* 美学的 měixué de

affair *n* (*business*) 事务 shìwù; (*love*) 暧昧关系 àimèi guānxì, 私通 sītōng

affect *v* 影响 yǐngxiǎng; **affection** *n* 喜爱 xǐ'ài, 感情 gǎnqíng

affiliate *v* (使) 附属 (shǐ) fùshǔ; **affiliation** *n* 所属单位 suǒshǔ dānwèi; 从属关系 cóngshǔ guānxì

affinity *n* 吸引力 xīyǐnlì; 密切关系 mìqiè guānxì

affirm *v* 确认 quèrèn; **affirmation** *n* 主张 zhǔzhāng; 认可 rènkě; **affirmative** *adj* 肯定的 kěndìng de

affix *v* (使) 附于 (shǐ) fù yú

afflict *v* (使) 痛苦 (shǐ) tòngkǔ

affluence *n* 富裕 fùyù; **affluent** *adj* 富裕的 fùyù de

afford *v* 提供 tígōng, 供应得起 gōngyìng de qǐ

afloat *adv* 漂浮着 piāofú zhe

afoot *adv* 在进行中 zài jìnxíng zhōng

aforesaid *adj* 上述的 shàngshù de

afraid *adj* 害怕 hàipà; 恐怕 kǒngpà

Africa *n* 非洲 fēizhōu; **African** *n* 非洲人 fēizhōurén; *adj* 非洲的 fēizhōu de

after *prep/conj* 在...之后 zài ... zhīhòu; **after all** 毕竟 bìjìng; **one after another** 一个接一个地 yīgè jiē yīgè de

afternoon *n* 下午 xiàwǔ

afterwards *adv* 然后 ránhòu, 后来 hòulái

again *adv* 再 zài, 又 yòu; **again and again** 反复 fǎnfù, 再三 zàisān; **now and again** 不时地 bùshí de

against *prep* 反对 fǎnduì; 靠着 kào zhe

age *n* 年龄 niánlíng; 时代 shídài; **of age** 成年的 chéngnián de; **under age** 未成年的 wèichéngnián de

agency *n* 代理机构 dàilǐ jīgòu; **agent** *n* 代理商 dàilǐshāng, 代理人 dàilǐrén

agenda *n* 议程 yìchéng

aggravate *v* (使) 恶化 (shǐ) èhuà, 加重 jiāzhòng; **aggravation** *n* 加剧 jiājù, 加重 jiāzhòng

aggregate *n* 合计 héjì, 总计 zǒngjì

aggression *n* 侵略 qīnlüè; **aggressive** *adj* 好斗的 hàodòu de, 有闯劲的 yǒu chuǎngjìn de

aghast *adj* 惊骇的 jīnghài de

agility *n* 敏捷 mǐnjié, 灵活 línghuó; **agile** *adj* 敏捷的 mǐnjié de

agitate *v* 激动 jīdòng; 煽动 shāndòng

ago *adv* 以前 yǐqián; **long ago** 很久以前 hěn jiǔ yǐqián

agonize *v* (使) 极度痛苦 (shǐ) jídù tòngkǔ; **agony** *n* 苦恼 kǔnǎo

agree *v* 同意 tóngyì, 赞成 zànchéng; **agreement** *n* 协议 xiéyì, 同意 tóngyì

agriculture *n* 农业 nóngyè; **agricultural** *adj* 农业的 nóngyè de

ahead *adv* 在前面 zài qiánmian; **go ahead** 前进 qiánjìn; 先走 xiān zǒu; 着手进行 zhuóshǒu jìnxíng

aid *v/n* 帮助 bāngzhù, 援助 yuánzhù; **first aid** 急救 jíjiù

aide *n* 助手 zhùshǒu

AIDS *abbr* 艾滋病 àizībìng

aim *v* 对 ... 瞄准 duì ... miáozhǔn; *n* 目标 mùbiāo, 目的 mùdì

air *n* 空气 kōngqì

airborne *adj* 在空中的 zài kōngzhōng de; 在飞行中的 zài fēixíng zhōng de

air-conditioner *n* 空调 kōngtiáo

aircraft *n* 飞机 fēijī; **aircraft-carrier** *n* 航空母舰 hángkōng mǔjiàn

airfare *n* 飞机票价 fēijī piàojià

airforce *n* 空军 kōngjūn

airline *n* 航空公司 hángkōng gōngsī

airliner *n* 客机 kèjī

airmail *n* 航空邮件 hángkōng yóujiàn

airplane *n* 飞机 fēijī

airport *n* 机场 jīchǎng

air-raid *n* 空袭 kōngxí

airtight *adj* 密封的 mìfēng de

airy *adj* 空中的 kōngzhōng de; 轻快的 qīngkuài de

aisle *n* 过道 guòdào

ajar *adv* 微开地 wēi kāi de

alarm *n* 警报 jǐngbào; **alarm clock** 闹钟 nàozhōng; **alarming** *adj* 吓人的 xiàrén de; 令人担心的 lìng rén dānxīn de

alas *interj* 唉 ài

Albania *n* 阿尔巴尼亚 ā'ěrbāníyà; **Albanian** *n* 阿尔巴尼亚人 ā'ěrbāníyàrén; *adj* 阿尔巴尼亚的 ā'ěrbāníyà de

albatross *n* 信天翁 xìntiānwēng

album *n* 影集 yǐngjí; 集邮本 jíyóuběn; 签名册 qiānmíngcè

alchemy *n* 炼金术 liànjīnshù; **alchemist** *n* 炼金术士 liànjīnshùshì

alcohol *n* 酒精 jiǔjīng; **alcohol-free** *adj* 无酒精的 wú jiǔjīng de; **alcoholic** *n* 酗酒者 xùjiǔzhě; **alcoholism** *n* 酗酒 xùjiǔ

ale *n* 麦芽酒 màiyájiǔ

alert *n* 警惕 jǐngtì; 警报 jǐngbào; *adj* 警觉的 jǐngjué de; 注意的 zhùyì de

algebra *n* 代数 dàishù

Algeria *n* 阿尔及利亚 ā'ěrjílìyà; **Algerian** *n* 阿尔及利亚人 ā'ěrjílìyàrén; *adj* 阿尔及利亚的 ā'ěrjílìyà de

alias *n* 别名 biémíng

alibi *n* 不在犯罪现场的证明 bù zài fànzuì xiànchǎng de zhèngmíng

alien *n* 外侨 wàiqiáo; *adj* 外国的 wàiguó de

align *v* 结盟 jiéméng; 对齐 duìqí; **alignment** *n* 结盟 jiéméng; 对齐 duìqí

alike *adj* 相似的 xiāngsì de

alimony *n* 赡养费 shànyǎngfèi

alive *adj* 活着的 huózhe de

all *adj* 所有的 suǒyǒu de, 全部的 quánbù de; *pron* 全体 quántǐ, 一切 yīqiè; **all right** 行 xíng, 好的 hǎo de; **all the more** 更加 gèngjiā

allay *v* 减轻 jiǎnqīng, 减少 jiǎnshǎo

allege *v* 断言 duànyán; 指控 zhǐkòng; **allegation** *n* 断言 duànyán, 指控 zhǐkòng

allegiance *n* 忠贞 zhōngzhēn, 效忠 xiàozhōng

allergy *n* 过敏症 guòmǐnzhèng; **allergic** *adj* 过敏的 guòmǐn de

alleviate *v* 减轻 jiǎnqīng; **alleviation** *n* 缓和 huǎnhé

alley *n* 胡同 hútòng, 小巷 xiǎoxiàng; **blind alley** 死胡同 sǐhútòng

alliance *n* 联盟 liánméng

alligator *n* 鳄鱼 èyú

allocate *v* 分配 fēnpèi; **allocation** *n* 分配 fēnpèi

allot *v* 分配 fēnpèi, **allotment** *n* 分配 fēnpèi

allow *v* 允许 yǔnxǔ; **allowance** *n* 津贴 jīntiē; 补贴 bǔtiē

alloy *n* 合金 héjīn

allude *v* 暗指 ànzhǐ; **allusion** *n* 暗指 ànzhǐ, 暗示 ànshì

allure *n* 诱惑 yòuhuò; **alluring** *adj* 诱人的 yòurén de

ally *n* 同盟国 tóngménguó; 盟友 méngyǒu

almanac *n* 年鉴 niánjiàn, 历书 lìshū

almond *n* 杏仁 xìngrén

almost *adv* 几乎 jīhū

aloft *adv* 在高处 zài gāochù; 在上面 zài shàngmian

alone *adv* 独自 dúzì; **leave alone** 不管 bùguǎn …

along *prep* 沿着 yánzhe; **along with** 和 … 一起 hé … yīqǐ; **come along** 一道来 yīdào lái, 进步 jìnbù; **alongside** *adv* 在旁边 zài pángbiān; *prep* 在 … 旁边 zài … pángbiān

aloof *adv* 远离地 yuǎnlí de, 避开 bìkāi; 漠不关心地 mòbù guānxīn de

aloud *adv* 大声地 dàshēng de

alphabet *n* 字母表 zìmǔbiǎo

Alps *n* 阿尔卑斯山 ā'ěrbēisīshān

already *adv* 已经 yǐjīng

alright *adv* 好吧 hǎo ba

also *adv* 也 yě

altar *n* 祭坛 jìtán

alter *v* 修改 xiūgǎi, 改变 gǎibiàn; **alteration** *n* 改变 gǎibiàn

alternate *v* 轮流 lúnliú, 交替 jiāotì; *adj* 轮流的 lúnliú de, 交替的 jiāotì de;

alternative *n* 可供选择的事物 kěgōng xuǎnzé de shìwù; **have no alternative but** 没有选择只得 méiyǒu xuǎnzé zhǐdé; *adj* 可供选择的 kěgōng xuǎnzé de

although *conj* 虽然 suīrán

altitude *n* 海拔高度 hǎibá gāodù

altogether *adv* 总共 zǒnggòng, 一共 yīgòng

aluminum *n* 铝 lǚ

always *adv* 总是 zǒngshì

amateur *n* 业余爱好者 yèyú àihàozhě; *adj* 业余的 yèyú de

amaze *v* (使) 吃惊 (shǐ) chījīng; **amazement** *n* 惊异 jīngyì; **amazing** *adj* 令人惊异的 lìng rén jīngyì de

ambassador *n* 大使 dàshǐ

ambidextrous *adj* 灵巧的 língqiǎo de, 多种才能的 duōzhǒng cáinéng de

ambiguity *n* 模糊 móhu; **ambiguous** *adj* 模糊的 móhu de

ambition *n* 野心 yěxīn, 抱负 bàofù; **ambitious** *adj* 野心勃勃的 yěxīn bóbó de

ambivalent *adj* 矛盾的 máodùn de

ambulance *n* 救护车 jiùhùchē

ambush *v/n* 埋伏 máifú

amend *v* 修正 xiūzhèng, 改进 gǎijìn; **make amends** 赔偿 péicháng; 道歉 dàoqiàn; **amendment** *n* 修正 xiūzhèng

America *n* (*U.S.*) 美国 měiguó; (*Americas*) 美洲 měizhōu; **American** *n* 美国人 měiguórén; *adj* 美国的 měiguó de

amiable *adj* 亲切的 qīnqiè de

amicable *adj* 友善的 yǒushàn de, 和平的 hépíng de

amid *prep* 在 ... 当中 zài ... dāngzhōng

amiss *adv* 错误的 cuòwù de

ammonia *n* 氨 ān

ammunition *n* 弹药 dànyào

amnesty *n* 特赦 tèshè

among *prep* 在 ... 之中 zài ... zhīzhōng

amount *n* 数量 shùliàng; **gross amount** 总额 zǒng'é; **net amount** 净总额 jìng zǒng'é

amphibian *adj* 两栖的 liǎngqī de; 水陆两用的 shuǐlù liǎngyòng de

amphitheatre *n* 阶梯教室 jiētī jiàoshì; 圆形剧场 yuánxíng jùchǎng

ample *adj* 充足的 chōngzú de

amplify *v* 放大 fàngdà, 增强 zēngqiáng; **amplifier** *n* 扩音器 kuòyīnqì

amputate *v* 截肢 jiézhī

amuse *v* (使) 发笑 (shǐ) fāxiào, 逗乐 dòulè; **amusement** *n* 娱乐 yúlè; **amusement park** 游乐园 yóulèyuán; **amusing** *adj* 有趣的 yǒuqù de

analogy *n* 类推 lèituī; **analogous** *adj* 可比拟的 kě bǐnǐ de

analyze *v* 分析 fēnxī; **analysis** *n* (*pl* **analyses**) 分析 fēnxī; **analyst** *n* 分析员 fēnxīyuán

anarchy *n* 无政府状态 wúzhèngfǔ zhuàngtài

anatomy *n* 解剖学 jiěpōuxué; **anatomical** *adj* 解剖学的 jiěpōuxué de

ancestor *n* 祖先 zǔxiān; **ancestral** *adj* 祖先的 zǔxiān de

anchor *n* 锚 máo

ancient *adj* 古代的 gǔdài de

ancillary *adj* 补助的 bǔzhù de, 副的 fù de

and *conj* 和 hé

anecdote *n* 轶事 yìshì, 奇闻 qíwén

anemia *n* 贫血 pínxuè; 贫血症 pínxuèzhèng

anesthesia *n* 麻醉 mázuì; **anesthetic** *n* 麻醉剂 mázuìjì; *adj* 麻醉的 mázuì de; **anesthetist** *n* 麻醉师 mázuìshī

anew *adv* 重新 chóngxīn, 再次 zàicì

angel *n* 天使 tiānshǐ

anger *n* 气愤 qìfèn; **angry** *adj* 愤怒的 fènnù de, 生气的 shēngqì de

angle *n* 角 jiǎo; 角度 jiǎodù

anguish *n* 痛苦 tòngkǔ, 苦恼 kǔnǎo

animal *n* 动物 dòngwù

animate *adj* 活泼的 huópo de; **animated** *adj* 精力旺盛的 jīnglì wàngshèng de, 热烈的 rèliè de; **animated cartoon** 漫画 mànhuà

animosity *n* 仇恨 chóuhèn

ankle *n* 脚腕 jiǎowàn

annals *n* 编年史 biānniánshǐ

annex *v* 附加 fùjiā; *n* 附加物 fùjiàwù

annihilate *v* 歼灭 jiānmiè

anniversary *n* 周年 zhōunián

annotate *v* 注释 zhùshì, 评注 píngzhù

announce *v* 宣布 xuānbù; **announcer** *n* 广播员 guǎng-bōyuán; **announcement** *n* 宣布 xuānbù, 通知 tōngzhī

annoy *v* 惹恼 rěnǎo, 骚扰 sāorǎo; **annoying** *adj* 恼人的 nǎorén de

annual *adj* 一年一次的 yīnián yīcì de, 年度的 niándù de

annul *v* 废除 fèichú

anomaly *n* 异常 yìcháng

anonymous *adj* 匿名的 nìmíng de

another *adj* 另一 lìngyī; **one after another** 一个接一个 yīgè jiē yīgè

answer *v* 回答 huídá; *n* 答案 dá'àn

ant *n* 蚂蚁 mǎyǐ

antagonize *v* (使) 对立 (shǐ) duìlì, (使) 对抗 (shǐ) duìkàng

antelope *n* 羚羊 língyáng

antenna *n* 天线 tiānxiàn

anthem *n* 圣歌 shènggē, 赞歌 zàngē; **national anthem** 国歌 guógē

anthology *n* 文集 wénjí

anthropology *n* 人类学 rénlèixué

anti- *pref* 反 fǎn; 抗 kàng

antibiotics *n* 抗生素 kàngshēngsù

antibody *n* 抗体 kàngtǐ

anticipate *v* 预见 yùjiàn, 预期 yùqī; **anticipation** *n* 预期 yùqī

anticlimax *n* 突降 tújiàng

antidote *n* 解毒剂 jiědújì

antifreeze *n* 防冻剂 fángdòngjì

antipathy *n* 憎恶 zèngwù, 反感 fǎngǎn

antique *n* 古董 gǔdǒng; *adj* 古时的 gǔshí de; **antique dealer** 古董商 gǔdǒngshāng; **antique shop** 古董店 gǔdǒngdiàn; **antiquity** *n* 古代 gǔdài

antisocial *adj* 反社会的 fǎn shèhuì de

antithesis *n* (*pl* **antitheses**) 对照 duìzhào; 对偶 duì'ǒu

antonym *n* 反义词 fǎnyìcí

anus *n* 肛门 gāngmén

anxiety *n* 焦虑 jiāolǜ; **anxious** *adj* 忧虑的 yōulǜ de, 渴望的 kěwàng de

any *adj* 任何的 rènhé de

anybody *pron* 任何人 rènhérén

anyhow *adv* 无论如何 wúlùn rúhé

anyone *pron* 任何人 rènhérén

anything *pron* 任何事物 rènhé shìwù

anyway *adv* 无论如何 wúlùn rúhé

anywhere *adv* 任何地方 rènhé dìfāng

apart *adv* 分开地 fēnkāi de; **apart from** 除 ... 以外 chú ... yǐwài

apartment *n* 公寓 gōngyù

apathy *n* 冷漠 lěngmò; **apathetic** *adj* 冷漠的 lěngmò de

ape *n* 猿 yuán

aperture *n* 孔 kǒng, 缝隙 fèngxì

apex *n* 顶点 dǐngdiǎn

apologize *v* 道歉 dàoqiàn; **apology** *n* 道歉 dàoqiàn

apostrophe *n* 省略符号 shěnglüè fúhào

appalling *adj* 骇人的 hàirén de

apparatus *n* 机构 jīgòu

apparent *adj* 明显的 míngxiǎn de; **apparently** *adv* 明显地 míngxiǎn de

appeal *v/n* 呼吁 hūyù; (*law*) 上诉 shàngsù; **appealing** *adj* 吸引人的 xīyǐnrén de

appear *v* 出现 chūxiàn; **appearance** *n* 出现 chūxiàn; 外观 wàiguān

appease *n* 平息 píngxī, 姑息 gūxī, 缓和 huǎnhé; **appeasement** *n* 平息 píngxī, 姑息 gūxī, 缓和 huǎnhé

append *v* 附加 fùjiā

appendix *n* 附录 fùlù; **appendicitis** *n* 阑尾炎 lánwěiyán

appetite *n* 食欲 shíyù, 胃口 wèikǒu; **have an appetite** 胃口好 wèikǒu hǎo

appetizer *n* 前菜 qiáncài, 冷盘 lěngpán

applaud *v* 鼓掌 gǔzhǎng; **applause** *n* 鼓掌 gǔzhǎng

apple *n* 苹果 píngguǒ

appliance *n* 用具 yòngjù; 电器 diànqì

apply *v* 申请 shēnqǐng; 应用 yìngyòng; **application** *n* 申请 shēnqǐng; 应用 yìngyòng; **applicable** *adj* 可适用的 kě shìyòng de

appoint *v* 任命 rènmìng; **be appointed as** 被任命为 bèi rènmìng wéi; **appointment** *n* 约会 yuēhuì, 预约 yùyuē; 任命 rènmìng; **make an appointment with** 和 ... 预约 hé ... yùyuē

apportion *v* 分配 fēnpèi

appraise *v* 评价 píngjià, 估价 gūjià; **appraisal** *n* 评价 píngjià, 估价 gūjià

appreciate *v* (*affection*) 感谢 gǎnxiè; (*understanding*) 赏识 shǎngshí; (*in value*) 增值 zēngzhí

apprehend *v* (*understand*) 领会 lǐnghuì, 理解 lǐjiě; **apprehension** *n* 理解 lǐjiě; **apprehensive** *adj* 有理解力的 yǒu lǐjiělì de

apprentice *n* 学徒 xuétú

approach *v* 接近 jiējìn; *n* 途径 tújìng, 方式 fāngshì

appropriate *adj* 适当的 shìdàng de; **appropriateness** *n* 妥当 tuǒdang

approve *v* 赞成 zànchéng; 批准 pīzhǔn; **approval** *n* 赞成 zànchéng; 批准 pīzhǔn

approximate *adj* 近似的 jìnsì de, 大约的 dàyuē de; **approximately** *adv* 近似地 jìnsì de, 大约地 dàyuē de

apricot *n* 杏 xìng

April *n* 四月 sìyuè

apron *n* 围裙 wéiqún

apt *adj* (*apt to*) 易于 ... 的 yìyú ... de

aptitude *n* 智能 zhìnéng, 自然倾向 zìrán qīngxiàng

aquarium *n* 养鱼池 yǎngyúchí; 水族馆 shuǐzúguǎn

aquatic *adj* 水生的 shuǐshēng de, 水上的 shuǐshàng de

Arab *n* 阿拉伯人 ālābórén; **Arabic** *n* 阿拉伯语 ālābóyǔ

arable *adj* 可耕的 kě gēng de

arbitrate *v* 公断 gōngduàn; **arbitration** *n* 仲裁 zhòngcái, 公断 gōngduàn; **arbitrary** *adj* 武断的 wǔduàn de

arch *n* (*shape*) 拱形 gǒngxíng; (*gate*) 拱门 gǒngmén

archaeology *n* 考古学 kǎogǔxué; **archaeologist** *n* 考古学家 kǎogǔxuéjiā

archaic *adj* 古老的 gǔlǎo de

archbishop *n* 大主教 dàzhǔjiào

archery *n* 箭术 jiànshù

architect *n* 建筑师 jiànzhùshī; **architecture** *n* 建筑 jiànzhù

archive *n* 档案 dàng'àn

arctic *adj* 北极的 běijí de; **the Arctic** *n* 北极 běijí

arduous *adj* 费劲的 fèijìn de, 辛勤的 xīnqín de, 险峻的 xiǎnjùn de

are. *See* **be**

area *n* 地区 dìqū; **area code** 电话区号 diànhuà qūhào

arena *n* 舞台 wǔtái

Argentina *n* 阿根廷 āgēntíng

argue *v* 争论 zhēnglùn, 辩论 biànlùn; **argument** *n* 争论 zhēnglùn, 辩论 biànlùn

arid *adj* 干旱的 gānhàn de

arise *v* (*arose, arisen*) 出现 chūxiàn, 发生 fāshēng

aristocracy *n* 贵族 guìzú; **aristocrat** *n* 贵族 guìzú; **aristocratic** *adj* 贵族的 guìzú de

arithmetic *n* 算术 suànshù

ark *n* 方舟 fāngzhōu

arm *v (with weapons)* 武装 wǔzhuāng; *n* 武器 wǔqì; *(limb)* 手臂 shǒubì; **take up arms** 拿起武器 náqǐ wǔqì; **armed** *adj* 武装的 wǔzhuāng de; **armed forces** 武装力量 wǔzhuāng lìliàng, 军队 jūnduì; **arm in arm** 手挽手 shǒu wǎn shǒu; **armchair** *n* 扶手椅 fúshǒuyǐ; **armpit** *n* 腋窝 yèwō

armistice *n* 停战 tíngzhàn

army *n* 军队 jūnduì

aroma *n* 香气 xiāngqì; **aromatic** *adj* 芳香的 fāngxiāng de

around *prep* 在 ... 周围 zài ... zhōuwéi; *adv* 大约 dàyuē

arouse *v* 唤醒 huànxǐng, 激发 jīfā

arrange *v* 安排 ānpái; **arrangement** *n* 安排 ānpái

array *n (range)* 排列 páiliè, 一系列 yīxìliè

arrest *v/n* 逮捕 dàibǔ; **under arrest** 被捕 bèibǔ

arrive *v* 到达 dàodá; **arrival** *n* 到达 dàodá

arrogance *n* 傲慢 àomàn; **arrogant** *adj* 傲慢的 àomàn de

arrow *n* 箭 jiàn; 箭头 jiàntóu

arson *n* 纵火 zònghuǒ

art *n* 艺术 yìshù; **art gallery** 画廊 huàláng

artery *n* 动脉 dòngmài

arthritis *n* 关节炎 guānjiéyán

article *n* 文章 wénzhāng

articulate *adj* 口才好的 kǒucái hǎo de; 发音清晰的 fāyīn qīngxī de; *v (unite)* 连接 liánjiē; *(utter)* 清晰明白地说 qīngxī míngbai de shuō

artifice *n* 技巧 jìqiǎo

artificial *adj* 人造的 rénzào de

artillery *n* 炮 pào

artisan *n* 工匠 gōngjiàng, 技工 jìgōng

artist *n* 艺术家 yìshùjiā; **artistic** *adj* 有艺术才能的 yǒu yìshù cáinéng de

as *conj* 当 ... 时 dāng ... shí; *prep* 作为 zuòwéi; **as far as** 就 ... 而言 jiù ... éryán; **as good as** 和 ... 一样 hé ... yīyàng; **as if** 好像 hǎoxiàng; **as soon as** 一 ... 就 yī ... jiù; **as soon as possible** 尽快 jǐnkuài; **as usual** 照常 zhàocháng; **as well** 也 yě

asbestos *n* 石棉 shímián

ascend *v* 攀登 pāndēng; 上升 shàngshēng

ash *n* 灰 huī

ashamed *adj* 惭愧的 cánkuì de, 羞耻的 xiūchǐ de

ashore *adv* 在岸上 zài ànshang; **go ashore** 上岸 shàng'àn

ashtray *n* 烟灰缸 yānhuīgāng

Asia *n* 亚洲 yàzhōu; **Asian** *n* 亚洲人 yàzhōurén; *adj* 亚洲的 yàzhōu de

aside *adv* 在旁边 zài pángbiān; **aside from** 除 ... 以外 chú ... yǐwài

ask *v* 问 wèn; **ask for** 请求 qǐngqiú

asleep *adj* 熟睡的 shúshuì de; **fall asleep** 睡着 shuìzháo

asparagus *n* 芦笋 lúsǔn

aspect *n* 方面 fāngmiàn; (*gram*) 态 tài

asphalt *n* 沥青 lìqīng

aspire *v* 热望 rèwàng, 立志 lìzhì; **aspiration** *n* 抱负 bàofù, 渴望 kěwàng

aspirin *n* 阿司匹林 āsīpǐlín

ass *n* 驴 lú

assail *v* 攻击 gōngjī; **assailant** *n* 攻击者 gōngjīzhě

assassinate *v* 暗杀 ànshā, 行刺 xíngcì; **assassin** *n* 刺客 cìkè; **assassination** *n* 暗杀 ànshā

assault *v/n* 攻击 gōngjī

assemble *v* (*people*) 集合 jíhé; (*machine*) 组装 zǔzhuāng; **assembly** *n* 集合 jíhé, 组装 zǔzhuāng; **assembly line** 装配线 zhuāngpèixiàn

assert *v* 断言 duànyán, 声称 shēngchēng; **assertion** *n* 断言 duànyán

assess *v* 评定 píngdìng, 评估 pínggū; **assessment** *n* 评估 pínggū

asset *n* 资产 zīchǎn, 财富 cáifù

assign *v* 指派 zhǐpài, 分配 fēnpèi; **assignment** *n* 任务 rènwu, 作业 zuòyè

assimilate *v* 吸收 xīshōu; **assimilation** *n* 同化 tónghuà

assist *v* 协助 xiézhù; **assistance** *n* 协助 xiézhù; **assistant** *n* 助手 zhùshǒu

associate *v* 结交 jiéjiāo; *n* 同事 tóngshì; **association** *n* 协会 xiéhuì

assorted *adj* 各种各样的 gèzhǒng gèyàng de

assume *v* 假定 jiǎdìng; **assumption** *n* 假定 jiǎdìng; **assumed** *adj* 装的 zhuāng de

assure *v* 保证 bǎozhèng, 担保 dānbǎo; **assurance** *n* 保证 bǎozhèng, 担保 dānbǎo

asthma *n* 哮喘 xiàochuǎn

astonish *v* (使) 吃惊 (shǐ) chījīng; **astonishment** *n* 惊讶 jīngyà

astound *v* (使) 惊骇 (shǐ) jīnghài, (使) 大吃一惊 (shǐ) dàchī yījīng

astray *adv* 迷路 mílù; **go astray** 迷路 mílù, 走失 zǒushī

astride *adv* 跨着 kuà zhe

astrology *n* 占星术 zhānxīngshù, 占星学 zhānxīngxué

astronaut *n* 宇航员 yǔhángyuán

astronomy *n* 天文学 tiānwénxué; **astronomical** *adj* 天文学的 tiānwénxué de

asylum *n* 收容所 shōuróngsuǒ, 避难所 bìnànsuǒ

at *prep* 在 zài; **at last** 终于 zhōngyú; **at least** 至少 zhìshǎo; **at once** 立刻 lìkè

ate. *See* eat

atheism *n* 无神论 wúshénlùn; **atheist** *n* 无神论者 wúshénlùnzhě

athlete *n* 运动员 yùndòngyuán; **athletic** *adj* 运动的 yùndòng de

Atlantic *n* 大西洋 dàxīyáng

atlas *n* 地图册 dìtúcè

atmosphere *n* 大气 dàqì; 气氛 qìfēn

atom *n* 原子 yuánzǐ; **atomic** *adj* 原子的 yuánzǐ de; **atomic bomb** 原子弹 yuánzǐdàn

atone *v* 弥补 míbǔ; **atonement** *n* 赎罪 shúzuì; 弥补 míbǔ

atrocity *n* 残暴 cánbào, 暴行 bàoxíng; **atrocious** *adj* 残暴的 cánbào de, 凶恶的 xiōng'è de

attach *v* 附上 fùshàng; **attachment** *n* 附件 fùjiàn

attaché *n* 大使馆专员 dàshǐguǎn zhuānyuán

attack *v/n* 攻击 gōngjī

attain *v* 获得 huòdé; **attainment** *n* 成就 chéngjiù; **attainable** *adj* 可以获得的 kěyǐ huòdé de

attempt *v/n* 尝试 chángshì, 企图 qǐtú

attend *v* 出席 chūxí, 参加 cānjiā; 照顾 zhàogù; **attendance** *n* 出席 chūxí; **attendant** *n* 服务员 fúwùyuán

attention *n* 注意 zhùyì; **pay attention** 注意 zhùyì; **call attention to** 引起对 … 的注意 yǐnqǐ duì … de zhùyì; **attentive** *adj* 专心的 zhuānxīn de

attic *n* 阁楼 gélóu

attire *n* 服装 fúzhuāng

attitude *n* 态度 tàidu

attorney *n* 律师 lǜshī

attract *v* 吸引 xīyǐn; **attraction** *n* 吸引力 xīyǐnlì; 吸引人的事物 xīyǐn rén de shìwù; **attractive** *adj* 吸引人的 xīyǐnrén de, 美貌的 měimào de

attribute *n* 属性 shǔxìng; 品质 pǐnzhì; 特征 tèzhēng

atypical *adj* 非典型的 fēi diǎnxíng de

auction *v/n* 拍卖 pāimài

audacity *n* 大胆 dàdǎn, 厚颜 hòuyán; **audacious** *adj* 大胆的 dàdǎn de, 卤莽的 lǔmǎng de

audible *adj* 听得见的 tīng de jiàn de

audience *n* 听众 tīngzhòng, 观众 guānzhòng

audiovisual *adj* 视听的 shìtīng de

audit *v* 查账 cházhàng; **auditor** *n* 审计员 shěnjìyuán

audition *v/n* 面试 miànshì

auditorium *n* 礼堂 lǐtáng

augment *v* 增加 zēngjiā; **augmentation** *n* 增加 zēngjiā

August *n* 八月 bāyuè

aunt *n* (*father's sister*) 姑妈 gūmā; (*mother's sister*) 阿姨 āyí; (*wife of father's older brother*) 伯母 bómǔ; (*wife of father's younger brother*) 婶婶 shěnshen; (*wife of mother's brother*) 舅母 jiùmǔ

auspicious *adj* 吉兆的 jízhào de, 幸运的 xìngyùn de

Australia *n* 澳大利亚 àodàlìyà; **Australian** *n* 澳大利亚人 àodàlìyàrén; *adj* 澳大利亚的 àodàlìyà de

Austria *n* 奥地利 àodìlì; **Austrian** *n* 奥地利人 àodìlìrén; *adj* 奥地利的 àodìlì de

authentic *adj* 真实的 zhēnshí de, 道地的 dàodì de

author *n* 作家 zuòjiā, 作者 zuòzhě

authority *n* 权威 quánwēi; **authorities** *n* 当局 dāngjú

authorize *v* 批准 pīzhǔn, 授权 shòuquán; **authorization** *n* 授权 shòuquán

autobiography *n* 自传 zìzhuàn

autocratic *adj* 独裁的 dúcái de, 专制的 zhuānzhì de

autograph *v* 署名 shǔmíng; *n* 亲笔签名 qīnbǐ qiānmíng

automatic *adj* 自动的 zìdòng de

automobile *n* 汽车 qìchē

autonomy *n* 自治 zìzhì; **autonomous** *adj* 自治的 zìzhì de

autopsy *n* 尸体解剖 shītǐ jiěpōu; 验尸 yànshī

autumn *n* 秋天 qiūtiān

auxiliary *adj* 辅助的 fǔzhù de, 补助的 bǔzhù de

avail *v* 有利 yǒulì; **avail oneself of** 利用 lìyòng; **to no avail** 不起作用 bù qǐ zuòyòng, 徒劳 túláo

available *adj* 可利用的 kě lìyòng de; 可获得的 kě huòdé de; **availability** *n* 可用性 kěyòngxìng; 获得的可能性 huòdé de kěnéngxìng

avalanche *n* 雪崩 xuěbēng

avenge *v* 为 ... 报复 wèi ... bàofù; **avenge oneself** 报仇 bàochóu

avenue *n* 大道 dàdào

average *n/v* 平均 píngjūn; *adj* 一般的 yībān de, 通常的 tōngcháng de; **on average** 平均 píngjūn

averse *adj* 不愿意的 bù yuànyì de; 反对的 fǎnduì de; **be averse to** 不愿意 bù yuànyì, 怕 pà; **aversion** *n* 讨厌的事和人 tǎoyàn de shì hé rén

avert *v* 转移 zhuǎnyí

aviation *n* 航空 hángkōng

avoid *v* 避免 bìmiǎn, 躲避 duǒbì

await *v* 等候 děnghòu

awake *v* (**awoke, awoken**) 醒 xǐng, 觉悟 juéwù; *adj* 醒的 xǐng de

award *v* 授予 shòuyǔ; *n* 奖 jiǎng

aware *adj* 明白的 míngbai de, 意识到的 yìshídào de

away *adv* 在远处 zài yuǎnchù; 到远处 dào yuǎnchù

awe *n* 敬畏 jìngwèi

awful *adj* 可怕的 kěpà de; **awfully** *adv* 非常 fēicháng

awkward *adj* 笨拙的 bènzhuō de, 为难的 wéi'nán de

awl *n* 锥子 zhuīzi, 尖钻 jiānzuān

awning *n* 遮阳篷 zhēyángpéng, 雨篷 yǔpéng

awoke. *See* **awake**

awoken. *See* **awake**

axe *n* 斧头 fǔtou

axis *n* 轴 zhóu

B

babble *v/n* 呀呀学语 yāyā xuéyǔ

baby *n* 婴儿 yīng'ér; **baby-sit** *v* 照管孩子 zhàoguǎn háizi; **baby-sitter** *n* 保姆 bǎomǔ

bachelor *n* (*of Arts or Science*) 学士 xuéshì; (*single*) 单身汉 dānshēnhàn

back *v* 支持 zhīchí; **back down** 后退 hòutuì, 让步 ràngbù; **back out** 退出 tuìchū; **back up** 倒退 dàotuì; 支持 zhīchí; *n* 后背 hòubèi; *adv* 在后面 zài hòumian; *adj* 后面的 hòumian de

backache *n* 背痛 bèitòng

backbone *n* 脊椎 jǐzhuī

backfire *v* 反弹 fǎntán

background *n* 背景 bèijǐng

backing *n* 支持 zhīchí

backlog *n* 积压 jīyā

backpack *n* 背包 bēibāo

backside *n* 后侧 hòucè; 背面 bèimiàn

backward *adj* 向后的 xiànghòu de, 落后的 luòhòu de; **backwards** *adv* 向后 xiànghòu

backyard *n* 后院 hòuyuàn

bacon *n* 腌肉 yānròu

bacteria *n* 细菌 xìjūn; **bacterial** *adj* 细菌的 xìjūn de

bad *adj* 坏的 huài de; **bad tempered** 坏脾气的 huài píqi de; **from bad to worse** 每况愈下 měikuàng yùxià; **badly** *adv* 非常 fēicháng, 严重地 yánzhòng de, 拙劣地 zhuōliè de

badge *n* 徽章 huīzhāng, 证章 zhèngzhāng

badminton *n* 羽毛球 yǔmáoqiú

baffle *v* 困惑 kùnhuò, 阻碍 zǔ'ài; **baffling** *adj* 令人困惑的 lìng rén kùnhuò de, 令人丧气的 lìng rén sàngqì de, (使)困惑的 (shǐ) kùnhuò de

bag *n* 袋 dài, 包 bāo

baggage *n* 行李 xíngli

baggy *adj* 袋状的 dàizhuàng de, 松垂的 sōngchuí de

bail *n* 取保金 qǔbǎojīn

bailiff *n* (*legal*) 执行官 zhíxíngguān

bait *n* 诱饵 yòu'ěr

bake *v* 烤 kǎo; **baker** *n* 面包师 miànbāoshī; **bakery** *n* 面包店 miànbāodiàn

balance *n* 平衡 pínghéng; 结余 jiéyú, 剩余部分 shèngyú bùfen

balcony *n* 阳台 yángtái

bald *adj* 秃的 tū de

ball *n* (*round object*) 球 qiú; **ball-point pen** 圆珠笔 yuánzhūbǐ; *n* (*dance*) 舞会 wǔhuì; **ballroom** *n* 舞厅 wǔtīng

ballad *n* 民谣 mínyáo

ballet *n* 芭蕾舞 bālěiwǔ

ballistic *adj* 弹道的 dàndào de; **ballistic missile** 弹道导弹 dàndào dǎodàn

balloon *n* 气球 qìqiú

ballot *n* 选票 xuǎnpiào; **ballot-box** *n* 投票箱 tóupiàoxiāng

bamboo *n* 竹子 zhúzi

ban *v/n* 禁止 jìnzhǐ

banana *n* 香蕉 xiāngjiāo

band *n* 群 qún, 帮 bāng; (*music*) 乐队 yuèduì; (*tape*) 带子 dàizi; **band-aid** *n* 创可贴 chuāngkětiē

bandage *n* 绷带 bēngdài

bandit *n* 强盗 qiángdào

bang *v* 猛击 měngjī; *n* 巨响 jùxiǎng

banish *v* 驱逐 qūzhú

bank *n* (*river*) 河岸 hé'àn; (*financial institution*) 银行 yínháng;
bank account 银行账户 yínháng zhànghù; **banker** *n*
银行家 yínhángjiā; **banknote** *n* 钞票 chāopiào

bankrupt *adj* 破产的 pòchǎn de; **go bankrupt** 破产 pòchǎn

banner *n* 旗帜 qízhì, 横幅 héngfú

banquet *n* 宴会 yànhuì

banter *n/v* 取笑 qǔxiào, 逗弄 dòunong

baptize *v* 施洗礼 shī xǐlǐ; **baptism** *n* 浸洗礼 jìnxǐlǐ

bar *n* 酒吧 jiǔbā; **bartender** *n* 酒吧伺者 jiǔbā cìzhě

barbarian *n* 粗鲁无礼的人 cūlǔ wúlǐ de rén, 野蛮人
yěmánrén; *adj* 野蛮的 yěmán de, 粗鲁的 cūlǔ de

barbecue *n* 烧烤肉的野餐 shāokǎoròu de yěcān

barber *n* 理发师 lǐfàshī; **barber's shop** 理发店 lǐfàdiàn

bare *adj* 赤裸的 chìluǒ de; **barely** *adv* 几乎不 jīhū bù,
几乎没有 jīhū méiyǒu; **barefoot** *adv* 赤脚 chìjiǎo

bargain *v* 讨价还价 tǎojià huánjià; *n* 便宜货 piányihuò

barge *n* 驳船 bóchuán, 游艇 yóutǐng

bark *v* 吠 fèi; *n* (*dog*) 吠声 fèishēng; (*tree*) 树皮 shùpí

barley *n* 大麦 dàmài

barn *n* 谷仓 gǔcāng; 畜棚 chùpéng

barometer *n* 气压计 qìyājì

barracks *n* 军营 jūnyíng

barrage *n* 密集火力 mìjí huǒlì

barrel *n* 桶 tǒng

barren *adj* 贫瘠的 pínjí de; 不孕的 bùyùn de

barricade *n* 路障 lùzhàng

barrier *n* 障碍 zhàng'ài

barrister *n* 律师 lǜshī

barter *v* 以物易物 yǐwù yìwù

base *n* 基础 jīchǔ, 基地 jīdì

baseball *n* 棒球 bàngqiú

basement *n* 地下室 dìxiàshì

bashful *adj* 害羞的 hàixiū de; **bashfulness** *n* 害羞 hàixiū

basic *adj* 基本的 jīběn de

basil *n* 罗勒 luólè

basin *n* (*wash-basin*) 盆 pén; (*geo*) 盆地 péndì

basis *n* 基础 jīchǔ; 根据 gēnjù

basket *n* 篮子 lánzi

basketball *n* 篮球 lánqiú

bass *n* (*voice*) 男低音 nándīyīn

bat *n* (*baseball, etc.*) 球棒 qiúbàng; (*zool*) 蝙蝠 biānfú

batch *n* 一批 yī pī

bath *n* 洗澡 xǐzǎo; **take a bath** 洗澡 xǐzǎo; **bathing suit** 游泳衣 yóuyǒngyī; **bathe** *v* 淋浴 línyù, 洗澡 xǐzǎo

bathrobe *n* 浴衣 yùyī

bathroom *n* 卫生间 wèishēngjiān, 厕所 cèsuǒ

bathtub *n* 浴缸 yùgāng

battalion *n* 军营 jūnyíng; 军队 jūnduì

battery *n* 电池 diànchí

battle *v* 战斗 zhàndòu; *n* 战斗 zhàndòu, 战役 zhànyì; **battle-field** *n* 战场 zhànchǎng; **battleship** *n* 战舰 zhànjiàn

bay *n* 海湾 hǎiwān

bayonet *n* 刺刀 cìdāo

bazaar *n* 集市 jíshì, 义卖 yìmài

be *v* (**was/were, been**) 是 shì; 在 zài

beach *n* 海滩 hǎitān

beacon *n* 灯塔 dēngtǎ

bead *n* 珠子 zhūzi

beak *n* 鸟嘴 niǎozuǐ

beam *n* (*arch*) 梁 liáng; (*light*) 光束 guāngshù

bean *n* 豆子 dòuzi

bear[1] *v* (**bore, born; borne**) 忍受 rěnshòu, 承受 chéngshòu; 带有 dàiyǒu; **bearable** *adj* 可忍受的 kě rěnshòu de

bear[2] *n* (*animal*) 熊 xióng

beard *n* 胡须 húxū

bearings *n* 关系 guānxì, 意义 yìyì, 方向 fāngxiàng

beast *n* 野兽 yěshòu

beat *v* (**beat, beaten/beat**) (*strike*) 打 dǎ; (*defeat*) 打败 dǎbài, 战胜 zhànshèng; (*stir*) 搅拌 jiǎobàn; *n* (*music*) 节拍 jiépāi

beauty *n* 美 měi; (*woman*) 美女 měinǚ; **beautiful** *adj* 美丽的 měilì de

beaver *n* 海狸 hǎilí

became. *See* **become**

because *conj* 因为 yīnwèi; **because of** *prep* 因为 yīnwèi, 由于 yóuyú

beckon *v* 招手 zhāoshǒu; 召唤 zhàohuàn

become *v* (**became, become**) 成为 chéngwéi, 变成 biànchéng

bed *n* 床 chuáng; **bedding** *n* 被褥 bèirù; **bedroom** *n* 卧室 wòshì

bedbug *n* 臭虫 chòuchóng

bee *n* 蜜蜂 mìfēng; **beeline** *n* 直线 zhíxiàn

been. *See* **be**

beef *n* 牛肉 niúròu

beer *n* 啤酒 píjiǔ

beetle *n* 甲虫 jiǎchóng

before *prep/conj* 在 ... 以前 zài ... yǐqián; *adv* 以前 yǐqián, 过去 guòqù; **beforehand** *adv* 提前 tíqián

befriend *v* 亲近 qīnjìn, 和 ... 交朋友 hé ... jiāo péngyou

beg *v* 乞求 qǐqiú; **beg your pardon** 对不起 duìbùqǐ; **beg the question** 回避问题实质 huíbì wèntí shízhì; **beggar** *n* 乞丐 qǐgài

began. *See* **begin**

begin *v* (**began, begun**) 开始 kāishǐ; **begin with** 首先 shǒuxiān; **beginner** *n* 初学者 chūxuézhě, 新手 xīnshǒu; **beginning** *n* 开始 kāishǐ

begun. *See* **begin**

behalf *n* 利益 lìyì; **on behalf of** 代表 dàibiǎo

behave *v* 表现 biǎoxiàn; **behavior** *n* 行为 xíngwéi

behead *v* 砍头 kǎntóu

behind *prep* 在 ... 后面 zài ... hòumian, 在 ... 背后 zài ... bèihòu; *adv* 在背后 zài bèihòu; 向背后 xiàng bèihòu; 在原处 zài yuánchù

behold *v* 看 kàn

beige *adj* 米色的 mǐsè de

being *n* 存在 cúnzài; 生命 shēngmìng; **human being** 人 rén; **well-being** *adj* 安宁 ānníng; **come into being** 出现 chūxiàn, 产生 chǎnshēng; **for the time being** 目前 mùqián, 暂时 zànshí

belated *adj* 误期的 wùqī de; 晚到的 wǎndào de

Belgium *n* 比利时 bǐlìshí; **Belgian** *n* 比利时人 bǐlìshírén; *adj* 比利时的 bǐlìshí de

believe *v* 相信 xiāngxìn; **belief** *n* 信仰 xìnyǎng, 信念 xìnniàn

bell *n* 钟 zhōng, 铃 líng

bellboy *n* (*hotel*) 行李员 xínglǐyuán

belligerent *adj* 好战的 hàozhàn de

belly *n* 肚子 dùzi

belong *v* 属于 shǔyú; **belongings** *n* 财物 cáiwù, 所有物 suǒyǒuwù

beloved *adj* 心爱的 xīn'ài de, 被热爱的 bèi rè'ài de

below *prep* 在 ... 下面 zài ... xiàmian, 低于 dīyú; *adv* 在下面 zài xiàmian; 到下面 dào xiàmian

belt *n* 带子 dàizi

bench *n* 长凳 chángdèng

bend *v* (**bent**, **bent**) 弯 wān

beneath *prep* 在 ... 下面 zài ... xiàmian

benefit *v* 有益于 yǒuyì yú, 有助于 yǒuzhù yú; *n* 利益 lìyì, 福利 fúlì, 好处 hǎochu

benevolence *n* 仁慈 réncí, 善行 shànxíng; **benevolent** *adj* 慈善的 císhàn de, 仁慈的 réncí de

benign *adj* (*med*) 良性的 liángxìng de

bequeath *v* 遗留 yíliú

bereaved *adj* 丧失的 sàngshī de

berry *n* 浆果 jiāngguǒ

berserk *adj* 狂暴的 kuángbào de; **go berserk** 发疯 fāfēng, 发狂 fākuáng

berth *n* 停泊处 tíngbóchù; (*boat, train, plane, etc.*) 卧铺 wòpù; **give a wide berth to** 远远离开 yuǎnyuǎn líkāi, 避开 bìkāi

beside *prep* 在 ... 旁边 zài ... pángbiān; **beside oneself** 极度兴奋 jídù xīngfèn; **beside the point** 离题 lítí; **besides** *adv* 此外 cǐwài; *prep* 除 ... 之外 chú ... zhīwài

besiege *v* 包围 bāowéi

best *adj* 最好的 zuìhǎo de; **at best** 至多 zhìduō; **do one's best** 尽力 jìnlì; **make the best of** 充分利用 chōngfèn lìyòng; **best seller** 畅销书 chàngxiāoshū; **better off** 生活优裕 shēnghuó yōuyù; 较幸运 jiào xìngyùn

bestow *v* 赐予 cìyǔ

bet *v* (**bet/betted**, **bet/betted**) 打赌 dǎdǔ; *n* 打赌 dǎdǔ; 赌钱 dǔqián

betray *v* 背叛 bèipàn

better *adj* 更好的 gèng hǎo de

between *prep* 在 ... 之间 zài ... zhījiān

beverage *n* 饮料 yǐnliào

beware *v* 小心 xiǎoxīn

bewilder *v* (使)迷惑 (shǐ) míhuò; **bewilderment** *n* 困惑 kùnhuò

beyond *prep* 在 ... 之外 zài ... zhīwài; 超过 chāoguò; **beyond doubt** 毫无疑问 háowú yíwèn

bias *n* 偏见 piānjiàn; *adj* 有偏见的 yǒu piānjiàn de

bib *n* 围兜 wéidōu

Bible *n* 圣经 shèngjīng

bibliography *n* 参考书目 cānkǎo shūmù

bicycle *n* 自行车 zìxíngchē

bid *v* (**bid/bade**, **bidden**) 投标 tóubiāo; *n* 出价 chūjià

big *adj* 大的 dà de

bigamy *n* 重婚 chónghūn; **bigamist** *n* 重婚者 chónghūnzhě; **bigamous** *adj* 重婚的 chónghūn de

bigot *n* 盲从者 mángcóngzhě, 顽固者 wángùzhě; **bigotry** *n* 偏执 piānzhí

bike *n* 自行车 zìxíngchē

bikini *n* 比基尼泳装 bǐjīní yǒngzhuāng

bilingual *adj* 双语的 shuāngyǔ de

bill *v* 开账单 kāi zhàngdān; *n* (*check*) 帐单 zhàngdān; (*law*) 法案 fǎ'àn; **billboard** *n* 广告牌 guǎnggàopái

billion *n* 十亿 shíyì

bin *n* 箱柜 xiāngguì

binary *adj* 二进位的 èrjìnwèi de, 二元的 èryuán de

bind *v* (**bound, bound**) 绑 bǎng; 装订 zhuāngdìng; 约束 yuēshù

binoculars *n* 望远镜 wàngyuǎnjìng

biography *n* 传记 zhuànjì; **biographical** *adj* 传记的 zhuànjì de

biology *n* 生物学 shēngwùxué; **biologist** *n* 生物学家 shēngwùxuéjiā

bird *n* 鸟 niǎo; **bird's eye view** 鸟瞰 niǎokàn; **birdcage** *n* 鸟笼 niǎolóng; **birdseed** *n* 鸟食 niǎoshí

birth *n* 出生 chūshēng; **give birth to** 生 shēng; **birth certificate** 出生证明 chūshēng zhèngmíng; **birth control pill** 避孕丸 bìyùnwán; **birthday** *n* 生日 shēngrì; **birthplace** *n* 出生地 chūshēngdì

biscuit *n* 饼干 bǐnggān

bishop *n* 主教 zhǔjiào

bit *n* 一小片 yīxiǎopiàn, 一点儿 yīdiǎnr

bite *v* (**bit, bitten**) 咬 yǎo; *n* 一口 yīkǒu

bitter *adj* 苦的 kǔ de

bizarre *adj* 怪异的 guàiyì de

black *adj* 黑色的 hēisè de; **black market** 黑市 hēishì

blackberry *n* 黑莓 hēiméi

blackboard *n* 黑板 hēibǎn

blackmail *v* 敲诈 qiāozhà

blackout *n* (*power*) 停电 tíngdiàn; (*faint*) 昏迷 hūnmí

blacksmith *n* 铁匠 tiějiàng

bladder *n* 膀胱 pángguāng

blade *n* 刀刃 dāorèn

blame *v* 责怪 zéguài; *n* 过错 guòcuò

blank *n* 空白 kòngbái; 空格 kònggé; *adj* 空白的 kòngbái de

blanket *n* 毯子 tǎnzi

blast *v/n* 爆炸 bàozhà

blaze *v* 燃烧 ránshāo; **blaze a trail** 开拓 kāituò; *n* 火焰 huǒyàn

bleach *v* 漂白 piǎobái; *n* 漂白剂 piāobáijì

bleak *adj* 寒冷的 hánlěng de, 荒凉的 huāngliáng de

bleed *v* (**bled, bled**) 出血 chūxiě, 流血 liúxiě

blemish *n* 污点 wūdiǎn, 瑕疵 xiácī

blend *v/n* 混合 hùnhé

bless *v* 祝福 zhùfú

blew. *See* **blow**

blight *n* (*plants*) 枯萎病 kūwěibìng

blind *adj* 瞎的 xiā de; 盲目的 mángmù de; **turn a blind eye** 无视 wúshì; **blindness** *n* 失明 shīmíng

blindfold *v* 将 ... 蒙起来 jiāng ... méng qǐlái; *n* 眼罩 yǎnzhào

blink *v* 眨眼 zhǎyǎn

bliss *n* 福气 fúqi, 极乐 jílè; **blissful** *adj* 极乐的 jílè de

blister *n* 水泡 shuǐpào

blizzard *n* 大风雪 dà fēngxuě

bloc *n* 集团 jítuán

block *n* (*street*) 街区 jiēqū; (*wood*) 木块 mùkuài

blockade *v/n* 阻塞 zǔsè; 封锁 fēngsuǒ

blonde *n* 金发女郎 jīnfā nǚláng; *adj* 金发的 jīnfà de

blood *n* 血 xuè *or* xiě; **blood donor** 捐血者 juānxuèzhě; **blood pressure** 血压 xuèyā; **blood test** 验血 yànxuè; **bloodshed** *n* 流血 liúxuè; **bloodthirsty** *adj* 嗜血如命 shìxuè rúmìng

bloom *v* 开花 kāihuā; *n* 花 huā; **in bloom** 开花 kāihuā; **blooming** *adj* 盛开的 shèngkāi de, 开着花的 kāi zhe huā de

blossom *v/n* 开花 kāihuā

blouse *n* 女式衬衫 nǚshì chènshān

blow *v* (**blew, blown**) 打击 dǎjī; 吹气 chuīqì; **blow away** 驱散 qūsàn; **blow out** 吹灭 chuīmiè; **blow up** 炸掉 zhà diào; *n* 打击 dǎjī

blue *adj* 蓝色的 lánsè de

blunder *n* 大错 dàcuò, 失误 shīwù

blunt *adj* 钝的 dùn de, 直言的 zhíyán de

blur *v* (使) 模糊不清 (shǐ) móhú bùqīng, 污损 wūsǔn

blush *v* 脸红 liǎnhóng

board *v* (*plane, ship, train, etc.*) 上 shàng; *n* (*wood*) 木板 mùbǎn; (*committee*) 董事会 dǒngshìhuì; (*bulletin*) 告示板 gàoshìbǎn; (*meal*) 膳食 shànshí; **boarding pass** 登机牌 dēngjīpái; **boarding school** 寄宿学校 jìsù xuéxiào; **chessboard** *n* 棋盘 qípán

boast *v* 自夸 zìkuā

boat *n* 船 chuán

body *n* 身体 shēntǐ; (*corpse*) 尸体 shītǐ; 主要部分 zhǔyào bùfen; **bodyguard** *n* 保镖 bǎobiāo

boil *v* 煮沸 zhǔfèi, 沸腾 fèiténg; **boiler** *n* 锅炉 guōlú; **boiling point** 沸点 fèidiǎn

boisterous *adj* 狂暴的 kuángbào de, 喧闹的 xuānnào de

bold *adj* 大胆的 dàdǎn de; **bold-faced** *adj* 黑体的 hēitǐ de; **bold-faced type** 黑体字 hēitǐzì

boldness *n* 大胆 dàdǎn

Bolivia *n* 玻利维亚 bōlìwéiyà; **Bolivian** *adj* 玻利维亚的 bōlìwéiyà de; *n* 玻利维亚人 bōlìwéiyàrén

bolster *v* 支持 zhīchí

bolt *n* 门闩 ménshuān, 螺栓 luóshuān

bomb *v* 轰炸 hōngzhà; *n* 炸弹 zhàdàn; **bomber** *n* 轰炸机 hōngzhàjī

bombard *v* 炮轰 pàohōng, 轰击 hōngjī; **bombardment** *n* 炮击 pàojī, 轰击 hōngjī

bona fide *adj* 真正的 zhēnzhèng de, 真诚的 zhēnchéng de

bond *n* (*tie*) 纽带 niǔdài; (*securities*) 债券 zhàiquàn

bone *n* 骨头 gútou; **all skin and bones** 骨瘦如柴 gǔshòu rúchái; **pick a bone with** 有争端 yǒu zhēngduān

bonfire *n* 篝火 gōuhuǒ

bonus *n* 奖金 jiǎngjīn

booby trap *n* 陷阱 xiànjǐng

book *v* 预订 yùdìng; *n* 书 shū; **bookcase** *n* 书橱 shūchú; **bookkeeper** *n* 簿记员 bùjìyuán; **booklet** *n* 小册子 xiǎocèzi; **bookmark** *n* 书签 shūqiān; **bookshelf** *n* 书架 shūjià; **bookshop** *n* 书店 shūdiàn; **bookstore** *n* 书店 shūdiàn

boom *v* 兴旺 xīngwàng; *n* 繁荣 fánróng

boost *v* 推进 tuījìn; 提高 tígāo

boot *n* 靴子 xuēzi; **get the boot** 被解雇 bèi jiěgù

booth *n* 货摊 huòtān, 售货亭 shòuhuòtíng, 摊位 tānwèi

border *n* 边界 biānjiè; *v* 邻接 línjiē; **borderline** *n* 边界线 biānjièxiàn

bore *v* see **bear**; (*drill*) 钻孔 zuànkǒng; (*to make sb. bored*) (使) 厌烦 (shǐ) yànfán; **bored** *adj* 无聊的 wúliáo de; **boring** *adj* 令人厌烦的 lìng rén yànfán de; 乏味的 fáwèi de

borne. See **bear**

born *adj* 出生的 chūshēng de; 天生的 tiānshēng de

borough *n* 行政区 xíngzhèngqū

borrow *v* 借 jiè

bosom *n* 胸 xiōng, 胸怀 xiōnghuái
boss *n* 老板 lǎobǎn
botany *n* 植物学 zhíwùxué; **botanist** *n* 植物学家 zhíwùxuéjiā;
    botanical *adj* 植物的 zhíwù de
both *adj/pron* 两者 liǎngzhě
bother *v* 打扰 dǎrǎo
bottle *n* 瓶子 píngzi; **bottle-opener** *n* 开瓶器 kāipíngqì
bottom *n* 底 dǐ
bought. *See* **buy**
boulevard *n* 干道 gàndào, 大街 dàjiē
bounce *v* 反弹 fǎntán, 弹跳 tántiào
bound *v* (*jump*) 跳跃 tiàoyuè; (*restrict*) 限制 xiànzhì;
    bounds *n* (*range*) 范围 fànwéi; (*limit*) 限度 xiàndù;
    within bounds 在限度之内 zài xiàndù zhīnèi; **bound for**
    前往 qiánwǎng
boundary *n* 分界线 fēnjièxiàn
bouquet *n* 花束 huāshù
bow *v* (*bend*) 鞠躬 jūgōng; *n* (*weapon*) 弓 gōng
bowels *n* 肠 cháng, 内脏 nèizàng
bowl *n* 碗 wǎn
box *n* 盒子 hézi, 箱子 xiāngzi; **box office** 票房 piàofáng,
    售票处 shòupiàochù
boxer *n* 拳击手 quánjīshǒu; **boxing** *n* 拳击 quánjī
boy *n* 男孩 nánhái
boycott *v/n* 抵制 dǐzhì
boyfriend *n* 男朋友 nánpéngyou
bra *n* 胸罩 xiōngzhào
bracelet *n* 手镯 shǒuzhuó
bracket *n* 括号 kuòhào; 支架 zhījià
brag *v* 吹牛 chuīniú
Braille *n* 盲字 mángzì
brain *n* 脑 nǎo; **rack one's brains** 绞尽脑汁 jiǎojìn nǎozhī;
    brainwash *v* 洗脑 xǐnǎo
brake *v* 刹车 shāchē; *n* 闸 zhá
branch *n* (*tree*) 树枝 shùzhī; (*company*) 分店 fēndiàn, (*office*)
    分部 fēnbù
brand *n* 商标 shāngbiāo; **brand-new** *adj* 崭新的 zhǎnxīn de
brandish *v* 挥舞 huīwǔ
brandy *n* 白兰地酒 báilándìjiǔ
brass *n* 黄铜 huángtóng
brassiere *n* 胸罩 xiōngzhào
brave *adj* 勇敢的 yǒnggǎn de; **bravery** *n* 英勇 yīngyǒng

brawl *n* 争吵 zhēngchǎo, 打架 dǎjià

Brazil *n* 巴西 bāxī; **Brazilian** *n* 巴西人 bāxīrén; *adj* 巴西的 bāxī de

breach *v* 突破 tūpò, 违背 wéibèi; *n* 违背 wéibèi; **breach of promise** 食言 shíyán

bread *n* 面包 miànbāo

breadth *n* 宽度 kuāndù, 幅度 fúdù

break *v* (**broke**, **broken**) 打破 dǎpò; **break away** 脱离 tuōlí; **break up** 打破 dǎpò, 分裂 fēnliè; **break down** (*mechanical*) 出故障 chū gùzhàng; (*emotional*) 崩溃 bēngkuì; *n* 休息 xiūxi; **breakthrough** *n* 突破 tūpò

breakdown *n* (*mechanical*) 故障 gùzhàng; (*emotional*) 崩溃 bēngkuì

breakfast *n* 早饭 zǎofàn

breast *n* 乳房 rǔfáng; **breaststroke** *n* 蛙式 wāshì

breath *n* 呼吸 hūxī; **breathalyzer** *n* 酒精测定计 jiǔjīng cèdìngjì

breathe *v* 呼吸 hūxī

breed *v* (**bred**, **bred**) 繁殖 fánzhí, 养殖 yǎngzhí

breeze *n* 微风 wēifēng

brew *v* 酿造 niàngzào; **brewery** *n* 酿酒厂 niàngjiǔchǎng

bribe *v* 贿赂 huìlù; **bribery** *n* 贿赂 huìlù

brick *n* 砖 zhuān

bride *n* 新娘 xīnniáng; **bridesmaid** 女傧相 nǔbīnxiàng

bridegroom *n* 新郎 xīnláng

bridge *n* 桥 qiáo; (*cards*) 桥牌 qiáopái

brief *v* 介绍情况 jièshào qíngkuàng, 通报 tōngbào; *adj* 简短的 jiǎnduǎn de; **briefly** *adv* 简要地 jiǎnyào de

briefcase *n* 公文包 gōngwénbāo

brigade *n* (*military*) 旅 lǔ, 队 duì

bright *adj* 明亮的 míngliàng de; 聪明的 cōngming de, 有才气的 yǒu cáiqì de; **brighten** *v* (使) 变亮 (shǐ) biàn liàng; **brightness** *n* 明亮 míngliàng

brilliant *adj* 灿烂的 cànlàn de, 杰出的 jiéchū de, 有才气的 yǒu cáiqì de

bring *v* (**brought**, **brought**) 带来 dài lái, 拿来 ná lái; **bring about** 导致 dǎozhì, 致使 zhìshǐ; **bring up** 培养 péiyǎng; 提出 tíchū

brink *n* 边缘 biānyuán

brisk *adj* 敏锐的 mǐnruì de, 轻快的 qīngkuài de

Britain *n* 英国 yīngguó; **British** *n* 英国人 yīngguórén; *adj* 英国的 yīngguó de; **Briton** *n* 英国人 yīngguórén

broad *adj* 宽广的 kuānguǎng de, 广大的 guǎngdà de

broadcast *v* (**broadcast/broadcasted, broadcast/broad-casted**) 广播 guǎngbō; *n* 广播节目 guǎngbō jiémù

broccoli *n* 椰菜 yēcài

brochure *n* 小册子 xiǎocèzi

broke *v see* **break**; *adj* 破产了的 pòchǎn le de

broken *v see* **break**; *adj* 坏了的 huài le de

broker *n* 经纪人 jīngjìrén

bronchitis *n* 支气管炎 zhīqìguǎnyán

bronze 青铜 qīngtóng

brook *n* 小溪 xiǎoxī

broom *n* 扫帚 sàozhou

broth *n* 肉汤 ròutāng

brothel *n* 妓院 jìyuàn

brother *n* (*older*) 哥哥 gēge; (*younger*) 弟弟 dìdi; **brother-in-law** *n* (*older sister's husband*) 姐夫 jiěfu; (*younger sister's husband*) 妹夫 mèifu; (*wife's older brother*) 内兄 nèixiōng; (*wife's younger brother*) 内弟 nèidì; **brotherly** *adj* 兄弟般的 xiōngdìbán de

brow *n* 眉毛 méimao

brown *adj* 棕色的 zōngsè de

bruise *n* 青肿 qīngzhǒng

brush *v* 刷 shuā; **brush aside** 不理睬 bù lǐcǎi; **brush off** 不客气地拒绝 bùkèqì de jùjué; *n* 刷子 shuāzi

brutal *adj* 残忍的 cánrěn de

bubble *n* 泡沫 pàomò, 气泡 qìpào

bucket *n* 桶 tǒng

buckle *v* 扣上 kòu shàng; *n* 带扣 dàikòu

bud *n* 芽 yá

Buddhism *n* 佛教 fójiào; **Buddhist** *n* 佛教徒 fójiàotú

budge *v* 移动 yídòng, 让步 ràngbù

budget *n* 预算 yùsuàn

buffalo *n* 水牛 shuǐniú

buffet *n* 自助餐 zìzhùcān

bug *n* 虫 chóng

build *v* (**built, built**) 建造 jiànzào; **building** *n* 建筑物 jiànzhùwù, 楼 lóu

built. *See* **build**

bulb *n* 灯泡 dēngpào

Bulgaria *n* 保加利亚 bǎojiālìyà; **Bulgarian** *n* (*people*) 保加利亚人 bǎojiālìyàrén; (*language*) 保加利亚语 bǎojiālìyàyǔ

bulge *n/v* 凸出 tūchū, 膨胀 péngzhàng; **bulging** *adj* 膨胀的 péngzhàng de, 凸出的 tūchū de

bulk *n* 大宗物件 dàzōng wùjiàn; 大部分 dàbùfen

bull *n* 公牛 gōngniú; **bullfight** *n* 斗牛 dòuniú; **bullfighter** *n* 斗牛士 dǒuniúshì

bulldozer *n* 推土机 tuītǔjī

bullet *n* 子弹 zǐdàn; **bulletproof** *adj* 防弹的 fángdàn de

bulletin *n* 公告 gōnggào, 报告 bàogào; **bulletin board** 布告板 bùgàobǎn

bully *n* 欺凌弱小者 qīlíng ruòxiǎo zhě

bump *v* 碰撞 pèngzhuàng; 颠簸 diānbǒ; *n* 颠簸 diānbǒ

bun *n* 小圆面包 xiǎo yuánmiànbāo

bunch *n* (*flowers*) 束 shù

bundle *n* 捆 kǔn, 束 shù

bungalow *n* 平房 píngfáng

bungle *v* 办糟 bànzāo; **bungling** *n* 失误 shīwù

bunker *n* 掩体 yǎntǐ, 地堡 dìbǎo

buoy *n* 浮标 fúbiāo; 救生圈 jiùshēngquān; **buoyancy** *n* 浮性 fúxìng, 浮力 fúlì

burden *v* 给 ... 增加负担 gěi ... zēngjiā fùdān; *n* 负担 fùdān

bureau *n* 局 jú, 署 shǔ

bureaucracy *n* 官僚作风 guānliáo zuòfēng; 官僚机构 guānliáo jīgòu; **bureaucrat** *n* 官僚 guānliáo; 官僚主义者 guānliáozhǔyìzhě; **bureaucratic** *adj* 官僚的 guānliáo de

burger *n* 汉堡包 hànbǎobāo

burglar *n* 小偷 xiǎotōu; **burglarize** *v* 盗窃 dàoqiè; **burglary** *n* 入室行窃 rùshì xíngqiè

bury *v* 埋 mái; **burial** *n* 埋葬 máizàng

burn *v* (**burned/burnt, burned/burnt**) 烧 shāo; *n* 烧伤 shāoshāng; **burning** *n* 燃烧 ránshāo

burst *v* (**burst, burst**) 爆裂 bàoliè, 破裂 pòliè

bus *n* 公共汽车 gōnggòng qìchē; **bus station** 公交车站 gōngjiāo chēzhàn; **bus stop** 公共汽车站 gōnggòng qìchēzhàn

bush *n* 灌木 guànmù; **bushy** *adj* 浓密的 nóngmì de

business *n* 商业 shāngyè, 生意 shēngyì; **business hours** 营业时间 yíngyè shíjiān; **mean business** 是认真的 shì rènzhēn de; **mind one's own business** 管自己的事 guǎn zìjǐ de shì; **businessman** *n* 商人 shāngrén; **businesswoman** *n* 女商人 nǚshāngrén; **businesslike** *adj* 公事公办的 gōngshì gōngbàn de

bust *n* 半身雕像 bànshēn diāoxiàng; *v* (*arrest*) 逮捕 dàibǔ;
(*bankrupt*) 破产 pòchǎn
busy *adj* 忙 máng; **busybody** *n* 爱管闲事的人 ài guǎnxiánshì
de rén
but *conj* 但是 dànshì, 可是 kěshì; **but for** 要不是 yàobùshì
butcher *n* 屠夫 túfū
butler *n* 男管家 nánguǎnjiā
butt *n* 臀部 túnbù; (*of a joke*) 笑柄 xiàobǐng
butter *n* 奶油 nǎiyóu
butterfly *n* 蝴蝶 húdié
buttocks *n* 臀部 túnbù
button *n* 纽扣 niǔkòu; **buttonhole** *n* 扣眼 kòuyǎn
buy *v* (**bought, bought**) 买 mǎi; **buyer** *n* 买主 mǎizhǔ
buzzer *n* 蜂鸣器 fēngmíngqì
by *prep* 乘 chéng; 被 bèi; 由 yóu; 用 yòng; **by all means**
务必 wùbì; **by and large** 大体上 dàtǐshang; **by the way**
顺便说 shùnbiàn shuō
bye *interj* 再见 zàijiàn
by-law *n* 章程 zhāngchéng
bypass *v* 绕过 ràoguò, 避开 bìkāi
by-product *n* 副产品 fùchǎnpǐn
bystander *n* 看热闹的人 kàn rènao de rén, 旁观者
pángguānzhě

C

cab *n* 出租车 chūzūchē
cabaret *n* 卡巴莱 kǎbālái
cabbage *n* 卷心菜 juǎnxīncài
cabin *n* (*aircraft, etc.*) 客舱 kècāng; 小屋 xiǎowū
cabinet *n* (*furniture*) 橱柜 chúguì; (*government*) 内阁 nèigé
cable *n* 电缆 diànlǎn; **cable TV** 有线电视 yǒuxiàn diànshì;
cable car 缆车 lǎnchē
cadet *n* 军校学生 jūnxiào xuésheng
cactus *n* 仙人掌 xiānrénzhǎng
café *n* 咖啡馆 kāfēiguǎn
cafeteria *n* 餐厅 cāntīng
caffeine *n* 咖啡因 kāfēiyīn
cage *n* 笼子 lóngzi
cake *n* 蛋糕 dàngāo; **a piece of cake** 容易的事 róngyì de shi
calamity *n* 灾难 zāinàn
calcium *n* 钙 gài

calculate *v* 计算 jìsuàn; **calculation** *n* 计算 jìsuàn; **calculator** *n* 计算器 jìsuànqì

calendar *n* 日历 rìlì

calf *n* (*pl* **calves**) 小牛 xiǎoniú

caliber *n* 能力 nénglì; 才干 cáigàn; 水准 shuǐzhǔn

call *v* 叫 jiào; 打电话 dǎ diànhuà; **call for** 要求 yāoqiú; **call off** 取消 qǔxiāo; **call on** 访问 fǎngwèn; **call up** 打电话 dǎ diànhuà; **on call** 随叫随到的 suíjiào suídào de, 听候召唤的 tīnghòu zhàohuàn de;

callous *adj* 无情的 wúqíng de, 冷淡的 lěngdàn de

calm *adj* 平静的 píngjìng de, 镇静的 zhènjìng de

calorie *n* 卡路里 kǎlùlǐ

calves. *See* **calf**

came. *See* **come**

camel *n* 骆驼 luòtuo

camera *n* 照像机 zhàoxiàngjī

camouflage *v/n* 伪装 wěizhuāng

camp *n* 营地 yíngdì

campaign *n* 战役 zhànyì; 竞选运动 jìngxuǎn yùndòng

campus *n* 校园 xiàoyuán

can *aux* 可以 kěyǐ, 能 néng; *n* 罐头 guàntou

Canada *n* 加拿大 jiānádà; **Canadian** *n* 加拿大人 jiānádàrén; *adj* 加拿大的 jiānádà de

canal *n* 运河 yùnhé

canary *n* 金丝雀 jīnsīquè

cancel *v* 取消 qǔxiāo; **cancellation** *n* 取消 qǔxiāo

cancer *n* 癌症 áizhèng

candid *adj* 坦率的 tǎnshuài de, 坦白的 tǎnbái de

candidate *n* 候选人 hòuxuǎnrén

candle *n* 蜡烛 làzhú; **burn the candle at both ends** 过分消耗精力 guòfèn xiāohào jīnglì

candy *n* 糖果 tángguǒ

cane *n* 手杖 shǒuzhàng

canine *adj* 犬的 quǎn de

cannibal *n* 食人者 shírénzhě; *adj* 食人的 shírén de; **cannibalism** *n* 嗜食同类 shìshí tónglèi; 食人 shírén

cannon *n* 大炮 dàpào

canoe *n* 独木舟 dúmùzhōu

canteen *n* 食堂 shítáng

canvas *n* (*fabric*) 帆布 fānbù

canyon *n* 峡谷 xiágǔ, 溪谷 xīgǔ

cap *n* 帽子 màozi; 盖子 gàizi

capable *adj* 有能力的 yǒu nénglì de

capacity *n* 容量 róngliàng; 身份 shēnfen; 能力 nénglì

cape *n* 斗篷 dǒupeng; 海角 hǎijiǎo

capital *n* (*city*) 首都 shǒudū; (*money*) 资本 zīběn; **capital punishment** 死刑 sǐxíng; **capitalism** *n* 资本主义 zīběnzhǔyì; **capitalist** *adj* 资本主义的 zīběnzhǔyì de; *n* 资本家 zīběnjiā

capitulate *v* 投降 tóuxiáng, 认输 rènshū; **capitulation** *n* 投降 tóuxiáng

capricious *adj* 反复无常的 fǎnfù wúcháng de

capsize *v* 倾覆 qīngfù

capsule *n* (*medicine*) 胶囊 jiāonáng; (*space*) 太空舱 tàikōngcāng

captain *n* (*ship*) 船长 chuánzhǎng; (*sports*) 球队队长 qiúduì duìzhǎng; (*plane*) 机长 jīzhǎng

caption *n* 标题 biāotí, 字幕 zìmù

capture *v* 捕获 bǔhuò; **captive** *n* 俘虏 fúlǔ

car *n* 小汽车 xiǎoqìchē; **dining car** 餐车 cānchē; **racing car** 赛车 sàichē; **sleeping car** 卧铺车厢 wòpù chēxiāng

carat *n* 克拉 kèlā

caravan *n* 大篷车 dàpéngchē

carbohydrate *n* 碳水化合物 tànshuǐ huàhéwù

carbon *n* 碳 tàn; **carbon dioxide** 二氧化碳 èryǎng huàtàn

carcass *n* 畜体 chùtǐ

card *n* 卡片 kǎpiàn; **cardboard** *n* 硬纸板 yìngzhǐbǎn

cardiac *adj* 心脏的 xīnzàng de

cardinal *n* (*church*) 红衣主教 hóngyī zhǔjiào; **cardinal number** 基数 jīshù

care *v* 关心 guānxīn, 在意 zàiyì; *n* 忧虑 yōulǜ, 关心 guānxīn; **medical care** 医疗保健 yīliáo bǎojiàn; **handle with care** 小心轻放 xiǎoxīn qīngfàng; **take care** 当心 dāngxīn; **take care of** 照顾 zhàogù, 处理 chǔlǐ; **careful** *adj* 小心的 xiǎoxīn de; **carefully** *adv* 仔细地 zǐxì de; **careless** *adj* 粗心的 cūxīn de

career *n* 事业 shìyè, 生涯 shēngyá

caress *n* 爱抚 àifǔ

cargo *n* 货物 huòwù

caricature *n* 讽刺画 fěngcìhuà

carnival *n* 狂欢节 kuánghuānjié

carpenter *n* 木匠 mùjiàng

carpet *n* 地毯 dìtǎn

carriage *n* 马车 mǎchē

carrier *n* 货运公司 huòyùn gōngsī; 邮递员 yóudìyuán

carrot *n* 胡萝卜 húluóbo

carry *v* 携带 xiédài; **carry on** 继续 jìxù; **carry out** 执行 zhíxíng

cart *n* 大车 dàchē

carton *n* 纸盒 zhǐhé, 纸箱 zhǐxiāng

cartoon *n* 漫画 mànhuà; 动画片 dònghuàpiān

cartridge *n* 套筒 tàotǒng

carve *v* 雕刻 diāokè, 刻 kè; **carve up** 把 ... 切成片 bǎ ... qiē chéng piàn

case *n* (*box*) 箱子 xiāngzi; (*situation*) 个案 gè'àn, 案例 ànlì; **in any case** 无论如何 wúlùn rúhé; **in case** 假使 jiǎshǐ; 以防 yǐfáng; **in case of** 假使 jiǎshǐ, 如果发生 rúguǒ fāshēng; **just in case** 以防万一 yǐfáng wànyī

cash *n* 现金 xiànjīn

cashier *n* 收款员 shōukuǎnyuán

cashmere *n* 开士米 kāishìmǐ, 山羊绒 shānyángróng

casino *n* 赌场 dǔchǎng

casket *n* 棺材 guāncai

cassette *n* 卡式磁带 kǎshì cídài; **cassette recorder** 盒式录音机 héshì lùyīnjī

cast *v* (**cast, cast**) 扔 rēng; 浇铸 jiāozhù; 投 tóu; **cast away** 丢掉 diū diào; **cast aside** 把 ... 丢一边 bǎ ... diū yībiān; **cast off** 抛弃 pāoqì

castle *n* 城堡 chéngbǎo

castrate *v* 阉割 yāngē

casual *adj* 随便的 suíbiàn de, 不经意的 bùjīngyì de; **casually** *adv* 随便地 suíbiàn de

casualty *n* 伤亡 shāngwáng

cat *n* 猫 māo

catalog *n* 目录册 mùlùcè

catalyst *n* 催化剂 cuīhuàjì

catapult *n* 弹弓 dàngōng

catastrophe *n* 大灾难 dà zāinàn

catch *v* (**caught, caught**) 抓 zhuā, 捉 zhuō; **catch up** 追上 zhuī shàng; **catch a train/bus** 赶车 gǎnchē; **catch on** 流行起来 liúxíng qǐlái

category *n* 类别 lèibié, 种类 zhǒnglèi

cater *v* 承办饮食服务 chéngbàn yǐnshí fúwù; 满足 mǎnzú, 迎合 yínghé; **caterer** *n* 承办饮食服务者 chéngbàn yǐnshí fúwùzhě caterpillar *n* 毛虫 máochóng

cathedral *n* 大教堂 dà jiàotáng

Catholic *n* 天主教徒 tiānzhǔjiàotú; *adj* 天主教的 tiānzhǔjiào de; **Catholicism** *n* 天主教教义 tiānzhǔjiào jiàoyì

cattle *n* 牛 niú

caught. *See* catch

cauliflower *n* 花菜 huācài

cause *v* 造成 zàochéng; *n* 原因 yuányīn

caution *v* 警告 jǐnggào; *n* 小心 xiǎoxīn; **cautious** *adj* 谨慎的 jǐnshèn de, 小心的 xiǎoxīn de

cave *n* 山洞 shāndòng, 岩洞 yándòng; **cave in** 坍塌 tāntā; 屈服 qūfú

cavity *n* 洞 dòng, 空穴 kōngxué

cease *v* 停止 tíngzhǐ; **cease-fire** *n* 停火 tínghuǒ

ceiling *n* 天花板 tiānhuābǎn

celebrate *v* 庆祝 qìngzhù; **celebration** *n* 庆祝 qìngzhù

celebrity *n* 名人 míngrén

celery *n* 芹菜 qíncài

celestial *adj* 天上的 tiānshang de

cell *n* 细胞 xìbāo; (*prison*) 牢房 láofáng; **cell phone** 手机 shǒujī

cellar *n* 地窖 dìjiào, 酒窖 jiǔjiào

cello *n* 大提琴 dàtíqín; **cellist** *n* 大提琴手 dàtíqínshǒu

cement *n* 水泥 shuǐní

cemetery *n* 墓地 mùdì

censor *n* 检查员 jiǎncháyuán; **censorship** *n* 新闻审查 xīnwén shěnchá

censure *v/n* 责难 zénàn

census *n* 人口普查 rénkǒu pǔchá

cent *n* 分 fēn

center *n* 中心 zhōngxīn; **central** *adj* 中心的 zhōngxīn de, 中央的 zhōngyāng de

centigrade *adj* 摄氏温度的 shèshìwēndù de

centimeter *n* 厘米 límǐ

century *n* 世纪 shìjì

ceramic *adj* 陶瓷的 táocí de; **ceramics** *n* 陶器 táoqì

cereal *n* 谷类食品 gǔlèi shípǐn

ceremony *n* 典礼 diǎnlǐ

certain *adj* 必然的 bìrán de, 一定的 yīdìng de, 肯定的 kěndìng de, 某一个 mǒu yī gè; **make certain** 弄确实 nòng quèshí; **certainty** *n* 确实 quèshí; **certainly** *adv* 的确 díquè, 当然 dāngrán

certify *v* 证明 zhèngmíng; **certificate** *n* 证书 zhèngshū; **birth certificate** 出生证 chūshēngzhèng; **death certificate** 死亡证 sǐwángzhèng; **marriage certificate** 结婚证 jiéhūnzhèng

cesspool *n* 污水坑 wūshuǐkēng, 化粪池 huàfènchí

chain *n* 链子 liànzi; **chain store** 连锁店 liánsuǒdiàn

chair *n* 椅子 yǐzi; 主席 zhǔxí

chairman *n* 主席 zhǔxí

chalk *n* 粉笔 fěnbǐ

challenge *v/n* 挑战 tiǎozhàn

chamber *n* 房间 fángjiān, 室 shì; **chamber music** 室内乐 shìnèiyuè; **chamber of commerce** 商会 shānghuì; **chambermaid** *n* 女服务员 nǚfúwùyuán

chameleon *n* 变色龙 biànsèlóng

champagne *n* 香槟酒 xiāngbīnjiǔ

champion *n* 冠军 guànjūn; **championship** *n* 锦标赛 jǐnbiāosài

chance *n* 机会 jīhuì; 可能性 kěnéngxìng

chancellor *n* 大臣 dàchén; 总理 zǒnglǐ; 校长 xiàozhǎng

change *v* 换 huàn, 兑换 duìhuàn; 找钱 zhǎoqián; *n* 变化 biànhuà; (*money*) 找回的零钱 zhǎohuí de língqián; **for a change** 为了改变一下 wèile gǎibiàn yīxià; **changeable** *adj* 多变的 duōbiàn de

channel *n* (*TV*) 频道 píndào; (*river*) 渠道 qúdào

chant *n* 圣歌 shènggē; 曲子 qǔzi

chaos *n* 混乱 hùnluàn; **chaotic** *adj* 混乱的 hùnluàn de

chapel *n* 小礼拜堂 xiǎo lǐbàitáng

chaperon *n* 陪伴 péibàn; 监护人 jiānhùrén

chaplain *n* 牧师 mùshī

chapter *n* (*book*) 章 zhāng; (*organization*) 分会 fēnhuì

character *n* 人物 rénwù; 人格 réngé; 特性 tèxìng; **characterize** *v* 描绘 miáohuì; **characteristic** *adj* 特有的 tèyǒu de, 典型的 diǎnxíng de

charcoal *n* 木炭 mùtàn

charge *v* (*bill*) 收费 shōufèi; (*accuse*) 指控 zhǐkòng; *n* 费用 fèiyòng; 指控 zhǐkòng; **in charge of** 负责 fùzé; **take charge of** 接管 jiēguǎn

charity *n* (*act*) 慈善行为 císhàn xíngwéi; (*org*) 慈善团体 císhàn tuántǐ

charm *n* 魅力 mèilì; **charming** *adj* 迷人的 mírén de

chart *v* 制图 zhìtú; *n* 图表 túbiǎo

charter *v* 包租 bāozū; *n* 宪章 xiànzhāng

chase *n* 追逐 zhuīzhú; *v* 追 zhuī; **chase away/off** 赶走 gǎn zǒu

chaste *adj* 贞洁的 zhēnjié de; **chastity** *n* 纯洁 chúnjié, 贞节 zhēnjié

chastise *v* 惩罚 chéngfá

chat *v/n* 聊天 liáotiān

chatter *v* 喋喋不休地说 diédiébùxiū de shuō; **chatterbox** *n* 喋喋不休者 diédié bùxiūzhě, 唠叨的人 láodao de rén

chauffeur *n* 司机 sījī

chauvinism *n* 沙文主义 shāwénzhǔyì; **chauvinist** *n* 沙文主义者 shāwénzhǔyìzhě; *adj* 沙文主义的 shāwénzhǔyì de

cheap *adj* 廉价的 liánjià de, 便宜的 piányi de; **dirt cheap** 极便宜 jí piányi

cheat *v* (*deceive*) 欺骗 qīpiàn; (*in exams*) 作弊 zuòbì

check *v* 核对 héduì, 检查 jiǎnchá; *n* 支票 zhīpiào; (*bill*) 账单 zhàngdān; **traveller's check** 旅行支票 lǚxíng zhīpiào; **checkbook** *n* 支票本 zhīpiàoběn; **checkpoint** *n* 检查站 jiǎncházhàn; **check-in** *n* 登记 dēngjì; **check-out** *n* 结账 jiézhàng; **check-up** *n* 体格检查 tǐgé jiǎnchá

cheek *n* 面颊 miànjiá; **cheeky** *adj* 厚脸皮的 hòuliǎnpí de

cheer *v* 喝彩 hècǎi, 欢呼 huānhū; (使) 振奋 (shǐ) zhènfèn; **cheer up** 振作起来 zhènzuò qǐlái; **cheers** *interj* (*toast*) 干杯 gānbēi; (*good-bye*) 再见 zàijiàn; **cheerful** *adj* 愉快的 yúkuài de

cheese *n* 奶酪 nǎilào

cheetah *n* 印度豹 yìndùbào

chef *n* 厨师 chúshī

chemist *n* 化学家 huàxuéjiā; **chemistry** *n* 化学 huàxué; **chemical** *adj* 化学的 huàxué de; 化学品 huàxuépǐn

cherish *v* 珍爱 zhēn'ài

cherry *n* (*fruit*) 樱桃 yīngtáo; (*tree*) 樱桃树 yīngtáoshù

chess *n* 象棋 xiàngqí; **chessboard** *n* 棋盘 qípán

chest *n* 胸 xiōng; **chest of drawers** 五斗橱 wǔdǒuchú

chestnut *n* 栗子 lìzi

chew *v* 嚼 jiáo; **chewing gum** 口香糖 kǒuxiāngtáng

chicken *n* 鸡 jī; **chickenpox** *n* 水痘 shuǐdòu; **chicken out** *v* 胆怯 dǎnqiè

chief *n* 领袖 lǐngxiù, 首脑 shǒunǎo, 首领 shǒulǐng, 长官 zhǎngguān; *adj* 首要的 shǒuyào de; **chiefly** *adv* 主要地 zhǔyào de

child *n* (*pl* **children**) 儿童 értóng; **childbirth** *n* 生育 shēngyù;

childhood *n* 童年 tóngnián; **childish** *adj* 幼稚的 yòuzhì de; **childless** *adj* 无子女的 wú zǐnǚ de

Chile *n* 智利 zhìlì; **Chilean** *n* 智利人 zhìlìrén; *adj* 智利的 zhìlì de

chilly *adj* 寒冷的 hánlěng de, 寒嗖嗖的 hánsōusōu de; **chilled to the bone** 寒气刺骨 hánqì cìgǔ

chimney *n* 烟囱 yāncōng

chimpanzee *n* 猩猩 xīngxīng

chin *n* 下巴 xiàba

China *n* 中国 zhōngguó; **Chinese** *n* (*people*) 中国人 zhōng-guórén; (*language*) 中文 zhōngwén; *adj* 中国的 zhōngguó de

china *n* 瓷器 cíqì

chip *n* 薄片 báopiàn; **chips** (*potato*) *n* 马铃薯条 mǎlíng-shǔtiáo; **chip in** *v* 共同出钱 gòngtóng chūqián, 共同出力 gòngtóng chūlì

chisel *v* 砍凿 kǎnzáo; *n* 凿子 záozi

chocolate *n* 巧克力 qiǎokèlì

choice *n* 选择 xuǎnzé

choir *n* 唱诗班 chàngshībān

choke *v* (*strangle*) (使) 窒息 (shǐ) zhìxī; (*block*) 堵塞 dǔsè

cholera *n* 霍乱 huòluàn

choose *v* (**chose, chosen**) 选择 xuǎnzé

chop *v* 剁 duò, 砍 kǎn

chopstick *n* 筷子 kuàizi

chord *n* 和音 héyīn

chore *n* 家务杂事 jiāwù záshì

choreography *n* 舞蹈设计 wǔdǎo shèjì

chorus *n* 合唱 héchàng

chose/chosen. *See* **choose**

Christian *n* 基督徒 jīdūtú; *adj* 基督教的 jīdūjiào de; **Christianity** *n* 基督教 jīdūjiào

Christmas *n* 圣诞节 shèngdànjié; **Christmas Day** 圣诞日 shèngdànri; **Christmas Eve** 圣诞夜 shèngdànyè

chronic *adj* 慢性的 mànxìng de; **chronic disease** 慢性病 mànxìngbìng

chronicle *n* 编年史 biānniánshǐ

chronological *adj* 按时间顺序排列的 àn shíjiān shùnxù páiliè de

chrysanthemum *n* 菊花 júhuā

chuckle *v* 暗笑 ànxiào

church *n* 教堂 jiàotáng

chute *n* 斜槽 xiécáo

cider *n* 苹果汁 píngguǒzhī

cigar *n* 雪茄 xuějiā

cigarette *n* 香烟 xiāngyān; **cigarette lighter** 香烟打火机 xiāngyān dǎhuǒjī

cinema *n* 电影院 diànyǐngyuàn

cinnamon *n* 肉桂 ròuguì, 桂皮 guìpí

circle *v* 环绕 huánrǎo; 画圈 huàquān; *n* 圆圈 yuánquān, 圈子 quānzi

circuit *n* 电路 diànlù; **short circuit** 短路 duǎnlù

circular *adj* 圆形的 yuánxíng de; 循环的 xúnhuán de

circulate *v* (使) 流通 (shǐ) liútōng; (使) 循环 (shǐ) xúnhuán; (使) 传播 (shǐ) chuánbō; **circulation** *n* 循环 xúnhuán; 流通 liútōng; 发行 fāxíng

circumcise *v* 环割包皮 huángē bāopí; **circumcision** *n* 环割包皮 huángē bāopí

circumference *n* 圆周 yuánzhōu, 周长 zhōucháng

circumstance *n* 环境 huánjìng; 境况 jìngkuàng; **under no circumstances** 决不 juébù; **under the circumstances** 在这种情况下 zài zhè zhǒng qíngkuàng xià; **circumstantial** *adj* 与环境有关的 yǔ huánjìng yǒuguān de; **circumstantial evidence** 间接证据 jiànjiē zhèngjù

circus *n* 马戏团 mǎxìtuán

cite *v* 引用 yǐnyòng, 列举 lièjǔ; **citation** *n* 引用 yǐnyòng; 嘉奖 jiājiǎng

citizen *n* 公民 gōngmín; **citizenship** *n* 公民身分 gōngmín shēnfèn

citrus *n* 柑橘类植物 gānjúlèi zhíwù; **citrus fruit** 柑橘 gānjú

city *n* 城市 chéngshì

civic *adj* 城市的 chéngshì de; 市民的 shìmín de, 公民的 gōngmín de

civil *adj* 公民的 gōngmín de; 文明的 wénmíng de; 民事的 mínshì de; **civil rights** 民权 mínquán; **civil servant** 公务员 gōngwùyuán; **civil service** 政府文职部门 zhèngfǔ wénzhíbùmén; **civil war** 内战 nèizhàn

civilian *n* 平民 píngmín; *adj* 平民的 píngmín de

civilization *n* 文明 wénmíng

claim *v* 声称 shēngchēng; 要求 yāoqiú; 认领 rènlǐng; *n* 要求 yāoqiú; 主张 zhǔzhāng

clam *n* 蛤 gé

clamp *v* 夹住 jiāzhù; *n* 夹子 jiāzi; **clamp down on** 对 ... 进行压制 duì ... jìnxíng yāzhì

clamor *v* 吵闹 chǎonào, 叫喊 jiàohǎn; *n* 喧闹 xuānnào

clan *n* 部落 bùluò, 宗族 zōngzú

clandestine *adj* 秘密的 mìmì de

clap *v* 拍手 pāishǒu

clarify *v* 澄清 chéngqīng; **clarity** *n* 清楚 qīngchu

clash *v/n* 冲突 chōngtū

clasp *v* (*grasp*) 紧握 jǐnwò; (*fasten*) 扣紧 kòujǐn

class *n* 班级 bānjí; 课 kè; 阶级 jiējí; 等级 děngjí

classic *n* 名著 míngzhù, 经典作品 jīngdiǎn zuòpǐn; *adj* 一流的 yīliú de; **classical** *adj* 古典的 gǔdiǎn de

classify *v* 分类 fēnlèi; **classification** *n* 分类 fēnlèi; **classified advertisement** 分类广告 fēnlèi guǎnggào

classmate *n* 同学 tóngxué

classroom *n* 教室 jiàoshì

clause *n* (*legal*) 条款 tiáokuǎn; (*gram*) 子句 zǐjù

claustrophobia *n* 幽闭恐怖症 yōubì kǒngbùzhēng

claw *n* 爪子 zhuǎzi

clay *n* 粘土 niántǔ

clean *adj* 干净的 gānjìng de, 整洁的 zhěngjié de; *v* 清洁 qīngjié, 打扫 dǎsǎo; **clean out** 把 ... 打扫干净 bǎ ... dǎsǎo gānjìng; **cleaner** *n* (*worker*) 清洁工 qīngjiégōng; (*chemical*) 清洁剂 qīngjiéjì; (*store*) 干洗店 gānxǐdiàn; **cleanliness** *n* 干净 gānjìng; **cleanse** *v* 清洗 qīngxǐ

clear *adj* 清楚的 qīngchu de; **clearly** *adv* 明显地 míngxiǎn de, 显然地 xiǎnrán de; **clearance sale** 清仓削价销售 qīngcāng xuējià xiāoshòu

clench *v* (*fist*) 握紧 wòjǐn; (*teeth*) 咬紧 yǎojǐn

clergy *n* 神职人员 shénzhí rényuán; **clergyman** *n* 神职人员 shénzhí rényuán

clerical *adj* 职员的 zhíyuán de, 文书的 wénshū de

clerk *n* 职员 zhíyuán

clever *adj* 聪明的 cōngming de

cliché *n* 陈词滥调 chéncí làndiào

click *v* 点击 diǎnjī

client *n* 客户 kèhù

cliff *n* 悬崖 xuányá

climate *n* 气候 qìhòu

climax *n* 高潮 gāocháo, 顶点 dǐngdiǎn

climb *v* 爬 pá

cling *v* (**clung, clung**) 紧贴 jǐntiē; 坚持 jiānchí

clinic *n* 诊所 zhěnsuǒ, 医务所 yīwùsuǒ

clip *v* (*cut*) 剪 jiǎn; *n* (*film*) 片断 piànduàn; (*newspaper*) 剪报 jiǎnbào

cloak *n* 斗蓬 dǒupéng; **cloak and dagger** 惊险场面 jīngxiǎn chǎngmiàn; **cloakroom** *n* 衣帽间 yīmàojiān

clock *n* 钟 zhōng; **alarm clock** 闹钟 nàozhōng; **against the clock** 争分夺秒地 zhēngfēn duómiǎo de; **around the clock** 日夜不停的 rìyè bùtíng de; **clockwise** *adv* 按顺时针地 àn shùnshízhēn de

clog *v* 堵塞 dǔsè

close *v* (*shut*) 关 guān; (*end*) 结束 jiéshù; **close in** 逼近 bījìn; **close up** (*advance*) 靠近 kàojìn; (*shut*) 关闭 guānbì; *adj* 亲近的 qīnjìn de, 近的 jìn de; 近距离地 jìnjùlí de

closet *n* 壁橱 bìchú

clot *n* (*blood*) 凝块 níngkuài

cloth *n* 布 bù

clothe *v* (**clothed/clad clothed/clad**) 给 ... 穿衣 gěi ... chuānyī; **clothes** *n* 衣服 yīfu; **clothing** *n* 衣服 yīfu

cloud *n* 云 yún; **cloudless** *adj* 无云的 wúyún de; **cloudy** *adj* 多云的 duōyún de

clown *n* 小丑 xiǎochǒu

club *n* 俱乐部 jùlèbù; 棍棒 gùnbàng; **clubfoot** *n* 畸形足 jīxíngzú

clue *n* 线索 xiànsuǒ

clumsy *adj* 笨拙的 bènzhuō de; **clumsiness** *n* 笨拙 bènzhuō

clung. *See* **cling**

cluster *v* 成群 chéngqún; *n* 串 chuàn, 丛 cóng

clutch *v* 抓住 zhuāzhù; *n* 离合器 líhéqì

clutter *v* 大声喧嚷 dàshēng xuānrǎng; *n* 混乱 hùnluàn

coach *v* (*tutor*) 辅导 fǔdǎo; *n* (*bus*) 长途汽车 chángtú qìchē; (*trainer*) 教练 jiàoliàn

coal *n* 煤 méi; **coal mine** 煤矿 méikuàng; **coal miner** 矿工 kuànggōng; **coalman** *n* 煤商 méishāng; 运煤工 yùnméigōng

coalesce *v* 合并 hébìng

coalition *n* 联盟 liánméng

coarse *adj* 粗糙的 cūcāo de

coast *n* 海岸 hǎi'àn; **coast guard** 海岸警卫队 hǎi'àn jǐngwèiduì; **coastal** *adj* 沿海的 yánhǎi de; **coastline** *n* 海岸线 hǎi'ànxiàn

coat *n* 大衣 dàyī, 外套 wàitào; **coat hanger** 衣架 yījià; **coat of paint** 涂层 túcéng; **coating** *n* 涂层 túcéng

coax *v* 哄骗 hǒngpiàn

cobra *n* 眼镜蛇 yǎnjìngshé

cobweb *n* 蜘蛛网 zhīzhūwǎng

cocaine *n* 可卡因 kěkǎyīn

cockpit *n* 座舱 zuòcāng

cockroach *n* 蟑螂 zhāngláng

cocktail *n* 鸡尾酒 jīwěijiǔ

cocoa *n* 可可粉 kěkěfěn, 可可豆 kěkědòu

coconut *n* 椰子 yēzi

cocoon *n* 茧 jiǎn

code *n* 密码 mìmǎ, 代号 dàihào

coeducation *n* 男女同校 nánnǚ tóngxiào

coerce *v* 强制 qiángzhì, 强迫 qiángpò; **coercion** *n* 强制 qiángzhì, 强迫 qiángpò

coexist *v* 共存 gòngcún, 共处 gòngchǔ

coffee *n* 咖啡 kāfēi; **coffee bean** 咖啡豆 kāfēidòu; **coffee pot** 咖啡壶 kāfēihú; **coffee shop** 咖啡馆 kāfēiguǎn; **coffee table** 咖啡桌 kāfēizhuō

coffin *n* 棺材 guāncai

cohabit *v* 同居 tóngjū; **cohabitation** *n* 同居 tóngjū

coherence *n* 连贯 liánguàn; **coherent** *adj* 连贯的 liánguàn de

coil *v* 盘绕 pánrǎo, 卷 juǎn

coin *n* 硬币 yìngbì

coincide *v* 相一致 xiāng yīzhì, 相符 xiāngfú; **coincidence** *n* 巧合 qiǎohé; 一致 yīzhì

cold *n* 感冒 gǎnmào, 伤风 shāngfēng; *adj* 冷的 lěng de; **cold front** 寒流 hánliú; **cold war** 冷战 lěngzhàn; **catch a cold** 感冒 gǎnmào; **cold-blooded** *adj* 冷血的 lěngxuè de

collaborate *v* 合作 hézuò; **collaboration** *n* 合作 hézuò

collapse *v/n* 倒塌 dǎotā, 崩溃 bēngkuì, 垮掉 kuǎdiào

collar *n* 衣领 yīlǐng

collate *v* 校对 jiàoduì

colleague *n* 同事 tóngshì

collect *v* 收 shōu; 收集 shōují, 收藏 shōucáng; **collection** *n* 收藏 shōucáng; (*rent, bills, etc.*) 追款 zhuīkuǎn, 收款 shōukuǎn; **collective** *adj* 集体的 jítǐ de

college *n* 学院 xuéyuàn

collide *v* 碰撞 pèngzhuàng; **collision** *n* 碰撞 pèngzhuàng

colloquial *adj* 口语的 kǒuyǔ de; 口语体的 kǒuyǔtǐ de

Colombia *n* 哥伦比亚 gēlúnbǐyà; **Colombian** *n* 哥伦比亚人 gēlúnbǐyàrén; *adj* 哥伦比亚的 gēlúnbǐyà de

colonel *n* 上校 shàngxiào

colony *n* 殖民地 zhímíndì; **colonist** *n* 殖民地开拓者 zhímíndì kāituòzhě; **colonialist** *n* 殖民主义者 zhímínzhǔyìzhě; **colonial** *adj* 殖民的 zhímín de

color *n* 颜色 yánsè; **color-blind** *adj* 色盲的 sèmáng de; **colorful** *adj* 多彩的 duōcǎi de

colossal *adj* 巨大的 jùdà de

column *n* (*newspaper, etc.*) 专栏 zhuānlán, 栏目 lánmù; (*pillar*) 圆柱 yuánzhù

coma *n* 昏迷 hūnmí

comb *v* 梳 shū; *n* 梳子 shūzi

combat *v/n* 战斗 zhàndòu

combine *v* 综合 zōnghé, 合并 hébìng; **combination** *n* 综合 zōnghé, 合并 hébìng

combustion *n* 燃烧 ránshāo; **combustible** *adj* 易燃的 yìrán de

come *v* (**came, come**) 来 lái; **come in** 进来 jìnlái; **come out** 出去 chūqù; (*publish*) 出版 chūbǎn

comedy *n* 喜剧 xǐjù; **comedian** *n* 喜剧演员 xǐjù yǎnyuán

comet *n* 彗星 huìxīng

comfort *n* 舒适 shūshì; **comfortable** *adj* 舒适的 shūshì de, 舒服的 shūfu de

comic *adj* 可笑的 kěxiào de, 滑稽的 huájī de

comma *n* 逗号 dòuhào

command *v/n* (*order*) 命令 mìnglìng, 指挥 zhǐhuī; (*mastery*) 掌握 zhǎngwò; **commander** *n* 司令员 sīlìngyuán, 指挥官 zhǐhuīguān; **commander-in-chief** *n* 最高统帅 zuìgāo tǒngshuài

commando *n* 突击队 tūjīduì

commemorate *v* 纪念 jìniàn; **commemoration** *n* 纪念 jìniàn; **commemorative** *adj* 纪念的 jìniàn de

commence *v* 开始 kāishǐ

commend *v* (*recommend*) 推荐 tuījiàn; (*praise*) 表扬 biǎoyáng; **commendation** *n* 表扬 biǎoyáng; **commendable** *adj* 值得称赞的 zhíde chēngzàn de

comment *v* 评论 pínglùn; *n* 评论 pínglùn, 意见 yìjian; **no comment** 无可奉告 wúkě fènggào; **commentary** *n* 评论 pínglùn

commerce *n* 商业 shāngyè; **commercial** *n* 广告 guǎnggào; *adj* 商业的 shāngyè de

commiserate *v* 怜悯 liánmǐn, 同情 tóngqíng

commission *v* 委托制作 wěituō zhìzuò; *n* 佣金 yòngjīn

commit *v* (*errors*) 犯 fàn; 承诺 chéngnuò; **commitment** *n* 承诺 chéngnuò; 承诺事项 chéngnuò shìxiàng; **committee** *n* 委员会 wěiyuánhuì

commodity *n* 商品 shāngpǐn

common *adj* 共同的 gòngtóng de, 普通的 pǔtōng de;
  commonplace *adj* 常见的事物 chángjiàn de shìwù;
  commonsense *adj* 具有常识的 jùyǒu chángshí de

commotion *n* 骚动 sāodòng, 暴乱 bàoluàn

communicate *v* 交际 jiāojì, 交流 jiāoliú; **communication** *n* 通信 tōngxìn; 交际 jiāojì

communism *n* 共产主义 gòngchǎnzhǔyì; **communist** *n* 共产主义者 gòngchǎnzhǔyìzhě; *adj* 共产党的 gòngchǎndǎng de

community *n* 社区 shèqū; 团体 tuántǐ

commute *v* (*travel*) 乘公交车上下班 chéng gōngjiāochē shàngxiàbān; **commuter** *n* 乘公交车上下班者 chéng gōngjiāochē shàngxiàbān zhě

compact *adj* 紧凑地 jǐncòu de, 小型的 xiǎoxíng de;
  compact disc 光盘 guāngpán

companion *n* 伴侣 bànlǚ

company *n* (*business*) 公司 gōngsī, (*companionship*) 陪伴 péibàn

compare *v* 比较 bǐjiào; **comparison** *n* 比较 bǐjiào;
  comparable *adj* 可比较的 kě bǐjiào de, 比得上的 bǐdé shàng de; **comparative** *adj* 比较的 bǐjiào de;
  comparatively *adv* 比较而言 bǐjiào éryán

compartment *n* 车厢 chēxiāng; 隔间 géjiān

compass *n* 指南针 zhǐnánzhēn

compassion *n* 同情 tóngqíng; **compassionate** *adj* 富于同情心的 fùyú tóngqíngxīn de

compatible *adj* 兼容的 jiānróng de; 一致的 yīzhì de; 协调的 xiétiáo de

compel *v* 强迫 qiǎngpò, 迫使 pòshǐ

compensate *v* 补偿 bǔcháng; 偿付 chángfù, 付报酬 fù bàochou; **compensation** *n* 补偿 bǔcháng, 报酬 bàochou

compete *v* 竞争 jìngzhēng, 比赛 bǐsài; **competition** *n* 比赛 bǐsài, 竞赛 jìngsài; **competitor** *n* 竞争者 jìngzhēngzhě, 竞争对手 jìngzhēng duìshǒu; **competitive** *adj* 竞争的 jìngzhēng de

competence *n* 能力 nénglì; **competent** *adj* 有能力的 yǒu nénglì de, 胜任的 shèngrèn de

compile *v* 编纂 biānzuǎn, 编辑 biānjí

complacence *n* 满足 mǎnzú, 自满 zìmǎn; **complacent** *adj* 自满的 zìmǎn de, 得意的 déyì de

complain *v* 抱怨 bàoyuàn; **complaint** *n* 抱怨 bàoyuàn, 诉苦 sùkǔ

complement *n* 补充 bǔchōng; (*gram*) 补语 bǔyǔ

complete *v* (*finish*) 完成 wánchéng; (*fill in*) 填写 tiánxiě; *adj* (*entire*) 全部的 quánbù de; (*whole*) 完整的 wánzhěng de; (*finished*) 完成的 wánchéng de; **completion** *n* 完成 wánchéng; **completely** *adv* 完全地 wánquán de, 彻底地 chèdǐ de

complex *n* 情结 qíngjié; *adj* 复杂的 fùzá de

complexion *n* 面色 miànsè; 肤色 fūsè

complicate *v* (使) 复杂 (shǐ) fùzá; **complicated** *adj* 复杂的 fùzá de

compliment *n* 称赞 chēngzàn, 恭维 gōngwéi; **complimentary** *adj* 赞美的 zànměi de

comply *v* 服从 fúcóng, 顺从 shùncóng

component *n* 成分 chéngfen

compose *v* (*music, etc.*) 创作 chuàngzuò; 组成 zǔchéng; **composer** 作曲家 zuòqǔjiā; **composition** *n* (*makeup*) 成分 chéngfen; (*essay*) 作文 zuòwén; **composed** *adj* 镇静的 zhènjìng de; **be composed of** 由 ... 组成 yóu ... zǔchéng; **composite** *adj* 合成的 héchéng de

compound *n* (*chem*) 混合物 hùnhéwù; (*enclosure*) 大院 dàyuàn

comprehend *v* 理解 lǐjiě; **comprehension** *n* 理解 lǐjiě; **comprehensible** *adj* 可理解的 kělǐjiě de

comprehensive *adj* 综合的 zōnghé de; 全面的 quánmiàn de

compress *v* 压缩 yāsuō

comprise *v* 包含 bāohán; 由 ... 组成 yóu ... zǔchéng

compromise *v/n* 妥协 tuǒxié

compulsory *adj* 强制的 qiángzhì de, 义务的 yìwù de; (*academic courses*) 必修的 bìxiū de

computer *n* 电脑 diànnǎo

comrade *n* 同志 tóngzhì

conceal *v* 隐瞒 yǐnmán, 隐藏 yǐncáng

concede *v* 让步 ràngbù; 承认 chéngrèn; **concession** *n* 让步 ràngbù

conceive *v* 怀孕 huáiyùn; 构思 gòusī; **conceive of** 构想出 gòuxiǎng chū; **conceivable** *adj* 可想象的 kě xiǎngxiàng de

concentrate *v* 专心致志 zhuānxīn zhìzhì; 浓缩 nóngsuō; 集中 jízhōng; **concentration** *n* 专心 zhuānxīn; 浓缩 nóngsuō; 浓度 nóngdù; 集中 jízhōng; **concentration camp** 集中营 jízhōngyíng

concept *n* 概念 gàiniàn

concern *n* 关心 guānxīn, 忧虑 yōulǜ; **concerned** *adj* 担心的 dānxīn de; 有关的 yǒuguān de

concert *n* 音乐会 yīnyuèhuì

concise *adj* 简明的 jiǎnmíng de

conciliate *v* 安慰 ānwèi; **conciliatory** *adj* 抚慰的 fǔwèi de

conclude *v* 结束 jiéshù, 终止 zhōngzhǐ; 下结论 xià jiélùn;
 conclusion *n* 结束 jiéshù; 结论 jiélùn; **conclusive** *adj*
 决定性的 juédìngxìng de

concrete *adj* 具体的 jùtǐ de

condemn *v* 谴责 qiǎnzé

condense *v* (使) 浓缩 (shǐ) nóngsuō; 精简 jīngjiǎn

condescend *v* 以恩赐态度对待 yǐ ēncì tàidu duìdài;
 condescending *adj* 以恩赐态度对待的 yǐ ēncì tàidu
 duìdài de

condition *n* 情况 qíngkuàng; 条件 tiáojiàn

condolences *n* 哀悼 āidào

condom *n* 避孕套 bìyùntào

condone *v* 容忍 róngrěn

conduct *v* 指导 zhǐdǎo; 指挥 zhǐhuī; 实施 shíshī; *n* (*tube*)
 行为 xíngwéi, 操行 cāoxíng; **conductor** *n* (*music*)
 乐队指挥 yuèduì zhǐhuī; (*bus*) 售票员 shòupiàoyuán;
 (*train*) 列车长 lièchēzhǎng

cone *n* 圆锥体 yuánzhuītǐ

confederate *n* 同盟者 tóngméngzhě, 同盟国 tóngméngguó;
 adj 同盟的 tóngméng de, 联合的 liánhé de;
 confederation *n* 同盟 tóngméng, 联盟 liánméng

confer *v* (*title, degree, etc.*) 授予 shòuyǔ, 赠与 zèngyǔ

conference *n* 会议 huìyì

confess *v* 坦白 tǎnbái, 招供 zhāogòng; **confession** *n* 坦白
 tǎnbái, 招供 zhāogòng

confide *v* 倾诉 qīngsù, 吐露 tǔlù

confidence *n* 信心 xìnxīn; **confident** *adj* 自信的 zìxìn de;
 confidential *adj* 机密的 jīmì de

confine *v* 限制 xiànzhì

confirm *v* 确认 quèrèn, 批准 pīzhǔn; **confirmation** *n* 确认
 quèrèn, 批准 pīzhǔn

confiscate *v* 没收 mòshōu; 征用 zhēngyòng

conflict *n* 冲突 chōngtū

conform *v* 遵照 zūnzhào

confound *v* (使) 混淆 (shǐ) hùnxiáo

confront *v* 对抗 duìkàng, 面对 miànduì; **confrontation** *n*
 对抗 duìkàng, 冲突 chōngtū

confuse *v* (使) 混乱 (shǐ) hùnluàn, (使) 困惑 (shǐ) kùnhuò,
 扰乱 rǎoluàn; **confusion** *n* 混乱 hùnluàn; **confused** *adj*

弄糊涂的 nòng hútu de, 困惑的 kùnhuò de; **confusing** *adj* 令人混淆的 lìng rén hùnxiáo de

congenial *adj* 令人愉快的 lìng rén yúkuài de, 适意的 shìyì de; (*pleasant*) 性格相似的 xìnggé xiāngsì de; (*suitable*) 适意的 shìyì de

congenital *adj* 天生的 tiānshēng de, 先天的 xiāntiān de

congested *adj* 拥挤的 yōngjǐ de

conglomeration *n* 混合体 hùnhétǐ

congratulate *v* 祝贺 zhùhè; **congratulation** *n* 祝贺 zhùhè; **congratulations!** *interj* 祝贺你! zhùhè nǐ

congregate *v* 聚集 jùjí; **congregation** *n* 集合 jíhé, 集会 jíhuì; (*religion*) 教堂会众 jiàotáng huìzhòng

congress *n* 代表大会 dàibiǎo dàhuì, 国会 guóhuì

conjecture *n* 推测 tuīcè, 猜想 cāixiǎng

conjugal *adj* 结婚的 jiéhūn de, 夫妻的 fūqī de

conjunction *n* 关联 guānlián; (*gram*) 连词 liáncí

connect *v* 联结 liánjié; **connection** *n* 连接 liánjiē, 联系 liánxì, 关系 guānxì

connoisseur *n* 鉴赏家 jiànshǎngjiā, 鉴定家 jiàndìngjiā, 内行 nèiháng

connotation *n* 含蓄 hánxù, 隐含意义 yǐnhán yìyì

conquer *v* 征服 zhēngfú, 克服 kèfú; **conquest** *n* 征服 zhēngfú

conscience *n* 良心 liángxīn, 道德心 dàodéxīn; **conscientiousness** *n* 认真 rènzhēn; **conscientious** *adj* 勤恳的 qínkěn de

conscious *adj* 有意识的 yǒu yìshíde, 有知觉的 yǒu zhījué de; **be conscious of** 知道 zhīdao, 意识到 yìshídào; **consciousness** *n* 意识 yìshí

conscript *n* 被征入伍的士兵 bèi zhēng rùwǔ de shìbīng

consecutive *adj* 连贯的 liánguàn de, 连续的 liánxù de

consecrate *v* (使) 神圣 (shǐ) shénshèng

consensus *n* 一致意见 yīzhì yìjian

consent *v/n* 同意 tóngyì

consequence *n* 后果 hòuguǒ; **consequently** *adv* 结果 jiéguǒ, 因此 yīncǐ

conserve *v* 保存 bǎocún, 保藏 bǎocáng; **conservation** *n* 保持 bǎochí, 保存 bǎocún; **conservatory** *n* 温室 wēnshì; (*music*) 音乐学校 yīnyuè xuéxiào

conservative *adj* 保守的 bǎoshǒu de

consider *v* 考虑 kǎolǜ; **consideration** *n* 考虑 kǎolǜ; 体谅 tǐliàng; **considerable** *adj* 可观的 kěguān de; **considerate** *adj* 考虑周到的 kǎolǜ zhōudào de

consist *v* 由 ... 组成 yóu ... zǔchéng; 在于 zàiyú

consolidate *v* 巩固 gǒnggù; **consolidation** *n* 巩固 gǒnggù, 合并 hébìng

console *n* 安慰 ānwèi, 慰藉 wèijié; **consolation** *n* 安慰 ānwèi, 慰藉 wèijié; **consolation prize** 安慰奖 ānwèijiǎng

consonant *n* 辅音 fǔyīn

consortium *n* 联盟 liánméng

conspicuous *adj* 显著的 xiǎnzhù de

conspire *v* 共谋 gòngmóu, 阴谋 yīnmóu; **conspiracy** *n* 阴谋 yīnmóu

constable *n* 警察 jǐngchá, 治安官 zhì'ānguān

constant *adj* 不变的 bùbiàn de, 持续的 chíxù de, 不断的 búduàn de

constipation *n* 便秘 biànmì

constitute *v* 组成 zǔchéng, 构成 gòuchéng; **constitution** *n* 宪法 xiànfǎ, 章程 zhāngchéng; 体格 tǐgé; **constitutional** *adj* 符合宪法的 fúhé xiànfǎ de

constraint *n* 约束 yuēshù, 限制 xiànzhì

constrict *v* 压缩 yāsuō; **constriction** *n* 压缩 yāsuō; **constricted** *adj* 收缩的 shōusuō de

construct *v* 建造 jiànzào; **construction** *n* 建设 jiànshè; 结构 jiégòu; **constructive** *adj* 建设性的 jiànshèxìng de

consul *n* 领事 lǐngshì

consulate *n* 领事馆 lǐngshìguǎn

consult *v/n* 咨询 zīxún; **consultant** *n* 顾问 gùwèn; **consultation** *n* 咨询 zīxún

consume *v* 消耗 xiāohào, 消费 xiāofèi, 花费 huāfèi; **consumer** *n* 消费者 xiāofèizhě; **consumer goods** 生活消费品 shēnghuó xiāofèipǐn; **consumption** *n* 消费 xiāofèi, 消耗 xiāohào

contact *v* 联系 liánxì; *n* 接触 jiēchù; 联系人 liánxìrén; **contact lens** 隐形眼镜 yǐnxíng yǎnjìng

contagious *adj* 传染的 chuánrǎn de

contain *v* 包含 bāohán; 牵制 qiānzhì; **container** *n* 容器 róngqì; (*package, receptacle transport*) 集装箱 jízhuāngxiāng

contaminate *v* 污染 wūrǎn; **contamination** *n* 污染 wūrǎn

contemplate *v* 沉思 chénsī

contemporary *adj* 当代的 dāngdài de

contempt *n* 蔑视 miǎoshì; **contempt of court** 蔑视法庭 mièshì fǎtíng

contend *v* (*compete*) 竞争 jìngzhēng; (*struggle*) 争斗

zhēngdòu; (*dispute*) 争辩 zhēngbiàn; *n* 争论 zhēnglùn;
论点 lùndiǎn; **contentious** *adj* 争论的 zhēnglùn de

content *n* (*substance*) 内容 nèiróng; (*table of contents*) 目录
mùlù; *adj* 满意的 mǎnyì de

contest *n* 竞赛 jìngsài

context *n* 上下文 shàngxiàwén, 语境 yǔjìng

continent *n* 大陆 dàlù; 陆地 lùdì; **the Continent (Europe)** *n*
欧洲大陆 ōuzhōu dàlù; **continental** *adj* 大陆的 dàlù de,
大陆性的 dàlùxìng de

contingency *n* 紧急情况 jǐnjí qíngkuàng, 意外 yìwài;
contingent *adj* (*accidental*) 意外的 yìwài de

continually *adv* 连续地 liánxù de, 不断地 bùduàn de

continue *v* 继续 jìxù; **continuous** *adj* 连续的 liánxù de,
持续的 chíxù de

contour *n* 轮廓 lúnkuò

contraband *n* 违禁品 wéijìnpǐn, 走私 zǒusī

contraception *n* 避孕 bìyùn; **contraceptive** *n* 避孕用具
bìyùn yòngjù

contract *v* (*shrink*) (使) 缩小 (shǐ) suōxiǎo; (*make a contract*)
签合同 qiān hétong; (*ailment*) 感染 gǎnrǎn; *n* 契约 qìyuē,
合同 hétong; **contractor** *n* 承包者 chéngbāozhě *adj*
契约的 qìyuē de

contradict *v* 反驳 fǎnbó; 与 ... 矛盾 yǔ ... máodùn;
contradiction *n* 反驳 fǎnbó; 矛盾 máodùn

contrary *n* 反面 fǎnmiàn; *adj* 相反的 xiāngfǎn de; **on the
contrary** 相反地 xiāngfǎn de

contrast *v* 对比 duìbǐ; *n* 对比 duìbǐ; **in contrast** 相反
xiāngfǎn

contribute *v* 贡献 gòngxiàn, 捐献 juānxiàn; (*write*) 投稿
tóugǎo; **contributor** *n* 投稿者 tóugǎozhě; 贡献者
gòngxiànzhě; **contribution** *n* 贡献 gòngxiàn, 捐献
juānxiàn; 投稿 tóugǎo

contrive *v* 设计 shèjì, 图谋 túmóu; **contrived** *adj* 人为的
rénwéi de, 做作的 zuòzuò de

control *v/n* 控制 kòngzhì, 支配 zhīpèi; **remote control** 遥控
yáokòng

controller *n* 审计官 shěnjìguān

controversial *adj* 有争议的 yǒu zhēngyì de

convenience *n* 便利 biànlì, 方便 fāngbiàn; **at your
convenience** 在你方便的时候 zài nǐ fāngbiàn de shíhou;
convenient *adj* 方便的 fāngbiàn de

convent *n* 女修道院 nǚxiūdàoyuàn

convention n (*meeting*) 大会 dàhuì; (*usage*) 惯例 guànlì; (*international agreement*) 公约 gōngyuē; **conventional** adj (*not original*) 常规的 chángguī de

converge v 聚集 jùjí, 会合 huìhé; **convergence** n 集中 jízhōng, 会合 huìhé

conversant adj 熟知的 shúzhī de, 熟悉的 shúxī de

converse v 谈话 tánhuà, 交谈 jiāotán; **conversation** n 会话 huìhuà, 交谈 jiāotán

convert v 转换 zhuǎnhuàn, 兑换 duìhuàn; **conversion** n 转变 zhuǎnbiàn, 转换 zhuǎnhuàn; **convertible** adj 可转换的 kě zhuǎnhuàn de 可兑换的 kě duìhuàn de; n 折篷汽车 zhépéng qìchē

convey v (*carry*) 搬运 bānyùn; (*relay*) 传达 chuándá; (*transmit*) 输送 shūsòng; **conveyance** n 运输 yùnshū

convict v 宣判 ... 有罪 xuānpàn ... yǒuzuì; n 罪犯 zuìfàn, 囚犯 qiúfàn

conviction n (*belief*) 确信 quèxìn; (*proving guilt*) 定罪 dìngzuì

convince v (使) ... 确信 (shǐ) ... quèxìn; (使) ... 信服 (shǐ) ... xìnfú

convoy n 车队 chēduì

cook v 做饭 zuòfàn; n 厨师 chúshī; **cooker** n 炊具 chuījù; **pressure cooker** 高压锅 gāoyāguō

cool adj 凉爽的 liángshuǎng de; (*excellent*) 极好的 jí hǎo de; **cooler** n 冷却器 lěngquèqì; **cooling** n 冷却 lěngquè; **cooling system** 冷却系统 lěngquè xìtǒng; **coolness** n 凉爽 liángshuǎng

cooperate v 合作 hézuò; **cooperation** n 合作 hézuò

coordinate v 协调 xiétiáo; **coordination** n 协调 xiétiáo; 协调员 xiétiáoyuán

cope v 应付 yìngfù

copious adj 很多的 hěn duō de, 丰富的 fēngfù de

copper n 铜 tóng; 铜币 tóngbì

copulate v 性交 xìngjiāo, 交配 jiāopèi

copy v 抄写 chāoxiě; 复印 fùyìn; n 副本 fùběn; **carbon copy** 副本 fùběn; **copy machine** 复印机 fùyìnjī

copyright n 版权 bǎnquán

cord n (*string, rope*) 绳索 shéngsuǒ; (*insulated wire*) 电线 diànxiàn; **spinal cord** 脊髓 jǐsuǐ; **umbilical cord** 脐带 qídài; **vocal cords** 声带 shēngdài

cordial adj 诚恳的 chéngkěn de, 热忱的 rèchén de

cordon n 警戒线 jǐngjièxiàn; **cordon off** 用警戒线隔离 yòng jǐngjièxiàn gélí

core n 核心 héxīn, 果核 guǒhé

cork *n* 瓶塞 píngsāi; *v* 用软木塞塞 yòng ruǎnmùsāi sāi;
  uncork *v* 拔去瓶塞 bá qù píngsāi; **corked** *adj* 塞着塞子的
  sāi zhe sāizi de; **corkscrew** *n* 瓶塞钻 píngsāi zuàn

corn *n* (*grain*) 玉米 yùmǐ; (*med*) 鸡眼 jīyǎn

corner *n* 角落 jiǎoluò; (*street*) 街角 jiējiǎo; **cut corners**
  抄近路 chāo jìnlù

coronary *adj* 花冠的 huāguān de, 冠状的 guānzhuàng de

corporal *adj* 肉体的 ròutǐ de, 身体的 shēntǐ de; **corporal**
  punishment 肉刑 ròuxíng, 体罚 tǐfá

corporation *n* 公司 gōngsī

corps *n* 军团 jūntuán; **diplomatic corps** 外交使团 wàijiāo
  shǐtuán

corpse *n* 尸体 shītǐ

correct *v* 改正 gǎizhèng; *adj* 正确的 zhèngquè de; **correction**
  n 更正 gēngzhèng

correlate *v* (使) 相互关联 (shǐ) xiānghù guānlián;
  correlation *n* 相互关系 xiānghù guānxì

correspond *n* (*write*) 通信 tōngxìn; **correspond with** 与 ...
  相当 yǔ ... xiāngdang; **correspondence** *n* 通信 tōngxìn;
  correspondent *n* 通讯员 tōngxùnyuán, 记者 jìzhě

corridor *n* 走廊 zǒuláng

corroborate *v* 证实 zhèngshí; **corroboration** *n* 确证
  quèzhèng, 旁证 pángzhèng

corrode *v* (使) 腐蚀 (shǐ) fǔshí; **corrosion** *n* 侵蚀 qīnshí

corruption *n* 腐败 fǔbài; **corrupt** *adj* 堕落的 duòluò de,
  腐败的 fǔbài de

cosmetics *n* 化妆品 huàzhuāngpǐn; **cosmetic** *adj* 化妆用的
  huàzhuāng yòng de, 美容的 měiróng de

cosmopolitan *adj* 世界性的 shìjièxìng de

cost *v* (**cost, cost**) 耗费 hàofèi; *n* 成本 chéngběn, 费用
  fèiyòng; **at all costs** 不惜代价 bùxī dàijià; **cost of living**
  生活费 shēnghuófèi; **costly** *adj* 昂贵的 ángguì de

Costa Rica *n* 哥斯达黎加 gēsīdálíjiā; **Costa Rican** *n*
  哥斯达黎加人 gēsīdálíjiārén; *adj* 哥斯达黎加的
  gēsīdálíjiā de

costume *n* 服装 fúzhuāng; 戏装 xìzhuāng

cot *n* 帆布床 fānbùchuáng, 轻便小床 qīngbiàn xiǎochuáng

cottage *n* 村舍 cūnshè

cotton *n* 棉花 miánhua

couch *n* 长沙发 cháng shāfā

cough *v/n* 咳嗽 késou

council *n* 议会 yìhuì, 理事会 lǐshìhuì, 委员会 wěiyuánhuì;
　　councilor *n* (*municiple*) 议员 yìyuán, 评议员 píngyìyuán
counsel *n* 商议 shāngyì, 忠告 zhōnggào; (*lawyer*) 律师 lùshī;
　　(*legal adviser*) 法律顾问 fǎlù gùwèn
count *v* 数 shǔ; **countdown** *n* 倒数计时 dàoshǔjìshí;
　　countless *adj* 无数的 wúshù de
countenance *n* 面容 miànróng, 脸色 liǎnsè; (*support*) 支持 zhīchí
counter *v* 反击 fǎnjī; *n* 柜台 guìtái
counterattack *n/v* 反击 fǎnjī, 反攻 fǎngōng
counterclockwise *adj* 逆时针的 nìshízhēn de
counterfeit *n* 赝品 yànpǐn; *adj* 伪造的 wěizào de
counterpart *n* 相对应的人 xiāngduì yīng de rén
country *n* 国家 guójiā; (*rural*) 乡村 xiāngcūn; **countryside** *n*
　　农村 nóngcūn
county *n* 县 xiàn
coup *n* 政变 zhèngbiàn
couple *n* 夫妻 fūqī, 一对 yīduì
coupon *n* 商家的优待券 shāngjiā de yōudàiquàn
courage *n* 勇气 yǒngqì
courier *n* 信使 xìnshǐ
course *n* (*direction*) 路线 lùxiàn; (*progress*) 进程 jìnchéng;
　　(*meal*) 一道菜 yī dào cài; **main course** 主菜 zhǔcài; **in**
　　due course 在一定的时候 zài yīdìng de shíhou; **of**
　　course 当然 dāngrán
court *n* (*royalty*) 宫廷 gōngtíng; (*law*) 法庭 fǎtíng; (*sport*)
　　球场 qiúchǎng; **court-martial** *n* 军事法庭 jūnshì fǎtíng;
　　courtship *n* 求爱 qiú'ài; **courtyard** *n* 院子 yuànzi
courtesy *n* 谦恭 qiāngōng, 礼貌 lǐmào; **courteous** *adj*
　　谦恭的 qiāngōng de, 有礼的 yǒulǐ de
cousin *n* 堂兄弟 tángxiōngdì; 堂姐妹 tángjiěmèi; 表兄弟
　　biǎoxiōngdì; 表姐妹 biǎojiěmèi
cover *v* 盖 gài; (*press*) 报道 bàodào; *n* (*book*) 封面 fēngmiàn;
　　(*lid*) 盖子 gàizi; **take cover** 隐蔽 yǐnbì
cow *n* 母牛 mǔniú; **cowboy** *n* 牛仔 niúzǎi
coward *n* 懦夫 nuòfū
coy *adj* 腼腆的 miǎntiǎn de, 怕羞的 pàxiū de
cozy *adj* 舒适的 shūshì de, 安逸的 ānyì de
crab *n* 螃蟹 pángxiè
crack *v* 破裂 pòliè, 打破 dǎpò; *n* 裂缝 lièfèng; **crack of**
　　dawn 破晓 pòxiǎo
cracker *n* (*food*) 饼干 bǐnggān; (*firecracker*) 爆竹 bàozhú
cradle *n* 摇篮 yáolán

craft *n* 工艺 gōngyì, 手艺 shǒuyì; **craftsman** *n* 工匠 gōngjiàng

cram *v* 填塞 tiánsāi

cramp *n* 抽筋 chōujīn

cranberry *n* 越橘 yuèjú

crane *n* (*bird*) 鹤 hè; (*machine*) 起重机 qǐzhòngjī

crash *v* (*collide*) 碰撞 pèngzhuàng, (*aeronautics*) 坠落 zhuìluò; *n* (*aeronautics*) 坠毁 zhuìhuǐ, (*collide*) 猛撞 měngzhuàng; **crash course** 速成班 sùchéngbān; **crash land** 强行着陆 qiángxíng zhuólù

crave *v* 渴望得到 kěwàng dédào; **craving** *n* 渴望 kěwàng

crawl *v* 爬 pá

crayon *n* 蜡笔 làbǐ

crazy *adj* 疯狂的 fēngkuáng de

cream *n* 奶油 nǎiyóu; **cream cheese** 奶油干酪 nǎiyóu gānlào

crease *n* 折缝 zhéfèng, 折痕 zhéhén; **crease-resistant** *adj* 抗皱的 kàngzhòu de

create *v* 创造 chuàngzào, 创作 chuàngzuò; **creation** *n* 创造 chuàngzào; 作品 zuòpǐn; **creator** *n* 创造者 chuàngzàozhě, 创作者 chuàngzuòzhě

creature *n* 生物 shēngwù

credential *n* 资格 zīgé

credibility *n* 可信性 kěxìnxìng; **credible** *adj* 可信的 kěxìn de

credit *n* 信用 xìnyòng; 功劳 gōngláo; **credit card** 信用卡 xìnyòngkǎ; **credit rating** 信用级别 xìnyòng jíbié; **on credit** 赊账 shēzhàng; **creditor** *n* 债权人 zhàiquánrén; **creditable** *adj* 可信的 kěxìn de

credulous *adj* 轻信的 qīngxìn de

creed *n* 宗教信条 zōngjiào xìntiáo, 教义 jiàoyì

creepy *adj* 令人毛骨悚然的 lìngrén máogǔsǒngrán de

cremate *v* 火葬 huǒzàng, 焚化 fénhuà; **cremation** *n* 火葬 huǒzàng

crest *n* 山顶 shāndǐng; **crest-fallen** *adj* 垂头丧气的 chuítóu sàngqì de

crew *n* (*plane*) 全体机务人员 quántǐ jīwùrényuán; (*ship*) 全体船员 quántǐ chuányuán; (*body of workers*) 全体人员 quántǐ rényuán; **ground crew** 地勤人员 dìqín rényuán

crib *n* 婴儿床 yīng'érchuáng

cricket *n* (*insect*) 蟋蟀 xīshuài; (*sport*) 板球 bǎnqiú

crime *n* 罪行 zuìxíng; **criminal** *n* 罪犯 zuìfàn; *adj* 犯罪的 fànzuì de

cringe *v* 畏缩 wèisuō

cripple *n* 跛子 bǒzi

crisis *n* (*pl* **crises**) 危机 wēijī

crisp *adj* 脆的 cuì de, 易碎的 yìsuì de

criterion *n* (*pl* **criteria**) 标准 biāozhǔn, 规范 guīfàn

critic *n* 批评者 pīpíngzhě; **critical** *adj* 持批评意见的 chí pīpíng yìjian de, 危急的 wēijí de

criticize *v* 批评 pīpíng; **criticism** *n* 批评 pīpíng

crockery *n* 陶器 táoqì, 瓦器 wǎqì

crocodile *n* 鳄鱼 èyú

crook *n* 骗子 piànzi

crooked *adj* 弯曲的 wānqū de, 歪斜的 wāixié de

crop *n* 庄稼 zhuāngjia

cross *v* 穿过 chuān guò; *n* 十字架 shízìjià; **cross one's mind** 想起 xiǎng qǐ; **cross out** 删去 shānqù; **crossbreeding** *n* 异种交配 yìzhǒng jiāopèi

cross-country *adj* 越野的 yuèyě de

crossfire *n* 交叉攻击 jiāochā gōngjī

crossing *n* (*road*) 人行横道 rénxíng héngdào; (*river*) 渡口 dùkǒu

crossroad *n* 十字路口 shízì lùkǒu

crouch *v* 蹲伏 dūnfú

crow *v* 啼叫 tíjiào; *n* 乌鸦 wūyā; **as the crow flies** 笔直地 bǐzhí de

crowd *n* 人群 rénqún; **crowded** *adj* 拥挤的 yōngjǐ de

crown *n* 王冠 wángguān; **crown jewels** 王冠 wángguān; **crown prince** 皇储 huángchǔ

crucial *adj* 至关重要的 zhìguān zhòngyào de, 关键的 guānjiàn de

crude *adj* 天然的 tiānrán de; 粗糙的 cūcāo de; 未加工的 wèi jiāgōng de

cruel *adj* 残酷的 cánkù de; **cruelty** *n* 残忍 cánrěn, 残酷 cánkù

cruise *v/n* 巡航 xúnháng, 漫游 mànyóu; **cruiser** *n* 巡洋舰 xúnyángjiàn

crumb *n* 碎屑 suìxiè

crumble *v* 崩溃 bēngkuì

crunch *n* 嘎吱嘎吱地咬嚼 gāzhīgāzhī de yǎojiáo; **crunchy** *adj* 松脆的 sōngcuì de

crusade *n* 宗教战争 zōngjiào zhànzhēng; 改革运动 gǎigé yùndòng

crush *v* 压碎 yāsuì, 粉碎 fěnsuì; **have a crush on** 迷恋 míliàn

crust *n* 外壳 wàiké; 面包皮 miànbāopí

crutch n 拐杖 guǎizhàng

crux n 症结 zhēngjié

cry v (*weep*) 哭 kū; (*call*) 喊 hǎn

crystal n 水晶 shuǐjīng; *adj* 晶莹的 jīngyíng de; **crystal clear** 极其明白的 jíqí míngbai de, 十分清楚的 shífēn qīngchu de; **crystallize** v 结晶 jiéjīng

Cuba n 古巴 gǔbā; **Cuban** n 古巴人 gǔbārén; *adj* 古巴的 gǔbā de

cube n 立方体 lìfāngtǐ; **cubic** *adj* 立方的 lìfāng de

cubicle n 小房间 xiǎo fángjiān

cuckoo n 杜鹃鸟 dùjuānniǎo, 布谷鸟 bùgǔniǎo

cucumber n 黄瓜 huángguā

cuddle v 依偎 yīwēi

cue n 暗示 ànshì, 提示 tíshì

cuff n 袖口 xiùkǒu; **cuff links** 袖口链扣 xiùkǒu liànkòu; **off the cuff** 即兴地 jíxìng de

cuisine n 烹饪 pēngrèn

culinary *adj* 烹饪的 pēngrèn de, 烹调用的 pēngtiáo yòng de

culminate v 达到顶点 dádào dǐngdiǎn; **culmination** n 顶点 dǐngdiǎn

culprit n 犯人 fànrén, 罪魁祸首 zuìkuí huòshǒu

cult n 邪教 xiéjiào; 狂热崇拜 kuángrè chóngbài

cultivate v (*person*) 培养 péiyǎng; (*land*) 耕作 gēngzuò; **cultivation** n (*person*) 培养 péiyǎng; (*land*) 耕作 gēngzuò

culture n 文化 wénhuà; **cultural** n 文化的 wénhuà de

cumbersome *adj* 麻烦的 máfan de, 笨重的 bènzhòng de

cunning *adj* 狡猾的 jiǎohuá de

cup n 杯子 bēizi

cupboard n 碗橱 wǎnchú

curator n 馆长 guǎnzhǎng, 展览策划人 zhǎnlǎn cèhuàrén

curb v 抑制 yìzhì; n 路边 lùbiān

curdle v 凝结 níngjié

cure v/n 治愈 zhìyù; **cure-all** n 万能药方 wànnéng yàofāng

curfew n 宵禁 xiāojìn

curious *adj* 好奇的 hàoqí de; **curiosity** n 好奇心 hàoqíxīn

curl v 卷曲 juǎnqū

currency n 货币 huòbì

current n (*elec*) 电流 diànliú; (*air*) 气流 qìliú; *adj* 目前的 mùqián de; **current affairs** 时事 shíshì; **currently** *adv* 目前 mùqián

curse v 诅咒 zǔzhòu; n 咒语 zhòuyǔ

curtail *v* 缩减 suōjiǎn; **curtailment** *n* 缩减 suōjiǎn, 缩短 suōduǎn

curtain *n* 帘子 liánzi; **curtain call** 谢幕 xièmù; **draw the curtain** 拉幕 lāmù

curve *n* 曲线 qūxiàn; **curved** *adj* 弯曲的 wānqū de, 曲线的 qūxiàn de

cushion *n* 垫子 diànzi

custody *n* 监护权 jiānhùquán; 看管 kānguǎn; **in custody** 被拘留 bèi jūliú; **take into custody** 拘留 jūliú; **custodian** *n* 监护人 jiānhùrén; 看门人 kānménrén

custom *n* 风俗 fēngsú; **custom-built** *adj* 定制的 dìngzhì de; **customer** *n* 顾客 gùkè; **customs** *n* 海关 hǎiguān; **customary** *adj* 习惯的 xíguàn de

cut *v* (**cut**, **cut**) 切 qiē, 割 gē; **cut off** 切断 qiēduàn; **cut short** (*shorten*) 缩短 suōduǎn; (*interrupt*) 中断 zhōngduàn; *n* (*wound*) 伤口 shāngkǒu; (*reduction*) 削减 xuējiǎn; 截止 jiézhǐ; **cut and dried** 呆板的 dāibǎn de; **shortcut** *n* 捷径 jiéjìng

cute *adj* 可爱的 kě'ài de

cutlery *n* 餐具 cānjù

cycle *n* 周期 zhōuqī, 循环 xúnhuán; **cycling** *n* 骑自行车 qí zìxíngchē; **cyclist** *n* 骑自行车者 qí zìxíngchē zhě; **cyclical** *adj* 循环的 xúnhuán de

cylinder *n* 圆柱 yuánzhù; 气缸 qìgāng

cynic *n* 愤世嫉俗者 fènshì jísú zhě; **cynicism** *n* 冷嘲热讽 lěngcháo rèfěng; **cynical** *adj* 愤世嫉俗的 fènshì jísú de

Czech *n* (*people*) 捷克人 jiékèrén; (*language*) 捷克语 jiékèyǔ; *adj* 捷克的 jiékè de; **Czech Republic** 捷克 jiékè

D

dad *n* 爸爸 bàba

dagger *n* 匕首 bǐshǒu

daily *n* (*newspaper*) 日报 rìbào; *adj* 每日的 měirì de, 日常的 rìcháng de

dairy *n* 乳制品 rǔzhìpǐn; **dairy farm** 乳牛场 rǔniúcháng; **dairy products** 乳制品 rǔzhìpǐn

dam *n* 水坝 shuǐbà

damage *v/n* 损害 sǔnhài

damn *v* (*condemn*) 谴责 qiǎnzé; (*curse*) 诅咒 zǔzhòu; **damned** *adj* 该死的 gāisǐ de

damp *adj* 潮湿的 cháoshī de; **put a damper on** (使) 扫兴 (shǐ) sǎoxìng

dance *v* 跳舞 tiàowǔ; *n* 舞蹈 wǔdǎo; **dancer** *n* 舞蹈家 wǔdǎojiā; **dance hall** 舞厅 wǔtīng

Dane *n* 丹麦人 dānmàirén; **Danish** *n* (*language*) 丹麦语 dānmàiyǔ; *adj* 丹麦的 dānmài de

danger *n* 危险 wēixiǎn; **dangerous** *adj* 危险的 wēixiǎn de

dangle *v* 悬吊 xuándiào

dare *v* 敢 gǎn; 挑战 tiǎozhàn; **daring** *adj* 大胆的 dàdǎn de

dark *adj* 黑暗的 hēi'àn de; **dark ages** 黑暗时代 hēi'àn shídài; **dark room** 暗室 ànshì; **be in the dark** 不知情 bù zhī qíng; **darken** *v* 涂黑 túhēi; **darkness** *n* 黑暗 hēi'àn

darling *n* 心爱的人 xīn'ài de rén

dash *v* 猛冲 měngchōng; *n* (*punctuation*) 破折号 pòzhéhào; **dash off** 匆忙完成 cōngmáng wánchéng; **dashboard** *n* (*cars, etc.*) 仪表盘 yíbiǎopán

data *n* 资料 zīliào, 数据 shùjù; **data processing** 数据处理 shùjù chǔlǐ; **database** *n* 数据库 shùjùkù

date *v* 写日期 xiě rìqī; 和 ... 谈恋爱 hé ... tánliàn'ài; *n* (*calendar*) 日期 rìqī; (*meeting*) 约会 yuēhuì; **up-to-date** 最新的 zuì xīn de; **out-of-date** 过时的 guòshí de

daughter *n* 女儿 nǚ'ér; **daughter-in-law** *n* 媳妇 xífù

daunt *v* 威吓 wēihè, 吓倒 xiàdǎo; **daunting** *adj* 令人望尔生畏的 lìng rén wàngěr shēngwèi de; **dauntless** *adj* 不屈不挠的 bùqū bùnáo de, 大胆的 dàdǎn de

dawn *v* 破晓 pòxiǎo; *n* 黎明 límíng; **from dawn to dusk** 从早到晚 cóng zǎo dào wǎn

day *n* 天 tiān, 日子 rìzi; **all day** 整天 zhěngtiān; **every day** 每天 měitiān; **the day after tomorrow** 后天 hòutiān; **the day before yesterday** 前天 qiántiān; **from day to day** 一天一天地 yī tiān yī tiān de; **daybreak** *n* 黎明 límíng; **daylight** *n* 白昼 báizhòu; **in broad daylight** 光天化日之下 guāngtiān huàrì zhīxià; **daydream** *n* 白日梦 báirìmèng

dazzle *v* (使) 眼花缭乱 (shǐ) yǎnhuā liáoluàn; 眩耀 xuànyào; **dazzling** *adj* 眼花缭乱的 yǎnhuā liáoluàn de; 耀眼的 yàoyǎn de

dead *adj* 死的 sǐ de; **deadly** *adj* 致命的 zhìmìng de

deadline *n* 截止时间 jiézhǐ shíjiān

deaf *adj* 聋的 lóng de; **turn a deaf ear** 充耳不闻 chōng'ěr bùwén; **deafening** *adj* 振耳欲聋的 zhèn'ěr yùlóng de; **deaf-mute** *n* 聋哑人 lóngyǎrén

deal *v* (**dealt, dealt**) (*business*) **deal in** 经营 jīngyíng; **deal with** (*discuss*) 论述 lùnshù; 对付 duìfu; 打交道 dǎjiāodao; (*treat*) 对待 duìdài, 处理 chǔlǐ; *n* (*business*) 交易 jiāoyì; (*treatment*) 待遇 dàiyù; (*amount*) 大量 dàliàng

dealer *n* 经销商 jīngxiāoshāng

dean *n* 院长 yuànzhǎng; 教务长 jiàowùzhǎng

dear *adj* 亲爱的 qīn'ài de

death *n* 死亡 sǐwáng; **death certificate** 死亡证明 sǐwáng zhèngmíng; **death penalty** 死刑 sǐxíng; **death rate** 死亡率 sǐwánglǜ

debase *v* 贬低 biǎndī, 降低 jiàngdī; **debasement** *n* 贬低 biǎndī, 降低 jiàngdī

debate *v/n* 辩论 biànlùn; **debatable** *adj* 可争议的 kě zhēngyì de

debit *v* 记入借方 jìrù jièfāng; *n* 借方 jièfāng, 借入 jièrù

debris *n* 碎片 suìpiàn; 残骸 cánhái

debt *n* 债 zhài; **run into debt** 债台高筑 zhàitái gāozhù; **debtor** *n* 债务人 zhàiwùrén

decade *n* 十年 shí nián

decadent *adj* 颓废 tuífèi

decapitate *v* 斩首 zhǎnshǒu

decay *v* 腐朽 fǔxiǔ, 衰退 shuāituì

decease *v* 死亡 sǐwáng; **deceased** *n* 死者 sǐzhě; *adj* 已故的 yǐgù de

deceive *v* 欺骗 qīpiàn; **deceit** *n* 欺骗 qīpiàn; **deceitful** *adj* 欺诈的 qīzhà de

December *n* 十二月 shí'èryuè

decency *n* 正派 zhèngpài, 得体 détǐ, 体面 tǐmiàn; **decent** *adj* 正派的 zhèngpài de, 得体的 détǐ de, 体面的 tǐmiàn de

deception *n* 欺骗 qīpiàn; **deceptive** *adj* 骗人的 piànrén de

decide *v* 决定 juédìng; **decision** *n* 决定 juédìng; **decisive** *adj* 决定性的 juédìngxìng de

decimal *adj* 十进位的 shíjìnwèi de; 小数的 xiǎoshù de; **decimal point** 小数点 xiǎoshùdiǎn

decipher *v* 译解 yìjiě

deck *n* 甲板 jiǎbǎn

declare *v* 宣布 xuānbù; **declaration** *n* 宣布 xuānbù

decline *v* (*an offer*) 谢绝 xièjué, 拒绝 jùjué; (*decrease*) 下降 xiàjiàng; (*med*) 衰退 shuāituì

decompose *v* 分解 fēnjiě; 腐烂 fǔlàn

decorate *v* 装饰 zhuāngshì; **decoration** *n* 装饰 zhuāngshì

decrease *v* 减少 jiǎnshǎo; *n* 减少 jiǎnshǎo; **decreasing** *adj* 减少的 jiǎnshǎo de

decree *n* 法令 fǎlìng, 判决 pànjué

dedicate *v* (*devote*) 致力 zhìlì; (*inscribe*) 题献 tíxiàn; **dedication** *n* (*devotion*) 奉献 fèngxiàn; (*inscription*) 献词 xiàncí

deduce *v* 推论 tuīlùn

deduct *v* (*discount*) 扣除 kòuchú; 演绎 yǎnyì; **deduction** *n* 演绎 yǎnyì; (*discount*) 扣除 kòuchú; **deductible** *n* 自付款 zìfùkuǎn

deed *n* 行为 xíngwéi, 作为 zuòwéi; (*law*) 契约 qìyuē

deep *adj* 深的 shēn de; **deep breathing** 深呼吸 shēnhūxī; **deep fry** 油炸 yóuzhà; **deep-sea** *adj* 深海的 shēnhǎi de

deer *n* 鹿 lù

default *n* 默认 mòrèn; (*debt*) 不履行责任 bù lǚxíng zérèn

defeat *v* 击败 jībài; *n* 失败 shībài

defect *n* 瑕疵 xiácī, 缺点 quēdiǎn; *v* 叛逃 pàntáo; **defective** *adj* 有缺点的 yǒu quēdiǎn de, 有毛病的 yǒu máobìng de

defend *v* 保卫 bǎowèi; **defendant** *n* 被告 bèigào; **defense** *n* 防御 fángyù; **self-defense** *n* 自卫 zìwèi; **defenseless** *adj* 无助的 wúzhù de; **on the defensive** 处于守势的 chùyú shǒushì de

defer *v* (*postpone*) 推迟 tuīchí; (*respect*) 听从 tīngcóng; **deference** *n* 顺从 shùncóng; 尊重 zūnzhòng; **in deference to** 服从 fúcóng; **deferential** *adj* 恭顺的 gōngshùn de

defiant *adj* 挑战的 tiǎozhàn de, 无畏的 wúwèi de, 蔑视的 mièshì de

deficient *adj* 不足的 bùzú de, 不完善的 bù wánshàn de

deficit *n* 不足额 bùzú'é, 赤字 chìzì

define *v* 下定义 xiàdìngyì, 阐明 chǎnmíng, 限定 xiàndìng

definite *adj* 明确的 míngquè de, 一定的 yīdìng de; **definitely** *adv* 明确地 míngquè de, 一定地 yīdìng de

deflate *v* 缩小 suōxiǎo, 紧缩 jǐnsuō

deform *v* (使) 变形 (shǐ) biànxíng; **deformation** *n* 变形 biànxíng

defrost *v* 解冻 jiědòng

defy *v* (*resist*) 违抗 wéikàng; (*challenge*) 藐视 miǎoshì

degenerate *v* 退化的 tuìhuà de; **degeneration** *n* 恶化 èhuà

degrade *v* (*rank*) (使) 降级 (shǐ) jiàngjí; (*quality*) (使) 退化 (shǐ) tuìhuà; **degradation** *n* (*rank*) 降级 jiàngjí; (*quality*) 退化 tuìhuà; **degrading** *adj* 可耻的 kěchǐ de

degree *n* (*academic*) 学位 xuéwèi; (*temperature*) 度 dù;

程度 chéngdù; **bachelor's degree** 学士 xuéshì; **doctor's degree** 博士 bóshì; **by degrees** 逐渐地 zhújiàn de

dehydrate v (使) 脱水 (shǐ) tuōshuǐ; **dehydration** n 脱水 tuōshuǐ

delay v/n (*postpone*) 推迟 tuīchí; (*make late*) 耽搁 dānge

delegate n 代表 dàibiǎo; **delegation** n 代表团 dàibiǎotuán

delete v 删除 shānchú

deliberate adj 故意的 gùyì de; **deliberately** adv 故意地 gùyì de

delicate adj 精巧的 jīngqiǎo de; (*health*) 脆弱的 cuìruò de

delicious adj 好吃的 hǎochī de

delight n 快乐 kuàilè, 愉快 yúkuài; **delightful** adj 令人愉快的 lìng rén yúkuài de

delinquency n (*conduct*) 行为不良 xíngwéi bùliáng, 错失 cuòshī; (*debt*) 拖欠债务 tuōqiàn zhàiwù; **delinquent** adj (*duty*) 失职的 shīzhí de; (*conduct*) 有过失的 yǒu guòshī de; (*law*) 违法的 wéifǎ de; (*debt*) 拖欠债务的 tuōqiàn zhàiwù de

delirious adj 神志昏迷的 shénzhì hūnmí de

deliver v (*goods, letters etc.*) 送 sòng; (*hand over*) 交付 jiāofù; (*speech*) 发表 fābiǎo; (*birth*) 接生 jiēshēng; **delivery** n (*goods*) 送货 sònghuò; (*birth*) 分娩 fēnmiǎn; (*speech*) 讲演 jiǎngyǎn

delve v 钻研 zuānyán; **delve into** 深入研究 shēnrù yánjiū

demand v/n 需求 xūqiú, 要求 yāoqiú

democracy n 民主 mínzhǔ; **Democrat** n 民主党人 mínzhǔdǎngrén; **democratic** adj 民主的 mínzhǔ de

demolish v 拆毁 chāihuǐ; **demolition** n 拆毁 chāihuǐ

demon n 邪魔 xiémó

demonstrate v (*show*) 示范 shìfàn; (*pol*) 示威 shìwēi; **demonstration** n (*show*) 示范 shìfàn; (*pol*) 示威 shìwēi

demoralize v 士气受挫 shìqì shòucuò

den n (*study*) 小室 xiǎoshì; (*of animals, etc.*) 兽穴 shòuxué

denial n 否认 fǒurèn

Denmark n 丹麦 dānmài

denomination n 名称 míngchēng; (*currency*) 面额 miàn'é; **denominator** n (*math*) 分母 fēnmǔ; 共同特性 gòngtóng tèxìng

denote v 表示 biǎoshì

denounce v 谴责 qiǎnzé, 抨击 pēngjī

dense adj 稠密的 chóumì de; **density** n 密度 mìdù

dent n 凹痕 āohén

dentist n 牙医 yáyī; **dental** adj 牙齿的 yáchǐ de

deny *v* 否认 fǒurèn

deodorant *n* 防臭剂 fángchòujì

depart *v* (*go away*) 离开 líkāi, (*set off*) 出发 chūfā;
    departure *n* 出发 chūfā, 离开 líkāi

department *n* (*college*) 系 xì, (*business*) 部门 bùmén;
    department store 百货公司 bǎihuò gōngsī

depend *v* 依靠 yīkào; **dependant** *n* 受抚养者 shòu fǔyǎng
    zhě, 家属 jiāshǔ; **dependable** *adj* 可靠的 kěkào de;
    dependent *adj* 依靠的 yīkào de, 取决于 ... 的 qǔjuéyú ... de

depict *v* 描述 miáoshù, 描写 miáoxiě; **depiction** *n* 描述
    miáoshù, 描写 miáoxiě

deplete *v* 耗尽 hàojìn, (使) 衰竭 (shǐ) shuāijié; **depletion** *n*
    耗尽 hàojìn

deplore *v* 对 ... 深感遗憾 duì ... shēngǎn yíhàn, 强烈反对
    qiángliè fǎnduì; **deplorable** *adj* 可悲的 kěbēi de, 悲惨的
    bēicǎn de, 应受谴责的 yīng shòu qiǎnzé de

deport *v* 驱逐出境 qūzhú chūjìng; **deportation** *n* 驱逐出境
    qūzhú chūjìng

depose *v* 罢免 bàmiǎn

deposit *v* (*bank*) 存款 cúnkuǎn; *n* (*security*) 押金 yājīn;
    (*money in account*) 存款 cúnkuǎn

depot *n* 仓库 cāngkù

deprave *v* 堕落 duòluò; **depravity** *n* 堕落 duòluò

depreciate *v* (*value*) 贬值 biǎnzhí, (*price*) 降低 jiàngdī;
    depreciation *n* 贬值 biǎnzhí

depression *n* 消沉 xiāochén, 萧条 xiāotiáo; **depressed** *adj*
    消沉的 xiāochén de, 沮丧的 jǔsàng de; **depressing** *adj*
    压抑的 yāyì de

deprive *v* 剥夺 bōduó; **deprivation** *n* 剥夺 bōduó

depth *n* 深度 shēndù; **out of one's depth** 不能理解的
    bùnéng lǐjiě de, 力所不及的 lìsuǒ bù jí de

deputy *n* 代表 dàibiǎo; 副手 fùshǒu

derail *v* 出轨 chūguǐ; **derailment** *n* 出轨 chūguǐ

derelict *adj* 失职的 shīzhí de

deride *v* 嘲笑 cháoxiào

derive *v* 起源于 qǐyuán yú, 取自 qǔzì

derogatory *adj* 贬损的 biǎnsǔn de

descend *v* 下降 xiàjiàng, 下落 xiàluò; **descendant** *n* 后代
    hòudài; **descent** *n* (*slope*) 降落 jiàngluò; (*lineage*) 血统
    xuètǒng

describe *v* 描写 miáoxiě; **description** *n* 描写 miáoxiě

desert *v* 离弃 líqì, 抛弃 pāoqì; *n* 沙漠 shāmò

deserve v 值得 zhíde, 应受 yīngshòu

design v/n 设计 shèjì; **designer** n 设计师 shèjìshī

designate v 指定 zhǐdìng, 指派 zhǐpài; **designation** n 指定 zhǐdìng, 选派 xuǎnpài

desire v 想要 xiǎng yào; n 欲望 yùwàng; **desirable** adj 合意的 héyì de, 可取的 kěqǔ de

desk n 书桌 shūzhuō

desolate adj 荒凉的 huāngliáng de

despair v/n 绝望 juéwàng

desperation n 绝望 juéwàng; **desperate** adj 不顾一切的 bùgù yīqiè de, 拼死的 pīnsǐ de

despise v 鄙视 bǐshì; **despicable** adj 卑劣的 bēiliè de

despite prep 尽管 jǐnguǎn

despot n 专制君主 zhuānzhì jūnzhǔ; **despotic** adj 专制的 zhuānzhì de, 暴虐 bàonüè de

dessert n 饭后甜点 fànhòu tiándiǎn

destination n 目的地 mùdìdì

destiny n 命运 mìngyùn

destitute adj 困穷的 kùnqióng de; **destitution** n 贫穷 pínqióng

destroy v 摧毁 cuīhuǐ; **destroyer** n 驱逐舰 qūzhújiàn; **destruction** n 破坏 pòhuài, 毁坏 huǐhuài

detach v 分开 fēnkāi, 分离 fēnlí; **detached** adj 分开的 fēnkāi de, 分离的 fēnlí de

detail n 细节 xìjié; **detailed** adj 详细的 xiángxì de

detain v 拘留 jūliú, 扣留 kòuliú; **detention** n 拘留 jūliú; **detention center** 拘留中心 jūliú zhōngxīn

detect v 察觉 chájué; **detection** n 察觉 chájué; **detective** n 侦探 zhēntàn; **detector** n 探测器 tàncèqì

deter v 阻止 zǔzhǐ, 阻骇 zǔhài; **deterrent** n 威慑 wēishè

detergent n 清洁剂 qīngjiéjì

deteriorate v 恶化 èhuà

determine v 决心 juéxīn, 决定 juédìng, 确定 quèdìng; **determination** n 决心 juéxīn, 决定 juédìng, 确定 quèdìng

detest v 憎恨 zēnghèn, 厌恨 yànhèn; **detestable** adj 可憎的 kězēng de

detonate v 引爆 yǐnbào; **detonation** n 爆炸 bàozhà

detour v/n 绕道 ràodào

detriment n 损害 sǔnhài; **detrimental** adj 有害的 yǒuhài de

devalue v 减值 jiǎnzhí, 贬值 biǎnzhí; **devaluation** n 贬值 biǎnzhí

devastate *v* 毁坏 huǐhuài, 摧毁 cuīhuǐ; **devastating** *adj* 破坏性的 pòhuàixìng de

develop *v* 发展 fāzhǎn, 开发 kāifā; **developer** *n* 开发商 kāifāshāng; **development** *n* 发展 fāzhǎn

deviate *v* 背离 bèilí, 偏离 piānlí; **deviation** *n* 背离 bèilí, 偏离 piānlí

device *n* 装置 zhuāngzhì

devil *n* 魔鬼 móguǐ; **devil's advocate** 故意唱反调的人 gùyì chàngfǎndiào de rén; **devilish** *adj* 恶魔般的 èmóbán de

devise *v* 设计 shèjì, 发明 fāmíng

devote *v* 致力 zhìlì; **devotion** *n* 献身精神 xiànshēnjīngshén

devour *v* 吞食 tūnshí, 吞没 tūnmò

dew *n* 露水 lùshuǐ

dexterity *n* 灵巧 língqiǎo; **dexterous** *adj* 灵巧的 língqiǎo de

diabetes *n* 糖尿病 tángniàobìng

diagnose *v* 诊断 zhěnduàn; **diagnosis** *n* 诊断 zhěnduàn

diagonal *adj* 斜的 xié de; **diagonally** *adv* 对角的 duìjiǎo de

diagram *n* 图表 túbiǎo

dial *v* 拨 bō; *n* 拨号盘 bōhàopán

dialect *n* 方言 fāngyán

dialogue *n* 对话 duìhuà

diameter *n* 直径 zhíjìng

diametrically *adv* 截然 jiérán, 完全 wánquán

diamond *n* 钻石 zuànshí

diaper *n* 尿布 niàobù

diarrhea *n* 腹泻 fùxiè

diary *n* 日记 rìjì

dice *n* 骰子 tóuzi

dictate *v* 口授 kǒushòu, 指令 zhǐlìng; **dictation** *n* 听写 tīngxiě

dictator *n* 独裁者 dúcáizhě; **dictatorship** *n* 专政 zhuānzhèng

dictionary *n* 字典 zìdiǎn

did. See **do**

die *v* 死 sǐ; **die away** 渐弱 jiàn ruò; **die down** 变弱 biàn ruò; **die out** 灭绝 mièjué

diesel *n* 柴油 cháiyóu; **diesel engine** 柴油机 cháiyóujī

diet *n* 饮食 yǐnshí, 食物 shíwù; **dietary** *adj* 饭食的 fànshí de; **dietician** *n* 营养师 yíngyǎngshī

differ *v* 不同 bùtóng; **difference** *n* 区别 qūbié, 分歧 fēnqí; **different** *adj* 不同的 bùtóng de

difficult *adj* 困难的 kùnnan de; **difficulty** *n* 困难 kùnnan

dig *v* (**dug, dug**) 挖 wā; **dig in** 挖进 wā jìn; **dig up** 掘起 jué qǐ

digest v 消化 xiāohuà; n (*summary*) 摘要 zhāiyào; **digestion** n 消化 xiāohuà

digit n 数字 shùzì; **digital** adj 数字的 shùzì de; 数码的 shùmǎ de

dignity n 尊严 zūnyán; **dignitary** n 贵宾 guìbīn; **dignified** adj 有威严的 yǒu wēiyán de

digress v 离题 lítí; **digression** n 离题 lítí

dilapidated adj 毁坏的 huǐhuài de, 破烂不堪的 pòlàn bùkān de

dilemma n 窘境 jiǒngjìng, 困境 kùnjìng

diligence n 勤勉 qínmiǎn; **diligent** adj 勤勉的 qínmiǎn de, 勤劳的 qínláo de

dilute v 稀释 xīshì

dim adj 昏暗的 hūn'àn de, 模糊的 móhu de

dimension n 尺寸 chǐcùn, 长宽高 chángkuāngāo; 方面 fāngmiàn

diminish v 变小 biàn xiǎo; 减少 jiǎnshǎo

diminutive n 爱称 àichēng, 昵称 nìchēng; adj 微小的 wēixiǎo de

dine v 用餐 yòngcān; **dining car** 餐车 cānchē; **dining room** 餐厅 cāntīng

dinner n 晚饭 wǎnfàn; **dinner table** 饭桌 fànzhuō

dinosaur n 恐龙 kǒnglóng

dip v 蘸 zhàn, 浸 jìn; (*drop*) 下降 xiàjiàng

diploma n 文凭 wénpíng

diplomacy n 外交 wàijiāo; **diplomat** n 外交官 wàijiāoguān; **diplomatic** adj 外交的 wàijiāo de; **diplomatic corps** 外交使团 wàijiāo shǐtuán; **diplomatic immunity** 外交豁免权 wàijiāo huōmiǎnquán

dire adj 可怕的 kěpà de

direct v 指挥 zhǐhuī; 指路 zhǐlù; 指导 zhǐdǎo; **direction** n 方向 fāngxiàng; **directions** n 指示 zhǐshì; **director** n 主任 zhǔrèn; (*movie*) 导演 dǎoyǎn; 主管 zhǔguǎn; **board of directors** 董事会 dǒngshìhuì; **directly** adv 直接地 zhíjiē de

directory n 通讯录 tōngxùnlù, 号码簿 hàomǎbù

dirt n 灰尘 huīchén, 泥土 nítǔ; **dirt cheap** adj 极便宜的 jí piányi de; **dirty** adj 脏的 zāng de; **dirty trick** 卑鄙行为 bēibǐ xíngwéi

disability n 伤残 shāngcán; **disabled** adj 伤残的 shāngcán de

disadvantage n 不利 bùlì, 劣势 lièshì; **be at a disadvantage** 处于劣势 chùyú lièshì

disagree v 不同意 bù tóngyì; **disagreement** n 分歧 fēnqí; **disagreeable** adj 令人厌恶的 lìng rén yànwù de

disappear v 消失 xiāoshī, 失踪 shīzōng; **disappearance** n 消失 xiāoshī, 失踪 shīzōng

disappoint v (使) 失望 (shǐ) shīwàng; **disappointment** n 失望 shīwàng; **disappointed** adj 失望的 shīwàng de

disapprove v 不赞成 bù zànchéng; **disapproval** n 不赞成 bù zànchéng

disarm v 裁军 cáijūn; 解除武装 jiěchú wǔzhuāng; **disarmament** n 裁军 cáijūn

disaster n 灾难 zāinàn; **disastrous** adj 灾难性的 zāinànxìng de

disband v 解散 jiěsàn

disbelief n 怀疑 huáiyí, 难以置信 nányǐ zhìxìn

disc n 圆盘 yuánpán; 唱片 chàngpiàn

discard v 丢弃 diūqì

discern v 辨别 biànbié; **discernible** adj 可辨别的 kě biànbié de; **discerning** adj 有辨别能力的 yǒu biànbié nénglì de

discharge v 卸下 xiè xià; (duty) 履行 lǚxíng; (dismiss) 解雇 jiěgù

disciple n 信徒 xìntú, 弟子 dìzǐ

discipline v 管教 guǎnjiào; n 纪律 jìlǜ; (subject of study) 学科 xuékē

disclaim v 放弃 fàngqì; **disclaimer** n 不承担责任的声明 bù chéngdān zérèn de shēngmíng

disclose v 揭露 jiēlù, 透露 tòulù, 公布 gōngbù; **disclosure** n 公布 gōngbù

discomfort n 不适 bùshì

disconnect v 分离 fēnlí, 断开 duànkāi; **disconnection** n 断开 duànkāi

discontinue v 停止 tíngzhǐ, 废止 fèizhǐ

discord n 不和 bùhé

discount n 折扣 zhékòu

discourage v (使) 气馁 (shǐ) qì'něi, 阻碍 zǔ'ài; **discouragement** n 气馁 qì'něi, 挫折 cuòzhé; **discouraging** adj 令人气馁的 lìng rén qì'něi de

discover v 发现 fāxiàn; **discovery** n 发现 fāxiàn

discredit v 怀疑 huáiyí

discretion n 判断力 pànduànlì; **at sb.'s discretion** 随 ... 意 suí ... yì; **discreet** adj 谨慎的 jǐnshèn de

discrepancy n 出入 chūrù, 矛盾 máodùn

discrete adj 不连续的 bù liánxù de, 离散的 lísàn de

discriminate v 歧视 qíshì, 区别 qūbié; **discriminate against** 歧视 qíshì; **discrimination** n 歧视 qíshì; **discriminatory** adj 有辨别力的 yǒu biànbiélì de

discuss *v* 讨论 tǎolùn; **discussion** *n* 讨论 tǎolùn

disease *n* 疾病 jíbìng

disembark *v* 下船 xiàchuán

disengage *v* 脱离 tuōlí

disfigure *v* 毁容 huǐróng

disgrace *v* 给 ... 丢脸 gěi ... diūliǎn; *n* 耻辱 chǐrǔ; **disgraceful** *adj* 可耻的 kěchǐ de; 不名誉的 bù míngyù de

disgruntled *adj* 不满的 bùmǎn de, 不高兴的 bù gāoxìng de

disguise *v* 伪装 wěizhuāng; *n* 伪装品 wěizhuāngpǐn

disgust *v* (使) 厌恶 (shǐ) yànwù; *n* 厌恶 yànwù; **disgusted** *adj* 厌恶的 yànwù de; **disgusting** *adj* 令人厌恶的 lìng rén yànwù de

dish *n* (*plate*) 盘子 pánzi; (*food*) 菜 cài; **dish out** 盛于盘中 chéng yú pán zhōng; (*fig*) 抛出 pāo chū; **dishwasher** *n* 洗碗机 xǐwǎnjī

dishearten *v* (使) 气馁 (shǐ) qì'něi; **disheartening** *adj* 使人沮丧的 shǐ rén jǔsàng de

dishonesty *n* 欺诈 qīzhà; **dishonest** *adj* 不诚实的 bù chéngshí de

disk *n* 磁盘 cípán

dislike *v* 不喜欢 bù xǐhuan

disillusion *v* 醒悟 xǐngwù

disinfect *v* 消毒 xiāodú; **disinfectant** *n* 消毒剂 xiāodújì

disintegrate *v* (使) 分解 (shǐ) fēnjiě; **disintegration** *n* 瓦解 wǎjiě

dislocate *v* 脱臼 tuōjiù

disloyal *adj* 不忠的 bù zhōng de

dismal *adj* 阴沉的 yīnchén de

dismantle *v* 拆除 chāichú

dismay *n* 沮丧 jǔsàng

dismiss *v* 开除 kāichú; 解散 jiěsàn; 下课 xiàkè; 打发 dǎfa; **dismissal** *n* 开除 kāichú; 解散 jiěsàn

disobey *v* 不服从 bù fúcóng; **disobedience** *n* 不服从 bù fúcóng, 违抗 wéikàng; **disobedient** *adj* 不服从的 bù fúcóng de

disorganize *v* 扰乱 rǎoluàn; **disorganization** *n* 瓦解 wǎjiě, 解体 jiětǐ

disparage *v* 蔑视 mièshì; **disparagement** *n* 轻蔑 qīngmiè

disparity *n* 不一致 bù yīzhì

dispassionate *adj* 平心静气的 píngxīn jìngqì de

dispel *v* 驱散 qūsàn

disprove *v* 反驳 fǎnbó

distaste *n* 嫌恶 xiánwù; **distasteful** *adj* 讨厌的 tǎoyàn de,
低级趣味的 dījí qùwèi de

disorder *n* 混乱 hùnluàn

dispatch *v* 派遣 pàiqiǎn

dispensary *n* 医务室 yīwùshì; 药房 yàofáng

dispense *v* 分发 fēnfā; **dispense with** 免除 miǎnchú;
dispensable *adj* 可有可无的 kěyǒu kěwú de

displace *v* (*move*) 移置 yízhì; (*replace*) 取代 qǔdài

display *v/n* 陈列 chénliè, 展览 zhǎnlǎn, 显示 xiǎnshì

displease *v* (使) 不快 (shǐ) bùkuài, 冒犯 màofàn

dispose *v* 处置 chǔzhì; **dispose of** 处理 chǔlǐ; **disposal** *n*
处置 chǔzhì; **disposable** *adj* 使用后即可抛弃的 shǐyòng
hòu jíkě pāoqì de, 一次性的 yīcìxìng de

dispute *n* 争论 zhēnglùn, 争执 zhēngzhí

disqualify *v* (使) 丧失资格 (shǐ) sàngshī zīgé, 取消资格
qǔxiāo zīgé

disregard *v* 忽视 hūshì, 不理睬 bù lǐcǎi

disrespect *n* 失礼 shīlǐ, 无礼 wúlǐ; **disrespectful** *adj* 无礼的
wúlǐ de

disrupt *v* 搅乱 jiǎoluàn, 干扰 gānrǎo, 中断 zhōngduàn;
disruption *n* 搅乱 jiǎoluàn, 打断 dǎduàn; **disruptive** *adj*
破坏性的 pòhuàixìng de

dissatisfy *v* (使) 不满 (shǐ) bùmǎn; **dissatisfaction** *n* 不满
bùmǎn

dissect *v* 把 ... 解剖 bǎ ... jiěpōu; **dissection** *n* 解剖 jiěpōu

dissent *n* 异议 yìyì; **dissident** *n* 持不同政见者 chí bùtóng
zhèngjiàn zhě

dissolve *v* (使) 溶解 (shǐ) róngjiě; 解散 jiěsàn

distance *n* 距离 jùlí; **distant** *adj* 远的 yuǎn de

distill *v* 蒸馏 zhēngliú; 提取 ... 的精华 tíqǔ ... de jīnghuá

distinct *adj* 清楚的 qīngchu de, 明显的 míngxiǎn de;
distinction *n* (*difference*) 差别 chābié, 区别 qūbié;
(*honor*) 显赫 xiǎnhè; **distinctive** *adj* 有特色的 yǒu tèsè de,
区别性的 qūbiéxìng de

distinguish *v* 区别 qūbié; **distinguished** *adj* 著名的
zhùmíng de, 高贵的 gāoguì de, 杰出的 jiéchū de

distort *v* 歪曲 wāiqū; **distortion** *n* 歪曲 wāiqū

distract *v* 转移 zhuǎnyí; **distraction** *n* 分心 fēnxīn

distraught *adj* 发狂的 fākuáng de

distress *n* (*grief*) 悲痛 bēitòng; (*trouble*) 危难 wēinàn;
distressed *adj* 哀伤的 āishāng de; **distressing** *adj*

令人痛苦的 lìng rén tòngkǔ de, 令人烦恼的 lìng rén fánnǎo de

distribute v 分发 fēnfā, 分布 fēnbù; 发行 fāxíng; **distribution** n 分发 fēnfā, 分布 fēnbù; 发行 fāxíng; **distributor** n 批发商 pīfāshāng

district n 区 qū

distrust v/n 不信任 bù xìnrèn

disturb v 打乱 dǎluàn, 干扰 gānrǎo; **disturbance** n 干扰 gānrǎo, 骚乱 sāoluàn; **disturbing** adj 令人不安的 lìng rén bù ān de

dissuade v 劝阻 quànzǔ

disuse n 废弃不用 fèiqì bùyòng

ditch n 沟 gōu

dive v (**dove/dived**, **dived**) 跳水 tiàoshuǐ; 潜水 qiánshuǐ; **diver** n 潜水员 qiánshuǐyuán; **diving** n 潜水 qiánshuǐ

diverge v 分歧 fēnqí; **divergence** n 分歧 fēnqí; **divergent** adj 分歧的 fēnqí de, 不同的 bùtóng de

diverse adj 不同的 bùtóng de, 多样化的 duōyànghuà de; **diversity** n 多样化 duōyànghuà

divert v 转移 zhuǎnyí, 转向 zhuǎnxiàng; **diversion** n 转移 zhuǎnyí; 消遣 xiāoqiǎn

divide v 分 fēn; **division** n 分割 fēngē; (*math*) 除法 chúfǎ; (*department*) 部门 bùmén; **dividend** n (*math*) 被除数 bèichúshù; (*investment*) 股息 gǔxī, 红利 hónglì

divine adj 神的 shén de

divorce v 与 ... 离婚 yǔ ... líhūn; n 离婚 líhūn; **divorced** adj 离了婚的 lí le hūn de

dizzy adj 眩晕的 xuànyūn de; **dizziness** n 眩晕 xuànyūn

do v (**did**, **done**) 做 zuò; **do away with** 废除 fèichú; **do without** 免除 miǎnchú; **how do you do**? 你好吗? nǐ hǎo ma; **make do with** 设法应付 shèfǎ yìngfù; 凑合 còuhe

docile adj 温顺的 wēnshùn de

dock n 船坞 chuánwù, 码头 mǎtou

doctor n (*medical*) 医生 yīshēng; (*university degree*) 博士 bóshì; **doctorate** n 博士学位 bóshì xuéwèi

doctrine n 教条 jiàotiáo, 学说 xuéshuō

document n 文件 wénjiàn; **documentary** n 纪录片 jìlùpiàn

dodge v 躲避 duǒbì

dog n 狗 gǒu; **dogged** adj 顽固的 wángù de

dogma n 教条 jiàotiáo; **dogmatic** adj 教条的 jiàotiáo de

dole n 施舍品 shīshěpǐn; **dole out** 少量发放 shǎoliàng fāfàng

doll n 洋娃娃 yángwáwa

dollar *n* 美元 měiyuán

dolphin *n* 海豚 hǎitún

domain *n* 领地 lǐngdì, 领域 lǐngyù

dome *n* 圆顶 yuándǐng

domestic *adj* (*home*) 家里的 jiālǐ de; (*country*) 国内的 guónèi de; **domestic animal** 家畜 jiāchù; **domestic help** 佣工 yōnggōng

dominate *v* 支配 zhīpèi, 占优势 zhàn yōushì; **domination** *n* 统治 tǒngzhì, 支配 zhīpèi; **dominant** *adj* 垄断的 lǒngduàn de

donate *v* 捐赠 juānzèng; **donation** *n* 捐赠品 juānzèngpǐn

done. *See* **do**

donkey *n* 驴 lǘ

donor *n* 捐赠者 juānzèngzhě

doom *n* 死亡 sǐwáng; 厄运 èyùn; **doomsday** *n* 世界末日 shìjiè mòrì

door *n* 门 mén; **next door** 隔壁 gébì; **doorbell** *n* 门铃 ménlíng; **doorknob** *n* 门把手 ménbǎshǒu; **doorstep** *n* 门阶 ménjiē; **doorway** *n* 门口 ménkǒu

dormant *adj* 静止的 jìngzhǐ de

dormitory *n* 宿舍 sùshè

dose *n* 剂量 jìliàng

dot *n* 点 diǎn, 圆点 yuándiǎn; **on the dot** 准时地 zhǔnshí de

dote *v* 溺爱 nì'ài; **doting** *adj* 溺爱的 nì'ài de

double *v* 加倍 jiābèi; *adj* 两倍的 liǎngbèi de; **double bed** 双人床 shuāngrénchuáng; **double room** 双人房 shuāngrénfáng

doubt *v/n* 怀疑 huáiyí; **no doubt** 无疑地 wúyí de; **doubtful** *adj* 可疑的 kěyí de; **doubtless** *adv* 无疑地 wúyí de

dough *n* 面团 miàntuán

dove *n* 鸽子 gēzi

down *n* (*fine hair*) 绒毛 róngmáo; *adv* 下 xià; 往下 wǎng xià; **down payment** 头款 tóukuǎn

downfall *n* 垮台 kuǎtái; (*rain*) 大雨 dàyǔ

downhill *adj* 下坡的 xiàpō de; *adv* 每况愈下 měikuàng yùxià

download *v* 下载 xiàzǎi

downpour *n* 倾盆大雨 qīngpén dàyǔ

downright *adj* 率直的 shuàizhí de, 显明的 xiǎnmíng de

downstairs *adv* 在楼下 zài lóuxià; 往楼下 wǎng lóuxià

downstream *adv* 在下游 zài xiàyóu; 向下游 xiàng xiàyóu

downward *adv* 向下地 xiàng xià de

dowry *n* 嫁妆 jiàzhuang

doze *v* 打瞌睡 dǎ kēshuì

dozen *n* 一打 yīdǎ, 十二个 shí'èr gè

draft *v* 起草 qǐcǎo; *n* 草稿 cǎogǎo

drag *v* 拖 tuō, 拉 lā

dragon *n* 龙 lóng

dragonfly *n* 蜻蜓 qīngtíng

drain *v* 排水 páishuǐ, 流失 liúshī, 耗尽 hàojìn; *n* 排水 páishuǐ; 负担 fùdān

drama *n* 戏剧 xìjù; **dramatic** *adj* 戏剧性的 xìjùxìng de

drank. *See* **drink**

drastic *adj* 猛烈的 měngliè de, 剧烈的 jùliè de

draught *v see* **draft**; *n* 通风气流 tōngfēng qìliú

draw *v* (**drew, drawn**) (*paint*) 画 huà; (*attract*) 吸引 xīyǐn; **drawing** *n* 图画 túhuà; **drawing board** 画板 huàbǎn

drawback *n* 缺点 quēdiǎn

drawer *n* 抽屉 chōuti

drawn. *See* **draw**

dread *v* 惧怕 jùpà, 担心 dānxīn; **dreadful** *adj* 可怕的 kěpà de, 讨厌的 tǎoyàn de

dream *v* (**dreamed/dreamt, dreamed/dreamt**) 做梦 zuòmèng; *n* 梦 mèng

dreary *adj* 沉闷的 chénmèn de; **dreariness** *n* 凄凉 qīliáng

drench *v* 湿透 shītòu

dress *v* 穿衣 chuānyī; **dress up** 打扮 dǎban; *n* 连衣裙 liányíqún; **dress rehearsal** 彩排 cǎipái; (*furniture*) **dresser** *n* 梳妆台 shūzhuāngtái; **dressmaker** *n* 裁缝 cáifeng

drift *v* 漂流 piāoliú

drill *v* 操练 cāoliàn, (*bore*) 钻孔 zuànkǒng; *n* (*practice*) 操练 cāoliàn

drink *v* (**drank, drunk**) 喝 hē; 喝酒 hē jiǔ; *n* 饮料 yǐnliào; 酒 jiǔ; **soft drink** 不含酒精的饮料 bù hán jiǔjīng de yǐnliào; **drinking water** 饮用水 yǐnyòngshuǐ

drip *v/n* 滴水 dīshuǐ

drive *v* (**drove, driven**) 开车 kāichē; **drive away** 赶走 gǎnzǒu; **driver** *n* 司机 sījī; **driving** *n* 驾驶 jiàshǐ; **driver's license** 驾驶执照 jiàshǐ zhízhào; **driving school** 驾驶学校 jiàshǐ xuéxiào

drizzle *v* 下毛毛雨 xià máomaoyǔ; *n* 细雨 xìyǔ

droop *v* 低垂 dīchuí

drop *v* 落下 luò xià, 下降 xiàjiàng; **drop behind** 落后 luòhòu; **drop dead** 倒毙 dǎobì; **drop in on** 顺道拜访

shùndào bàifǎng; **drop off** 下降 xiàjiàng; **dropout** *n* 退学生 tuìxué xuésheng

drought *n* 干旱 gānhàn

drove. *See* **drive**

drown *v* 淹死 yānsǐ

drowsy *adj* 昏昏欲睡的 hūnhūn yùshuì de

drug *n* (*narcotics*) 毒品 dúpǐn; (*medicine*) 药 yào; **drug addiction** 毒瘾 dúyǐn; **drugstore** *n* 药房 yàofáng

drum *n* 鼓 gǔ; **drummer** *n* 鼓手 gǔshǒu

drunk *adj* 喝醉的 hēzuì de; **get drunk** 喝醉 hēzuì

dry *v* 弄干 nònggān; **dry-clean** *v* 干洗 gānxǐ; *adj* 干的 gān de; **dryer** *n* 烘干机 hōnggānjī

dual *adj* 双的 shuāng de, 二重的 èrchóng de; **dual-purpose** *adj* 两用的 liǎngyòng de

dub *v* (*film*) 配音 pèiyīn

dubious *adj* 疑惑的 yíhuò de, 靠不住的 kàobuzhù de

duck *v* 躲避 duǒbì; *n* 鸭子 yāzi

due *adj* 应得的 yīngdé de; 到期的 dàoqī de; **due to** 由于 yóuyú, 因为 yīnwèi; **dues** *n* (*membership*) 会员费 huìyuánfèi

duel *n* 决斗 juédòu

duet *n* 二重奏 èrchóngzòu

dug. *See* **dig**

dull *adj* (*object*) 钝的 dùn de; (*person*) 呆笨的 dāibèn de

dumb *adj* (*mute*) 哑的 yǎ de; (*stupid*) 笨的 bèn de; **dumbfound** *v* (使) 发愣 (shǐ) fālèng; **dumbfounded** *adj* 目瞪口呆的 mùdèng kǒudāi de

dummy *n* 哑巴 yǎba; 笨人 bènrén; 虚设物 xūshèwù

dump *v* 丢弃 diūqì, 倾卸 qīngxiè; *n* 垃圾场 lājīchǎng

dumpling *n* 饺子 jiǎozi

dung *n* 粪便 fènbiàn

duplicate *v* 复制 fùzhì; *n* 复制品 fùzhìpǐn, 完全一样的东西 wánquán yīyàng de dōngxi

durable *adj* 持久的 chíjiǔ de, 耐用的 nàiyòng de; **durability** *n* 耐久力 nàijiǔlì

duration *n* 期间 qījiān

during *prep* 在 ... 期间 zài ... qījiān

dusk *n* 黄昏 huánghūn

dust *n* 尘土 chéntǔ; **dustbin** *n* 垃圾箱 lājīxiāng; **dustpan** *n* 簸箕 bòji

Dutch *n* 荷兰人 hélánrén; *adj* 荷兰的 hélán de

duty *n* (*responsibility*) 职责 zhízé; (*tax*) 税 shuì; **off duty**

不当班的 bù dāngbān de; **on duty** 当班的 dāngbān de, 值班的 zhíbān de; **dutiful** *adj* 忠实的 zhōngshí de; **duty-free** *adj* 免税的 miǎnshuì de

dwarf *n* 矮子 ǎizi

dwell *v* (**dwelt/dwelled**, **dwelt/dwelled**) 居住 jūzhù; **dwell on** 详述 xiángshù; **dwelling** *n* 住宅 zhùzhái

dwindle *v* 缩小 suōxiǎo

dye *v* 染 rǎn; *n* 染料 rǎnliào

dying *adj* 垂死的 chuísǐ de, 快死的 kuàisǐ de

dyke *n* 堤坝 dībà

dynamic *adj* 有活力的 yǒu huólì de, 动态的 dòngtài de

dynasty *n* 朝代 cháodài, 王朝 wángcháo

E

each *adj* 各 gè; **each other** 互相 hùxiāng

eager *adj* 热切的 rèqiè de, 急切的 jíqiè de; **eagerness** *n* 热心 rèxīn

eagle *n* 鹰 yīng

ear *n* 耳朵 ěrduo; **earache** *n* 耳痛 ěrtòng; **eardrum** *n* 耳膜 ěrmó; **earring** *n* 耳环 ěrhuán

early *adj/adv* 早 zǎo

earn *v* 赚 zhuàn, 挣 zhèng; **earnings** *n* 收入 shōurù, 所得 suǒdé

earnest *adj* 认真的 rènzhēn de; **in earnest** 认真地 rènzhēn de, 诚挚地 chéngzhì de

earring *n* 耳环 ěrhuán

earth *n* (*globe*) 地球 dìqiú; (*dirt*) 泥土 nítǔ

earthquake *n* 地震 dìzhèn

ease *n* 轻松 qīngsōng, 安心 ānxīn; **easiness** *n* 容易 róngyì; **easy** *adj* 容易的 róngyì de; **easy-going** *adj* 脾气随和的 píqi suíhe de; **take it easy**! 别急! bié jí; **easily** *adv* 容易地 róngyì de, 轻易地 qīngyì de

east *n* 东边 dōngbian, 东方 dōngfāng, 东部 dōngbù; **eastern** *adj* 东方的 dōngfāng de, 东部的 dōngbù de

Easter *n* 复活节 fùhuójié

eastward *adv* 向东方 xiàng dōngfāng

eat *v* (**ate**, **eaten**) 吃 chī; **eat up** 吃光 chī guāng; **eatable** *adj* 可以吃的 kěyǐ chī de

eavesdrop *v* 偷听 tōutīng

ebb *v/n* 落潮 luòcháo, 退潮 tuìcháo

eccentric *adj* 古怪的 gǔguài de; **eccentricity** *n* 古怪 gǔguài

echo *v* 发出回声 fāchū huíshēng, 作出反响 zuòchū fǎnxiǎng; *n* 回声 huíshēng, 反响 fǎnxiǎng

eclipse *n* 日蚀 rìshí, 月蚀 yuèshí

ecology *n* 生态 shēngtài; 生态学 shēngtàixué; **ecological** *adj* 生态学的 shēngtàixué de

economy *n* 经济 jīngjì; **economics** *n* 经济学 jīngjìxué; **economist** *n* 经济学家 jīngjìxuéjiā; **economic** *adj* 经济的 jīngjì de, 经济学的 jīngjìxué de; **economical** *adj* 节约的 jiéyuē de, 经济的 jīngjì de; **economize** *v* 节约 jiéyuē, 节省 jiéshěng

ecstasy *n* 狂喜 kuángxǐ; **ecstatic** *adj* 狂喜的 kuángxǐ de, 入迷的 rùmí de

Ecuador *n* 厄瓜多尔 èguāduō'ěr; **Ecuadorian** *n* 厄瓜多尔人 èguāduō'ěrrén; *adj* 厄瓜多尔的 èguāduō'ěr de

edge *n* 边缘 biānyuán; (*knife*) 刀口 dāokǒu; **have the edge on** 占优势 zhàn yōushì; **be on edge** 紧张不安 jǐnzhāng bù ān; **edgy** *adj* 烦躁的 fánzào de

edible *adj* 可食用的 kě shíyòng de

edit *v* 编辑 biānjí; **editor** *n* 编辑 biānjí; **editorial** *n* 社论 shèlùn

edition *n* 版本 bǎnběn

educate *v* 教育 jiàoyù; **education** *n* 教育 jiàoyù; **educational** *adj* 教育的 jiàoyù de; 有教育意义的 yǒu jiàoyù yìyì de

eel *n* 鳗鱼 mányú

effect *n* 效应 xiàoyìng, 作用 zuòyòng; **side effect** 副作用 fùzuòyòng; **take effect** 生效 shēngxiào; **effectiveness** *n* 效力 xiàolì; **effective** *adj* 有效的 yǒuxiào de

efficiency *n* 效率 xiàolǜ; **efficient** *adj* 有效率的 yǒu xiàolǜ de

effort *n* 努力 nǔlì; **effortless** *adj* 不费力的 bù fèilì de

egg *n* 蛋 dàn, 卵子 luǎnzǐ

eggplant *n* 茄子 qiézi

Egypt *n* 埃及 āijí; **Egyptian** *n* 埃及人 āijírén; *adj* 埃及的 āijí de

eight *num* 八 bā; **eighth** *num* 第八 dì bā

eighteen *num* 十八 shíbā; **eighteenth** *num* 第十八 dì shíbā

eighty *num* 八十 bāshí; **eightieth** *num* 第八十 dì bāshí

either *adj* 任一的 rènyī de; *conj* 或者 huòzhě; **either ... or ...** 或 ... 或 ... huò ... huò ...

eject *v* 弹出 tán chū, 射出 shè chū

elaboration *n* 详尽的细节 xiángjìn de xìjié; **elaborate** *adj* 精心制作的 jīngxīn zhìzuò de; 详尽的 xiángjìn de; **elaborately** *adv* 精巧的 jīngqiǎo de

elapse *v/n* 流逝 liúshì

elastic *adj* 有弹性的 yǒutánxìng de; **elastic band** 松紧带 sōngjǐndài; **elasticity** *n* 弹性 tánxìng

elation *n* 兴高采烈 xìnggāo cǎiliè; **elated** *adj* 兴高采烈的 xìnggāo cǎiliè de

elbow *n* 肘 zhǒu; **elbow room** 宽裕的空间 kuānyù de kōngjiān

elder *n* 年长者 niánzhǎngzhě; *adj* 年长的 niánzhǎng de; **elderly** *adj* 上年纪的 shàngniánji de; **eldest** *adj* 最年长的 zuì niánzhǎng de

elect *v* 选举 xuǎnjǔ; **election** *n* 选举 xuǎnjǔ; **electoral** *adj* 选举的 xuǎnjǔ de

electric *adj* 电的 diàn de; **electrician** *n* 电工 diàngōng; **electricity** *n* 电 diàn

electrocute *v* 电死 diànsǐ

electronics *n* 电子学 diànzǐxué; **electronic** *adj* 电子的 diànzǐ de

elegance *n* 高雅 gāoyǎ; **elegant** *adj* 优雅的 yōuyǎ de, 雅致的 yǎzhì de

element *n* 要素 yàosù, 成分 chéngfen

elementary *adj* 初级的 chūjí de; **elementary school** 小学 xiǎoxué

elephant *n* 大象 dàxiàng

elevate *v* (*raise*) 提高 tígāo; (*promote*) 提拔 tíbá; **elevation** *n* 提高 tígāo; 高度 gāodù; 海拔 hǎibá

elevator *n* 电梯 diàntī

eleven *num* 十一 shíyī; **eleventh** *num* 第十一 dì shíyī

eligibility *n* 资格 zīgé; **eligible** *adj* 合格的 hégé de, 有资格的 yǒu zīgé de

eliminate *v* 排除 páichú, 淘汰 táotài; **elimination** *n* 排除 páichú, 淘汰 táotài

elite *n* 精华 jīnghuá, 精英 jīngyīng

ellipsis *n* 省略 shěnglüè; **elliptical** *adj* 省略的 shěnglüè de

eloquent *adj* 雄辩的 xióngbiàn de, 有口才的 yǒu kǒucái de

else *adj* 其他的 qítā de, 别的 bié de; **or else** 否则 fǒuzé, 不然 bùrán; **elsewhere** *adv* 在别处 zài biéchù

email *n* 电子邮件 diànzǐ yóujiàn

emancipate *v* 解放 jiěfàng; **emancipation** *n* 解放 jiěfàng

embargo *n* 禁运 jìnyùn

embark *v* 上船 shàng chuán; **embark on** 从事 cóngshì; **embark upon** 开始进行 kāishǐ jìnxíng; **embankment** *n* 堤防 dīfáng

embarrass *v* (使) 尴尬 (shǐ) gāngà; **embarrassment** *n* 困窘

kùnjiǒng, 尴尬 gāngà; **embarrassed** *adj* 难为情的
nánwéiqíng de, 尴尬的 gāngà de; **embarrassing** *adj*
令人困窘的 lìng rén kùnjiǒng de

embassy *n* 大使馆 dàshǐguǎn

embellish *v* 修饰 xiūshì; **embellishment** *n* 装饰 zhuāngshì,
修饰 xiūshì

embezzle *v* 盗用 dàoyòng, 挪用 nuóyòng; **embezzlement** *n*
盗用 dàoyòng, 侵占 qīnzhàn

emblem *n* 象征 xiàngzhēng; 徽章 huīzhāng; **emblematic**
adj 象征性的 xiàngzhēngxing de

embrace *v/n* 拥抱 yōngbào, 接受 jiēshòu, 信奉 xìnfèng

embroidery *n* 刺绣 cìxiù

embryo *n* 胚胎 pēitāi; **in embryo** 在酝酿中 zài yùnniàng
zhōng

emerge *v* 出现 chūxiàn

emergency *n* 紧急情况 jǐnjí qíngkuàng; **emergency exit**
紧急出口 jǐnjí chūkǒu; **emergency landing** 紧急着陆
jǐnjí zhuólù

emigrate *v* 移居外国 yíjū wàiguó; **emigrant** *n* 移居外国者
yíjū wàiguó zhě; **emigration** *n* 移民 yímín

eminent *adj* 显赫的 xiǎnhè de, 杰出的 jiéchū de

emission *n* (*light, heat*) 散发 sànfā

emit *v* 发出 fāchū, 放射 fàngshè

emotion *n* 情感 qínggǎn; **emotional** *adj* 动感情的 dòng
gǎnqíng de

emperor *n* 皇帝 huángdì; **empress** *n* 皇后 huánghòu

emphasize *v* 强调 qiángdiào; **emphasis** *n* (*pl* **emphases**)
强调 qiángdiào; **emphatic** *adj* 强调的 qiángdiào de

empiricism *n* 经验主义 jīngyànzhǔyì; **empirical** *adj* 经验的
jīngyàn de

empire *n* 帝国 dìguó

employ *v* 雇用 gùyòng; **employee** *n* 雇员 gùyuán;
employer *n* 雇主 gùzhǔ; **employment** *n* 就业 jiùyè;
employment agency 职业介绍所 zhíyè jièshàosuǒ

empower *v* 授权予 shòuquán yǔ, 赋予 ... 权力 fùyù ... quánlì

empty *adj* 空的 kōng de; **empty-handed** *adv* 空手地 kōng-
shǒu de; **emptiness** *n* 空 kōng

enable *v* (使) 能够 (shǐ) nénggòu

enact *v* 制定法律 zhìdìng fǎlǜ; **enactment** *n* 制定 zhìdìng

enamor *n* 迷住 mízhù; **be enamored of** 倾心于 qīngxīn yú

enchantment *n* 着迷 zháomí; **enchanting** *adj* 迷人的 mírén de

encircle *v* 环绕 huánrǎo

enclose *v* 附寄 fùjì, 装入 zhuāngrù; **enclosure** *n* 围栏 wéilán; 附件 fùjiàn; **enclosed** *adj* 被附上的 bèi fù shàng de

encore *interj* 再来一个! zài lái yī gè

encroach *v* 侵占 qīnzhàn; **encroachment** *n* 侵占 qīnzhàn

encounter *v* 遇到 yùdào; *n* 邂逅 xièhòu

encourage *v* 鼓励 gǔlì; **encouragement** *n* 鼓励 gǔlì

encyclopedia *n* 百科全书 bǎikē quánshū

end *v* 结束 jiéshù; *n* 结束 jiéshù; 末端 mòduān; **make ends meet** 收支相抵 shōuzhī xiāngdǐ; **ending** *n* 结尾 jiéwěi; **endless** *adj* 无尽的 wújìn de, 无休止的 wúxiūzhǐ de

endanger *v* 危及 wēijí, 危害 wēihài

endeavor *v/n* 尽力 jìnlì, 努力 nǔlì, 尝试 chángshì

endorse *v* (*checks, etc.*) 在背面签名 zài bèimiàn qiānmíng, 背书 bèishū, 认可 rènkě; **endorsement** *n* 票据签字 piàojù qiānzì, 背书 bèishū, 认可 rènkě

endow *v* 赋予 fùyǔ; **endowment** *n* 天资 tiānzī; 捐赠 juānzèng

endure *v* 忍耐 rěnnài; **endurance** *n* 耐力 nàilì

enemy *n* 敌人 dírén

energy *n* 精力 jīnglì, 能量 néngliàng; 能源 néngyuán; **energetic** *adj* 精力充沛的 jīnglì chōngpèi de

enforce *v* 强制执行 qiángzhì zhíxíng

engage *v* (*employ*) 雇佣 gù, 聘聘 pìn; (*keep busy*) 占用 zhànyòng; **get engaged** 订婚 dìnghūn; **engagement** *n* (*betrothal*) 订婚 dìnghūn; (*appointment*) 约会 yuēhuì; **engagement ring** 订婚戒指 dìnghūn jièzhi

engine *n* 发动机 fādòngjī

engineer *n* 工程师 gōngchéngshī; **engineering** *n* 工程学 gōngchéngxué

England *n* 英国 yīngguó; **English** *n* 英文 yīngwén, 英语 yīngyǔ; *adj* 英国的 yīngguó de

enigma *n* 谜 mí; **enigmatic** *adj* 谜一般的 mí yībān de

enjoy *v* 享受 xiǎngshòu; **enjoyment** *n* 享受 xiǎngshòu; **enjoyable** *adj* 令人愉快的 lìng rén yúkuài de

enlarge *v* 扩大 kuòdà, 放大 fàngdà

enlighten *v* 启发 qǐfā, 启蒙 qǐméng; **enlightenment** *n* 启迪 qǐdí, 教化 jiàohuà

enlist *v* 征募 zhēngmù, 谋取 móuqǔ

enmity *n* 敌意 díyì

enormity *n* 巨大 jùdà; **enormous** *adj* 巨大的 jùdà de; **enormously** *adv* 巨大地 jùdà de

enough *adj* 足够的 zúgòu de

enquire *v* 询问 xúnwèn

enrage *v* 激怒 jīnù

enrich *v* 丰富 fēngfù; **enrichment** *n* 丰富 fēngfù

enroll *v* 注册 zhùcè, 报名 bàomíng; **enrollment** *n* 登记 dēngjì, 注册 zhùcè

ensue *v* 跟着发生 gēn zhe fāshēng; **ensuing** *adj* 接着的 jiē zhe de

ensure *v* 保证 bǎozhèng, 确保 quèbǎo

entail *v* 需要 xūyào; 引致 yǐnzhì

enter *v* 进入 jìnrù; **entry** *n* 进入 jìnrù

enterprise *n* 企业 qǐyè; **enterprising** *adj* 有进取心的 yǒu jìnqǔxīn de

entertain *v* 招待 zhāodài, 款待 kuǎndài; (*thoughts, etc.*) 抱有 bàoyǒu; **entertainment** *n* 娱乐 yúlè; **entertaining** *adj* 愉快的 yúkuài de, 有趣的 yǒuqù de

enthusiasm *n* 热情 rèqíng; **enthusiastic** *adj* 热情的 rèqíng de

entice *v* 诱惑 yòuhuò; **enticing** *adj* 迷人的 mírén de

entire *adj* 整个的 zhěnggè de; **entirely** *adv* 完全地 wánquán de

entitle *v* 给... 权力 gěi ... quánlì; **be entitled** 叫做 jiàozuò, 称为 chēngwéi

entity *n* 实体 shítǐ

entrance *n* 入口 rùkǒu; **entrance examination** 入学考试 rùxué kǎoshì

entrée *n* 主菜 zhǔcài

entrepreneur *n* 企业家 qǐyèjiā

entrust *v* 委托 wěituō

enunciate *v* 阐明 chǎnmíng; **enunciation** *n* 阐明 chǎnmíng

envelope *n* 信封 xìnfēng

environment *n* 环境 huánjìng; **environmental** *adj* 环境的 huánjìng de

envoy *n* 外交使节 wàijiāo shǐjié, 特使 tèshǐ

envy *v* 羡慕 xiànmù, 忌妒 jídù; *n* 忌妒 jídù; **envious** *adj* 忌妒的 jídù de, 羡慕的 xiànmù de

enzyme *n* 酶 méi

epic *n* 史诗 shǐshī; *adj* 英雄的 yīngxióng de, 壮丽的 zhuànglì de, 史诗般的 shǐshī bān de

epidemic *n* 流行病 liúxíngbìng; *adj* 流行性的 liúxíngxìng de, 传染的 chuánrǎn de

episode *n* 一段情节 yī duàn qíngjié, 插曲 chāqǔ

epitomize *v* 成为 ... 的缩影 chéngwéi ... de suōyǐng; **epitome** *n* 缩影 suōyǐng

epoch *n* 新纪元 xīnjìyuán, 时代 shídài

equal *v* 等于 děngyú; *adj* 相等的 xiāngděng de, 平等的 píngděng de; **equality** *n* 平等 píngděng

equate *v* (使) 相等 (shǐ) xiāngděng; **equation** *n* 相等 xiāngděng, 等式 děngshì

equator *n* 赤道 chìdào

equip *v* 装备 zhuāngbèi, 配备 pèibèi; 赋予 fùyǔ; **equipment** *n* 设备 shèbèi

equivalent *n* 相等物 xiāngděngwù, 相对应物 xiāng duìyīngwù; *adj* 相等的 xiāngděng de

era *n* 时代 shídài

eradicate *v* 根除 gēnchú, 消除 xiāochú; **eradication** *n* 根除 gēnchú

erase *v* 擦掉 cā diào; **eraser** *n* 橡皮 xiàngpí

erect *v* 建立 jiànlì, 竖起 shùqǐ

erode *v* 侵蚀 qīnshí, 腐蚀 fǔshí; **erosion** *n* 侵蚀 qīnshí, 腐蚀 fǔshí

erotic *adj* 性爱的 xìng'ài de, 色情的 sèqíng de

err *v* 犯错 fàncuò; **error** *n* 错误 cuòwù

errand *n* 差事 chāishi; **run an errand** 办事 bànshì

erupt *v* 爆发 bàofā; **eruption** *n* 爆发 bàofā

erudition *n* 博学 bóxué; **erudite** *adj* 博学的 bóxué de

escalate *v* 逐步升级 zhúbù shēngjí; **escalation** *n* 升级 shēngjí; **escalator** *n* 自动扶梯 zìdòng fútī

escape *v/n* 逃脱 táotuō; **fire escape** 防火梯 fánghuǒtī

escort *v/n* 护送 hùsòng, 陪同 péitóng

especial *adj* 特别的 tèbié de, 特殊的 tèshū de; **especially** *adv* 特别地 tèbié de

essay *n* 文章 wénzhāng, 散文 sǎnwén

essence *n* 精华 jīnghuá, 本质 běnzhì

essential *adj* 基本的 jīběn de, 精华的 jīnghuá de

establish *v* 建立 jiànlì, 成立 chénglì; **establishment** *n* 建立 jiànlì; 机构 jīgòu

estate *n* 庄园 zhuāngyuán, 不动产 bùdòngchǎn, 财产 cáichǎn

esteem *v/n* 尊重 zūnzhòng, 敬重 jìngzhòng

estimate *v/n* 估计 gūjì; 估价 gūjià

estuary *n* 河口 hékǒu

eternal *adj* 永恒的 yǒnghéng de; **eternity** *n* 永恒 yǒnghéng

ethics *n* 道德规范 dàodé guīfàn; **ethical** *adj* 有道德的 yǒu dàodé de

ethnic *adj* 种族的 zhǒngzú de; **ethnic minority** 少数民族 shǎoshù mínzú

etiquette *n* 礼节 lǐjié

etymology *n* 语源 yǔyuán; 语源学 yǔyuánxué

euphemism *n* 委婉语 wěiwǎnyǔ; **euphemistic** *adj* 委婉的 wěiwǎn de

euro *n* 欧元 ōuyuán

Europe *n* 欧洲 ōuzhōu; **European** *n* 欧洲人 ōuzhōurén; *adj* 欧洲的 ōuzhōu de; **European Union** 欧盟 ōuméng

evacuate *v* 撤离 chèlí; **evacuation** *n* 撤离 chèlí; **evacuee** *n* 被疏散者 bèi shūsàn zhě

evade *v* 逃避 táobì; **evasion** *n* 逃避 táobì; **evasive** *adj* 逃避的 táobì de, 推托的 tuītuō de

evangelist *n* 福音传道者 fúyīn chuándàozhě; **evangelical** *adj* 福音的 fúyīn de

evaluate *v* 评价 píngjià, 鉴定 jiàndìng; **evaluation** *n* 评价 píngjià

evaporate *v* 蒸发 zhēngfā

eve *n* 前夕 qiánxī, 前夜 qiányè; **Christmas Eve** 圣诞夜 shèngdànyè; **New Year's Eve** 新年除夕 xīnnián chúxī; **on the eve of** 在 ... 的前夕 zài ... de qiánxī

even *adj* 相等的 xiāngděng de; 平坦的 píngtǎn de; 均匀的 jūnyún de; 偶数的 ǒushù de; **break even** 不盈不亏 bù yíng bù kuī; **get even** 扯平 chěpíng; *adv* 甚至 shènzhì; **even if** *conj* 即使 jíshǐ; **even though** *conj* 即使 jíshǐ; **evenly** *adv* 均匀的 jūnyún de

evening *n* 晚上 wǎnshang

event *n* 活动 huódòng; **in the event of** 如果 ... 发生 rúguǒ ... fāshēng; **eventful** *adj* 多事的 duōshì de; **eventually** *adv* 最终 zuìzhōng

ever *adv* 曾经 céngjīng; 永远 yǒngyuǎn; 在任何时候 zài rènhé shíhou; **ever since** 自从 zìcóng

evergreen *adj* 常青的 chángqīng de

everlasting *adj* 永久的 yǒngjiǔ de

every *adj* 每一 měi yī; **everybody** *pron* 每个人 měi ge rén; **everyone** *pron* 每个人 měi ge rén; **everything** *pron* 一切 yīqiè; **everywhere** *adv* 到处 dàochù

evict *v* 驱逐 qūzhú, 逐出 zhúchū; **eviction** *n* 逐出 zhúchū

evidence *n* 证据 zhèngjù; **evident** *adj* 明显的 míngxiǎn de

evil *n* 邪恶 xié'è; *adj* 邪恶的 xié'è de; **evildoer** *n* 为恶者 wéi'èzhě

evolve *v* 演变 yǎnbiàn, 演化 yǎnhuà; **evolution** *n* 演变 yǎnbiàn, 演化 yǎnhuà

exacerbate *v* 激怒 jīnù, 加剧 jiājù; **exacerbation** *n* 激怒 jīnù, 恼怒 nǎonù

exact *adj* 确切的 quèqiè de; **exactly** *adv* 确切地 quèqiè de; 的确如此 díquè rúcǐ

exaggerate *v* 夸张 kuāzhāng; **exaggeration** *n* 夸张 kuāzhāng

exam *n* 考试 kǎoshì 检查 jiǎnchá; **take an exam** 参加考试 cānjiā kǎoshì; **written exam** 笔试 bǐshì; **examination** *n* 考试 kǎoshì, 检查 jiǎnchá

examine *v* 检查 jiǎnchá, 调查 diàochá, 考试 kǎoshì; **examiner** *n* 主考官 zhǔkǎoguān

example *n* 例子 lìzi; 榜样 bǎngyàng; **follow someone's example** 效仿 xiàofǎng; **for example** 例如 lìrú; **set an example** 树立榜样 shùlì bǎngyàng

excavate *v* 挖掘 wājué; **excavation** *n* 挖掘 wājué; 出土文物 chūtǔ wénwù

exceed *v* 超过 chāoguò; **exceedingly** *adv* 极其 jíqí

excel *v* 出类拔萃 chūlèibácuì; **excellence** *n* 优秀 yōuxiù; **excellent** *adj* 优秀的 yōuxiù de, 极好的 jí hǎo de

except *prep* 除 ... 之外 chú ... zhīwài; **except for** 除了 chúle

exception *n* 例外 lìwài; **take exception to** 反对 fǎnduì; **exceptional** *adj* 例外的 lìwài de, 异常的 yìcháng de

excerpt *n* 摘录 zhāilù

excess *n* 过量 guòliàng, 超额 chāo'é; **excessive** *adj* 过多的 guòduō de, 过分的 guòfèn de; **excessively** *adv* 过多地 guòduō de, 过分地 guòfèn de

exchange *v/n* 交换 jiāohuàn, 交流 jiāoliú; **stock exchange** 股票交易所 gǔpiào jiāoyìsuǒ

excite *v* 刺激 cìjī, (使) 兴奋 (shǐ) xīngfèn; **get excited** 兴奋起来 xīngfèn qǐlái; **excitement** *n* 兴奋 xīngfèn, 激动 jīdòng; **exciting** *adj* 令人兴奋的 lìng rén xīngfèn de

exclaim *v* 呼喊 hūhǎn, 惊叫 jīngjiào; **exclamation** *n* 惊呼 jīnghū; 惊叹词 jīngtàncí; **exclamation mark** 感叹号 gǎntànháo

exclude *v* 排除 páichú; **exclusive** *adj* 排外的 páiwài de; 独家的 dújiā de

excursion *n* 游玩 yóuwán, 远足 yuǎnzú

excruciate *v* 施酷刑 shī kùxíng, 折磨 zhémó; **excruciating** *adj* 极痛苦的 jí tòngkǔ de

excuse *v* 原谅 yuánliàng; **excuse me** 对不起 duìbùqǐ; *n* 借口 jièkǒu

execute *v* (*carry out*) 执行 zhíxíng; (*death penalty*) 处死 chǔsǐ; **execution** *n* (*carrying out*) 执行 zhíxíng; (*death penalty*) 死刑 sǐxíng

executive *adj* 执行的 zhíxíng de; *n* 主管人员 zhǔguǎn rényuán; **Chief Executive Officer (CEO)** 首席执行官 shǒuxí zhíxíngguān

exemplify *v* 例证 lìzhèng, 例示 lìshì; **exemplification** *n* 范例 fànlì

exempt *v* 免除 miǎnchú, 豁免 huòmiǎn; **exemption** *n* 解除 jiěchú, 免除 miǎnchú

exercise *v* 锻炼 duànliàn, 行使 xíngshǐ; *n* 练习 liànxí, 锻炼 duànliàn; **exercise book** 练习本 liànxíběn

exert *v* 用力 yònglì, 尽力 jìnlì; **exertion** *n* 尽力 jìnlì, 费力 fèilì

exhale *v* 吐气 tǔqì

exhaust *v* 用尽 yòngjìn; *n* 排气口 páiqìkǒu; **exhaust pipe** 排气管 páiqìguǎn; **exhaustion** *n* 筋疲力尽 jīnpí lìjìn; **exhausted** *adj* 筋疲力尽的 jīnpí lìjìn de

exhibit *v* 展览 zhǎnlǎn; *n* 展览品 zhǎnlǎnpǐn, 陈列品 chénlièpǐn; **exhibition** *n* 展览 zhǎnlǎn

exile *v/n* 流放 liúfàng; **go into exile** 逃亡 táowáng

exist *v* 存在 cúnzài, 生存 shēngcún; **existence** *n* 存在 cúnzài, 生存 shēngcún; **existing** *adj* 现有的 xiànyǒu de

exit *v* 出去 chūqù, 离去 líqù, 退出 tuìchū; *n* 出口 chūkǒu, 离去 líqù, 退出 tuìchū

exonerate *v* 证明无罪 zhèngmíng wúzuì

exorbitant *adj* 过度的 guòdù de, 过高的 guògāo de

exotic *adj* 异国情调的 yìguó qíngdiào de

expand *v* 扩展 kuòzhǎn, 扩张 kuòzhāng; **expansion** *n* 扩展 kuòzhǎn, 扩张 kuòzhāng

expatriate *n* 移居国外者 yíjū guówài zhě, 侨民 qiáomín

expect *v* 期望 qīwàng, 期待 qīdài; **expectant mother** 孕妇 yùnfù; **expectation** *n* 期望 qīwàng, 期待 qīdài

expedience *n* 方便 fāngbiàn, 合算 hésuàn, 得当 dédàng; **expedient** *adj* 方便的 fāngbiàn de, 得当的 dédàng de, 合算的 hésuàn de

expedition *n* 远征 yuǎnzhēng

expel *v* 驱逐 qūzhú; 开除 kāichú

expense *n* 费用 fèiyòng, 开支 kāizhī; **at the expense of** 由 ... 付费 yóu ... fùfèi; 在损害 ... 的情况下 zài sǔnhài ... de qíngkuàng xià; **expenditure** *n* 开支 kāizhī; **expensive** *adj* 贵的 guì de

experience *v* 体验 tǐyàn; *n* 经验 jīngyàn, 经历 jīnglì; **experienced** *adj* 有经验的 yǒu jīngyàn de

experiment *n* 试验 shìyàn; **experimental** *adj* 试验性的 shìyànxìng de

expert *n* 专家 zhuānjiā; **expertise** *n* 专业知识 zhuānyè zhīshi

expire *v* 到期 dàoqī, 过期 guòqī; **expiration** *n* 到期 dàoqī, 过期 guòqī

explain *v* 解释 jiěshì; **explanation** *n* 解释 jiěshì

explicit *adj* 清楚的 qīngchu de, 直率的 zhíshuài de, 无掩饰的 wú yǎnshì de

explode *v* 爆炸 bàozhà; *n* 爆炸物 bàozhàwù, 炸药 zhàyào; **explosion** *n* 爆炸 bàozhà; **explosive** *adj* 易爆炸的 yì bàozhà de, 爆炸性的 bàozhàxìng de

exploit *v* 开发 kāifā; 剥削 bōxuē; **exploitation** *n* 开发 kāifā; 剥削 bōxuē

explore *v* 勘探 kāntàn, 探索 tànsuǒ; **exploration** *v* 探索 tànsuǒ; **explorer** *n* 探险家 tànxiǎnjiā

export *v* 出口 chūkǒu, 输出 shūchū; *n* 出口 chūkǒu, 输出 shūchū; **exporter** *n* 出口商 chūkǒushāng

expose *v* 暴露 bàolù, 揭露 jiēlù; **exposure** *n* 暴露 bàolù; 曝光 bàoguāng

express *v* 表示 biǎoshì; *adj* 急速的 jísù de; 明确的 míngquè de; **express mail** 快件 kuàijiàn; **express train** 快车 kuàichē; **expression** *n* 表达 biǎodá, 表示 biǎoshì; 表情 biǎoqíng; 词语 cíyǔ

exquisite *adj* 精致的 jīngzhì de, 优美的 yōuměi de

extend *v* 延长 yáncháng, 伸展 shēnzhǎn, 延伸 yánshēn; **extension** *n* 延长 yáncháng, 伸展 shēnzhǎn; (*telephone*) 分机 fēnjī; **extensive** *adj* 广泛的 guǎngfàn de

extent *n* 范围 fànwéi, 程度 chéngdù

exterior *adj* 外部的 wàibù de

exterminate *v* 灭绝 mièjué, 消灭 xiāomiè

external *adj* 外部的 wàibù de; **for external use only** 仅限外用 jǐn xiàn wàiyòng

extinct *adj* 绝种的 juézhǒng de, 灭绝的 mièjué de; **extinction** *n* 绝种 juézhǒng, 灭绝 mièjué

extinguish *v* 熄灭 xīmiè, 扑灭 pūmiè; **extinguisher** *n* 灭火器 mièhuǒqì

extort *v* 敲诈 qiāozhà; **extortion** *n* 敲诈 qiāozhà

extra *adj* 额外的 éwài de

extract *v* 抽出 chōuchū, 取出 qǔchū, 榨取 zhàqǔ; **extraction** *n* 抽出 chōuchū, 取出 qǔchū

extradite *v* 引渡 yǐndù; **extradition** *n* 引渡 yǐndù

extraordinary *adj* 非凡的 fēifán de, 卓越的 zhuōyuè de

extravagant *adj* 奢侈的 shēchǐ de

extreme *adj* 极度的 jídù de, 极端的 jíduān de, 偏激的 piānjī de; **go to extremes** 走极端 zǒu jíduān; **extremely** *adv* 极端地 jíduān de; **extremist** *n* 极端主义者 jíduānzhǔyìzhě

extrovert *n* 性格外向者 xìnggé wàixiàng zhě

exuberance *n* 生气勃勃 shēngqì bóbó; **exuberant** *adj* 兴高采烈的 xìnggāo cǎiliè de

eye *n* 眼睛 yǎnjing; **an eye for an eye** 以眼还眼 yǐ yǎn huán yǎn; **see eye to eye with** 与 ... 看法完全一致 yǔ ... kànfa wánquán yīzhì; **turn a blind eye** 视而不见 shì'ér bùjiàn; **with the naked eye** 用肉眼 yòng ròuyǎn

eyeball *n* 眼珠 yǎnzhū

eyebrow *n* 眉毛 méimao

eye-catching *adj* 引人注目的 yǐnrénzhùmù de

eyeglasses *n* 眼镜 yǎnjìng

eyelash *n* 睫毛 jiémáo

eyelid *n* 眼睑 yǎnjiǎn

eyesight *n* 视力 shìlì

eyesore *n* 眼中钉 yǎnzhōngdīng

eyewitness *n* 目击者 mùjīzhě

F

fable *n* 寓言 yùyán

fabric *n* 布 bù, 料子 liàozi

fabricate *v* 编造 biānzào, 伪造 wěizào; **fabrication** *n* 捏造 niēzào

fabulous *adj* 惊人的 jīngrén de, 难以置信的 nányǐ zhìxìn de

facade *n* 正面 zhèngmiàn, 外表 wàibiǎo

face *v* 面对 miànduì, 面临 miànlín; *n* 脸 liǎn; **facelift** *n* 整容 zhěngróng; **face to face** 面对面地 miàn duì miàn de; **on the face of it** 从表面判断 cóng biǎomiàn pànduàn; **fly in the face of** 公然抗拒 gōngrán kàngjù; **in the face of** 面临 miànlín; **lose face** 丢脸 diūliǎn; **save face** 顾及面子 gùjí miànzi; **face value** 面值 miànzhí

facility *n* 设施 shèshī; 灵巧 língqiǎo

fact *n* 事实 shìshí; **as a matter of fact** 事实上 shìshí shang

faction *n* 派别 pàibié

factor *n* 因素 yīnsù

factory *n* 工厂 gōngchǎng

faculty *n* (*university*) 全体教员 quántǐ jiàoyuán; (*gift*) 才能 cáinéng

fad *n* 时尚 shíshàng

faddish *adj* 喜欢赶时髦的 xǐhuan gǎnshímáo de

fade *v* 褪色 tuìsè; 逐渐消失 zhújiàn xiāoshī

fail *v* (*not succeed*) 失败 shībài; (*exams*) 不及格 bù jígé; (*weaken*) 衰竭 shuāijié; **failure** *n* 失败 shībài 失灵 shīlíng; 衰竭 shuāijié

faint *v* 昏倒 hūn dǎo; *adj* 微弱的 wēiruò de

fair *adj* 公平的 gōngpíng de; **fairly** *adv* 公平地 gōngpíng de; (*reasonably*) 相当地 xiāngdāng de

fair *n* (*trade fair*) 交易会 jiāoyìhuì, (*market*) 集市 jíshì; (*amusement*) 游乐园 yóulèyuán

faith *n* 信仰 xìnyǎng, 信念 xìnniàn; **faithful** *adj* 忠实的 zhōngshí de

fake *n* 赝品 yànpǐn; *adj* 假的 jiǎ de

fall *v* (**fell, fallen**) 跌倒 diē dǎo, 摔倒 shuāi dǎo, 落下 luò xià; *n* 摔倒 shuāi dǎo, 倒台 dǎotái; (*autumn*) 秋天 qiūtiān

false *adj* 错误的 cuòwù de, 假的 jiǎ de

fame *n* 名声 míngshēng

familiar *adj* 熟悉的 shúxī de

family *n* 家庭 jiātíng

famine *n* 饥荒 jīhuāng

famous *adj* 有名的 yǒumíng de

fan *n* (*hand*) 扇子 shànzi; (*machine*), 电扇 diànshàn, (*admirer*) 爱好者 àihàozhě, 迷 mí; *v* 煽动 shāndòng

fanatic *n* 狂热者 kuángrèzhě

fancy *v* 想象 xiǎngxiàng; *adj* 精美的 jīngměi de, 别致的 biézhi de

fanfare *n* 声势 shēngshì, 炫耀 xuànyào

fantastic *adj* 奇异的 qíyì de, 美妙的 měimiào de

fantasy *n* 幻想 huànxiǎng, 白日梦 báirìmèng

far *adj* 远的 yuǎn de; **far-sighted** *adj* 有远见的 yǒu yuǎnjiàn de

farce *n* 闹剧 nàojù 笑剧 xiàojù; **farcical** *adj* 滑稽的 huájī de

fare *n* 旅费 lǚfèi, 车费 chēfèi

farewell *n* 告别 gàobié, 离别 líbié

farm *n* 农场 nóngchǎng, 农庄 nóngzhuāng; **farmer** *n* 农民 nóngmín; **farming** *n* 农业 nóngyè, 耕作 gēngzuò

farther *adj* 更远的 gèng yuǎn de; **farthest** *adj* 最远的 zuìyuǎn de

fascinate *v* 迷住 mízhù; **fascinating** *adj* 迷人的 mírén de, 醉人的 zuìrén de, 美妙的 měimiào de

fascism *n* 法西斯主义 fǎxīsīzhǔyì; **fascist** *adj* 法西斯主义的 fǎxīsīzhǔyì de

fashion *n* 时尚 shíshàng; **fashionable** *adj* 时髦的 shímáo de

fast n 绝食 juéshí, 斋戒 zhāijiè; adj (rapid) 快的 kuài de; (secure) 牢的 láo de

fasten v 扎牢 zā láo, 系 jì; **fastener** n 扣件 kòujiàn; **zip fastener** 拉链 lālián

fat adj 胖的 pàng de, 肥的 féi de

fatal adj 致命的 zhìmìng de

fate n 命运 mìngyùn

father n 父亲 fùqīn; **father-in-law** n (wife's father) 岳父 yuèfù; (husband's father) 公公 gōnggong

fathom v 测量深度 cèliáng shēndù

fatigue n 疲劳 píláo

fault n 缺点 quēdiǎn, 过错 guòcuò; **faulty** adj 有缺点的 yǒu quēdiǎn de, 不完美的 bù wánměi de

favor v 喜爱 xǐ'ài, 偏爱 piān'ài; n 恩惠 ēnhuì, 帮忙 bāngmáng; **favorite** n 特别喜爱的人或物 tèbié xǐ'ài de rén huò wù; adj 特别喜爱的 tèbié xǐ'ài de; **favorable** adj 有利的 yǒulì de

fax v 发传真 fā chuánzhēn; n 传真 chuánzhēn; **fax machine** 传真机 chuánzhēnjī

fear v 惧怕 jùpà; n 恐惧 kǒngjù; **fearless** adj 无畏的 wúwèi de

feasible adj 可行的 kěxíng de

feast n 盛宴 shèngyàn, 大餐 dàcān

feat n 技艺 jìyì

feather n 羽毛 yǔmáo

feature n 特点 tèdiǎn, 特色 tèsè, 特征 tèzhēng, (face) 容貌 róngmào; **feature film** 故事片 gùshìpiān

February n 二月 èryuè

fed v see **feed**; adj (fed up) 极其厌烦的 jíqí yànfán de

federal adj 联邦的 liánbāng de, 联邦政府的 liánbāng zhèngfǔ de; **federation** n 联邦 liánbāng, 联盟 liánméng

fee n 费 fèi

feeble adj 虚弱的 xūruò de

feed v (fed, fed) 喂 wèi, 喂养 wèiyǎng

feel v (felt, felt) 感觉 gǎnjué, 觉得 juéde; **feeling** n 感觉 gǎnjué, 感情 gǎnqíng

feet. See **foot**

fell. See **fall**

fellow n 男人 nánrén; 家伙 jiāhuo; 小伙子 xiǎohuǒzi; adj 同伴的 tóngbàn de, 同事的 tóngshì de

felony n 重罪 zhòngzuì

felt v see **feel**; n (material) 毡 zhān, 毡制品 zhānzhìpǐn

female *n* 女性 nǚxìng; *adj* 女的 nǚ de

feminine *adj* 女性的 nǚxìng de; (*gram*) 阴性的 yīnxìng de; **feminism** *n* 女权主义 nǚquánzhǔyì; **feminist** *n* 女权主义者 nǚquánzhǔyìzhě

fence *n* 篱笆 líba, 栅栏 zhàlan

fend *v* 抵挡 dǐdǎng, 击退 jītuì; **fend for oneself** 自己谋生 zìjǐ móushēng; **fend off** 挡开 dǎngkāi

ferocity *n* 凶猛 xiōngměng; **ferocious** *adj* 凶恶的 xiōng'è de, 凶猛的 xiōngměng de

ferret *n* 雪貂 xuědiāo

ferry *n* (*boat*) 渡船 dùchuán; (*crossing*) 渡口 dùkǒu

fertilize *v* 施肥 shīféi; (使) 受精 (shǐ) shòujīng; **fertility** *n* 肥沃 féiwò, 生育力 shēngyùlì; **fertile** *adj* 肥沃的 féiwò de

fervor *n* 热情 rèqíng; **fervent** *adj* 炽热的 chìrè de, 狂热的 kuángrè de

festival *n* 节日 jiérì

festivity *n* 欢庆 huānqìng; 庆祝活动 qìngzhù huódòng; **festive** *adj* 喜庆的 xǐqìng de

fetch *v* 取来 qǔlái

feud *n* 世仇 shìchóu

feudalism *n* 封建制度 fēngjiàn zhìdù; **feudal** *adj* 封建制度的 fēngjiàn zhìdù de

fever *n* 发烧 fāshāo, 发热 fārè, 狂热 kuángrè

few *n* 极少数 jíshǎoshù; *adj* 很少 hěn shǎo

fiancé *n* 未婚夫 wèihūnfū; **fiancée** *n* 未婚妻 wèihūnqī

fiasco *n* 惨败 cǎnbài

fiber *n* 纤维 xiānwéi

fiction *n* (*stories*) 小说 xiǎoshuō; (*invention*) 虚构 xūgòu

fiddle *n* 小提琴 xiǎotíqín; **fiddle with** 乱动 luàndòng; **fiddling** *adj* 无足轻重的 wúzúqīngzhòng de, 无用的 wúyòng de

field *n* 田 tián, 原野 yuányě, 野外 yěwài; (*sphere*) 领域 lǐngyù

fierce *adj* 凶猛的 xiōngměng de, 猛烈的 měngliè de

fiery *adj* 火的 huǒ de, 炽热的 chìrè de

fifteen *num* 十五 shíwǔ; **fifteenth** *num* 第十五 dì shíwǔ

fifth *num* 第五 dì wǔ

fifty *num* 五十 wǔshí; **fiftieth** *num* 第五十 dì wǔshí

fig *n* 无花果 wúhuāguǒ

fight *v/n* (*fought, fought*) 打架 dǎjià, 打仗 dǎzhàng; **fighter** *n* (*soldier*) 战士 zhànshì; (*plane*) 战斗机 zhàndòujī

figure n (*number*) 数字 shùzì; (*table*) 图表 túbiǎo; (*body*)
体形 tǐxíng; **figure skating** 花样滑冰 huāyàng huábīng

file v (*documents*) 把 ... 归档 bǎ ... guīdàng; (*news*) 发送 fāsòng;
(*application, etc.*) 提交 tíjiāo; n (*archive*)文件夹 wénjiànjiā,
档案 dàng'àn, 卷宗 juànzōng; (*tool*) 锉刀 cuòdāo

filial adj 子女的 zǐnǚ de, 孝顺的 xiàoshùn de

fill v 装满 zhuāngmǎn; (*form*) 填写 tiánxiě; (*hole*) 填 tián;
filling station 加油站 jiāyóuzhàn

film n (*movie*) 电影 diànyǐng; (*camera*) 胶卷 jiāojuǎn

filter v 过滤 guòlǜ; n 过滤器 guòlǜqì

filth n 污秽 wūhuì, 肮脏 āngzāng; **filthy** adj 污秽的 wūhuì
de, 肮脏的 āngzāng de

final n (*competition*) 决赛 juésài; (*exam*) 期终考试 qīzhōng
kǎoshì; adj 最后的 zuìhòu de, 决定性的 juédìngxìng de;
finalist n 决赛选手 juésài xuǎnshǒu; **finally** adv 最后
zuìhòu, 终于 zhōngyú

finance n 财政 cáizhèng, 金融 jīnróng; **financial** adj 财政的
cáizhèng de, 金融的 jīnróng de, 经济的 jīngjì de

find v (**found, found**) 找到 zhǎo dào; **find out** 发现 fāxiàn;
findings n (*legal*) 裁决 cáijué

fine v 罚款 fákuǎn; n 罚金 fájīn; adj 好的 hǎo de, 精细的
jīngxì de; **fine arts** 美术 měishù

finger n 手指 shǒuzhǐ; **fingernail** n 手指甲 shǒuzhǐjia;
fingerprint n 指纹 zhǐwén; **fingertip** n 指尖 zhǐjiān;
have at one's fingertips 对 ... 了如指掌 duì ... liǎorú
zhǐzhǎng

finish v/n 结束 jiéshù, 完成 wánchéng; **finish line** 终点线
zhōngdiǎnxiàn; **finishing touch** 最后的润色 zuìhòu de rùnsè

finite adj 有限的 yǒuxiàn de

Finland n 芬兰 fēnlán; **Finn** n 芬兰人 fēnlánrén; **Finnish** n
(*language*) 芬兰语 fēnlányǔ; adj 芬兰的 fēnlán de

fire n 火 huǒ; **catch fire** 着火 zháohuǒ; **set on fire** 放火烧
fàng huǒ shāo; **set fire to** 点燃 diǎnrán

fire alarm n 火警 huǒjǐng

firearm n 火器 huǒqì, 武器 wǔqì

fire brigade n 消防队 xiāofángduì

fire drill n 消防训练 xiāofáng xùnliàn; 火灾避难训练 huǒzāi
bìnàn xùnliàn

fire engine n 消防车 xiāofángchē

fire escape n 防火梯 fánghuǒtī

fire-extinguisher n 灭火器 mièhuǒqì

firefighter n 消防员 xiāofángyuán

firefly *n* 萤火虫 yínghuǒchóng

fireman *n* 消防员 xiāofángyuán

fireplace *n* 壁炉 bìlú

fireproof *adj* 耐火的 nàihuǒ de, 防火的 fánghuǒ de

fire station *n* 消防站 xiāofángzhàn

firewood *n* 木柴 mùchái

fireworks *n* 焰火 yānhuǒ

firing squad *n* 行刑队 xíngxíngduì

firm *n* 公司 gōngsī; *adj* 坚固的 jiāngù de, 坚定的 jiāndìng de; **firmness** *n* 坚定 jiāndìng, 稳固 wěngù

first *num* 第一 dìyī; *adj* 第一的 dìyī de; **first aid** 急救 jíjiù; **first name** 名 míng; **first-class** *adj* 第一流的 dìyīliú de, 头等的 tóuděng de; **at first** 最初 zuìchū; **in the first place** 首先 shǒuxiān

fiscal *adj* 财政的 cáizhèng de

fish *n* 鱼 yú; **fish sauce** 鱼露 yúlù; **fishy** *adj* 可疑的 kěyí de; **fisherman** *n* 渔民 yúmín; **fishing** *n* 钓鱼 diàoyú; **go fishing** 钓鱼 diàoyú; **fishing line** 钓线 diàoxiàn; **fishing net** 渔网 yúwǎng; **fishing rod** 钓杆 yúgān

fist *n* 拳头 quántou

fit *v* (**fitted/fit, fitted/fit**) (*suit*) 适合 shìhé, 符合 fúhé; (*install*) 安装 ānzhuāng; *adj* (*suitable*) 合适的 héshì de, (*healthy*) 健康的 jiànkāng de; **see fit** 觉得合适 juéde héshì; **fitness** *n* (*health*) 健康 jiànkāng; (*suitability*) 适当 shìdàng; **fitting room** 试衣室 shìyīshì

five *num* 五 wǔ

fix *v* (*repair*) 修理 xiūlǐ, (使)固定 (shǐ) gùdìng; (*prepare*) 准备 zhǔnbèi; *n* 困境 kùnjìng

flag *v* 变弱 biànruò; *n* 旗 qí; **flagship** 旗舰 qíjiàn; **flagging** 衰弱的 shuāiruò de

flagrant *adj* 公然的 gōngrán de

flamboyant *adj* 浮夸的 fúkuā de, 炫耀的 xuànyào de

flame *n* 火焰 huǒyàn; **flammable** *adj* 易燃的 yìrán de

flap *v* 拍打 pāida, 飘动 piāodòng

flare *v* 闪光 shǎnguāng; **flare up** 突然发出火焰 tūrán fāchū huǒyàn

flash *n* 闪光 shǎnguāng; (*photo*) 闪光灯 shǎnguāngdēng; **flashback** *n* 倒叙 dàoxù; **flashlight** *n* 手电筒 shǒudiàntǒng

flask *n* 长颈瓶 chángjǐngpíng

flat *adj* (*level*) 平坦的 píngtǎn de; (*boring*) 枯燥的 kūzào de;

flat-footed *adj* 平足的 píngzú de; **flatly** *adv* 断然地 duànrán de

flavor *n* 味道 wèidao

flaw *n* 缺点 quēdiǎn; **flawed** *adj* 有缺陷的 yǒu quēxiàn de; **flawless** *adj* 无瑕疵的 wúxiácī de

flea *n* 跳蚤 tiàozǎo; **flea market** 跳蚤市场 tiàozǎo shìchǎng, 旧货市场 jiùhuò shìchǎng

flee *v* (**fled, fled**) 逃跑 táopǎo

fleece *n* 羊毛 yángmáo

fleet *n* 舰队 jiànduì

flesh *n* 肉 ròu; **flesh-eating** *adj* 食肉的 shí ròu de; **in the flesh** 亲自 qīnzì

flew. *See* **fly**

flexibility *n* 灵活性 línghuóxìng, 机动性 jīdòngxìng; **flexible** *adj* 灵活的 línghuó de

flight *n* 航班 hángbān; **flight crew** 机组人员 jīzǔ rényuán; **flight deck** 飞行甲板 fēixíng jiǎbǎn; **flight of stairs** 楼梯的一段 lóutī de yī duàn

flick *v* 轻弹 qīngtán; **flick through** 浏览 liúlǎn

flimsy *adj* 脆弱的 cuìruò de; **flimsiness** *n* 脆弱 cuìruò

flinch *v* 畏缩 wèisuō

fling *v* (**flung, flung**) 抛 pāo, 掷 zhī

flip *v* 翻 fān

flirt *v* 调情 tiáoqíng; **flirtation** *n* 调情 tiáoqíng

float *v* 漂浮 piāofú

flock *n* 群 qún

flog *v* 鞭打 biāndǎ; **flogging** *n* 鞭打 biāndǎ

flood *v* 淹没 yānmò, 淹水 yānshuǐ; *n* 水灾 shuǐzāi, 洪水 hóngshuǐ

floor *n* 楼 lóu, 层 céng; 地板 dìbǎn

flop *v* 彻底失败 chèdǐ shībài

florist *n* 花商 huāshāng; **florist's shop** 花店 huādiàn

flour *n* 面粉 miànfěn

flourish *v* 繁荣 fánróng, 兴旺 xīngwàng; **flourishing** *adj* 繁荣的 fánróng de

flow *v/n* 流动 liúdòng; **flow chart** 流程图 liúchéngtú

flower *n* 花 huā; **flower bed** 花坛 huātán; **flowerpot** *n* 花盆 huāpén; **flower show** 花展 huāzhǎn; **flowery** *adj* 像花一样的 xiàng huā yīyàng de

flown. *See* **fly**

flu *n* 流行性感冒 liúxíngxìng gǎnmào

fluctuate *v* 波动 bōdòng, 涨落 zhǎngluò; **fluctuation** *n* 波动 bōdòng

fluency *n* 流利 liúlì; **fluent** *adj* 流利的 liúlì de; **fluently** *adv* 流利地 liúlì de

fluid *n* 液体 yètǐ; *adj* 流动的 liúdòng de

flung. See **fling**

fluorescence *n* 荧光 yíngguāng; **fluorescent** *adj* 荧光的 yíngguāng de

flush *v* (*face*) 脸红 liǎnhóng; (*flow*) 冲 chōng; **flush the toilet** 冲抽水马桶 chōng chōushuǐmǎtǒng; *adj* 丰足的 fēngzú de, 泛滥的 fànlàn de

flutter *v* 乱跳 luàn tiào

flute *n* 笛子 dízi

flux *n* 变迁 biànqiān

fly *v* (*flew, flown*) 飞 fēi; *n* 苍蝇 cāngyíng; **fly swatter** 苍蝇拍 cāngyíngpāi; **flying saucer** 飞碟 fēidié

focal *adj* 焦点的 jiāodiǎn de; **focal point** 焦点 jiāodiǎn, 召集人 zhàojírén

focus *v* 聚焦 jùjiāo; *n* 焦点 jiāodiǎn, 注视点 zhùshìdiǎn; **in focus** 焦点对准 jiāodiǎn duìzhǔn; **out of focus** 焦点没对准 jiāodiǎn méi duìzhǔn

foe *n* 敌人 dírén

fog *n* 雾 wù

foil *v* 挫败 cuòbài

fold *v* 折叠 zhédié; *n* 折 zhé; **folding** *adj* 折叠的 zhédié de; **folding chair** 折叠椅 zhédiéyǐ

folder *n* 文件夹 wénjiànjiā

folk *n* (*people*) 人们 rénmen; (*relatives*) 亲属 qīnshǔ; *adj* 民间的 mínjiān de; **folk art** 民间艺术 mínjiān yìshù; **folk dance** 民间舞蹈 mínjiān wǔdǎo; **folklore** *n* 民间传说 mínjiān chuánshuō; **folk music** 民乐 mínyuè; **folk song** 民歌 míngē

follow *v* 跟随 gēnsuí, 遵循 zūnxún; **follow up** 采取进一步行动 cǎiqǔ jìnyíbù xíngdòng; **follower** *n* 追随者 zhuīsuízhě; **following** *adj* 下面的 xiàmian de

folly *n* 愚蠢 yúchǔn

fond *adj* 喜爱的 xǐ'ài de, 温柔的 wēnróu de, 温馨的 wēnxīn de; **fondly** *adv* 亲爱地 qīn'ài de; **fondness** *n* 爱好 àihào

fondle *v* 抚弄 fǔnòng

font *n* 字体 zìtǐ

food *n* 食物 shíwù; **food poisoning** 食物中毒 shíwù zhòngdú; **foodstuff** *n* 食品 shípǐn

fool v 愚弄 yúnòng, 欺骗 qīpiàn; n 傻瓜 shǎguā; **fool about/around** 干蠢事 gàn chǔnshì; **foolishness** n 愚蠢 yúchǔn; **foolhardy** adj 有勇无谋的 yǒuyǒng wúmóu de; **foolish** adj 愚蠢的 yúchǔn de; **foolproof** adj 十分简单的 shífēn jiǎndān de

foot n (pl **feet**) (anat) 脚 jiǎo; (measure) 英尺 yīngchǐ; **get cold feet** 临阵萎缩 línzhèn wěisuō; **foothold** n 立足处 lìzúchù; **footnote** n 脚注 jiǎozhù; **footprint** n 足迹 zújī, 脚印 jiǎoyìn; **footstep** n 脚步 jiǎobù

football n 足球 zúqiú, 橄榄球 gǎnlǎnqiú

footing n 立足处 lìzúchù, (social) 地位 dìwèi; **on an equal footing** 处于同等地位 chǔyú tóngděng dìwèi

for prep 为 wèi, 给 gěi, 对 duì; **for example** 例如 lìrú

forbear v 忍受 rěnshòu; **forbearance** n 忍耐 rěnnài

forbid v (**forbade, forbidden**) 禁止 jìnzhǐ

force v 强迫 qiángpò; n 力量 lìliang, 武力 wǔlì; **join forces with ...** 携手合作 yǔ ... xiéshǒu hézuò; **forceful** adj 强有力的 qiángyǒulì de

fore n 前部 qiánbù; (ship) 船头 chuántóu; **to the fore** 在前面 zài qiánmian

forefather n 祖先 zǔxiān

forefront n 最前线 zuìqiánxiàn

foregone adj 过去的 guòqù de; **foregone conclusion** 不可避免的结果 bù kě bìmiǎn de jiéguǒ

forecast v/n (**forecast, forecast**) 预报 yùbào; **weather forecast** 天气预报 tiānqì yùbào

foreground n 前景 qiánjǐng; 最显著的位置 zuì xiǎnzhù de wèizhi

forehead n 前额 qián'é

foreign adj 外国的 wàiguó de; **foreign affairs** 外交事务 wàijiāo shìwù; **foreign exchange** (money) 外汇 wàihuì; **foreign minister** 外交部长 wàijiāo bùzhǎng; **foreign ministry** 外交部 wàijiāobù; **foreign trade** 外贸 wàimào; **foreigner** n 外国人 wàiguórén

foreman n 领班 lǐngbān

foremost adj 最重要的 zuì zhòngyào de, 首要的 shǒuyào de; adv 首要地 shǒuyào de; **first and foremost** 首先 shǒuxiān

forensic adj 法院的 fǎyuàn de, 法医的 fǎyī de

forerunner n 前驱 qiánqū

foresee v (**foresaw, foreseen**) 预见 yùjiàn

foresight n 远见 yuǎnjiàn

forest *n* 森林 sēnlín

forever *adv* 永远 yǒngyuǎn

foreword *n* 前言 qiányán, 序 xù

forfeit *v* 丧失 sàngshī

forgave. *See* **forgive**

forge *v* 伪造 wěizào; 铸造 zhùzào; **forgery** *n* 伪造 wěizào

forgo *v* (**forwent, forgone**) 放弃 fàngqì, 作罢 zuòbà

forget *v* (**forgot, forgotten**) 忘记 wàngjì; **forgetfulness** *n* 健忘 jiànwàng; **forgetful** *adj* 健忘的 jiànwàng de

forgive *v* (**forgave, forgiven**) 原谅 yuánliàng; **forgiveness** *n* 原谅 yuánliàng; **forgiving** *adj* 宽容的 kuānróng de

forgot. *See* **forget**

fork *n* 叉子 chāzi

form *v* 形成 xíngchéng, 构成 gòuchéng; *n* 形式 xíngshì; (*table*) 表格 biǎogé

formal *adj* 正式的 zhèngshì de; 形式上的 xíngshì shang de; **formality** *n* 礼节 lǐjié; 手续 shǒuxù; **formally** *adv* 正式地 zhèngshì de

format *n* 版式 bǎnshì

formation *n* 形成 xíngchéng, 构成 gòuchéng; (*mil*) 编队 biānduì

former *adj* 以前的 yǐqián de, 前任的 qiánrèn de; **formerly** *adv* 以前 yǐqián

formidable *adj* 强大的 qiángdà de, 令人敬畏的 lìng rén jìngwèi de

formula *n* (*pl* **formulae**) 公式 gōngshì

formulate *v* 阐述 chǎnshù, 规划 guīhuà; **formulation** *n* 公式化 gōngshìhuà, 配制 pèizhì

forsake *v* (**forsook, forsaken**) 放弃 fàngqì, 抛弃 pāoqì

fort *n* 堡垒 bǎolěi

forth *adv* 往前 wǎngqián, 向外 xiàngwài; **forthcoming** *adj* (*approaching*) 即将到来的 jíjiāng dàolái de; (*candid*) 坦诚的 tǎnchéng de; **and so forth** 等等 děngděng

fortify *v* 加强 jiāqiáng

fortress *n* 堡垒 bǎolěi, 要塞 yàosài

fortuitous *adj* 幸运的 xìngyùn de

fortunate *adj* 幸运的 xìngyùn de; **fortunately** *adv* 幸运地 xìngyùn de

fortune *n* 运气 yùnqì, 财富 cáifù; **fortune-teller** *n* 算命先生 suànmìng xiānsheng

forty *num* 四十 sìshí; **forties** *num* 第四十 dì sìshí

forum *n* 论坛 lùntán

forward *v* 转送 zhuǎnsòng, 转交 zhuǎnjiāo; *adv* 向前 xiàngqián

forwent. *See* **forgo**

fossil *n* 化石 huàshí; **fossilized** *adj* 僵化的 jiānghuà de

foster *v* 养育 yǎngyù, 培养 péiyǎng

fought. *See* **fight**

foul *n* 犯规 fànguī; *adj* 污秽的 wūhuì de; **foul play** 不公平的比赛 bù gōngpíng de bǐsài

found *v see* **find**; 创建 chuàngjiàn; **founder** *n* 创立者 chuànglìzhě, 缔造者 dìzàozhě

foundation *n* (*organization*) 基金会 jījīnhuì; 基础 jīchǔ

fountain *n* 喷泉 pēnquán; **fountainhead** *n* 源泉 yuánquán; **fountain pen** 钢笔 gāngbǐ

four *num* 四 sì; **fourth** *num* 第四 dì sì

fourteen *num* 十四 shísì; **fourteenth** *num* 第十四 dì shísì

fox *n* 狐狸 húli

fraction *n* 分数 fēnshù; **fractional** *adj* 部分的 bùfen de, 分数的 fēnshù de

fracture *v* 破裂 pòliè; *n* 骨折 gǔzhé

frail *adj* 虚弱的 xūruò de; **frailty** *n* 虚弱 xūruò

fragile *adj* (*object*) 易碎的 yìsuì de; (*person*) 虚弱的 xūruò de

fragment *n* 碎片 suìpiàn

fragrance *n* 芬芳 fēnfāng, 香味 xiāngwèi; **fragrant** *adj* 芬芳的 fēnfāng de, 香的 xiāng de

frame *n* 框架 kuàngjià; **frame of mind** 心情 xīnqíng; **framework** *n* 结构 jiégòu, 框架 kuàngjià

France *n* 法国 fǎguó

franchise *n* (*business*) 特许经营权 tèxǔ jīngyíngquán; (*vote*) 选举权 xuǎnjǔquán

frank *adj* 坦白的 tǎnbái de, 率直的 shuàizhí de; **frankly** *adv* 坦白地 tǎnbái de, 真诚的 zhēnchéng de; **frankness** *n* 率直 shuàizhí

fraud *n* 诈骗 zhàpiàn; **fraudulent** *adj* 欺诈的 qīzhà de

fraught *adj* (*fraught with*) 充满的 chōngmǎn de

freak *n* 畸形 jīxíng, 怪物 guàiwù

free *adj* (*unrestricted*) 自由的 zìyóu de; (*time*) 有空的 yǒukòng de; (*money*) 免费的 miǎnfèi de; **free of charge** 免费的 miǎnfèi de; **free trade** 自由贸易 zìyóu màoyì; **freedom** *n* 自由 zìyóu; **freedom of speech** 言论自由 yánlùn zìyóu; **freedom of the press** 出版自由 chūbǎn zìyóu; **freely** *adv* 自由地 zìyóu de; **freestyle** *n* 自由式 zìyóushì; **freelance** *n* 自由职业者 zìyóu zhíyè zhě

freeze *v* (**froze, frozen**) (*ice*) 结冰 jiébīng; (*asset*) 冻结 dòngjié; **freezer** *n* 冰柜 bīngguì

freight *n* 货物 huòwù; **freighter** *n* 货船 huòchuán

French *n* (*people*) 法国人 fǎguórén; (*language*) 法语 fǎyǔ; *adj* 法国的 fǎguó de

frequency *n* 频率 pínlǜ; **frequent** *adj* 频繁的 pínfán de; **frequently** *adv* 频繁地 pínfán de

fresh *adj* 新鲜的 xīnxiān de; **freshwater** *n* 淡水 dànshuǐ; **freshen up** (使) 精神饱满 (shǐ) jīngshén bǎomǎn; **freshness** *n* 气味清新 qìwèi qīngxīn

friction *n* 摩擦 mócā

Friday *n* 星期五 xīngqīwǔ

fridge *n* 冰箱 bīngxiāng

friend *n* 朋友 péngyou; **make friends with** 与 ... 交朋友 yǔ ... jiāo péngyou; **friendship** *n* 友谊 yǒuyì; **friendliness** *n* 友善 yǒushàn; **friendly** *adj* 友好的 yǒuhǎo de

fright *n* 惊吓 jīngxià; **frighten** *v* 吓唬 xiàhu, 恐吓 kǒnghè; **frightened** *adj* 受惊的 shòujīng de, 受恐吓的 shòu kǒnghè de; **frightening** *adj* 令人恐惧的 lìng rén kǒngjù de

frigid *adj* 寒冷的 hánlěng de

fringe *n* 边缘 biānyuán; **fringe benefits** 附加福利 fùjiā fúlì

frivolity *n* 轻薄 qīngbó; **frivolous** *adj* 无聊的 wúliáo de

fro *adv* 向后 xiànghòu; **to and fro** 来来回回 láilái huíhuí

frog *n* 青蛙 qīngwā

from *prep* 从 cóng

front *n* 前面 qiánmian, 前线 qiánxiàn; **in front of** 在 ... 前面 zài ... qiánmian

frontier *n* 边境 biānjìng, 边疆 biānjiāng

frost *n* 霜 shuāng; **frostbite** *n* 冻伤 dòngshāng

froze. *See* **freeze**

frozen *v* see **freeze**; *adj* 结冰的 jiébīng de; **frozen food** 冷冻食物 lěngdòng shíwù

frown *v* 皱眉头 zhòu méitóu; **frown on/upon** 表示不赞成 biǎoshì bù zànchéng

frugality *n* 节俭 jiéjiǎn; **frugal** *adj* 节俭的 jiéjiǎn de, 朴素的 pǔsù de

fruit *n* 水果 shuǐguǒ; **fruit cake** 水果蛋糕 shuǐguǒ dàngāo; **fruit salad** 水果沙拉 shuǐguǒ shālā; **fruitful** *adj* 多产的 duōchǎn de, 富有成效的 fùyǒu chéngxiào de; **fruitless** *adj* 不结果的 bù jiéguǒ de, 无效的 wúxiào de

frustrate *v* 挫败 cuòbài, 阻止 zǔzhǐ; **frustration** *n* 挫败

cuòbài, 失望 shīwàng, 失意 shīyì; **frustrated** *adj* 挫败的 cuòbài de, 失望的 shīwàng de, 泄气的 xièqì de

fry *v* 油炸 yóuzhà, 炒 chǎo; **frying pan** 煎锅 jiānguō

fuel *v* 加燃料 jiā ránliào; *n* 燃料 ránliào; **fuel gauge** 燃油计 rányóujì; **fuel pump** 燃油泵 rányóubèng

fugitive *n* 逃亡者 táowángzhě

fulfill *v* (*promise or obligation*) 履行 lǚxíng; (*wishes*) 满足 mǎnzú; (*ambition*) 实现 shíxiàn; **fulfillment** *n* 实行 shíxíng; 满足 mǎnzú; 实现 shíxiàn

full *adj* (*filled*) 满的 mǎn de; (*whole*) 完全的 wánquán de; (*appetite satisfied*) 饱的 bǎo de; **full house** 客满 kèmǎn; **full-time** 全职的 quánzhí de; **fully** *adv* 完全地 wánquán de; 充分地 chōngfèn de

fun *n* 乐趣 lèqù; *adj* 有趣的 yǒuqù de; **make fun of** 取笑 qǔxiào

function *v* 起作用 qǐ zuòyòng; 行使职责 xíngshǐ zhízé; *n* (*role, feature*) 功能 gōngnéng, (*use*) 作用 zuòyòng; (*occasion*) 仪式 yíshì; **functional** *adj* 功能的 gōngnéng de

fund *v* 拨款 bōkuǎn; *n* 基金 jījīn, 资金 zījīn; **funding** *n* 资助 zīzhù, 基金 jījīn, 专款 zhuānkuǎn

fundamental *adj* 根本的 gēnběn de

funeral *n* 葬礼 zànglǐ

fungus *n* 菌类 jūnlèi

funny *adj* 好笑的 hǎoxiào de, 滑稽的 huájī de

fur *n* 毛皮 máopí; **fur coat** 皮大衣 pídàyī

furious *adj* 狂怒的 kuángnù de

furnace *n* 熔炉 rónglú

furnish *v* 提供 tígòng; **furnishings** *n* 家具 jiājù

furniture *n* 家具 jiājù

further *v* 增进 zēngjìn; *adj* 更远的 gèng yuǎn de; **furthermore** *adv* 此外 cǐwài; 而且 érqiě; 进一步地 jìnyíbù de

fury *n* 暴怒 bàonù

fuse *n* 保险丝 bǎoxiǎnsī; **fuse box** 保险丝盒 bǎoxiǎnsīhé

fuss *n* 大惊小怪 dàjīng xiǎoguài; **a lot of fuss about nothing** 大惊小怪 dàjīng xiǎoguài; **fussy** *adj* 爱挑剔的 ài tiāotī de, 难取悦的 nán qǔyuè de

futile *adj* 无用的 wúyòng de, 无效果的 wú xiàoguǒ de

future *n* 未来 wèilái, 前途 qiántú

G

gadget *n* 小配件 xiǎo pèijiàn, 小玩艺 xiǎo wányì

gag *v* 限制言论 xiànzhì yánlùn

gain *v* 得到 dédào, 获利 huòlì; *n* 收获 shōuhuò, 获益 huòyì

gala *n* 盛会 shènghuì

galaxy *n* 星系 xīngxì

gall *n* 胆汁 dǎnzhī; **gall-bladder** *n* 膀胱 pángguāng

gallery *n* 画廊 huàláng, 美术馆 měishùguǎn

gallon *n* 加仑 jiālún

gallow *v* 恐吓 kǒnghè; **gallows** *n* 绞刑架 jiǎoxíngjià

galvanize *v* (使) 振奋 (shǐ) zhènfèn

gamble *v* 赌博 dǔbó; **gambler** *n* 赌徒 dǔtú; **gambling** *n* 赌博 dǔbó

game *n* (*play*) 游戏 yóuxì; (*competition*) 比赛 bǐsài

gang *n* 团伙 tuánhuǒ, 帮派 bāngpài; **gangster** *n* 歹徒 dǎitú

gap *n* 缺口 quēkǒu, 间断 jiànduàn

garage *n* 车库 chēkù

garbage *n* 垃圾 lājī; **garbage can** 垃圾桶 lājītǒng

garble *v* 混淆不清 hùnxiáo bù qīng; **garbled** *adj* 混乱不清的 hùnluàn bù qīng de

garden *n* 花园 huāyuán; **gardener** *n* 园丁 yuándīng; **gardening** *n* 园艺 yuányì

garlic *n* 大蒜 dàsuàn

garment *n* 衣服 yīfu

garnish *v* 装饰 zhuāngshì

garrison *n* 驻军 zhùjūn

gas *n* 汽油 qìyóu; **gasmask** *n* 防毒面具 fàngdù miànjù; **gas station** 加油站 jiāyóuzhàn; **gas tank** 油箱 yóuxiāng; **gas stove** 煤气炉 méiqìlú; **gasoline** *n* 汽油 qìyóu

gash *n* 很深的伤口 hěn shēn de shāngkǒu

gasp *v* 喘息 chuǎnxī, 喘气 chuǎnqì

gastronomy *n* 美食法 měishífǎ, 烹饪法 pēngrènfǎ; **gastronomic** *adj* 美食的 měishí de

gate *n* 大门 dàmén; **gate-keeper** *n* 看门人 kānménrén; **gatepost** *n* 门柱 ménzhù; **gateway** *n* 通路 tōnglù

gather *v* 聚集 jùjí, 采集 cǎijí; **gathering** *n* 聚会 jùhuì

gauge *v* 测量 cèliáng; **pressure gauge** 压力计 yālìjì

gave. *See* **give**

gay *n* 同性恋者 tóngxìngliànzhě; *adj* (*happy*) 快乐的 kuàilè de; (*homosexual*) 同性恋的 tóngxìngliàn de

gaze *v* 盯 dīng, 凝视 níngshì

gear *v* (使) 适合 (shǐ) shìhé; *n* 齿轮 chǐlún

geese. *See* **goose**

gem *n* 宝石 bǎoshí

gender *n* 性别 xìngbié

genealogy *n* 系谱 xìpǔ, 家谱 jiāpǔ

general *adj* 一般的 yībān de, 总的 zǒng de; **general election** 大选 dàxuǎn; **in general** 通常 tōngcháng; **generally** *adv* 一般 yībān; **generally speaking** 一般来说 yībān láishuō, 总的来说 zǒngde láishuō; **generalize** *v* 概括 gàikuò, 归纳 guīnà

generate *v* 产生 chǎnshēng; **generator** *n* 发电机 fādiànjī

generation *n* (*procreation*) 产生 chǎnshēng; (*people*) 一代 yīdài, 一代人 yīdàirén

generic *adj* 一般的 yībān de, 普通的 pǔtōng de

generosity *n* 慷慨 kāngkǎi; **generous** *adj* 慷慨的 kāngkǎi de

genetic *adj* 遗传的 yíchuán de, 基因的 jīyīn de; **genetics** *n* 遗传学 yíchuánxué

genital *n* 生殖器 shēngzhíqì

genitive *n* 所有格 suǒyǒugé

genius *n* 天才 tiāncái

genocide *n* 种族灭绝 zhǒngzú mièjué

gentle *adj* 温和的 wēnhé de, 文雅的 wényǎ de

gentleman *n* 绅士 shēnshì, 先生 xiānsheng

genuine *adj* 真正的 zhēnzhèng de

geography *n* 地理 dìlǐ; **geographical** *adj* 地理的 dìlǐ de

geology *n* 地质学 dìzhìxué

geometry *n* 几何学 jǐhéxué; **geometrical** *adj* 几何学的 jǐhéxué de

germ *n* 细菌 xìjūn

Germany *n* 德国 déguó; **German** *n* (*people*) 德国人 déguórén; (*language*) 德语 déyǔ; *adj* 德国的 déguó de

gesture *n* (*hand*) 手势 shǒushì; (*demonstration*) 姿态 zītài

get *v* (**got, gotten**) 得到 dédào; **get away** 离开 líkāi, 逃离 táolí; **get back** (*return*) 回来 huílái; (*recover*) 重新得到 chóngxīn dédào; **get married** 结婚 jiéhūn; **get off** 下车 xiàchē; **get on** 上车 shàngchē; **get out** 出去 chūqù; (*escape*) 逃脱 táotuō; **get ready** 准备好 zhǔnbèi hǎo; **get together** 聚会 jùhuì; **get up** 起床 qǐchuáng; **get-together** *n* 聚会 jùhuì, 联欢会 liánhuānhuì

ghastly *adj* 恐怖的 kǒngbù de

ghetto *n* 贫民区 pínmínqū

ghost *n* 鬼 guǐ; **ghost writer** 捉刀人 zhuōdāorén; **ghostly** *adj* 可怕的 kěpà de

giant *n* 巨人 jùrén; *adj* 庞大的 pángdà de; **gigantic** *adj* 巨大的 jùdà de

gift *n* 礼物 lǐwù; **gifted** *adj* 有天赋的 yǒu tiānfù de

giggle n 傻笑 shǎxiào

gimmick n 花招 huāzhāo, 骗局 piànjú

ginger n 生姜 shēngjiāng

Gypsy n 吉卜赛人 jíbǔsàirén; adj 吉卜赛人的 jíbǔsàirén de

giraffe n 长颈鹿 chángjǐnglù

girl n 女孩 nǚhái; **girlfriend** n 女朋友 nǚpéngyou

gist n 要点 yàodiǎn

give v (**gave, given**) 给 gěi; **give away** 泄漏 xièlòu; **give back** 归还 guīhuán; **give in** 屈服 qūfú, 让步 ràngbù; **give up** 放弃 fàngqì; **give birth** 生孩子 shēng háizi; **give sb. a hand** 帮 bāng

glacier n 冰河 bīnghé

glad adj 高兴的 gāoxìng de; **gladly** adv 高兴地 gāoxìng de

glamour n 魅力 mèilì; **glamorous** adj 迷人的 mírén de

glance v 扫视 sǎoshì; n 扫视 sǎoshì, 一瞥 yīpiē

glare n 炫目的光 xuànmù de guāng

glass n (container) 杯子 bēizi; (substance) 玻璃 bōli

glasses. See **eyeglasses**

gleam v 闪烁 shǎnshuò; n 闪光 shǎnguāng, 微光 wēiguāng

glean v 搜集 sōují

glide v 滑行 huáxíng; **glider** n 滑翔机 huáxiángjī

glimmer n 闪光 shǎnguāng

glimpse v 瞥见 piējiàn; n 一瞥 yīpiē; **catch a glimpse of** 瞥见 piējiàn

glisten v 闪光 shǎnguāng; **glistening** adj 闪耀的 shǎnyào de

glitter v 闪光 shǎnguāng

globe n 地球 dìqiú; **global** adj 全球的 quánqiú de

gloom n 阴暗 yīn'àn; **gloomy** adj 令人沮丧的 lìng rén jǔsàng de, 阴郁的 yīnyù de

glory n 光荣 guāngróng; **glorious** adj 光荣的 guāngróng de

gloss v 发光 fāguāng; n 光泽 guāngzé, 色泽 sèzé; **gloss over** 掩盖 yǎngài

glossary n 词表 cíbiǎo

glove n 手套 shǒutào; **hand in glove with** 亲密地 qīnmì de

glow v 发热 fārè, 发光 fāguāng, 光亮 guāngliàng, 光辉 guānghuī

glue v 粘贴 zhāntiē; n 胶水 jiāoshuǐ

gnash v (one's teeth) 咬牙切齿 yǎoyá qièchǐ

gnaw v 啃 kěn

go v (**went, gone**) 去 qù; **go ahead** 前进 qiánjìn; 先走 xiān zǒu; 着手进行 zhuóshǒu jìnxíng; **go away** 走开 zǒu kāi; **go back** 回去 huí qù; 变质 biànzhì; **go down** 下去 xiàqù,

下降 xiàjiàng; **go in** (*enter*) 进入 jìnrù; (*join*) 参加 cānjiā;
go into 进入 jìnrù; **go on** 继续 jìxù; **go out** (*set out*)
出门 chūmén; (*fire, light*) 熄灭 xīmiè; **go over** (*inspect*)
察看 chákàn; (*review*) 温习 wēnxí; **go through** (*undergo*)
经历 jīnglì, (*examine*) 详查 xiángchá; **go up** 上升
shàngshēng, 增长 zēngzhǎng; **go with** 伴随 bànsuí; **go to
a doctor** 看医生 kàn yīshēng; **go to bed** 上床
shàngchuáng; **go to school** 上学 shàngxué; **go to the
movies** 看电影 kàn diànyǐng; **go to work** 上班 shàngbān;
go home 回家 huí jiā; **go bad** 变坏 biàn huài

goal *n* (*purpose*) 目标 mùbiāo; (*ball game*) 球门 qiúmén;
goalkeeper *n* 守门员 shǒuményuán; **goalpost** *n* 球门柱
qiúménzhù

goat *n* 山羊 shānyáng

god *n* 神 shén; **God** *n* 上帝 shàngdì; **goddess** *n* 女神 nǔshén

goggles *n* 风镜 fēngjìng, 护目镜 hùmùjìng

gold *n* 黄金 huángjīn; *adj* 金的 jīn de; **golden** *adj* 金色的
jīnsè de

goldfish *n* 金鱼 jīnyú

golf *n* 高尔夫球 gāo'ěrfūqiú; **golf course** 高尔夫球场
gāo'ěrfūqiúchǎng

gone. *See* go

good *adj* 好的 hǎo de; **good-looking** *adj* 好看的 hǎokàn de;
good-tempered *adj* 脾气好的 píqi hǎo de; **goodness** *n*
善良 shànliáng; **goods** *n* 货物 huòwù; **good afternoon**
interj 下午好 xiàwǔ hǎo; **good evening** *interj* 晚上好
wǎnshang hǎo; **good morning** *interj* 早上好 zǎoshang
hǎo; **good night** *interj* 晚安 wǎn'ān; **good-bye** *interj*
再见 zàijiàn; **goodwill** *n* 善意 shànyì, 友善 yǒushàn

goose *n* (*pl* **geese**) 鹅 é

gorge *n* 峡谷 xiágǔ

gorgeous *adj* 华丽的 huálì de, 美妙的 měimiào de

gossip *v* 说长道短 shuōcháng dàoduǎn, 闲聊 xiánliáo; *n*
流言蜚语 liúyán fēiyǔ, 闲话 xiánhuà

got. *See* get

govern *v* 统治 tǒngzhì, 支配 zhīpèi; **governess** *n*
女家庭教师 nǔ jiātíngjiàoshī; **government** *n* 政府
zhèngfǔ; **governor** *n* 统治者 tǒngzhìzhě; (*of a state*) 州长
zhōuzhǎng

gown *n* 长袍 chángpáo, 睡袍 shuìpáo

grab *v* 抢 qiǎng, 夺 duó

graceful *adj* 优美的 yōuměi de

grade *n* (*year in school*) 年级 niánjí; (*mark*) 分数 fēnshù

gradual *adj* 逐渐的 zhújiàn de, 渐进的 jiànjìn de; **gradually**
adv 逐渐地 zhújiàn de, 渐进地 jiànjìn de

graduate *v* 毕业 bìyè; *n* 毕业生 bìyèshēng; **graduate school**
研究生院 yánjiūshēngyuàn; **graduate student** 研究生
yánjiūshēng

grain *n* 谷物 gǔwù, 粮食 liángshi

gram *n* 克 kè

grammar *n* 语法 yǔfǎ; **grammatical** *adj* 语法的 yǔfǎ de,
合语法的 hé yǔfǎ de

grand *adj* 盛大的 shèngdà de; **grandchild** *n* 孙辈 sūnbèi;
grandfather *n* (*father's father*) 爷爷 yéye; (*mother's
father*) 外公 wàigōng; **grandmother** *n* (*father's mother*)
奶奶 nǎinai; (*mother's mother*) 外婆 wàipó; **grandparents**
n (*paternal*) 祖父母 zǔfùmǔ; (*maternal*) 外祖父母
wàizǔfùmǔ

granite *n* 花岗岩 huāgāngyán

grant *v* 同意 tóngyì, 准予 zhǔnyǔ; *n* 资助款 zīzhùkuǎn

grape *n* 葡萄 pútáo

grapefruit *n* 柚子 yòuzi

graph *n* 图表 túbiǎo; **graphic** *adj* 图解的 tújiě de, 图表的
túbiǎo de; **graphic arts** 平面造型艺术 píngmiàn zàoxíng
yìshù; **graphic designer** 美术设计员 měishù shèjì yuán

grasp *v* (*seize*) 抓住 zhuāzhù; (*comprehend*) 领会 lǐnghuì; *n*
掌握 zhǎngwò

grass *n* 草 cǎo

grateful *adj* 感谢的 gǎnxiè de, 感激的 gǎnjī de

gratify *v* (使) 满足 (shǐ) mǎnzú; **gratifying** *adj* 令人满意的
lìng rén mǎnyì de

gratitude *n* 感激 gǎnjī

gratuity *n* 小费 xiǎofèi

grave *n* 坟墓 fénmù; **graveyard** *n* 墓地 mùdì; *adj* 严重的
yánzhòng de

gravity *n* (*force*) 地心引力 dìxīnyǐnlì; (*seriousness*) 严重性
yánzhòngxìng

gravy *n* 肉汁 ròuzhī

gray. *See* **grey**

grease *n* 油脂 yóuzhī; **greasy** *adj* 油腻的 yóunì de

great *adj* 大的 dà de, 伟大的 wěidà de; **greatly** *adv* 很 hěn,
非常 fēicháng

Great Britain *n* 英国 yīngguó

Greece *n* 希腊 xīlà; **Greek** *n* (*people*) 希腊人 xīlàrén; (*language*) 希腊语 xīlàyǔ; *adj* 希腊的 xīlà de

greed *n* 贪婪 tānlán; **greedy** *adj* 贪婪的 tānlán de

green *adj* 绿色的 lǜsè de; **greens** *n* 青菜 qīngcài

greenhouse *n* 温室 wēnshì

greet *v* 打招呼 dǎzhāohu; **greeting** *n* 问候 wènhòu

grew. *See* **grow**

grey *adj* 灰色的 huīsè de

grid *n* 格子 gézi

grief *n* 悲痛 bēitòng, 忧伤 yōushāng; **grief-stricken** *adj* 悲痛欲绝的 bēitòng yùjué de

grieve *v* 伤心 shāngxīn, 感到悲痛 gǎndào bēitòng

grievous *adj* 令人忧伤的 lìng rén yōushāng de

grill *v* 烧烤 shāokǎo

grim *adj* 严酷的 yánkù de

grind *v* (**ground, ground**) 磨碎 mósuì, 碾碎 niǎnsuì

grip *n* 紧握 jǐnwò

groan *v* 呻吟 shēnyín

grocer *n* 杂货店 záhuòdiàn, 食品店 shípǐndiàn; **groceries** *n* 杂货 záhuò, 食品 shípǐn

groom *n* 新郎 xīnláng

groove *n* 凹槽 āocáo

grope *v* 摸索 mōsuǒ

ground *v see* **grind**; *n* 地 dì, 地面 dìmiàn; **grounds** *n* 根据 gēnjù, 理由 lǐyóu; *adj* 地面的 dìmiàn de, 靠地面的 kào dìmiàn de; **ground floor** *n* 底层 dǐcéng; **groundwork** *n* 基础 jīchǔ

group *v* 使 ... 形成组 shǐ ... xíngchéng zǔ, 将 ... 归于一类 jiāng ... guīyú yīlèi; *n* 团 tuán, 组 zǔ, 群 qún

gross *adj* (*total*) 总的 zǒngde; (*not net*) 毛重的 máozhòng de

grow *v* (**grew, grown**) 生长 shēngzhǎng, 成长 chéngzhǎng; (*plant*) 种植 zhòngzhí; **grow up** 长大 zhǎng dà

growl *v* 咆哮 páoxiāo

grown-up *n* 成年人 chéngniánrén; *adj* 成年的 chéngnián de

growth *n* 生长 shēngzhǎng, 成长 chéngzhǎng, 增长 zēngzhǎng

grudge *v* 怨恨 yuànhèn, 嫌恶 xiánwù; *n* 不满 bùmǎn, 嫌隙 xiánxì; **bear a grudge** 对 ... 怀有积怨 duì ... huáiyǒu jīyuàn; **grudgingly** *adv* 勉强地 miǎnqiǎng de

gruesome *adj* 可怕的 kěpà de, 可憎的 kězēng de

guarantee *v/n* 担保 dānbǎo, 保证 bǎozhèng

guard *v* 保卫 bǎowèi, 看守 kānshǒu, 守卫 shǒuwèi; *n* 警戒

jǐngjiè, 警惕 jǐngtì, 警卫 jǐngwèi; **be on guard** 警惕
jǐngtì; **guard against** 防备 fángbèi

guardian *n* 监护人 jiānhùrén

guerrilla *n* 游击队员 yóujīduìyuán; **guerrilla war** 游击战
yóujīzhàn

guess *v/n* 猜测 cāicè

guest *n* 客人 kèrén, 宾馆 bīnguǎn; **guest of honor** 贵宾
guìbīn; **guesthouse** *n* 招待所 zhāodàisuǒ, 宾馆 bīnguǎn;
guest room 客房 kèfáng

guidance *n* 指导 zhǐdǎo

guide *v* 指导 zhǐdǎo; *n* 导游 dǎoyóu, 向导 xiàngdǎo;
guidebook *n* 旅行指南 lǚxíng zhǐnán

guilt *n* (*offense*) 罪行 zuìxíng (*remorse*) 内疚 nèijiù; **guilty**
adj 有罪的 yǒuzuì de; 内疚的 nèijiù de; **plead guilty**
认罪 rènzuì

guinea pig *n* (*animal*) 天竺鼠 tiānzhúshǔ; (*experiment*)
实验品 shíyànpǐn

guitar *n* 吉它 jítā; **guitarist** *n* 吉他手 jítāshǒu

gulf *n* 海湾 hǎiwān

gum *n* 口香糖 kǒuxiāngtáng; **gums** *n* 牙龈 yáyín

gun *n* (*pistol, rifle*) 枪 qiāng; (*cannon*) 炮 pào; **gunfire** *n*
炮火 pàohuǒ; **gunman** *n* 枪手 qiāngshǒu; **gunpowder** *n*
火药 huǒyào

guts *n* (*entrails*) 内脏 nèizàng; (*determination*) 胆量 dǎnliàng

guy *n* (*fellow*) 家伙 jiāhuo; (*man*) 男人 nánrén

gym *n* 体育馆 tǐyùguǎn, 健身房 jiànshēnfáng

gymnasium *n* 体育馆 tǐyùguǎn; **gymnast** *n* 体操运动员
tǐcāo yùndòngyuán; **gymnastics** *n* 体操 tǐcāo

gynecology *n* 妇科学 fùkēxué; **gynecological** *adj* 妇科的
fùkē de; **gynecologist** *n* 妇科医生 fùkē yīshēng

H

habit *n* 习惯 xíguàn; **habitat** *n* 生活环境 shēnghuó huánjìng;
habitual *adj* 习惯性的 xíguànxìng de

hack *v* 砍 kǎn, 劈 pī

had. *See* **have**

hail *v* 致敬 zhìjìng; **hail from** 来自 lái zì; *n* 冰雹 bīngbáo;
hailstone *n* 冰雹 bīngbáo; **hailstorm** *n* 雹暴 báobào

hair *n* (*body*) 毛 máo; (*head*) 发 fà; **split hairs** 吹毛求疵
chuīmáo qiúcī; **hairbrush** *n* 发刷 fàshuā; **haircut** *n* 理发
lǐfà; **hairdresser** *n* 美发师 měifàshī; **hairdryer** *n* 吹风机

chuīfēngjī; **hairpiece** *n* 假发 jiǎfà; **hairpin** *n* 发夹 fàjiā;
hairstyle *n* 发型 faxing; **hairy** *adj* 多毛的 duōmáo de
Haiti *n* 海地 hǎidì; **Haitian** *n* 海地人 hǎidìrén; *adj* 海地的
hǎidì de
half *n* (*pl* **halves**) 一半 yībàn; **half an hour** 半小时 bàn
xiǎoshí; **half-price** *n* 半价 bànjià; **half-time** *n* 中场休息
zhōngchǎng xiūxi; **halfway** *adv* 半路上 bànlù shang
hall *n* 大堂 dàtáng, 大厅 dàtīng, 门厅 méntīng; (*corridor*)
走廊 zǒuláng
hallmark *n* 特点 tèdiǎn
hallucination *n* 幻觉 huànjué
halt *v/n* 停止 tíngzhǐ, 中止 zhōngzhǐ
halve *v* 平分 píngfēn, 减半 jiǎnbàn
halves. *See* half
ham *n* 火腿 huǒtuǐ
hamburger *n* 汉堡包 hànbǎobāo
hammer *v* 锤打 chuídǎ; *n* 锤子 chuízi
hand *n* 手 shǒu; **handful** *n* 少数 shǎoshù; **at hand** 在手头
zài shǒutóu; **hand in hand** 携手 xiéshǒu; **on the other
hand** 在另一方面 zài lìngyī fāngmiàn; **hand down**
传下来 chuán xiàlái; **hand in** 交上 jiāo shàng; **hand over**
移交 yíjiāo
handbag *n* 手提包 shǒutíbāo
handbook *n* 手册 shǒucè
handcuffs *n* 手铐 shǒukào
handicap *n* 障碍 zhàng'ài
handicraft *n* 手工艺 shǒugōngyì
handkerchief *n* 手帕 shǒupà
handle *v* 处理 chǔlǐ, 操作 cāozuò; *n* 把手 bǎshou; **handle
with care** 小心轻放 xiǎoxīn qīngfàng
handmade *adj* 手工制作的 shǒugōng zhìzuò de
handout *n* 传单 chuándān
handshake *n* 握手 wòshǒu
handsome *adj* 英俊的 yīngjùn de
handwriting *n* 书写体 shūxiětǐ, 笔迹 bǐjī
handy *adj* 便利的 biànlì de, 手边的 shǒubiān de
hang *v* (**hung, hung**) 挂 guà; **hang on** 坚持 jiānchí,
紧紧抓住 jǐnjǐn zhuāzhù; **hang up** (*telephone*) 挂 guà;
(*suspend*) 吊 diào; (*kill*) 吊死 diào sǐ, 绞死 jiǎo sǐ;
hangar *n* 飞机棚 fēijīpéng
hanger *n* 衣架 yījià
hangman *n* 刽子手 guìzishǒu

hangover *n* 宿醉 sùzuì

happen *v* 发生 fāshēng

happy *adj* 快乐的 kuàilè de, 幸福的 xìngfú de; **happiness** *n* 幸福 xìngfú

harass *v* 骚扰 sāorǎo; **harassment** *n* 骚扰 sāorǎo

harbor *v* 庇护 bìhù, 心怀 xīnhuái; *n* 港口 gǎngkǒu

hard *adv* 努力 nǔlì; *adj* 硬的 yìng de; **hard disk** 硬盘 yìngpán; **hard-and-fast** *adj* 严格的 yángé de; **hard-hearted** *adj* 无情的 wúqíng de; **hard labor** 强迫劳役 qiǎngpò láoyì; **harden** *v* (使) 变硬 (shǐ) biàn yìng; **hardship** *n* 艰难 jiānnán, 困苦 kùnkǔ; **hardly** *adv* 几乎不 jīhū bù, 几乎没有 jīhū méiyǒu

hardware *n* 硬件 yìngjiàn

hare *n* 野兔 yětù; **hare-brained** *adj* 轻率的 qīngshuài de

harm *v* 伤害 shānghài; *n* 伤害 shānghài, 害处 hàichu; **harmful** *adj* 有害的 yǒuhài de; **harmless** *adj* 无害的 wúhài de

harmony *n* 和谐 héxié, 融洽 róngqià; **harmonious** *adj* 和谐的 héxié de

harp *n* 竖琴 shùqín; **harpist** *n* 竖琴师 shùqínshī

harsh *adj* 严厉的 yánlì de

harvest *v/n* 收获 shōuhuò

has. *See* **have**

hassle *n* 麻烦 máfan, 争吵 zhēngchǎo

haste *n* 匆忙 cōngmáng; **hasten** *v* 急忙 jímáng, 赶紧 gǎnjǐn; **hasty** *adj* 匆忙的 cōngmáng de, 草率的 cǎoshuài de

hat *n* 帽子 màozi; **take one's hat off to** 向 ... 致敬 xiàng ... zhìjìng

hate *v* 恨 hèn; **hatred** *n* 仇恨 chóuhèn, 憎恨 zēnghèn; **hateful** *adj* 可恶的 kěwù de

haughty *adj* 傲慢的 àomàn de; **haughtiness** *n* 傲慢 àomàn

haunt *v* 神鬼出没 shénguǐ chūmò; **haunted** *adj* 闹鬼的 nàoguǐ de, 鬼魂出没的 guǐhún chūmò de

have *v* (**had**, **had**) 有 yǒu

havoc *n* 大破坏 dàpòhuài; **wreak havoc on** (使) 陷入大混乱 (shǐ) xiànrù dàhùnluàn

hawk *n* 鹰 yīng

hay *n* 干草 gāncǎo; **make hay while the sun shines** 趁热打铁 chènrè dǎtiě; **haystack** *n* 干草堆 gāncǎoduī

hazard *n* 危险 wēixiǎn; **hazardous** *adj* 危险的 wēixiǎn de, 有害的 yǒuhài de

he *pron* 他 tā

head *v* 居 ... 之首 jū ... zhī shǒu, 率领 shuàilǐng; **head for**

向 ... 行进 xiàng ... xíngjìn; *n (body)* 头 tóu; *(chief)* 领导
lǐngdǎo ; **headlight** *n* 前灯 qiándēng; **headache** *n* 头痛
tóutòng; **headline** *n* 大字标题 dàzì biāotí; **headmaster** *n*
男校长 nánxiàozhǎng; **headmistress** *n* 女校长 nǚxi-
àozhǎng; **headphones** *n* 耳机 ěrjī; **headquarters** *n*
总部 zǒngbù; **head-on** *adj* 正面的 zhèngmiàn de;
迎面的 yíngmiàn de; *adv* 正面地 zhèngmiàn de; 迎面地
yíngmiàn de
heal *v* 治愈 zhìyù
health *n* 医疗 yīliáo, 健康 jiànkāng; **health certificate**
健康证明书 jiànkāng zhèngmíngshū; **healthcare** *n*
卫生保健 wèishēng bǎojiàn; **healthy** *adj* 健康的 jiànkāng
de
heap *v/n* 堆 duī
hear *v (heard, heard)* 听到 tīng dào, 听见 tīngjiàn; **hear**
from 接到 ... 的信 jiē dào ... de xìn; **hear about/of** 听说
tīngshuō; **hearing** *n (sense)* 听力 tīnglì; *(law)* 听证会
tīngzhènghuì; **hearing aid** 助听器 zhùtīngqì
heart *n* 心 xīn; **heart attack** 心脏病发作 xīnzàngbìng fāzuò;
by heart 熟记 shújì; **set one's heart on** 决心得到 juéxīn
dédào, 决心做 juéxīn zuò; **to one's heart's content**
尽情地 jìnqíng de; **heartbeat** *n* 心跳 xīntiào; **heart-**
breaking *adj* 令人悲伤的 lìng rén bēishāng de; **heart-**
broken *adj* 悲伤的 bēishāng de; **heartfelt** *adj* 衷心的
zhōngxīn de; **heart-to-heart** *adj* 率直的 shuàizhí de,
诚实的 chéngshí de; **have a heart-to-heart talk**
倾心交谈 qīngxīn jiāotán; **heartless** *adj* 无情的 wúqíng
de; **hearten** *v* 振奋 zhènfèn; **hearty** *adj* 丰盛的 fēng-
shèng de, 热情的 rèqíng de
heat *v* 加热 jiārè; *n* 热 rè; **in the heat of the moment**
一时激动之下 yīshí jīdòng zhīxià; **heater** *n* 加热器
jiārèqì, 取暖器 qǔnuǎnqì; **heated** *adj* 激烈的 jīliè de;
heating *n* 暖气 nuǎnqì
heave *v (sigh)* 发出 fāchū
heaven *n* 天堂 tiāntáng, 天空 tiānkōng; **heavenly** *adj*
神圣的 shénshèng de
heavy *adj* 重的 zhòng de; **heaviness** *n* 沉重 chénzhòng;
heavyweight *n* 有影响的人物 yǒu yǐngxiǎng de rénwù
Hebrew *n (people)* 希伯莱人 xībóláirén; *(language)*
希伯莱语 xībóláiyǔ
hectare *n* 公顷 gōngqǐng
hectic *adj* 忙碌的 mánglù de

hedge *n* 树篱 shùlí

hedgehog *n* 刺猬 cìwei

heed *v* 留意 liúyì, 注意 zhùyì, 听从 tīngcóng; **heedless** *adj* 不注意的 bù zhùyì de

heel *n* 脚跟 jiǎogēn

hefty *adj* 重的 zhòng de; 可观的 kěguān de

height *n* 高度 gāodù; **heighten** *v* 提高 tígāo

heir *n* 继承人 jìchéngrén; **heiress** *n* 女继承人 nǚjìchéngrén; **heirloom** *n* 传家宝 chuánjiābǎo; **go to hell!** 见你的鬼! jiàn nǐde guǐ; **to hell with it!** 见鬼去吧! jiàn guǐ qù ba

helicopter *n* 直升飞机 zhíshēng fēijī

hell *n* 地狱 dìyù

hello! *interj* 你好! nǐ hǎo

helm *n* 舵 duò; **be at the helm** 掌舵 zhǎngduò, 掌权 zhǎngquán

helmet *n* 头盔 tóukuī

help *v/n* 帮助 bāngzhù; **help yourself!** 请随便用! qǐng suíbiàn yòng; **helper** *n* 帮手 bāngshou; **helpful** *adj* 有用的 yǒuyòng de, 有助的 yǒuzhù de; **helpless** *adj* 无助的 wúzhù de; **it can't be helped!** 实在没法儿! shízài méi fǎr; **helping** *n* (*of food*) 一份 yī fèn

hemisphere *n* 半球 bànqiú

hen *n* 母鸡 mǔjī; **henpecked** *adj* 惧内的 jùnèi de

hence *adv* 因此 yīncǐ, 从此 cóngcǐ

henceforth *adv* 从今以后 cóng jīn yǐhòu

her *pron* 她 tā

herb *n* 药草 yàocǎo

herd *n* 牧群 mùqún

here *adv* 这里 zhèlǐ, 这儿 zhè'r

hereditary *adj* 世袭的 shìxí de, 遗传的 yíchuán de

heritage *n* 遗产 yíchǎn

hernia *n* 疝气 shànqì

hero *n* 英雄 yīngxióng (*main male character in a story*, *play*, *film*); 男主角 nánzhǔjué; **heroine** *n* 女英雄 nǚyīngxióng; (*main female character in a story*, *play*, *film*) 女主角 nǚzhǔjué; **heroic** *adj* 英勇的 yīngyǒng de

hers *pron* 她的 tāde

herself *pron* 她自己 tā zìjǐ

hesitate *v* 犹豫 yóuyù; **hesitation** *n* 犹豫 yóuyù; **hesitant** *adj* 犹豫的 yóuyù de

heterosexual *n* 异性恋者 yìxìngliànzhě; *adj* 异性恋的 yìxìngliàn de

hibernate *v* 冬眠 dōngmián; **hibernation** *n* 冬眠 dōngmián
hiccup *v/n* 打嗝 dǎgé
hid. *See* **hide**
hidden *adj* 隐藏的 yǐncáng de; *v see* **hide**
hide *v* (**hid, hidden**) 隐藏 yǐncáng, 隐瞒 yǐnmán; *n* 兽皮
shòupí; **hide-and-seek** *n* 捉迷藏 zhuōmícáng; **hideout** *n*
隐藏处 yǐncángchù; **hiding** *n* 躲藏 duǒcáng; 躲藏处
duǒcáng chù
hideous *adj* 丑恶的 chǒu'è de, 令人惊骇的 lìng rén jīnghài de
hierarchy *n* 等级系统 děngjí xìtǒng; **hierarchical** *adj*
分等级的 fēn děngjí de
high *adj* 高 gāo, 高等的 gāoděng de; **high-class** *adj* (*first-
rate*) 高级的 gāojí de (*upper class*) 上流社会
shàngliúshèhuì; **high court** 高等法院 gāoděng fǎyuàn;
high jump 跳高 tiàogāo; **high school** 高中 gāozhōng;
highly *adv* 高度 gāodù; **high-heeled** *adj* 高跟的 gāogēn de
highland *n* 高地 gāodì, 高原 gāoyuán
highlight *v* 突出 tūchū, 强调 qiángdiào; *n* 精彩场面 jīngcǎi
chǎngmiàn, 高潮 gāocháo, 亮点 liàngdiǎn
highway *n* 公路 gōnglù
hijack *v* 劫持 jiéchí, 胁迫 xiépò
hike *v* 远足 yuǎnzú
hilarious *adj* 欢闹的 huānnào de, 狂欢的 kuánghuān de
hill *n* 小山 xiǎoshān, 丘陵 qiūlíng; **hilly** *adj* 多小山的 duō
xiǎoshān de
him *pron* 他 tā
himself *pron* 他自己 tā zìjǐ
hind *adj* 后面的 hòumian de; **hindsight** *n* 后见之明 hòujiàn
zhīmíng
hinder *v* 阻碍 zǔ'ài; **hinderance** *n* 阻碍 zǔ'ài
Hindu *adj* 印度人的 yìndùrén de; 印度教的 yìndùjiào de;
Hinduism *n* 印度教 yìndùjiào
hinge *v* 铰链 jiǎoliàn; **hinge on** 取决于 qǔjué yú
hint *v/n* 暗示 ànshì
hip *n* 臀部 túnbù
hippopotamus *n* 河马 hémǎ
hire *v* 租 zū, 雇用 gùyòng; *n* 租用 zūyòng; **for hire** 供出租
gōng chūzū, 供雇用 gōng gùyòng
his *pron* 他的 tāde
history *n* 历史 lìshǐ; **historic** *adj* 有历史意义的 yǒu lìshǐ
yìyì de; **historical** *adj* 历史的 lìshǐ de; **historian** *n*
历史学家 lìshǐxuéjiā

hit *v* (**hit, hit**) (*strike*) 打 dǎ, 打击 dǎjī, (*collide*) 碰撞 pèngzhuàng; (*reach*) 到达 dàodá

hitch *n* 故障 gùzhàng; **without a hitch** 顺利地 shùnlì de; **hitchhike** *v* 搭便车 dā biànchē

hoard *v* 储藏 chǔcáng; **hoarding** *n* 囤积 túnjī

hoarse *adj* 嘶哑的 sīyǎ de; **hoarseness** *n* 嘶哑 sīyǎ

hoax *n* 骗局 piànjú

hog *n* 猪 zhū

hoist *v* 提升 tíshēng

hold *v* (**held, held**) 拿 ná, 持 chí, 拥有 yōngyǒu; (*events, etc.*) 举行 jǔxíng, (*restrain*) 抑制 yìzhì; (*hinder*) 止住 zhǐzhù; (*detain*) 拘留 jūliú; **hold back** 阻挡 zǔdǎng; 抑制 yìzhì; (*hide*) 隐瞒 yǐnmán; **hold on** (*phone*) 不挂断 bù guà duàn; (*stop*) 停止 tíngzhǐ; **hold out** 伸出 shēnchū; **hold up** (*raise*) 举起 jǔ qǐ; (*support*) 支撑 zhīchēng; (*hinder*) 阻碍 zǔ'ài; (*stop*) 拦截 lánjié; (*delay*) 耽搁 dānge; **holder** *n* 持有人 chíyǒurén

hole *n* 洞 dòng

holiday *n* 假日 jiàrì

Holland *n* 荷兰 hélán

hollow *adj* 空心的 kōngxīn de, 空洞的 kōngdòng de

holy *adj* 神圣的 shénshèng de

home *n* 家 jiā; **at home** 在家 zài jiā; **make yourself at home** 请别拘束 qǐng bié jūshù; **homeland** *n* 祖国 zǔguó; (*hometown*) 故乡 gùxiāng; **homeless** *adj* 无家可归的 wújiā kěguī de; **homemade** *adj* 自制的 zìzhì de; **homemaker** *n* 主妇 zhǔfù; **homesick** *adj* 想家的 xiǎng jiā de; **hometown** *n* 故乡 gùxiāng; **homework** *n* 家庭作业 jiātíng zuòyè

homicide *n* 杀人 shārén

homogeneous *adj* 同类的 tónglèi de

homosexual *n* 同性恋者 tóngxìngliànzhě; *adj* 同性恋的 tóngxìngliàn de; **homosexuality** *n* 同性恋 tóngxìngliàn

honest *adj* 诚实的 chéngshí de; **honesty** *n* 诚实 chéngshí; **honestly** *adv* 真诚地 zhēnchéng de

honey *n* 蜂蜜 fēngmì

honeymoon *n* 蜜月 mìyuè

honk *v* 鸣笛 míngdí, 按喇叭 àn lǎba

honor *v* 尊敬 zūnjìng, 礼待 lǐdài, 承诺 chéngnuò; *n* 荣誉 róngyù, 荣幸 róngxìng; **honored** *adj* 尊敬的 zūnjìng de; **honorable** *adj* 尊敬的 zūnjìng de, 荣誉的 róngyù de, 光荣的 guāngróng de, 荣幸的 róngxìng de, 体面的 tǐmiàn de

hood *n* (*hat*) 风帽 fēngmào; (*car*) 汽车发动机罩 qìchē fādòngjīzhào

hook *n* 钩子 gōuzi; **get hooked on** 迷上 mí shàng

hooligan *n* 流氓 liúmáng

hop *v* 单脚跳 dānjiǎotiào

hope *v/n* 希望 xīwàng; **hopeful** *adj* 有希望的 yǒuxīwàng de; **hopeless** *adj* 没有希望的 méiyǒu xīwàng de

horde *n* 群 qún, 帮 bāng, 伙 huǒ

horizon *n* 地平线 dìpíngxiàn, 眼界 yǎnjiè; **horizontal** *adj* 水平的 shuǐpíng de, 横的 héng de

horn *n* 喇叭 lǎba

horoscope *n* 占星 zhānxīng

hors d'oeuvres *n* 开胃小吃 kāiwèi xiǎochī

horrible *adj* 恐怖的 kǒngbù de, 可怕的 kěpà de

horrid *adj* 恐怖的 kǒngbù de

horrify *v* (使) 恐惧 (shǐ) kǒngjù

horror *n* 恐怖 kǒngbù

horse *n* 马 mǎ; **horse racing** 赛马 sàimǎ

horseback *n* 马背 mǎbèi

horsepower *n* 马力 mǎlì

horticulture *n* 园艺 yuányì; **horticultural** *adj* 园艺的 yuányì de

hose *n* 水龙带 shuǐlóngdài

hospital *n* 医院 yīyuàn

hospitality *n* 好客 hàokè; **hospitable** *adj* 好客的 hàokè de

host *v* 作主人 zuò zhǔrén, 作东道主 zuò dōngdàozhǔ, 主办 zhǔbàn; *n* 主人 zhǔrén, 东道主 dōngdàozhǔ

hostage *n* 人质 rénzhì

hostel *n* 客栈 kèzhàn

hostile *adj* 敌对的 díduì de, 有敌意的 yǒu díyì de; **hostility** *n* 敌意 díyì

hot *adj* 热的 rè de; **hot dog** 热狗 règǒu; **hotplate** *n* 电热锅 diànrèguō; **hot-tempered** *adj* 易怒的 yìnù de

hotel *n* 旅馆 lǚguǎn

hour *n* 小时 xiǎoshí; **after hours** 办公时间以后 bàngōng shíjiān yǐhòu; **by the hour** 按钟点的 àn zhōngdiǎn de; **peak hours** 高峰时间 gāofēng shíjiān; **rush hour** 上下班时间 shàngxiàbān shíjiān; **hourly** *adv* 每小时一次地 měi xiǎoshí yī cì de; *adj* 每小时的 měi xiǎoshí de, 每小时一次的 měi xiǎoshí yī cì de

House *n* 议院 yìyuàn; **House of Commons** 下议院 xiàyìyuàn; **House of Lords** 上议院 shàngyìyuàn; **House of Representatives** 众议院 zhòngyìyuàn

house *n* 房子 fángzi; **household** *n* 家庭 jiātíng; **housing** *n* 住房 zhùfáng

housekeeper *n* 主妇 zhǔfù, 女管家 nǚguǎnjiā; **housekeeping** *n* 家务管理 jiāwù guǎnlǐ

housewife *n* 家庭主妇 jiātíng zhǔfù

how *adv* 怎么 zěnme, 怎样 zěnyàng, 如何 rúhé, 多么 duōme

however *conj* 然而 rán'ér; *adv* 无论如何 wúlùn rúhé, 可是 kěshì

howl *v/n* 嚎叫 háojiào

hub *n* 枢纽 shūniǔ, 中心 zhōngxīn

hug *v/n* 拥抱 yōngbào

huge *adj* 巨大的 jùdà de

hum *n* 哼曲子 hēng qǔzi

human *n* 人 rén; *adj* 人的 rén de; 人类的 rénlèi de; 通人情的 tōng rénqíng de; **human being** 人 rén; **human resources** 人力资源 rénlì zīyuán; **human rights** 人权 rénquán; **humankind** *n* 人类 rénlèi; **humanity** *n* (*humankind*) 人类 rénlèi; (*human nature*) 人性 rénxìng

humane *adj* 人道的 réndào de

humanism *n* 人道主义 réndàozhǔyì, 人文主义 rénwénzhǔyì

humanitarian *adj* 人道主义的 réndàozhǔyì de, 慈善的 císhàn de

humanities *n* 人文学科 rénwén xuékē

humble *adj* 谦逊的 qiānxùn de, 卑微的 bēiwēi de

humid *adj* 潮湿的 cháoshī de

humiliate *v* 羞辱 xiūrǔ; (使) 丢脸 (shǐ) diūliǎn; **humiliation** *n* 羞辱 xiūrǔ, 耻辱 chǐrǔ

humility *n* 谦逊 qiānxùn, 卑微 bēiwēi

humor *n* 幽默 yōumò; **humorous** *adj* 幽默的 yōumò de, 诙谐的 huīxié de

hunch *n* 预感 yùgǎn, 直觉 zhíjué; **hunchback** *n* 驼背 tuóbèi

hundred *num* 百 bǎi; **hundredth** *num* 第一百 dì yībǎi

hung. *See* **hang**

Hungary *n* 匈牙利 xiōngyálì; **Hungarian** *n* (*people*) 匈牙利人 xiōngyálìrén; (*language*) 匈牙利语 xiōngyálìyǔ; *adj* 匈牙利的 xiōngyálì de

hunger *n* 饥饿 jī'è; **hunger for** 渴望 kěwàng; **hungry** *adj* 饿的 è de

hunt *v* 打猎 dǎliè; (*search*) 搜寻 sōuxún; *n* 狩猎 shòuliè; **hunter** *n* 猎人 lièrén; **hunting** *n* 狩猎 shòuliè

hurdle *n* 障碍 zhàng'ài

hurricane *n* 飓风 jùfēng

hurry *v* 催 cuī, 赶紧 gǎnjǐn; *n* 仓促 cāngcù, 匆忙 cōngmáng;
   be in a hurry 匆忙地 cōngmáng de; **hurried** *adj* 匆忙的
   cōngmáng de; **hurriedly** *adv* 仓促地 cāngcù de

hurt *v* (**hurt, hurt**) 伤害 shānghài; **hurtful** *adj* 伤人的
   shāngrén de, 伤感情的 shānggǎnqíng de

husband *n* 丈夫 zhàngfu

hush *v* 安静下来 ānjìng xiàlái; **hush up** 隐瞒 yǐnmán, 遮掩
   zhēyǎn; **hushed** *adj* 安静的 ānjìng de, 寂静的 jìjìng de

hustle *v* 挤 jǐ, 推 tuī; *n* 忙碌 mánglù; **hustle and bustle**
   忙乱 mángluàn; 熙熙攘攘 xīxī rǎngrǎng

hut *n* 小屋 xiǎowū

hybrid *adj* 混合的 hùnhé de, 杂种的 zázhǒng de

hygiene *n* 卫生 wèishēng, 卫生学 wèishēngxué; **hygienic**
   adj 卫生的 wèishēng de

hydraulic *adj* 水力的 shuǐlì de

hydro-electric *adj* 水电的 shuǐdiàn de

hymn *n* 赞美诗 zànměishī

hyphen *n* 连字号 liánzìhào

hypocrisy *n* 虚伪 xūwěi; **hypocrite** *n* 伪君子 wěijūnzǐ;
   hypocritical *adj* 虚伪的 xūwěi de

hypodermic *n* 皮下的 píxià de; **hypodermic syringe**
   皮下注射器 píxià zhùshèqì

hypothesis *n* (*pl.* **hypotheses**) 假设 jiǎshè, 假说 jiǎshuō;
   hypothetical *adj* 假设的 jiǎshè de

hysterical *adj* 歇斯底里的 xiēsīdǐlǐ de

I

I *pron* 我 wǒ

ice *n* 冰 bīng; **ice cream** 冰淇淋 bīngqílín; **ice hockey** 冰球
   bīngqiú; **iceberg** *n* 冰山 bīngshān; **icebreaker** *n* 破冰船
   pòbīngchuán; **ice-cold** *adj* 寒冷的 hánlěng de; **ice-skate**
   冰鞋 bīngxié; **icy** *adj* 冰冷的 bīnglěng de, 冷淡的
   lěngdàn de

Iceland *n* 冰岛 bīngdǎo; **Icelandic** *adj* 冰岛的 bīngdǎo de

icon *n* 偶像 ǒuxiàng; (*computer*) 图标 túbiāo

idea *n* 想法 xiǎngfa, 主意 zhǔyi

ideal *n* 理想 lǐxiǎng; *adj* 理想的 lǐxiǎng de; **idealist** *n*
   理想主义者 lǐxiǎngzhǔyìzhě

identical *adj* 同一的 tóngyī de, 完全相同的 wánquán
   xiāngtóng de

identify v 辨认 biànrèn, 鉴定 jiàndìng, 识别 shíbié; **identify with** 与 ... 认同 yǔ ... rèntóng

identity n 身份 shēnfen; **identification** n 辨认 biànrèn; (proof of identity) 身份证明 shēnfen zhèngmíng; **identification card** 身份证 shēnfènzhèng

ideology n 意识形态 yìshí xíngtài

idiom n 成语 chéngyǔ, 习语 xíyǔ; **idiomatic** adj 合乎语言习惯的 héhū yǔyán xíguàn de

idiot n 笨蛋 bèndàn, 白痴 báichī

idle adj 空闲的 kòngxián de, 停顿的 tíngdùn de, 懒散的 lǎnsǎn de, 无所事事的 wúsuǒshìshì de; (engine) 空转的 kōngzhuàn de

idol n 偶像 ǒuxiàng; **idolize** v 偶像化 ǒuxiànghuà; 把 ... 当偶像崇拜 bǎ ... dāng ǒuxiàng chóngbài

if conj 如果 rúguǒ, 假如 jiǎrú, 要是 yàoshi, 是否 shìfǒu; **if not** 否则 fǒuzé; **if only** 只要 zhǐyào

ignite v 点燃 diǎnrán, 点火 diǎnhuǒ

ignition n 点火 diǎnhuǒ; (device) 发火装置 fāhuǒ zhuāngzhì; **ignition key** 点火开关钥匙 diǎnhuǒ kāiguān yàoshi

ignorance n 无知 wúzhī, 愚昧 yúmèi; **ignorant** adj 无知的 wúzhī de, 愚昧的 yúmèi de

ignore v 忽视 hūshì, 不理睬 bù lǐcǎi

ill adj 有病的 yǒubìng de, 坏的 huài de, 邪恶的 xié'è de, 困难的 kùnnan de; **ill-advised** adj 不明智的 bù míngzhì de; **ill-mannered** adj 无礼的 wúlǐ de, 粗鲁的 cūlǔ de; **ill treatment** 虐待 nüèdài, 折磨 zhémo

illegal adj 违法的 wéifǎ de, 不合法的 bù héfǎ de; **illegally** adv 非法地 fēifǎ de, 不合法地 bù héfǎ de

illegible adj 模糊的 móhu de, 难以辨认的 nányǐ biànrèn de

illegitimacy n 不法 bùfǎ; **illegitimate** adj 非法的 fēifǎ de, 不合法的 bù héfǎ de; (born out of wedlock) 私生的 sī shēng de

illicit adj 违法的 wéifǎ de

illiterate n 文盲 wénmáng; adj 不识字的 bù shízì de; **illiteracy** n 文盲 wénmáng

illness n 病 bìng, 疾病 jíbìng

illogical adj 不合逻辑的 bùhé luójí de

illuminate v (light up) 照亮 zhàoliàng; (make clear) 阐明 chǎnmíng; (enlighten) 启迪 qǐdí; **illumination** n 照明 zhàoming; 阐明 chǎnmíng; 启发 qǐfā

illusion n 错觉 cuòjué, 幻想 huànxiǎng

illustrate *v* (*drawing*) 插图 chātú; (*exemplify*) 阐明 chǎnmíng; **illustration** *n* 插图 chātú; 例证 lìzhèng

image *n* 形象 xíngxiàng, 图像 túxiàng; **imaginary** *adj* 想象的 xiǎngxiàng de, 虚构的 xūgòu de

imagine *v* 想象 xiǎngxiàng; **imagination** *n* 想象力 xiǎngxiànglì

imitate *v* 模仿 mófǎng, 效仿 xiàofǎng; **imitation** *n* 仿制品 fǎngzhìpǐn, 赝品 yànpǐn, 模仿 mófǎng

immaculate *adj* 无瑕的 wúxiá de

immediate *adj* 立即的 lìjí de, 直接的 zhíjiē de, 最贴近的 zuì tiējìn de 当前的 dāngqián de; **immediately** *adv* 立即 lìjí, 立刻 lìkè, 马上 mǎshàng, 直接地 zhíjiē de, 贴近地 tiējìn de

immense *adj* 巨大的 jùdà de

immerse *v* 沉浸 chénjìn; **immersion** *n* 沉浸 chénjìn; **immersion method** 沉浸式训练 chénjìn shì xùnliàn

immigrate *v* 移民 yímín; **immigrant** *n* 移民 yímín; **immigration** *n* 移民 yímín

imminent *adj* 即将到来的 jíjiāng dàolái de

immoral *adj* 不道德的 bù dàodé de

immortal *adj* 不朽的 bùxiǔ de

immune *adj* 免除的 miǎnchú de; (*diplomatic*) 豁免的 huòmiǎn de; 不受影响的 bù shòu yǐngxiǎng de; **immunity** *n* 免除 miǎnchú; (*diplomatic*) 豁免 huòmiǎn; **immunize** *v* (使) 免疫 (shǐ) miǎnyì

impact *n* 冲击 chōngjī, 影响 yǐngxiǎng

impair *v* 削弱 xuēruò; **impairment** *n* 损害 sǔnhài

impartial *adj* 公平的 gōngpíng de; **impartiality** *n* 公平 gōngpíng, 公正 gōngzhèng

impatient *adj* 不耐烦的 bù nàifán de; **impatience** *n* 急躁 jízào

impeach *v* 弹劾 tánhé; **impeachment** *n* 弹劾 tánhé

impeccable *adj* 没有缺点的 méiyǒu quēdiǎn de, 完美的 wánměi de

imperative *adj* 必要的 bìyào de, 极重要的 jí zhòngyào de; (*gram*) 祈使的 qíshǐ de, 命令的 mìnglìng de

imperfect *adj* 有缺点的 yǒu quēdiǎn de, 有缺陷的 yǒu quēxiàn de, 不完美的 bù wánměi de

imperial *adj* 帝国的 dìguó de; 帝国主义的 dìguózhǔyì de; **imperialism** *n* 帝国主义 dìguózhǔyì

impersonal *adj* 非个人的 fēigèrén de, 冷漠的 lěngmò de

impersonate *v* 模仿 mófǎng, 扮演 bànyǎn; **impersonation** *n* 扮演 bànyǎn

impertinence *n* 相关性 xiāngguānxìng; **impertinent** *adj* 无关的 wúguān de

impetus *n* 推动力 tuīdònglì

impinge *v* 撞击 zhuàngjī; **impinge on** 侵犯 qīnfàn

implement *v* 贯彻 guànchè, 实施 shíshī; *n* 工具 gōngjù, 用具 yòngjù

implicate *v* 牵连 qiānlián, 涉及 shèjí; **implication** *n* 含意 hányì

implicit *adj* 暗示的 ànshì de, 含蓄的 hánxù de

imply *v* 暗示 ànshì; **implied** *adj* 暗指的 ànzhǐ de

impolite *adj* 无礼的 wúlǐ de, 粗鲁的 cūlǔ de

import *v/n* 进口 jìnkǒu, 输入 shūrù

important *adj* 重要的 zhòngyào de; **importance** *n* 重要 zhòngyào, 重要性 zhòngyàoxìng

impose *v* 强加 qiángjiā, **impose on** 强加于 qiángjiā yú; **imposing** *adj* 使人难忘的 shǐ rén nánwàng de, 威严的 wēiyán de

impossible *adj* 不可能的 bù kěnéng de

impotent *adj* 阳痿的 yángwěi de, 无力的 wúlì de

impress *v* 给 ... 深刻印象 gěi ... shēnkè yìnxiàng; 盖印 gàiyìn; **impression** *n* 印象 yìnxiàng; **impressive** *adj* 给人深刻印象的 gěi rén shēnkè yìnxiàng de; 感人的 gǎnrén de

imprison *v* 监禁 jiānjìn; **imprisonment** *n* 囚禁 qiújìn

impregnate *v* (使) 怀孕 (shǐ) huáiyùn, 注入 zhùrù

improper *adj* 不适当的 bù shìdàng de

improbable *adj* 不可能的 bù kěnéng de

improve *v* 改善 gǎishàn; **improvement** *n* 改善 gǎishàn

impulse *n* 冲动 chōngdòng; **impulsive** *adj* 冲动的 chōngdòng de, 心血来潮的 xīnxuè láicháo de

impure *adj* 不纯的 bù chún de; **impurity** *n* 不纯 bù chún

in *prep* 在 ... 里 zài ... lǐ, 在 ... 内 zài ... nèi, 在 ... 期间 zài ... qījiān, 在 ... 方面 zài ... fāngmiàn, 用 yòng; 穿着 chuān zhe, 戴着 dài zhe; **in order to** 为了 wèile

inability *n* 无能 wúnéng, 无力 wúlì

inaccessible *adj* 达不到的 dá bù dào de, 难以接近的 nányǐ jiējìn de

inaccuracy *n* 错误 cuòwù; **inaccurate** *adj* 不准确的 bù zhǔnquè de

inactive *adj* 不活动的 bù huódòng de, 不活跃的 bù huóyuè de, 停止的 tíngzhǐ de; **inaction** *n* 无为 wúwéi

inadequate *adj* 不充分的 bù chōngfèn de, 不够的 bù gòu de

inadvertent *adj* 不小心的 bù xiǎoxīn de, 疏忽的 shūhu de;
  inadvertently *adv* 不小心地 bù xiǎoxīn de

inappropriate *adj* 不适当的 bù shìdàng de, 不妥当的 bù
  tuǒdang de

inaugurate *v* 开始 kāishǐ, 开展 kāizhǎn; (*hold a ceremony*)
  为 ... 举行就职典礼 wèi ... jǔxíng jiùzhí diǎnlǐ;
  inauguration *n* 就职典礼 jiùzhí diǎnlǐ

incapable *adj* 不能的 bù néng de

incentive *n* 刺激 cìjī, 奖励 jiǎnglì

incessantly *adv* 不断地 bùduàn de, 不停地 bù tíng de

incest *n* 乱伦 luànlún; **incestuous** *adj* 乱伦的 luànlún de

inch *n* 英寸 yīngcùn; **inch forward** 缓慢地前进 huǎnmàn de
  qiánjìn

incident *n* 事件 shìjiàn; **incidentally** *adv* 顺便说 shùnbiàn
  shuō, 附带说 fùdài shuō

incinerate *v* 焚化 fénhuà; **incinerator** *n* 焚化炉 fénhuàlú;
  incineration *n* 焚化 fénhuà

incite *v* 煽动 shāndòng

inclination *n* 倾向 qīngxiàng, 意向 yìxiàng, 偏好 piānhào

incline *v* 倾斜 qīngxié, 倾向 qīngxiàng; **inclined** *adj* 倾向于
  qīngxiàng yú; 有 ... 意向的 yǒu ... yìxiàng de

include *v* 包括 bāokuò; **including** *prep* 包括 bāokuò;
  inclusion *n* 包括 bāokuò, 包容 bāoróng; **inclusive** *adj*
  包含的 bāohán de

incoherent *adj* 不连贯的 bù liánguàn de; **incoherence** *n*
  语无伦次 yǔwúlúncì

income *n* 收入 shōurù; **income tax** 所得税 suǒdéshuì

incoming *adj* 进来的 jìnlái de, 新来的 xīnlái de, 继任的
  jìrèn de

incompatibility *n* 不相容 bù xiāngróng; **incompatible** *adj*
  矛盾的 máodùn de, 不调和的 bù tiáohé de

incompetence *n* 无能 wúnéng; **incompetent** *adj* 不胜任的
  bù shèngrèn de, 不称职的 bù chènzhí de

incomplete *adj* 不完全的 bù wánquán de, 不完整的 bù
  wánzhěng de

incomprehensible *adj* 不能理解的 bù néng lǐjiě de

inconceivable *adj* 难以置信的 nányǐ zhìxìn de

inconclusive *adj* 非决定性的 fēi juédìngxìng de, 无结论的
  wú jiélùn de

inconsiderate *adj* 不顾他人的 bùgù tārén de

inconsistency *n* 矛盾 máodùn; **inconsistent** *adj* 不一致的
  bù yīzhì de, 矛盾的 máodùn de

inconvenience *n* 不便 bùbiàn; **inconvenient** *adj* 不方便的 bù fāngbiàn de

incorporate *v* 合并 hébìng, 并入 bìngrù; (*form into a corporation*) 组成公司 zǔchéng gōngsī

incorrect *adj* 不正确的 bù zhèngquè de, 错的 cuò de

increase *v* 增加 zēngjiā, 增长 zēngzhǎng; **increasing** *adj* 渐增的 jiànzēng de; **increasingly** *adv* 愈加 yùjiā, 越来越 yuèláiyuè

incredible *adj* 难以置信的 nányǐzhìxìn de

incriminate *v* 连累 liánlěi, 牵连 qiānlián

incur *v* 招致 zhāozhì, 引起 yǐnqǐ

incurable *adj* 无可救药的 wúkě jiùyào de, 不能治愈的 bù néng zhìyù de

indecency *n* 下流 xiàliú; **indecent** *adj* 下流的 xiàliú de, 猥亵的 wěixiè de

indeed *adv* 的确 díquè, 真正地 zhēnzhèng de

indefinitely *adv* 不确定地 bù quèdìng de, 不限期地 bù xiànqī de

indent *n* 缩进 suōjìn

independence *n* 独立 dúlì; **independent** *adj* 自主的 zìzhǔ de, 独立的 dúlì de

index *n* 索引 suǒyǐn; **index finger** 食指 shízhǐ

India *n* 印度 yìndù; **Indian** *n* 印度人 yìndùrén; *adj* 印度的 yìndù de; 印度人的 yìndùrén de

indicate *v* 指出 zhǐchū, 表明 biǎomíng; **indication** *n* 指出 zhǐchū, 表明 biǎomíng; **indicator** *n* 标志 biāozhì

indict *v* 起诉 qǐsù, 控告 kònggào; **indictment** *n* 控告 kònggào

indifferent *adj* 不关心的 bù guānxīn de, 冷淡的 lěngdàn de

indigenous *adj* 本土的 běntǔ de

indigestion *n* 消化不良 xiāohuà bù liáng; **indigestible** *adj* 不消化的 bù xiāohuà de

indignation *n* 愤怒 fènnù; **indignant** *adj* 愤怒的 fènnù de

indirectly *adj* 间接的 jiànjiē de; **indirectly** *adv* 间接地 jiànjiē de

indiscreet *adj* 轻率的 qīngshuài de, 不慎重的 bù shènzhòng de

indiscriminate *adj* 不加鉴别的 bù jiā jiànbié de

indispensable *adj* 不可缺少的 bùkě quēshǎo de

individual *n* 个人 gèrén; *adj* 个别的 gèbié de, 个人的 gèrén de; **individuality** *n* 个性 gèxìng

indoor *adj* 室内的 shìnèi de, 户内的 hùnèi de; **indoors** *adv* 户内 hùnèi

indulge *v* 纵容 zòngróng, 沉溺 chénnì; **indulge in** 沉湎于 chénmiǎn yú; **indulgence** *n* 放任 fàngrèn

industry *n* 工业 gōngyè; **industrial** *adj* 工业的 gōngyè de; **industrialized** *adj* 工业化的 gōngyèhuà de; **industrious** *adj* 勤勉的 qínmiǎn de

inefficient *adj* 无效率的 wúxiàolǜ de, 无效用的 wúxiàoyòng de

inequality *n* 不平等 bù píngděng

inertia *n* 惯性 guànxìng; **inert** *adj* 惰性的 duòxìng de

inevitability *n* 必然性 bìránxìng; **inevitable** *adj* 不可避免的 bù kě bìmiǎn de

inexpensive *adj* 便宜的 piányi de

inexperienced *adj* 无经验的 wú jīngyàn de

infallible *adj* 没有错误的 méiyǒu cuòwù de

infancy *n* 婴儿期 yīng'érqī; (*early stage*) 初始期 chūshǐqī

infant *n* 婴儿 yīng'ér

infantry *n* 步兵 bùbīng

infatuate *v* 冲昏头脑 chōnghūn tóunǎo; **be infatuated with** 迷恋 míliàn; **infatuation** *n* 醉心 zuìxīn

infect *v* 传染 chuánrǎn; **infection** *n* 传染 chuánrǎn, 感染 gǎnrǎn; **infectious** *adj* (*of disease*) 传染的 chuánrǎn de; (*spreading*) 有感染力的 yǒu gǎnrǎnlì de

infer *v* 推断 tuīduàn; **inference** *n* 推论 tuīlùn

inferior *n* 部下 bùxià, 下级 xiàjí; *adj* 低等的 dīděng de, 差的 chà de; **inferiority** *n* 自卑 zìbēi; **inferiority complex** 自卑情结 zìbēi qíngjié

infest *v* 大批滋生 dàpī zīshēng; **infestation** *n* 侵扰 qīnrǎo

infiltrate *v* 渗透 shèntòu; **infiltration** *n* 渗透 shèntòu

infinity *n* 无限 wúxiàn; **infinite** *adj* 无限的 wúxiàn de

infirmary *n* 医务室 yīwùshì

inflame *v* 燃烧 ránshāo; **inflammation** *n* 炎症 yánzhèng; **inflammable** *adj* 易燃的 yìrán de; **inflammatory** *adj* 煽动性的 shāndòngxìng de

inflate *v* 充气 chōngqì, 膨胀 péngzhàng; **inflation** *n* 膨胀 péngzhàng; (*currency*) 通货膨胀 tōnghuò péngzhàng

inflict *v* 造成 zàochéng, 施加 shījiā; **infliction** *n* 施加 shījiā

influence *v/n* 影响 yǐngxiǎng; **under the influence** 喝醉酒 hē zuì jiǔ; **influential** *adj* 有影响的 yǒu yǐngxiǎng de

influenza *n* 流行性感冒 liúxíngxìng gǎnmào

inform *v* 通知 tōngzhī, 告诉 gàosu; **informer** *n* 告密者 gàomìzhě; **information** *n* 消息 xiāoxi, 信息 xìnxī; **informative** *adj* 内容翔实的 nèiróng xiángshí de; **information desk** 问询处 wènxúnchù

informal *adj* 非正式的 fēizhèngshì de

infringe *v* 侵犯 qīnfàn; **infringe on** 违反 wéifǎn; **infringement** *n* 侵犯 qīnfàn

infuriate *v* 激怒 jīnù; **infuriating** *adj* 令人发怒的 lìng rén fānù de

ingenuity *n* 独创性 dúchuàngxìng; **ingenious** *adj* 有独创性的 yǒu dúchuàngxìng de

ingredient *n* 成分 chéngfèn

inhabit *v* 居住于 jūzhù yú; **inhabitant** *n* 居民 jūmín

inhale *v* 吸入 xīrù

inherent *adj* 固有的 gùyǒu de, 内在的 nèizài de, 天生的 tiānshēng de

inherit *v* 继承 jìchéng; **inheritance** *n* 遗传 yíchuán, 遗产 yíchǎn

inhibit *v* 抑制 yìzhì; **inhibition** *n* 压抑 yāyì

inhuman *adj* 野蛮的 yěmán de; **inhumane** *adj* 不人道的 bù réndào de

initial *n* 姓名首字母 xìngmíng shǒuzìmǔ; *adj* 初始的 chūshǐ de; **initially** *adv* 最初 zuìchū

initiate *v* 开始 kāishǐ, 发起 fāqǐ; **initiation** *n* 开始 kāishǐ, 发起 fāqǐ

initiative *n* 主动 zhǔdòng, 倡议 chàngyì

inject *v* 注射 zhùshè, 注入 zhùrù; **injection** *n* 注射 zhùshè, 注入 zhùrù

injure *v* 损害 sǔnhài, 伤害 shānghài; **injury** *n* 伤 shāng, 伤害 shānghài

injustice *n* 不公平 bù gōngpíng, 不公正 bù gōngzhèng

ink *n* 墨水 mòshuǐ

inkling *n* 模糊感觉 móhu gǎnjué

inmate *n* 监犯 jiānfàn; 囚犯 qiúfàn

inn *n* 客栈 kèzhàn

inner *adj* 内部的 nèibù de; **inner city** (*city center*) 市中心 shìzhōngxīn, (*poor area*) 市中心贫民区 shìzhōngxīn pínmínqū

innocence *n* 无辜 wúgū, 清白 qīngbái; **innocent** *adj* 无罪的 wúzuì de, 无辜的 wúgū de, 清白的 qīngbái de

innocuous *adj* 无害的 wúhài de

innovate *v* 创新 chuàngxīn; **innovation** *n* 创新 chuàngxīn

innuendo *n* 影射 yǐngshè

innumerable *adj* 无数的 wúshù de

input *v* 输入 shūrù; *n* (*computer*) 输入 shūrù; (*comment*) 意见 yìjian

inquire *v* 询问 xúnwèn, 调查 diàochá; **inquire into** 探究 tànjiū; **inquiry** *n* 询问 xúnwèn, 调查 diàochá

inquisitive *adj* 好奇的 hàoqí de

insanity *n* 疯狂 fēngkuáng, 精神错乱 jīngshén cuòluàn; **insane** *adj* 疯狂的 fēngkuáng de, 愚蠢的 yúchǔn de

insatiable *adj* 不满足的 bù mǎnzú de

insect *n* 昆虫 kūnchóng; **insecticide** *n* 杀虫剂 shāchóngjì

insecure *adj* 不安全的 bù ānquán de

insensitive *adj* 感觉迟钝的 gǎnjué chídùn de

inseparable *adj* 不能分的 bù néng fēn de

insert *v* 插入 chārù; **insertion** *n* 插入 chārù

inside *adv* 在里面 zài lǐmiàn; **inside-out** *adv* 里朝外地 lǐ cháo wài de

insidiousness *n* 阴险 yīnxiǎn; **insidious** *adj* 阴险的 yīnxiǎn de

insight *n* 洞察力 dòngchálì, 见识 jiànshi

insignificance *n* 无意义 wú yìyì; **insignificant** *adj* 无关紧要的 wúguān jǐnyào de

insincerity *n* 伪善 wěishàn; **insincere** *adj* 虚假的 xūjiǎ de

insinuate *v* 含沙射影地说 hánshā shèyǐng de shuō; **insinuation** *n* 暗示 ànshì

insist *v* 坚持 jiānchí, 执意 zhíyì; **insistent** *adj* 坚持的 jiānchí de

insolent *adj* 傲慢无礼的 àomàn wúlǐ de

insomnia *n* 失眠 shīmián

inspect *v* 检查 jiǎnchá, 视察 shìchá, 检验 jiǎnyàn; **inspection** *n* 检查 jiǎnchá, 视察 shìchá, 检验 jiǎnyàn; **inspector** *n* 检查员 jiǎncháyuán, 督察员 dūcháyuán

inspire *v* 鼓舞 gǔwǔ, 鼓励 gǔlì; **inspiration** *n* 灵感 línggǎn; **inspirational** *adj* 有灵感的 yǒu línggǎn de

instability *n* 不稳定 bù wěndìng

install *v* 安装 ānzhuāng; **installation** *n* 安装 ānzhuāng, 装置 zhuāngzhì

installment *n* 分期付款 fēnqī fùkuǎn

instance *n* 实例 shílì; **for instance** 例如 lìrú

instant *n* 时刻 shíkè, 瞬间 shùnjiān; *adj* 立即的 lìjí de, 即刻的 jíkè de; **instantly** *adv* 立刻 lìkè; **instantaneous** *adj* 瞬间的 shùnjiān de

instead *adv* 作为代替 zuòwéi dàitì, 反尔 fǎn' ěr; **instead of** 代替 dàitì, 而不是 érbùshì

instigate *v* 煽动 shāndòng; **instigation** *n* 煽动 shāndòng

instinct *n* 本能 běnnéng

institute *n* 学院 xuéyuàn, 研究所 yánjiūsuǒ; **institution** *n* 机构 jīgòu

instruct *v* 教 jiāo, 指示 zhǐshì; **instruction** *n* 说明 shuōmíng, 说明书 shuōmíngshū, 指令 zhǐlìng; **instructor** *n* 教员 jiàoyuán

instrument *n* (*musical*) 乐器 yuèqì; (*tool*) 工具 gōngjù, 仪器 yíqì; **instrumental** *adj* 有帮助的 yǒu bāngzhù de

insubordination *n* 不顺从 bù shùncóng; **insubordinate** *adj* 不顺从的 bù shùncóng de, 不听话的 bù tīnghuà de;

insufficient *adj* 不足的 bùzú de, 不够的 bù gòu de

insulate *v* (使) 绝缘 (shǐ) juéyuán, 隔离 gélí; **insulation** *n* 绝缘 juéyuán

insult *v/n* 侮辱 wǔrǔ

insure *v* 给 ... 保险 gěi ... bǎoxiǎn; **insurance** *n* 保险 bǎoxiǎn; **insurance policy** 保险单 bǎoxiǎndān

intact *adj* 完整无缺的 wánzhěng wúquē de, 未经触动的 wèijīng chùdòng de

integral *adj* 整体的 zhěngtǐ de, 组成的 zǔchéng de

integrate *v* 结合 jiéhé; **integration** *n* 结合 jiéhé, 融合 rónghé

integrity *n* (*honesty*) 正直 zhèngzhí; (*entirety*) 完整 wánzhěng

intellect *n* 智力 zhìlì; **intellectual** *n* 知识分子 zhīshi fènzǐ; *adj* 智力的 zhìlì de

intelligence *n* (*capacity*) 智力 zhìlì; (*information*) 情报 qíngbào; **intelligent** *adj* 聪明的 cōngming de, 有才智的 yǒu cáizhì de

intelligible *adj* 可理解的 kě lǐjiě de, 明白易懂的 míngbai yìdǒng de

intend *v* 打算 dǎsuan

intensify *v* 强化 qiánghuà

intensity *n* 强度 qiángdù; **intense** *adj* 强烈的 qiángliè de, 强化的 qiánghuà de; **intensive** *adj* 密集的 mìjí de, 强化的 qiánghuà de; **intensive care** 重病特别护理 zhòngbìng tèbié hùlǐ

intent *n* 意图 yìtú; *adj* 专心的 zhuānxīn de

intention *n* 意图 yìtú, 目的 mùdì; **intentional** *adj* 故意的 gùyì de

interact *v* 互动 hùdòng; **interaction** *n* 交互作用 jiāohù zuòyòng, 互动 hùdòng

intercept *v* 拦截 lánjié; **interception** *n* 拦截 lánjié

interchange *v* 互换 hùhuàn; **interchangeable** *adj* 可互换的 kě hùhuàn de

intercourse *n* 交往 jiāowǎng; **sexual intercourse** 性交 xìngjiāo

interest *n* (*curiosity*) 兴趣 xìngqù; (*advantage*) 利益 lìyì; (*banking*) 利息 lìxī; **be interested** 感兴趣 gǎnxìngqù; **interest-free** *adj* 无利息的 wú lìxī de

interfere *v* (*interfere with*) 干涉 gānshè, 打扰 dǎrǎo; **interference** *n* 干涉 gānshè

interior *n* 内部 nèibù; *adj* 内部的 nèibù de; **interior design** 室内装饰 shìnèi zhuāngshì

interjection *n* 感叹词 gǎntàncí

intermediate *adj* 中级的 zhōngjí de, 中间的 zhōngjiān de; **intermediary** *n* 调解者 tiáojiě zhě, 中间人 zhōngjiānrén

interminable *adj* 冗长的 rǒngcháng de

intermittent *adj* 断断续续的 duànduàn xùxù de; **intermittently** *adv* 断断续续地 duànduàn xùxù de

intermission *n* 中场休息 zhōngchǎng xiūxi

intern *v* 实习 shíxí; *n* 实习生 shíxíshēng

internal *adj* 内部的 nèibù de

international *adj* 国际的 guójì de; **international dateline** 国际日期变更线 guójì rìqī biàngēngxiàn

interpret *v* (*translate*) 口译 kǒuyì; (*explain*) 解释 jiěshì, 说明 shuōmíng; **interpretation** *n* 口译 kǒuyì; 解释 jiěshì, 说明 shuōmíng; **interpreter** *n* 口译员 kǒuyìyuán

interrogate *v* 审问 shěnwèn; **interrogation** *n* 审问 shěnwèn; **interrogative** *adj* 疑问的 yíwèn de

interrupt *v* 中断 zhōngduàn, 打断 dǎduàn; **interruption** *n* 中断 zhōngduàn, 打断 dǎduàn

intersection *n* 十字路口 shízì lùkǒu

interval *n* 间隔 jiàngé

intervene *v* 干预 gānyù; **intervention** *n* 干预 gānyù, 调停 tiáotíng

interview *v/n* 面谈 miàntán, 面试 miànshì; (*press*) 采访 cǎifǎng; **interviewer** *n* 采访者 cǎifǎngzhě

intestines *n* 肠子 chángzi

intimacy *n* 亲密 qīnmì; **intimate** *adj* 亲密的 qīnmì de

intimidate *v* 胁迫 xiépò, 吓唬 xiàhu; **intimidation** *n* 恐吓 kǒnghè

into *prep* 进 jìn, 入 rù, 到 ... 里面 dào ... lǐmiàn, 成为 chéngwéi, 转为 zhuǎnwéi

intolerable *adj* 无法容忍的 wúfǎ róngrěn de

intolerance *n* 不容忍 bù róngrěn, 偏执 piānzhí

intoxicate v (使) 陶醉 (shǐ) táozuì, (使) 喝醉 (shǐ) hēzuì;
  intoxicated adj 喝醉的 hē zuì de, 陶醉的 táozuì de
intricate adj 复杂的 fùzá de
intrigue v 激起兴趣 jīqǐ xìngqù, 迷住 mízhù; n 阴谋 yīnmóu
introduce v 介绍 jièshào, 引进 yǐnjìn; **introduction** n 介绍
  jièshào, 引进 yǐnjìn
introspection n 反省 fǎnxǐng; **introspective** adj 反省的
  fǎnxǐng de
introvert n 性格内向的人 xìnggé nèixiàng de rén
intrude v 闯入 chuǎngrù, 侵入 qīnrù; **intruder** n 闯入者
  chuǎngrùzhě, 入侵者 rùqīnzhě; **intrusion** n 闯入
  chuǎngrù, 侵扰 qīnrǎo
intuitive adj 直觉的 zhíjué de
inundate v 淹没 yānmò; **inundation** n 洪水 hóngshuǐ
invade v 侵略 qīnlüè; **invader** n 侵略者 qīnlüèzhě; **invasion**
  n 侵略 qīnlüè
invalid n 病残者 bìngcánzhě; adj 无效的 wúxiào de
invaluable adj 无价的 wújià de, 宝贵的 bǎoguì de
invent v 发明 fāmíng; **invention** n 发明 fāmíng; **inventor** n
  发明者 fāmíngzhě
invest v 投资 tóuzī; **investment** n 投资 tóuzī; **investment**
  bank 投资银行 tóuzī yínháng; **investor** n 投资者 tóuzīzhě
investigate v 调查 diàochá; **investigation** n 调查 diàochá
invisibility n 看不清 kàn bù qīng; **invisible** adj 看不见的 kàn
  bù jiàn de, 无形的 wúxíng de
invite v 邀请 yāoqǐng; **invitation** n 邀请 yāoqǐng; **invitation**
  letter 邀请信 yāoqǐngxìn
invoice v 开发票 kāi fāpiào; n 发票 fāpiào
involuntary adj 非自愿的 fēi zìyuàn de, 无意的 wúyì de;
  involuntarily adv 不知不觉地 bùzhī bùjué de
involve v 包括 bāokuò, 牵涉 qiānshè, (使) 卷入 (shǐ) juǎnrù,
  (使) 参与 (shǐ) cānyù; **involved** adj (complicated) 棘手的
  jíshǒu de; (participating) 参与的 cānyù de; **involvement**
  n 参与 cānyù, 牵涉 qiānshè
Ireland n 爱尔兰 ài'ěrlán; **Irish** n 爱尔兰人 ài'ěrlánrén; adj
  爱尔兰的 ài'ěrlán de
irk v (使) 厌倦 (shǐ) yànjuàn; **irksome** adj 令人厌烦的 lìng
  rén yànfán de
iron v 熨 yùn, 熨平 yùnpíng; n (metal) 铁 tiě; (for pressing)
  熨斗 yùndǒu; **iron out** 消除 xiāochú; **ironing board**
  熨衣板 yùnyībǎn

irony *n* 反话 fǎnhuà, 嘲弄 cháonòng; **ironic** *adj* 讽刺的 fěngcì de

irrational *adj* 无理性的 wú lǐxìng de

irregularity *n* 不规则 bù guīzé; **irregular** *adj* 不规则的 bù guīzé de

irrelevant *adj* 不相关的 bù xiāngguān de, 不切题的 bù qiètí de

irreparable *adj* 不可挽回的 bù kě wǎnhuí de

irresistible *adj* 不可抵抗的 bù kě dǐkàng de

irrespective *adj* 不顾的 bùgù de, 不考虑的 bù kǎolǜ de; **irrespective of** 不管 bùguǎn

irresponsible *adj* 不负责任的 bù fù zérèn de

irrigate *v* 灌溉 guàngài; **irrigation** *n* 灌溉 guàngài

irritate *v* 激怒 jīnù; **irritation** *n* 激怒 jīnù, 恼怒 nǎonù; **irritating** *adj* 令人愤怒的 lìng rén fènnù de

is. *See* **be**

island *n* 岛 dǎo

isolate *v* (使) 隔离 (shǐ) gélí, (使) 孤立 (shǐ) gūlì; **isolation** *n* 孤立 gūlì

issue *v* (*distribute*) 发 fā, 发放 fāfàng; (*publish*) 发行 fāxíng, 出版 chūbǎn; *n* (*magazines, etc.*) 期 qī; (*problem*) 问题 wèntí; (*contention*) 争议 zhēngyì; **take issue with** 持异议 chí yìyì

it *pron* 它 tā

italics *n* 斜体字 xiétǐzì

Italy *n* 意大利 yìdàlì; **Italian** *n* (*people*) 意大利人 yìdàlìrén; (*language*) 意大利语 yìdàlìyǔ; *adj* 意大利的 yìdàlì de

itch *v* 痒 yǎng; **itchy** *adj* 使人发痒的 shǐ rén fāyǎng de

item *n* 项目 xiàngmù, 条目 tiáomù, 条款 tiáokuǎn

itemize *v* 逐条列记 zhútiáo lièjì

itinerary *n* 旅行路线 lǚxíng lùxiàn, 旅行计划 lǚxíng jìhuà

its *pron* 它的 tāde

itself *pron* 它自己 tā zìjǐ

ivory *n* 象牙 xiàngyá

J

jacket *n* 上衣 shàngyī, 夹克 jiákè

jackpot *n* 头奖 tóujiǎng, 巨额奖金 jù'é jiǎngjīn

jail *v* 监禁 jiānjìn; *n* 监狱 jiānyù; **jailer** *n* 狱卒 yùzú

jam *v* 堵塞 dǔsè, 卡住 kǎzhù; *n* (*preserved fruit*) 果酱 guǒjiàng; (*dense crowd*) 堵塞 dǔsè

January *n* 一月 yīyuè

Japan *n* 日本 rìběn; **Japanese** *n* (*people*) 日本人 rìběnrén; (*language*) 日语 rìyǔ; *adj* 日本的 rìběn de

jar *n* 罐子 guànzi

jaw *n* 颌 hé

jazz *n* 爵士乐 juéshìyuè; **jazz band** 爵士乐队 juéshìyuèduì

jealousy *n* 嫉妒 jídù; **jealous** *adj* 嫉妒的 jídù de

jeans *n* 牛仔裤 niúzǎikù

jeep *n* 吉普车 jípǔchē

jelly *n* 果冻 guǒdòng; **jellyfish** *n* 水母 shuǐmǔ

jeopardize *v* 危害 wēihài, 危及 wēijí, (使) 处于危险境地 (shǐ) chǔyú wēixiǎn jìngdì; **jeopardy** *n* 危险 wēixiǎn

jersey *n* 运动衫 yùndòngshān

jest *n* 笑话 xiàohua, 俏皮话 qiàopíhuà; **jester** *n* 讲笑话的人 jiǎng xiàohua de rén, 小丑 xiǎochǒu

jet *n* 喷气式飞机 pēnqìshì fēijī

Jew *n* 犹太人 yóutàirén; **Jewish** *adj* 犹太人的 yóutàirén de

jewel *n* 宝石 bǎoshí; **jeweler** *n* 珠宝商 zhūbǎoshāng; **jewelry** *n* 珠宝 zhūbǎo

job *n* 工作 gōngzuò, 活儿 huór

jog *v* 慢跑 mànpǎo; **jogging** *n* 慢跑 mànpǎo

join *v* (*connect*) 连接 liánjiē; (*participate*) 参加 cānjiā, 加入 jiārù

joint *n* 关节 guānjié; *adj* 共同的 gòngtóng de, 联合的 liánhé de; **jointly** *adv* 共同地 gòngtóng de, 联合地 liánhé de

joke *v* 开玩笑 kāi wánxiào; *n* 玩笑 wánxiào, 笑话 xiàohua; **joker** *n* 爱开玩笑的人 ài kāiwánxiào de rén

jolly *adj* 欢乐的 huānlè de, 快活的 kuàihuo de

journal *n* (*magazine*) 杂志 zázhì; (*diary*) 日记 rìjì; **journalism** *n* 新闻业 xīnwényè; **journalist** *n* 新闻记者 xīnwén jìzhě

journey *v/n* 旅行 lǚxíng

joy *n* 快乐 kuàilè, 喜悦 xǐyuè; **joyful** *adj* 快乐的 kuàilè de, 兴高采烈的 xìnggāocǎiliè de

jubilant *adj* 喜悦的 xǐyuè de

jubilee *n* 五十周年纪念 wǔshí zhōunián jìniàn

judge *v* 判断 pànduàn, 裁判 cáipàn; *n* (*law*) 法官 fǎguān; (*competition*) 裁判 cáipàn; **judgment** *n* 判断 pànduàn; (*law*) 判决 pànjué; **judging by** 根据 ... 判断 gēnjù ... pànduàn

judicial *adj* (*law*) 司法的 sīfǎ de; (*discriminating*) 考虑慎密的 kǎolǜ shènmì de, 明断的 míngduàn de

jug *n* 水壶 shuǐhú

juggle *v* 尽力应付 jìnlì yìngfù; **juggling** *n* 杂耍 záshuǎ

juice *n* 果汁 guǒzhī

July *n* 七月 qīyuè

jump *v/n* 跳 tiào, 跃 yuè; **jump at** 欣然接受 xīnrán jiēshòu, 抓住 zhuāzhù; **jumpy** *adj* 神经质的 shénjīngzhì de

junction *n* 连接点 liánjiēdiǎn, 交叉点 jiāochādiǎn

juncture *n* 接合点 jiēhédiǎn; **at this juncture** 在这个当口 zài zhè gè dāngkǒu

June *n* 六月 liùyuè

jungle *n* 丛林 cónglín

junior *n* 下级 xiàjí; 年少者 niánshàozhě; (*college*) 大学三年级学生 dàxué sānniánjí xuésheng; *adj* (*rank*) 下级的 xiàjí de; (*age*) 年少的 niánshào de

junk *n* 垃圾 lājī

jurisdiction *n* 管辖地 guǎnxiádì, 管辖范围 guǎnxiá fànwéi

jury *n* 陪审团 péishěntuán; **juror** *n* 陪审员 péishěnyuán

just *adv* (*a moment ago*) 刚刚 gānggāng; (*only*) 仅仅 jǐnjǐn; (*just right*) 正好 zhènghǎo; (*precisely*) 正是 zhèngshì; (*nothing but*) 只是 zhǐshì; *adj* 正义的 zhèngyì de, 公正的 gōngzhèng de

justice *n* 正义 zhèngyì, 公平 gōngpíng

justify *v* 证明 ... 有理 zhèngmíng ... yǒulǐ; **justifiable** *adj* 有理由的 yǒu lǐyóu de; **justification** *n* 理由 lǐyóu

juvenile *n* 少年 shàonián; *adj* 少年的 shàonián de, 幼稚的 yòuzhì de; **juvenile delinquent** 少年犯 shǎoniánfàn

juxtapose *v* 并置 bìngzhì; **juxtaposition** *n* 并置 bìngzhì

K

kangaroo *n* 袋鼠 dàishǔ

kebab *n* 烤肉串 kǎoròuchuàn

keen *adj* (*of acumen*) 敏锐的 mǐnruì de, (*eager*) 渴望的 kěwàng de, 热心的 rèxīn de; **keenly** *adv* 敏锐地 mǐnruì de

keep *v* (**kept, kept**) 保持 bǎochí, 保存 bǎocún, 维持 wéichí; **keep away from** 远离 yuǎnlí, 避开 bìkāi; **keep on** 继续 jìxù, 坚持 jiānchí; **keep out of** 置身于外 zhìshēn yú wài; **keep up with** 跟上 gēn shàng; **keeper** *n* 保管人 bǎoguǎnrén, 看守人 kānshǒurén

kettle *n* 壶 hú

key *n* (*for a lock*) 钥匙 yàoshi; (*answer*) 答案 dá'àn; (*crucial element*) 关键 guānjiàn; **keyboard** *n* (*computer*) 键盘 jiànpán; (*music instrument*) 键盘乐器 jiànpán yuèqì

kick v 踢 tī; **kick off** 开始 kāishǐ; **kick out** 开除 kāichú, 逐出 zhúchū

kid v 戏弄 xì'nòng; n 小孩 xiǎohái

kidnap v 绑架 bǎngjià; **kidnapper** n 绑匪 bǎngfěi; **kidnapping** n 绑架 bǎngjià

kidney n 肾 shèn

kill v 杀死 shāsǐ; **killer** n 杀手 shāshǒu, 凶手 xiōngshǒu; **killing** n 杀害 shāhài, 杀戮 shālù

kilogram n 公斤 gōngjīn

kilometer n 公里 gōnglǐ

kin n 血缘关系 xuèyuán guānxì, 家属 jiāshǔ, 亲属 qīnshǔ; **kinship** n 亲属关系 qīnshǔ guānxì

kind n 种类 zhǒnglèi; **in kind** 以货代款 yǐhuò dàikuǎn; adj 和蔼的 hé'ǎi de, 善良的 shànliáng de; **kindness** n 亲切 qīnqiè, 善意 shànyì, 仁慈 réncí

kindergarten n 幼儿园 yòu'éryuán

kindle v 点燃 diǎnrán

king n 国王 guówáng; **kingdom** n 王国 wángguó; **king size** 超大号 chāodàhào

kiosk n (grocery) 售货亭 shòuhuòtíng; (telephone) 电话亭 diànhuàtíng; (newspaper) 售报亭 shòubàotíng

kiss v/n 吻 wěn

kit n 成套物品 chéngtào wùpǐn, 工具箱 gōngjùxiāng

kitchen n 厨房 chúfáng

kite n 风筝 fēngzheng

kitten n 小猫 xiǎomāo

knack n 诀窍 juéqiào; **get the knack of** 掌握技巧 zhǎngwò jìqiǎo

knee n 膝盖 xīgài

kneel v (knelt/kneeled, knelt/kneeled) 跪 guì

knew. See **know**

knickers n 灯笼裤 dēnglóngkù

knife n (pl **knives**) 刀 dāo

knight n 骑士 qíshì

knit v (knitted/knit, knitted/knit) 编织 biānzhī; **knitting** n 编织品 biānzhīpǐn; **knitting machine** 编织机 biānzhījī

knives. See **knife**

knob n 旋钮 xuánniǔ

knock v 敲 qiāo; **knock out** (defeat) 击倒 jī dǎo; (damage) 毁坏 huǐhuài; (render unconscious) (使) 失去知觉 (shǐ) shīqù zhījué; **knock down** 击倒 jī dǎo

knot n 结 jié

know *v* (**knew, known**) 知道 zhīdao; **know how to** 会 huì;
   know-how *n* 技术 jìshù
knowledge *n* 知识 zhīshi; **knowledgeable** *adj* 知识渊博的
   zhīshí yuānbó de
knuckle *n* 关节 guānjié; **knuckle under** 认输 rènshū

L

lab. *See* **laboratory**
label *v* 标注 biāozhù; *n* 标签 biāoqiān
labor *v* 劳动 láodòng; *n* (*work*) 劳动 láodòng, (*body of*
   persons) 劳工 láogōng, (*childbirth*) 分娩 fēnmiǎn; **labor**
   camp 劳改营 láogǎiyíng; **laborious** *adj* 艰苦的 jiānkǔ
   de, 费力的 fèilì de; **laborer** *n* 劳工 láogōng
laboratory *n* 实验室 shíyànshì
lack *v/n* 缺乏 quēfá
lacquer *n* 漆 qī
lad *n* 小伙子 xiǎohuǒzi
ladder *n* 梯子 tīzi
lady *n* 女士 nǚshì; **ladies and gentleman!** 女士们, 先生们!
   nǚshìmen xiānshengmen; **ladylike** *adj* 雍容温雅的
   yōngróng wēnyǎ de
lag *v/n* 落后 luòhòu
laid. *See* **lay**
lain. *See* **lie**
lake *n* 湖 hú
lamb *n* (*animal*) 羊羔 yánggāo, (*meat*) 羊肉 yángròu
lame *adj* 跛足的 bǒzú de
lament *v/n* 哀悼 āidào; **lamentable** *adj* 可悲的 kěbēi de,
   不幸的 búxìng de
laminate *v* 覆盖层压塑料 fùgài céngyā sùliào; **laminated**
   adj 包层压塑料的 bāo céngyā sùliào de
lamp *n* 灯 dēng; **lamp-post** *n* 路灯柱 lùdēngzhù
land *v* 着陆 zhuólù; *n* 陆地 lùdì, 土地 tǔdì; **landing** *n* 着陆
   zhuólù, 登陆 dēnglù; **landlady** *n* 女房东 nǚfángdōng;
   landlord *n* 房东 fángdōng; **landmark** *n* 陆标 lùbiāo,
   里程碑 lǐchéngbēi; **landscape** *n* 风景 fēngjǐng
lane *n* (*alley*) 小巷 xiǎoxiàng; (*highway*) 车道 chēdào
language *n* 语言 yǔyán
languish *v* 憔悴 qiáocuì, 衰退 shuāituì, 遭冷落 zāo lěngluò
lantern *n* 灯 dēng, 灯笼 dēnglong
lap *n* (*anat*) 膝头 xītóu; (*track*) 一圈 yī quān

lapse *n* (*time*) 流逝 liúshì; (*error*) 失误 shīwù

laptop *n* 便携式电脑 biànxiéshì diànnǎo

larder *n* 食品库 shípǐnkù

large *adj* 大的 dà de; **at large** 逍遥法外的 xiāoyáo fǎwài de; **large scale** 大规模 dàguīmó

larynx *n* 喉 hóu

laryngitis *n* 喉炎 hóuyán

laser *n* 激光 jīguāng; **laser printer** 激光打印机 jīguāng dǎyìnjī

lash *v* 鞭打 biāndǎ; **lash out** 猛烈抨击 měngliè pēngjī

last *v* 持续 chíxù, 维持 wéichí; *adj* (*previous*) 上一个 shàng yī gè, 前一个 qián yī gè; (*final*) 最后一个 zuìhòu yī gè; **last minute** 最后一刻 zuìhòu yī kè; **last night** 昨夜 zuóyè; **lastly** *adv* 最后 zuìhòu; **lasting** *adj* 持久的 chíjiǔ de, 永恒的 yǒnghéng de, 耐久的 nàijiǔ de

late *adj* 迟的 chí de, 晚的 wǎn de; **lately** *adv* 最近 zuìjìn; **later** *adv* 后来 hòulái; **see you later** 再见 zàijiàn; **latest** *adj* 最近的 zuìjìn de, 最新的 zuì xīn de

Latin *n* 拉丁文 lādīngwén, 拉丁语 lādīngyǔ; *adj* 拉丁文的 lādīngwén de, 拉丁语的 lādīngyǔ de

Latin America *n* 拉丁美洲 lādīng měizhōu; **Latin American** *n* 拉丁美洲人 lādīng měizhōurén; *adj* 拉丁美洲的 lādīng měizhōu de

latitude *n* 纬度 wěidù

lateral *adj* 横向的 héngxiàng de, 侧面的 cèmiàn de

latter *n* 后者 hòuzhě; *adj* 后面的 hòumian de

laugh *v* 笑 xiào; **laughable** *adj* 可笑的 kěxiào de; **laughter** *n* 笑声 xiàoshēng; **laugh at** 嘲笑 cháoxiào; **laughing stock** 笑柄 xiàobǐng

launch *v* 发射 fāshè, 发起 fāqǐ

laundry *n* 洗衣店 xǐyīdiàn; 要洗的衣服 yào xǐ de yīfu; **launderette** *n* 自助洗衣店 zìzhù xǐyīdiàn;

lava *n* 熔岩 róngyán

lavatory *n* 盥洗室 guànxǐshì

lavish *adj* (*generous*) 非常大方的 fēicháng dàfāng de; (*wasteful*) 浪费的 làngfèi de, 挥霍的 huīhuò de

law *n* 法律 fǎlù; **law court** *n* 法院 fǎyuàn; **law abiding** 守法的 shǒufǎ de; **lawsuit** *n* 诉讼 sùsòng; **lawful** *adj* 合法的 héfǎ de; **lawyer** *n* 律师 lùshī

lawn *n* 草坪 cǎopíng

lax *adj* (*loose*) 松的 sōng de; (*of bowels*) 腹泻的 fùxiè de

laxative *n* 泻药 xièyào

lay *v* (**laid**, **laid**) 放置 fàngzhì; **lay eggs** 下蛋 xiàdàn; **lay off** 解雇 jiěgù; **lay-out** *n* 布局 bùjú, 设计 shèjì; *See* **lie**

layer *n* 层 céng

lazy *adj* 懒惰的 lǎnduò de; **laziness** *n* 懒惰 lǎnduò

lead *v* (**led**, **led**) 领导 lǐngdǎo, 引导 yǐndǎo; 致使 zhìshǐ, **lead up to** 作为 ... 的准备 zuòwéi ... de zhǔnbèi; **leader** *n* 领导者 lǐngdǎozhě, 领袖 lǐngxiù; **leadership** *n* 领导地位 lǐngdǎo dìwèi; 领导阶层 lǐngdǎo jiēcéng; **leading** *adj* 主要的 zhǔyào de; *n* (*chemical element*) 铅 qiān

leaf *n* (*pl* **leaves**) 叶子 yèzi; **leaflet** *n* 传单 chuándān

league *n* 联盟 liánméng, 联合会 liánhéhuì; **in league with** 与 ... 联合 yǔ ... liánhé

leak *v* 漏 lòu, 泄漏 xièlòu; *n* 漏洞 lòudòng, 泄漏 xièlòu

lean *v* 靠 kào, 依 yī, 倾向于 qīngxiàng yú; **lean on** 依赖 yīlài; **leaning** *n* 倾向 qīngxiàng; **lean back** 向后仰 xiàng hòu yǎng; *adj* (*thin*) 瘦的 shòu de; (*poor*) 贫乏的 pínfá de

leap *v* (**leaped/leapt**, **leaped/leapt**) 跳跃 tiàoyuè; *n* 跳跃 tiàoyuè; **by leaps and bounds** 突飞猛进地 tūfēi měngjìn de; **leap-year** *n* 闰年 rùnnián

learn *v* (**learned/learnt**, **learned/learnt**) 学习 xuéxí; **learn about/of** 获悉 huòxī, 得知 dézhī; **learn from** 向 ... 学习 xiàng ... xuéxí; **learn how to** 学会 xuéhuì; **learner** *n* 学习者 xuéxízhě, 学生 xuésheng; **learning** *n* (*study*) 学习 xuéxí; (*scholarship*) 学识 xuéshí, 学问 xuéwen; **learned** *adj* 有学问的 yǒuxuéwèn de

learnt. *See* **learn**

lease *v* 出租 chūzū, 租 zū; *n* 租约 zūyuē

least *adj* 最小的 zuìxiǎo de, 最少的 zuìshǎo de; **at least** 至少 zhìshǎo

leather *n* 皮革 pígé

leave *v* (**left**, **left**) (*depart*) 离开 líkāi; (*set out*) 出发 chūfā; (*give up*) 放弃 fàngqì; (*allow to stay*) 留下 liúxià, 丢下 diūxià; (*remain*) 剩余 shèngyú; **leave alone** 让 ... 独自待着 ràng ... dúzì dài zhe, 不打扰 bù dǎrǎo, 不干预 bù gānyù; **leave behind** 留下 liúxià, 不带 bù dài, 忘了带 wàng le dài; **leave out** 省去 shěngqù, 不考虑 bù kǎolǜ; *n* 假期 jiàqī, 休假 xiūjià, 告别 gàobié; **be on leave** 请假中 qǐngjià zhōng, 休假中 xiūjià zhōng; **take leave of** 离开 líkāi

leaves. *See* **leaf**

lecture *v* 演讲 yǎnjiǎng; *n* 讲座 jiǎngzuò; **lecturer** *n* 讲师 jiǎngshī, 讲演人 jiǎngyǎnrén

led. *See* **lead**

left *v see* **leave**; *n* (*remainder*) 剩余物 shèngyúwù, 剩菜 shèngcài; (*direction*) 左 zuǒ; **left over** *adj* 剩下的 shèngxià de, 吃剩的 chī shèng de; **left-handed** *adj* 左撇子 zuǒpiězi; **left-wing** *adj* 左翼的 zuǒyì de

leg *n* (*anat*) 腿 tuǐ; (*travel*) 一段行程 yī duàn xíngchéng, 一站 yī zhàn

legacy *n* 遗产 yíchǎn

legal *adj* 法律的 fǎlǜ de, 合法的 héfǎ de; **legalize** *v* (使) 合法化 (shǐ) héfǎhuà

legend *n* 传奇 chuánqí, 传说 chuánshuō; **legendary** *adj* 传奇的 chuánqí de

legible *adj* 清晰的 qīngxī de, 易读的 yìdú de; **legibility** *n* 易读性 yìdúxìng

legislate *v* 制定法律 zhìdìng fǎlǜ, 立法 lìfǎ; **legislation** *n* 立法 lìfǎ; **legislative** *adj* 立法的 lìfǎ de; **legislature** *n* 立法机构 lìfǎ jīgòu

legitimacy *n* 合法 héfǎ; **legitimate** *adj* 合法的 héfǎ de

leisure *n* 闲暇 xiánxiá, 休闲 xiūxián; **leisurely** *adj* 闲暇的 xiánxiá de, 从容的 cōngróng de

lemon *n* 柠檬 níngméng; **lemonade** *n* 柠檬汁 níngméngzhī

lend *v* (**lent**, **lent**) 借 jiè

length *n* 长度 chángdù; **lengthen** *v* 加长 jiācháng; **lengthy** *adj* 冗长的 rǒngcháng de

lenient *adj* 宽容的 kuānróng de

lens *n* 镜头 jìngtóu; **contact lens** 隐形眼镜 yǐnxíng yǎnjìng

lent. *See* **lend**

lesbian *n* 女同性恋 nǚtóngxìngliàn; **lesbianism** *n* 女同性恋关系 nǚtóngxìngliàn guānxì

less *adj* 较少的 jiàoshǎo de, 较小的 jiàoxiǎo de; **lessen** *v* (*reduce*) 减少 jiǎnshǎo; (*lighten*) 减轻 jiǎnqīng; **lesser** *adj* 较少的 jiàoshǎo de, 较小的 jiàoxiǎo de

lesson *n* 课 kè

lest *conj* 以免 yǐmiǎn

let *v* (**let**, **let**) 让 ràng, 使 shǐ; **let alone** 不管 bùguǎn, 不用说 bùyòng shuō; **let down** (*slacken*) 松劲 sōngjìn; (*disappoint*) 辜负 gūfù; **let in** 放进 fàng jìn; **let off** 放出 fàng chū; **let up** (*stop*) 停止 tíngzhǐ; (*slacken*) 放松 fàngsōng

lethal *adj* 致命的 zhìmìng de

letter *n* (*message*) 信 xìn; (*symbol*) 字母 zìmǔ; **letter-box** *n* 信箱 xìnxiāng

lettuce *n* 生菜 shēngcài

leukemia *n* 白血病 báixuèbìng

level *n* 水平 shuǐpíng; *adj* 水平的 shuǐpíng de, 平的 píng de; **be level with** 对 ... 说实话 duì ... shuō shíhuà; **level-headed** *adj* 头脑冷静的 tóunǎo lěngjìng de

lever *n* 杠杆 gànggǎn; **leverage** *n* 优势 yōushì

levy *v* 征税 zhēngshuì

lewd *adj* 猥亵的 wěixiè de

liable *adj* 有责任的 yǒu zérèn de; **liable to** 易受 yìshòu; **liability** *n* (*responsibility*) 责任 zérèn; (*debt*) 债务 zhàiwù

liaison *n* 联络 liánluò

liar *n* 说谎者 shuōhuǎngzhě, 骗子 piànzi

libel *v/n* 诽谤 fěibàng

liberal *n* 自由主义者 zìyóuzhǔyìzhě; *adj* 自由主义的 zìyóuzhǔyì de

liberate *v* 解放 jiěfàng; **liberation** *n* 解放 jiěfàng

liberty *n* 自由 zìyóu; **at liberty** 随意 suíyì

library *n* 图书馆 túshūguǎn

lice *n* 虱子 shīzi

license *n* 执照 zhízhào

lick *v* 舔 tiǎn

lid *n* 盖子 gàizi

lie *v* (**lay, lain**) 躺 tǎng; **lie down** 躺下 tǎng xià; (**lied, lied**) 说谎 shuōhuǎng; *n* 谎言 huǎngyán

lieutenant *n* (*military*) 中尉 zhōngwèi; (*deputy*) 副职 fùzhí

life *n* 生命 shēngmìng, 生活 shēnghuó; **life insurance** 人寿保险 rénshòu bǎoxiǎn; **life jacket** 救生衣 jiùshēngyī; **lifebelt** *n* 救生圈 jiùshēngquān; **lifeboat** *n* 救生艇 jiùshēngtǐng; **lifeless** *adj* 无生命的 wúshēngmìng de, 无活力的 wúhuólì de; **lifestyle** *n* 生活方式 shēnghuó fāngshì; **lifetime** *n* 一生 yīshēng; **lifelong** *adj* 终身的 zhōngshēn de; **lifeguard** *n* 救生员 jiùshēngyuán

lift *v* 举 jǔ, 举起 jǔqǐ, 提高 tígāo

light *v* (**lighted/lit, lit**) 点着 diǎn zháo, 点燃 diǎnrán; *n* 光 guāng, 灯 dēng; **lightbulb** *n* 电灯泡 diàndēngpào; **light year** 光年 guāngnián; **lighthouse** *n* 灯塔 dēngtǎ; **lighter** *n* 打火机 dǎhuǒjī; **lightning** *n* 闪电 shǎndiàn; **lighten** *v* 减轻 jiǎnqīng; *adj* (*not heavy*) 轻的 qīng de; **lightheaded** *adj* 头晕的 tóuyūn de; **lighthearted** 无忧无虑的 wúyōuwúlǜ de; **lightweight** *n* 不能胜任者 bùnéng shèngrèn zhě

like *v* 喜欢 xǐhuan; **liking** *n* 喜爱 xǐ'ài; **likeable** *adj* 讨人喜爱的 tǎo rén xǐ'ài de; *prep* 像 xiàng; **liken** *v* 把 ...

比作 bǐ ... bǐzuò; **likeness** *n* 相像 xiāngxiàng; **likewise** *adv* 同样地 tóngyàng de; **look like** 看起来像 kàn qǐlái xiàng

likely *adj* 很可能的 hěn kěnéng de; **be likely to** 可能 kěnéng; **likelihood** *n* 可能 kěnéng, 可能性 kěnéngxìng

limb *n* 肢 zhī

lime *n* 石灰 shíhuī; **limestone** *n* 石灰石 shíhuīshí

limelight *n* 众人注意的中心 zhòngrén zhùyì de zhōngxīn

limp *v* 跛行 bǒxíng

limit *v* 限制 xiànzhì; *n* 极限 jíxiàn, 局限 júxiàn; **limitation** *n* 限制 xiànzhì, 局限 júxiàn; **limitless** *adj* 无限的 wúxiàn de

limousine *n* 豪华轿车 háohuá jiàochē

line *v* 排成行 pái cheng háng, 排队 páiduì; *n* (*mark*) 线 xiàn; (*queue*) 队 duì; **line up** 排队 páiduì; **on line** (*Internet*) 在网上 zài wǎng shang

linen *n* 亚麻布 yàmábù, 亚麻制品 yàmázhìpǐn

liner *n* 班轮 bānlún

lingerie *n* 女内衣 nǚnèiyī

linguist *n* 语言学家 yǔyánxuéjiā; **linguistic** *adj* 语言学的 yǔyánxué de; **linguistics** *n* 语言学 yǔyánxué

link *v* 连接 liánjiē, 联系 liánxì; *n* 链接 liànjiē, 链环 liànhuán

linoleum *n* 油布 yóubù

lion *n* 狮子 shīzi

lip *n* 嘴唇 zuǐchún; **lip-read** *v* 唇读 chúndú; **lipstick** *n* 口红 kǒuhóng

liquid *n* 液体 yètǐ; *adj* 液体的 yètǐ de

liquidate *v* 清算 qīngsuàn; **liquidation** *n* 清算 qīngsuàn, 清仓 qīngcāng

liquor *n* 酒 jiǔ; **liquor store** 酒店 jiǔdiàn

list *v* 列单 lièdān, 列出 lièchū; *n* 单子 dānzi

listen *v* 听 tīng; **listener** *n* 听者 tīngzhě

lit. *See* **light**

literacy *n* 读写能力 dúxiě nénglì

literally *adv* (*word for word*) 逐字地 zhúzì de; (*without exaggeration*) 不加夸张地 bùjiā kuāzhāng de

literary *adj* 文学的 wénxué de, 精通文学的 jīngtōng wénxué de, 文艺的 wényì de; **literate** *adj* 有文化的 yǒu wénhuà de

literature *n* 文学 wénxué, 文献 wénxiàn

litter *v* 乱丢 luàndiū

little *adj* 少的 shǎo de, 小的 xiǎo de

live *v* 住 zhù; **live up to** 不辜负 ... 的希望 bù gūfù ... de xīwàng; *adj* (*alive*) 活的 huó de; (*broadcast*) 实况的 shíkuàng de

livelihood *n* 生计 shēngjì

lively *adj* 活泼的 huópo de, 生动的 shēngdòng de

liver *n* 肝脏 gānzàng

living *n* 生计 shēngjì; *adj* 活的 huó de, 生活的 shēnghuó de; **living room** 客厅 kètīng

lizard *n* 蜥蜴 xīyì

load *v* 装载 zhuāngzài; *n* 负载 fùzài

loaf *n* (*pl* **loaves**) 一块面包 yī kuài miànbāo

loan *v* 借出 jièchū; *n* 贷款 dàikuǎn

loathe *v* 憎恶 zēngwù; **loathing** *n* 讨厌 tǎoyàn; **loathsome** *adj* 讨厌的 tǎoyàn de

lobby *v* 游说支持 yóushuì zhīchí; *n* 大厅 dàtīng

lobster *n* 龙虾 lóngxiā

local *adj* 当地的 dāngdì de, 地方的 dìfāng de; **the locals** 当地人 dāngdìrén; **locality** *n* 位置 wèizhi; **locally** *adv* 在本地 zài běndì; 当地地 dāngdì de

locate *v* 查找地点 cházhǎo dìdiǎn; **be located at or in** 位于 wèiyú; **location** *n* 位置 wèizhi, 地点 dìdiǎn

lock *v* 锁 suǒ; *n* 锁 suǒ; **lock in** 锁住 suǒ zhù; **locker** *n* 锁柜 suǒguì; **lock out** 把 ... 关在外面 bǎ ... guān zài wàimian; **lock up** 锁上 suǒ shàng

locomotion *n* 运动 yùndòng, 运转 yùnzhuàn; **locomotive** *n* 机车 jīchē, 火车头 huǒchētóu

lodge *v* 寄宿 jìsù; *n* 门房 ménfáng, 旅馆 lǚguǎn; **lodgings** *n* 寄宿处 jìsùchù

lofty *adj* 崇高的 chónggāo de

log *n* (*tree*) 圆木 yuánmù; (*records*) 日志 rìzhì; **log in** *v* 注册 zhùcè, 登录 dēnglù

loggerheads *n* 傻子 shǎzi; **be at loggerheads** 不和 bùhé

logic *n* 逻辑 luójí; **logical** *adj* 合逻辑的 hé luójí de

lonely *adj* 孤独的 gūdú de, 寂寞的 jìmò de; **loneliness** *n* 寂寞 jìmò, 孤独 gūdú

long *v* 渴望 kěwàng; **longing** *n* 期盼 qīpàn, 渴望 kěwàng; *adj* 长的 cháng de; **as long as** 只要 zhǐyào; **long-lasting** *adj* 持久的 chíjiǔ de; **long-range** *adj* 长期的 chángqī de, 远程的 yuǎnchéng de; **long-sighted** *adj* 有远见的 yǒu yuǎnjiàn de; **long-term** *adj* 长期的 chángqī de

longevity *n* 长寿 chángshòu

longitude *n* 经度 jīngdù

look *v* 看 kàn; (*appear, seem*) 显得 xiǎnde, 看上去 kàn shàngqù; **look after** 照顾 zhàogù; **look ahead** 展望未来 zhǎnwàng wèilái; **look at** 看 kàn; **look back** 回顾 huígù;

look for 找 zhǎo; **look forward to** 期待 qīdài; **look into** 调查 diàochá; **look like** 看起来像 kàn qǐlái xiàng; **look out!** 小心! xiǎoxīn; **look over** 检查 jiǎnchá; **look up** 仰视 yǎngshì; (*search for*) 查阅 cháyuè; **look up to** 敬仰 jìngyǎng, 钦佩 qīnpèi; *n* 表情 biǎoqíng

loop *n* 环 huán

loose *v* 释放 shìfàng; *adj* 宽松的 kuānsōng de; **loosen** *v* 松开 sōngkāi, 解开 jiěkāi; **loose leaf** 活页的 huóyè de; **loosely** *adv* 松散地 sōngsǎn de

loot *v* 掠夺 lüèduó, 抢劫 qiǎngjié; **looter** *n* 掠夺者 lüèduózhě, 抢劫者 qiǎngjiézhě; **looting** *n* 掠夺 lüèduó, 抢劫 qiǎngjié

lopsided *adj* 倾向一方的 qīngxiàng yīfāng de

lord *n* (*ruler*) 统治者 tǒngzhìzhě; **Lord** *n* 上帝 shàngdì

lorry *n* 卡车 kǎchē

lose *v* (**lost**, **lost**) (*fail to retain*) 丢 diū; (*fail to win*) 输 shū; **lose one's way** 迷路 mílù; **lose weight** 减轻体重 jiǎnqīng tǐzhòng; **loser** *n* 失败者 shībàizhě, 输者 shūzhě

loss *n* 损失 sǔnshī; **be at a loss** 茫然不知所措 mángrán bùzhī suǒcuò

lost *adj* 失去的 shīqù de; *v see* **lose**

lot *n* (*drawing*) 抽签 chōuqiān; (*fate*) 命运 mìngyùn; (*ground*) 场地 chǎngdì; **a lot** 很 hěn; **quite a lot** 相当多 xiāngdāng duō; **lots of** 许多 xǔduō

lotion *n* 洗液 xǐyè, 涂剂 tújì

lottery *n* 抽彩给奖法 chōucǎi gěijiǎngfǎ, 抽签法 chōuqiānfǎ; **lottery ticket** 彩票 cǎipiào

loud *adj* 大声的 dàshēng de; **loudly** *adv* 大声地 dàshēng de; **loudness** *n* 大声 dàshēng, 喧闹 xuānnào

loudspeaker *n* 扩音器 kuòyīnqì, 喇叭 lǎba

lounge *n* 休息室 xiūxīshì

love *v/n* 爱 ài; **fall in love with** 爱上 ài shàng; **make love** 做爱 zuò'ài; **lovable** *adj* 可爱的 kě'ài de; **lovely** *adj* 可爱的 kě'ài de; **lover** *n* 爱人 àiren; 情人 qíngrén; **loving** *adj* 钟爱的 zhōng'ài de, 钟情的 zhōngqíng de

low *adj* 低的 dī de; **lowland** *n* 低地 dīdì; **low-lying** *adj* 低地的 dīdì de; **lowly** *adv* 地位低地 dìwèi dī de; **lower** *v* 降低 jiàngdī; *adj* 较低的 jiào dī de; **lower oneself** 降低自己的身份 jiàngdī zìjǐ de shēnfen

loyal *adj* 忠诚的 zhōngchéng de; **loyalty** *n* 忠诚 zhōngchéng

lubricant *n* 润滑剂 rùnhuájì; **lubricate** *v* 加润滑油 jiā rùnhuáyóu; **lubrication** *n* 润滑 rùnhuá

luck *n* 运气 yùnqì; **bad luck** 霉运 méiyùn; **good luck** 好运 hǎoyùn; **lucky** *adj* 幸运的 xìngyùn de; **luckily** *adv* 幸运地 xìngyùn de

lucrative *adj* 有利可图的 yǒulì kětú de

luggage *n* 行李 xíngli

lukewarm *adj* 冷淡的 lěngdàn de, 不冷不热的 bù lěng bù rè de

lumber *n* 木材 mùcái

lump *n* 块 kuài; *v* 把 ... 归并在一起 bǎ ... guībìng zài yīqǐ

lunar *adj* (*of the moon*) 月亮的 yuèliang de; (*of the lunar calendar*) 农历的 nónglì de

lunatic *n* 疯子 fēngzi; *adj* 精神失常的 jīngshén shīcháng de; **lunacy** *n* 精神错乱 jīngshén cuòluàn

lunch *n* 午饭 wǔfàn, 中饭 zhōngfàn; **lunchtime** *n* 午餐时间 wǔcān shíjiān

lung *n* 肺 fèi

lurch *n* 困境 kùnjìng; **leave in the lurch** 致 ... 于困境 zhì ... yú kùnjìng

lure *v* 引诱 yǐnyòu

lust *n* 性欲 xìngyù

luxury *n* (*condition*) 奢侈 shēchǐ; (*products*) 奢侈品 shēchǐpǐn; **luxurious** *adj* 奢侈的 shēchǐ de; **luxuriant** *adj* 丰产的 fēngchǎn de, 茂盛的 màoshèng de

lynch *v* 处私刑 chǔ sīxíng; *n* 私刑 sīxíng

lyrics *n* 歌词 gēcí; **lyricist** *n* 歌词作者 gēcí zuòzhě

M

machine *n* 机器 jīqì; **machine-gun** *n* 机关枪 jīguānqiāng; **machinery** *n* 机械 jīxiè

mad *adj* (*insane*) 疯狂的 fēngkuáng de; (*angry*) 生气的 shēngqì de; **madden** *v* 发狂 fākuáng; **madness** *n* 疯狂 fēngkuáng; **madly** *adv* 发狂地 fākuáng de

madam *n* 女士 nǔshì, 夫人 fūren

made. *See* **make**

magazine *n* 杂志 zázhì

magic *n* 魔法 mófǎ; *adj* 有魔力的 yǒu mólì de; **magical** *adj* 不可思议的 bùkěsīyì de; **magician** *n* 魔术师 móshùshī; **magistrate** *n* 地方法官 dìfāng fǎguān

magnet *n* 磁体 cítǐ, 磁铁 cítiě; **magnetic** *adj* 磁的 cí de, 有吸引力的 yǒu xīyǐnlì de

magnificent *adj* 宏伟的 hóngwěi de, 华丽的 huálì de

magnify *v* 放大 fàngdà, 扩大 kuòdà; **magnifying glass** 放大镜 fàngdàjìng; **magnificence** *n* 雄伟壮观 xióngwěi zhuàngguān

magnanimous *adj* 宽宏大量的 kuānhóng dàliàng de; **magnanimity** *n* 宽宏大量 kuānhóng dàliàng

maid *n* (*girl*) 少女 shàonǚ; (*servant*) 女仆 nǚpú

maiden *n* 少女 shàonǚ, 处女 chǔnǚ; **maiden name** 婚前姓 hūnqiánxìng, 娘家姓 niángjiāxìng

mail *v* 邮寄 yóujì; *n* 邮件 yóujiàn; **mail order** 邮购 yóugòu; **mailbox** *n* 邮箱 yóuxiāng; **mailman** *n* 邮差 yóuchāi

main *adj* 主要的 zhǔyào de; **in the main** 大体上 dàtǐ shang; **mainland** *n* 大陆 dàlù

maintain *v* (*preserve*) 维持 wéichí; (*service*) 维修 wéixiū; (*state*) 主张 zhǔzhāng; **maintenance** *n* 维持 wéichí, 维修 wéixiū

majesty *n* 雄伟 xióngwěi, 壮丽 zhuànglì, 威严 wēiyán; **majestic** *adj* 宏伟的 hóngwěi de, 庄严的 zhuāngyán de

major *v* 主修 zhǔxiū; *n* 主修 zhǔxiū, 专业 zhuānyè

majority *n* 多数 duōshù

make *v* (**made, made**) (*manufacture*) 制造 zhìzào, (*produce, do*) 做 zuò, (*form*) 构成 gòuchéng, (*cause to be or become*) 使 shǐ; *n* 牌子 páizi, 型号 xínghào; **make believe** 伪装 wěizhuāng, 假装 jiǎzhuāng; **make do** 勉强使用 miǎnqiǎng shǐyòng; **make of** 推断 tuīduàn; 理解 lǐjiě; **make off** (*walk away*) 走开 zǒukāi; (*escape*) 逃走 táozǒu; **make out** (*fill out*) 填写 tiánxiě; (*decipher*) 辨认出 biànrèn chū; **make up** 补充 bǔchōng, 补偿 bǔcháng, 弥补 míbǔ; (*concoct*) 捏造 niēzào, (*invent*) 虚构 xūgòu; (*constitute*) 组成 zǔchéng, 构成 gòuchéng; (*exam*) 补考 bǔkǎo; **maker** *n* 制造者 zhìzàozhě; **makeup** *n* 化妆品 huàzhuāngpǐn

malaria *n* 疟疾 nüèjí

male *n* 男人 nánrén; *adj* 男的 nán de

malfunction *v/n* 故障 gùzhàng

malice *n* 恶意 èyì; **malicious** *adj* 恶毒的 èdú de

malignant *adj* 恶意的 èyì de; 恶性的 èxìng de

malnutrition *n* 营养不良 yíngyǎng bùliáng

maltreat *v* 虐待 nüèdài; **maltreatment** *n* 虐待 nüèdài

mammal *n* 哺乳动物 bǔrǔ dòngwù

man *n* (*pl* **men**) 男人 nánrén; (*mankind*) 人类 rénlèi; **manhood** *n* 男子气概 nánzǐ qìgài; **manly** *n* 有男子气概的 yǒu nánzǐqìgài de

manage v 管理 guǎnlǐ; **manageable** adj 易管理的 yì guǎnlǐ de; **managerial** adj 管理的 guǎnlǐ de; **management** n 管理 guǎnlǐ; **manager** n 经理 jīnglǐ; **managing director** n 常务董事 chángwù dǒngshì

Mandarin n 普通话 pǔtōnghuà; **mandarin orange** 橘子 júzi

mandate n 授权 shòuquán; **mandatory** adj 强制的 qiángzhì de

maneuver v/n (*movement*) 调遣 diàoqiǎn; (*mil excercises*) 演习 yǎnxí; (*manipulate*) 操纵 cāozòng

mania n 狂热 kuángrè; **maniac** n 疯子 fēngzi, 狂人 kuángrén

manicure v 修剪 xiūjiǎn; n 修指甲 xiūzhǐjia

manifest adj 显然的 xiǎnrán de; **manifestation** n 表现 biǎoxiàn

manipulate v 操纵 cāozòng; **manipulation** n 操纵 cāozòng

mankind n 人类 rénlèi

man-made adj 人造的 rénzào de, 人为的 rénwéi de

manner n 方式 fāngshì; **manners** n 礼貌 lǐmào

manor n 庄园 zhuāngyuán

manpower n 人力 rénlì

mansion n 豪宅 háozhái

manslaughter n 过失杀人 guòshī shārén

manual adj 手工的 shǒugōng de; **manually** n 手册 shǒucè; adv 手工地 shǒugōng de

manufacture v 制造 zhìzào; **manufacturer** n 制造商 zhìzàoshāng

manure n 肥料 féiliào

manuscript n 手稿 shǒugǎo

many adj 许多的 xǔduō de; **as many as** 多达 duō dá; **how many** 多少 duōshao

map n 地图 dìtú; **map out** 制定 zhìdìng

marathon n 马拉松赛跑 mǎlāsōng sàipǎo

marble n 大理石 dàlǐshí

March n 三月 sānyuè

march v 前进 qiánjìn, 游行 yóuxíng; n 行军 xíngjūn; (*demonstration*) 示威游行 shìwēi yóuxíng

margarine n 人造黄油 rénzào huángyóu

margin n 边缘 biānyuán; **marginal** adj 边缘的 biānyuán de

marijuana n 大麻 dàmá

marine n 海军陆战队 hǎijun lùzhànduì; adj 海的 hǎi de

maritime adj 海事的 hǎishì de

mark v 做记号 zuò jìhao (*give a grade*) 打分数 dǎ fēnshù; n (*trace*) 记号 jìhao; (*school*) 分数 fēnshù; **marksman** n 神射手 shénshèshǒu

market *n* 市场 shìchǎng; **marketing** *n* 营销 yíngxiāo

marriage *n* 婚姻 hūnyīn; **marriage certificate** 结婚证 jiéhūnzhèng

marry *v* 与 ... 结婚 yǔ ... jiéhūn; **married** *adj* 已婚的 yǐhūn de

Mars *n* 火星 huǒxīng; **Martian** *adj* 火星的 huǒxīng de

marsh *n* 沼泽 zhǎozé

marshmallow *n* 药属葵 yàoshǔkuí

marshal *n* 元帅 yuánshuài

martial *adj* 军事的 jūnshì de; **martial law** 戒严法 jièyánfǎ

martyr *n* 烈士 lièshì

marvelous *adj* 奇妙的 qímiào de, 了不起的 liǎobuqǐ de

masculine *adj* 男子气概的 nánzǐqìgài de; (*gram*) 阳性的 yángxìng de

mask *v* 掩饰 yǎnshì; *n* 面具 miànjù

mason *n* 泥瓦匠 níwǎjiàng; **masonry** *n* 石匠职业 shíjiang zhíyè

mass *adj* 大规模的 dàguīmó de; **mass media** 大众传媒 dàzhòng chuánméi; **mass meeting** 群众集会 qúnzhòng jíhuì; **mass produce** 大批生产 dàpī shēngchǎn; **mass production** 大批生产 dàpī shēngchǎn

massacre *n* 大屠杀 dàtúshā, 集体屠杀 jítǐ túshā

massage *v/n* 按摩 ànmó

massive *adj* 巨大的 jùdà de, 大量的 dàliàng de, 大规模的 dàguīmó de

master *v* 掌握 zhǎngwò; *n* (*owner*) 主人 zhǔrén; (*expert*) 大师 dàshī; (*skilled worker*) 师傅 shīfu; **master of ceremonies** 司仪 sīyí; **masterpiece** *n* 杰作 jiézuò; **mastery** *n* 掌握 zhǎngwò

mat *n* 垫席 diànxí

match *v* 比赛 bǐsài, 敌得过 dí de guò, 比得上 bǐ de shàng, 和 ... 相配 hé ... xiāngpèi; *n* 对手 duìshǒu, 配对物 pèiduìwù; (*competition*) 比赛 bǐsài; (*lighter*) 火柴 huǒchái; **matchless** *adj* 无敌的 wúdí de; **matchbox** *n* 火柴盒 huǒcháihé

mate *n* (*partner*) 伙伴 huǒbàn; (*spouse*) 配偶 pèi'ǒu

material *n* 材料 cáiliao, 原料 yuánliào; **materialize** *v* 实现 shíxiàn

maternal *adj* 母亲的 mǔqīn de, 母方的 mǔfāng de

maternity *adj* 产妇的 chǎnfù de, 孕妇的 yùnfù de; **maternity clinic** 产科诊所 chǎnkē zhěnsuǒ; **maternity hospital**

产科医院 chǎnkē yīyuàn; **maternity leave** 产假 chǎnjià;
maternity nurse 助产士 zhùchǎnshì

mathematics *n* 数学 shùxué; **mathematician** *n* 数学家
shùxuéjiā; **mathematical** *adj* 数学的 shùxué de

matinee *n* 日场演出 rìchǎng yǎnchū

matrimonial *adj* 婚姻的 hūnyīn de

matter *v* 有关系 yǒu guānxì, 要紧 yàojǐn; *n* (*thing*) 事 shì;
(*substance*) 物质 wùzhì; **as a matter of fact** 事实上
shìshí shang; **matter of fact** 事实 shìshí; **what's the
matter?** 怎么了 zěnme le; **it doesn't matter** 没关系 méi
guānxi

mattress *n* 席梦思 xímèngsī

mature *v* 成熟 chéngshú; *adj* (*ripe, fully developed*) 成熟的
chéngshú de; (*payable, due*) 到期的 dàoqī de

maximize *v* 使增加到最大限度 shǐ zēngjiā dào zuìdà xiàndù,
最大限度地利用 zuìdà xiàndù de lìyòng; **maximum** *n*
最大量 zuìdàliàng; *adj* 最高的 zuìgāo de, 最大的 zuìdà de

May *n* 五月 wǔyuè

may *aux* (*might*) 可能 kěnéng, 可以 kěyǐ

maybe *adv* 也许 yěxǔ

mayonnaise *n* 蛋黄酱 dànhuángjiàng

mayor *n* 市长 shìzhǎng

me *pron* 我 wǒ

meal *n* 餐 cān, 饭 fàn

mean *v* (**meant, meant**) 意思是 yìsi shì, 意味着 yìwèi zhe;
n (*math*) 平均数 píngjūnshù; *adj* (*unkind*) 卑鄙的 bēibǐ
de, (*stingy*) 吝啬的 lìnsè de

meaning *n* 意义 yìyì; **meaningless** *adj* 无意义的 wúyìyì de;
meaningful *adj* 意味深长的 yìwèi shēncháng de

means *n* 工具 gōngjù, 手段 shǒuduàn; **by all means**
尽一切方法 jìn yīqiè fāngfǎ; **by means of** 凭借 píngjiè;
by no means 决不 juébù

meant. *See* **mean**

meanwhile *n* 其时 qíshí, 其间 qíjiān; *adv* 其间 qíjiān,
与此同时 yǔcǐ tóngshí

measure *v* 测量 cèliáng; *n* 措施 cuòshī; **made to measure**
定做的 dìngzuò de; **measurement** *n* 度量 dùliàng, 尺寸
chǐcùn

meat *n* 肉 ròu; **meatball** *n* 肉丸 ròuwán

mechanic *n* 技工 jìgōng, 修理工 xiūlǐgōng; **mechanical** *adj*
机械的 jīxiè de; **mechanics** *n* 力学 lìxué, 结构 jiégòu;

mechanism *n* 机构 jīgòu, 机制 jīzhì, 途径 tújìng, 技巧 jìqiǎo

medal *n* 奖章 jiǎngzhāng, 勋章 xūnzhāng

meddle *v* 管闲事 guǎn xiánshì; **meddle with** 干涉 gānshè; **meddlesome** *adj* 爱管闲事的 ài guǎn xiánshì de

media *n* 媒体 méitǐ

mediate *v* 调停 tiáotíng, 调解 tiáojiě; **mediation** *n* 调停 tiáotíng, 调解 tiáojiě; **mediator** *n* 调停者 tiáotíngzhě

medical *adj* 医学的 yīxué de; **medical school** 医学院 yīxuéyuàn

medicine *n* (*science*) 医学 yīxué; (*drug*) 药 yào; **medicinal** *adj* 药的 yào de

medieval *adj* 中世纪的 zhōngshìjì de

mediocre *adj* 平庸的 píngyōng de

meditate *v* 沉思 chénsī, 考虑 kǎolǜ; **meditation** *n* 沉思 chénsī

medium *adj* 中等的 zhōngděng de; **medium-sized** *n* 媒介 méijiè, 媒体 méitǐ, 手段 shǒuduàn, 工具 gōngjù; *adj* 中等大小的 zhōngděng dàxiǎo de

meek *adj* 温顺的 wēnshùn de

meet *v* (**met, met**) (*see*) 和 ... 见面 hé ... jiànmiàn; (*have a meeting*) 开会 kāihuì; (*pick up*) 接 jiē; **meeting** *n* 会 huì, 会议 huìyì

melancholy *n* 忧郁 yōuyù

melodrama *n* 情节剧 qíngjiéjù; **melodramatic** *adj* 情节剧的 qíngjiéjù de

melody *n* 曲调 qǔdiào

melon *n* 瓜 guā

melt *v* 融化 rónghuà

member *n* 成员 chéngyuán; **membership** *n* 全体会员 quántǐ huìyuán

memo. *See* **memorandum**

memoirs *n* 回忆录 huíyìlù

memorable *adj* 难忘的 nánwàng de

memorandum *n* 备忘录 bèiwànglù

memorial *n* 纪念馆 jìniànguǎn; *adj* 纪念性的 jìniànxìng de

memory *n* 记忆 jìyì, 记忆力 jìyìlì; **memorize** *v* 记住 jìzhù

men. *See* **man**

menace *v/n* 威胁 wēixié

mend *v* (*improve*) 改进 gǎijìn; (*repair*) 修理 xiūlǐ

menstruation *n* 月经 yuèjīng

mental *adj* 脑力的 nǎolì de, 精神的 jīngshén de, 心理的 xīnlǐ de; **mental hospital** 精神病院 jīngshénbìngyuàn;

mentality n 心理 xīnlǐ, 智力 zhìlì, 心态 xīntài; **mentally** adv 精神上地 jīngshén shang de

mention v/n 提及 tíjí; **don't mention it** 不客气 bùkèqì

menu n 菜单 càidān

mercenary n 雇佣兵 gùyōng bīng; adj (working for money) 唯利是图的 wéilì shìtú de; (for hire in a foreign army) 雇佣的 gùyōng de

merchandise n 商品 shāngpǐn, 货物 huòwù

merchant n 商人 shāngrén

mercury n 水银 shuǐyín

mercy n 仁慈 réncí, 怜悯 liánmǐn; **at the mercy of** 受 ... 的支配 shòu ... de zhīpèi; **merciful** adj 仁慈的 réncí de; **merciless** adj 残忍的 cánrěn de

mere adj 仅仅的 jǐnjǐn de

merge v 合并 hébìng, 融合 rónghé

merit n 优点 yōudiǎn, 功劳 gōngláo

merry adj 快乐的 kuàilè de

mess n 混乱 hùnluàn, 脏乱 zāngluàn; **messy** v 把 ... 弄脏 bǎ ... nòng zāng, 把 ... 弄乱 bǎ ... nòng luàn; adj 凌乱的 língluàn de

message n 信息 xìnxī, 留言 liúyán; **messenger** n 信使 xìnshǐ, 信差 xìnchāi

met. See **meet**

metal n 金属 jīnshǔ

metaphor n 隐喻 yǐnyù; **metaphorical** adj 隐喻的 yǐnyù de, 比喻的 bǐyù de

meteor n 流星 liúxīng; **meteoric** adj 流星似的 liúxīngshì de

meteorology n 气象学 qìxiàngxué; **meteorological** adj 气象的 qìxiàng de

meter n 公尺 gōngchǐ, 米 mǐ

metric adj 公制的 gōngzhì de

method n 方法 fāngfǎ

meticulous adj 一丝不苟的 yīsī bùgǒu de

metropolis n 都市 dūshì

metropolitan adj 大城市的 dàchéngshì de, 大都会的 dàdūhuì de

Mexico n 墨西哥 mòxīgē; **Mexican** n 墨西哥人 mòxīgērén; adj 墨西哥的 mòxīgē de

mice. See **mouse**

microphone n 麦克风 màikèfēng

microscope n 显微镜 xiǎnwēijìng

microwave *n* 微波 wēibō; (*oven*) 微波炉 wēibōlú

mid *adj* 中间的 zhōngjiān de, 中部的 zhōngbù de, 中央的 zhōngyāng de

midday *n* 正午 zhèngwǔ

middle *adj* 中间的 zhōngjiān de; **in the middle** 在 ... 中间 zài ... zhōngjiān; **the middle ages** 中世纪 zhōngshìjì; **middle class** 中产阶级 zhōngchǎn jiējí; **Middle East** 中东 zhōngdōng; **middle-aged** *adj* 中年的 zhōngnián de

midnight *n* 午夜 wǔyè

midst *n* 中间 zhōngjiān; **in the midst of** 在 ... 当中 zài ... dāngzhōng

midsummer *n* 仲夏 zhòngxià

midway *adv* 中途 zhōngtú

midweek *n* 一周的中间 yīzhōu de zhōngjiān

midwife *n* 助产士 zhùchǎnshì

might *v see* **may**; *n* 威力 wēilì

mighty *adj* 强大的 qiángdà de, 有势力的 yǒu shìlì de

migraine *n* 偏头痛 piāntóutòng

migrate *v* 移居 yíjū, 迁徙 qiānxǐ; **migration** *n* 移居 yíjū, 迁徙 qiānxǐ

mild *adj* 温和的 wēnhé de

mile *n* 英里 yīnglǐ; **mileage** *n* 英里数 yīnglǐshù; **milestone** *n* 里程碑 lǐchéngbēi

militant *adj* 好战的 hàozhàn de, 好斗的 hàodòu de

military *n* 军队 jūnduì; *adj* 军事的 jūnshì de

milk *n* 牛奶 niúnǎi

Milky Way *n* 银河 yínhé

mill *n* 磨坊 mòfāng, 工厂 gōngchǎng

millennium *n* 一千年 yīqiān nián

million *n* 百万 bǎiwàn; **millionaire** *n* 百万富翁 bǎiwàn fùwēng

mince *v* 切碎 qiēsuì; **mince words** 说话兜圈子 shuōhuà dōu quānzi

mind *v* (*pay attention to*) 注意 zhùyì; (*care about*) 介意 jièyì; (*look after*) 照看 zhàokàn; *n* 头脑 tóunǎo, 智力 zhìlì, 理智 lǐzhì, 心情 xīnqíng, 精神 jīngshén; **bear in mind** 记住 jì zhù; **go out of one's mind** 发疯 fāfēng; **keep in mind** 记住 jìzhù; **make up one's mind** 下决心 xià juéxīn; **to my mind** 在我看来 zài wǒ kànlái; **never mind** 算了 suàn le

mine *v* 采矿 cǎikuàng; 布地雷 bù dìléi; *n* (*excavation*) 矿 kuàng; (*explosive*) 地雷 dìléi; **mine detector** 探雷器 tànléiqì; **mine disposal** 除雷 chúléi; **minefield** *n* 布雷区

bùléiqū; **miner** *n* 矿工 kuànggōng; **mining** *n* 采矿 cǎikuàng; *pron* 我的 wǒde

mineral *n* 矿物 kuàngwù; **mineral water** 矿泉水 kuàngquánshuǐ

minimize *v* 使减少到最低限度 shǐ jiǎnshǎo dào zuìdī xiàndù, 极度轻视 jídù qīngshì; **minimum** *n* 最小值 zuìxiǎozhí; **minimal** *adj* 最小的 zuìxiǎo de, 最少的 zuìshǎo de

minister *n* (*government*) 部长 bùzhǎng; (*diplomat*) 公使 gōngshǐ; (*clergy*) 牧师 mùshī; **ministry** *n* (*government*) 部 bù

minor *n* (*course of study*) 副修科目 fùxiū kēmù, (*under age*) 未成年的人 wèichéngnián de rén; *adj* (*of size*) 较小的 jiàoxiǎo de; (*not important*) 次要的 cìyào de, 不重要的 bù zhòngyào de; (*under age*) 未成年的 wèichéngnián de

minority *n* 少数 shǎoshù; (*ethnic group*) 少数民族 shǎoshù mínzú

mint *v* 铸造 zhùzào; *n* (*factory*) 铸币厂 zhùbìchǎng; (*herb*) 薄荷 bòhe

minus *prep* 减 jiǎn

minute *n* 分钟 fēnzhōng; *adj* (*tiny*) 微小的 wēixiǎo de, (*detailed*) 细微的 xìwēi de; **minutes** *n* 会议记录 huìyìjìlù

miracle *n* 奇迹 qíjī; **miraculous** *adj* 奇迹的 qíjī de

mirror *n* 镜子 jìngzi

misbehave *v* 行为不当 xíngwéi búdàng, 举止失礼 jǔzhǐ shīlǐ; **misbehavior** *n* 不当行为 búdàng xíngwéi

miscalculate *v* 误算 wùsuàn, 错算 cuòsuàn

miscarriage *n* 流产 liúchǎn

miscellaneous *adj* 混杂的 hùnzá de, 各种各样的 gèzhǒng gèyàng de

mischief *n* 恶作剧 èzuòjù; **mischievous** *adj* 恶作剧的 èzuòjù de, 顽皮的 wánpí de, 淘气的 táoqì de

misconduct *n* 不当行为 bùdāng xíngwéi

miserable *adj* 悲惨的 bēicǎn de, 可怜的 kělián de

misery *n* 痛苦 tòngkǔ, 穷困 qióngkùn

miser *n* 吝啬鬼 lìnsèguǐ; **miserly** *adj* 吝啬的 lìnsè de

misfire *v* (*weapon, engine, etc.*) 不发火 bù fāhuǒ, 失败 shībài

misfortune *n* 不幸 bùxìng, 灾祸 zāihuò

misguided *adj* 误入歧途的 wùrù qítú de

misinterpret *v* 曲解 qūjiě; **misinterpretation** *n* 曲解 qūjiě

misjudge *v* 错误判断 cuòwù pànduàn

mislead *v* (*misled, misled*) 误导 wùdǎo

misplace *v* 放错地方 fàngcuò dìfāng

misprint *n* 错印 cuòyìn

Miss *n* 小姐 xiǎojie

miss *v* (*long for*) 思念 sīniàn; (*fail to catch*) 错过 cuòguò;
　missing *adj* 失踪的 shīzōng de, 丢失的 diūshī de

missile *n* 导弹 dǎodàn; **guided missile** 导弹 dǎodàn

mission *n* 使命 shǐmìng, 宗旨 zōngzhǐ; (*diplomatic*) 代表团
　dàibiǎotuán; **missionary** *n* 传教士 chuánjiàoshì

mist *n* 薄雾 báowù; **misty** *adj* 薄雾笼罩的 báowù lǒngzhào
　de, 模糊的 móhu de

mistake *n* 错误 cuòwù; **by mistake** 错误地 cuòwù de; **make
　a mistake** 犯错误 fàn cuòwù; *v* (**mistook, mistaken**)
　误解 wùjiě, 误会 wùhuì; **mistaken** *adj* 错误的 cuòwù de

mistress *n* (*of the house*) 女主人 nǚzhǔrén; (*lover*) 情妇
　qíngfù

mistrust *v/n* 不信任 bù xìnrèn

misunderstand *v* (**misunderstood, misunderstood**) 误会
　wùhuì; **misunderstanding** *n* 误会 wùhuì

misuse *v* 误用 wùyòng, 错用 cuòyòng, 滥用 lànyòng

mix *v* 混合 hùnhé; **mix-up** *n* 混乱 hùnluàn, 弄错 nòngcuò,
　混淆 hùnxiáo; **mixer** *n* 搅拌器 jiǎobànqì; **mixture** *n*
　混合物 hùnhéwù; **mixed feelings** 矛盾的心情 máodùn
　de xīnqíng

moan *v* 呻吟 shēnyín; *n* 呻吟声 shēnyínshēng

mob *n* 暴民 bàomín, 乌合之众 wūhé zhīzhòng

mobile *adj* 移动的 yídòng de; **mobile phone** 移动电话
　yídòngdiànhuà, 手机 shǒujī; **mobilize** *v* 动员 dòngyuán;
　mobility *n* 机动性 jīdòngxing, 晋升可能 jìnshēng kěnéng

mock *v* (*ridicule*) 嘲笑 cháoxiào; (*mimic*) 模仿 mófǎng;
　mockery *n* 嘲笑 cháoxiào; **mocking** *adj* 嘲笑的 cháoxiào
　de

mode *n* 方式 fāngshì

model *v* 模仿 mófǎng, 仿效 fǎngxiào; *n* 模型 móxíng, 模式
　móshì, (*person*) 模特儿 mótèr;

moderate *adj* 适度的 shìdù de, 温和的 wēnhé de;
　moderately *adv* 适度地 shìdù de; **moderation** *n* 适度 shìdù;
　in moderation 适度 shìdù

modern *adj* 现代的 xiàndài de; **modernize** *v* (使) 现代化
　(shǐ) xiàndàihuà; **modernization** *n* 现代化 xiàndàihuà

modesty *n* 谦逊 qiānxùn; **modest** *adj* 谦逊的 qiānxùn de,
　适度的 shìdù de

modify *v* 修改 xiūgǎi, 更改 gēnggǎi; **modification** *n* 修改 xiūgǎi, 更改 gēnggǎi

moist *adj* 潮湿的 cháoshī de; **moisture** *n* 湿气 shīqì; **moisturize** *v* (使) 潮湿 (shǐ) cháoshī

mold *v* (*make a pattern*) 塑造 sùzào; *n* (*pattern*) 模子 múzǐ; (*fungus*) 霉菌 méijūn

mole *n* (*med*) 胎块 tāi kuài; *n* (*zool*) 鼹鼠 yǎnshǔ; (*spy*) 双重间谍 shuāngchóng jiàndié; **molehill** *n* 无意义的事 wú yìyì de shì

molecule *n* 分子 fēnzǐ

molest *v* 调戏 tiáoxì, 猥亵 wěixiè

moment *n* 时刻 shíkè; **at the moment** 此刻 cǐkè; **momentary** *adj* 瞬间的 shùnjiān de; **momentarily** *adv* 立刻 lìkè

momentum *n* 势头 shìtóu

mommy *n* (*coll: mother*) 妈妈 māma

monarch *n* 君主 jūnzhǔ; **monarchy** *n* 君主政体 jūnzhǔ zhèngtǐ

monastery *n* 修道院 xiūdàoyuàn

Monday *n* 星期一 xīngqīyī

money *n* 钱 qián

monitor *n* 监视器 jiānshìqì, 电脑显示器 diànnǎo xiǎnshìqì

monk *n* 和尚 héshang

monkey *n* 猴子 hóuzi

monogamy *n* 一夫一妻制 yīfū yīqī zhì; **monogamous** *adj* 一夫一妻制的 yīfū yīqī zhì de

monopolize *v* 垄断 lǒngduàn, 独占 dúzhàn; **monopoly** *n* 垄断 lǒngduàn

monosyllable *n* 单音节字 dānyīnjiézì; **monosyllabic** *adj* 单音节的 dānyīnjié de

monotony *n* 单调 dāndiào; **monotonous** *adj* 单调的 dāndiào de

monsoon *n* 雨季 yǔjì

monster *n* 怪物 guàiwù; **monstrosity** *n* 畸形 jīxíng

month *n* 月 yuè; **monthly** *n* 月刊 yuèkān; *adj* 每月一次的 měiyuè yīcì de

monument *n* 纪念碑 jìniànbēi; **monumental** *adj* 不朽的 bùxiǔ de

mood *n* (*gram*) 语气 yǔqì; (*humor*) 心情 xīnqíng; **moody** *adj* 喜怒无常的 xǐnù wúcháng de

moon *n* 月亮 yuèliang; **moonlight** *n* 月光 yuèguāng

moral *n* 寓意 yùyì; *adj* 道德的 dàodé de; 有道德的 yǒu

dàodé de, 精神上的 jīngshén shang de; **morals** *n* 道德 dàodé

morale *n* 士气 shìqì

more *adj* 更多的 gèngduō de; **all the more** 更加 gèngjiā; **and what's more** 另外 lìngwài; **more and more** 越来越多的 yuèláiyuè duō de; **more than ever** 比任何时候都更 bǐ rènhé shíhou dōu gèng; **once more** 再一次 zài yī cì

moreover *adv* 而且 érqiě, 此外 cǐwài

morning *n* 早上 zǎoshang, 上午 shàngwǔ

mortal *n* 凡人 fánrén; *adj* 必死的 bìsǐ de; **mortality** *n* 死亡 sǐwáng

mortgage *n* 抵押 dǐyā

mortuary *n* 太平间 tàipíngjiān, 停尸房 tíngshīfáng

mosque *n* 清真寺 qīngzhēnsì

mosquito *n* 蚊子 wénzi

most *adv* 最 zuì; **at most** 至多 zhìduō; **make the most of** 充分利用 chōngfèn lìyòng; **mostly** *adv* 大多 dàduō

motel *n* 汽车旅馆 qìchē lǚguǎn

moth *n* 蛾子 ézi; **mothball** *n* 樟脑球 zhāngnǎoqiú

mother *n* 母亲 mǔqīn, 妈妈 māma; **mother-in-law** *n* (*wife's mother*) 岳母 yuèmǔ; (*husband's mother*) 婆婆 pópo; **mother tongue** 母语 mǔyǔ; **motherly** *adj* 母亲的 mǔqīn de

motion *n* 运动 yùndòng; **motionless** *adj* 不动的 bùdòng de, 静止的 jìngzhǐ de

motivate *v* 激发 jīfā, (使) 产生动力 (shǐ) chǎnshēng dònglì; **motivation** *n* 动力 dònglì

motive *n* 动机 dòngjī

motor *n* 发动机 fādòngjī; **motorist** *n* 驾驶员 jiàshǐyuán; **motorway** *n* 高速公路 gāosù gōnglù

motto *n* 座右铭 zuòyòumíng

mound *n* 土墩 tǔdūn

mount *v* (*climb*) 登上 dēng shàng, 爬上 pá shàng; (*install*) 安放 ānfàng; *n* 山 shān

mountain *n* 山 shān; **mountaineer** *n* 登山者 dēngshānzhě; **mountainous** *adj* 多山的 duōshān de

mourn *v* 哀悼 āidào; **mourner** *n* 哀悼者 āidàozhě; **mourning** *n* 服丧 fúsāng

mouse *n* (*pl* **mice**) (*zool*) 老鼠 lǎoshǔ; (*computer*) 鼠标 shǔbiāo

moustache *n* 髭 zī, 小胡子 xiǎohúzi

mouth *n* 嘴 zuǐ; **mouthpiece** *n* 话筒 huàtǒng; **mouthwash** *n* 漱口水 shùkǒushuǐ

move *v* 搬 bān, 动 dòng; **movement** *n* 运动 yùndòng; **moving** *adj* 感人的 gǎnrén de

movie *n* 电影 diànyǐng; **movie theater** 电影院 diànyǐngyuàn

mow *v* (**mowed, mowed/mown**) 割 gē

Mr. *n* 先生 xiānsheng

Mrs. *n* 太太 tàitai

much *adj* 许多的 xǔduō de, 大量的 dàliàng de, 很大程度的 hěn dà chéngdù de; **how much?** 多少? duōshao

mud *n* 泥 ní; **muddy** *adj* 泥泞的 nínìng de; **mudguard** *n* 挡泥板 dǎngníbǎn

muddle *n* 糊涂 hútu, 困惑 kùnhuò; **muddleheaded** *adj* 精神混乱的 jīngshén hùnluàn de

mug *v* 行凶抢劫 xíngxiōng qiǎngjié; *n* 杯子 bēizi

multilingual *adj* 会多种语言的 huì duōzhǒng yǔyán de, 多种语言的 duōzhǒng yǔyán de

multiple *adj* 多种的 duōzhǒng de; **multiple sclerosis** 多发性硬化 duōfāxìng yìnghuà

multiply *v* (*math*) 乘 chéng; (*increase*) 增加 zēngjiā; **multiplication** *n* (*math*) 乘法 chéngfǎ; (*proliferation*) 增殖 zēngzhí

multitude *n* 众多 zhòngduō, 群众 qúnzhòng

mummy *n* 木乃伊 mùnǎiyī

municipal *adj* 市政的 shìzhèng de; **municipality** *n* 市政府 shìzhèngfǔ, 市 shì

murder *v/n* 谋杀 móushā; **murderer** *n* 凶手 xiōngshǒu

murmur *v* 低声说 dīshēng shuō

muscle *n* 肌肉 jīròu; **muscular** *adj* 肌肉发达的 jīròu fādá de

museum *n* 博物馆 bówùguǎn

mushroom *n* 蘑菇 mógu

music *n* 音乐 yīnyuè; **musical** *n* 音乐剧 yīnyuèjù; *adj* 音乐的 yīnyuè de; **musical instrument** 乐器 yuèqì; **musician** *n* 音乐家 yīnyuèjiā

Muslim *n* 穆斯林 mùsīlín

must *aux* 必须 bìxū

muster *v* 召集 zhāojí; **pass muster** 合格 hégé

mustard *n* 芥末 jièmò

mute *n* 哑巴 yǎba; *adj* 沉默的 chénmò de, 哑的 yǎ de

mutilate *v* 毁伤 huǐshāng; **mutilation** *n* 毁损 huǐsǔn

mutiny *v/n* 兵变 bīngbiàn

mutter *v* 咕哝 gūnong

mutton *n* 羊肉 yángròu

mutual *adj* 相互的 xiānghù de, 共同的 gòngtóng de

my *pron* 我的 wǒde

myself *pron* 我自己 wǒ zìjǐ

mystery *n* 谜 mí; **mysterious** *adj* 神秘的 shénmì de

mystify *v* 迷惑 míhuò, (使) 神秘化 (shǐ) shénmì huà

myth *n* 神话 shénhuà; **mythical** *adj* 神话的 shénhuà de;
  mythology *n* 神话学 shénhuàxué

N

nail *v* 钉 dìng; *n* (*finger*) 指甲 zhǐjia; (*metal*) 钉子 dīngzi

naive *adj* 天真的 tiānzhēn de; **naivety** *n* 天真 tiānzhēn

naked *adj* 裸体的 luǒtǐ de, 无遮盖的 wú zhēgài de,
  赤裸裸的 chìluǒluǒ de

name *v* 给 ... 起名 gěi ... qǐmíng, 给 ... 命名 gěi ...
  mìngmíng; *n* 名字 míngzi, 名称 míngchēng; **namely** *adv*
  即 jí

nanny *n* 保姆 bǎomǔ

nap *n* 睡 xiǎoshuì, 午觉 wǔjiào

napkin *n* 餐巾纸 cānjīnzhǐ

nappy *n* 尿布 niàobù

narcotic *n* (*med*) 麻醉药 mázuìyào; (*drug*) 毒品 dúpǐn; *adj*
  麻醉的 mázuì de, 毒品的 dúpǐn de

narrate *v* 叙述 xùshù; **narration** *n* 叙述 xùshù; **narrator** *n*
  叙述者 xùshùzhě; **narrative** *n* 叙述 xùshù

narrow *adj* 狭窄的 xiázhǎi de; **narrow-minded** *adj*
  心胸狭窄的 xīnxiōng xiázhǎi de; **narrowly** *adv* 勉强地
  miǎnqiǎng de, 险些儿 xiǎnxiēr

nasty *adj* 令人厌恶的 lìng rén yànwù de, 态度恶劣的 tàidu
  èliè de

nation *n* 国家 guójiā; **national** *adj* 国家的 guójiā de, 全国的
  quánguó de; **national anthem** 国歌 guógē; **nationalism**
  n 民族主义 mínzúzhǔyì; **nationalist** *n* 民族主义者
  mínzúzhǔyìzhě; *adj* 民族主义的 mínzúzhǔyì de;
  nationality *n* 国籍 guójí, 民族 mínzú; **nationalization** *n*
  国有化 guóyǒuhuà; **nationalize** *n* (使) 国有化 (shǐ)
  guóyǒuhuà

native *adj* 土生的 tǔshēng de, 本族的 běnzú de; **native**
  country 祖国 zǔguó; **native speaker** 说本族语者 shuō
  běnzúyǔ zhě

natural *adj* 自然的 zìrán de; **naturally** *adv* 自然地 zìrán de, 天生地 tiānshēng de

nature *n* (*universe*) 自然 zìrán; (*character*) 本性 běnxìng, 天性 tiānxìng; (*property*) 性质 xìngzhì

naught *n* 零 líng

naughty *adj* 淘气的 táoqì de

nausea *n* 作呕 zuò'ǒu; 恶心 ěxin

nautical *adj* 航海 hánghǎi, 海上的 hǎishang de

naval *adj* 海军的 hǎijūn de

navigate *v* 航海 hánghǎi; **navigation** *n* 航海 hánghǎi; **navigator** *n* 航海家 hánghǎijiā; **navigable** *adj* 适于航行的 shìyú hángxíng de

navy *n* 海军 hǎijūn; **navy blue** 海军蓝 hǎijūnlán

near *adj* 近 jìn; **near-sighted** *adj* 近视的 jìnshì de; **nearby** *adv* 附近 fùjìn; **nearly** *adv* 几乎 jīhū

neat *adj* 整洁的 zhěngjié de; **neatly** *adv* 整洁地 zhěngjié de; **neatness** *n* 整洁 zhěngjié

necessary *adj* 必要的 bìyào de, 必需的 bìxū de; **necessity** *n* 必需 bìxū, 必需品 bìxūpǐn

neck *n* 脖子 bózi; **neck and neck** 并驾齐驱 bìngjià qíqū; **necklace** *n* 项链 xiàngliàn

need *v/n* 需要 xūyào; **needless** *adj* 不必要的 bù bìyào de; **needy** *adj* 贫穷的 pínqióng de

needle *n* 针 zhēn

negative *adj* 否定的 fǒudìng de, 负面的 fùmiàn de, 阴性的 yīnxìng de

neglect *v/n* 疏忽 shūhu; **neglected** *adj* 被忽视的 bèi hūshì de

negligence *n* 疏忽 shūhu; **negligent** *adj* 疏忽的 shūhu de

negotiate *v* 谈判 tánpàn; **negotiation** *n* 谈判 tánpàn; **negotiable** *adj* 可谈判的 kě tánpàn de; 可磋商的 kě cuōshāng de

neighbor *n* 邻居 línjū; **neighborhood** *n* 街道 jiēdào, 邻里 línlǐ; **neighboring** *adj* 邻近的 línjìn de

neither *pron* 两者都不 liǎngzhě dōu bù

neon *n* 氖 nǎi

nephew *n* (*brother's son*) 侄子 zhízi; (*sister's son*) 外甥 wàisheng

nepotism *n* 裙带关系 qúndài guānxì

nerve *n* 神经 shénjīng; **get on someone's nerves** 惹人心烦 rě rén xīnfán; **lose one's nerve** 心里发慌 xīnlǐ fāhuāng; **nerve-wracking** *adj* 伤脑筋的 shāngnǎojīn de; **nervous** *adj* 紧张的 jǐnzhāng de

nest *n* 巢 cháo

net *n* 网 wǎng; (*Internet*) 互联网 hùliánwǎng; *adj* 净余的 jìngyú de; **network** *n* 网络 wǎngluò

Netherlands *n* 荷兰 hélán

neurosis *n* 神经官能症 shénjīng guānnéngzhèng

neutral *adj* 中立的 zhōnglì de, 中性的 zhōngxing de

never *adv* 从不 cóngbù, 决不 juébù; **never mind** 算了 suàn le; **never-ending** *adj* 永无止境的 yǒngwú zhǐjìng de

nevertheless *conj* 然而 rán'ér

new *adj* 新的 xīn de

New Testament *n* 新约全书 xīnyuē quánshū

New Year *n* 新年 xīnnián; **New Year's Eve** 除夕 chúxī

New Zealand *n* 新西兰 xīnxīlán; **New Zealander** *n* 新西兰人 xīnxīlánrén

new-born *adj* 新生的 xīnshēng de

newcomer *n* 新来者 xīnláizhě

news *n* 新闻 xīnwén; **news agency** 通讯社 tōngxùnshè; **newscast** *n* 新闻广播 xīnwén guǎngbō; **newscaster** *n* 新闻播音员 xīnwén bōyīnyuán; **newspaper** *n* 报纸 bàozhǐ; **newsstand** *n* 报摊 bàotān, 报亭 bàotíng

next *adj* 下一 xià yī, 紧邻的 jǐnlín de; **next door** 隔壁 gébì; **next to** 在 ... 旁边 zài ... pángbiān

nice *adj* 好的 hǎo de; **nicely** *adv* 精细地 jīngxì de; **nicety** *n* 精确 jīngquè

nick *n* 关键时刻 guānjiàn shíkè; **in the nick of time** 在关键时刻 zài guānjiàn shíkè

nickname *n* 绰号 chuòhào

niece *n* (*brother's daughter*) 侄女 zhínǔ; (*sister's daughter*) 外甥女 wàishēngnǔ

night *n* 夜里 yèlǐ; **good night!** 晚安! wǎn'ān; **last night** 昨天晚上 zuótiān wǎnshang; **night school** 夜校 yèxiào; **night shift** 夜班 yèbān; **nightclub** *n* 夜总会 yèzǒnghuì; **nightmare** *n* 恶梦 èmèng

nil *n* 零 líng

nimble *adj* 敏捷的 mǐnjié de

nine *num* 九 jiǔ; **ninth** *num* 第九 dì jiǔ

nineteen *num* 十九 shíjiǔ; **nineteenth** *num* 第十九 dì shíjiǔ

ninety *num* 九十 jiǔshí; **ninetieth** *num* 第九十 dì jiǔshí

nip *v* 捏 niē

nipple *n* 乳头 rǔtóu

no *adv* 不 bù; **no longer** 不再 bù zài; **no more** 不再 bù zài; **no one** 没有人 méiyǒu rén

noble *adj* 贵族的 guìzú de, 高尚的 gāoshàng de; **nobility** *n*
贵族 guìzú, 高尚 gāoshàng

nobody *pron* 无人 wúrén

nod *v* 点头 diǎntóu

noise *n* 噪声 zàoshēng, 吵声 chǎoshēng; **noisy** *adj* 嘈杂的
cáozá de, 喧闹的 xuānnào de

nomad *n* 游牧民 yóumùmín; **nomadic** *adj* 游牧的 yóumù de

nominate *v* 提名 tímíng, 任命 rènmìng; **nomination** *n* 提名
tímíng

none *pron* 一个也没有 yī gè yě méiyǒu; **nonetheless** *adv*
虽然如此 suīrán rúcǐ

non-existent *adj* 不存在的 bù cúnzài de

nonsense *n* 废话 fèihuà, 胡说 húshuō; **nonsensical** *adj*
荒谬的 huāngmiù de

non-stop *adj* 不停的 bùtíng de; *adv* 不停地 bùtíng de

noodles *n* 面条 miàntiáo

noon *n* 中午 zhōngwǔ

nor *conj* 也不 yě bù

norm *n* 准则 zhǔnzé, 规范 guīfàn

normal *adj* 正常的 zhèngcháng de

north *n* 北边 běibian, 北方 běifāng, 北部 běibù; **northern**
adj 北方的 běifāng de; **northeast** *n* 东北 dōngběi; *adj*
东北的 dōngběi de; **northwest** *n* 西北 xīběi; *adj* 西北的
xīběi de

North America *n* 北美洲 běiměizhōu; **North American** *n*
北美洲人 běiměizhōurén

Norway *n* 挪威 nuówēi; **Norwegian** *n* (*people*) 挪威人
nuówēirén; (*language*) 挪威语 nuówēiyǔ; *adj* 挪威的
nuówēi de

nose *n* 鼻子 bízi; **blow one's nose** 擤鼻涕 xǐng bítì; **nosey**
adj 爱管闲事的 ài guǎn xiánshì de

nostalgia *n* 怀旧 huáijiù; **nostalgic** *adj* 怀旧的 huáijiù de

nostril *n* 鼻孔 bíkǒng

not *adv* 不 bù; **not yet** 尚未 shàngwèi; **not at all** 一点也不
yīdiǎn yě bù

notable *adj* 显著的 xiǎnzhù de, 著名的 zhùmíng de

notary *n* 公证人 gōngzhèngrén

note *v* (*record*) 记录 jìlù; (*heed*) 注意 zhùyì; *n* (*record*) 笔记
bǐjì; (*message*) 短信 duǎnxìn; (*music*) 音符 yīnfú; **notebook** *n* 笔记本 bǐjìběn; **noteworthy** *adj* 显著的 xiǎnzhù
de; **noted** *adj* 著名的 zhùmíng de

nothing *pron* 什么也没有 shénme yě méiyǒu; **nothing but** 只有 zhǐyǒu

notice *v* 注意到 zhùyì dào; *n* 通知 tōngzhī; **at short notice** 临时 línshí; **noticeable** *adj* 显而易见的 xiǎn'éryìjiàn de; **notice-board** *n* 布告牌 bùgàopái

notify *v* 通知 tōngzhī; **notification** *n* 通知 tōngzhī

notion *n* 观念 guānniàn, 概念 gàiniàn

notorious *adj* 臭名昭著的 chòumíng zhāozhù de

notwithstanding *prep* 尽管 jǐnguǎn

noun *n* 名词 míngcí

nourish *n* 滋养 zīyǎng; **nourishing** *adj* 有营养的 yǒu yíngyǎng de; **nourishment** *n* 营养 yíngyǎng

novel *n* 小说 xiǎoshuō; *adj* 新颖的 xīnyǐng de, 新奇的 xīnqí de; **novelist** *n* 小说家 xiǎoshuōjiā; **novelty** *n* 新颖 xīnyǐng, 新奇 xīnqí

November *n* 十一月 shíyīyuè

novice *n* 新手 xīnshǒu, 初学者 chūxuézhě

now *adv* 现在 xiànzài; **from now on** 从现在开始 cóng xiànzài kāishǐ; **up to now** 到目前为止 dào mùqián wéizhǐ; **nowadays** *adv* 现今 xiànjīn

nowhere *adv* 无处 wúchù

nuance *n* 细微差别 xìwēi chābié

nuclear *adj* 原子核的 yuánzǐhé de, 原子能的 yuánzǐnéng de; **nuclear weapon** 核武器 héwǔqì

nude *adj* 裸体的 luǒtǐ de

nuisance *n* (*thing*) 讨厌的东西 tǎoyàn de dōngxi; (*person*) 讨厌的人 tǎoyàn de rén

numb *adj* 麻木的 mámù de; **numbness** *n* 麻木 mámù

number *n* 数字 shùzì, 号码 hàomǎ

numeral *n* 数字 shùzì

numerous *adj* 无数的 wúshù de

nun *n* 修女 xiūnǚ, 尼姑 nígū

nurse *v* 护理 hùlǐ, 照料 zhàoliào; *n* 护士 hùshi; **nursing** *n* 护理 hùlǐ; **nursing home** 养老院 yǎnglǎoyuàn

nursery *n* 托儿所 tuō'érsuǒ; **nursery rhyme** 童谣 tóngyáo

nut *n* 干果 gānguǒ, 果仁 guǒrén; **in a nutshell** 简短地说 jiǎnduǎn de shuō

nutrition *n* 营养 yíngyǎng; **nutritious** *adj* 有营养的 yǒu yíngyǎng de

O

O.K. *interj* 好的 hǎo de, 行 xíng

oak *n* (*tree*) 橡树 xiàngshù; (*wood*) 像木 xiàngmù

oar *n* 桨 jiǎng; **oarsman** *n* 桨手 jiǎngshǒu

oasis *n* 绿洲 lǜzhōu

oat *n* 燕麦 yànmài; **oats** *n* 燕麦 yànmài; **oatmeal** *n* 燕麦片 yànmàipiàn

oath *n* (*promise*) 誓言 shìyán; (*swearword*) 诅咒语 zǔzhòuyǔ; **oath of office** 就职宣誓 jiùzhí xuānshì; **take the oath** 宣誓 xuānshì

obedient *adj* 服从的 fúcóng de, 顺从的 shùncóng de; **obedience** *n* 服从 fúcóng, 顺从 shùncóng

obese *adj* 肥胖的 féipàng de; **obesity** *n* 肥胖症 féipàngzhèng

obey *v* 服从 fúcóng

obituary *n* 讣告 fùgào

object *v* 反对 fǎnduì; *n* (*thing*) 物体 wùtǐ; (*target*) 目标 mùbiāo; (*goal*) 目的 mùdì; **objection** *n* 反对 fǎnduì, 异议 yìyì; **objective** *adj* 客观的 kèguān de

oblige *v* (*compel*) 强迫 qiǎngpò, 强制 qiángzhì; (*put under debt of gratitude*) (使) 感激 (shǐ) gǎnjī; **be obliged to** 被迫做 bèipò zuò; **obligation** *n* 义务 yìwù; **obligatory** *adj* 义务的 yìwù de, 必须的 bìxū de, 强制的 qiángzhì de

oblivion *n* 遗忘 yíwàng; **oblivious** *adj* 遗忘的 yíwàng de

obnoxious *adj* 讨厌的 tǎoyàn de, 可憎的 kězēng de

obscenity *n* 猥亵 wěixiè; **obscene** *adj* 淫秽的 yínhuì de, 下流的 xiàliú de

obscure *v* 遮掩 zhēyǎn, 混淆 hùnxiáo; *adj* 费解的 fèijiě de, 晦涩的 huìsè de, 默默无闻的 mòmò wúwén de; **obscurity** *n* 晦涩 huìsè, 默默无闻 mòmò wúwén

observe *v* (*watch*) 观察 guānchá; (*obey*) 遵守 zūnshǒu; (*comment*) 评论 pínglùn; **observant** *adj* 留意的 liúyì de, 观察力敏锐的 guānchálì mǐnruì de; **observation** *n* 观察 guānchá

obsess *v* 迷住 mízhù, (使) 着迷 (shǐ) zháomí; **obsession** *n* 着迷 zháomí, 着魔 zháomó

obsolete *adj* 过时的 guòshí de, 已废弃的 yǐ fèiqì de

obstacle *n* 障碍 zhàng'ài

obstinate *adj* 顽固的 wángù de; **obstinancy** *n* 顽固 wángù

obstruct *v* 阻塞 zǔsè, 妨碍 fáng'ài; **obstruction** *n* 障碍 zhàng'ài

obtain *v* 获得 huòdé

obvious *adj* 明显的 míngxiǎn de
occasion *n* 场合 chǎnghé; **occasional** *adj* 偶然的 ǒurán de;
   occasionally *adv* 偶尔地 ǒu'ěr de
occupy *v* (*control*) 占领 zhànlǐng, 占据 zhànjù; (*keep busy*)
   (使) 忙碌 (shǐ) mánglù; **occupation** *n* (*work*) 职业 zhíyè;
   (*control*) 占领 zhànlǐng; **occupational** *adj* 职业的 zhíyè de
occur *v* 发生 fāshēng; **occurrence** *n* (*event*) 事件 shìjiàn;
   (*happening*) 发生 fāshēng
o'clock *adv* 点钟 diǎnzhōng
October *n* 十月 shíyuè
octopus *n* 章鱼 zhāngyú
odd *adj* (*strange*) 奇怪的 qíguài de; (*of numbers*) 奇数的
   jīshù de; **odd number** 奇数 jīshù; **odd jobs** 零活
   línghuó; **oddity** *n* 怪癖 guàipǐ; **odds** *n* 可能的机会
   kěnéng de jīhuì; **be at odds with** 与 ... 不和 yǔ ... bùhé;
   odds and ends 零碎东西 língsuì dōngxi
odor *n* 气味 qìwèi
of *prep* 的 de
off *adj*; *adv*; *prep* (离) 开 (lí) kāi, (走) 开 (zǒu) kāi; **take off** *v*
   (*clothes, etc.*) 脱去 tuō qù; (*plane*) 起飞 qǐfēi
offend *v* 冒犯 màofàn; **offence** *n* 冒犯 màofàn, 进攻
   jìngōng; **take offence** 生气 shēngqì, 见怪 jiànguài;
   offensive *n* 进攻 jìngōng; *adj* 无礼的 wúlǐ de
offer *v* 提供 tígòng, 提出 tíchū
offhand *adj* 草率的 cǎoshuài de; *adv* 草率地 cǎoshuài de
office *n* 办公室 bàngōngshì; **take office** 就职 jiùzhí; **officer**
   n 官员 guānyuán; (*mil*) 军官 jūnguān
official *adj* 官方的 guānfāng de, 正式的 zhèngshì de; *n* 官员
   guānyuán
off-peak *adj* 非高峰的 fēigāofēng de
off-season *n* 淡季 dànjì
offshore *adj* 近海的 jìnhǎi de
offspring *n* 子孙 zǐsūn, 后裔 hòuyì
often *adv* 常常 chángcháng; **as often as not** 时常 shícháng;
   every so often 时常 shícháng
oil *n* 油 yóu; **oil painting** 油画 yóuhuà; **oil well** 油井 yóujǐng;
   oily *adj* 油滑的 yóuhuá de
oilfield *n* 油田 yóutián
old *adj* 老的 lǎo de; **old age** 晚年 wǎnnián; **old-fashioned**
   adj 传统的 chuántǒng de
olive *n* 橄榄 gǎnlǎn; **olive oil** 橄榄油 gǎnlǎnyóu

Olympic *adj* 奥林匹克的 àolínpǐkè de; **Olympic Games** 奥林匹克运动会 àolínpǐkè yùndònghuì

omelet *n* 煎蛋饼 jiāndànbǐng

omen *n* 征兆 zhēngzhào, 预兆 yùzhào

ominous *adj* 预示的 yùshì de, 不祥的 bùxiáng de

omit *v* 遗漏 yílòu, 省略 shěnglüè; **omission** *n* 遗漏 yílòu, 省略 shěnglüè

on *prep* 在 ... 上 zài ... shang; **on time** 准时 zhǔnshí; **on top of** 在 ... 之上 zài ... zhīshàng, 除 ... 之外 chú zhīwài; **oncoming** *adj* 即将来临的 jíjiāng láilín de

once *adv* 一次 yī cì; *conj* 一旦 yīdàn; **once again** 再一次 zài yī cì; **once and for all** 一劳永逸的 yīláo yǒngyì de

one *num* 一 yī; **one by one** 一个接一个地 yī gè jiē yī gè de; **one-sided** *adj* 单方面的 dānfāngmiàn de; **one-way** *adj* 单程的 dānchéng de; 单向道的 dānxiàngdào de; **oneself** *pron* 自己 zìjǐ

onion *n* 洋葱 yángcōng

online *adj* 在线的 zàixiàn de, 在网上的 zài wǎngshang de

onlooker *n* 旁观者 pángguānzhě

only *adj* 唯一的 wéiyī de; *adv* 只 zhǐ, 仅仅 jǐnjǐn

onto *prep* 到 ... 上 dào ... shang

open *v* 开 kāi, 打开 dǎkāi; *adj* 开着的 kāi zhe de, 开放的 kāifàng de; **open-air** *adj* 户外的 hùwài de, 露天的 lùtiān de

opening *n* (*aperture*) 开口 kāikǒu; (*ceremony*) 开幕式 kāimùshì; (*job*) 空缺 kòngquē; *adj* 开头的 kāitóu de

opera *n* 歌剧 gējù; **opera house** 歌剧院 gējùyuàn

operate *v* (*perform*) 操作 cāozuò; (*surgical*) 动手术 dòng shǒushù; **operation** *n* (*surgical*) 手术 shǒushù; (*process*) 操作 cāozuò, 运作 yùnzuò; (*mil*) 军事行动 jūnshì xíngdòng; **operator** *n* (*worker*) 操作者 cāozuòzhě; (*telephone*) 电话接线员 diànhuà jiēxiànyuán

opinion *n* 意见 yìjian; **public opinion** 公众舆论 gōngzhòng yúlùn

opium *n* 鸦片 yāpiàn

opponent *n* 对手 duìshǒu

opportunity *n* 机会 jīhuì

oppose *v* 反对 fǎnduì

opposite *prep* 在 ... 对面 zài ... duìmiàn

opposition *n* 相反 xiāngfǎn, 对立面 duìlìmiàn; **opposition party** 反对党 fǎnduìdǎng

oppress *v* 压迫 yāpò; **oppressive** *adj* 压迫的 yāpò de; **oppression** *n* 压迫 yāpò

opt *v* 选择 xuǎnzé; **opt for** 选择 xuǎnzé; **opt out** 选择不参加 xuǎnzé bù cānjiā

optical *adj* 视觉的 shìjué de, 光学的 guāngxué de; **optician** *n* 眼镜商 yǎnjìng shāng, 眼睛配制师 yǎnjing pèizhì shī

optimism *n* 乐观 lèguān; **optimist** *n* 乐观的人 lèguān de rén; **optimistic** *adj* 乐观的 lèguān de

optimum *adj* 最适宜的 zuì shìyí de, 最理想的 zuì lǐxiǎng de

option *n* 选择 xuǎnzé; **optional** *adj* 可选择的 kě xuǎnzé de, 任选的 rènxuǎn de

or *conj* 或者 huòzhě; **or else** 否则 fǒuzé

oral *adj* 口头的 kǒutóu de, 口用的 kǒuyòng de

orator *n* 演说家 yǎnshuōjiā; **oration** *n* 演说 yǎnshuō; **oratory** *n* 演说术 yǎnshuōshù

orange *n* (*color*) 橙色 chéngsè; (*fruit*) 橙子 chéngzi; **orange juice** 橙汁 chéngzhī

orbit *v* 绕轨道运行 rào guǐdào yùnxíng; *n* 轨道 guǐdào

orchard *n* 果园 guǒyuán

orchestra *n* 管弦乐队 guǎnxián yuèduì

orchid *n* 兰花 lánhuā

ordeal *n* 折磨 zhémó, 严峻的考验 yánjùn de kǎoyàn

order *v* (*purchase*) 定购 dìnggòu; (*subscribe, reserve*) 预定 yùdìng; (*command*) 命令 mìnglìng; *n* (*sequence*) 次序 cìxù; 顺序 shùnxù; (*condition*) 秩序 zhìxù; (*purchase form*) 定单 dìngdān; **in order** 整齐的 zhěngqí de; **in order to** 为了 wèile; **out of order** 混乱的 hùnluàn de; (*malfunctioning*) 坏了的 huài le de; **orderly** *adj* 有秩序的 yǒu zhìxù de, 有条理的 yǒu tiáolǐ de

ordinal *adj* 顺序的 shùnxù de; **ordinal number** 序数词 xùshùcí

ordinary *adj* 平常的 píngcháng de, 普通的 pǔtōng de

ore *n* 矿石 kuàngshí

organ *n* (*anat*) 器官 qìguān; (*organization*) 机关 jīguān; (*musical instrument*) 风琴 fēngqín; **organist** *n* 风琴师 fēngqínshī

organic *adj* 有机的 yǒujī de

organism *n* 有机体 yǒujītǐ

organize *v* 组织 zǔzhī; **organizer** *n* 组织者 zǔzhīzhě; **organization** *n* 组织 zǔzhī

orient *v* (使) 熟悉情况 (shǐ) shúxī qíngkuàng; **orientation** *n* (*position*) 方位 fāngwèi; (*introduction*) 迎新情况介绍 yíngxīn qíngkuàng jièshào

origin *n* 起源 qǐyuán, 发端 fāduān, 起因 qǐyīn; **originate**

from 起源于 qǐyuán yú; **original** n 原作 yuánzuò, 原文 yuánwén; adj 原始的 yuánshǐ de, 独创的 dúchuàng de; **originally** adv 最初 zuìchū, 原先 yuánxiān

ornament n 装饰 zhuāngshì, 装饰物 zhuāngshìwù; **ornamental** adj 装饰的 zhuāngshì de

orphan n 孤儿 gū'ér; **orphanage** n 孤儿院 gū'éryuàn

orthodox adj 正统的 zhèngtǒng de; **orthodoxy** n 正统 zhèngtǒng

oscillation n 摇摆 yáobǎi

ostrich n 鸵鸟 tuóniǎo

other adj 别的 biéde; **the other** 另一 lìng yī; **other than** 除了 chúle; **otherwise** adv 否则 fǒuzé, 不然 bùrán

ought aux (ought to) 应该 yīnggāi

our pron 我们的 wǒmende

ours pron 我们的 wǒmende

ourselves pron 我们自己 wǒmen zìjǐ

out adv 向外 xiàngwài, 出 chū, 在外 zàiwài, 出外 chūwài; **out of date** 过时的 guòshí de; **out of work** 失业的 shīyè de

outbreak n 爆发 bàofā

outcome n 结果 jiéguǒ, 后果 hòuguǒ

outcry n 喊叫 hǎnjiào, 强烈抗议 qiángliè kàngyì

outdoor adj 户外的 hùwài de; **outdoors** adv 户外 hùwài

outer adj 外部的 wàibù de, 远离中心的 yuǎnlí zhōngxīn de; **outer space** 太空 tàikōng

outfit n 全套服装 quántào fúzhuāng

outgoing adj (departing) 外出的 wàichū de; (sociable) 开朗的 kāilǎng de

outing n 远足 yuǎnzú

outlet n (elec) 电源插座 diànyuán chāzuò; (exit) 出口 chūkǒu; (store) 直销店 zhíxiāodiàn

outline v 画轮廓 huà lúnkuò; 概述 gàishù; n 轮廓 lúnkuò, 大纲 dàgāng

outlook n 景色 jǐngsè, 前景 qiánjǐng

outnumber v 数量超过 shùliàng chāoguò

output n 产量 chǎnliàng, 输出 shūchū

outrage n 暴行 bàoxíng; **outrageous** adj 残暴的 cánbào de, 不可容忍的 bùkě róngrěn de

outright adj 直率的 zhíshuài de; adv 直率地 zhíshuài de

outset n 开端 kāiduān; **at the outset** 起初 qǐchū

outside adv 外面 wàimian; prep 在 ... 外面 zài ... wàimian; **outsider** n 外人 wàirén

outsize n 特大号 tèdàhào; adj 特大的 tèdà de

outskirts *n* 郊区 jiāoqū

outspoken *adj* 坦率直言的 tǎnshuài zhíyán de

outstanding *adj* 杰出的 jiéchū de, 显著的 xiǎnzhù de

outward *adj* 向外的 xiàngwài de, 外面的 wàimian de; **outwards** *adv* 向外 xiàngwài

oval *adj* 椭圆的 tuǒyuán de

oven *n* 烤箱 kǎoxiāng

over *prep* 在 ... 上 zài ... shang; **over there** 在那边 zài nàbiān

overall *adj* (*whole*) 全部的 quánbù de; (*all-around*) 全面的 quánmiàn de

overboard *adv* 向船外 xiàng chuánwài; **go overboard** 走极端 zǒu jíduān

overcast *adj* 阴沉的 yīnchén de, 多云的 duōyún de

overcharge *v* 收费过高 shōufèi guògāo, 乱讨价 luàn tǎojià

overcoat *n* 大衣 dàyī

overcome *v* (**overcame, overcome**) 克服 kèfú

overcrowded *adj* 过度拥挤的 guòdù yōngjǐ de; **overcrowding** *n* 过度拥挤 guòdù yōngjǐ

overdo *v* (**overdid, overdone**) 做得过火 zuò de guòhuǒ

overdose *n* 服药过量 fúyào guòliàng

overdue *adj* (*to be paid*) 过期未付的 guòqī wèi fù de; (*to be returned*) 过期未还的 guòqī wèi huán de

overestimate *v* 过高估计 guògāo gūjì

overflow *v* 溢出 yìchū

overhang *v* 悬于 ... 之上 xuán yú ... zhīshàng; **overhanging** *adj* 悬垂的 xuánchuí de

overhaul *v* 彻底检修 chèdǐ jiǎnxiū, 大修 dàxiū

overhead *n* 经营费用 jīngyíng fèiyòng; *adj* 在头顶上的 zài tóudǐng shang de

overhear *v* (**overheard, overheard**) 无意中听到 wúyìzhōng tīngdào, 偷听 tōutīng

overjoyed *adj* 狂喜的 kuángxǐ de

overland *adj* 陆路的 lùlù de; *adv* 通过陆路 tōngguò lùlù

overlap *v* 部分重叠 bùfen chóngdié

overload *v* 超载 chāozài

overlook *v* (*look down*) 俯瞰 fǔkàn; (*neglect*) 忽视 hūshì

overnight *adv* 一夜之间 yīyè zhījiān

overpower *v* 压倒 yādǎo, 制服 zhìfú

overrule *v* 批驳 pībó, 驳回 bóhuí

overseas *adj* 海外的 hǎiwài de; *adv* 在海外 zài hǎiwài

oversight *n* 失察 shīchá, 疏忽 shūhū

overt *adj* 明显的 míngxiǎn de, 公开的 gōngkāi de

overtake *v* (**overtook, overtaken**) 追上 zhuī shàng

overthrow *v* (**overthrew, overthrown**) 推翻 tuīfān

overtime *n* 加班 jiābān

overturn *v* 推翻 tuīfān, 颠倒 diāndǎo

overwhelm *v* (*of floodwater*) 淹没 yānmò; (*overpower*) 压倒 yādǎo, 制伏 zhìfú

overwork *v* 工作过劳 gōngzuò guòláo

owe *v* 欠 qiàn; **owing to** *prep* 由于 yóuyú

owl *n* 猫头鹰 māotóuyīng

own *v* 拥有 yōngyǒu; *adj* 自己的 zìjǐ de; **own up** 承认 chéngrèn; **on one's own** 自己做 zìjǐ zuò; **owner** *n* 所有者 suǒyǒuzhě, 业主 yèzhǔ; **ownership** *n* 所有权 suǒyǒuquán

ox *n* (*pl* **oxen**) 公牛 gōngniú

oxygen *n* 氧气 yǎngqì

oyster *n* 牡蛎 mǔlì

P

pace *v* 踱步 duóbù; *n* (*steps*) 步 bù; (*speed*) 速度 sùdù; **keep pace with** 跟上 gēn shàng

Pacific Ocean *n* 太平洋 tàipíngyáng

pacify *v* (使) 平静 (shǐ) píngjìng, 平定 píngdìng, 安抚 ānfǔ

pack *v* 打包 dǎbāo; *n* 一包 yībāo

package *n* 包裹 bāoguǒ; **package tour** 包办旅行 bāobàn lǚxíng

packet *n* 小包 xiǎobāo

pact *n* 契约 qìyuē, 公约 gōngyuē

pad *n* 衬垫 chèndiàn

padlock *n* 挂锁 guàsuǒ

page *n* 页 yè

paid. *See* **pay**

pain *v* (使) 痛苦 (shǐ) tòngkǔ; *n* 痛苦 tòngkǔ; **painful** *adj* 疼痛的 téngtòng de, 痛苦的 tòngkǔ de; **painkiller** *n* 止痛药 zhǐtòngyào; **painless** *adj* 无痛的 wútòng de; 不痛的 bù tòng de

paint *v* (*cover with paint*) 涂油漆 tú yóuqī; (*draw*) 画 huà; *n* 油漆 yóuqī; **paintbrush** *n* (*for drawing as art*) 画笔 huàbǐ; (*for applying paint*) 漆刷 qīshuā; **painter** *n* 画家 huàjiā; **painting** *n* 画 huà

pair *v* 配对 pèiduì; **pair off** 配成对 pèi chéng duì; *n* 一对 yīduì, 一双 yīshuāng, 一副 yīfù

pajamas *n* 睡衣 shuìyī

palace *n* 宫殿 gōngdiàn

pale *adj* 苍白的 cāngbái de

palm *n* (*hand*) 手掌 shǒuzhǎng; (*tree*) 棕榈 zōnglú

pamphlet *n* 小册子 xiǎocèzi

pan *n* 平底锅 píngdǐguō

Panama *n* 巴拿马 bānámǎ

pancake *n* 薄煎饼 báojiānbǐng

panel *n* (*board*) 面板 miànbǎn; (*conference*) 讨论组 tǎolùnzǔ

panic *v/n* 恐慌 kǒnghuāng

panorama *n* 全景 quánjǐng; **panoramic** *adj* 全景的 quánjǐng de

pant *v* 喘息 chuǎnxī

pantry *n* 食品室 shípǐnshì

pants *n* 裤子 kùzi

papal *adj* 罗马教皇的 luōmǎ jiàohuáng de

paper *n* 纸 zhǐ; (*newspaper*) 报纸 bàozhǐ; **paperback** *n* 平装书 píngzhuāngshū; **paperwork** *n* 文件 wénjiàn

par *n* 同等 tóngděng; **on a par with** 与 ... 同等重要 yǔ ... tóngděng zhòngyào

parachute *v* 跳伞 tiàosǎn; *n* 降落伞 jiàngluòsǎn

parade *n* 游行 yóuxíng

paradise *n* 天堂 tiāntáng

paragraph *n* 段落 duànluò

parallel *adj* 平行的 píngxíng de

paralyze *v* (使) 麻痹 (shǐ) mábì; **paralysis** *n* 麻痹 mábì

paranoia *n* 偏执狂 piānzhíkuáng, 妄想狂 wàngxiǎngkuáng

paranoid *adj* 多疑的 duōyí de

paraphrase *v/n* 解释 jiěshì

parasite *n* 寄生虫 jìshēngchóng; **parasitic** *adj* 寄生的 jìshēng de

paratrooper *n* 伞兵 sǎnbīng

parcel *v* 分割 fēngē; *n* 包裹 bāoguǒ

pardon *v/n* 原谅 yuánliàng, 赦免 shèmiǎn; **pardon?** 你说什么? nǐ shuō shénme; **I beg your pardon?** 对不起,你说什么? duìbùqǐ nǐ shuō shénme

parenthesis *n* 圆括号 yuánkuòhào; **in parentheses** 在括号里 zài kuòhào li

parents *n* 父母 fùmǔ; **parental** *adj* 父母的 fùmǔ de

parish *n* 教区 jiàoqū; **parishioner** *n* 教区居民 jiàoqū jūmín

park *v* 停车 tíngchē; *n* 公园 gōngyuán; **parking** *n* 停车 tíngchē; **parking lot** 停车场 tíngchēchǎng

parliament *n* 议会 yìhuì; **parliamentary** *adj* 议会的 yìhuì de

parody *n* 拙劣的模仿 zhuōliè de mófǎng

parrot *n* 鹦鹉 yīngwǔ

part *n* 部分 bùfen, 零件 língjiàn; **part-time** *adj* 半职的 bànzhí de, 兼职的 jiānzhí de; **partly** *adv* 部分地 bùfen de

partake *v* 分担 fēndān; **partake of** 参与 cānyù

partial *adj* 部分的 bùfen de; **be partial to** 对 ... 偏爱 duì ... piān'ài

participate *v* 参加 cānjiā; **participant** *n* 参加者 cānjiāzhě, 与会者 yùhuìzhě; **participation** *n* 参与 cānyù

particle *n* 粒子 lìzǐ

particular *adj* 特别的 tèbié de, 具体的 jùtǐ de; **in particular** 特别地 tèbié de

partner *n* 合伙人 héhuǒrén, 合作伙伴 hézuò huǒbàn; **partnership** *n* 合伙 héhuǒ

party *n* (*social*) 社交聚会 shèjiāo jùhuì; (*political*) 党派 dǎngpài; **partisan** *n* 党徒 dǎngtú

pass *v* 通过 tōngguò, 经过 jīngguò, 过去 guòqù; *n* 通行证 tōngxíngzhèng; **pass away** 去世 qùshì; **pass out** 晕厥 yūnjué; **pass round** 传发 chuánfā; **pass up** 放弃 fàngqì

passage *n* (*way*) 通道 tōngdào; (*text*) 一段文章 yī duàn wénzhāng

passenger *n* 乘客 chéngkè

passer-by *n* 过路人 guòlùrén, 行人 xíngrén

passion *n* 激情 jīqíng; **passionate** *adj* 充满激情的 chōngmǎn jīqíng de

passive *adj* 被动的 bèidòng de; 消极的 xiāojí de

passport *n* 护照 hùzhào

password *n* 口令 kǒulìng, 暗号 ànhào

past *n* 过去 guòqù

pasta *n* 意大利面食 yìdàlì miànshí

paste *n* 面团 miàntuán, 糨糊 jiànghu

pastime *n* 消遣 xiāoqiǎn

pasture *n* 牧场 mùchǎng, 草地 cǎodì

pat *v* 轻拍 qīngpāi

patch *v* 修补 xiūbǔ; *n* 补丁 bǔdīng; **patchwork** *n* 拼凑物 pīncòuwù

path *n* 小路 xiǎolù, 路径 lùjìng

pathetic *adj* 可怜的 kělián de, 可悲的 kěbēi de

pathology *n* 病理学 bìnglǐxué; **pathological** *adj* 病理的 bìnglǐ de

patient *n* 病人 bìngrén; *adj* 耐心的 nàixīn de; **patience** *n* 耐心 nàixīn

patriot *n* 爱国者 àiguózhě; **patriotic** *adj* 爱国的 àiguó de;
    patriotism *n* 爱国主义 àiguózhǔyì

patrol *v/n* 巡逻 xúnluó

patron *n* 赞助人 zànzhùrén, 主顾 zhǔgù; **patronize** *v* 光顾
    guānggù

pattern *n* 式样 shìyàng, 模式 móshì

pause *v/n* 暂停 zàntíng

pave *v* 铺 pū; **pave the way for** 为 ... 铺平道路 wèi ...
    pūpíng dàolù; **pavement** *n* 人行道 rénxíngdào

pavilion *n* 亭子 tíngzi

paw *n* 爪子 zhuǎzi

pawn *n* 当 dàng; **pawnshop** *n* 当铺 dàngpu

pay *v* (**paid, paid**) 付钱 fùqián; *n* 工资 gōngzī; **pay back**
    偿付 chángfù; 报复 bàofù; **payment** *n* 付款 fùkuǎn; **pay
    off** 付清 fùqīng; **payday** *n* 发工资日 fā gōngzī rì; **pay-
    roll** *n* 薪金名册 xīnjīn míngcè

pea *n* 豌豆 wāndòu

peace *n* 和平 hépíng, 平静 píngjìng; **peaceful** *adj* 和平的
    hépíng de, 宁静的 níngjìng de

peach *n* 桃子 táozi

peacock *n* 孔雀 kǒngquè

peak *v* 达到顶点 dádào dǐngdiǎn; *n* 山顶 shāndǐng; **peak
    hours** 高峰时间 gāofēng shíjiān

peanut *n* 花生 huāshēng

pear *n* 梨子 lízi

pearl *n* 珍珠 zhēnzhū

peasant *n* 农民 nóngmín

peck *v* 啄 zhuó

peculiar *adj* 奇怪的 qíguài de, 特有的 tèyǒu de; **peculiarity**
    n 特性 tèxìng

pedal *v* 踩踏板 cǎi tàbǎn; *n* 踏板 tàbǎn

peddle *v* 兜售 dōushòu, 叫卖 jiàomài

pedestrian *n* 行人 xíngrén; *adj* 步行 bùxíng; **pedestrian
    crossing** 人行横道 rénxíng héngdào

pediatric *adj* 儿科的 érkē de; **pediatrics** *n* 儿科学 érkēxué;
    pediatrician *n* 儿科医师 érkē yīshī

peel *v* 剥 bāo, 削 xiāo; **peel off** 剥落 bōluò

peep *v* 偷看 tōukàn; **peeping Tom** 偷看者 tōukànzhě

peer *n* 同辈 tóngbèi

peg *n* 拴 shuān, 钉子 dīngzi, 销 xiāo

pen *n* 钢笔 gāngbǐ; **pen-name** *n* 笔名 bǐmíng

penal *adj* 刑罚的 xíngfá de; **penalize** *v* 惩罚 chéngfá;
　penalty *n* 惩罚 chéngfá; (*in a game*) 罚球 fáqiú

pencil *n* 铅笔 qiānbǐ

penetrate *v* 穿透 chuāntòu, 渗透 shèntòu, 打入 dǎrù;
　penetration *n* 渗透 shèntòu, 打入 dǎrù

penguin *n* 企鹅 qǐ'é

penicillin *n* 青霉素 qīngméisù, 盘尼西林 pánníxīlín

peninsula *n* 半岛 bàndǎo

penis *n* 阴茎 yīnjīng

penitence *n* 悔罪 huǐzuì; **penitent** *adj* 悔过的 huǐguò de

penknife *n* 小折刀 xiǎozhédāo

penny *n* 一分钱 yī fēn qián

pension *n* 退休金 tuìxiūjīn

people *n* 人 rén; (*of a nation*) 民族 mínzú

pepper *n* 辣椒 làjiāo

per *prep* 每一 měiyī

percent *n* 百分之 bǎifēnzhī

perceive *v* 察觉 chájué, 看出 kànchū, 领悟 lǐngwù

perception *n* 感知 gǎnzhī, 感觉 gǎnjué

perfect *v* (使) 完美 (shǐ) wánměi; *adj* 完美的 wánměi de;
　perfection *n* 完美 wánměi

perform *v* (*execute*) 执行 zhíxíng; (*act*) 表演 biǎoyǎn; (*of investments*) 表现 biǎoxiàn; **performance** *n* 表演 biǎoyǎn;
　表现 biǎoxiàn

perfume *n* 香水 xiāngshuǐ

perhaps *adv* 也许 yěxǔ

peril *n* 危险 wēixiǎn; **perilous** *adj* 危险的 wēixiǎn de

period *n* 时期 shíqī, 周期 zhōuqī; (*women's*) 月经 yuèjīng;
　periodic *adj* 周期的 zhōuqī de; **periodical** *adj* 定期的
　dìngqī de

perish *v* 死亡 sǐwáng; **perishable** *adj* 容易腐烂的 róngyì
　fǔlàn de

perjure *v* 作伪证 zuò wěizhèng; **perjury** *n* 伪证 wěizhèng

permanent *adj* 永久的 yǒngjiǔ de; **permanently** *adv*
　永久地 yǒngjiǔ de; **permanence** *n* 永久 yǒngjiǔ

permit *v* 允许 yǔnxǔ; *n* 许可证 xǔkězhèng; **permission** *n*
　许可 xǔkě, 允许 yǔnxǔ; **permissive** *adj* 放任的 fàngrèn
　de, 放纵的 fàngzòng de

perpetrate *v* 犯罪 fànzuì

perpetual *adj* 永久的 yǒngjiǔ de

perpetuate *v* (使) 永存 (shǐ) yǒngcún, (使) 永恒 shǐ
　yǒnghéng, (使) 不朽 (shǐ) bùxiǔ

persecute *v* 迫害 pòhài; **persecution** *n* 迫害 pòhài

persevere *v* 坚持 jiānchí; **perseverance** *n* 不屈不挠 bùqū bùnáo, 坚持不懈 jiānchí bùxiè

persist *v* 坚持 jiānchí, 持续 chíxù; **persistence** *n* 持续 chíxù; **persistent** *adj* 坚持的 jiānchí de, 持续的 chíxù de, 顽固的 wángù de

person *n* 人 rén; **personal** *adj* 个人的 gèrén de; 私人的 sīrén de; **personality** *n* 个性 gèxìng, 性格 xìnggé; **personally** *adv* 亲自地 qīnzì de

personify *v* 拟人 nǐrén; **personification** *n* 拟人 nǐrén

personnel *n* 人员 rényuán; (*admin division*) 人事 rénshì

perspective *n* (*angle*) 角度 jiǎodù; (*prospect*) 远景 yuǎnjǐng

perspire *v* 出汗 chūhàn; **perspiration** *n* 汗 hàn

persuade *v* 说服 shuōfú; **persuasion** *n* 说服 shuōfú; **persuasive** *adj* 有说服力的 yǒu shuōfúlì de

pertain *v* 属于 shǔyú

pertinent *adj* 相关的 xiāngguān de

Peru *n* 秘鲁 bìlǔ; **Peruvian** *n* 秘鲁人 bìlǔrén; *adj* 秘鲁的 bìlǔ de

pervade *v* 弥漫 mímàn, 遍及 biànjí

pervert *n* 行为反常者 xíngwéi fǎncháng zhě, 性变态者 xìngbiàntàizhě

pessimism *n* 悲观 bēiguān; **pessimist** *n* 悲观主义者 bēiguānzhǔyìzhě; **pessimistic** *adj* 悲观的 bēiguān de

pest *n* 害虫 hàichóng; **pesticide** *n* 杀虫剂 shāchóngjì

pester *v* 纠缠 jiūchán

pet *n* 宠物 chǒngwù

petal *n* 花瓣 huābàn

petition *v* 请求 qǐngqiú; *n* 请愿 qǐngyuàn

petrol *n* 汽油 qìyóu; **petrol station** 汽车加油站 qìchē jiāyóuzhàn

petroleum *n* 石油 shíyóu

petty *adj* 次要的 cìyào de, 渺小的 miǎoxiǎo de; **petty cash** 零用钱 língyòngqián; **petty officer** (*military*) 士官 shìguān; (*civil*) 公务员 gōngwùyuán

phantom *n* 幽灵 yōulíng, 幻影 huànyǐng

pharmacy *n* 药房 yàofáng; **pharmaceutical** *adj* 制药的 zhìyào de; **pharmacist** *n* 药剂师 yàojìshī

phase *n* 阶段 jiēduàn; **phase in** 逐步采用 zhúbù cǎiyòng; **phase out** 逐步停止 zhúbù tíngzhǐ; 逐步淘汰 zhúbù táotài

phenomenon *n* (*pl* **phenomena**) 现象 xiànxiàng;
  phenomenal *adj* 显著的 xiǎnzhù de
philanthropy *n* 慈善 císhàn; **philanthropic** *adj* 慈善的
  císhàn de; **philanthropist** *n* 慈善家 císhànjiā
philosophy *n* 哲学 zhéxué; **philosopher** *n* 哲学家 zhéxuéjiā
phone *v* 打电话 dǎ diànhuà; *n* 电话 diànhuà
phonetic *adj* 语音的 yǔyīn de; **phonetics** *n* 语音学
  yǔyīnxué
phony *n* (*person*) 骗子 piànzi; (*object*) 假货 jiǎhuò; *adj* 假的
  jiǎ de, 伪造的 wěizào de
photo *n* 照片 zhàopiàn
photocopy *v* 影印 yǐngyìn; *n* 影印件 yǐngyìnjiàn; **photocopier** *n* 影印机 yǐngyìnjī
photograph *n* 照片 zhàopiàn; **photograph album** 影集
  yǐngjí; **photographer** *n* 摄影师 shèyǐngshī; **photography**
  n 摄影 shèyǐng
phrase *n* 短语 duǎnyǔ
physical *n* 体格检查 tǐgé jiǎnchá; *adj* (*of the body*) 身体的
  shēntǐ de; (*of matter*) 物理的 wùlǐ de
physician *n* 内科医师 nèikē yīshī
physics *n* 物理学 wùlǐxué; **physicist** *n* 物理学家 wùlǐxuéjiā
physiotherapy *n* 物理疗法 wùlǐ liáofǎ; **physiotherapist** *n*
  理疗师 lǐliáoshī
piano *n* 钢琴 gāngqín; **pianist** *n* 钢琴家 gāngqínjiā
pick *v* 采摘 cǎizhāi, 挑选 tiāoxuǎn; **pick up** 捡起 jiǎn qǐ;
  (*meet*) 接 jiē; **pickpocket** *n* 扒手 páshǒu
picnic *n* 野餐 yěcān
picture *n* 图画 túhuà, 照片 zhàopiàn
picturesque *adj* 如画的 rúhuà de
pie *n* 馅饼 xiànbǐng
piece *n* 片 piàn, 块 kuài, 张 zhāng, 个 gè; **piecemeal** *adv*
  零碎地 língsuì de; **piece together** 拼凑起来 pīncòu qǐlái
pier *n* (*bridge*) 桥墩 qiáodūn; (*wharf*) 码头 mǎtou
pierce *v* 刺穿 cìchuān
pig *n* 猪 zhū; **pigsty** *n* 猪圈 zhūjuàn
pigeon *n* 鸽子 gēzi
pile *n* 堆 duī; **pile up** 堆积 duījī
pilgrimage *v/n* 朝圣 cháoshèng
pill *n* 药丸 yàowán
pillar *n* 柱子 zhùzi
pillow *n* 枕头 zhěntou; **pillowcase** *n* 枕头套 zhěntóutào
pilot *n* 飞行员 fēixíngyuán

pin *n* 大头针 dàtóuzhēn, 别针 biézhēn; **pinpoint** *v* 精确地确定 ... 的位置 jīngquè de quèdìng ... de wèizhi; **on pins and needles** 如坐针毡般的 rú zuò zhēnzhānbān de

pinch *v* 捏 niē, 掐 qiā

pineapple *n* 菠萝 bōluó

ping-pong *n* 乒乓球 pīngpāngqiú

pink *adj* 粉红色的 fěnhóngsè de

pioneer *n* 先锋 xiānfēng, 开辟者 kāipìzhě

pious *adj* 虔诚的 qiánchéng de

pip *n* 果仁 guǒrén, 种子 zhǒngzi

pipe *n* (*tube*) 管子 guǎnzi; (*tobacco*) 烟斗 yāndǒu; **pipeline** *n* 管道 guǎndào

piss *v* 小便 xiǎobiàn; **pissed** *adj* 愤怒的 fènnù de; **be pissed off** 被惹怒 bèi rěnù

pistachio *n* 开心果 kāixīnguǒ

pistol *n* 手枪 shǒuqiāng

pit *n* 坑 kēng; **pit oneself against** 与 ... 争斗 yǔ ... zhēngdòu

pitch *v* 投掷 tóuzhì; **pitch in** 协力 xiélì; *n* (*toss*) 投掷 tóuzhì; (*voice*) 音高 yīngāo; **pitch-black** *adj* 漆黑的 qīhēi de

pitfall *n* 陷阱 xiànjǐng, 缺陷 quēxiàn

pity *v/n* 同情 tóngqíng; **take pity on** 怜悯 liánmǐn; **what a pity!** 真可惜! zhēn kěxī; **pitiful** *adj* 可怜的 kělián de

place *v* 置 zhì, 放 fàng; *n* 地方 dìfāng; **in place** 就位 jiùwèi; **in place of** 代替 dàitì; **out of place** 不适合 bù shìhé; 不相称 bù xiāngchèn; **take place** 发生 fāshēng

plagiarize *v* 剽窃 piāoqiè, 抄袭 chāoxí; **plagiarism** *n* 剽窃 piāoqiè; **plagiarist** *n* 剽窃者 piāoqièzhě

plague *n* 瘟疫 wēnyì, 疫病 yìbìng

plain *adj* (*simple*) 简单的 jiǎndān de; (*clear*) 明白的 míngbai de; (*common*) 普通的 pǔtōng de; **plain-clothes** *n* 便服 biànfú

plan *v/n* 计划 jìhuà, 打算 dǎsuan

plane *n* 飞机 fēijī

planet *n* 行星 xíngxīng

plant *v* 种 zhòng; *n* (*zool*) 植物 zhíwù; (*factory*) 工厂 gōngchǎng; **plantation** *n* 种植园 zhòngzhíyuán

plaster *v* 涂灰泥 tú huīní; *n* 石膏 shígāo, 膏药 gāoyao

plastic *n* 塑料 sùliào; *adj* 塑料的 sùliào de; **plastic surgery** 整容手术 zhěngróng shǒushù

plate *n* 盘子 pánzi

platform *n* 月台 yuètái, 平台 píngtái

plausible *adj* 似是而非的 sìshì érfēi de

play *v* 玩 wán; (*records, etc.*) 放 fàng; (*sports*) 参加 cānjiā; (*ball*) 打 dǎ; (*an instrument*) 演奏 yǎnzòu; *n* 话剧 huàjù, 戏剧 xìjù; **player** *n* (*theater*) 表演者 biǎoyǎnzhě; (*sports*) 选手 xuǎnshǒu

playback *v* 重播 chóngbō

playground *n* 操场 cāochǎng, 运动场 yùndòngchǎng

playing card *n* 扑克牌 pūkèpái

playwright *n* 剧作家 jùzuòjiā

plea *n* (*appeal*) 恳求 kěnqiú, 请求 qǐngqiú; (*law*) 辩解 biànjiě

plead *v* (**pleaded/pled, pleaded/pled**) (*law*) 辩护 biànhù; (*appeal*) 恳求 kěnqiú, 以 ... 为理由 yǐ ... wèi lǐyóu

pleasant *adj* 愉快的 yúkuài de

please *v* (使) 高兴 (shǐ) gāoxìng, (使) 满意 (shǐ) mǎnyì; *adv* 请 qǐng; **pleased** *adj* 高兴的 gāoxìng de, 愉快的 yúkuài de; **pleasing** *adj* 令人高兴的 lìng rén gāoxìng de

pleasure *n* 愉快 yúkuài, 乐趣 lèqù

pledge *n* 誓言 shìyán, 保证 bǎozhèng

plenty *n* 丰富 fēngfù, 充足 chōngzú; **plenty of** 大量的 dàliàng de, 丰富的 fēngfù de; **plentiful** *adj* 大量的 dàliàng de, 丰富的 fēngfù de

plot *v* 密谋 mìmóu; *n* (*storyline*) 情节 qíngjié; (*scheme*) 密谋 mìmóu

plough *v* 耕地 gēngdì; *n* 犁 lí

pluck *v* (*plants*) 采摘 cǎizhāi; (*feather, etc.*) 拔 bá; **pluck up courage** 鼓起勇气 gǔqǐ yǒngqì

plug *v* (*stop*) 堵 dǔ; (*insert*); 插上 chā shàng; **plug in** 插上电源 chā shàng diànyuán; *n* 塞子 sāizi; (*elec*) 插头 chātóu

plum *n* 李子 lǐzi

plumb *v* 探测 tàncè; *n* 铅锤 qiānchuí; *adj* 垂直的 chuízhí de; **plumbing** *n* 水暖设备 shuǐnuǎn shèbèi; **plumber** *n* 水管工 shuǐguǎngōng

plunder *v* 抢劫 qiǎngjié; **plundering** *n* 抢劫 qiǎngjié

plunge *v* 跳入 tiàorù, 陷入 xiànrù

plural *n* 复数 fùshù; *adj* 复数的 fùshù de

plus *prep* 加 jiā

pneumonia *n* 肺炎 fèiyán

pocket *v* 私吞 sītūn; *n* 口袋 kǒudài; **pocket-money** *n* 零花钱 línghuāqián

poem *n* 诗 shī

poet *n* 诗人 shīrén; **poetic** *adj* 有诗意的 yǒu shīyì de; **poetry** *n* 诗 shī

point *n* 尖 jiān, 点 diǎn; **beside the point** 离题 lítí, 不相关 bù xiāngguān; **point out** 指出 zhǐ chū; **make a point (of)** 打定主意做 dǎdìng zhǔyi zuò, 重视 zhòngshì; 表明自己的意图 biǎomíng zìjǐ de yìtú; **point-blank** *adv* (*directly*) 直截了当地 zhíjié liǎodàng de; (*at close range*) 近距离地 jìnjùlí de; **pointless** *adj* 无意义的 wúyìyì de

poison *v* 下毒 xiàdú; *n* 毒药 dúyào; **poisonous** *adj* 有毒的 yǒudú de; **poisoning** *n* 中毒 zhòngdú

poke *v* 戳 chuō, 捅 tǒng

poker *n* 扑克牌戏 pūkèpáixì

Poland *n* 波兰 bōlán; **Polish** *n* (*people*) 波兰人 bōlánrén; (*language*) 波兰语 bōlányǔ; *adj* 波兰的 bōlán de

polar *adj* 极地的 jídì de, 截然对立的 jiérán duìlì de; **polar bear** 北极熊 běijíxióng; **polarize** *v* (使)极化 (shǐ) jíhuà

pole *n* 杆 gǎn; **the North Pole** 北极 běijí; **the South Pole** 南极 nánjí

police *n* 警察 jǐngchá; **police officer** 警察 jǐngchá; **police station** 警察局 jǐngchájú; **policeman** *n* 警察 jǐngchá; **policewoman** *n* 女警察 nǚjǐngchá

policy *n* 政策 zhèngcè

polio *n* 小儿麻痹症 xiǎo'ér mábìzhèng

polish *v* 擦亮 cāliàng, 润色 rùnsè; *n* 上光 shàngguāng

polite *adj* 有礼貌的 yǒu lǐmào de; **politeness** *n* 礼貌 lǐmào

politics *n* 政治 zhèngzhì; **political** *adj* 政治的 zhèngzhì de; **politician** *n* 政治家 zhèngzhìjiā, 政客 zhèngkè

poll *n* 民意测验 mínyì cèyàn; **polling booth** 投票亭 tóupiàotíng; **polling station** 投票站 tóupiàosuǒ

pollen *n* 花粉 huāfěn; **pollen count** 空中散布的花粉量 kōngzhōng sànbù de huāfěn liàng

pollute *v* 污染 wūrǎn; **pollution** *n* 污染 wūrǎn

polygamy *n* 一夫多妻 yīfū duōqī

pomp *n* 盛况 shèngkuàng; **pompous** *adj* 华而不实的 huá ér bùshí de

pond *n* 池塘 chítáng

pony *n* 小马 xiǎomǎ; **ponytail** *n* 马尾辫 mǎwěibiàn

pool *v* (*money, etc.*) 集中 jízhōng, 汇集 huìjí; *n* (*for water*) 水池 shuǐchí; (*for swimming*) 游泳池 yóuyǒngchí

poor *adj* (*having little money*) 穷的 qióng de; (*inferior*) 差的 chà de; **poorly** *adv* 不足地 bùzú de, 拙劣地 zhuōliè de

pop *v* 突然出现 tūrán chūxiàn, 跳出 tiào chū; **pop in**

突然进来 tūrán jìnlái; *adj* 通俗的 tōngsú de, 流行的 liúxíng de; **pop quiz** 突袭测验 tūxí cèyàn; **pop music** 流行音乐 liúxíng yīnyuè

pope *n* 教皇 jiàohuáng

popular *adj* 流行的 liúxíng de, 受欢迎的 shòu huānyíng de; **popularity** *n* 流行 liúxíng, 普及 pǔjí, 大众化 dàzhònghuà

population *n* 人口 rénkǒu

porcelain *n* (*material*) 瓷 cí, (*product*) 瓷器 cíqì

porch *n* 门廊 ménláng

pork *n* 猪肉 zhūròu

pornography *n* 色情描写 sèqíng miáoxiě, 色情作品 sèqíng zuòpǐn; **pornographic** *adj* 色情的 sèqíng de

porridge *n* 粥 zhōu

port *n* 港口 gǎngkǒu

portable *adj* 便携式的 biànxiéshì de

porter *n* 行李搬运工 xíngli bānyùngōng

portion *n* 部分 bùfen, 一份 yī fèn

portrait *n* 肖像 xiāoxiàng

portray *v* 描绘 miáohuì

Portugal *n* 葡萄牙 pútáoyá; **Portuguese** *n* (*people*) 葡萄牙人 pútáoyárén; (*language*) 葡萄牙语 pútáoyáyǔ; *adj* 葡萄牙的 pútáoyá de

pose *v* (*assume stance*) 摆姿势 bǎi zīshì; (*present*) 造成 zàochéng; (*questions, etc.*) 提出 tíchū; *n* 样子 yàngzi, 姿势 zīshì

posh *adj* 豪华的 háohuá de

position *n* (*location*) 位置 wèizhi; (*stand*) 立场 lìchǎng; (*job*) 职位 zhíwèi

positive *adj* 肯定的 kěndìng de, 积极的 jījí de; (*med*) 阳性的 yángxìng de

possess *v* 拥有 yōngyǒu; **possession** *n* 拥有 yōngyǒu; 所有 suǒyǒu; 财产 cáichǎn; **possessive** *adj* 有占有欲的 yǒu zhānyǒuyù de

possible *adj* 可能的 kěnéng de; **possibility** *n* 可能性 kěnéngxìng; **possibly** *adv* 可能地 kěnéng de

post *v* (*put up*) 张贴 zhāngtiē; (*mail*) 邮递 yóudì; *n* (*job*) 岗位 gǎngwèi, (*position*) 职位 zhíwèi; (*mail*) 邮政 yóuzhèng; **post code** 邮政编码 yóuzhèng biānmǎ; **post office** 邮局 yóujú; **postage** *n* 邮资 yóuzī; **postcard** *n* 明信片 míngxìnpiàn

poster *n* 海报 hǎibào

postgraduate *n* 博士后 bóshìhòu

postman *n* 邮递员 yóudìyuán

postmark *n* 邮戳 yóuchuō

postmaster *n* 邮政局长 yóuzhèng júzhǎng

postpone *v* 推迟 tuīchí; **postponement** *n* 推迟 tuīchí

pot *n* 罐 guàn, 壶 hú, 锅 guō

potato *n* (*pl* **potatoes**) 马铃薯 mǎlíngshǔ, 土豆 tǔdòu

potent *adj* 有力的 yǒulì de, 有效的 yǒuxiào de

potential *n* 潜力 qiánlì; *adj* 潜在的 qiánzài de

potter *n* 陶工 táogōng

pottery *n* 陶器 táoqì

pouch *n* 小袋 xiǎodài

poultry *n* 家禽 jiāqín

pound *v* 捣烂 dǎolàn, 强烈打击 qiángliè dǎjī; *n* (*weight*) 磅 bàng; (*British currency*) 英镑 yīngbàng

pour *v* 倒 dào, 灌注 guànzhù

poverty *n* 贫困 pínkùn

powder *n* 粉 fěn

power *n* 力量 lìliàng; (*elec*) 电力 diànlì; **power plant** 发电厂 fādiànchǎng; **power station** 发电站 fādiànzhàn; **powerful** *adj* 强大的 qiángdà de; **powerless** *adj* 无力的 wúlì de

practical *adj* 实用的 shíyòng de, 实际的 shíjì de; **practical joke** 恶作剧 èzuòjù

practice *v/n* 实践 shíjiàn, 练习 liànxí

pragmatic *adj* 实用的 shíyòng de, 实际的 shíjì de

praise *v/n* 称赞 chēngzàn; **praiseworthy** *adj* 值得称赞的 zhíde chēngzàn de

prank *n* 恶作剧 èzuòjù, 玩笑 wánxiào

prawn *n* 对虾 duìxiā

pray *v* 祈求 qíqiú, 祷告 dǎogào; **prayer** *n* 祷告 dǎogào

preach *v* 布道 bùdào, 说教 shuōjiào; **preacher** *n* 传教士 chuánjiàoshì; **preaching** *n* 讲道 jiǎngdào

precaution *n* 防范 fángfàn, 预防措施 yùfáng cuòshī

precede *v* 先于 xiān yú; 处在 ... 之前 chǔ zài ... zhīqián

precinct *n* (*election*) 选区 xuǎnqū; (*police*) 警区 jǐngqū

precious *adj* 宝贵的 bǎoguì de

precision *n* 精确 jīngquè; **precise** *adj* 精确的 jīngquè de

predecessor *n* 前任 qiánrèn

predict *v* 预报 yùbào, 预言 yùyán; **prediction** *n* 预言 yùyán, 预见 yùjiàn; **predictable** *adj* 可预见的 kě yùjiàn de

predominate *v* 支配 zhīpèi, 占优势 zhàn yōushì; **predominance** *n* 优势 yōushì; **predominant** *adj* 卓越的 zhuōyuè de, 突出的 tūchū de

pre-eminence *n* 卓越 zhuōyuè; **pre-eminent** *adj* 卓越的 zhuōyuè de, 优秀的 yōuxiù de

preface *n* 序 xù, 前言 qiányán

prefer *v* 偏爱 piān'ài; **preference** *n* 偏爱 piān'ài, 优先选择 yōuxiān xuǎnzé; **preferable** *adj* 更可取的 gèng kěqǔ de, 最好的 zuìhǎo de

prefix *n* 前缀 qiánzhuì

pregnancy *n* 怀孕 huáiyùn; **pregnant** *adj* 怀孕的 huáiyùn de

prehistoric *adj* 史前的 shǐqián de

prejudice *n* 偏见 piānjiàn; **prejudiced** *adj* 怀偏见的 huái piānjiàn de

preliminary *adj* 初步的 chūbù de

premature *adj* 过早的 guòzǎo de, 未成熟的 wèi chéngshú de

premeditate *v* 预谋 yùmóu

premier *n* 总理 zǒnglǐ

premiere *n* 首演 shǒuyǎn

premises *n* 前提 qiántí

premium *n* (*insurance*) 保险费 bǎoxiǎnfèi; (*prize*) 奖金 jiǎngjīn; **at a premium** 以高价 yǐ gāojià

prepare *v* 准备 zhǔnbèi; **preparation** *n* 准备 zhǔnbèi; **preparatory** *adj* 预备的 yùbèi de

preposition *n* 介词 jiècí

prescribe *v* 指示 zhǐshì, 规定 guīdìng; (*med*) 开处方 kāi chǔfāng; **prescription** *n* 处方 chǔfāng

presence *n* 出席 chūxí, 到场 dàochǎng

present *v* (*give*) 赠送 zèngsòng; (*propose*) 提出 tíchū; (*submit*) 递交 dìjiāo; (*introduce*) 介绍 jièshào; *n* 礼物 lǐwù; *adj* 出席的 chūxí de, 在场的 zàichǎng de, 现在的 xiànzài de; **presently** *adv* 目前 mùqián, 不久 bùjiǔ; **at present** 现在 xiànzài, 目前 mùqián; **presentable** *adj* 像样的 xiàngyàng de, 拿得出手的 ná de chūshǒu de; **presentation** *n* (*introduction*) 介绍 jièshào; (*statement*) 陈述 chénshù; (*gifting*) 赠送 zèngsòng

preserve *v* 保存 bǎocún; **preservation** *n* 保存 bǎocún

preside *v* (*preside over*) 主持 zhǔchí

president *n* (*state*) 总统 zǒngtǒng; (*university*) 校长 xiàozhǎng; (*business*) 总裁 zǒngcái; **presidency** *n* 总统职位 zǒngtǒng zhíwèi; **presidential** *adj* 总统的 zǒngtǒng de

press *v* (*push, weigh on*) 压 yā, 按 àn; (*force*) 逼迫 bīpò; *n* 出版社 chūbǎnshè; **The Press** 新闻界 xīnwénjiè; **press**

agency 通讯社 tōngxùnshè; **press conference** 记者招待会 jìzhě zhāodàihuì

pressure n 压力 yālì; **pressure cooker** 高压锅 gāoyāguō; **pressure gauge** 压力计 yālìjì

prestige n 威望 wēiwàng, 美名 měimíng; **prestigious** adj 负有盛名的 fùyǒu shèngmíng

presume v 假定 jiǎdìng, 认定 rèndìng

presumptuous adj 放肆的 fàngsì de, 冒昧的 màomèi de

pretend v 假装 jiǎzhuāng; **pretence** n 借口 jièkǒu

pretty adj 漂亮的 piàoliang de; adv 非常 fēicháng

prevail v 流行 liúxíng; (defeat) 战胜 zhànshèng; **prevailing** adj 占优势的 zhàn yōushì de, 流行的 liúxíng de; **prevalent** adj 普遍的 pǔbiàn de, 流行的 liúxíng de

prevent v 防止 fángzhǐ, 预防 yùfáng; **prevention** n 防止 fángzhǐ, 预防 yùfáng; **preventive/preventative** adj 预防性的 yùfángxìng de

preview n (of a movie, play, etc.) 预演 yùyǎn; (of an exhibition) 预展 yùzhǎn

previous adj 先前的 xiānqián de, 以前的 yǐqián de; **previously** adv 以前 yǐqián, 先前 xiānqián

prey n 猎物 lièwù; **prey on** 捕食 bǔshí, 掠夺 lüèduó

price n 价格 jiàgé; **priceless** adj 无价的 wújià de

prick v 戳 chuō; **prick up one's ears** 竖起耳朵 shù qǐ ěrduo

pride n 自豪 zìháo, 自尊心 zìzūnxīn

priest n 牧师 mùshī

primary adj (main) 主要的 zhǔyào de; (original) 原始的 yuánshǐ de; **primary school** 小学 xiǎoxué

prime adj (main) 主要的 zhǔyào de; (best) 最好的 zuìhǎo de; **prime minister** 总理 zǒnglǐ; **primer** n 入门书 rùménshū

primitive adj 原始的 yuánshǐ de

prince n 王子 wángzǐ; **princess** n 公主 gōngzhǔ

principal n 校长 xiàozhǎng; adj 主要的 zhǔyào de

principle n 原理 yuánlǐ, 原则 yuánzé

print v 印刷 yìnshuā; n 印刷字体 yìnshuā zìtǐ; **out of print** 绝版 juébǎn; **printed matter** 印刷品 yìnshuāpǐn; **printer** n (person) 印刷工 yìnshuāgōng; (machine) 打印机 dǎyìnjī

priority n 优先 yōuxiān; **prior** adj 优先的 yōuxiān de, 在前的 zài qián de; **prior to** prep 在 ... 之前 zài ... zhīqián

prison n 监狱 jiānyù; **prisoner** n 囚犯 qiúfàn; **prisoner of war (POW)** 战俘 zhànfú

privacy n 隐私 yǐnsī; **private** adj 私人的 sīrén de, 秘密的

mìmì de; **private detective/investigator** 私人侦探 sīrén zhēntàn; **privately** *adv* 私下地 sīxià de; 秘密地 mìmì de

privilege *n* 特权 tèquán; **privileged** *adj* 有特权的 yǒu tèquán de

prize *n* 奖品 jiǎngpǐn

probability *n* 可能性 kěnéngxìng, 概率 gàilǜ; **probable** *adj* 很可能的 hěn kěnéng de; **probably** *adv* 很可能地 hěn kěnéng de

probation *n* 见习 (期) jiànxí (qī), 试用 (期) shìyòng (qī); **on probation** 试用中 shìyòng zhōng; **probationary** *adj* 试用的 shìyòng de

probe *v/n* 调查 diàochá

problem *n* 难题 nántí, 问题 wèntí, 麻烦 máfan; **problematic** *adj* 有问题的 yǒu wèntí de

proceed *v* 进行 jìnxíng; **proceedings** *n* (*conference*) 议项 yìxiàng; (*legal*) 诉讼程序 sùsòng chéngxù; 会议录 huìyìlù; **procedure** *n* 程序 chéngxù, 手续 shǒuxù

process *v* 加工 jiāgōng; *n* 过程 guòchéng; **in the process of** 在 ... 的过程中 zài ... de guòchéng zhōng

procession *n* 队伍 duìwu, 行列 hángliè

proclaim *v* 宣布 xuānbù; **proclamation** *n* 宣布 xuānbù

produce *v* 生产 shēngchǎn; **producer** *n* (*maker*) 生产者 shēngchǎnzhě; (*of movies*, *plays*, *etc.*) 制片人 zhìpiànrén; **product** *n* 产品 chǎnpǐn; **productive** *adj* 多产的 duōchǎn de, 有效率的 yǒu xiàolǜ de; **productivity** *n* 生产力 shēngchǎnlì, 效率 xiàolǜ; **production** *n* 生产 shēngchǎn

profession *n* 职业 zhíyè, 行业 hángyè; **professional** *n* 专业人士 zhuānyè rénshì; *adj* 职业的 zhíyè de, 专业的 zhuānyè de

professor *n* 教授 jiàoshòu

proficiency *n* 熟练 shúliàn, 精通 jīngtōng, 水平 shuǐpíng; **proficient** *adj* 熟练的 shúliàn de

profile *n* 侧面 cèmiàn, 轮廓 lúnkuò; (*biography*) 人物介绍 rénwù jièshào

profit *n* 利润 lìrùn; **profitable** *adj* 盈利的 yínglì de, 有利可图的 yǒulì kětú de

profound *adj* 深刻的 shēnkè de, 渊博的 yuānbó de; **profoundly** *adv* 深刻地 shēnkè de, 渊博地 yuānbó de

program *n* 节目 jiémù, 计划 jìhuà, 项目 xiàngmù; **programmer** *n* 程序员 chéngxùyuán

progress *v/n* 前进 qiánjìn, 进步 jìnbù; **progression** *n* 进步

jìnbù, 级数 jíshù; **progressive** *adj* 进步的 jìnbù de, 渐进的 jiànjìn de

prohibit *v* 禁止 jìnzhǐ; **prohibition** *n* 禁止 jìnzhǐ

project *n* 工程 gōngchéng, 项目 xiàngmù; **projection** *n* 投射 tóushè (*prediction*) 预测 yùcè; **projector** *n* (*film*) 放映机 fàngyìngjī; (*computer*) 投影机 tóuyǐngjī

prolific *adj* 多产的 duōchǎn de

prolong *v* 延长 yáncháng

prominence *n* 卓著 zhuōzhù; **prominent** *adj* 突出的 tūchū de, 卓越的 zhuōyuè de, 著名的 zhùmíng de

promiscuity *n* 混杂 hùnzá; (*sex*) 乱交 luàn jiāo; **promiscuous** *adj* 混杂的 hùnzá de; (*sex*) 男女乱交的 nánnǚ luànjiāo de

promise *v/n* 允诺 yǔnnuò, 许诺 xǔnuò; **promising** *adj* 有前途的 yǒu qiántú de, 有希望的 yǒuxīwàng de

promote *v* (*advance in rank*) 提拔 tíbá; (*encourage*) 促进 cùjìn; **promotion** *n* (*advance in rank*) 晋升 jìnshēng; (*sale*) 推销 tuīxiāo

prompt *adj* 迅速的 xùnsù de, 及时的 jíshí de

pronoun *n* 代词 dàicí

pronounce *v* 发音 fāyīn; **pronunciation** *n* 发音 fāyīn

proof *n* 证据 zhèngjù; **proof-read** *v* 校对 jiàoduì; **proof-reading** *n* 校对 jiàoduì

prop *v* 支撑 zhīchēng

propaganda *n* 宣传 xuānchuán

propel *v* 推进 tuījìn, 驱使 qūshǐ; **propeller** *n* 螺旋桨 luóxuánjiǎng

proper *adj* 适当的 shìdàng de, 正确的 zhèngquè de; **properly** *adv* 适当地 shìdàng de

property *n* (*possessions*) 财产 cáichǎn; (*attribute*) 性质 xìngzhì

prophet *n* 先知 xiānzhī, 预言者 yùyánzhě

proportion *n* 比例 bǐlì; **in proportion to** 与 ... 成比例 yǔ ... chéng bǐlì; **out of proportion** 不成比例 bù chéng bǐlì; **proportional** *adj* 成比例的 chéng bǐlì de

propose *v* 建议 jiànyì, 提议 tíyì; **proposal** *n* 建议 jiànyì, 提议 tíyì; **proposition** *n* 主张 zhǔzhāng

proprietor *n* 所有者 suǒyǒuzhě, 业主 yèzhǔ

prosecute *v* 起诉 qǐsù; **prosecution** *n* 起诉 qǐsù; **prosecutor** *n* 检察官 jiǎncháguān, 公诉人 gōngsùrén

prospect *n* 展望 zhǎnwàng, 期望 qīwàng; **prospective** *adj* 预期的 yùqī de, 未来的 wèilái de

prospectus *n* 内容说明书 nèiróng shuōmíngshū

prosper *v* 繁荣 fánróng, 兴旺 xīngwàng; **prosperity** *n* 繁荣 fánróng, 兴旺 xīngwàng; **prosperous** *adj* 繁荣的 fánróng de, 兴旺的 xīngwàng de

prostitute *n* 妓女 jìnǚ; **prostitution** *n* 卖淫 màiyín

protect *v* 保护 bǎohù; **protection** *n* 保护 bǎohù; **protective** *adj* 保护性的 bǎohùxìng de

protein *n* 蛋白质 dànbáizhì

protest *v/n* 抗议 kàngyì; **protester** *n* 抗议者 kàngyìzhě

Protestant *adj* 新教徒的 xīnjiàotú de, 新教的 xīnjiào de

protocol *n* 礼仪 lǐjié; (*diplomatic*) 外交礼节 wàijiāo lǐjié

prototype *n* 原型 yuánxíng

protrude *v* 突出 tūchū, 伸出 shēnchū

proud *adj* 自豪的 zìháo de, 骄傲的 jiāo'ào de

prove *v* (**proved, proved/proven**) 证明 zhèngmíng

proverb *n* 谚语 yànyǔ

provide *v* 提供 tígòng; **provide for** 提供生计 tígòng shēngjì, 赡养 shànyǎng; **provided that** *conj* 倘若 tǎngruò, 条件是 tiáojiàn shì

province *n* 省 shěng; **provincial** *adj* (*of a province*) 省的 shěng de; (*rustic*) 乡下的 xiāngxià de

provision *n* (*supplying*) 供应 gōngyìng; (*stipulation*) 规定 guīdìng; (*clause*) 条款 tiáokuǎn; **provisions** *n* 粮食 liángshi; **provisional** *adj* 临时的 línshí de

provoke *v* 挑衅 tiǎoxìn; **provocative** *adj* 挑衅的 tiǎoxìn de

prudent *adj* 审慎的 shěnshèn de; **prudence** *n* 审慎 shěnshèn

pseudonym *n* 笔名 bǐmíng

psychiatry *n* 精神病学 jīngshénbìngxué

psycho *n* 精神变态者 jīngshén biàntàizhě

psychologist *n* 心理学家 xīnlǐxuéjiā; **psychological** *adj* 心理学的 xīnlǐxué de

psychology *n* 心理学 xīnlǐxué

pub *n* 酒吧 jiǔbā

puberty *n* 青春期 qīngchūnqī

pubic *adj* 阴部的 yīnbù de

public *n* 公众 gōngzhòng, 民众 mínzhòng; *adj* 公开的 gōngkāi de, 公共的 gōnggòng de, 公立的 gōnglì de; **public relations** *n* 公共关系 gōnggòng guānxì

publication *n* 出版 chūbǎn; (*books, etc.*) 出版物 chūbǎnwù

publicize *v* 宣传 xuānchuán, 宣扬 xuānyáng; **publicity** *n* 宣传 xuānchuán, 宣扬 xuānyáng

publish *v* 出版 chūbǎn, 发表 fābiǎo; **publisher** *n* 出版者

chūbǎnzhě, 发行人 fāxíngrén; **publishing** *n* 出版业
chūbǎnyè; **publishing house** 出版社 chūbǎnshè

pudding *n* 布丁 bùdīng

puddle *n* 水坑 shuǐkēng

Puerto Rico *n* 波多黎各 bōduōlígè; **Puerto Rican** *n*
波多黎各人 bōduōlígèrén

puff *v* 喷气 pēnqì, 喷烟 pēnyān

pull *v* 拉 lā, 扯 chě; **pull back** 撤退 chètuì, 紧缩 jǐnsuō; **pull
through** 渡过难关 dùguò nánguān

pullover *n* 套头毛衣 tàotóu máoyī

pulp *n* 果肉 guǒròu, 纸浆 zhǐjiāng

pulse *n* 脉搏 màibó, 脉冲 màichōng

pump *v* 用泵抽 yòng bèng chōu; *n* 泵 bèng

pumpkin *n* 南瓜 nánguā

pun *n* 双关语 shuāngguānyǔ

punch *v* (*make a hole*) 打孔 dǎkǒng; (*strike*) 用拳猛击 yòng
quán měngjī; *n* (*tool*) 打孔机 dǎkǒngjī; (*drink*) 潘趣酒
pānqùjiǔ

punctuality *n* 准时 zhǔnshí, 守时 shǒushí; **punctual** *adj*
准时的 zhǔnshí de, 守时的 shǒushí de

punctuate *v* 加标点 jiā biāodiǎn; **punctuation** *n* 标点符号
biāodiǎn fúhào

puncture *v* 刺穿 cìchuān, 刺破 cìpò; *n* 穿孔 chuānkǒng

punish *v* 处罚 chǔfá; **punishment** *n* 处罚 chǔfá

pupil *n* (*student*) 学生 xuésheng; (*eye*) 瞳孔 tóngkǒng

puppet *n* (*artificial figure*) 木偶 mù'ǒu; (*person controlled
by another*) 傀儡 kuǐlěi

puppy *n* 小狗 xiǎogǒu

purchase *v* 购买 gòumǎi

purify *v* 净化 jìnghuà; **purity** *n* 纯净 chúnjìng, 纯洁 chúnjié;
pure *adj* 纯的 chún de, 纯净的 chúnjìng de

purple *adj* 紫色的 zǐsè de

purpose *n* 目的 mùdì, 用途 yòngtú; **on purpose** 故意地 gùyì
de; **purposeful** *adj* 有目的的 yǒu mùdì de, 故意的 gùyì de

purse *n* 钱包 qiánbāo

pursue *v* 追求 zhuīqiú; **pursuit** *n* 追求 zhuīqiú

push *v* 推 tuī; (*promote*) 推行 tuīxíng; (*urge*) 催促 cuīcù

put *v* (put, put) 放 fàng; **put away** 放好 fàng hǎo; 放起来
fàng qǐlái; **put back** 放回原处 fànghuí yuánchù; **put
down** 放下 fàng xià; (*note down*) 记下 jì xià; **put off**
推迟 tuīchí; **put on** 穿上 chuān shàng; **put out** 扑灭
pūmiè, 熄灭 xīmiè; **put up with** 忍受 rěnshòu

puzzle *v* (使) 迷惑 (shǐ) míhuò; *n* 难题 nántí; 谜 mí;
puzzling *adj* 令人迷惑的 lìng rén míhuò de

Q

quaint *adj* 离奇有趣的 líqí yǒuqù de

quake *v* 地震 dìzhèn

qualify *v* (使) 获得资格 (shǐ) huòdé zīgé; **qualification** *n*
资格 zīgé; **qualified** *adj* 有资格的 yǒu zīgé de

quality *n* 质量 zhìliàng

quantity *n* 数量 shùliàng

quarantine *v* 隔离 gélí; *n* 隔离检疫 gélí jiǎnyì

quarrel *v/n* 吵架 chǎojià; **quarrelsome** *adj* 好争论的 hào
zhēnglùn de

quarter *n* (*one fourth*) 四分之一 sì fēn zhīyī; (*calendar*)
季度 jìdù; **quarters** *n* 住处 zhùchù; **quarterly** *n* 季刊
jìkān; *adj* 每季的 měi jì de; *adv* 季度地 jìdù de

queen *n* 女王 nǚwáng

queer *adj* 奇怪的 qíguài de

quench *v* (*put out*) 熄灭 xīmiè (*suppress*); 抑制 yìzhì; (*cool
down*) 冷却 lěngquè

query *n* 询问 xúnwèn

quest *n* 搜寻 sōuxún

question *v* 提问 tíwèn, 问 wèn; *n* 问题 wèntí; **beside the
question** 离题的 lítí de; **out of the question** 不可能的
bù kěnéng de; **question mark** 问号 wènhào;
questionable *adj* 可疑的 kěyí de; **questionnaire** *n* 问卷
wènjuàn, 调查表 diàochábiǎo

queue *n* 队 duì

quick *adj* 迅速的 xùnsù de, 快的 kuài de; **quicken** *v* 加快
jiākuài, 加速 jiāsù; **quickly** *adv* 迅速地 xùnsù de

quiet *adj* 安静的 ānjìng de; **quietly** *adv* 悄悄地 qiǎoqiǎo de;
quietness *n* 平静 píngjìng, 寂静 jìjìng

quilt *n* 被子 bèizi

quit *v* (**quit/quitted, quit/quitted**) (*from a position*) 辞职
cízhí; (*stop*) 停止 tíngzhǐ

quite *adv* 相当 xiāngdāng, 完全 wánquán

quiz *v* 盘问 pánwèn, 对 ... 测验 duì ... cèyàn; *n* 测验 cèyàn

quota *n* 配额 pèi'é, 限额 xiàn'é

quote *v* 引用 yǐnyòng; *n* (*state a price*) 报价 bàojià; (*cite
from a book, author, etc.*) 引语 yǐnyǔ; **quotation** *n*
(*citation from a book, author, etc.*) 引文 yǐnwén;

(*statement of a price*) 报价 bàojià; **quotation marks** 问号 wènhào

R

race *v* 赛跑 sàipǎo; *n* (*sports*) 赛跑 sàipǎo; (*ethnic*) 种族 zhǒngzú; **race horse** 赛马 sàimǎ; **racism** *n* 种族主义 zhǒngzúzhǔyì; **racist** *n* 种族主义者 zhǒngzúzhǔyìzhě; **racial** *adj* 种族的 zhǒngzú de

rack *v* 榨取 zhàqǔ; *n* 架子 jiàzi; **rack one's brains** 绞尽脑汁 jiǎojìn nǎozhī

radiate *v* 放射 fàngshè; **radiation** *n* 辐射 fúshè; **radiator** *n* 散热器 sànrèqì

radio *n* 收音机 shōuyīnjī; **radio station** 无线电台 wúxiàn diàntái

radioactive *adj* 放射性的 fàngshèxìng de

radiology *n* 放射学 fàngshèxué

radium *n* 镭 léi

raft *n* 木筏 mùfá, 木排 mùpái

rag *n* 破布 pòbù, 抹布 mābù

rage *v* 发怒 fānù; *n* 愤怒 fènnù; **raging** *adj* 狂怒的 kuángnù de

raid *v/n* 袭击 xíjī

rail *n* (*fence*) 围栏 wéilán; (*stairs*) 扶手 fúshǒu; (*train*) 铁轨 tiěguǐ; **by rail** 乘火车 chéng huǒchē; **railway/railroad** *n* 铁路 tiělù

railing *n* 扶手 fúshǒu

rain *v* 下雨 xiàyǔ; *n* 雨 yǔ; **rainbow** *n* 彩虹 cǎihóng; **raincoat** *n* 雨衣 yǔyī; **rainy** *adj* 多雨的 duōyǔ de, 下雨的 xiàyǔ de

raise *v* (*lift*) 举起 jǔ qǐ, (*grow, breed, care for*) 养 yǎng, (*collect money*) 筹 chóu, (*ask a question*) 提出 tíchū; *n* 加薪 jiāxīn

raisin *n* 葡萄干 pútáogān

rally *v* 集结 jíjié; *n* 集会 jíhuì

rampage *n* 狂暴行径 kuángbào xíngjìng; **be on the rampage** 横冲直闯 héngchōng zhíchuǎng

ran. *See* **run**

ranch *n* 大农场 dà nóngchǎng

random *adj* 随便的 suíbiàn de, 任意的 rènyì de; **at random** 任意地 rènyì de

rang. *See* **ring**

range *n* (*scope*) 范围 fànwéi; (*shooting*) 射击场 shèjīchǎng; **mountain range** 山脉 shānmài

rank *n* (*position*) 等级 děngjí; (*military*) 军衔 jūnxián; (*graded body*) 行列 hángliè; *v* 把 … 分等 bǎ ... fēndēng, 给 ... 评定等级 gěi ... píngdìng děngjí

ransom *n* 赎金 shújīn

rap *v* 敲击 qiāojī; *n* 说唱音乐 shuōchàng yīnyuè, 嚼舌音乐 jiáoshé yīnyuè

rape *v/n* 强奸 qiángjiān; **rapist** *n* 强奸犯 qiángjiānfàn

rapid *adj* 迅速的 xùnsù de; **rapidity** *n* 急速 jísù, 迅速 xùnsù

rapture *n* 狂喜 kuángxǐ; **go into raptures over** 对 … 狂喜 duì … kuángxǐ

rare *adj* 罕见的 hǎnjiàn de, 稀有的 xīyǒu de; **rarely** *adv* 很少地 hěn shǎo de, 罕见地 hǎnjiàn de

rash *n* 皮疹 pízhěn; *adj* 鲁莽的 lǔmǎng de, 急躁的 jízào de

raspberry *n* 树莓 shùméi

rate *n* (*amount, quantity*) 比率 bǐlǜ; (*price*) 价格 jiàgé; (*grade, class*) 等级 děngjí; (*speed*) 速度 sùdù; **at any rate** 无论如何 wúlùn rúhé

rather *adv* (*more readily*) 宁愿 nìngyuàn; (*to a certain degree*) 相当 xiāngdāng

ratify *v* 批准 pīzhǔn, 认可 rènkě; **ratification** *n* 批准 pīzhǔn

ratio *n* 比率 bǐlǜ

ration *v/n* 定量配给 dìngliáng pèijǐ

rational *adj* 理性的 lǐxìng de

rattle *v* 喋喋不休地说 diédié bùxiū de shuō

ravage *v* 蹂躏 róulìn, 毁坏 huǐhuài

rave *v* 热情地赞美 rèqíng de zànměi

raw *adj* 生的 shēng de, 未加工的 wèi jiāgōng de; **raw materials** 原材料 yuáncáiliào

ray *n* 光线 guāngxiàn

razor *n* 剃刀 tìdāo; **razor-blade** *n* 剃刀刀片 tìdāo dāopiàn

reach *v* (*arrive*) 到达 dàodá; (*extend*) 延伸 yánshēn; (*stretch to touch*) 够到 gòudào; **out of reach** 够不着 gòu bù zháo; **within reach** 够得着 gòu de zháo

react *v* 作出反应 zuòchū fǎnyìng; **reaction** *n* 反应 fǎnyìng

read *v* (**read, read**) 读 dú, 看书 kàn shū; **reader** *n* (*person*) 读者 dúzhě; (*book*) 读物 dúwù; **reading** *n* 阅读 yuèdú

ready *adj* (*willing*) 乐意的 lèyì de; (*prepared*) 准备好的 zhǔnbèi hǎo de; **get ready** 准备好 zhǔnbèi hǎo; **ready-made** *adj* 现成的 xiànchéng de, 做好的 zuò hǎo de; **readily** *adv* 乐意地 lèyì de, 欣然 xīnrán

real *adj* 真实的 zhēnshí de; **reality** *n* 真实 zhēnshí, 现实

xiànshí; **in reality** 实际上 shíjìshang; **really** *adv* 真正地 zhēnzhèng de; **really?** 真的吗? zhēnde ma

real estate *n* 房地产 fángdìchǎn

realize *v* (*understand*) 意识到 yìshí dào; (*achieve*) 实现 shíxiàn; **realization** *n* 实现 shíxiàn

realism *n* 现实主义 xiànshízhǔyì

realist *n* 现实主义者 xiànshízhǔyìzhě

realm *n* 领域 lǐngyù

reap *v* (*harvest*) 收割 shōugē; (*gain*) 获得 huòdé

rear *n* 后面 hòumian, 后方 hòufāng; *adj* 后面的 hòumian de, 后方的 hòufāng de; **bring up the rear** 处在最后的位置 chǔzài zuìhòu de wèizhi, 殿后 diànhòu

rearrange *v* 重新整理 chóngxīn zhěnglǐ; **rearrangement** *n* 重新整理 chóngxīn zhěnglǐ

reason *n* 理由 lǐyóu; **reasoning** *n* 推理 tuīlǐ; **reasonable** *adj* 合理的 hélǐ de

reassure *v* (使) 放心 (shǐ) fàngxīn

rebate *n* (*partial refund*) 回扣 huíkòu, (*discount*) 折扣 zhékòu

rebel *v* 反叛 fǎnpàn, 造反 zàofǎn; *n* 反叛者 fǎnpànzhě, 造反者 zàofǎnzhě; **rebellion** *n* 叛乱 pànluàn, 谋反 móufǎn; **rebellious** *adj* 叛逆的 pànnì de

rebuild *v* (**rebuilt, rebuilt**) 重建 chóngjiàn

rebuke *v* 指责 zhǐzé

recall *v* (*call back*) 召回 zhàohuí; (*recollect*) 回忆 huíyì

recapture *v* 夺回 duóhuí, 收复 shōufù

recede *v* 后退 hòutuì

receipt *n* 收据 shōujù, 发票 fāpiào

receive *v* 收到 shōu dào

recent *adj* 新近的 xīnjìn de, 最近的 zuìjìn de; **recently** *adv* 最近 zuìjìn

reception *n* (*receiving*) 接待 jiēdài; (*function, occasion*) 招待会 zhāodàihuì; **receptionist** *n* 接待员 jiēdàiyuán

recess *n* (*vacation*) 假期 jiàqī; (*rest*) 休息 xiūxi; (*court*) 休庭 xiūtíng

recession *n* 不景气 bùjǐngqì, 萧条 xiāotiáo

recharge *v* 充电 chōngdiàn

recipe *n* 菜谱 càipǔ

recipient *n* (*receiver*) 接受者 jiēshòuzhě; (*letter*) 收信人 shōuxìnrén

reciprocate *v* 酬答 chóudá, 互换 hùhuàn; **reciprocal** *adj* 互惠的 hùhuì de

recite v 背诵 bèisòng; **recital** n (*music*) 独奏会 dúzòuhuì; (*reading from memory*) 背诵 bèisòng

reckless adj 鲁莽的 lǔmǎng de

reckon v (*guess*) 猜想 cāixiǎng; (*calculate*) 计算 jìsuàn

reclaim v (*claim*) 收回 shōuhuí; (*land*) 开垦 kāikěn

recognize v (*identify*) 认出 rènchū; (*acknowledge*) 认可 rènkě; **recognition** n (*emphasis*) 重视 zhòngshì; (*acknowledgment*) 承认 chéngrèn, 认可 rènkě

recollect v 回忆 huíyì; **recollection** n 回忆 huíyì

recommend v 推荐 tuījiàn; **recommendation** n 推荐 tuījiàn; **recommendation letter** 推荐信 tuījiànxìn

recompense v/n 报酬 bàochou

reconcile v (使) 和解 (shǐ) héjiě, (使) 一致 (shǐ) yīzhì; **reconciliation** n 和解 héjiě

reconstruct v 重建 chóngjiàn; **reconstruction** n 重建 chóngjiàn

record v 记录 jìlù, 录制 lùzhì; n 记录 jìlù; (*music*) 唱片 chàngpiàn; **recording** n 记录 jìlù; (*music*) 唱片 chàngpiàn, 录音 lùyīn

recount v 叙述 xùshù, 细述 xìshù

recoup v 重获 chónghuò, 偿还 chánghuán

recover v (*get well*) 痊愈 quányù; (*get back*) 找回 zhǎohuí; **recovery** n 恢复 huīfù; 找回 zhǎohuí

recreation n 消遣 xiāoqiǎn, 娱乐 yúlè

recruit v 招募 zhāomù; n (*soldier*) 新兵 xīnbīng; (*member*) 新成员 xīn chéngyuán; **recruitment** n 招募 zhāomù

rectangle n 长方形 chángfāngxíng; **rectangular** adj 长方形的 chángfāngxíng de

rectify v 校正 jiàozhèng, 修正 xiūzhèng

recuperate v 恢复 huīfù; **recuperation** n 恢复 huīfù

recur v 复发 fùfā; **recurrence** n 复发 fùfā

red adj 红色的 hóngsè de; **red tape** 繁文缛节 fánwén rùjié; **in the red** 亏空 kuīkòng, 赤字 chìzì; **red-handed** adj 当场 dāngchǎng; **red-hot** adj 炽热的 chìrè de

redeem v 赎回 shúhuí, 兑出 duìchū

reduce v 减少 jiǎnshǎo; **reduction** n 减少 jiǎnshǎo

redundancy n 冗余 rǒngyú; **redundant** adj 多余的 duōyú de

reduplicate v 重复 chóngfù, 复制 fùzhì

reef n 礁石 jiāoshí

refer v (*mention*) 提到 tídào; (*introduce*) 介绍 jièshào; **reference** n 参考 cānkǎo; (*person*) 推荐人 tuījiànrén;

reference book 参考书 cānkǎoshū; **make reference to** 提到 tídào, 参考 cānkǎo; **with reference to** 关于 guānyú

referee *n* 裁判员 cáipànyuán

referendum *n* 公民投票 gōngmín tóupiào

refill *v* 再装满 zài zhuāngmǎn, 加满 jiā mǎn

refine *v* 精炼 jīngliàn; **refinery** *n* 精炼厂 jīngliànchǎng

reflect *v* (*cast back*) 反映 fǎnyìng, (*think*) 反思 fǎnsī; **reflection** *n* (*feedback*) 反映 fǎnyìng; (*thought*) 反思 fǎnsī; (*image*) 倒影 dàoyǐng

reflex *n* 反射作用 fǎnshè zuòyòng

reform *v/n* 改革 gǎigé

refrain *v* 克制 kèzhì; *n* 叠句 diéjù

refresh *v* (使) 振作 (shǐ) zhènzuò, 重温 chóngwēn; **refreshments** *n* 点心 diǎnxin; **refreshing** *adj* 提神的 tíshén de, 清新的 qīngxīn de

refrigerator *n* 冰箱 bīngxiāng; **refrigeration** *n* 冷藏 lěngcáng

refuel *v* 加油 jiāyóu

refuge *n* 避难 bìnàn, 避难所 bìnànsuǒ; **refugee** *n* 难民 nànmín

refund *v/n* 退款 tuìkuǎn

refuse *v* 拒绝 jùjué; *n* 垃圾 lājī; **refusal** *n* 拒绝 jùjué

regain *v* 收复 shōufù, 收回 shōu huí

regard *v* 视为 shìwéi, 看待 kàndài; *n* 方面 fāngmiàn; **regards** *n* 致意 zhìyì; **regarding** *prep* 关于 guānyú; **regardless** *adv* 不管 bùguǎn; **regardless of** 不顾 bùgù, 不管 bùguǎn

regime *n* 政权 zhèngquán

regiment *n* (*military*) 团 tuán

region *n* 地区 dìqū; **regional** *adj* 地域性的 dìyùxìng de

register *v/n* 登记 dēngjì; **registration** *n* 登记 dēngjì

regret *v* 遗憾 yíhàn, 后悔 hòuhuǐ; *n* 遗憾 yíhàn, 歉意 qiànyì; **regrettable** *adj* 令人遗憾的 lìng rén yíhàn de

regular *adj* 规则的 guīzé de, 定期的 dìngqī de, 经常的 jīngcháng de, 正常的 zhèngcháng de; **regularity** *n* 规律性 guīlǜxìng

regulate *v* 规定 guīdìng, 调节 tiáojié, 管制 guǎnzhì; **regulation** *n* 规定 guīdìng, 规则 guīzé

rehabilitate *v* 修复 xiūfù, 康复 kāngfù

rehearse *v* 排演 páiyǎn; **rehearsal** *n* 排演 páiyǎn

reign *v/n* 统治 tǒngzhì

reimburse *v* 偿还 chánghuán, 报销 bàoxiāo; **reimbursement** *n* 偿还 chánghuán, 报销 bàoxiāo

rein *v* 止住 zhǐzhù; *n* 缰绳 jiāngsheng

reinforce *v* 增援 zēngyuán, 加强 jiāqiáng; **reinforcement** *n* 增援 zēngyuán, 加固 jiāgù

reject *v* 拒绝 jùjué, 否决 fǒujué; **rejection** *n* 拒绝 jùjué, 否决 fǒujué

rejoice *v* 感到高兴 gǎndào gāoxìng, 喜悦 xǐyuè

relapse *n* 复发 fùfā

relate *v* (*tell*) 叙述 xùshù; (*bring into connection*) (使) 联系 (shǐ) liánxì; **related** *adj* 有关系的 yǒu guānxi de; (*of kinship*) 有亲属关系的 yǒu qīnshǔ guānxi de

relation *n* 关系 guānxi; (*relatives*) 亲戚 qīnqi; **diplomatic relations** 外交关系 wàijiāo guānxi; **relationship** *n* 关系 guānxi, 关联 guānlián

relative *n* 亲戚 qīnqi; **relatively** *adv* 相对地 xiāngduì de

relax *v* 放松 fàngsōng, 休息 xiūxi; **relaxation** *n* 放松 fàngsōng, 消遣 xiāoqiǎn; **relaxing** *adj* 使人轻松的 shǐrén qīngsōng de

relay *v* 传递 chuándì, 转播 zhuǎnbō

release *v* 释放 shìfàng; (*information, film, etc.*) 发布 fābù

relevant *adj* 有关的 yǒuguān de; **relevance/relevancy** *n* 关联 guānlián

reliability *n* 可靠性 kěkàoxìng; **reliable** *adj* 可靠的 kěkào de

reliance *n* 信任 xìnrèn, 依靠 yīkào

relic *n* (*object*) 遗物 yíwù; (*site*) 遗迹 yíjī

relief *n* (*alleviation*) 安慰 ānwèi; (*food, money, etc.*) 救济 jiùjì; (*release from a post*) 换班 huànbān; (*removal*) 免除 miǎnchú

relieve *v* 救济 jiùjì; (*release from a post*) 换班 huànbān; (*removal*) 免除 miǎnchú, 解除 jiěchú

religion *n* 宗教 zōngjiào; **religious** *adj* 宗教的 zōngjiào de, 信教的 xìnjiào de

relish *v* 欣赏 xīnshǎng, 品味 pǐnwèi; *n* 美味 měiwèi

reluctance *n* 勉强 miǎnqiǎng; **reluctant** *adj* 勉强的 miǎnqiǎng de; **reluctantly** *adv* 勉强地 miǎnqiǎng de

rely *v* (*rely on*) 依赖 yīlài

remain *v* (*left to be done*) 剩余 shèngyú; (*continue to be*) 保持 bǎochí; (*stay behind*) 留下 liúxià; **remainder** *n* 剩余物 shèngyúwù, 其余的 qíyú de; **remains** *n* 残余 cányú; (*site*) 遗迹 yíjī; (*body*) 遗体 yítǐ

remark *v* 评论 pínglùn, 发言 fāyán; *n* 评论 pínglùn, 备注 bèizhù; **remarkable** *adj* 不平常的 bù píngcháng de, 显著的 xiǎnzhù de

remarry *v* 再婚 zàihūn

remedy *v* 补救 bǔjiù, 矫正 jiǎozhèng; *n* 补救办法 bǔjiùbànfǎ, 救药 jiùyào; **remedial** *adj* 补救的 bǔjiù de

remember *v* 记住 jì zhù, 记得 jìde

remind *v* 提醒 tíxǐng; **reminder** *n* 提示 tíshì, 提醒 tíxǐng

reminisce *v* 回忆 huíyì; **reminiscence** *n* 回想 huíxiǎng

remit *v* 汇款 huìkuǎn; **remittance** *n* 汇款 huìkuǎn

remorse *n* 后悔 hòuhuǐ; **remorseful** *adj* 忏悔的 chànhuǐ de; **remorseless** *adj* 无悔意的 wúhuǐyì de

remote *adj* 遥远的 yáoyuǎn de; **remote control** 遥控器 yáokòngqì

remove *v* (*of an object*) 移走 yízǒu; (*from a post*) 免职 miǎnzhí; (*rid*) 去除 qùchú; **removal** *n* 移走 yízǒu; 免职 miǎnzhí; 去除 qùchú

remunerate *v* 报酬 bàochou; **remuneration** *n* 报酬 bàochou

renaissance *n* 复兴 fùxīng

render *v* (*perform*) 给予 jǐyǔ; (*translate*) 翻译 fānyì

renew *v* (*begin*) 更新 gēngxīn; (*extend*) 续借 xùjiè; **renewal** *n* 更新 gēngxīn; 续借 xùjiè

renounce *v* 断绝关系 duànjué guānxì

renovate *v* 整修 zhěngxiū; **renovation** *n* 整修 zhěngxiū

renown *n* 声誉 shēngyù; **renowned** *adj* 著名的 zhùmíng de, 有声誉的 yǒu shēngyù de

rent *v* 租 zū; *n* 租金 zūjīn; **rental** *n* 租费 zūfèi, 租贷 zūdài

reorganize *v* 改组 gǎizǔ

repair *v/n* 修理 xiūlǐ

repatriate *v* 遣返 qiǎnfǎn; **repatriation** *n* 遣返 qiǎnfǎn

repay *v* (**repaid, repaid**) 偿还 chánghuán; **repayment** *n* 偿还 chánghuán

repeal *v* 废除 fèichú, 撤销 chèxiāo, 作废 zuòfèi

repeat *v* 重复 chóngfù; **repetition** *n* 重复 chóngfù; **repeatedly** *adv* 再三地 zàisān de, 反复地 fǎnfù de; **repetitive** *adj* 重复的 chóngfù de

repel *v* 击退 jītuì; **repellent** *adj* 排斥的 páichì de, 令人厌恶的 lìng rén yànwù de

repent *v* 后悔 hòuhuǐ, 忏悔 chànhuǐ; **repentance** *n* 后悔 hòuhuǐ, 忏悔 chànhuǐ; **repentant** *adj* 后悔的 hòuhuǐ de, 有悔改表现的 yǒu huǐgǎi biǎoxiàn de

replace *v* (*substitute*) 取代 qǔdài; (*put back*) 将 ... 放回原处 jiāng ... fàng huí yuánchù; **replacement** *n* 取代 qǔdài, 替换 tìhuan

replenish *v* 补充 bǔchōng; **replenishment** *n* 补充 bǔchōng

reproach *v* 责备 zébèi; **reproachful** *adj* 责备的 zébèi de

replica *n* 复制品 fùzhìpǐn
reply *v/n* 答复 dáfù
report *v/n* 报告 bàogào; **reporter** *n* 记者 jìzhě
represent *v* 代表 dàibiǎo **representation** *n* 表现 biǎoxiàn, 代表 dàibiǎo
representative *n* 代表 dàibiǎo
reprieve *v/n* 缓刑 huǎnxíng, 暂缓 zànhuǎn
reprimand *v/n* 申斥 shēnchì, 责备 zébèi
reprint *v* 重印 chóngyìn
reproduce *v* (*duplicate*) 复制 fùzhì; (*biology*) 繁殖 fánzhí, 生育 shēngyù; **reproduction** *n* 复制 fùzhì, 复制品 fùzhìpǐn; 繁殖 fánzhí, 生育 shēngyù
reptile *n* 爬行动物 páxíng dòngwù
republic *n* 共和国 gònghéguó; **Republican** *n* 共和党人 gònghédǎngrén; *adj* 共和党的 gònghédǎng de
repulsive *adj* 排斥的 páichì de, 令人作呕的 lìng rén zuò'ǒu de
reputation *n* 名誉 míngyù, 名声 míngshēng; **reputable** *adj* 著名的 zhùmíng de
request *v/n* 请求 qǐngqiú; **at the request of** 依照 ... 要求 yīzhào ... yāoqiú
require *v* 需要 xūyào, 要求 yāoqiú; **requirement** *n* 需要 xūyào, 要求 yāoqiú
rescue *v/n* 援救 yuánjiù, 营救 yíngjiù
research *v/n* 研究 yánjiū, 调查 diàochá; **researcher** *n* 研究员 yánjiūyuán
resemble *v* 像 xiàng, 相似 xiāngsì; **resemblance** *n* 相似 xiāngsì, 相像 xiāngxiàng
resent *v* 愤恨 fènhèn, 怨恨 yuànhèn; **resentment** *n* 愤恨 fènhèn, 怨恨 yuànhèn
reserve *v* (*keep*) 保留 bǎoliú; (*book*) 预订 yùdìng; **reservation** *n* 保留 bǎoliú; 订位 dìngwèi; **reserved** *adj* 保留的 bǎoliú de, 矜持的 jīnchí de
reservoir *n* (*for water*) 水库 shuǐkù; (*reserve*) 储积 chǔjī
reset *v* (**reset, reset**) 重新安放 chóngxīn ānfàng, 重新调整 chóngxīn tiáozhěng
reside *v* 居住 jūzhù; **residence** *n* 住宅 zhùzhái, 居住 jūzhù; **resident** *n* 居民 jūmín; **residential** *adj* 住宅的 zhùzhái de, 居民的 jūmín de
residue *n* 残余 cányú, 剩余物 shèngyúwù; **residual** *adj* 残留的 cánliú de, 剩余的 shèngyú de
resign *v* 辞职 cízhí; **resignation** *n* 辞职 cízhí

resilience *n* 复原力 fùyuánlì, 活力 huólì; **resilient** *adj*
富有活力的 fùyǒu huólì de

resist *v* 抵抗 dǐkàng; **resistance** *n* 抵抗 dǐkàng; **resistant** *adj*
反抗的 fǎnkàng de; 抵抗的 dǐkàng de

resolve *v* (*determine*) 决定 juédìng, 决意 juéyì; (*solve*) 解决
jiějué; **resolution** *n* (*decision*) 决议 juéyì, (*determination*)
决心 juéxīn

resound *v* 回响 huíxiǎng; **resounding** *adj* 洪亮的
hóngliàng de

resort *n* 度假胜地 dùjià shèngdi; **as a last resort**
作为最后的一招 zuòwéi zuìhòu de yī zhāo; **resort to**
诉诸 sùzhū

resource *n* 资源 zīyuán; **resourceful** *adj* 足智多谋的 zúzhì
duōmóu de

respect *v/n* 尊敬 zūnjìng; **respectable** *adj* 可敬的 kějìng de;
respectful *adj* 尊敬的 zūnjìng de; **respective** *adj* 各自的
gèzì de, 分别的 fēnbié de

respond *v* 回答 huídá, 反应 fǎnyìng; **response** *n* 回答 huídá,
反应 fǎnyìng

responsibility *n* 责任 zérèn; **responsible** *adj* 负责的 fùzé de

rest *v* 休息 xiūxi; *n* 休息 xiūxi; (*remainder*) 其余的 qíyúde;
restless *adj* 不安宁的 bù ānníng de

restaurant *n* 餐馆 cānguǎn

restore *v* (*return*) 归还 guīhuán; (*bring up*) 恢复 huīfù; (*repair*) 修复 xiūfù; **restoration** *n* 归还 guīhuán; 恢复 huīfù;
修复 xiūfù, 重建 chóngjiàn

restrain *v* 抑制 yìzhì; **restraint** *n* 抑制 yìzhì, 克制 kèzhì

restrict *v* 限制 xiànzhì; **restriction** *n* 限制 xiànzhì; **restricted**
adj 受限制的 shòu xiànzhì de, 有限的 yǒuxiàn de

result *v* 产生 chǎnshēng; *n* 结果 jiéguǒ; **result in** 导致
dǎozhì; **resultant** *adj* 从而产生的 cóng'ér chǎnshēng de

resume *v* 重新开始 chóngxīn kāishǐ; **resumption** *n*
重新开始 chóngxīn kāishǐ

résumé *n* 简历 jiǎnlì, 学历 xuélì

resurrect *v* 复兴 fùxīng; **resurrection** *n* 复苏 fùsū

retail *v/n* 零售 língshòu; **retailer** *n* 零售商 língshòushāng

retain *v* 保留 bǎoliú

retaliate *v* 报复 bàofù; **retaliation** *n* 报复 bàofù

retarded *adj* 发展迟缓的 fāzhǎn chíhuǎn de

reticence *n* 沉默寡言 chénmò guǎyán; **reticent** *adj*
沉默寡言的 chénmò guǎyán de

retire v 退休 tuìxiū; **retirement** n 退休 tuìxiū; **retired** adj 退休的 tuìxiū de

retreat v/n 撤退 chètuì, 后退 hòutuì

retrieve v 收回 shōu huí, 领回 lǐng huí; **retrieval** n 收回 shōu huí, 领回 lǐng huí

retrospect n 回顾 huígù; **in retrospect** 回想起来 huíxiǎng qǐlái; **retrospective** adj 回顾的 huígù de

return v (go back) 回 huí; (take back) 归还 guīhuán; **return ticket** 往返票 wǎngfǎnpiào; **in return** 反过来 fǎn guòlái, 作为回报 zuòwéi huíbào

reunite v 重聚 chóngjù, 团圆 tuányuán; **reunion** n 重聚 chóngjù, 团圆 tuányuán

reveal v 显示 xiǎnshì, 揭露 jiēlù; **revelation** n 启示 qǐshì; **revealing** adj 有启迪作用的 yǒu qǐdí zuòyòng de

revenge v 为 ... 复仇 wèi ... fùchóu; n 复仇 fùchóu

revenue n 收入 shōurù; (tax) 税收 shuìshōu

revere v 尊敬 zūnjìng, 敬畏 jìngwèi; **reverence** n 尊敬 zūnjìng; **reverent** adj 尊敬的 zūnjìng de, 虔诚的 qiánchéng de

reverse v 倒转 dàozhuǎn, 倒退 dàotuì; n 反面 fǎnmiàn; adj 相反的 xiāngfǎn de; **reversal** n 颠倒 diāndǎo, 反转 fǎnzhuǎn, 撤销 chèxiāo

review v/n (go over) 复习 fùxí; (inspect) 审阅 shěnyuè; (discuss) 评论 pínglùn

revise v 校订 jiàodìng, 修改 xiūgǎi; **revision** n 校订 jiàodìng, 修改 xiūgǎi

revive v 复苏 fùsū, 苏醒 sūxǐng, 复原 fùyuán, 复兴 fùxīng; **revival** n 苏醒 sūxǐng, 复兴 fùxīng

revolt v 反叛 fǎnpàn, 憎恶 zēngwù; n 叛乱 pànluàn; **revolting** adj 使人厌恶的 shǐ rén yànwù de

revolution n 旋转 xuánzhuǎn; (political) 革命 gémìng; **revolutionary** n 革命者 gémìngzhě; adj 革命的 gémìng de

revolve v 旋转 xuánzhuǎn; **revolver** n 左轮手枪 zuǒlún shǒuqiāng; **revolving door** 旋转门 xuánzhuànmén

reward v/n 报酬 bàochou, 奖赏 jiǎngshǎng

rewind v (rewound, rewound) 重绕 chóngrào, 重上发条 chóngshàng fātiáo, 倒回 dào huí

rewrite v (rewrote, rewritten) 重写 chóngxiě

rhetoric n 修辞学 xiūcíxué; **rhetorical** adj 修辞学的 xiūcíxué de; **rhetorical question** 反问句 fǎnwènjù

rheumatism n 风湿病 fēngshībìng; **rheumatic** adj 风湿的 fēngshī de

rhinoceros n 犀牛 xīniú

rhyme *n* 押韵 yāyùn

rhythm *n* 节奏 jiézòu; **rhythmic** *adj* 有节奏的 yǒu jiézòu de

rib *n* 肋骨 lèigǔ

ribbon *n* 缎带 duàndài

rice *n* (*raw*) 米 mǐ; (*cooked*) 米饭 mǐfàn

rich *adj* 有钱的 yǒu qián de, 富有的 fùyǒu de; **riches** *n* 财富 cáifù

rid *v* (**rid, rid**) (使) 摆脱 (shǐ) bǎituō; **get rid of** 摆脱 bǎituō, 除去 chúqù

ridden. *See* **ride**

riddle *n* 谜 mí, 谜语 míyǔ

ride *v* (**rode, ridden**) 骑 qí; **rider** *n* 骑手 qíshǒu

ridicule *v* 嘲笑 cháoxiào, 愚弄 yúnòng; **ridiculous** *adj* 荒谬的 huāngmiù de, 可笑的 kěxiào de

rifle *n* 步枪 bùqiāng

rig *v* 装置 zhuāngzhì, 操纵 cāozòng

right *n* 权利 quánlì; 右边 yòubian; *adj* 正确的 zhèngquè de; **right-hand** *n* 右手 yòushǒu; **right-handed** *adj* 惯用右手的 guànyòng yòushǒu de; **right-winger** *n* 右翼成员 yòuyì chéngyuán; **right-wing** *adj* 右翼的 yòuyì de

rigidity *n* 严格 yángé; 死板 sǐbǎn; **rigid** *adj* 坚硬的 jiānyìng de; 死板的 sǐbǎn de

rigorous *adj* 严格的 yángé de

rim *n* 边缘 biānyuán

ring *v* (**rang, rung**) (*bell*) 鸣 míng, 响 xiǎng; (*phone*) 打电话 dǎ diànhuà; *n* 环 huán, 圈 quān; (*finger*) 戒指 jièzhi; **ringleader** *n* 罪魁 zuìkuí; **ring a bell** 引起回忆 yǐnqǐ huíyì, 想起 xiǎngqǐ

rink *n* 溜冰场 liūbīngchǎng

rinse *v* 冲洗 chōngxǐ, 淘 táo

riot *v/n* 暴乱 bàoluàn; **rioter** *n* 暴乱者 bàoluànzhě

rip *n* 裂口 lièkǒu; *v* 撕裂 sīliè; (*rip off*) 欺骗 qīpiàn, 巧取豪夺 qiǎoqǔ háoduó

ripe *adj* 成熟的 chéngshú de; **ripen** *v* 成熟 chéngshú

ripple *n* 波纹 bōwén

rise *v* (**rose, risen**) 上升 shàngshēng; (*get up*) 起床 qǐchuáng; (*revolt*) 起义 qǐyì; *n* 上升 shàngshēng; **give rise to** 引起 yǐnqǐ, 导致 dǎozhì; **rising** *adj* 上升的 shàngshēng de, 崛起的 juéqǐ de

risk *v* 冒风险 mào fēngxiǎn; *n* 风险 fēngxiǎn; **at risk** 在危险中 zài wēixiǎn zhōng; **risky** *adj* 危险的 wēixiǎn de, 冒险的 màoxiǎn de

rite *n* 仪式 yíshì

ritual *n* 仪式 yíshì; *adj* 仪式的 yíshì de

rival *v* 竞争 jìngzhēng; *n* 对手 duìshǒu; **rivalry** *n* 竞争 jìngzhēng, 敌对 díduì

river *n* 河 hé

road *n* 路 lù; **road sign** 路牌 lùpái; **roadside** *n* 路旁 lùpáng

roam *v* 漫步 mànbù, 漫游 mànyóu

roar *v/n* 咆哮 páoxiāo, 吼叫 hǒujiào

roast *v* 烤 kǎo

rob *v* 抢劫 qiǎngjié; **robber** *n* 强盗 qiángdào; **robbery** *n* 抢劫 qiǎngjié

robe *n* 长袍 chángpáo

robot *n* 机器人 jīqìrén

robust *adj* 强壮的 qiángzhuàng de, 精力充沛的 jīnglì chōngpèi de

rock *v* 摇 yáo, 动摇 dòngyáo; *n* 石头 shítou

rocket *n* 火箭 huǒjiàn

rod *n* 杆 gān, 棒 bàng

rode. *See* **ride**

role *n* 角色 juésè

roll *v* 滚动 gǔndòng; *n* 名单 míngdān; **roll-call** *n* 点名 diǎnmíng; **roller coaster** *n* 过山车 guòshānchē

romance *n* 浪漫故事 làngmàn gùshi; **romantic** *adj* 浪漫的 làngmàn de

Rome *n* 罗马 luómǎ; **Roman Catholic** *n* 天主教徒 tiānzhǔjiàotú; *adj* 天主教的 tiānzhǔjiào de; **Roman numeral** 罗马数字 luómǎ shùzì

roof *n* 屋顶 wūdǐng

room *n* (*house*) 房间 fángjiān; (*space*) 空间 kōngjiān; **make room for** 为 ... 让地方 wèi ... ràng dìfang; **room and board** 膳宿 shànsù; **roommate** *n* 室友 shìyǒu; **roomy** *adj* 宽敞的 kuānchang de

roost *v* 栖息 qīxī; *n* 栖息所 qīxīsuǒ, 卧室 wòshì; **rooster** *n* 公鸡 gōngjī

root *n* 根 gēn

rope *n* 绳子 shéngzi; **know the ropes** 知道内情 zhīdao nèiqíng; **learn the ropes** 摸窍门 mō qiàomén, 了解内幕 liǎojiě nèimù

rose *v see* **rise**; *n* 玫瑰 méiguī

rot *v* 腐烂 fǔlàn; **rotten** *adj* 腐烂的 fǔlàn de

rotate *v* (*cause to turn around*) (使) 旋转 (shǐ) xuánzhuǎn; (*take turns*) 轮流 lúnliú; **rotation** *n* 旋转 xuánzhuǎn; 轮流 lúnliú

rough *adj* (*coarse*) 粗糙的 cūcāo de; (*rude*) 粗暴的 cūbào

de; (*not fully detailed*) 粗略的 cūlüè de; **roughly** *adv*
(*rudely*) 粗暴地 cūbào de; (*approximately*) 大约 dàyuē

round *n* 回合 huíhé, 一轮 yī lún; *adj* 圆的 yuán de; *adv*
成圆圈地 chéng yuánquān de, 围绕地 wéirào de, 在四处
zài sìchù, 到处 dàochù; *prep* 围绕 wéirào, 环绕 huánrǎo

roundabout *n* (*fair*) 旋转木马 xuánzhuǎn mùmǎ; (*roads*)
环状交叉路 huánzhuàng jiāochālù

route *n* 路线 lùxiàn

routine *n* 常规 chángguī; *adj* 常规的 chángguī de

row *v* 划船 huáchuán; *n* 排 pái, 行 háng

royal *adj* 王室的 wángshì de, 皇家的 huángjiā de; **royalty** *n*
王室成员 wángshì chéngyuán; **royalties** *n* (*author*) 版税
bǎnshuì

rub *v* 擦 cā

rubber *n* 橡胶 xiàngjiāo, 橡皮 xiàngpí; **rubber band** 橡皮圈
xiàngpíquān; **rubber stamp** 橡皮图章 xiàngpí túzhāng

rubbish *n* 垃圾 lājī

rude *adj* 粗鲁的 cūlǔ de; **rudeness** *n* 粗鲁 cūlǔ

rudiment *n* 基础 jīchǔ; **rudimentary** *adj* 基础的 jīchǔ de

rug *n* 地毯 dìtǎn

rugged *adj* 崎岖的 qíqū de

ruin *v* 毁坏 huǐhuài, 破坏 pòhuài; *n* 毁灭 huǐmiè; **ruins** *n*
废墟 fèixū

rule *v* 统治 tǒngzhì; *n* (*code*) 规则 guīzé; (*control, government*)
统治 tǒngzhì; **as a rule** 通常 tōngcháng; **ruler** *n* (*person*)
统治者 tǒngzhìzhě; (*measuring*) 直尺 zhíchǐ; **ruling** *n*
裁决 cáijué; *adj* 统治的 tǒngzhì de

rum *n* 朗姆酒 lǎngmǔjiǔ

rummage *v* 到处翻寻 dàochù fānxún; *n* 翻箱倒柜的寻找
fānxiāng dǎoguì de xúnzhǎo

rumor *n* 谣言 yáoyán

run *v* (**ran, run**) 跑 pǎo; **run away** 逃跑 táopǎo; **run into**
遇见 yùjiàn; **run out** 用完 yòngwán; **run over** 碾过 niǎn
guò; **in the long run** 长久看来 chángjiǔ kànlái, 最后
zuìhòu

rung *v* see **ring**; *n* (*position*) 地位 dìwèi; (*ladder*) 横档
héngdǎng

runner *n* 赛跑者 sàipǎozhě; **runner-up** *n* 亚军 yàjūn

runway *n* 跑道 pǎodào

rural *adj* 乡下的 xiāngxià de, 农村的 nóngcūn de

rush *v* 匆忙 cōngmáng; 仓促 cāngcù; *n* 匆促 cōngcù; **rush**

hour 高峰时间 gāofēng shíjiān, 上下班时间 shàngxiàbān shíjiān

Russia *n* 俄国 éguó; **Russian** *n* (*people*) 俄国人 éguórén; (*language*) 俄语 éyǔ; *adj* 俄国的 éguó de

rusty *adj* 生锈的 shēngxiù de, (*fig.*) 荒疏的 huāngshū de

ruthless *adj* 无情的 wúqíng de

S

sabbatical *adj* 安息日的 ānxīrì de; **sabbatical leave** (*university*) 休假 xiūjià

sabotage *v/n* 阴谋破坏 yīnmóu pòhuài

sack *v* 解雇 jiěgù; *n* 袋子 dàizi; **get sacked** 被解雇 bèi jiěgù

sacred *adj* 神圣的 shénshèng de

sacrifice *v/n* 牺牲 xīshēng

sad *adj* 悲伤的 bēishāng de; **sadden** *v* (使) 悲哀 (shǐ) bēiāi; **sadness** *n* 悲伤 bēishāng

saddle *n* 马鞍 mǎ'ān

sadistic *adj* 虐待狂的 nüèdàikuáng de

safe *adj* 安全的 ānquán de; **safely** *adv* 安全地 ānquán de; **safety** *n* 安全 ānquán

safeguard *v* 保护 bǎohù

said. See **say**

sail *v* 航行 hángxíng; *n* 帆 fān; **set sail** 起航 qǐháng; **sailing** *n* 航行 hángxíng; **sailboat** *n* 帆船 fānchuán; **sailor** *n* 海员 hǎiyuán; 水手 shuǐshǒu

saint *n* 圣人 shèngrén

sake *n* 缘故 yuángù, 理由 lǐyóu; **for the sake of** 为了 wèile, 出于 ... 的缘故 chūyú ... de yuángù

salad *n* 沙拉 shālā

salary *n* 工资 gōngzī

sale *n* 销售 xiāoshòu; (*discount*) 减价销售 jiǎnjià xiāoshòu; **salesman** *n* 售货员 shòuhuòyuán

saline *adj* 含盐的 hányán de

saliva *n* 唾液 tuòyè, 口水 kǒu shuǐ

salmon *n* 鲑鱼 guīyú

saloon *n* 客厅 kètīng, 沙龙 shālóng

salt *n* 盐 yán; **salty** *adj* 咸的 xián de

salute *v* 向 ... 敬礼 xiàng ... jìnglǐ; *n* 敬礼 jìnglǐ

salvage *v* 抢救 qiǎngjiù

salvation *n* 拯救 zhěngjiù

same *adj* 相同的 xiāngtóng de; **at the same time** 与此同时 yǔcǐ tóngshí

sample *n* 样品 yàngpǐn

sanction *v* (*ratify*) 批准 pīzhǔn; (*approval*) 认可 rènkě; *n* (*approval*) 认可 rènkě; (*punishment*) 制裁 zhìcái

sand *n* 沙子 shāzi; **sandpaper** *n* 砂纸 shāzhǐ; **sandy** *adj* 沙状的 shāzhuàng de

sandal *n* 凉鞋 liángxié

sandwich *n* 三明治 sānmíngzhì

sane *adj* 理智的 lǐzhì de; **sanity** *n* 神志正常 shénzhì zhèngcháng

sang. *See* **sing**

sanitation *n* 卫生 wèishēng; **sanitary** *adj* 卫生的 wèishēng de

sarcasm *n* 讽刺 fěngcì, 嘲笑 cháoxiào; **sarcastic** *adj* 讽刺的 fěngcì de

sardine *n* 沙丁鱼 shādīngyú

sat. *See* **sit**

satellite *n* 卫星 wèixīng

satire *n* 讽刺 fěngcì; **satirical** *adj* 讽刺的 fěngcì de; **satirize** *v* 讽刺性描写 fěngcìxìng miáoxiě

satisfy *v* (使) 满意 (shǐ) mǎnyì, 满足 mǎnzú, **be satisfied with** 对 ... 满意 duì ... mǎnyì; **satisfaction** *n* 满意 mǎnyì; **satisfactory** *adj* 令人满意的 lìng rén mǎnyì de

saturate *v* 浸 jìn, (使) 饱和 (shǐ) bǎohé; **saturation** *n* 浸透 jìntòu; **saturation point** 饱和点 bǎohédiǎn

Saturday *n* 星期六 xīngqīliù

sauce *n* 调味汁 tiáowèizhī, 佐料 zuǒliào

saucer *n* 茶托 chátuō; **flying saucer** 飞碟 fēidié

sausage *n* 香肠 xiāngcháng

savage *adj* 野蛮的 yěmán de, 残忍的 cánrěn de; **savagery** *n* 野性 yěxìng

save *v* (*deposit*) 存 cún; (*economize*) 节省 jiéshěng; (*rescue*) 救 jiù; **savings** *n* 存款 cúnkuǎn; **savings bank** 储蓄银行 chǔxù yínháng

savor *v* 品尝 pǐncháng; **savory** *adj* 开胃的 kāiwèi de

saw *v see* **see**; (**sawed**, **sawn/sawed**) 锯 jù; *n* 锯子 jùzi

sawn. *See* **saw**

say *v* (**said**, **said**) 说 shuō; **saying** *n* 谚语 yànyǔ, 俗话 súhuà; **have no say** 没有说话的资格 méiyǒu shuōhuà de zīgé

scaffolding *n* 脚手架 jiǎoshǒujià

scale *v* 攀登 pāndēng; *n* (*proportion*) 比例 bǐlì; (*size*) 规模 guīmó; (*music*) 音阶 yīnjiē; **scale down** 缩减 suōjiǎn

scales *n* 天平 tiānpíng; **fish scales** 鱼鳞 yúlín

scallop *n* 干贝 gānbèi

scalp *n* 头皮 tóupí

scan *v* 浏览 liúlǎn, 扫描 sǎomiáo; *n* 扫描仪 sǎomiáoyí

scandal *n* 丑闻 chǒuwén

Scandinavia *n* 斯堪的纳维亚 sīkāndí'nàwéiyà;
  Scandinavian *n* 斯堪的纳维亚人 sīkāndí'nàwéiyàrén;
  adj 斯堪的纳维亚的 sīkāndí'nàwéiyà de

scant *adj* 不足的 bùzú de, 欠缺的 qiànquē de; **scanty** *adj*
  缺乏的 quēfá de, 不足的 bùzú de; **scantily** *adv* 缺乏地
  quēfá de, 吝啬地 lìnsè de

scapegoat *n* 替罪羊 tìzuìyáng

scar *n* 伤疤 shāngbā

scarce *adj* 缺乏的 quēfá de, 稀有的 xīyǒu de; **scarcely** *adv*
  几乎不 jīhū bù, 几乎没有 jīhū méiyǒu; **scarcity** *n* 稀少
  xīshǎo, 缺乏 quēfá

scare *v* 吓唬 xiàhu; *n* 恐慌 kǒnghuāng; **scared** *adj* 恐惧的
  kǒngjù de; **scary** *adj* 令人恐慌的 lìng rén kǒnghuāng de,
  吓人的 xiàrén de; **scarecrow** *n* 稻草人 dàocǎorén

scarf *n* 围巾 wéijīn

scarlet *adj* 猩红的 xīnghóng de

scatter *v* 撒 sā, 散 sàn

scene *n* 情景 qíngjǐng, 景色 jǐngsè; **scenic** *adj* 景色优美的
  jǐngsè yōuměi de; **scenery** *n* 风景 fēngjǐng

scent *n* 气味 qìwèi, 香味 xiāngwèi

schedule *v* 约时间 yuē shíjiān, 安排时间 ānpái shíjiān; *n*
  时间表 shíjiānbiǎo

scheme *n* (*plan*) 计划 jìhuà; (*intrigue*) 阴谋 yīnmóu

schizophrenia *n* 精神分裂症 jīngshén fēnlièzhèng;
  schizophrenic *adj* 精神分裂症的 jīngshén fēnlièzhèng de

scholar *n* 学者 xuézhě; **scholarship** *n* (*money*) 奖学金
  jiǎngxuéjīn; (*learning*) 学问 xuéwen; **scholarly** *adj*
  有学者气质的 yǒu xuézhě qìzhì de, 学术的 xuéshù de

school *n* 学校 xuéxiào; **schoolboy** *n* 男生 nánshēng;
  schoolgirl *n* 女生 nǚshēng; **schoolteacher** *n* 教师 jiàoshī

science *n* 科学 kēxué; **scientist** *n* 科学家 kēxuéjiā; **scientific**
  adj 科学的 kēxué de

scissors *n* 剪刀 jiǎndāo

scold *v* 责骂 zémà, 训斥 xùnchì

scooter *n* 单脚滑行车 dānjiǎo huáxíngchē

scope *n* 范围 fànwéi

score *v* 得分 défēn; *n* 分数 fēnshù, 比分 bǐfēn; **scorer** *n* 记分员
  jìfēnyuán

scorn v 鄙视 bǐshì; n 轻蔑 qīngmiè; **scornful** adj 轻蔑的 qīngmiè de

Scotland n 苏格兰 sūgélán; **Scot** n 苏格兰人 sūgélánrén; **Scotch** n (people) 苏格兰人 sūgélánrén; (language) 苏格兰语 sūgélányǔ; adj (people) 苏格兰人的 sūgélánrén de; **Scottish** adj 苏格兰的 sūgélán de

scout n 侦察员 zhēncháyuán

scramble v (climb) 攀登 pāndēng; (compete) 争夺 zhēngduó; (move hastily) 仓促行动 cāngcù xíngdòng; (eggs) 炒蛋 chǎodàn

scrap v (discard) 扔弃 rēngqì; (destroy) 拆毁 chāihuǐ; n 碎片 suìpiàn, 废料 fèiliào; **scrap paper** 草稿纸 cǎogǎozhǐ

scratch v 抓破 zhuāpò; n 抓痕 zhuāhén

scream v/n 尖叫 jiānjiào

screen n 筛选 shāixuǎn; n 屏幕 píngmù, 银幕 yínmù

screw v 上螺丝 shàng luósī; n 螺丝钉 luósīdīng; **screwdriver** n 螺丝刀 luósīdāo; **screw up** 搞砸 gǎozá

script n (movie, play) 剧本 jùběn; (text) 文字稿 wénzìgǎo

scrutinize v 详细审查 xiángxì shěnchá; **scrutiny** n 详细审查 xiángxì shěnchá

sculpt v 雕刻 diāokè; **sculptor** n 雕刻家 diāokèjiā; **sculpture** n 雕塑 diāosù

scum n 糟粕 zāopò

scruple n (moral standards) 审慎 shěnshèn; (hesitation) 犹豫 yóuyù; **scrupulous** adj 小心谨慎的 xiǎoxīnjǐnshèn de

sea n 海 hǎi; **sea-level** n 海平面 hǎipíngmiàn; **seafood** n 海味 hǎiwèi; **seagull** n 海鸥 hǎi'ōu; **seahorse** n 海马 hǎimǎ; **sea-lion** n 海狮 hǎishī; **seaman** n (pl seamen) 海员 hǎiyuán; **sea shell** n 贝壳 bèiké; **seashore** n 海岸 hǎi'àn; **seasick** adj 晕船的 yùnchuán de; **seaside** n 海滨 hǎibīn

seal v (stamp) 盖印 gàiyìn; (close) 密封 mìfēng; n (stamp) 印章 yìnzhāng; (zool) 海豹 hǎibào

search v/n 搜寻 sōuxún, 搜索 sōusuǒ; **searchlight** n 探照灯 tànzhàodēng; **search warrant** n 搜查令 sōucháling

season n 季节 jìjié; **seasonal** adj 季节性的 jìjiéxìng de

seat n 座位 zuòwèi; **seat belt** n 安全带 ānquándài

seclude v 隔离 gélí; **secluded** adj 隐退的 yǐntuì de, 隐蔽的 yǐnbì de; **seclusion** n 隔离 gélí

second n (time) 秒钟 miǎozhōng; num 第二 dì'èr, 第二的 dì èr de; **second class** 二等 èrděng; **second-hand** adj 二手的 èrshǒu de

secondary *adj* 次要的 cìyào de, 二级的 èrjí de; **secondary school** 中学 zhōngxué

secret *n* 秘密 mìmì; *adj* 秘密的 mìmì de; **secret agent** 特务 tèwu; **secret service** 特工 tègōng; **secrecy** *n* 秘密 mìmì; **secretly** *adv* 秘密地 mìmìde

secretary *n* 秘书 mìshū; **secretary of state** 国务卿 guówùqīng; **secretarial** *adj* 秘书的 mìshū de

sect *n* 教派 jiàopài; **sectarian** *adj* 宗派主义的 zōngpàizhǔyì de

section *n* (*part*) 部分 bùfen; (*department*) 部门 bùmén

sector *n* 部门 bùmén, 行业 hángyè

secular *adj* (*non-religious*) 非宗教的 fēizōngjiào de; (*worldly*) 现世的 xiànshì de, 世俗的 shìsú de; (*long-standing*) 长期的 chángqī de

secure *v* (*protect*) 保护 bǎohù; (*obtain*) 获取 huòqǔ; *adj* 安全的 ānquán de; **security** *n* 安全 ānquán; (*deposit*) 押金 yājīn

sedate *adj* 安详的 ānxiáng de, 沉着的 chénzhuó de; **sedative** *adj* 镇定的 zhèndìng de

seduce *v* 引诱 yǐnyòu; **seduction** *n* 诱惑 yòuhuò; **seductive** *adj* 诱人的 yòurén de

see *v* (**saw**, **seen**) 看见 kànjiàn; **see off** 送行 sòngxíng; **see through** 识破 shípò; **see you later!** 再见! zàijiàn

seed *n* 种子 zhǒngzi; **seedling** *n* 秧苗 yāngmiáo; **seedless** *adj* 无籽的 wúzǐ de

seek *v* (**sought**, **sought**) 寻求 xúnqiú

seem *v* 好像 hǎoxiàng; **seemingly** *adv* 表面上 biǎomiàn shàng

seethe *v* 发怒 fānù; **seething** *adj* 极度恼怒的 jídù nǎonù de

seen. *See* **see**

segment *n* 段 duàn; 片段 piànduàn

segregate *v* 隔离 gélí; **segregation** *n* 隔离 gélí

seize *v* (*grasp*) 抓住 zhuāzhù; (*capture*) 夺取 duóqǔ; (*confiscate*) 没收 mòshōu; **seizure** *n* 夺取 duóqǔ

seldom *adv* 不常 bù cháng, 很少 hěn shǎo

select *v* 选择 xuǎnzé; **selection** *n* 选择 xuǎnzé; **selective** *adj* 有选择的 yǒu xuǎnzé de

self *n* (*pl* **selves**) 自己 zìjǐ

self-adhesive *adj* 自粘的 zìzhān de

self-centered *adj* 自我中心的 zìwǒ zhōngxīn de

self-conscious *adj* 自觉的 zìjué de; (*shy*) 害羞的 hàixiū de; **self-consciousness** *n* 自觉 zìjué; 害羞 hàixiū

self-confidence *n* 自信 zìxìn; **self-confident** *adj* 自信的 zìxìn de

self-control *n* 自制 zìzhì

self-defense *n* 自卫 zìwèi

self-employed *adj* 自雇的 zìgù de

self-esteem *n* 自尊 zìzūn

self-explanatory *adj* 自明的 zìmíng de

self-government *n* 自治 zìzhì

self-interest *n* 私利 sīlì

selfish *adj* 自私的 zìsī de; **selfishness** *n* 自私 zìsī

selfless *adj* 无私的 wúsī de

self-made *adj* 自制的 zìzhì de, 自力更生的 zìlì gēngshēng de

self-respect *n* 自尊 zìzūn

self-righteous *adj* 自以为是的 zì yǐ wéi shì de; **self-righteousness** *n* 自以为是 zì yǐ wéi shì

self-rule *n* 自治 zìzhì

self-service *n* 自助式销售 zìzhùshì xiāoshòu

self-sufficiency *n* 自给自足 zì jǐ zì zú; **self-sufficient** *adj* 自给自足的 zì jǐ zì zú de

sell *v* (**sold, sold**) 卖 mài; **sell out** 售完 shòuwán; **seller** *n* 卖方 màifāng; **best-seller** *n* 畅销书 chàngxiāoshū

semantic *adj* 语义的 yǔyì de; **semantics** *n* 语义学 yǔyìxué

semblance *n* 外表 wàibiǎo

semen *n* 精液 jīngyè

semicolon *n* 分号 fēnhào

semifinal *n* 半决赛 bànjuésài

seminar *n* 研讨会 yántǎohuì

senate *n* 参议院 cānyìyuàn; **senator** *n* 参议员 cānyìyuán

send *v* (**sent, sent**) (*take to*) 送 sòng; (*mail*) 寄 jì

senile *adj* 衰老的 shuāilǎo de; **senility** *n* 高龄 gāolíng, 老态龙钟 lǎotài lóngzhōng

senior *n* (*old people*) 老人 lǎorén; (*university*) 大学四年级学生 dàxué sìniánjí xuésheng; *adj* 年长的 niánzhǎng de, 资深的 zīshēn de; **seniority** *n* 资历 zīlì

sensation *n* (*feeling*) 感觉 gǎnjué; (*excitement*) 轰动 hōngdòng; **sensational** *adj* 耸人听闻的 sǒng rén tīngwén de

sense *v* 感觉 gǎnjué, 觉察 juéchá; *n* 感觉 gǎnjué, 官能 guānnéng; **senseless** *adj* (*feeling*) 无感觉的 wú gǎnjué de; (*meaning*) 无意义的 wúyìyì de

sensible *adj* 明智的 míngzhì de, 有判断力的 yǒu pànduànlì de

sensitive *adj* 敏感的 mǐngǎn de; **sensitivity** *n* 敏感性 mǐngǎnxìng

sensual *adj* 肉欲的 ròuyù de, 感官的 gǎnguān de

sent. *See* send

sentence *v* 宣判 xuānpàn, 判决 pànjué; *n* (*gram*) 句子 jùzi; (*law*) 判决 pànjué

sentiment *n* 情感 qínggǎn; **sentimental** *adj* 感伤性的 gǎnshāngxìng de; 感情脆弱的 gǎnqíng cuìruò de

sentry *n* 岗哨 gǎngshào

separate *v* 分开 fēnkāi; *v*; *adj* 分开的 fēnkāi de; **separation** *n* 分离 fēnlí

September *n* 九月 jiǔyuè

septic *adj* 腐败的 fǔbài de

sequel *n* 续集 xùjí

sequence *n* 顺序 shùnxù

sergeant *n* (*mil*) 中士 zhōngshì; (*police*) 警察小队长 jǐngchá xiǎoduìzhǎng

serial *n* 连续剧 liánxùjù; *adj* 连续的 liánxù de; **serial killer** 连环杀手 liánhuán shāshǒu

series *n* 系列 xìliè

serious *adj* 严肃的 yánsù de, 认真的 rènzhēn de

sermon *n* 布道 bùdào, 说教 shuōjiào

serpent *n* 蛇 shé; (*fig. person*) 阴险的人 yīnxiǎn de rén

servant *n* 佣人 yòngrén

serve *v* 服务 fúwù; 供应 gōngyìng; 担任 dānrèn; (*tennis, volleyball, etc.*) 发球 fāqiú; **service** *n* 服务 fúwù; **service station** 加油站 jiāyóuzhàn

session *n* (*meeting*) 会议 huìyì; (*court*) 开庭 kāitíng

set *v* (**set, set**) (put) 摆放 bǎifàng (*post, appoint*) 安置 ānzhì; (*fix*) 确定 quèdìng; *n* 一套 yī tào; *adj* 固定的 gùdìng de; **set fire to** 放火烧 fàng huǒ shāo; **set free** 释放 shìfàng; **set off/out** 出发 chūfā; **set sail** 启航 qǐháng; **set up** 设立 shèlì; 装配 zhuāngpèi; **setback** *n* 挫折 cuòzhé; **setting** *n* (*surroundings*) 环境 huánjìng; (*locale*) 场景 chǎngjǐng

settle *v* (*reside*) 定居 dìngjū; (*solve*) 解决 jiějué; **settlement** *n* 定居 dìngjū; 解决 jiějué, 和解 héjiě; (*community*) 小村落 xiǎocūnluò; (*colony*) 殖民 zhímín

seven *num* 七 qī; **seventh** *num* 第七 dì qī

seventeen *num* 十七 shíqī; **seventeenth** *num* 第十七 dì shíqī

seventy *num* 七十 qīshí; **seventies** *num* 第七十 dì qīshí

sever *v* 切断 qiēduàn, 中断 zhōngduàn, 中止 zhōngzhǐ

several *adj* 几 (个) jǐ (gè)

severe *adj* 严厉的 yánlì de, 严重的 yánzhòng de; **severity** *n* 严厉 yánlì, 严重 yánzhòng, 严重性 yánzhòngxìng

sew *v* (**sewed, sewn/sewed**) 缝 féng; **sewing** *n* 缝纫 féngrèn; **sewing machine** 缝纫机 féngrènjī

sewage *n* 污水 wūshuǐ

sex *n* 性 xìng; **sexuality** *n* 性事 xìngshì, 性活动 xìnghuódòng; **sexual** *adj* 性的 xìng de; **sexy** *adj* 性感的 xìnggǎn de

shabby *adj* 破烂的 pòlàn de, 邋遢的 lāta de

shade *n* 荫 yìn

shadow *n* 影子 yǐngzi; **shadowy** *adj* 阴凉的 yīnliáng de, 模糊的 móhu de

shake *v* (**shook, shaken**) 摇 yáo, 撼 hàn; (*hand*) 握 wò; **shake off** 摆脱 bǎituō; **shaky** *adj* 颤抖的 chàndǒu de, 不安的 bù'ān de, 摇晃的 yáohuàng de, 不牢的 bùláo de

shaken. *See* **shake**

shall (**should**). *See* **be**

shallow *adj* 浅的 qiǎn de, 肤浅的 fūqiǎn de

shame *n* 羞耻 xiūchǐ, 耻辱 chǐrǔ; **shameful** *adj* 可耻的 kěchǐ de; **shameless** *adj* 无耻的 wúchǐ de

shampoo *n* 洗发液 xǐfàyè

shape *v* (使) 成形 (shǐ) chéngxíng; *n* 形状 xíngzhuàng

share *v* 共有 gòngyǒu, 共用 gòngyòng, 共享 gòngxiǎng

shark *n* 鲨鱼 shāyú

sharp *adj* 锋利的 fēnglì de; **sharpen** *v* (使) 锋利 (shǐ) fēnglì

shatter *v* 打碎 dǎsuì, 粉碎 fěnsuì

shave *v* (**shaved, shaved/shaven**) 剃 tì

she *pron* 她 tā

shed *v* (**shed, shed**) (使) 脱落 (shǐ) tuōluò, 散发 sànfā; **shed blood** 流血 liúxuè; *n* 棚 péng

sheep *n* (*pl* **sheep**) 绵羊 miányáng; **sheepdog** *n* 牧羊犬 mùyángquǎn

sheer *adj* 纯粹的 chúncuì de, 完全的 wánquán de

sheet *n* (*bed*) 被单 bèidān; (*paper*) 纸张 zhǐzhāng

shelf *n* (*pl* **shelves**) 架子 jiàzi

shell *v* 炮击 pàojī; *n* (*sea*) 贝壳 bèiké; (*egg*) 蛋壳 dànké; (*cannon*) 炮弹 pàodàn; **shellfish** *n* 有壳水生动物 yǒuké shuǐshēng dòngwù

shelter *v* 掩蔽 yǎnbì, 庇护 bìhù; *n* 避难处 bìnánchù, 掩蔽处 yǎnbìchù

shelve *v* 搁置 gēzhì

sheriff *n* 郡治安官 jùnzhì'ānguān

shield *v* 保护 bǎohù, 庇护 bìhù; *n* 盾 dùn

shift *v* (*change*) 改变 gǎibiàn; (*transfer*) 转移 zhuǎnyí; (*transform*) 变换 biànhuàn; *n* (*transfer*) 转移 zhuǎnyí; (*period of work*) 轮班 lúnbān

shine *v* (**shined/shone**, **shined/shone**) 发光 fāguāng; *n* 光泽 guāngzé; **shiny** *adj* 发光的 fāguāng de

ship *v* 运输 yùnshū, 运送 yùnsòng; *n* 船 chuán; **shipping** *n* 海运 hǎiyùn; 运送 yùnsòng; **shipwreck** *n* 海难 hǎinàn

shipment *n* 出货 chūhuò, 运送 yùnsòng

shirt *n* 衬衫 chènshān

shiver *v* 哆嗦 duōsuō, 颤抖 chàndǒu

shock *v* (使) 震惊 (shǐ) zhènjīng; *n* 震惊 zhènjīng, 休克 xiūkè; **shocking** *adj* 令人震惊的 lìng rén zhènjīng de

shoddy *adj* (*inferior in quality*) 劣质的 lièzhì de, (*rude*) 卑鄙的 bēibǐ de

shoe *n* 鞋子 xiézi; **shoe-string** *n* 鞋带 xiédài

shone. *See* **shine**

shook. *See* **shake**

shoot *v* (**shot, shot**) 射击 shèjī, 开枪 kāiqiāng; *n* (*sprout*) 嫩芽 nènyá; (*firearm*) 射击 shèjī; **shooting** *n* 射击 shèjī, 开枪 kāiqiāng

shop *v* 购物 gòuwù; *n* 商店 shāngdiàn; **shop assistant** *n* 售货员 shòuhuòyuán

shopkeeper *n* 店主 diànzhǔ

shoplifting *n* 入店行窃 rùdiàn xíngqiè

shopping *n* 购物 gòuwù; **shopping center/mall** 购物中心 gòuwù zhōngxīn

shore *n* 海岸 hǎi'àn

short *adj* (*of people*) 矮 ǎi; (*of objects*) 短 duǎn; **in short** 简而言之 jiǎn ér yán zhī; **shorten** *v* 缩短 suōduǎn; **shortage** *n* 短缺 duǎnquē; **shortly** *adv* 不久 bù jiǔ, 很快 hěn kuài

shortcoming *n* 缺点 quēdiǎn

shortcut *n* 捷径 jiéjìng

short-circuit *n* 短路 duǎnlù; *v* (使) 短路 (shǐ) duǎnlù

short-lived *adj* 短命的 duǎnmìng de

shorts *n* 短裤 duǎnkù

short-sighted *adj* 眼光短浅的 yǎnguāng duǎnqiǎn de

short story *n* 短篇小说 duǎnpiān xiǎoshuō

short-term *adj* 短期的 duǎnqī de

short wave *n* 短波 duǎnbō

shot *v see* shoot; *n* (*gun*) 射击 shèjī, (*gun*) 开枪 kāiqiāng; (*injection*) 注射 zhùshè; (*basketball*) 投篮 tóulán

should *v see* **shall**; *aux* 应该 yīnggāi
shoulder *n* 肩膀 jiānbǎng
shout *v* 叫 jiào, 喊 hǎn
shove *v* 推 tuī
shovel *v* 铲 chǎn; *n* 铁铲 tiěchǎn
show *v* (**showed**, **shown/showed**) 表示 biǎoshì, 显示 xiǎnshì, 给 ... 看 gěi ... kàn; *n* (*exhibition*) 展览 zhǎnlǎn; (*performance*) 演出 yǎnchū; **show off** 炫耀 xuànyào, 卖弄 màinòng; **show up** 露面 lòumiàn, 出席 chūxí; **show sb. around** 领人参观 lǐng rén cānguān; **show business** 娱乐行业 yúlè hángyè
shower *n* 淋浴 línyù
showroom *n* 陈列室 chénlièshì
shrimp *n* 虾 xiā
shrine *n* 神祠 shéncí, 神龛 shénkān
shrink *v* (**shrank**, **shrunk**) 收缩 shōusuō, 缩小 suōxiǎo
shrug *v* 耸肩 sǒngjiān
shudder *v* 战栗 zhànlì, 发抖 fādǒu
shuffle *v* (*cards*) 洗牌 xǐ pái; (*reorganize*) 改组 gǎizǔ
shut *v* (**shut**, **shut**) 关闭 guānbì; **shut out** 关在外面 guān zài wàimian, 排除在外 páichú zàiwài; **shut up** 闭嘴 bìzuǐ
shutter *n* (*window*) 百叶窗 bǎiyèchuāng; (*camera*) 快门 kuàimén
shuttle *v* 穿梭 chuānsuō; *n* (*loom*) 梭子 suōzi; (*space*) 航天飞机 hángtiān fēijī; (*bus, train, etc.*) 穿梭往返的车辆 chuānsuō wǎngfǎn de chēliàng
shy *adj* 腼腆的 miǎntiǎn de, 害羞的 hàixiū de
sick *adj* (*ill*) 有病的 yǒubìng de; (*nausea*) 恶心的 ěxin de; **sick leave** 病假 bìngjià; **sicken** *v* (*make disgusted*) (使)人厌恶 (shǐ) rén yànwù; (*make ill*) 生病 shēngbìng; **sickness** *n* 疾病 jíbìng
side *n* 边 biān, 面 miàn, 方 fāng, 方面 fāngmiàn; **side dish** 配菜 pèicài; **side effect** 副作用 fùzuòyòng; **sideways** *adv* 向旁边地 xiàng pángbiān de, 横向地 héngxiàng de
siege *n* 包围 bāowéi, 围困 wéikùn, 围攻 wéigōng
sigh *v/n* 叹息 tànxī
sight *n* (*vision*) 视力 shìlì; (*view*) 视野 shìyě; (*scene*) 景象 jǐngxiàng; **sightseeing** *n* 观光 guānguāng
sign *v* 签名 qiānmíng; *n* 标记 biāojì, 标志 biāozhì; **sign language** 手语 shǒuyǔ
signal *v* 发信号 fā xìnhào; *n* 信号 xìnhào
signature *n* 签名 qiānmíng

signify *v* 表示 biǎoshì; **significance** *n* 意义 yìyì, 重要性 zhòngyàoxìng; **significant** *adj* 有意义的 yǒu yìyì de, 重要的 zhòngyào de

silence *n* 沉默 chénmò, 寂静 jìjìng; **silent** *adj* 沉默的 chénmò de, 寂静的 jìjìng de

silk *n* 丝绸 sīchóu

silly *adj* 傻的 shǎ de, 愚蠢的 yúchǔn de

silver *n* 银 yín, 银色 yínsè; *adj* 银的 yín de, 银色的 yínsè de

similar *adj* 相似的 xiāngsì de; **similarity** *n* 相似 xiāngsì

simple *adj* 简单的 jiǎndān de, 朴素的 pǔsù de; **simplicity** *n* 简单 jiǎndān; **simplify** *v* 简化 jiǎnhuà; **simply** *adv* 简单地 jiǎndān de; 仅仅 jǐnjǐn; 简直 jiǎnzhí

simulate *v* 模拟 mónǐ; **simulation** *n* 模拟 mónǐ, 模仿 mófǎng

simultaneous *adj* 同时的 tóngshí de

sin *v* 犯过错 fàn guòcuò; *n* 罪孽 zuìniè

since *conj* (*time*) 自 ... 以来 zì ... yǐlái; (*because*) 既然 jìrán

sincere *adj* 真诚的 zhēnchéng de; **sincerity** *n* 真挚 zhēnzhì

sing *v* (**sang**, **sung**) 唱 chàng; **singer** *n* 歌手 gēshǒu; **singing** *n* 歌唱 gēchàng

single *v* (*single out*) 挑出 tiāo chū; **single** *adj* (*unmarried*) 单身的 dānshēn de; (*one*) 单一的 dānyī de; **single-minded** *adj* 一心一意的 yī xīn yī yì de

singular *n* 单数 dānshù; *adj* (*gram*) 单数的 dānshù de; (*extraordinary*) 非凡的 fēifán de; (*only one*) 唯一的 wéiyī de; (*rare*) 罕有的 hǎnyǒu de

sinister *adj* 险恶的 xiǎn'è de

sink *v* (**sank**, **sunk**) 下沉 xiàchén, 沉没 chénmò; **sink in** 被理会 bèi lǐhuì, 被理解 bèi lǐjiě; *n* 水池 shuǐchí

sinus *n* 窦 dòu; **sinusitis** *n* 窦炎 dòuyán

siphon *v* 虹吸管 hóngxīguǎn; **siphon off** 吸出 xī chū

sir *n* 先生 xiānsheng

siren *n* 警报器 jǐngbàoqì, 警笛 jǐngdí

sister *n* (*older*) 姐姐 jiějie; (*younger*) 妹妹 mèimei; **sister-in-law** *n* 嫂子 sǎozi (*older brother's wife*) sǎozi; (*husband's sister*) 姑子 gūzi; (*younger brother's wife*) 弟媳 dìxí; (*wife's sister*) 姨子 yízi

sit *v* (**sat**, **sat**) 坐 zuò; **sit down** 坐下 zuò xià; **baby-sit** *v* 照看婴儿 zhàokàn yīng'ér, 担任保姆 dānrèn bǎomǔ

site *n* 地点 dìdiǎn

situate *v* (*使*) 位于 (shǐ) wèiyú; **be situated at/in** 位于 wèiyú; **situation** *n* 情形 qíngxíng, 情况 qíngkuàng

six *num* 六 liù; **sixth** *num* 第六 dì liù

sixteen *num* 十六 shíliù; **sixteenth** *num* 第十六 dì shíliù

sixty *num* 六十 liùshí; **sixties** *num* 第六十 dì liùshí

size *n* 尺寸 chǐcùn, 大小 dàxiǎo; **size up** 估量 gūliàng, 鉴定 jiàndìng; **sizeable** *adj* 相当大的 xiāngdāng dà de

skate *v* 溜冰 liūbīng; *n* 溜冰鞋 liūbīngxié; **skating** *n* 溜冰 liūbīng

skeleton *n* 骨骼 gǔgé

skeptic *n* 怀疑者 huáiyízhě; **skeptical** *adj* 怀疑的 huáiyí de

sketch *v* 作素描 zuò sùmiáo, 勾画 gōuhuà; *n* (*drawing, design*) 草图 cǎotú; (*outline*) 梗概 gěnggài; **sketchy** *adj* 粗略的 cūlüè de

ski *v* 滑雪 huáxuě; *n* 雪撬 xuěqiāo; **skiing** *n* 滑雪 huáxuě

skid *v* 打滑 dǎhuá

skill *n* 技巧 jìqiǎo, 技能 jìnéng; **skillful** *adj* 熟练的 shúliàn de; **skilled** *adj* 熟练的 shúliàn de

skin *v* 去皮 qùpí; *n* 皮肤 pífū; **skinny** *adj* 瘦的 shòu de

skip *v* 跳 tiào; 跳过 tiàoguò

skirt *n* 短裙 duǎnqún

skull *n* 头骨 tóugǔ

skunk *n* 臭鼬 chòuyòu

sky *n* 天空 tiānkōng; **skyscraper** *n* 摩天大楼 mótiān dàlóu

slack *adj* (*loose*) 松弛的 sōngchí de; (*sluggish*) 不景气的 bù jǐngqì de; (*negligent*) 疏忽的 shūhu de; **slacken** *v* 松弛 sōngchí, 懈怠 xièdài

slam *v* 猛放 měngfàng

slang *n* 俚语 lǐyǔ

slant *v/n* 倾斜 qīngxié

slap *v/n* 掴 guāi, 掌击 zhǎngjī

slash *v* 乱砍 luàn kǎn, 大幅度削减 dàfúdù xuējiǎn

slaughter *v* 屠宰 túzǎi, 屠杀 túshā; *n* 屠宰 túzǎi, 屠杀 túshā; **slaughterhouse** *n* 屠宰场 túzǎichǎng

slave *n* 奴隶 núlì; **slavery** *n* 奴隶制 núlìzhì

slay *v* (**slew/slayed, slain/slayed**) 杀死 shāsǐ

sled/sledge *n* 雪橇 xuěqiāo

sleep *v* (**slept, slept**) 睡 shuì; **sleeper** *n* (*train*) 卧铺 wòpù, 卧铺车厢 wòpù chēxiāng; **sleepless** *adj* 失眠的 shīmián de, 不眠的 bù mián de; **sleepy** *adj* 困的 kùn de

sleeve *n* 袖子 xiùzi

sleigh *n* 雪橇 xuěqiāo

slender *adj* 苗条的 miáotiao de

slice *n* 薄片 báopiàn

slick *adj* 圆滑的 yuánhuá de
slide *v* (**slid, slid**) 滑动 huádòng, 滑行 hoaxing; *n* 幻灯片 huàndēngpiàn
slight *adj* 轻微的 qīngwēi de, 些微的 xiēwēi de; **slightly** *adv* 轻微地 qīngwēi de, 些微地 xiēwēi de
slim *adj* 苗条的 miáotiao de, 纤细的 xiānxì de
slimy *adj* 粘糊糊的 niánhuhu de
slip *v* 滑倒 huá dǎo; *n* (*fall*) 滑倒 huá dǎo; (*error*) 失误 shīwù; (*paper*) 纸片 zhǐpiàn
slipper *n* 拖鞋 tuōxié
slippery *adj* 滑的 huá de
slit *v* (**slit, slit**) 撕裂 sīliè; *n* 裂缝 lièfèng
slogan *n* 口号 kǒuhào
slope *n* 斜坡 xiépō
sloppy *adj* (*loose*) 宽松的 kuānsōng de; (*wet*) 潮湿的 cháoshī de; (*careless*) 草率的 cǎoshuài de; **sloppiness** *n* 草率 cǎoshuài
slot *n* (*time*) 时段 shíduàn; (*coin*) 投币口 tóubìkǒu
Slovak *n* (*people*) 斯洛伐克人 sīluòfákèrén; **Slovakia** *n* 斯洛伐克 sīluòfákè; **Slovakian** *n* 斯洛伐克人 sīluòfákèrén; *adj* 斯洛伐克的 sīluòfákè de
slow *v* (*slow down*) 慢下来 màn xiàlái; **slow** *adj* 慢的 màn de; **slowly** *adv* 缓慢地 huǎnmàn de
sluggish *adj* (*slow*) 迟缓的 chíhuǎn de; (*lazy*) 懒散的 lǎnsǎn de; (*slack*) 呆滞的 dāizhì de
slum *n* 贫民窟 pínmínkū
slump *v/n* 暴跌 bàodiē
sly *adj* 狡猾的 jiǎohuá de
smack *v* 带有 ... 味道 dàiyǒu ... wèidao; *n* 滋味 zīwèi
small *adj* 小的 xiǎo de
smart *adj* 聪明的 cōngming de
smash *v* 打碎 dǎsuì, 粉碎 fěnsuì
smear *v* 弄脏 nòngzàng, 涂 tú
smell *v* (**smelled/smelt smelled/smelt**) 闻 wén; **smelly** *adj* 发臭的 fāchòu de
smile *v/n* 微笑 wēixiào
smoke *v* 抽烟 chōuyān, 吸烟 xīyān; *n* 烟 yān; **smoking** *n* 吸烟 xīyān; **no smoking** 请勿吸烟 qǐngwù xīyān; **smoker** *n* 吸烟者 xīyānzhě
smooth *adj* 光滑的 guānghuá de, 平稳的 píngwěn de, 顺利的 shùnlì de; **smoothly** *adv* 光滑地 guānghuá de, 平稳地 píngwěn de, 顺利地 shùnlì de

smuggle *v* 走私 zǒusī; **smuggler** *n* 走私者 zǒusīzhě;
　smuggling *n* 走私活动 zǒusī huódòng

snack *n* 点心 diǎnxin, 小吃 xiǎochī; **snack bar** 小吃店
　xiǎochīdiàn

snail *n* 蜗牛 wōniú

snake *n* 蛇 shé

snap *v* 突然折断 tūrán zhéduàn, 突然崩溃 tūrán bēngkuì;
　snapshot *n* 快照 kuàizhào

snatch *v* 抢 qiǎng

sneak *v* 偷偷摸摸地做 tōutōumōmō de zuò; **sneak in/out**
　偷偷溜进去/出来 tōutōu liū jìn qu/chu lai

sneer *v* 讥讽 jīfěng, 嘲笑 cháoxiào

sneeze *v* 打喷嚏 dǎ pēntì; *n* 喷嚏 pēntì

sniff *v* (*smell*) 嗅 xiù; (*inhale*) 吸气 xīqì

snip *v* 剪 jiǎn, 剪断 jiǎnduàn; *n* 碎片 suìpiàn

snipe *v* 狙击 jūjī; **sniper** *n* 狙击手 jūjīshǒu

snob *n* 势利小人 shìlì xiǎorén, 自命不凡者 zìmìng bùfán zhě;
　snobbish *adj* 势力的 shìlì de

snore *v* 打鼾 dǎhān

snorkel *n* 通气管 tōngqìguǎn

snow *v* 下雪 xiàxuě; *n* 雪 xuě; **snowy** *adj* 下雪的 xiàxuě de;
　snowball *v* (*increase*) 滚雪球般地增长 gǔn xuěqiúbān de
　zēngzhǎng; *n* 雪球 xuěqiú; **snowball fight** 打雪仗 dǎ
　xuězhàng; **snowfall** *n* 降雪 jiàngxuě; **snowflake** *n* 雪花
　xuěhuā; **snowstorm** *n* 暴风雪 bàofēngxuě

so *adv* 如此 rúcǐ, 这么 zhème, 那么 nàme; **so-called** *adj*
　所谓的 suǒwèi de; **so long as** 只要 zhǐyào; **so that** 所以
　suǒyǐ, 因此 yīncǐ, 以便 yǐbiàn, 为使 wèishǐ; **and so on**
　等等 děngděng; **if so** 如果这样的话 rúguǒ zhèyàng de huà

soak *v* 浸 jìn, 泡 pào

soap *n* 肥皂 féizào; **soap opera** 肥皂剧 féizàojù

soar *v* 飞 fēi, 翱翔 áoxiáng

sob *v* 啜泣 chuòqì

sober *adj* 清醒的 qīngxǐng de, 冷静的 lěngjìng de

soccer *n* 足球 zúqiú

sociable *adj* 好交际的 hào jiāojì de, 随和的 suíhe de

social *adj* (*of society*) 社会的 shèhuì de; (*friendly*) 社交的
　shèjiāo de; **social worker** 社会工作者 shèhuì
　gōngzuòzhě; **social science** 社会科学 shèhuì kēxué;
　Social Security 社会保险 shèhuì bǎoxiǎn

socialism *n* 社会主义 shèhuìzhǔyì; **socialist** *n* 社会主义者
　shèhuìzhǔyìzhě; *adj* 社会主义的 shèhuìzhǔyì de

society *n* 社会 shèhuì; (*association*) 社团 shètuán

sociology *n* 社会学 shèhuìxué; **sociologist** *n* 社会学家 shèhuìxuéjiā; **sociological** *adj* 社会学的 shèhuìxué de

sock *n* 短袜 duǎnwà

socket *n* 插座 chāzuò; **eye socket** 眼窝 yǎnwō

soda *n* 苏打 sūdá

sofa *n* 沙发 shāfā

soft *adj* 软的 ruǎn de; **soften** *v* (使) 软化 (shǐ) ruǎnhuà

soil *v* 弄脏 nòngzàng; *n* 土壤 tǔrǎng

solar *adj* 太阳的 tàiyáng de, 日光的 rìguāng de; **solar power** 太阳能 tàiyángnéng

sold. *See* **sell**

soldier *n* 士兵 shìbīng, 军人 jūnrén

sole *n* (*of foot*) 脚掌 jiǎozhǎng; (*of shoe*) 鞋底 xiédǐ; *adj* 唯一的 wéiyī de

solemn *adj* 庄严的 zhuāngyán de, 严肃的 yánsù de

solicit *v* 募捐 mùjuān, 恳求 kěnqiú, 征求 zhēngqiú, 招揽 zhāolǎn

solid *n* 固体 gùtǐ; *adj* 固体的 gùtǐ de, 坚固的 jiāngù de

solitary *adj* 孤独的 gūdú de

solitude *n* 孤独 gūdú

solo *n* 独唱 dúchàng; *adj* 单独的 dāndú de

solution *n* 解决办法 jiějué bànfǎ; (*chem.*) 溶解 róngjiě

solve *v* 解决 jiějué

some *pron*; *adj* 一些 yīxiē, 大约 dàyuē; **somebody** *pron* 某人 mǒurén; 重要人物 zhòngyào rénwù; **somehow** *adv* 以某种方式 yǐ mǒuzhǒng fāngshì, 不知怎的 bù zhī zěnde; **someone** *pron* 某人 mǒurén; **something** *pron* 某事 mǒushì; 某物 mǒuwù; **sometime** *adv* 在某时 zài mǒushí; **sometimes** *adv* 有时 yǒushí; **somewhat** *adv* 有些 yǒuxiē, 稍微 shāowēi; **somewhere** *adv* 在某处 zài mǒuchù

son *n* 儿子 érzi; **son-in-law** *n* 女婿 nǚxù

song *n* 歌 gē

soon *adv* 不久 bùjiǔ, 很快 hěn kuài; **as soon as** 一 ... 就 yī ... jiù; **sooner or later** 迟早 chízǎo

soothe *v* (使) 平息 (shǐ) píngxī, 安慰 ānwèi; **soothing** *adj* 安慰性的 ānwèixìng de, 缓和的 huǎnhé de

sophisticated *adj* 老练的 lǎoliàn de, 有修养的 yǒu xiūyǎng de, 复杂的 fùzá de

soprano *n* 女高音 nǚgāoyīn

sore 痛 tòng, 痛处 tòngchù; *adj* 疼的 téng de; **sorely** *adv* 强烈的 qiángliè de, 非常 fēicháng

sorrow *n* 悲伤 bēishāng; **sorrowful** *adj* 悲伤的 bēishāng de

sorry *adj* 抱歉 bàoqiàn, 对不起 duìbùqǐ

sort *v* 分类 fēnlèi; *n* 种类 zhǒnglèi

so-so *adj* 马马虎虎的 mǎma hūhu de, 一般的 yībān de

sought. See **seek**

soul *n* 灵魂 línghún

sound *v* 听起来 tīng qilai; *n* 声音 shēngyīn; *adj* 健全的 jiànquán de, 合理的 hélǐ de; **sound-track** *n* 音带 yīndài; **soundproof** *adj* 隔音的 géyīn de

soup *n* 汤 tāng

sour *adj* 酸的 suān de

source *n* 来源 láiyuán

south *n* 南边 nánbian, 南方 nánfāng, 南部 nánbù; **southerly** *adj* 向南方的 xiàng nánfāng de; **southern** *adj* 南方的 nánfāng de; **southeast** *n* 东南 dōngnán; *adj* 东南的 dōngnán de; **southwest** *n* 西南 xīnán; *adj* 西南的 xīnán de

South America *n* 南美洲 nánměizhōu; **South American** *n* 南美洲人 nánměizhōurén

souvenir *n* 纪念品 jìniànpǐn

sovereign *n* 君主 jūnzhǔ; *adj* 主权的 zhǔquán de; **sovereign state** 主权国家 zhǔquán guójiā

sow *v* (**sowed**, **sown/sowed**) 播种 bōzhǒng

spa *n* 矿泉 kuàngquán, 温泉疗养地 wēnquán liáoyǎngdì

space *n* 空间 kōngjiān; **spaceman** *n* 宇航员 yǔhángyuán; **spaceship** *n* 太空船 tàikōngchuán; **space shuttle** 航天飞机 hángtiān fēijī; **spacious** *adj* 宽敞的 kuānchàng de

spade *n* 锹 qiāo

spades *n* (*playing cards*) 黑桃 hēitáo

spaghetti *n* 意大利面条 yìdàlì miàntiáo

Spain *n* 西班牙 xībānyá; **Spaniard** *n* 西班牙人 xībānyárén; **Spanish** *n* (*language*) 西班牙语 xībānyáyǔ; (*people*) 西班牙人 xībānyárén; *adj* 西班牙的 xībānyá de

span *n* 跨度 kuàdù, 范围 fànwéi

spanner *n* 扳手 bānshou

spare *v* 省掉 shěngdiào, 节约 jiéyuē; *adj* (*reserve*) 备用的 bèiyòng de; (*free*) 空闲的 kòngxián de; **spare time** 业余时间 yèyú shíjiān; **spare part** 备件 bèijiàn **spareribs** *n* 排骨 páigǔ; **spare tire** 备用胎 bèiyòngtāi; **sparing** *adj* 节俭的 jiéjiǎn de

spark *n* 火星 huǒxīng, 闪光 shǎnguāng; **spark plug** 火花塞 huǒhuāsāi

sparrow *n* 麻雀 máquè

sparse *adj* 稀疏的 xīshū de, 稀少的 xīshǎo de; **sparsely** *adv* 稀疏地 xīshū de, 稀少地 xīshǎo de

spasm *n* 痉挛 jìngluán, 抽搐 chōuchù

spat. *See* spit

spatial *adj* 空间的 kōngjiān de

speak *v* (**spoke, spoken**) 说 shuō, 发言 fāyán; **speaker** *n* 说话者 shuōhuàzhě, 演讲人 yǎnjiǎngrén; (*elec*) 扬声器 yángshēngqì; **speak up** 大声说 dàshēng shuō

spear *n* 矛 máo

special *adj* 特别的 tèbié de, 专门的 zhuānmén de; **specialize** *v* 专攻 zhuāngōng; 擅长于 shàncháng yú; **specialist** *n* 专家 zhuānjiā; **specialty** *n* 专业 zhuānyè, 特长 tècháng

species *n* 种类 zhǒnglèi

specify *v* 指定 zhǐdìng, 说明 shuōmíng; **specification** *n* 规格 guīgé; **specific** *adj* 明确的 míngquè de, 特定的 tèdìng de

specimen *n* 样品 yàngpǐn, 标本 biāoběn

spectacle *n* 奇观 qíguān; **spectacles** *n* 眼镜 yǎnjìng

spectacular *adj* 壮观的 zhuàngguān de

spectator *n* 观众 guānzhòng

speculate *v* (*guess*) 猜测 cāicè; (*business*) 投机 tóujī; **speculation** *n* 猜测 cāicè; 投机活动 tóujī huódòng; **speculative** *adj* 猜测的 cāicè; 投机的 tóujī de

speech *n* 演说 yǎnshuō, 发言 fāyán; **speechless** *adj* 说不出话的 shuō bù chū huà de

speed *v* (**sped/speeded, sped/speeded**) 超速 chāosù; **speed up** 加速 jiāsù; *n* 速度 sùdù; **speed limit** 限速 xiànsù; **speedy** *adj* 快速的 kuàisù de

spell *v* 拼写 pīnxiě; **spelling** *n* 拼写 pīnxiě; **spelling bee** 拼写比赛 pīnxiě bǐsài

spend *v* (**spent, spent**) (*time, money*) 花 huā, (*time, vacation*) 度过 dùguò

sperm *n* 精子 jīngzǐ, 精液 jīngyè

sphere *n* 范围 fànwéi, 领域 lǐngyù

spice *n* 调味品 tiáowèipǐn; **spicy** *adj* 辣的 là de

spider *n* 蜘蛛 zhīzhū

spike *n* 长钉 chángdīng

spill *v* (**spilt/spilled, spilt/spilled**) 溢出 yìchū, 溅出 jiànchū

spin *v* (**spun, spun**) 旋转 xuánzhuǎn; (*yarn*) 纺纱 fǎngshā

spinach *n* 菠菜 bōcài

spine *n* 脊椎的 jǐzhuī de; **spinal** *adj* 脊椎的 jǐzhuī de; **spinal cord** 脊椎 jǐzhuī

spiral *n* 螺旋 luóxuán; *adj* 螺旋的 luóxuán de

spirit *n* 精神 jīngshén, 灵魂 línghún; **spirits** *n* 情绪 qíngxù

spit *v* (**spit/spat, spit/spat**) 吐出 tǔ chū; *n* 唾液 tuòyè

spite *n* 恶意 èyì; **in spite of** 不管 bùguǎn, 尽管 jǐnguǎn; **spiteful** *adj* 恶意的 èyì de

splash *v* 溅 jiàn; *n* 飞溅 fēijiàn

splendor *n* 壮丽 zhuànglì, 壮观 zhuàngguān; **splendid** *adj* 壮丽的 zhuànglì de

split *v* (**split, split**) 裂开 lièkāi, 分离 fēnlí; *n* 裂口 lièkǒu, 裂缝 lièfèng

spoil *v* (**spoilt/spoiled, spoilt/spoiled**) (*damage*) 弄坏 nòng huài; (*indulgence*) 宠坏 chǒng huài

spoke. *See* **speak**

spokesman *n* 发言人 fāyánrén

sponge *n* 海绵 hǎimián; **spongy** *adj* 像海绵的 xiàng hǎimián de, 吸水的 xīshuǐ de

sponsor *v* 发起 fāqǐ, 赞助 zànzhù; *n* 主办人 zhǔbànrén, 赞助人 zànzhùrén

spontaneity *n* 自发性 zìfāxìng; **spontaneous** *adj* 自发的 zìfā de

spool *n* 线轴 xiànzhóu

spoon *n* 汤匙 tāngchí, 勺子 sháozi

sport *n* 运动 yùndòng; **sportsman** *n* 运动员 yùndòngyuán; **sportswoman** *n* 女运动员 nǚ yùndòngyuán

spot *v* 认出 rènchū, 发现 fāxiàn; *n* (*stain*) 斑点 bāndiǎn; (*place*) 地点 dìdiǎn; **on the spot** 当场 dāngchǎng; **spotless** *adj* 一尘不染的 yīchén bùrǎn de; **spotlight** *n* 聚光灯 jùguāngdēng

spouse *n* 配偶 pèi'ǒu

spout *n* 喷口 pēnkǒu

spur *v* 刺激 cìjī; **on the spur of the moment** 一时冲动之下 yīshí chōngdòng zhīxià

spray *v* 喷射 pēnshè; *n* 喷雾 pēnwù

spread *v* (**spread, spread**) (*stretch*) 伸展 shēnzhǎn; (*distribution*) 传播 chuánbō; *n* 伸展 shēnzhǎn; 传播 chuánbō

spring *v* (**sprang, sprung**) 跳 tiào, 跃 yuè; *n* (*season*) 春天 chūntiān; (*coil*) 弹簧 tánhuáng; (*water*) 源泉 yuánquán

sprinkle *v* 喷洒 pēnsǎ; **sprinkler** *n* 喷水装置 pēnshuǐ zhuāngzhì

sprint *v* 疾跑 jípǎo, 短跑 duǎnpǎo, 冲刺 chōngcì

spy *v* 侦察 zhēnchá, 暗中监视 ànzhōng jiānshì; *n* 间谍 jiàndié; **spying** *n* 侦察 zhēnchá, 监视 jiānshì

squad *n* 班 bān, 小队 xiǎoduì

squalid *adj* 污秽的 wūhuì de

squander *v* 浪费 làngfèi, 挥霍 huīhuò

square *n* (*shape*) 正方形 zhèngfāngxíng; (*place*) 广场 guǎngchǎng; *adj* 正方形的 zhèngfāngxíng de; **square kilometer** 平方公里 píngfāng gōnglǐ; **square meter** 平方米 píngfāngmǐ

squash *v* 挤压 jǐyā, 压扁 yābiǎn; *n* 挤 jǐ, 压 yā

squat *v* 蹲 dūn

squeak *v* 尖叫 jiānjiào

squeeze *v* 压榨 yāzhà, 挤 jǐ

squid *n* 鱿鱼 yóuyú

squirrel *n* 松鼠 sōngshǔ

stab *v* 刺 cì

stabilize *v* (使) 稳定 (shǐ) wěndìng

stable *n* 马房 mǎfáng; *adj* 稳定的 wěndìng de; **stability** *n* 稳定 wěndìng

stack *v/n* 堆 duī

stadium *n* 体育场 tǐyùchǎng

staff *n* 员工 yuángōng

stage *n* (*theater*) 舞台 wǔtái; (*point*) 阶段 jiēduàn

stagnation *n* 停滞 tíngzhì; **stagnant** *adj* 停滞的 tíngzhì de, 迟钝的 chídùn de

stain *v* 染污 rǎnwū; *n* 污点 wūdiǎn; **stainless** *adj* 无瑕疵的 wú xiácī de, 不锈的 bù xiù de

stair *n* 楼梯 lóutī; **staircase** *n* 楼梯 lóutī

stake *v* 以 ... 打赌 yǐ ... dǎdǔ; *n* (*post*) 桩 zhuāng; (*interest, share, etc.*) 利害关系 lìhài guānxì; **at stake** 在危险中 zài wēixiǎn zhōng, 成问题 chéng wèntí

stale *adj* 陈腐的 chénfǔ de

stalemate *n* 僵持 jiāngchí, 僵局 jiāngjú

stalk *v* 悄悄地追踪 qiǎoqiāo de zhuīzōng; *n* 茎 jīng

stall *v* (*engine*) 熄火 xīhuǒ, (使) 停止 (shǐ) tíngzhǐ; *n* 摊位 tānwèi

stamina *n* 耐力 nàilì, 持久力 chíjiǔlì

stamp *v* (*seal*) 盖图章 gài túzhāng; (*foot*) 跺脚 duòjiǎo; *n* (*post*) 邮票 yóupiào; (*seal*) 图章 túzhāng

stand *v* (**stood, stood**) 站 zhàn; **stand down** 退出 tuìchū; **stand for** 代表 dàibiǎo, 象征 xiàngzhēng; **stand out** 突出 tūchū; **stand up** 站起来 zhàn qǐlái; (*remain strong*) 坚持 jiānchí; (*resist*) 抵抗 dǐkàng; *n* (*position*) 立场 lìchǎng; (*rack*) 架子 jiàzi; (*platform*) 台子 táizi; **standstill** *n* 停顿 tíngdùn, 停止 tíngzhǐ

standard n 标准 biāozhǔn; **standard of living** 生活水平 shēnghuó shuǐpíng; **standardize** v (使) 标准化 (shǐ) biāozhǔnhuà

stank. *See* **stink**

staple v 用钉书钉钉 yòng dīngshūdīng dìng; n (*food*) 主要食品 zhǔyàoshípǐn; (*product*) 主要产品 zhǔyào chǎnpǐn; (*papers*) 订书钉 dìngshūdīng; *adj* 主要的 zhǔyào de; **stapler** n 订书机 dìngshūjī

star n 星 xīng

starch n 淀粉 diànfěn; **starchy** *adj* 含淀粉的 hán diànfěn de

stare v 凝视 níngshì, 盯着看 dīng zhe kàn

start v/n 开始 kāishǐ, 出发 chūfā

startle v (使) 震惊 (shǐ) zhènjīng; **startling** *adj* 令人吃惊的 lìng rén chījīng de

starve v 饿极 èjí; **starvation** n 饥饿 jī'è, 饿死 èsǐ

state v 声明 shēngmíng, 陈述 chénshù; n (*country*) 国家 guójiā; (*condition*) 状态 zhuàngtài; **statesman** n 政治家 zhèngzhìjiā; **statement** n 陈述 chénshù, 声明 shēngmíng; **stately** *adj* 庄严的 zhuāngyán de

static *adj* 静态的 jìngtài de, 静电的 jìngdiàn de

station n (*bus, train*) 车站 chēzhàn; (*post*) 岗位 gǎngwèi; (*radio, TV*) 台 tái

stationary *adj* 静止的 jìngzhǐ de, 固定的 gùdìng de

stationer n 文具商 wénjùshāng; **stationer's** n 文具店 wénjùdiàn; **stationery** n 文具 wénjù

statistics n 统计数字 tǒngjì shùzì; 统计学 tǒngjìxué; **statistical** *adj* 统计的 tǒngjì de

statue n 雕像 diāoxiàng

stature n 身高 shēngāo, 高度 gāodù

status n 身份 shēnfen, 地位 dìwèi

statute n 法令 fǎlìng; **statutory** *adj* 法定的 fǎdìng de

staunch *adj* 坚定的 jiāndìng de

stay v (*spend time*) 停留 tíngliú, 住 zhù; (*restrain*) 抑制 yìzhì; (*halt*) 延缓 yánhuǎn; **stay up** 熬夜 áoyè; n 逗留 dòuliú

steadfast *adj* (*firm*) 坚定的 jiāndìng de; (*fixed*) 固定的 gùdìng de

steady *adj* (*even*) 稳定的 wěndìng de; (*firm*) 坚定的 jiāndìng de; **steadily** *adv* 稳定地 wěndìng de

steak n 牛排 niúpái

steal v (**stole, stolen**) 偷 tōu

stealthy *adj* 偷偷的 tōutōu de, 秘密的 mìmì de

steam *v* 蒸 zhēng; *n* 蒸汽 zhēngqì

steel *n* 钢 gāng

steep *adj* 陡的 dǒu de

steer *v* 驾驶 jiàshǐ; **steering wheel** *n* 方向盘 fāngxiàngpán

stem *v* 遏制 èzhì; **stem from** 起源于 qǐyuán yú; *n* (*plant*) 茎 jīng; (*word*) 词干 cígàn

step *v* 走 zǒu; *n* (*foot*) 步 bù; (*stairs*) 台阶 táijiē; (*move*) 步骤 bùzhòu

stepbrother *n* (*with the same biological mother*) 异父兄弟 yìfù xiōngdì; (*with the same biological father*) 异母兄弟 yìmǔ xiōngdì

stepdaughter *n* 继女 jìnǚ

stepfather *n* 继父 jìfù

stepmother *n* 继母 jìmǔ

stepsister *n* (*with the same biological mother*) 异父姐妹 yìfù jiěmèi; (*with the same biological father*) 异母姐妹 yìmǔ jiěmèi

stepson *n* 继子 jìzǐ

stereo *n* 立体声 lìtǐshēng; *adj* 立体声的 lìtǐ shēng de

stereotype *n* 老套 lǎotào, 陈规 chénguī

sterile *adj* (*barren*) 贫瘠的 pínjí de; (*infertile*) 不育的 bùyù de; (*disinfected*) 消过毒的 xiāo guò dú de; **sterility** *n* (*freedom from germs*) 无菌状态 wújùn zhuàngtài; (*infertility*) 不育 bù yù

sterilize *v* 消毒 xiāodú; **sterilization** *n* (*germs*) 杀菌 shājūn; (*reproduction*) 绝育 juéyù

stern *n* 船尾 chuánwěi; *adj* 严厉的 yánlì de

stethoscope *n* 听诊器 tīngzhěnqì

stew *v* 炖 dùn, 焖 mèn

steward *n* 乘务员 chéngwùyuán; **stewardess** *n* 女乘务员 nǚchéngwùyuán

stick *v* (**stuck, stuck**) (*poke*) 戳 chuō; (*paste*) 贴 tiē; **stick to** 坚持 jiānchí; **stick out** 伸出 shēnchū; **sticky** *adj* 粘的 nián de; *n* 棍 gùn, 棒 bang

stiff *adj* (*of objects*) 硬的 yìng de; (*of manner*) 拘谨的 jūjǐn de; **stiffen** *v* (使) 硬 (shǐ) yìng; **stiffness** *n* 僵硬 jiāngyìng; 拘谨 jūjǐn

still *adv* 仍然 réngrán, 还 hái, 更 gèng; *adj* 静止的 jìngzhǐ de

stimulate *v* 刺激 cìjī, 激励 jīlì; **stimulation** *n* 刺激 cìjī; **stimulant** *n* 兴奋剂 xīngfènjì

sting *v* (**stung, stung**) 蜇 zhē, 刺 cì

stink *v* (**stunk/stank, stunk**) 发臭味 fā chòuwèi; *n* 臭味 chòuwèi

stipulate *v* 规定 guīdìng; **stipulation** *n* 约定 yuēdìng, 契约 qìyuē

stir *v* 搅动 jiǎodòng, 激起 jīqǐ

stitch *v* 缝合 fénghé; *n* 缝针 féngzhēn

stock *v* (*lay up*) 贮存 zhùcún; (*furnish*) 进货 jìnhuò; *n* (*inventory*) 库存 kùcún; (*share*) 股票 gǔpiào; **stock exchange** 证券交易所 zhèngquàn jiāoyìsuǒ; **stock market** 股票市场 gǔpiào shìcháng; **stockbroker** *n* 股票经纪人 gǔpiào jīngjìrén

stocking *n* 长袜 chángwà

stole/stolen. *See* **steal**

stomach *n* 胃 wèi, 肚子 dùzi; **stomachache** *n* 胃痛 wèitòng

stone *n* (*rock*) 石头 shítou; (*gem*) 宝石 bǎoshí

stood. *See* **stand**

stool *n* (*seat*) 凳子 dèngzi; (*feces*) 大便 dàbiàn

stop *v* 停 tíng, 停止 tíngzhǐ, 终止 zhōngzhǐ; *n* 车站 chēzhàn

store *v* 储藏 chǔcáng; *n* 商店 shāngdiàn; **storage** *n* 储藏 chǔcáng

storey *n* 楼层 lóucéng

storm *n* 风暴 fēngbào; **stormy** *adj* 暴风雨的 bàofēngyǔ de, 激烈的 jīliè de

story *n* (*tale*) 故事 gùshì; (*fabrication*) 假话 jiǎhuà, 谎话 huǎnghuà

stove *n* 炉子 lúzi

straight *adv* 一直 yīzhí, *adj* 直的 zhí de, 齐的 qí de; **straightaway** *adj* (*plain*) 明白易懂的 míngbai yìdǒng de; (*right away*) 立即的 lìjí de; *adv* 立刻 lìkè, 马上 mǎshàng; **straightforward** *adj* (*frank*) 坦率的 tǎnshuài de; (*simple*) 简单的 jiǎndān de; **straighten** *v* 弄直 nòngzhí; (*clean up*) 整理 zhěnglǐ

strain *v* (使) 紧张 (shǐ) jǐnzhāng, 拉紧 lājǐn; *n* 紧张 jǐnzhāng

straits *n* 海峡 hǎixiá

strand *v* 搁浅 gēqiǎn

strange *adj* 奇怪的 qíguài de; **stranger** *n* 陌生人 mòshēngrén

strangle *v* 扼死 èsǐ, 勒死 lè sǐ

strap *n* 带子 dàizi, 皮带 pídài

strategy *n* 策略 cèlüè; **strategic** *adj* 战略的 zhànlüè de

straw *n* 稻草 dàocǎo; (*tube*) 吸管 xīguǎn

strawberry *n* 草莓 cǎoméi

stray *v* 走失 zǒushī; 迷路 mílù

streak *n* 条纹 tiáowén

stream *v* 流动 liúdòng; *n* 小溪 xiǎoxī; **streamlined** *adj* 流线型的 liúxiànxíng de

street *n* 街 jiē; **streetlamp/light** *n* 路灯 lùdēng

strength *n* 力量 lìliàng, 力气 lìqi; **strengthen** *v* 加强 jiāqiáng

stress *v* 强调 qiángdiào; *n* (*pressure*) 压力 yālì; (*emphasis*) 重点 zhòngdiǎn; (*phonetics*) 重音 zhòngyīn

stretch *v* 伸展 shēnzhǎn, 伸长 shēncháng, 舒展 shūzhǎn; *n* (*time*) 一段时间 yī duàn shíjiān; (*distance*) 一段路程 yī duàn lùchéng

strict *adj* 严格的 yángé de; **strictly** *adv* 严格地 yángé de; **strictly speaking** 严格地说 yángé de shuō

stride *v* (**strode**, **stridden**) 大步走 dàbù zǒu, 跨过 kuà guo; *n* 大步 dàbù

strife *n* 争吵 zhēngchǎo, 冲突 chōngtū

strike *v* (**struck**, **struck/stricken**) 罢工 bàgōng; (*blow*) 打击 dǎjī; *n* (*stoppage*) 罢工 bàgōng; (*attack*) 袭击 xíjī; **striking** *adj* 醒目的 xǐngmù de, 显著的 xiǎnzhù de

string *n* 串 chuàn; 线 xiàn; **string bean** 刀豆 dāodòu

strip *v* (*clothing*) 脱去衣服 tuō qu yīfu; (*peel off*) 剥去 bō qu; *n* 条状物 tiáozhuàngwù

stripe *n* 条纹 tiáowén; **striped** *adj* 有条纹的 yǒu tiáowén de

strive *v* (**strove/strived**, **strove/strived**) 努力 nǔlì, 奋斗 fèndòu, 力争 lìzhēng

stroke *v* 抚摸 fǔmō; *n* (*characters*) 笔划 bǐhuà; (*med*) 中风 zhòngfēng

stroll *n* 散步 sànbù, 闲逛 xiánguàng

strong *adj* 强壮的 qiángzhuàng de, 强大的 qiángdà de; **stronghold** *n* 要塞 yàosài, 据点 jùdiǎn

struck. *See* **strike**

structure *n* 结构 jiégòu; **structural** *adj* 结构的 jiégòu de

struggle *v* 搏斗 bódòu, 奋斗 fèndòu, 挣扎 zhēngzhá; *n* 斗争 dòuzhēng, 奋斗 fèndòu

stubborn *adj* 顽固的 wángù de

stuck. *See* **stick**

student *n* 学生 xuésheng

studio *n* (*broadcast*) 演播室 yǎnbōshì; (*work*) 工作室 gōngzuòshì; (*painting*) 画室 huàshì

study *v* 学习 xuéxí, 研究 yánjiū; *n* 学习 xuéxí, 研究 yánjiū; (*room*) 书房 shūfáng; **studious** *adj* 勤学的 qínxué de

stuff *v* 塞满 sāimǎn; *n* (*material*) 材料 cáiliao; (*things*) 东西 dōngxi; **stuffy** *adj* 闷热的 mēnrè de; (*nose*) 塞的 sāi de

stumble *v* (*trip*) 绊倒 bàn dǎo; (*walk*) 跌跌撞撞地走 diēdiē zhuàngzhuàng de zǒu

stun *v* 将... 打昏 jiāng ... dǎhūn, (使) 震惊 (shǐ) zhènjīng

stung. *See* **sting**

stunk. *See* **stink**

stunt *n* 特技 tèjì; **stunt man** 替身演员 tìshēn yǎnyuán, 特技演员 tèjì yǎnyuán

stupid *adj* 愚蠢的 yúchǔn de, 笨的 bèn de; **stupidity** *n* 愚蠢 yúchǔn

sturdy *adj* 强壮的 qiángzhuàng de, 牢固的 láogù de

stutter *n* 口吃 kǒuchī, 结巴 jiēba, 结结巴巴地说 jiējiebābā de shuō

sty *n* 猪圈 zhūjuàn

style *n* 风格 fēnggé, 样式 yàngshì; **stylish** *adj* 时髦的 shímáo de

subconscious *adj* 下意识的 xiàyìshí de

subdue *v* 征服 zhēngfú; **subdued** *adj* (*quiet*) 低沉的 dīchén de; (*repressed*) 抑郁的 yìyù de; (*controlled*) 被制服的 bèi zhìfú de

subject *v* (使) 服从 (shǐ) fúcóng, (使) 隶属 (shǐ) lìshǔ; *n* (*theme*) 主题 zhǔtí; (*gram*) 主语 zhǔyǔ; (*study*) 学科 xuékē; **subjective** *adj* 主观的 zhǔguān de

submarine *n* 潜艇 qiántǐng; *adj* 水下的 shuǐxià de

submerge *v* 淹没 yānmò

submission *n* 驯从 xùncóng; **submissive** *adj* 驯从的 xùncóng de

submit *v* 递交 dìjiāo, 提交 tíjiāo

subordinate *n* 下级 xiàjí, 下属 xiàshǔ; *adj* (*secondary*) 次要的 cìyào de; (*rank*) 下级的 xiàjí de; (*subservient*) 从属的 cóngshǔ de

subscribe *v* (*subscribe to*) 订 dìng; **subscriber** *n* 订户 dìnghù; **subscription** *n* 订阅 dìngyuè

subsequent *adj* 随后的 suíhòu de; **subsequent to** 继 ... 之后 jì ... zhīhòu

subside *v* 下沉 xiàchén, 退去 tuìqù

subsidiary *adj* 辅助的 fǔzhù de, 次要的 cìyào de; **subsidiary company** 子公司 zǐgōngsī

subsidize *v* 资助 zīzhù, 补助 bǔzhù; **subsidy** *n* 补贴 bǔtiē

substance *n* (*matter*) 物质 wùzhì; (*content*) 内容 nèiróng;

substantial *adj* 实在的 shízài de, 真实的 zhēnshí de, 充实的 chōngshí de

substandard *adj* 低于标准的 dīyú biāozhǔn de, 次等的 cìděng de

substitute *v* 代替 dàitì 替换 tìhuàn; *n* (*person*) 替代人 tìdàirén; (*thing*) 替代物 tìdàiwù; **substitution** *n* 代替 dàitì

subtitle *v* 字幕 zìmù

subtle *adj* 微妙的 wēimiào de; **subtlety** *n* 微妙 wēimiào

subtract *v* 减 jiǎn; **subtraction** *n* 减法 jiǎnfǎ

suburb *n* 郊区 jiāoqū; **suburban** *adj* 郊区的 jiāoqū de

subvert *v* 颠覆 diānfù; **subversive** *adj* 颠覆性的 diānfùxìng de

subway *n* 地铁 dìtiě

succeed *v* (*accomplish*) 成功 chénggōng; (*follow*, *replace*) 接替 jiētì, 承袭 chéngxí; **success** *n* 成功 chénggōng; **succession** *n* (*sequence*) 连续 liánxù, 接续 jiēxù; (*transmission of throne, office, etc.*) 继任 jìrèn; **successor** *n* 继承者 jìchéngzhě; **successful** *adj* 成功的 chénggōng de; **successive** *adj* 连续的 liánxù de

succinct *adj* 简明的 jiǎnmíng de, 简洁的 jiǎnjié de

such *adj* 这样的 zhèyàng de, 此类的 cǐlèi de; *pron* (*person*) 这样的人 zhèyàng de rén; (*thing*) 这样的物 zhèyàng de wù; **such and such** 某某 mǒumǒu, 这样那样的 zhèyàng nàyàng de; **such as** 诸如 zhūrú

suck *v* 吸 xī

sudden *adj* 突然的 tūrán de; **all of a sudden** 突然 tūrán

sue *v* 控告 kònggào

suffer *v* 遭受 zāoshòu, 忍受 rěnshòu, 经历 jīnglì; **suffering** *n* 痛苦 tòngkǔ

sufficient *adj* 足够的 zúgòu de; **sufficiently** *adv* 足够地 zúgòu de

suffix *v* 后缀 hòuzhuì

suffocate *v* (使) 窒息 (shǐ) zhìxī, 窒息 zhìxī

sugar *n* 糖 táng; **sugarcane** 甘蔗 gānzhè

suggest *v* 建议 jiànyì; **suggestion** *n* 建议 jiànyì

suicide *n* 自杀 zìshā; **commit suicide** 自杀 zìshā; **suicidal** *adj* 有自杀倾向的 yǒu zìshā qīngxiàng de

suit *v* 符合 fúhé, 适合 shìhé; *n* 套装 tàozhuāng, 西装 xīzhuāng; **suitcase** *n* 手提箱 shǒutíxiāng; **suitable** *adj* 适合的 shìhé de

suite *n* 套房 tàofáng

sum *v* (*sum up*) 总结 zǒngjié; *n* 总数 zǒngshù

summarize *v* 总结 zǒngjié; **summary** *n* 摘要 zhāiyào, 总结 zǒngjié

summer *n* 夏天 xiàtiān

summit *n* 山顶 shāndǐng, 顶峰 dǐngfēng; **summit meeting** 高峰会议 gāofēng huìyì

summon *v* 召唤 zhāohuàn, 传唤 chuánhuàn

summons *n* 传票 chuánpiào

sun *n* 太阳 tàiyáng; **sunny** *adj* 晴朗的 qínglǎng de

sunbathe *v* 沐日光浴 mù rìguāngyù

sunburn *n* 晒斑 shàibān, 晒伤 shàishāng; **sunburnt** *adj* 晒伤的 shàishāng de

Sunday *n* 星期天 xīngqītiān

sunflower *n* 向日葵 xiàngrìkuí

sunglasses *n* 太阳镜 tàiyángjìng

sunk. *See* **sink**

sunlight *n* 阳光 yángguāng

sunrise *n* 日出 rìchū

sunset *n* 日落 rìluò

sunshine *n* 阳光 yángguāng

sunstroke *n* 中暑 zhòngshǔ

suntan *n* 晒黑 shàihēi; **suntan lotion** 防晒露 fángshàilù

super *adj* 极好的 jí hǎo de

superb *adj* 卓越的 zhuōyuè de

superficial *adj* 表面的 biǎomiàn de, 肤浅的 fūqiǎn de

superfluous *adj* 多余的 duōyú de

superhuman *adj* 超人的 chāorén de

superintendent *n* (*supervisor*) 督导 dūdǎo; (*custodian*) 管理人 guǎnlǐrén

superior *n* 上级 shàngjí; *adj* 优越的 yōuyuè de; (*rank*) 上级的 shàngjí de; **superiority** *n* 优越 yōuyuè, 优势 yōushì

supermarket *n* 超市 chāoshì

supernatural *adj* 超自然的 chāozìrán de

superpower *n* 超级大国 chāojí dàguó

superstar *n* 超级明星 chāojí míngxīng

superstition *n* 迷信 míxìn; **superstitious** *adj* 迷信的 míxìn de

supervise *v* 监督 jiāndū, 领导 lǐngdǎo, 指导 zhǐdǎo; **supervision** *n* 监督 jiāndū, 指导 zhǐdǎo; **supervisor** *n* 监督人 jiāndūrén, 上司 shàngsī, 指导者 zhǐdǎozhě

supper *n* 晚饭 wǎnfàn

supplement *n* 补充 bǔchōng, 附录 fùlù; **supplementary** *adj* 补充的 bǔchōng de

supply *v* 供给 gōngjǐ, 提供 tígòng; *n* 供给品 gōngjǐpǐn;

(*office, etc.*) 用品 yòngpǐn; **supplier** *n* 供应商 gōngyìngshāng

support *v* 支持 zhīchí; *n* 支持 zhīchí; **supporter** *n* 支持者 zhīchízhě, 拥护者 yōnghùzhě

suppose *v* 假设 jiǎshè, 倘若 tǎngruò; **be supposed to** 应该 yīnggāi, 被期望 bèi qīwàng; **supposition** *n* 假定 jiǎdìng, 推测 tuīcè; **supposedly** *adv* 据称 jùchēng; **supposing** *conj* 假如 jiǎrú

suppress *v* (*crack down*) 镇压 zhènyā,; (*check*) 抑制 yìzhì; **suppression** *n* 镇压 zhènyā; 抑制 yìzhì

supreme *adj* 最高的 zuìgāo de; **supremacy** *n* 至高无上 zhìgāo wúshàng, 霸权 bàquán

surcharge *n* 增收费 zēngshōufèi

sure *adj* 必定的 bìdìng de; *adv* 确实 quèshí; **surely** *adv* 的确 díquè; 一定 yīdìng; 当然 dāngrán

surf *v* 冲浪 chōnglàng; **surfing** *n* 冲浪 chōnglàng

surface *n* 表层 biǎocéng, 浮面 fúmiàn; **on the surface** 表面上 biǎomiàn shang

surge *v/n* (*waves*) 汹涌 xiōngyǒng, 激增 jīzēng

surgeon *n* 外科医生 wàikēyīshēng; **surgery** *n* 手术 shǒushù; **surgical** *adj* 外科的 wàikē de, 手术的 shǒushù de

surmount *v* (*overcome*) 克服 kèfú; (*scale*) 登上 dēng shàng

surname *n* 姓 xìng

surpass *v* 超过 chāoguo, 胜过 shèngguo

surplus *n* 盈余 yíngyú

surprise *v* (使) 吃惊 (shǐ) chījīng; *n* 惊奇 jīngqí, 惊喜 jīngxǐ; **surprising** *adj* 令人吃惊的 lìng rén chījīng de

surrender *v/n* (*yield*) 投降 tóuxiáng; (*relinquish*) 交出 jiāochū

surround *v* 包围 bāowéi; **surrounding** *adj* 周围的 zhōuwéi de; **surroundings** *n* 环境 huánjìng

survey *v/n* 调查 diàochá, 测量 cèliáng; **surveyor** *n* 调查员 diàocháyuán

survive *v* 生存 shēngcún, 幸存 xìngcún; **survival** *n* 幸存 xìngcún; **survivor** *n* 幸存者 xìngcúnzhě

susceptible *adj* 易受影响的 yì shòu yǐngxiǎng de

suspect *v* 怀疑 huáiyí; *n* 嫌疑犯 xiányífàn; *adj* 可疑的 kěyí de

suspend *v* (*hang*) 悬挂 xuánguà; (*stop*) 中止 zhōngzhǐ; **suspense** *n* 悬念 xuánniàn; **suspension** *n* 悬挂 xuánguà; 中止 zhōngzhǐ; (*rhetoric*) 悬念 xuánniàn

suspicion *n* 怀疑 huáiyí, 猜疑 cāiyí; **suspicious** *adj* 可疑的 kěyí de, 有疑心的 yǒu yíxīn de

sustain *v* (*support*) 支撑 zhīchēng; (*keep going*) 持续 chíxù

swallow *v* 吞咽 tūnyàn; *n* 燕子 yànzi

swam. *See* **swim**

swamp *n* 沼泽 zhǎozé; **swampy** *adj* 多沼泽的 duōzhǎozé de

swan *n* 天鹅 tiān'é

swap *v* 交换 jiāohuàn

swear *v* (**swore, sworn**) 发誓 fāshì, 赌咒 dǔzhòu

sweat *v* 出汗 chūhàn; *n* 汗 hàn

sweater *n* 毛线衣 máoxiànyī

Sweden *n* 瑞典 ruìdiǎn; **Swede** *n* 瑞典人 ruìdiǎnrén; **Swedish** *n* (*people*) 瑞典人 ruìdiǎnrén; (*language*) 瑞典语 ruìdiǎnyǔ; *adj* 瑞典的 ruìdiǎn de

sweep *v* (**swept, swept**) 扫扫 sǎo, 扫荡 sǎodàng; **make a clean sweep** 大获全胜 dàhuò quánshèng; **sweeping** *adj* 彻底的 chèdǐ de, 广泛的 guǎngfàn de; **sweeping statement** 总括性的说法 zǒngkuòxìng de shuōfa

sweet *adj* 甜的 tián de; **sweet potato** 甘薯 gānshǔ, 山芋 shānyù; **sweets** *n* 糖果 tángguǒ; **sweetheart** *n* 恋人 liànrén

swell *v* (**swelled, swollen/swelled**) (*of objects*) 膨胀 péngzhàng; (*of body*) 肿 zhǒng; **swelling** *n* 肿 zhǒng

swept. *See* **sweep**

swift *adj* 迅速的 xùnsù de; **swiftness** *n* 迅速 xùnsù

swim *v* (**swam, swum**) 游泳 yóuyǒng; **swimsuit** *n* 泳衣 yǒngyī; **swimming** *n* 游泳 yóuyǒng; **swimming pool** 游泳池 yóuyǒngchí

swindle *v* 诈骗 zhàpiàn

swine *n* 猪 zhū

swing *v* (**swung, swung**) 摇摆 yáobǎi; *n* (*amusement*) 秋千 qiūqiān; (*shift*) 摇摆 yáobǎi; **in full swing** 正如火如荼 zhèng rúhuǒ rútú

Swiss *n* 瑞士人 ruìshìrén; *adj* 瑞士的 ruìshì de

switch *v* 转换 zhuǎnhuàn; *n* (*elec*) 开关 kāiguān; (*change*) 变换 biànhuàn, 转换 zhuǎnhuàn; **switch off** 切断 qiēduàn, 关 guān; **switch on** 接通 jiē tōng, 开 kāi; **switchboard** *n* 电话总机 diànhuà zǒngjī

Switzerland *n* 瑞士 ruìshì

swollen *v see* **swell**; *adj* 肿胀的 zhǒngzhàng de

swoop *v* 猛扑 měngpū

sword *n* 剑 jiàn

swum. *See* **swim**
syllable *n* 音节 yīnjié; **syllabic** *adj* 音节的 yīnjié de
syllabus *n* 课程提纲 kèchéng tígāng
symbol *n* (*sign*) 符号 fúhào; (*token*) 象征 xiàngzhēng;
　　symbolize *v* 象征 xiàngzhēng; **symbolism** *n* 象征主义
　　xiàngzhēngzhǔyì; **symbolic** *adj* 象征的 xiàngzhēng de
symmetry *n* 对称 duìchèn; **symmetrical** *adj* 对称的 duìchèn
　　de
sympathy *n* 同情 tóngqíng; **sympathetic** *adj* 同情的
　　tóngqíng de; **sympathize** *v* 同情 tóngqíng
symphony *n* 交响乐 jiāoxiǎngyuè; **symphonic** *adj*
　　交响乐的 jiāoxiǎngyuè de
symposium *n* 研讨会 yántǎohuì, 座谈会 zuòtánhuì
symptom *n* 症状 zhèngzhuàng
synagogue *n* 犹太教会堂 yóutàijiàohuìtáng
syndicate *n* 辛迪加 xīndíjiā, 财团 cáituán
synonym *n* 同义词 tóngyìcí; **synonymous** *adj* 同义的
　　tóngyì de
synopsis *n* (*pl* **synopses**) 梗概 gěnggài, 概要 gàiyào
syntax *n* 句法 jùfǎ
synthesize *v* 综合 zōnghé; **synthesis** *n* 综合 zōnghé
synthetic *adj* 合成的 héchéng de, 人造的 rénzào de
syringe *n* 注射器 zhùshèqì
syrup *n* 糖浆 tángjiāng
system *n* 系统 xìtǒng, 制度 zhìdù, 体系 tǐxì

T

table *n* (*furniture*) 桌子 zhuōzi; (*form*) 表格 biǎogé;
　　tablecloth *n* 桌布 zhuōbù; **set the table** 摆餐具 bǎi cānjù
tablet *n* (*steel*) 碑 bēi; (*pill*) 药片 yàopiàn
tabloid *n* 小报 xiǎobào
taboo *n* 禁忌 jìnjì; *adj* 忌讳的 jìhuì de
tackle *v* 应付 yìngfù, 处理 chǔlǐ
tact *n* 机敏 jīmǐn, 手法 shǒufǎ; **tactful** *adj* 机智的 jīzhì de,
　　策略的 cèlüè de
tactic *n* 策略 cèlüè; **tactical** *adj* 战术的 zhànshù de
tadpole *n* 蝌蚪 kēdǒu
tag *n* 标签 biāoqiān
tail *n* 尾巴 wěiba
tailor *n* 裁缝 cáifeng
take *v* (**took, taken**) 拿 ná, 取 qǔ; **take back** (*return*) 送还

sòng huán; (claim) 取回 qǔ huí, 收回 shōu huí; **take care of** 照顾 zhàogù; **take notice of** 注意到 zhùyì dào; **take off** (clothes, etc.) 脱去 tuō qù; (plane) 起飞 qǐfēi; **take over** 接管 jiēguǎn, 取代 qǔdài; **take place** 发生 fāshēng; **take up** 拿起 náqǐ, 开始从事 kāishǐ cóngshì

tale n 故事 gùshì; **fairytale** n 童话 tónghuà, 神话故事 shénhuà gùshì

talent n 才能 cái'néng; **talented** adj 有才能的 yǒu cáinéng de

talk v 谈 tán; **talk back** 顶嘴 dǐngzuǐ, 回嘴 huízuǐ; n 讲话 jiǎnghuà; **talking** n 说话 shuōhuà; **talking point** 话题 huàtí, 论点 lùndiǎn; **talkative** adj 话多的 huà duō de

tall adj 高的 gāo de

tamper v (tamper with) (text) 篡改 cuàngǎi; (spoil) 胡乱摆弄 húluàn bǎinòng

tampon n 月经棉塞 yuèjīng miánsāi

tan v 晒黑 shàihēi; n 棕褐色 zōnghèsè

tangerine n 柑橘 gānjú

tangible adj 有形的 yǒuxíng de, 有实体的 yǒu shítǐ de

tank n (water) 水箱 shuǐxiāng; (mil) 坦克 tǎnkè; **tanker** n (truck) 罐车 guànchē; (ship) 油轮 yóulún

tantamount adj (tantamount to) 相当于的 xiāngdāngyú de

tap v 轻拍 qīngpāi; n (water) 水龙头 shuǐlóngtóu; (hit) 轻拍 qīngpāi

tape v 录音 lùyīn; n 带子 dàizi, 胶带 jiāodài; **tape recorder** 录音机 lùyīnjī (audio) 录音带 lùyīndài; (video) 录像带 lùxiàngdài

target n 目标 mùbiāo, 对象 duìxiàng; (shooting) 靶子 bǎzi

tart n 果馅饼 guǒxiànbǐng

task n 任务 rènwu; **task force** 特遣部队 tèqiǎn bùduì

taste v 品尝 pǐncháng; n 味道 wèidao; **tasteful** adj 有鉴赏力的 yǒu jiànshǎnglì de, 有品味的 yǒu pǐnwèi de; **tasteless** adj 没味道的 méi wèidao de, 无品味的 wú pǐnwèi de; **tasty** adj 好吃的 hǎochī de

tattoo n 纹身 wénshēn

taught. See **teach**

tavern n 酒馆 jiǔguǎn

tax n 税 shuì; **tax-free** adj 免税的 miǎnshuì de; **taxpayer** n 纳税人 nàshuìrén; **taxation** n 征税 zhēngshuì; **taxable** adj 应纳税的 yīng nàshuì de

taxi n 出租车 chūzūchē; **taxi driver** 出租车司机 chūzūchē sījī

tea n 茶 chá; **teapot** n 茶壶 cháhú

teaspoon *n* 茶匙 cháchí

teach *v* (**taught**, **taught**) 教 jiāo; **teacher** *n* 老师 lǎoshī; **teaching** *n* 教学 jiàoxué, 教诲 jiàohuì

team *n* 队 duì, 组 zǔ; **team up** 结成一队 jié chéng yī duì; 齐力合作 qílì hézuò

tear *v* (**tore**, **torn**) 撕 sī, 撕破 sī pò; *n* (*rip*) 破处 pòchù, 裂缝 lièfèng; (*crying*) 眼泪 yǎnlèi; **tear gas** 催泪瓦斯 cuīlèi wǎsī

tease *v* 嘲弄 cháonòng; **teasing** *n* 嘲弄 cháonòng

technique *n* 技术 jìshù, 技巧 jìqiǎo; **technology** *n* 技术 jìshù; **technician** *n* 技术员 jìshùyuán; **technical** *adj* 技术的 jìshù de; **technological** *adj* 技术的 jìshù de

tedious *adj* 冗长的 rǒngcháng de, 沉闷的 chénmèn de

teenager *n* 少年 shàonián; **teens** *n* 少年 shàonián

tee-shirt *n* T恤衫 T xùshān

teeth. *See* **tooth**

telecommunications *n* 电信 diànxìn

telegram *n* 电报 diànbào

telegraph *n* 电报 diànbào

telepathic *adj* 心灵感应的 xīnlíng gǎnyìng de

telephone *n* 电话 diànhuà; **telephone booth** 电话亭 diànhuàtíng; **telephone call** 电话 diànhuà; **telephone directory** 电话簿 diànhuàbù

telescope *n* 望远镜 wàngyuǎnjìng

television *n* 电视 diànshì; **television set** 电视机 diànshìjī

tell *v* (**told**, **told**) 告诉 gàosu

temper *n* 脾气 píqi; **lose one's temper** 发脾气 fāpíqi; **temperament** *n* 性情 xìngqíng; **temperamental** *adj* 易兴奋的 yì xīngfèn de, 易激动的 yì jīdòng de

temperature *n* 温度 wēndù

temple *n* (*rel*) 庙 miào; *n* (*anat*) 太阳穴 tàiyangxuè

temporary *adj* 暂时的 zànshí de, 临时的 línshí de; **temporary worker** 临时工 línshígōng

tempt *v* 诱惑 yòuhuò, (使) 感兴趣 (shǐ) gǎn xìngqù; **temptation** *n* 诱惑 yòuhuò

ten *num* 十 shí; **tenth** *num* 第十 dì shí

tenacious *adj* 顽强的 wánqiáng de; **tenacity** *adj* 顽强 wánqiáng

tenant *n* 租户 zūhù, 房客 fángkè

tend *v* (*look after*) 照管 zhàoguǎn, (*attend to*) 护理 hùlǐ; (*inclined to*) 趋向 qūxiàng; **tendency** *n* 倾向 qīngxiàng, 趋势 qūshì

tender *v* 投标 tóubiāo; *n* 投标 tóubiāo; *adj* 嫩的 nèn de,
温柔的 wēnróu de; **tenderness** *n* 嫩 nèn, 柔和 róuhé

tennis *n* 网球 wǎngqiú; **tennis court** 网球场 wǎngqiúchǎng

tenor *n* 男高音 nángāoyīn

tense *n* (*gram*) 时态 shítài; *adj* 紧张的 jǐnzhāng de; **tension**
n 紧张 jǐnzhāng, 压力 yālì

tent *n* 帐篷 zhàngpeng

tenterhooks *n* 张布钩 zhāngbùgōu; **be on tenterhooks**
提心吊胆 tíxīn diàodǎn

tentative *adj* 尝试的 chángshì de, 试验性的 shìyànxìng de

term *n* 期限 qīxiàn, (*office*) 任期 rènqī; (*school*) 学期 xuéqī;
(*language*) 术语 shùyǔ; **terms** *n* 条件 tiáojiàn; **to be on
good terms with** 和 ... 关系好 hé ... guānxì hǎo

terminal *n* (*bus, train, etc.*) 终点站 zhōngdiǎnzhàn; (*point*)
终端 zhōngduān; *adj* 末期的 mòqī de; **terminal disease**
不治之症 bùzhì zhī zhēng

terminate *v* 终止 zhōngzhǐ, 停止 tíngzhǐ; (*fire*) 解雇 jiěgù;
termination *n* 终止 zhōngzhǐ, 停止 tíngzhǐ; 解雇 jiěgù

terminology *n* 术语 shùyǔ

terminus *n* 终点站 zhōngdiǎnzhàn

terrace *n* 阳台 yángtái

terrible *adj* 糟糕的 zāogāo de, 可怕的 kěpà de; **terribly** *adv*
十分 shífēn, 非常 fēicháng

terrify *v* (使) 恐惧 (shǐ) kǒngjù, 恐吓 kǒnghè; **terrific** *adj*
极好的 jí hǎo de

territory *n* 领土 lǐngtǔ; **territorial** *adj* 领土的 lǐngtǔ de

terror *n* 恐怖 kǒngbù; **terrorism** *n* 恐怖主义 kǒngbùzhǔyì;
terrorist *n* 恐怖分子 kǒngbùfēnzǐ

terse *adj* 简洁的 jiǎnjié de

test *v/n* 测试 cèshì, 试验 shìyàn

testify *v* 作证 zuòzhèng

text *n* 正文 zhèngwén, 课文 kèwén, 文本 wénběn; **textbook**
n 教科书 jiàokēshū, 教材 jiàocái

textile *n* 纺织品 fǎngzhīpǐn

texture *n* 质地 zhìdì

than *conj* 比 bǐ

thank *v* 谢谢 xièxie; **thanks** *n* 感谢 gǎnxiè; **thanks to** 由于
yóuyú; **thankful** *adj* 感激的 gǎnjī de; **thankless** *adj*
忘恩负义的 wàng'ēn fùyì de

that *pron* 那 nà; **that is** (*i.e.*) 即 jí

thaw *v/n* 解冻 jiědòng, 融化 rónghuà

theater *n* 剧场 jùchǎng; **movie theater** 电影院 diànyǐngyuàn;

theater room 阶梯教室 jiētī jiàoshì; **theatrical** *adj* 戏剧的 xìjù de

theft *n* 盗窃 dàoqiè

their *pron* (*human*) 他们的 tāmen de; (*nonhuman*) 它们的 tāmen de; **theirs** *pron* (*human*) 他们的 tāmen de; (*nonhuman*) 它们的 tāmen de

them *pron* (*human*) 他们 tāmen; (*nonhuman*) 它们 tāmen; **themselves** *pron* (*human*) 他们自己 tāmen zìjǐ; (*nonhuman*) 它们自己 tāmen zìjǐ

theme *n* 主题 zhǔtí; **thematic** *adj* 主题的 zhǔtí de

then *adv* 然后 ránhòu, 那么 nàme

theology *n* 神学 shénxué, 宗教 zōngjiào; **theological** *adj* 神学的 shénxué de

theory *n* 理论 lǐlùn

therapy *n* 治疗 zhìliáo, 疗法 liáofǎ; **therapist** *n* 理疗师 lǐliáoshī

there *adv* 在那里 zài nàlǐ; **there is/are** 有 yǒu, 存在 cúnzài; **therefore** *adv* 因此 yīncǐ, 所以 suǒyǐ

thermometer *n* 温度计 wēndùjì

these *pron* 这些 zhèxiē

thesis *n* (*pl* **theses**) 论文 lùnwén

they *pron* (*human*) 他们 tāmen; (*nonhuman*) 它们 tāmen

thick *adj* 厚的 hòu de; (*dense*) 稠密的 chóumì de; **thicken** *v* 变厚 biàn hòu; **thickness** *n* 厚度 hòudù

thief *n* (*pl* **thieves**) 小偷 xiǎotōu

thigh *n* 大腿 dàtuǐ

thin *adj* (*of people*) 瘦的 shòu de; (*of things*) 薄的 báo de; **thinness** *n* 瘦 shòu; 薄 báo

thing *n* (*affair*) 事 shì; (*object*) 物 wù, 东西 dōngxi; **things** *n* 情况 qíngkuàng

think *v* (**thought, thought**) 想 xiǎng, 认为 rènwéi

third *num* 第三 dìsān

thirst *n* 口渴 kǒukě; **thirsty** *adj* 口渴的 kǒukě de

thirteen *num* 十三 shísān; **thirteenth** *num* 第十三 dì shísān

thirty *num* 三十 sānshí; **thirtieth** *num* 第三十 dì sānshí

this *pron* 这 zhè

thorn *n* 荆棘 jīngjí; **thorny** *adj* 多刺的 duōcì de, 棘手的 jíshǒu de

thorough *adj* 彻底的 chèdǐ de; **thoroughly** *adv* 彻底地 chèdǐ de

those *pron* 那些 nàxiē

though *conj* 虽然 suīrán, 尽管 jǐnguǎn

thought *n* 想法 xiǎngfa, 思想 sīxiǎng; **thoughtful** *adj* 体贴的 tǐtiē de, 有思想的 yǒu sīxiǎng de; **thoughtless** *adj* 欠考虑的 qiàn kǎolǜ de

thousand *num* 千 qiān; **thousandth** *num* 第一千 dì yīqiān

thread *n* 线 xiàn

threat *n* 威胁 wēixié; **threaten** *v* 威胁 wēixié

three *num* 三 sān

threshold *n* 门槛 ménkǎn

threw. *See* **throw**

thrift *n* 节俭 jiéjiǎn; **thrifty** *adj* 节俭的 jiéjiǎn de

thrill *v* (使) 兴奋 (shǐ) xīngfèn, (使) 激动 (shǐ) jīdòng; *n* 兴奋 xīngfèn, 激动 jīdòng; **thriller** *n* 惊险小说 jīngxiǎn xiǎoshuō

thrive *v* 兴旺 xīngwàng; **thriving** *adj* 兴旺的 xīngwàng de

throat *n* 喉咙 hóulóng

throne *n* 王座 wángzuò

through *prep* 穿过 chuānguò, 通过 tōngguò; **throughout** *prep* 遍及 biànjí, 贯穿 guànchuān

throw *v* (**threw, thrown**) 扔 rēng, 投 tóu; **throw away** 扔掉 rēngdiào; **throw off** 抛弃 pāoqì; **throw up** 呕吐 ǒutù

thrust *v* (**thrust, thrust**) 猛推 měngtuī

thumb *n* 拇指 mǔzhǐ

thunder *n* 雷 léi; **thunderstorm** *n* 雷暴 léibào

Thursday *n* 星期四 xīngqīsì

thus *adv* 因此 yīncǐ

tick *v* (*sound*) 发出滴答声 fā chū dīdáshēng; (*mark*) 打勾 dǎgōu; *n* (*sound*) 滴答声 dīdáshēng; (*mark*) 勾号 gōuhào

ticket *n* 票 piào; (*fine*) 罚单 fádān; **ticket inspector** 查票员 chápiàoyuán; **ticket office** 票房 piàofáng, 售票处 shòupiàochù

tickle *v* 呵痒 hēyǎng; **ticklish** *adj* 易痒的 yì yǎng de

tide *n* 潮汐 cháoxī, 潮水 cháoshuǐ; **tidal** *adj* 潮汐的 cháoxī de; **tidal wave** 潮波 cháobō, 浪潮 làngcháo

tidy *v* 整理 zhěnglǐ; *adj* 整洁的 zhěngjié de

tie *v* (*fasten*) 系 jì, 打结 dǎjié; (*game*) 打成平局 dǎ chéng píngjú; *n* (*necktie*) 领带 lǐngdài; 纽带 niǔdài; (*game*) 平局 píngjú

tier *n* (*row*) 排 pái; (*layer*) 层 céng; (*rank*) 等级 děngjí

tiger *n* 老虎 lǎohǔ

tight *adj* 紧的 jǐndi; (*difficult*) 困难的 kùnnan de; **tight-fisted** *adj* 吝啬的 lìnsè de, 小气的 xiǎoqi de; **tight-lipped** *adj* 沉默的 chénmò de, 嘴唇紧闭的 zuǐchún jǐnbì de; **tighten** *v* 绷紧 bēngjǐn, 拉紧 lājǐn

tile *v* 铺瓷砖 pū cízhuān; *n* 瓷砖 cízhuān

till *prep See* **until**; *v* 耕种 gēngzhòng; *n* 钱柜 qiánguì; *prep* 直到 zhídào

timber *n* 木材 mùcái

time *v* 计时 jìshí, 记录 ... 时间 jìlù ... shíjiān; *n* 时间 shíjiān, 时候 shíhou; (*era*) 时代 shídài; (*occurrence*) 次数 cìshù; (*situation*) 形势 xíngshì; **at the same time** 同时 tóngshí; **from time to time** 有时 yǒushí; **in time** 及时 jíshí; **on time** 准时 zhǔnshí; **timeless** *adj* 永恒的 yǒnghéng de; **timely** *adj* 及时的 jíshí de; **time zone** 时区 shíqū; **times** *prep* 乘以 chéngyǐ; **timetable** *n* 时间表 shíjiānbiǎo

timid *adj* 胆小的 dǎnxiǎo de; **timidity** *n* 胆怯 dǎnqiè

tin *n* (*metal*) 锡 xī; (*container*) 罐头 guàntou; **tinfoil** *n* 锡纸 xīzhǐ

tiny *adj* 微小的 wēixiǎo de

tip *v* (*for service*) 给小费 gěi xiǎofèi; (*hint*) 暗示 ànshì; **tip off** 透露消息 tòulù xiāoxi; *n* (*gratuity*) 小费 xiǎofèi; (*hint*) 提示 tíshì; (*point*) 尖 jiān, 梢 shāo; **on tiptoe** 踮着脚尖走 diǎn zhe jiǎojiān zǒu

tire *v* (使) 疲倦 (shǐ) píjuàn; *n* 轮胎 lúntāi; **tired** *adj* 疲倦的 píjuàn de, 累的 lèi de; **be tired of** 厌烦的 yànfán de; **tiresome** *adj* 无聊的 wúliáo de

tissue *n* 擦手纸 cāshǒu zhǐ; **tissue paper** 薄纸 báozhǐ; (*toilet*) 卫生纸 wèishēngzhǐ

title *n* (*book, etc.*) 标题 biāotí; (*job*) 头衔 tóuxián

to *prep* 向 xiàng, 到 dào, 对 duì

toad *n* 蟾蜍 chánchú

toast *v* (*wine*) 敬酒 jìngjiǔ; (*bread*) 烤 kǎo; *n* (*wine*) 敬酒 jìngjiǔ; (*bread*) 土司面包 tǔsī miànbāo; **toaster** *n* 祝酒的人 zhùjiǔ de rén

tobacco *n* 烟草 yāncǎo

today *n/adv* 今天 jīntiān

toe *n* 脚趾 jiǎozhǐ; **toe the line** 服从 fúcóng, 听从 tīngcóng; **toenail** *n* 脚趾甲 jiǎozhǐjiǎ

together *adv* 一起 yīqǐ, 共同 gòngtóng

toilet *n* 厕所 cèsuǒ; **toilet paper** 卫生纸 wèishēngzhǐ

token *n* 象征 xiàngzhēng, 标志 biāozhì, 表示 biǎoshì; **as a token of** 作为 ... 的表示 zuòwéi ... de biǎoshì

told. *See* **tell**

tolerate *v* 容忍 róngrěn; **toleration** *n* 宽容 kuānróng, 忍受 rěnshòu; **tolerant** *adj* 宽容的 kuānróng de, 容忍的 róngrěn de

toll *n* (*fee*) 过路费 guòlùfèi, 过桥费 guòqiáofèi; (*total*) 代价 dàijià; **death toll** 死亡人数 sǐwáng rénshù

tomato *n* 西红柿 xīhóngshì

tomb *n* 坟墓 fénmù; **tombstone** *n* 墓碑 mùbēi

tomorrow *n/adv* 明天 míngtiān; **the day after tomorrow** 后天 hòutiān

ton *n* 吨 dūn

tone *n* (*music*) 音调 yīndiào; (*phonetics*) 声调 shēngdiào; (*manner of expression*) 语气 yǔqì; (*mood*) 气氛 qìfēn

tongue *n* (*anat*) 舌头 shétou; (*language*) 语言 yǔyán; **tongue-tied** *adj* 无话可说的 wúhuà kěshuō de, 哑口无言的 yǎkǒu wúyán de

tonight *n/adv* 今夜 jīnyè, 今晚 jīnwǎn

too *adv* (*very, excessively*) 太 tài; (*also*) 也 yě

took. *See* **take**

tool *n* 工具 gōngjù

tooth *n* (*pl* **teeth**) 牙齿 yáchǐ; **toothbrush** *n* 牙刷 yáshuā; **toothpaste** *n* 牙膏 yágāo

top *n* 顶 dǐng; *adj* 顶上的 dǐngshàng de, 最高的 zuìgāo de, 头等的 tóuděng de; **top-secret** *adj* 绝密的 juémì de

topic *n* 题目 tímù, 话题 huàtí; **topical** *adj* 题目的 tímù de, 话题的 huàtí de

topple *v* 倾倒 qīngdào, 推翻 tuīfān

torch *n* 火炬 huǒjù

tore/torn. *See* **tear**

torment *n* 痛苦 tòngkǔ, 折磨 zhémo

tornado *n* 龙卷风 lóngjuǎnfēng

torrent *n* 急流 jíliú, 洪流 hóngliú

torso *n* 躯干 qūgàn

torture *v/n* 拷打 kǎodǎ, 折磨 zhémo

toss *v* 抛 pāo, 投 tóu, 扔 rēng

total *v* 合计 héjì, 总数达 zǒngshù dá; *n* 总数 zǒngshù; **totalitarian** *adj* 极权主义的 jíquánzhǔyì de

touch *v* 触摸 chùmō, 触及 chùjí, 感动 gǎndòng, 碰 pèng; *n* (*contact*) 接触 jiēchù, 联系 liánxì; (*polish*) 润色 rùnsè; **touching** *adj* 动人的 dòngrén de

tough *adj* (*strong*) 坚强的 jiānqiáng de; (*hard*) 艰苦的 jiānkǔ de, 困难的 kùnnan de; **toughness** *n* 坚强 jiānqiáng

tour *v* 旅游 lǚyóu; *n* 旅游 lǚyóu; **tour group** 旅游团 lǚyóutuán; **tour guide** 导游 dǎoyóu; **tourism** *n* 旅游业 lǚyóuyè; **tourist** *n* 观光客 guānguāngkè; **tourist industry** 旅游业 lǚyóuyè; **tourist season** 旅游季节 lǚyóu jìjié

tournament *n* 锦标赛 jǐnbiāosài

tow *v* 拖 tuō, 拽 zhuài

toward/**towards** *prep* 向 xiàng, 朝 cháo, 往 wǎng

towel *n* 毛巾 máojīn

tower *n* 塔 tǎ

town *n* 城镇 chéngzhèn; **town council** 镇议会 zhèn yìhuì; **town hall** 市政厅 shìzhèngtīng

toxic *adj* 有毒的 yǒudú de

toy *n* 玩具 wánjù

trace *v* 追踪 zhuīzōng, 映描 yìngmiáo; *n* 踪迹 zōngjì, 痕迹 hénjī

track *v* 追踪 zhuīzōng; *n* (*trace*) 轨迹 guǐjī; (*race*) 跑道 pǎodào; (*train*) 轨道 guǐdào

tractor *n* 拖拉机 tuōlājī

trade *v* 交换 jiāohuàn; *n* 贸易 màoyì; **trade fair** 交易会 jiāoyìhuì; **trade(s) union** 工会 gōnghuì; **trader** *n* 商人 shāngrén; 证券交易人 zhèngquàn jiāoyìrén

tradition *n* 传统 chuántǒng; **traditional** *adj* 传统的 chuántǒng de

traffic *n* 交通 jiāotōng; **traffic jam** 交通堵塞 jiāotōng dǔsè; **traffic light** 交通灯 jiāotōngdēng

tragedy *n* 悲剧 bēijù; **tragic** *adj* 悲惨的 bēicǎn de, 悲剧的 bēijù de

trail *n* (*path*) 小道 xiǎodào; (*trace*) 踪迹 zōngjì; **trailer** *n* 拖车 tuōchē; **trailer park** (*housing*) 活动住屋集中地 huódòng zhùwū jízhōngdì

train *v* (*teach*) 训练 xùnliàn; *n* 火车 huǒchē; **train station** 火车站 huǒchēzhàn; **trainer** *n* 教练员 jiàoliànyuán, 培训员 péixùnyuán; **training** *n* 训练 xùnliàn, 培训 péixùn

trait *n* 特性 tèxìng, 特点 tèdiǎn

traitor *n* 叛徒 pàntú

tram *n* 电车 diànchē

tramp *n* 流浪者 liúlàngzhě

trance *n* 恍惚 huǎnghū

tranquil *adj* 宁静的 níngjìng de; **tranquility** *n* 宁静 níngjìng; **tranquilizer** *n* 镇定剂 zhèndìngjì

transact *v* 交易 jiāoyì; **transaction** *n* 交易 jiāoyì

transcribe *v* 转录 zhuǎnlù; **transcription** *n* 抄写本 chāoxiěběn

transfer *v/n* (*work*) 调动 diàodòng; (*things*) 转移 zhuǎnyí; (*transportation*) 转车 zhuǎnchē; **transferable** *adj* 可转移的 kě zhuǎnyí de, 可转让的 kě zhuǎnràng de

transform *v* 改变 gǎibiàn, 转变 zhuǎnbiàn; **transformation** *n* 变化 biànhuà; **transformer** *n* 变压器 biànyāqì

transfusion *n* 输血 shūxuè

transit *n* 经过 jīngguò, 通行 tōngxíng; **in transit** 过路 guòlù, 过境 guòjing

transition *n* 过渡 guòdù; **transitional** *adj* 过渡的 guòdù de

translate *v* 翻译 fānyì; **translation** *n* 翻译 fānyì; **translator** *n* 译员 yìyuán

transmit *v* 传输 chuánshū, 传送 chuánsòng; **transmission** *n* 传输 chuánshū, 传送 chuánsòng; **transmitter** *n* 发射机 fāshèjī

transparent *adj* 透明的 tòumíng de; **transparency** *n* 透明 tòumíng

transplant *v/n* 移植 yízhí

transport *v/n* 运输 yùnshū; **transportation** *n* 运输 yùnshū

trap *v* 设陷阱 shè xiànjǐng; *n* 陷阱 xiànjǐng

trash *n* 垃圾 lājī

trauma *n* 外伤 wàishāng; **traumatic** *adj* 创伤的 chuāngshāng de, 痛苦万分的 tòngkǔ wànfēn de

travel *n/v* 旅行 lǚxíng; **travel agency** 旅行社 lǚxíngshè; **travel industry** 旅游业 lǚyóuyè; **travel insurance** 旅行保险 lǚxíng bǎoxiǎn; **travel sickness** (*car, bus, train*) 晕车 yùnchē; (*ship*) 晕船 yùnchuán; (*plane*) 晕机 yùnjī; **traveler** *n* 旅行者 lǚxíngzhě; **traveler's check** 旅行支票 lǚxíng zhīpiào

tray *n* 托盘 tuōpán

treachery *n* 背信弃义 bèixìn qìyì, 叛逆行为 pànnì xíngwéi

tread *v* (**trod, trodden/trod**) 踏 tà, 履 lǚ, 踩 cǎi

treason *n* 叛逆 pànnì, 叛国 pànguó, 谋反 móufǎn

treasure *n* 财宝 cáibǎo; **treasurer** *n* 财务掌管者 cáiwù zhǎngguǎnzhě; **treasury** *n* 财政部 cáizhèngbù; 国库 guókù

treat *v* 请客 qǐngkè, 招待 zhāodài, 对待 duìdài; **treatment** *n* (*benefit*) 待遇 dàiyù; (*med*) 治疗 zhìliáo

treaty *n* 条约 tiáoyuē

treble *v* 增为三倍 zēngwéi sānbèi; *adj* 三倍的 sānbèi de, 三重的 sānchóng de

tree *n* 树 shù

tremble *v* 颤抖 chàndǒu

tremendous *adj* 巨大的 jùdà de

tremor *n* 颤动 chàndòng

trend *n* 趋势 qūshì; **trendy** *adj* 流行的 liúxíng de, 时髦的 shímáo de

trespass *v/n* 侵入 qīnrù, 冒犯 màofàn

trial *n* 试验 shìyàn; (*law*) 审判 shěnpàn

triangle *n* 三角形 sānjiǎoxíng; **triangular** *adj* 三角形的 sānjiǎoxíng de

tribe *n* 部落 bùluò; **tribal** *adj* 部落的 bùluò de

tribunal *n* 法庭 fǎtíng

tribute *n* (*gifts*) 贡品 gòngpǐn; (*compliment*) 颂词 sòngcí

trick *v* 欺骗 qīpiàn; *n* 诡计 guǐjì, 诀窍 juéqiào; **tricky** *adj* 狡猾的 jiǎohuá de

tricycle *n* 三轮车 sānlúnchē

trifle *n* 琐事 suǒshì; **trifle with** *v* 视同儿戏 shìtóng érxì; **trifling** *adj* 不重要的 bù zhòngyào de

trigger *v* 引发 yǐnfā; *n* 扳机 bānjī

trim *v* 修剪 xiūjiǎn

trip *n* 旅行 lǚxíng

triple *v* 增至三倍 zēngzhì sānbèi; *adj* 三倍的 sānbèi de

tripod *n* 三脚架 sānjiǎojià

triumph *v* 取得胜利 qǔdé shènglì; *n* 胜利 shènglì; **triumphant** *adj* 胜利的 shènglì de, 成功的 chénggōng de

trivial *adj* 琐碎的 suǒsuì de, 微不足道的 wēibùzúdào de

trod/trodden. *See* tread

troops *n* 部队 bùduì

trophy *n* 奖品 jiǎngpǐn, 战利品 zhànlìpǐn

tropic *n* 热带 rèdài; **tropical** *adj* 热带的 rèdài de

trot *v* 小跑 xiǎopǎo

trouble *v* 麻烦 máfan, 打扰 dǎrǎo; *n* 麻烦 máfan; **troublesome** *adj* 麻烦的 máfan de; **troublemaker** *n* 惹麻烦的人 rě máfan de rén, 捣乱者 dǎoluànzhě

trough *n* 槽 cáo

trousers *n* 裤子 kùzi

truce *n* 停战 tíngzhàn

truck *n* 卡车 kǎchē

true *adj* 真实的 zhēnshí de, 真的 zhēnde; **truly** *adv* 真实地 zhēnshí de, 真正地 zhēnzhèng de

trumpet *n* 喇叭 lǎba

trunk *n* (*tree*) 树干 shùgàn; (*person*) 躯干 qūgàn; (*box*) 箱子 xiāngzi; (*car*) 汽车后箱 qìchē hòuxiāng; (*elephant*) 象鼻子 xiàngbízi

trust *v/n* 信任 xìnrèn, 信赖 xìnlài; **trustworthy** *adj* 可信赖的 kě xìnlài de; **trustee** *n* 理事 lǐshì, 托管人 tuōguǎnrén

truth n 事实 shìshí, 真理 zhēnlǐ; **truthfulness** n 真实 zhēnshí;
  truthful adj 诚实的 chéngshí de, 真实的 zhēnshí de
try v (*taste*) 尝 cháng; 试 shì
T-shirt. *See* **tee-shirt**
tub n 浴盆 yùpén
tube n 管子 guǎnzi; **inner tube** 内胎 nèitāi
tuberculosis n 结核病 jiéhébìng, 肺结核 fèijiéhé
tuck v 塞进 sāijìn
Tuesday n 星期二 xīngqī'èr
tug v 猛拉 měnglā; **tug of war** 拔河 báhé
tuition n 学费 xuéfèi
tumult n 吵闹 chǎonào, 骚动 sāodòng; **tumultuous** adj
  喧嚣的 xuānxiāo de
tune n 曲调 qǔdiào, 曲子 qǔzi; **in tune** 合调子 hé diàozi,
  一致 yīzhì; **out of tune** 走调 zǒudiào, 不一致 bù yīzhì
tunnel n 隧道 suìdào
turbulent adj 骚乱的 sāoluàn de, 动荡的 dòngdàng de;
  turbulence n (*turmoil*) 骚乱 sāoluàn, 动荡 dòngdàng;
  (*air*) 气流 qìliú
turf n 草皮 cǎopí, 地盘 dìpán
turkey n 火鸡 huǒjī
Turkey n 土耳其 tǔ'ěrqí; **Turkish** n 土耳其语 tǔ'ěrqíyǔ; adj
  土耳其的 tǔ'ěrqí de
turmoil n 骚动 sāodòng, 混乱 hùnluàn
turn v (*rotate*) (使) 转动 (shǐ) zhuǎndòng; (*bend*) 转弯
  zhuǎnwān; **turn against** 与 ... 为敌 yǔ ... wéidí; **turn
  around** 转向 zhuǎnxiàng, 好转 hǎozhuǎn; **turn back** (*go
  back*) 往回走 wǎng huí zǒu; (*push back*) 挡回 dǎng huí;
  turn down 拒绝 jùjué, 回绝 huíjué, 否决 fǒujué; **turn
  into** (使) 变为 (shǐ) biàn wéi; **turn off** 关 guān; **turn on**
  开 kāi; **turn up** 露面 lòumiàn, 出席 chūxí; n (*bend*) 转弯
  zhuǎnwān; (*in rotation*) 一次机会 yīcì jīhuì; **turnover** n
  营业额 yíngyè'é, 周转 zhōuzhuǎn
turtle n 乌龟 wūguī; **turtleneck** n 套领衫 tàolǐngshān
tutor n 辅导 fǔdǎo; 家庭教师 jiātíng jiàoshī, 私人教师 sīrén
  jiàoshī
twelve num 十二 shí'èr; **twelfth** num 第十二 dì shí'èr
twenty num 二十 èrshí; **twentieth** num 第二十 dì èrshí
twice adv 两次 liǎngcì, 两倍 liǎngbèi
twinkle v 闪烁 shǎnshuò
twins n 双胞胎 shuāngbāotāi

twist *v* 拧 nǐng; (*distort*) 歪曲 wāiqū; *n* 曲折 qūzhé, 周折 zhōuzhé

two *num* 二 èr; **two-faced** *adj* 两面派的 liǎngmiànpài de

type *v* 打字 dǎzì; *n* 种类 zhǒnglèi; **typewriter** *n* 打字机 dǎzìjī; **typist** *n* 打字员 dǎzìyuán

typhoon *n* 台风 táifēng

typical *adj* 典型的 diǎnxíng de

tyrant *n* 暴君 bàojūn; **tyranny** *n* 暴政 bàozhèng; **tyrannical** *adj* 暴虐的 bàonüè de

U

ugly *adj* 丑陋的 chǒulòu de, 丑的 chǒu de; **ugliness** *n* 丑陋 chǒulòu

ulterior *adj* 不可告人的 bùkě gàorén de; **ulterior motive** 不可告人的动机 bùkě gàorén de dòngjī

ultimate *adj* 最终的 zuìzhōng de; **ultimately** *adv* 最后 zuìhòu, 最终 zuìzhōng; **ultimatum** *n* 最后通牒 zuìhòu tōngdié

ultra- *pref* 极端 jíduān, 过度 guòdù

umbrella *n* 伞 sǎn

umpire *n* 裁判员 cáipànyuán

unable *adj* 不能 bù néng; **be unable to** 不能 bù néng

unacceptable *adj* 不能接受的 bù néng jiēshòu de

unaccompanied *adj* 无人陪伴的 wú rén péibàn de, 独自的 dúzì de

unanimous *adj* 一致同意的 yīzhì tóngyì de

unarmed *adj* 未武装的 wèi wǔzhuāng de, 徒手的 túshǒu de

unattractive *adj* 不引人注意的 bù yǐnrén zhùyì de

unauthorized *adj* 未经授权的 wèijīng shòuquán de, 未经批准的 wèijīng pīzhǔn de

unavoidable *adj* 不可避免的 bùkě bìmiǎn de

unaware *adj* 不知道的 bù zhīdao de

unbearable *adj* 难以忍受的 nányǐ rěnshòu de

unbelievable *adj* 难以置信的 nányǐ zhìxìn de

unbiased *adj* 没有偏见的 méiyǒu piānjiàn de

uncanny *adj* 离奇的 líqí de, 怪异的 guàiyì de

uncertain *adj* 不确定的 bù quèdìng de, 无常的 wúcháng de; **uncertainty** *n* 不定 bùdìng

uncle *n* (*father's younger brother*) 叔叔 shūshu; (*father's older brother*) 伯伯 bóbo; (*mother's brother*) 舅舅 jiùjiu

uncomfortable *adj* 不舒服的 bù shūfu de

uncommon *adj* 不凡的 bùfán de, 罕有的 hǎnyǒu de

unconditional *adj* 无条件的 wútiáojiàn de, 绝对的 juéduì de

unconscious *adj* 失去知觉的 shīqù zhījué de, 无意识的 wúyìshí de

unconventional *adj* 非常规的 fēichángguī de

uncouth *adj* 笨拙的 bènzhuō de, 粗俗的 cūsú de

uncover *v* 揭露 jiēlù, 揭开 jiēkāi

undecided *adj* 未定的 wèidìng de

undeniable *adj* 不可否认的 bùkě fǒurèn de

under *prep* 在 ... 之下 zài ... zhīxià, 在 ... 下面 zài ... xiàmian, 在 ... 下方 zài ... xiàfāng, 在 ... 底下 zài ... dǐxia

underclothes *n* 内衣 nèiyī

undercover *adj* 暗中进行的 ànzhōng jìnxíng de, 秘密的 mìmì de

underdeveloped *adj* 不发达的 bù fādá de

underestimate *v* 低估 dīgū

undergo *v* (**underwent, undergone**) 经历 jīnglì

undergraduate *n* 大学生 dàxuéshēng, 本科生 běnkēshēng

underground *adj* 地下的 dìxià de

underlie *v* 成为 ... 的基础 chéngwéi ... de jīchǔ; **underlying** *adj* 潜在的 qiánzài de, 根本的 gēnběn de

underline *v* (*draw line*) 在 ... 下面画线 zài ... xiàmian huàxiàn; (*emphasize*) 强调 qiángdiào

undermine *v* 暗中破坏 ànzhōng pòhuài

underneath *prep* 在 ... 下面 zài ... xiàmian; *adv* 在下面 zài xiàmian

underpants *n* 内裤 nèikù

underpass *n* 地下通道 dìxià tōngdào

underprivileged *adj* 被剥夺基本权力的 bèi bōduó jīběn quánlì de, 下层社会的 xiàcéng shèhuì de

understand *v* (**understood, understood**) 懂 dǒng, 理解 lǐjiě; **understandable** *adj* 可以理解的 kěyǐ lǐjiě de; **understanding** *n* 理解 lǐjiě, 谅解 liàngjiě; *adj* 谅解的 liàngjiě de; 理解的 lǐjiě de

understate *v* 保守地说 bǎoshǒu de shuō; **understatement** *n* 轻描淡写的陈述 qīngmiáo dànxiě de chénshù

undertake *v* (**undertook, undertaken**) 承担 chéngdān, 担负 dānfù; **undertaking** *n* 任务 rènwu, 事业 shìyè, 承诺 chéngnuò

underwater *adj* 在水下的 zài shuǐ xià de

underwrite *v* (**underwrote, underwritten**) 承诺支付 chéngnuò zhīfù

undesirable *adj* 不受欢迎的 bùshòu huānyíng de, 不合意的 bù héyì de

undo *v* (**undid**, **undone**) (*untie*) 解开 jiěkāi, 松开 sōngkāi; (*cancel*) 取消 qǔxiāo, 撤销 chèxiāo

undoubted *adj* 无疑的 wúyí de

undress *v* 脱衣服 tuō yīfu

unearth *v* 挖出 wā chū, 掘出 jué chū

uneasy *adj* 不安宁的 bù ānníng de, 焦虑的 jiāolǜ de

uneducated *adj* 没有教育的 méiyǒu jiàoyù de, 未受教育的 wèi shòu jiàoyù de

unemployed *adj* 失业的 shīyè de; **unemployment** *n* 失业 shīyè

unenthusiastic *adj* 不热心的 bù rèxīn de

unequal *adj* 不相等的 bù xiāngděng de, 不平等的 bù píngděng de

uneven *adj* 不平坦的 bù píngtǎn de, 不平均的 bù píngjūn de

uneventful *adj* 平静无事的 píngjìng wúshì de

unexpected *adj* 意外的 yìwài de

unfair *adj* 不公平的 bù gōngpíng de

unfaithful *adj* 不忠实的 bù zhōngshí de; **unfaithfulness** *n* 不忠 bù zhōng

unfamiliar *adj* 不熟悉的 bù shúxī de

unfasten *v* 解开 jiěkāi

unfavorable *adj* 不顺利的 bù shùnlì de, 不宜的 bùyí de, 不利的 bù lì de

unfinished *adj* 未完成的 wèiwánchéng de

unfit *adj* 不适宜的 bù shìyí de

unfold *v* 打开 dǎkāi, 展开 zhǎnkāi, 显露 xiǎnlù

unforeseen *adj* 无法预料的 wúfǎ yùliào de

unforgivable *adj* 不可原谅的 bùkě yuánliàng de

unfortunate *adj* 不幸的 bùxìng de; **unfortunately** *adv* 不幸地 bùxìng de

unfounded *adj* 没有理由的 méiyǒu lǐyóu de, 没有根据的 méiyǒu gēnjù de

unfriendly *adj* 不友好的 bù yǒuhǎo de

ungrateful *adj* 忘恩负义的 wàng'ēn fùyì de

unhappy *adj* 不高兴的 bù gāoxìng de

unhealthy *adj* 不健康的 bù jiànkāng de

unheard-of *adj* 空前的 kōngqián de, 前所未闻的 qiánsuǒ wèiwén de

unhurt *adj* 没有受伤的 méiyǒu shòushāng de

uniform *n* 制服 zhìfú; *adj* 一致的 yīzhì de, 统一的 tǒngyī de

unify *v* 统一 tǒngyī; **unification** *n* 统一 tǒngyī
unilateral *adj* 单方面的 dānfāngmiàn de
unimportant *adj* 不重要的 bù zhòngyào de
uninhabited *adj* 无人居住的 wúrén jūzhù de
uninhibited *adj* 不受约束的 bùshòu yuēshù de
unintentional *adj* 无心的 wúxīn de
uninteresting *adj* 无趣的 wúqù de
union *n* 联合 liánhé, 联盟 liánméng
unique *adj* 独特的 dútè de
unisex *adj* 男女通用的 nánnǚ tōngyòng de
unison *n* 一致 yīzhì; **in unison** 一致 yīzhì
unit *n* 单位 dānwèi, 单元 dānyuán
unite *v* 联合 liánhé; **united** *adj* 团结的 tuánjié de, 联合的 liánhé de
United Kingdom *n* 英国 yīngguó
United Nations *n* 联合国 liánhéguó
United States of America *n* 美国 měiguó
unity *n* 团结 tuánjié
universe *n* 宇宙 yǔzhòu; **universal** *adj* 普遍的 pǔbiàn de, 通用的 tōngyòng de
university *n* 大学 dàxué
unjust *adj* 不公平的 bù gōngpíng de, 非正义的 fēizhèngyì de
unkempt *adj* 不整洁的 bù zhěngjié de, 蓬乱的 péngluàn de
unknown *adj* 未知的 wèizhī de, 不知的 bùzhī de
unlawful *adj* 非法的 fēifǎ de
unleash *v* 释放 shìfàng, 发动 fādòng
unless *conj* 除非 chúfēi
unlike *adj* 不相似的 bù xiāngsì de; *prep* 不像 bùxiàng
unlikely *adj* 不太可能的 bù tài kěnéng de
unlimited *adj* 无限的 wúxiàn de
unload *v* 卸货 xièhuò
unlock *v* 开锁 kāisuǒ, 开启 kāiqǐ
unlucky *adj* 不幸的 bùxìng de
unmarried *adj* 未婚的 wèihūn de
unmistakable *adj* 不会弄错的 bùhuì nòngcuò de
unnatural *adj* 不自然的 bù zìrán de
unnecessary *adj* 不必要的 bù bìyào de
unnoticed *adj* 未被注意的 wèi bèi zhùyì de, 被忽视的 bèi hūshì de
unofficial *adj* 非正式的 fēizhèngshì de, 非官方的 fēiguān-fāng de
unpack *v* 打开包裹 dǎkāi bāoguǒ, 打开箱子 dǎkāi xiāngzi

unpaid *adj* 未付款的 wèifùkuǎn de
unpleasant *adj* 令人不愉快的 lìng rén bù yúkuài de
unpopular *adj* 不流行的 bù liúxíng de, 不受欢迎的 bùshòu huānyíng de
unprecedented *adj* 空前的 kōngqián de
unpredictable *adj* 不可预知的 bùkě yùzhī de
unqualified *adj* 不合格的 bù hégé de, 无资格的 wúzīgé de
unreal *adj* 不真实的 bù zhēnshí de
unreasonable *adj* 不合理的 bù hélǐ de
unreliable *adj* 不可靠的 bù kěkào de
unrest *n* 不安 bù'ān, 动荡 dòngdàng
unruly *adj* 不守规矩的 bùshǒu guīju de
unsafe *adj* 不安全的 bù ānquán de
unsatisfactory *adj* 不能令人满意的 bù néng lìng rén mǎnyì de
unscrew *v* 拧开 nǐng kāi
unselfish *adj* 无私的 wúsī de
unskilled *adj* 不熟练的 bù shúliàn de, 无技能的 wújìnéng de
unstable *adj* 不稳定的 bù wěndìng de
unsteady *adj* 不稳固的 bù wěngù de
unsuccessful *adj* 不成功的 bù chénggōng de, 失败的 shībài de
unsuitable *adj* 不适合的 bù shìhé de
untidy *adj* 不整洁的 bù zhěngjié de
untie *v* 解开 jiě kāi
until *prep/conj* 直到 zhídào
untrue *adj* 不真实的 bù zhēnshí de
unusual *adj* 不寻常的 bù xúncháng de
unwind *v* (**unwound, unwound**) 展开 zhǎnkāi, 解开 jiěkāi, 放松 fàngsōng
unwise *adj* 不明智的 bù míngzhì de
unwrap *v* 打开 dǎkāi, 解开 jiěkāi, 展开 zhǎnkāi
up *adv* 上 shàng, 起来 qǐlái; (*get up*) 起床 qǐchuáng; *adv* 向上 xiàng shàng, 在上 zài shàng; *adj* 向上的 xiàng shàng de; **up close** 近距离地 jìn jùlí de; **up to** (*reaching*) 达到 dádào, 接近于 jiējìn yú; (*depending on*) 取决于 qǔjué yú
upbringing *n* 养育 yǎngyù, 教养 jiàoyǎng
update *v* 提供最新的情况 tígòng zuìxīn de qíngkuàng; *n* 新的情况 xīn de qíngkuàng, 新的信息 xīn de xìnxī
upheaval *n* 剧变 jùbiàn, 动乱 dòngluàn
uphill *adj* 上坡的 shàngpō de; (*hard*) 艰难的 jiānnán de
uphold *v* (**upheld, upheld**) (*lift*) 举起 jǔqǐ; (*support*) 支持 zhīchí; (*approve of*) 赞成 zànchéng; (*maintain*) 维持 wéichí

uplift v (*raise*) 举起 jǔqǐ; (*exalt*) 振奋 zhènfèn

upon prep 在 ... 上面 zài ... shàngmian

upper adj 上面的 shàngmian de, 上部的 shàngbù de, 较高的 jiàogāo de, 较上的 jiàoshàng de, 高等的 gāoděng de, 上等的 shàngděng de; **upper class** 上层阶级 shàngcéng jiējí; **upper hand** 优势 yōushì, 上风 shàngfēng

upright adj 直立的 zhílì de; adv 直立地 zhílì de

uprising n 起义 qǐyì

uproar n 喧嚣 xuānxiāo, 哗然 huárán

uproot v 连根拔起 liángēn báqǐ, 根除 gēnchú

upset v (**upset, upset**) 打翻 dǎfān, 扰乱 rǎoluàn

upside down adj 颠倒的 diāndǎo de

upstairs adv 在楼上 zài lóushàng, 往楼上 wǎng lóushàng

upstream adv 向上游 xiàng shàngyóu, 逆流地 nìliú de

up-to-date adj 最近的 zuìjìn de

upward; upwards adv 向上 xiàngshàng; **upward of** ... 以上 ... yǐshàng, 多于 ... duōyú ...

uranium n 铀 yóu

urban adj 城市的 chéngshì de

urge v 敦促 dūncù; n 冲动 chōngdòng, 推动力 tuīdònglì

urgent adj 紧急的 jǐnjí de, 急迫的 jípò de; **urgency** n 急迫 jípò

urine n 尿 niào, 小便 xiǎobiàn

Uruguay n 乌拉圭 wūlāguī; **Uruguayan** n 乌拉圭人 wūlāguīrén; adj 乌拉圭的 wūlāguī de

us pron 我们 wǒmen

usage n 用法 yòngfǎ

use v/n 用处 yòngchu, 用途 yòngtú; v 使用 shǐyòng; **use up** 用完 yòng wán; **user** n 用户 yònghù, 使用者 shǐyòngzhě; **used** adj 旧的 jiù de, 二手的 èrshǒu de; **used to (sth.)** 习惯于 xíguàn yú; **useful** adj 有用的 yǒuyòng de; **useless** adj 无用的 wúyòng de

usher v 引座 yǐnzuò; **usher in** 迎接 yíngjiē; n 引座员 yǐnzuòyuán

usual adj 通常的 tōngcháng de; **usually** adv 通常 tōngcháng, 往往 wǎngwǎng

utensil n 器具 qìjù

utility n (*usefulness*) 功用 gōngyòng, 效用 xiàoyòng; (*public service*) 公用事业 gōngyòng shìyè

utilize v 利用 lìyòng

utmost adj 极度的 jídù de

utter *v* 说 shuō, 发声 fāshēng; *adj* 完全的 wánquán de, 绝对的 juéduì de

utterance *n* 说话 shuō huà, 言语 yányǔ

U-turn *n* 180度转弯 180 dù zhuǎnwān

V

vacant *adj* 空的 kōng de; **vacancy** *n* (*space*) 空位 kòngwèi; (*position*) 空缺 kòngquē

vacation *n* 假期 jiàqī

vaccine *n* 疫苗 yìmiáo; **vaccinate** *v* 给 ... 接种疫苗 gěi ... jiēzhòng yìmiáo

vacillate *v* 犹豫不定 yóuyù bùdìng; **vacillation** *n* 犹豫不定 yóuyù bùdìng

vacuum *n* 真空 zhēnkōng; *v* 用真空吸尘器打扫 yòng zhēnkōng xīchénqì dǎsǎo; **vacuum cleaner** 真空吸尘器 zhēnkōng xīchénqì

vagina *n* 阴道 yīndào

vagrant *n* 流浪者 liúlàngzhě

vague *adj* 含糊的 hánhu de, 模糊的 móhu de

vain *adj* (*of vanity*) 虚荣的 xūróng de; (*futile*) 徒劳的 túláo de; **in vain** 徒劳的 túláo de

valiant *adj* 勇敢的 yǒnggǎn de

valid *adj* 有效的 yǒuxiào de; **validity** *n* 有效性 yǒuxiàoxìng

valley *n* 山谷 shāngǔ

value *v* 重视 zhòngshì; *n* 价值 jiàzhí; **valuable** *adj* 有价值的 yǒu jiàzhí de; 贵重的 guìzhòng de; **valuables** *n* 贵重物品 guìzhòng wùpǐn

valve *n* 阀门 fámén

vampire *n* 吸血鬼 xīxuèguǐ

van *n* 面包车 miànbāochē

vandal *n* 破坏他人财产者 pòhuài tārén cáichǎn zhě; **vandalism** *n* 破坏他人财产 pòhuài tārén cáichǎn

vanilla *n* 香草 xiāngcǎo

vanish *v* (*disappear*) 消失 xiāoshī; (*go away*) 离开 líkāi

vanity *n* 虚荣心 xūróngxīn

vapor *n* 蒸气 zhēngqì; **vaporize** *v* (使) 蒸发 (shǐ) zhēngfā

variety *n* 多样性 duōyàngxìng, 种类 zhǒnglèi; **a variety of** 各种各样的 gèzhǒnggèyàng de

various *adj* 各种各样的 gèzhǒng gèyàng de

vary *v* 更改 gēnggǎi, (使) 不同 (shǐ) bùtóng; **variant** *n* 变种

biànzhǒng, 变量 biànliàng, 变体 biàntǐ; **variation** *n* 变异 biànyì

vase *n* 花瓶 huāpíng

vast *adj* 巨大的 jùdà de, 辽阔的 liáokuò de; **vastly** *adv* 广大地 guǎngdà de, 极大的 jídà de

Vatican *n* 梵蒂冈 fàndìgāng

vault *n* (*arch*) 拱顶 gǒngdǐng; (*chamber*) 地下室 dìxiàshì

veal *n* 小牛肉 xiǎoniúròu

vegetable *n* 蔬菜 shūcài; **vegetarian** *n* 素食者 sùshízhě; *adj* 素食的 sùshí de; **vegetation** *n* 植物 zhíwù, 草木 cǎomù

vehement *adj* 激烈的 jīliè de; **vehemence** *n* 激烈 jīliè, 强烈 qiángliè; **vehemently** *adj* 强烈地 qiángliè de

vehicle *n* (*cars, etc.*) 车辆 chēliàng; (*means*) 手段 shǒuduàn

veil *n* 面纱 miànshā

vein *n* 静脉 jìngmài, 血管 xuèguǎn

velocity *n* 速度 sùdù

velvet *adj* 柔软的 róuruǎn de

vending machine *n* 自动售货机 zìdòng shòuhuòjī

vendor *n* 小贩 xiǎofàn, 卖主 màizhǔ, 商家 shāngjiā

venereal *adj* (*of intercourse*) 性交的 xìngjiāo de; (*of disease*) 性病的 xìngbìng de; **venereal disease** 性病 xìngbìng

venerate *v* 崇敬 chóngjìng; **venerable** *adj* 值得尊敬的 zhíde zūnjìng de, 庄严的 zhuāngyán de

Venezuela *n* 委内瑞拉 wěinèiruìlā, **Venezuelan** *n* 委内瑞拉人 wěinèiruìlārén; *adj* 委内瑞拉的 wěinèiruìlā de

vengeance *n* 复仇 fùchóu, 报仇 bàochóu

venom *n* (*fluid*) 毒液 dúyè; (*malice*) 怨恨 yuànhèn; **venomous** *adj* (*poisonous*) 有毒的 yǒudú de; (*malicious*) 恶毒的 èdú de

vent *n* 通风孔 tōngfēngkǒng; **give vent to** 发泄 fāxiè

ventilate *v* 通风 tōngfēng; **ventilation** *n* 通风 tōngfēng; **ventilator** *n* 通风设备 tōngfēng shèbèi

venture *v* 冒险 màoxiǎn; *n* 冒险行动 màoxiǎn xíngdòng; (*business*) 商业冒险 shāngyè màoxiǎn

venue *n* 活动场地 huódòng chǎngdì

veranda *n* 走廊 zǒuláng

verb *n* 动词 dòngcí; **verbal** *adj* (*spoken*) 口头的 kǒutóu de; (*of words*) 词语的 cíyǔ de

verdict *n* 裁决 cáijué, 判决 pànjué

verge *n* 边缘 biānyuán; **on the verge of** 濒临于 bīnlín yú, 接近于 jiējìn yú

verify *v* 核实 héshí; **verification** *n* 核实 héshí

vermin *n* (*pest*) 害虫 hàichóng; (*person*) 歹徒 dǎitú

verse *n* 韵文 yùnwén, 诗句 shījù

version *n* 版本 bǎnběn; (*translation*) 译本 yìběn

versus *prep* 对 duì

vertebrate *n* 脊椎动物 jǐzhuī dòngwù

vertical *adj* 垂直的 chuízhí de, 竖的 shù de

very *adv* 很 hěn; **very much** *adj* 很 hěn, 非常 fēicháng

vessel *n* (*ship*) 船 chuán; (*utensil*) 器皿 qìmǐn; (*artery*) 脉管 màiguǎn

vest *n* 背心 bèixīn

vet *n* (*veterinarian*) 兽医 shòuyī

veteran *n* 退伍军人 tuìwǔ jūnrén

veterinary *n* 兽医 shòuyī; **veterinary medicine** 兽医学 shòuyīxué

veto *v/n* (*pl* **vetoes**) 否决 fǒujué

vex *v* (使) 恼怒 (shǐ) nǎonù

viable *adj* 可行的 kěxíng de; **viability** *n* 生存能力 shēngcún nénglì

vibrate *v* (使) 振动 (shǐ) zhèndòng; **vibration** *n* 振动 zhèndòng; **vibrant** *adj* 振动的 zhèndòng de, 精力充沛的 jīnglì chōngpèi de

vice *n* (*habit*) 恶习 èxí; (*tool*) 老虎钳 lǎohǔqián; (*deputy*) 副 fù; **vice president** (*of a country*) 副总统 fùzǒngtǒng

vicinity *n* 邻近 línjìn; **in the vicinity of** 在附近 zài fùjìn

vicious *adj* 恶意的 èyì de, 恶毒的 èdú de; **vicious circle** 恶性循环 èxìng xúnhuán; **viciousness** *n* 恶毒 èdú

victim *n* 受害人 shòuhàirén; **victimize** *v* (使) 受害 (shǐ) shòuhài, (使) 受骗 (shǐ) shòupiàn

victory *n* 胜利 shènglì; **victorious** *adj* 获胜的 huòshèng de, 胜利的 shènglì de

view *n* (*scene*) 风景 fēngjǐng; (*opinion*) 观点 guāndiǎn; **viewer** *n* 观察者 guāncházhě; **viewpoint** *v* 观点 guāndiǎn

vigil *n* 守夜 shǒuyè; **vigilance** *n* 警惕 jǐngtì; **vigilant** *adj* 警惕的 jǐngtì de

vigor *n* 活力 huólì; **vigorous** *adj* 精力旺盛的 jīnglì wàngshèng de

villa *n* 别墅 biéshù

village *n* 乡村 xiāngcūn, 村子 cūnzi; **villager** *n* 村民 cūnmín

villain *n* 坏人 huàirén, 恶棍 ègùn

vindicate *v* 证明无辜 zhèngmíng wúgū

vinegar *n* 醋 cù

vineyard *n* 葡萄园 pútáoyuán

vintage *adj* 上等的 shàngděng de; (*of wine*) 佳酿的 jiāniàng de

violate *v* 违犯 wéifàn, 侵害 qīnhài; **violation** *n* 违犯 wéifàn, 侵害 qīnhài

violence *n* 暴力 bàolì; **violent** *adj* 猛烈的 měngliè de, 暴烈的 bàoliè de, 暴力的 bàolì de

violet *n* 紫罗兰 zǐluōlán

violin *n* 小提琴 xiǎotíqín; **violinist** *n* 小提琴手 xiǎotíqínshǒu

virgin *n* 处女 chǔnǚ

virility *n* 生殖力 shēngzhílì, 男子气 nánzǐqì

virtual *adj* (*actual*) 事实上的 shìshíshang de; (*computer*) 虚拟的 xūnǐ de; *adv* 事实上 shìshí shang, 实质上 shízhì shang

virtue *n* 美德 měidé; **by virtue of** 由于 yóuyú; **virtuous** *adj* (*moral*) 有道德的 yǒu dàodé de, (*of women*) 贞节的 zhēnjié de

virus *n* 病毒 bìngdú

visa *n* 签证 qiānzhèng

visible *adj* 看得见的 kàn de jiàn de, 明显的 míngxiǎn de; **visibility** *n* 可见性 kějiànxing, 能见度 néngjiàndù

vision *n* (*sight*) 视力 shìlì; (*farsightedness*) 远见 yuǎnjiàn

visit *v/n* 访问 fǎngwèn, 参观 cānguān; **visitor** *n* 访客 fǎngkè

visual *adj* 视觉的 shìjué de; **visualize** *v* 想象 xiǎngxiàng

vital *adj* 至关重要的 zhìguān zhòngyào de; **vitality** *n* 生命力 shēngmìnglì, 活力 huólì

vitamin *n* 维生素 wéishēngsù

vivid *adj* 生动的 shēngdòng de; **vividness** *n* 生动 shēngdòng

vocabulary *n* 词汇 cíhuì

vocal *adj* (*of voice*) 声音的 shēngyīn de; (*of singing*) 歌唱的 gēchàng de; (*outspoken*) 直言的 zhíyán de; **vocalist** *n* 歌手 gēshǒu, 声乐家 shēnyuèjiā

vocation *n* 职业 zhíyè, 行业 hángyè; **vocational** *adj* 职业的 zhíyè de

vodka *n* 伏特加酒 fútèjiājiǔ

vogue *n* 时尚 shíshàng; **in vogue** 流行 liúxíng

voice *v* 表达 biǎodá; *n* 声音 shēngyīn

void *n* 空虚 kōngxū; *adj* (*empty*) 空的 kōng de; (*invalid*) 无效的 wúxiào de

volatile *adj* 易挥发的 yì huīfā de, 不稳定的 bù wěndìng de

volcano *n* 火山 huǒshān

volt *n* 伏特 fútè; **voltage** *n* 电压 diànyā

volume *n* (*books*) 册 cè; (*space*) 体积 tǐjī; (*quantity*) 大量

dàliàng; (*sound*) 音量 yīnliàng; **voluminous** *adj*
卷数多的 juàn shù duō de

volunteer *n* 志愿者 zhìyuànzhě; **voluntary** *adj* 自愿的
zìyuàn de, 义务的 yìwù de

vomit *v* 呕吐 ǒutù

vote *v* 投票 tóupiào; *n* 选票 xuǎnpiào; **voter** *n* 投票人
tóupiàorén, 选举人 xuǎnjǔrén

vouch *v* (*vouch for*) 作证 zuòzhèng, 担保 dānbǎo, 保证
bǎozhèng

voucher *n* 凭证 píngzhèng, 优惠购物券 yōuhuì gòuwùquàn

vow *v* 发誓 fāshì; *n* 誓言 shìyán

vowel *n* 元音 yuányīn

voyage *n* 航海 hánghǎi

vulgar *adj* 粗俗的 cūsú de

vulnerability *n* 弱点 ruòdiǎn; **vulnerable** *adj* 易受攻击的
yìshòu gōngjī de

vulture *n* 秃鹫 tūjiù

W

wade *v* 涉水 shèshuǐ

wag *v* 摇动 yáodòng

wage *v* (*war, etc.*) 发动 fādòng; *n* 工资 gōngzī; **wage earner**
挣工资的人 zhèng gōngzī de rén; **wage freeze** 工资冻结
gōngzī dòngjié; **wage raise** 加薪 jiāxīn

wagon *n* 货车 huòchē

wail *v* 嚎啕 háotáo

waist *n* 腰 yāo; **waistcoat** *n* 背心 bèixīn

wait *v* 等 děng, 等候 děnghòu, 等待 děngdài; **waiter** *n*
服务员 fúwùyuán; **waitress** *n* 女服务员 nǚfúwùyuán;
waiting room 等候室 děnghòushì; (*doctor's office,
hospital*) 候诊室 hòuzhěnshì

waive *v* (*give up*) 放弃 fàngqì; (*exempt*) 免除 miǎnchú

wake *v* (**woke/waked, woken/waked**) 醒 xǐng; **wake up**
醒来 xǐng lái

waken. *See* **wake**

Wales *n* 威尔士 wēi'ěrshì

walk *v* 步行 bùxíng, 走 zǒu; **walkout** *n* 罢工 bàgōng;
walking *n* 步行 bùxíng; **walking stick** 拐杖 guǎizhàng

wall *n* 墙 qiáng

wallet *n* 钱包 qiánbāo

wallpaper *n* 墙纸 qiángzhǐ

walnut *n* 胡桃 hútáo

waltz *n* 华尔兹舞 huá'ěrzīwǔ, 圆舞曲 yuánwǔqǔ

wander *v* 漫步 mànbù

want *v* (*need*) 要 yào; (*be short of*) 短缺 duǎnquē; *n* (*need*) 需要 xūyào; (*shortage*) 短缺 duǎnquē; **for want of** 因缺乏 yīn quēfá; **wanted** *adj* 被通缉的 bèi tōngjī de; **wanting** *adj* 缺乏的 quēfá de

war *n* 战争 zhànzhēng; **war crime** 战争罪行 zhànzhēng zuìxíng; **war criminal** 战犯 zhànfàn; **war game** 军事演习 jūnshì yǎnxí; **warfare** *n* 战争 zhànzhēng; **warship** *n* 军舰 jūnjiàn, 战船 zhànchuán; **wartime** *n* 战时 zhànshí

ward *n* (*hospital*) 病房 bìngfáng; (*prison*) 牢房 láofáng; **ward off** 避开 bìkāi, 挡住 dǎngzhù

warden *n* 监狱长 jiānyùzhǎng

warder *n* 监狱看守 jiānyù kānshǒu

wardrobe *n* 衣橱 yīchú

warehouse *n* 仓库 cāngkù

warm *adj* 温暖的 wēnnuǎn de; **warm up** 热身 rèshēn; **warmth** *n* 温暖 wēnnuǎn

warn *v* 警告 jǐnggào; **warning** *n* 警告 jǐnggào

warrant *n* (*authorization*) 授权 shòuquán; (*law*) 令状 lìngzhuàng; (*justification*) 理由 lǐyóu; **warranty** *n* 保证 bǎozhèng, 担保 dānbǎo, 保修 bǎoxiū; **under warranty** 在保修期内 zài bǎoxiūqī nèi

warrior *n* 战士 zhànshì, 勇士 yǒngshì

was. *See* **be**

wash *v* 洗 xǐ; **wash up** 洗餐具 xǐ cānjù; **washing** *n* 洗涤 xǐdí; **washing powder** 洗衣粉 xǐyīfěn; **wash basin** 洗脸盆 xǐliǎnpén; **washing machine** 洗衣机 xǐyījī

washroom *n* 厕所 cèsuǒ, 盥洗室 guànxǐshì

wasp *n* 黄蜂 huángfēng

waste *v* 浪费 làngfèi; *n* 废物 fèiwù; **wasteful** *adj* 浪费的 làngfèi de; **wasteland** *n* 荒地 huāngdì; **wastepaper** *n* 废纸 fèizhǐ; **wastepaper basket** 废纸篓 fèizhǐ lǒu

watch *v* 观看 guānkàn, 注视 zhùshì; *n* 手表 shǒubiǎo; **watchdog** *n* (*dog*) 看门狗 kànméngǒu; (*person*) 监督人员 jiāndū rényuán

water *v* 给 ... 浇水 gěi ... jiāoshuǐ; *n* 水 shuǐ; **by water** 乘船 chéng chuán, 由水路 yóu shuǐlù; **water buffalo** 水牛 shuǐniú; **water chestnut** 荸荠 bíqí; **waterfall** *n* 瀑布 pùbù; **waterproof** *adj* 防水的 fángshuǐ de

watermelon *n* 西瓜 xīguā

wave *v* 挥手 huīshǒu; *n* 波浪 bōlàng; **wavelength** *n* 波长 bōcháng

waver *v* 犹豫 yóuyù, 动摇 dòngyáo; **wavering** *adj* 摇摆的 yáobǎi de

wax *n* 蜡 là

way *n* (*method*) 方式 fāngshì, 办法 bànfǎ; (*road*) 道路 dàolù; **way of life** 生活方式 shēnghuó fāngshì; **by the way** 顺便说一句 shùnbiàn shuō yī jù; **give way** 退让 tuìràng (*give in*) 屈服 qūfú; (*collapse*) 倒塌 dǎotā; **on the way** 在路上 zài lùshang; **this way** 这边请 zhèbiān qǐng, 这边走 zhèbiān zǒu; **under way** 正在进行 zhèngzài jìnxíng; **way in** 入口 rùkǒu

we *pron* 我们 wǒmen

weak *adj* 弱的 ruò de, 虚弱的 xūruò de; **weaken** *v* 削弱 xuēruò; **weakness** *n* 虚弱 xūruò, 弱点 ruòdiǎn

wealth *n* 财富 cáifù; (*quantity*) 众多 zhòngduō, 大量 dàliàng; **wealthy** *adj* 富有的 fùyǒu de

weapon *n* 武器 wǔqì

wear *v* (**wore**, **worn**) 穿 chuān, 戴 dài; (*deteriorate*) 磨损 mósǔn; **wear out** (*of clothes*) 穿破 chuān pò; (*deteriorate*) 磨损 mósǔn; (*fatigue*) 疲劳 píláo; **wear and tear** 磨损 mósǔn; 损耗 sǔnhào

weary *adj* 疲倦的 píjuàn de, 消沉的 xiāochén de, 厌倦的 yànjuàn de

weasel *n* 黄鼠狼 huángshǔláng

weather *n* 天气 tiānqì, 气象 qìxiàng; **weather forecast** 天气预报 tiānqì yùbào; **weather station** 气象站 qìxiàngzhàn; **in all weathers** 风雨无阻 fēngyǔ wú zǔ, 不论在什么情况下 bùlùn zài shénme qíngkuàng xià; **under the weather** 不舒服 bù shūfu, 生病 shēngbìng

weave *v* (**wove/weaved**, **woven/weaved**) 编织 biānzhī

web *n* 网 wǎng

wed *v* (**wed/wedded**, **wed/wedded**) 结婚 jiéhūn; **wedding** *n* 婚礼 hūnlǐ

Wednesday *n* 星期三 xīngqīsān

weed *n* 野草 yěcǎo, 杂草 zácǎo

week *n* 星期 xīngqī; **weekend** *n* 周末 zhōumò; **weekly** *n* 周刊 zhōukān; *adj* 每周一次的 měi zhōu yī cì de; *adv* 每周一次地 měi zhōu yī cì de

weep *v* (**wept**, **wept**) 哭泣 kūqì

weigh *v* 重量为 zhòngliàng wéi; 称 chēng; **weight** *n* 重量 zhòngliàng; **weightlifting** *n* 举重 jǔzhòng

weird *adj* 怪异的 guàiyì de; **weirdness** *n* 怪异 guàiyì

welcome *v/n* 欢迎 huānyíng; **you're welcome** 不客气 bù kèqì

welfare *n* 福利 fúlì, 福利事业 fúlì shìyè

well *adv* 很好地 hěnhǎo de; *adj* 健康的 jiànkāng de

well-behaved *adj* 行为端正的 xíngwéi duānzhèng de, 听话的 tīnghuà de

well-being *n* 安宁 ānníng, 健康 jiànkāng

well-dressed *adj* 穿着入时的 chuānzhuó rùshí de

well-informed *adj* 消息灵通的 xiāoxī língtōng de

well-known *adj* 众所周知的 zhòngsuǒ zhōuzhī de, 著名的 zhùmíng de

well-to-do *adj* 富有的 fùyǒu de

Welsh *adj* 威尔士的 wēi'ěrshì de

went. *See* **go**

wept. *See* **weep**

were. *See* **be**

west *n* 西边 xībian, 西方 xīfāng, 西部 xībù; **Western** *adj* 西方的 xīfāng de; **Westerner** *n* 西方人 xīfāngrén

wet *adj* 湿的 shī de

whale *n* 鲸 jīng

wharf *n* 码头 mǎtou

what *pron* 什么 shénme; **what about** 又怎样 yòu zěnyàng

whatever *pron* 无论什么 wúlùn shénme

wheat *n* 小麦 xiǎomài

wheel *n* 轮子 lúnzi; **wheelchair** *n* 轮椅 lúnyǐ

when *adv* 什么时候 shénme shíhou; **whenever** *conj* 无论何时 wúlùn héshí

where *adv* 在哪儿 zài nǎr; **whereabouts** *n* 下落 xiàluò, 行踪 xíngzōng, 所在 suǒzài; **whereas** *conj* 然而 rán'ér, 但是 dànshì; **wherever** *adv* 无论哪里 wúlùn nǎli

whether *conj* 是否 shìfou, 不管 bùguǎn

which *pron* 哪 (个) nǎ (gè); **whichever** *pron* 无论哪 (个) wúlùn nǎ (gè)

while *n* 一会儿 yīhuìr; *conj* (*when*) 当 ... 时 dāng ... shí; (*although*) 虽然 suīrán; **while away** 消磨 xiāomó

whisker *n* 胡须 húxū

whiskey/whisky *n* 威士忌 wēishìjì

whisper *v* 小声说 xiǎoshēng shuō; *n* 耳语 ěryǔ

whistle *v* 吹口哨 chuī kǒushào; *n* 口哨 kǒushào

white *adj* 白色的 báisè de
who *pron* 谁 shuí/shéi; **whoever** *pron* 无论谁 wúlùn shuí/shéi, 不管是谁 bùguǎn shì shuí/shéi
whole *n* 全部 quánbù; 整个 zhěnggè; **on the whole** 总体来说 zǒngtǐ láishuō; *adj* 完全的 wánquán de, 完整的 wánzhěng de, 全部的 quánbù de; **wholehearted** *adj* 一心一意的 yīxīn yīyì de; **wholeheartedly** *adv* 一心一意地 yīxīn yīyì de; **wholesome** *adj* 健康的 jiànkāng de, 有益的 yǒuyì de
wholesale *n* 批发 pīfā; **wholesaler** *n* 批发商 pīfāshāng
whom *pron* 谁 shuí/shéi
whose *pron* 谁的 shuíde/shéide
why *adv* 为什么 wèishénme
wicked *adj* 邪恶的 xié'è de
wide *adj* 宽的 kuān de; **widespread** *adj* 普遍的 pǔbiàn de, 广泛的 guǎngfàn de
widow *n* 寡妇 guǎfù; **widower** *n* 鳏夫 guānfū
width *n* 宽度 kuāndù
wield *v* 挥动 huīdòng, 挥 huī
wife *n* (*pl* **wives**) 妻子 qīzi
wig *n* 假发 jiǎfà
wild *adj* (*plants, etc.*) 野生的 yěshēng de; (*savage*) 野蛮的 yěmán de; **wildlife** *n* 野生动植物 yěshēng dòngzhíwù; **wildly** *adv* 野生地 yěshēng de; 野蛮地 yěmán de
wilderness *n* 荒野 huāngyě
will *v* (*would*) See **be**; *n* (*volition*) 意志 yìzhì; (*law*) 遗嘱 yízhǔ
willing *adj* 自愿的 zìyuàn de, 愿意的 yuànyì de; **willingly** *adv* 自愿地 zìyuàn de
willow *n* 柳树 liǔshù
win *v* (**won, won**) 赢 yíng, 胜 shèng; **winner** *n* 获胜者 huòshèngzhě; **winning** *adj* 得胜的 déshèng de, 胜利的 shènglì de
wind *v* (**wound, wound**) 缠绕 chánrào, 上发条 shàng fātiáo; **wind up** 结束 jiéshù; **winding** *adj* 蜿蜒的 wānyán de; *n* (*air*) 风 fēng; **wind force** 风力 fēnglì; **wind instrument** 吹奏乐器 chuīzòu yuèqì; **windmill** *n* 风车 fēngchē; **windpipe** *n* 气管 qìguǎn; **wind storm** 风暴 fēngbào; **windy** *adj* 有风的 yǒu fēng de
window *n* 窗子 chuāngzi; **window blind** 遮光帘 zhēguānglián; **window shopping** 看橱窗 kàn chúchuāng, 逛商店 guàng shāngdiàn

windshield *n* 挡风玻璃 dǎngfēng bōli; **windshield wiper** 风档雨刷 fēngdàng yǔshuā

wine *n* 葡萄酒 pútáojiǔ; **winery** *n* 葡萄酒酿造厂 pútáojiǔ niàngzàochǎng

wing *n* (*birds*) 翅膀 chìbǎng; (*faction*) 派别 pàibié

wink *v* 眨眼 zhǎyǎn

winter *n* 冬天 dōngtiān

wipe *v* 擦 cā; **wipe out** 消灭 xiāomiè

wire *n* 金属线 jīnshǔxiàn, 电线 diànxiàn; **wireless** *n* 无线的 wúxiàn de

wise *adj* 明智的 míngzhì de; **wisdom** *n* 智慧 zhìhuì; **wisdom tooth** 智齿 zhìchǐ

wish *v* 希望 xīwàng, 想要 xiǎngyào; *n* 愿望 yuànwàng; **wishful** *adj* 想望的 xiǎngwàng de; **wishful thinking** 痴心妄想 chīxīn wàngxiǎng

wit *n* 机智 jīzhì, 智慧 zhìhuì; **be at one's wits' end** 智穷计尽 zhìqióng jìjìn

witch *n* 女巫 nǚwū; **witchcraft** *n* 魔法 mófǎ; **witch hunt** 政治迫害 zhèngzhì pòhài

with *prep* 和 hé, 跟 gēn

withdraw *v* (**withdrew**, **withdrawn**) (*take back*) 取回 qǔ huí; (*pull out*) 撤出 chè chū; (*retreat*) 撤退 chètuì; (*money*) 取 qǔ; **withdrawal** *n* 撤出 chè chū; 撤退 chètuì; **withdrawn** *adj* 孤僻的 gūpì de, 性格内向的 xìnggé nèixiàng de

withhold *v* (**withheld**, **withheld**) 拒给 jùgěi, 扣发 kòufā

within *prep* 在 ... 之内 zài ... zhīnèi; *adv* 在内部 zài nèibù

without *prep* 没有 méiyǒu

withstand *v* (**withstood**, **withstood**) 抵挡 dǐdǎng

witness *v* 目击 mùjī; *n* 目击者 mùjīzhě, 证人 zhèngrén

wizard *n* (*sorcerer*) 男巫 nánwū; (*person of amazing skill*) 奇才 qícái

woke/woken. *See* **wake**

wolf *n* (*pl* **wolves**) 狼 láng

woman *n* (*pl* **women**) 女人 nǚrén

womb *n* 子宫 zǐgōng

won. *See* **win**

wonder *v* 想知道 xiǎng zhīdao; *n* 奇迹 qíjī; **no wonder** 难怪 nánguài; **wonderful** *adj* 美妙的 měimiào de, 极好的 jíhǎo de

woo *v* (*court*) 求婚 qiúhūn; (*seek to win*) 争取 zhēngqǔ

wood *n* 木柴 mùchái, 木头 mùtou; **wooden** *adj* 木制的 mùzhì de

woodpecker *n* 啄木鸟 zhuómùniǎo

wool *n* 羊毛 yángmáo, 毛线 máoxiàn

word *n* 词 cí; **wording** *n* 措辞 cuòcí; **wordy** *adj* 冗长的 rǒngcháng de

wore. *See* **wear**

work *v* 工作 gōngzuò; **work out** (*exercise*) 锻炼 duànliàn; (*solve*) 解决 jiějué; *n* 工作 gōngzuò; (*product*) 作品 zuòpǐn; **work force** 职工总数 zhígōng zǒngshù, 劳动人口 láodòng rénkǒu; **work permit** 工作许可 gōngzuò xǔkě

workable *adj* 可行的 kěxíng de

working-class *adj* 劳工阶级的 láogōng jiējí de

workings *n* 运行 yùnxíng, 运作 yùnzuò

worker *n* 工人 gōngrén

workman *n* 工匠 gōngjiàng; **workmanship** *n* (*skill*) 手艺 shǒuyì; (*products*) 工艺品 gōngyìpǐn

workplace *n* 工作场所 gōngzuò chǎngsuǒ, 单位 dānwèi

workshop *n* (*work room*) 车间 chējiān; (*seminar*) 讲习会 jiǎngxíhuì

world *n* 世界 shìjiè; **worldwide** *adj* 全世界的 quán shìjiè de

worm *n* 虫 chóng, 蚯蚓 qiūyǐn

worn. *See* **wear**

worry *v* 发愁 fāchóu, 担心 dānxīn; *n* 烦恼 fánnǎo; **worried** *adj* 担心的 dānxīn de

worse *adj* 更坏的 gènghuài de; **to make matters worse** 使情况更糟 shǐ qíngkuàng gèngzāo

worship *v/n* 崇拜 chóngbài

worst *adj* 最坏的 zuìhuài de

worth *n* 价值 jiàzhí; *adj* 值... zhí ...; **worthless** *adj* 无价值的 wú jiàzhí de; **worthwhile** *adj* 值得的 zhídé de; **worthy** *adj* 值得的 zhídé de, 有价值的 yǒu jiàzhí de, 可敬的 kějìng de

would. *See* **will**

wound *v* (*twist*) *See* **wind**; (*hurt*) 伤害 shānghài; **wounded** *adj* 受伤的 shòushāng de; *n* 创伤 chuāngshāng;

wove/woven. *See* **weave**

wrap *v* 包 bāo, 缠绕 chánrǎo; **wrap up** 完成 wánchéng, 结束 jiéshù

wreath *n* 花环 huāhuán, (*for funeral*) 花圈 huāquān

wreck *v* (*crash*) 失事 shīshì; (*demolish*) 拆毁 chāihuǐ; *n* 失事 shīshì; **wreckage** *n* 遇难 yùnàn, 残骸 cánhái

wrench *v* 猛扭 měng niǔ; *n* 扳手 bānshou

wrestle *v* 摔跤 shuāijiāo; **wrestling** *n* 摔跤 shuāijiāo

wriggle *v* 蠕动 rúdòng

wrinkle *n* 皱纹 zhòuwén

wrist *n* 手腕 shǒuwàn

write *v* (**wrote, written**) 写 xiě; **writer** *n* 作家 zuòjiā, 作者 zuòzhě; **writing** *n* (*books, etc.*) 作品 zuòpǐn; (*handwriting*) 手迹 shǒujì

written *v see* **write**; *adj* 书面的 shūmiàn de

wrong *v* 冤枉 yuānwang, 错怪 cuòguài; *adj* 错误的 cuòwù de; **wrongful** *adj* 不正当的 bù zhèngdāng de, 不公允的 bù gōngyǔn de

wrote. *See* **write**

X

xenophobia *n* 仇外 chóuwài, 惧外 jùwài; **xenophobic** *adj* 仇外的 chóuwài de, 惧外的 jùwài de

Xerox *v* 复印 fùyìn; *n* 复印机 fùyìnjī

X-ray *n* X光 X guāng

Y

yacht *n* 游艇 yóutǐng

yard *n* (*ground*) 院子 yuànzi; (*unit of measure*) 码 mǎ

yarn *n* 纱 shā, 线 xiàn

yawn *v* 打哈欠 dǎ hāqian; *n* 哈欠 hāqian

year *n* 年 nián, 岁 suì

yearn *v* 渴望 kěwàng

yell *v* 大叫 dàjiào; *n* 大叫声 dàjiàoshēng

yellow *adj* 黄色的 huángsè de

yes *adv* 是 shì, 对 duì

yesterday *n*; *adv* 昨天 zuótiān; **the day before yesterday** 前天 qiántiān

yet *adv* 仍 réng, 更 gèng, 还 hái; *conj* 然而 rán'ér, 但是 dànshì

yield *v* (*give in*) 让步 ràngbù, 屈从 qūcóng; (*produce*) 出产 chūchǎn, 产生 chǎnshēng; *n* 产量 chǎnliàng

yoga *n* 瑜珈 yújiā

yogurt *n* 酸奶 suānnǎi

yolk *n* 蛋黄 dànhuáng

you *pron* 你 nǐ

young *adj* 年轻的 niánqīng de; **youngster** *n* 少年 shàonián

your *pron* (*sing*) 你的 nǐde; (*pl*) 你们的 nǐmende; **yours** *pron* (*sing*) 你的 nǐde; (*pl*) 你们的 nǐmende; **yourself** *pron* (*pl* **yourselves**) 你自己 nǐ zìjǐ

youth *n* 青春 qīngchūn, 青年 qīngnián

Yugoslavia *n* 南斯拉夫 nánsīlāfū; **Yugoslavian** *n* 南斯拉夫人 nánsīlāfūrén; *adj* 南斯拉夫的 nánsīlāfū de

Z

zebra *n* 斑马 bānmǎ

zero *n* 零 líng

zigzag *n* 之字形 zhīzìxíng, 曲折 qūzhé

zip *n* 拉链 lāliàn; **zip code** 邮编 yóubiān

zipper *n* 拉链 lāliàn

zodiac *n* 黄道 huángdào

zone *n* 区 qū; **time zone** 时区 shíqū

zoo *n* 动物园 dòngwùyuán

zoology *n* 动物学 dòngwùxué; **zoological** *adj* 动物学的 dòngwùxué de; **zoologist** *n* 动物学家 dòngwùxuéjiā

zoom *n* 急剧上升 jíjù shàngshēng, 猛增 měngzēng; (*photography*) 缩放 suōfàng; **zoom lens** 变焦透镜 biànjiāo tòujìng

Chinese Character Index
(By Number of Strokes)

1

一 yī

2

八 bā
厂 chǎng
刀 dāo
儿 er, ér
二 èr
几 jǐ, jī
九 jiǔ
力 lì
七 qī
人 rén
入 rù
十 shí
又 yòu

3

才 cái
叉 chā
大 dà, dài
凡 fán

飞 fēi
干 gàn, gān
个 gè
工 gōng
弓 gōng
广 guǎng
久 jiǔ
口 kǒu
马 mǎ
门 mén
女 nǚ
乞 qǐ
千 qiān
三 sān
山 shān
上 shàng
勺 sháo
尸 shī
士 shì
土 tǔ
卫 wèi
习 xí
下 xià
乡 xiāng
小 xiǎo
也 yě

已 yǐ
义 yì
于 yú
与 yǔ
丈 zhàng
之 zhī
子 zi

亿 yì

4

巴 bā
办 bàn
贝 bèi
比 bǐ
币 bì
不 bù
车 chē, jū
尺 chǐ
丑 chǒu
丹 dān
斗 dòu, dǒu
乏 fá
反 fǎn
方 fāng

分 fēn
丰 fēng
风 fēng
夫 fū
父 fù
公 gōng
勾 gōu
互 hù
户 hù
幻 huàn
火 huǒ
及 jí
见 jiàn
斤 jīn
井 jǐng
巨 jù
开 kāi
六 liù
毛 máo
木 mù
内 nèi
牛 niú
片 piàn
气 qì
欠 qiàn
切 qiē
区 qū
日 rì
少 shǎo, shào

升 shēng
手 shǒu
书 shū
水 shuǐ
太 tài
天 tiān
王 wáng
为 wèi, wéi
文 wén
乌 wū
无 wú
五 wǔ
午 wǔ
心 xīn
凶 xiōng
牙 yá
以 yǐ
尤 yóu
友 yǒu
元 yuán
月 yuè
云 yún
匀 yún
允 yǔn
长 cháng, zhǎng
爪 zhǎo, zhuǎ
支 zhī
止 zhǐ

中 zhōng
专 zhuān

═══

历 lì
仇 chóu
化 huà
仅 jǐn
仆 pū
仁 rén
仍 réng
什 shí, shén
从 cóng, cōng
仓 cāng
介 jiè
今 jīn
冗 rǒng
订 dìng
讥 ji
计 jì
认 rèn
劝 quàn
双 shuāng
队 duì
艺 yì
引 yǐn
扎 zā

5

白	bái	民	mín	占	zhàn
半	bàn	目	mù	正	zhèng, zhēng
包	bāo	母	mǔ		
北	běi	鸟	niǎo	主	zhǔ
本	běn	皮	pí	左	zuǒ
必	bì	卡	qiǎ, kǎ		
布	bù	平	qiú	买	mǎi
斥	chì	去	shǎn	写	xiě
出	chū	申	shēn	归	guī
处	chù, chǔ	圣	shèng	召	zhào
丛	cóng	生	shēng	刊	kān
匆	cōng	石	shí	加	jiā
电	diàn	示	shì	幼	yòu
东	dōng	世	shì	代	dài
冬	dōng	市	shì	付	fù
发	fā, fà	失	shī	他	tā
甘	gān	术	shù	仪	yí
古	gǔ	司	sī	仔	zǐ, zǎi
瓜	guā	丝	sī	印	yìn
击	jī	四	tǎo	厉	lì
甲	jiǎ	田	tián	对	duì
句	jù	头	tóu	奶	nǎi
可	kě	外	wài	孕	yùn
乐	lè, yuè	未	xùn	记	jì
立	lì	业	yìn	让	ràng
龙	lóng	用	yòng	讨	tǎo
矛	máo	永	yǒng	训	xùn
灭	miè	由	yóu	议	yì
		右	yòu	汉	hàn
		玉	yù	汇	huì

汁 zhī
犯 fàn
号 hào, háo
叫 jiào
另 lìng
台 tái
叹 tàn
叶 yè
只 zhī, zhǐ
囚 qiú
奴 nú
宁 níng,
  nìng
它 tā
功 gōng
巧 qiǎo
扒 pá
扒 bā
打 dǎ, dá
扔 rēng
纠 jiū
节 jié
边 biān
闪 shǎn
饥 jī
旧 jiù
礼 lǐ

6

百 bǎi
并 bìng
产 chǎn
成 chéng
虫 chóng
充 chōng
此 cǐ
存 cún
当 dāng,
  dàng
丢 diū
多 duō
而 ér
耳 ěr
负 fù
各 gè
共 gòng
光 guāng
后 hòu
华 huá, huà
灰 huī
夹 jiā
考 kǎo
老 lǎo
米 mǐ
名 míng
年 nián
农 nóng

乒 pīng
曲 qū, qǔ
肉 ròu
色 sè, shǎi
舌 shé
式 shì
死 sǐ
同 tóng
网 wǎng
危 wēi
西 xī
先 xiān
向 xiàng
血 xiě, xuě,
  xuè
兴 xīng,
  xìng
寻 xún
羊 yáng
页 yè
异 yì
衣 yī
有 yǒu
杂 zá
再 zài
在 zài
兆 zhào
争 zhēng
至 zhì
州 zhōu

竹 zhú
自 zì

冰 bīng
冲 chōng, chòng
次 cì
决 jué
关 guān
合 hé
会 huì, kuài
企 qǐ
全 quán
伞 sǎn
众 zhòng
创 chuàng, chuāng
刚 gāng
划 huà
列 liè
刘 liú
动 dòng
毕 bì
协 xié
传 chuán, zhuàn
仿 fǎng
伙 huǒ
价 jià
件 jiàn

伦 lún
任 rèn, rén
伤 shāng
伪 wěi
休 xiū
仰 yǎng
伊 yī
优 yōu
仲 zhòng
压 yā
厌 yàn
观 guān,
欢 huān
戏 xì
那 nà
邪 xié
防 fáng
阶 jiē
阳 yáng
阴 yīn
导 dǎo
交 jiāo
军 jūn
芝 zhī
访 fǎng
讽 fěng
讲 jiǎng
诀 jué
论 lùn, lún
设 shè

许 xǔ
池 chí
汗 hàn
江 jiāng
汤 tāng
污 wū
羽 yǔ
行 xíng, háng
吃 chī
吐 tǔ, tù
吓 xià
吉 jí
壮 zhuàng
夸 kuā
回 huí
团 tuán
因 yīn
妇 fù
好 hǎo, hào
奸 jiān
妈 mā
如 rú
她 tā
她 tā
孙 sūn
安 ān
守 shǒu
宇 yǔ
字 zì

尖 jiān
巩 gǒng
帆 fān
庆 qìng
庄 zhuāng
场 cháng,
　　chǎng
尘 chén
地 de, dì
扛 káng
扣 kòu
扩 kuò
扫 sǎo
托 tuō
扬 yáng
执 zhí
忙 máng
红 hóng
纪 jì
纤 qiàn
约 yuē
达 dá
过 guò
巡 xún
迅 xùn
迂 yū
闭 bì
闯 chuǎng
问 wèn
收 shōu

劣 liè
尽 jìn, jǐn
早 zǎo
肌 jī
肋 lèi
机 jī
朴 pò
权 quán
杀 shā
氖 nǎi
灯 dēng
爷 yé
轨 guǐ

7

兵 bīng
步 bù
赤 chì
串 chuàn
岛 dǎo
弟 dì
豆 dòu
兑 duì
否 fǒu
更 gèng,
　　gēng
角 jiǎo, jué
局 jú
君 jūn

克 kè
来 lái
里 lǐ
良 liáng
两 liǎng
卵 luǎn
麦 mài
每 měi
免 miǎn
弃 qì
求 qiú
系 xì, jì

伴 bàn
伯 bó
但 dàn
低 dī
佛 fó, fú
估 gū
你 nǐ
别 bié, biè
利 lì
判 pàn
努 nǔ
劫 jié
冻 dòng
冷 lěng
词 cí
评 píng
即 jí

邻 lín
阿 ā, ē
陈 chén
附 fù
陆 lù
宏 hóng
牢 láo
芭 bā
苍 cāng
芳 fāng
芬 fēn
花 huā
劳 láo
狂 kuáng
改 gǎi
攻 gōng
贡 gòng
庇 bì
床 chuáng
库 kù
纯 chún
纺 fǎng
级 jí
纽 niǔ
吵 chǎo
吹 chuī
吨 dūn
吠 fèi
告 gào
谷 gǔ

吼 hǒu
呕 ǒu
呆 dāi, ái
驳 bó
驴 lǘ
间 jiān, jiàn
妨 fáng
妓 jì
沉 chén
沟 gōu
沥 lì
没 méi, mò
汽 qì
层 céng
尿 niào
屁 pì
饭 fàn
壳 ké, qiào
怀 huái
快 kuài
彻 chè
把 bǎ
扳 bān
扮 bàn
报 bào
抄 chāo
扯 chě
抖 dǒu
扼 è
扶 fú

抚 fǔ
护 hù
技 jì
拒 jù
抗 kàng
抛 pāo
批 pī
抢 qiǎng
坟 fén
坏 huài
均 jūn
块 kuài
坚 jiān
迟 chí
还 hái, huán
进 jìn
近 jìn
连 lián
财 cái
困 kùn
奸 jiān
戒 jiè
启 qǐ
灵 líng
含 hán
罕 hǎn
材 cái
村 cūn
杆 gān, gǎn
杠 gàng

试	shì	呻	shēn	岸	àn
诗	shī	味	wèi	岩	yán
详	xiáng	知	zhī	岳	yuè
询	xún	垄	lǒng	底	dǐ
迪	dí	幸	xìng	店	diàn
迫	pò, pǎi	奔	bēn	废	fèi
波	bō	奋	fèn	庙	miào
法	fǎ	契	qì	庞	páng
河	hé	奇	qí, jī	垃	lā
沮	jǔ	固	gù	坡	pō
泪	lèi	国	guó	坦	tǎn
泥	ní, nì	图	tú	拖	tuō
泡	pào	姑	gū	拌	bàn
浅	qiǎn	姐	jiě	抱	bào
泄	xiè	妹	mèi	拨	bō
泻	xiè	妻	qī	拆	chāi
沿	yán	委	wěi	抽	chōu
泳	yǒng	姓	xìng	担	dān, dàn
油	yóu	孤	gū	抵	dǐ
沾	zhān	享	xiǎng	拐	guǎi
沼	zhǎo	学	xué	拘	jū
治	zhì	宝	bǎo	拉	lā, lá
注	zhù	宠	chǒng	拦	lán
往	wǎng	定	dìng	抹	mǒ, mā, mò
征	zhēng	官	guān		
狗	gǒu	审	shěn	拇	mǔ
狐	hú	实	shí	拧	nǐng, níng, nìng
咖	gā	宗	zōng		
呼	hū	居	jū		
咆	páo	屈	qū	拍	pāi

购 gòu
货 huò
贫 pín
贪 tān
责 zé
账 zhàng
质 zhì
贮 zhù
轰 hōng
轮 lún
转 zhuǎn,
zhuàn
畅 chàng
的 de, dì, dí
盲 máng
矿 kuàng
码 mǎ
和 hé, huò,
huó, hè
季 jì
空 kōng,
kòng
帘 lián
衬 chèn
钓 diào
凭 píng
取 qǔ
卧 wò
虎 hǔ

9

复 fù
革 gé
骨 gǔ
鬼 guǐ
面 miàn
甚 shèn
食 shí
是 shì
首 shǒu
威 wēi
咸 xián
音 yīn
幽 yōu
重 zhòng
奏 zòu

孩 hái
厘 lí
厚 hòu
除 chú
陡 dǒu
院 yuàn
陨 yǔn
勉 miǎn
勇 yǒng
建 jiàn
说 shuō,
shuì

误 wù
诱 yòu
语 yǔ
亮 liàng
罚 fá
剑 jiàn
前 qián
剃 tì
削 xiāo, xuē
卸 xiè
临 lín
保 bǎo
便 biàn,
pián
促 cù
俄 é
俘 fú
俚 lǐ
侵 qīn
侮 wǔ
信 xìn
修 xiū
南 nán
冠 guān
郡 jùn
独 dú
狠 hěn
狮 shī
狩 shòu
狭 xiá

羞 xiū
紧 jǐn
素 sù
索 suǒ
虔 qián
耕 gēng
耗 hào
蚕 cán
蚊 wén
躯 qū
配 pèi
起 qǐ
赶 gǎn

11

巢 cháo
率 shuài
象 xiàng

随 suí
隐 yǐn
凑 còu
减 jiǎn
剪 jiǎn
谎 huǎng
谋 móu
谢 xiè
谚 yàn
商 shāng

副 fù
偿 cháng
假 jiǎ, jià
健 jiàn
偶 ǒu
偏 piān
停 tíng
偷 tōu
做 zuò
兽 shòu
猜 cāi
猎 liè
猫 māo
猛 měng
猪 zhū
奢 shē
屠 tú
弹 dàn, tán
寂 jì
寄 jì
密 mì
宿 sù, xiǔ,
　　 xiù
阐 chǎn
堵 dǔ
堆 duī
堕 duò
基 jī
婚 hūn
婆 pó

婴 yīng
馄 hún
馅 xiàn
菜 cài
黄 huáng
萧 xiāo
营 yíng
著 zhù
鹿 lù
麻 má
庸 yōng
措 cuò
掉 diào
捷 jié
接 jiē
据 jù
控 kòng
描 miáo
排 pái
捧 pěng
授 shòu
探 tàn
推 tuī
掩 yǎn
惭 cán
惊 jīng
惧 jù
情 qíng
骑 qí, jì
崩 bēng

479

chéng
笨 bèn
笛 dí
第 dì
笼 lóng
船 chuán
袋 dài
袭 xí
聋 lóng
聊 liáo
职 zhí
票 piào
领 lǐng
粗 cū
粒 lì
粘 zhān,
    nián
着 zhe, zhāo,
    zháo,
    zhuó
虚 xū
甜 tián
蛋 dàn
蛇 shé
萤 yíng
断 duàn
距 jù
野 yě
酗 xù
斜 xié

雪 xuě
梦 mèng
勘 kān
新 xīn

12

奥 ào
曾 céng
鲁 lǔ
童 tóng
凿 záo
最 zuì

博 bó
厨 chú
隔 gé
寒 hán
谦 qiān
谣 yáo
割 gē
剩 shèng
傲 ào
傍 bàng
储 chǔ
猴 hóu
猩 xīng
属 shǔ, zhǔ
强 qiáng,
    jiàng,

qiǎng
粥 zhōu
圈 quān,
    juàn
富 fù
寓 yù
阑 lán
堡 bǎo
堤 dī
塔 tǎ
媒 méi
嫂 sǎo
董 dǒng
落 luò, lào,
    là
葡 pú
葬 zàng
插 chā
搅 jiǎo
揭 jiē
搂 lǒu
搜 sōu
提 tí, dī
握 wò
援 yuán
愤 fèn
惯 guàn
慌 huāng
愉 yú
骗 piàn

餐 cān

17

爵 jué
赢 yíng

藏 cáng, zàng
藐 miǎo
擦 cā
懦 nuò
嚎 háo
臂 bì, bèi
臀 tún
赡 shàn
戴 dài
瞳 tóng
瞩 zhǔ
礁 jiāo
癌 ái
黏 nián
糟 zāo
繁 fán
螺 luó
蟋 xī

蟑 zhāng
辫 biàn
鼾 hān

18

鹰 yīng
瀑 pù
戳 chuō
翻 fān
糨 jiàng
鳏 guān
鞭 biān

19

蘑 mó
攀 pān
蟾 chán
颤 chàn
蹲 dūn
警 jǐng

20

魔 mó
嚼 jiáo, jué
灌 guàn
籍 jí
蠕 rú

21

蠢 chǔn
露 lù

22

蘸 zhàn

23

罐 guàn

Also available from Hippocrene Books

Beginner's Chinese with 2 Audio CDs
Second Edition
$32.00 pb · 978-0-7818-1257-3

Intermediate Chinese with Audio CD
Second Edition
$29.95 pb · 978-0-7818-1311-2

Chinese through Tone and Color
A Unique Visual Method for Learning over 100 Basic Chinese Characters
$24.95pb · 978-0-7818-1204-7

Hippocrene Children's Illustrated Chinese (Mandarin) Dictionary
$14.95 pb · 0-7818-0848-4

Chinese-English/English-Chinese Pocket Legal Dictionary
$19.95 pb · 0-7818-1215-1

Chinese-English/English-Chinese Dictionary & Phrasebook (Mandarin)
$13.95 pb · 0-7818-1135-X

Concise Chinese-English Usage Dictionary
A Study Reference to the 500 Most Essential Mandarin Characters
$19.95 pb · 978-0-7818-1293-1

Emergency Chinese Phrasebook
$5.95 pb · 0-7818-0975-4

Prices subject to change without prior notice.
To purchase Hippocrene Books contact your local bookstore,
visit www.hippocrenebooks.com, call (212) 685-4373,
or write to: HIPPOCRENE BOOKS, 171 Madison Avenue,
New York, NY 10016.